CHILDREN AND YOUTH
Social Problems and Social Policy

CHILDREN AND YOUTH
Social Problems and Social Policy

HOMES OF HOMELESS CHILDREN

William P[ryor] Letchworth

ARNO PRESS
A New York Times Company
New York — 1974

Reprint Edition 1974 by Arno Press Inc.

Reprinted from a copy in
The Princeton University Library

CHILDREN AND YOUTH
Social Problems and Social Policy
ISBN for complete set: 0-405-05940-X
See last pages of this volume for titles.

Publisher's Note: The Chromographic Chart has been reproduced in black and white for this edition.

Manufactured in the United States of America

Library of Congress Cataloging in Publication Data

Letchworth, William Pryor, 1823-1910.
Homes of homeless children.

(Children and youth: social problems and social policy)
Reprint of the 1903 ed.
1. Orphans and orphan asylums--New York (State)
2. Children--Institutional care--New York (State)
I. Title. II. Series.
HV883.N68L4 1974 362.7'32'09747 74-1693
ISBN 0-405-05969-8

HOMES OF HOMELESS CHILDREN

HOMES OF HOMELESS CHILDREN

A report on orphan asylums and other institutions for the care of children

BY

WILLIAM P. LETCHWORTH

COMMISSIONER OF THE NEW YORK STATE BOARD OF CHARITIES

Transmitted to the Legislature with the annual report of the Board January 14th, 1876.

To this is appended a report on "Pauper and Destitute Children," also a report on "Pauper Children in New York County."

EXPLANATORY NOTE.

"Homes of Homeless Children" is the title given to an extra edition of a report made by the writer to the State Board of Charities in 1875 and presented to the Legislature with the annual report of the Board in January of the following year. The report, upon which much time and labor were bestowed in its preparation, embraces a history and description of the various charitable institutions then existing in the state for the care of homeless children, in which there were 17,791 beneficiaries.

In addition to visiting these institutions and describing their different systems, another object had in view was to confer with their managers respecting the execution of the law requiring the removal of children from the poorhouses and almshouses. The statute was enacted April 24th, 1875, and became operative January 1st, 1876. It was thought that the adoption by the orphan asylums of an active system of placing out children in families would make room for the admission into the asylums of the children from the poorhouses without enlarging or inconveniencing the asylums.

The action of the Legislature requiring the removal of the children from the poorhouses and almshouses of the state and prohibiting their admission into these establishments was based upon a report on the condition of the children in the poorhouses and almshouses, which was made by the writer in connection with an inquiry into the causes of pauperism and crime made by the State Board of Charities in 1874. The report was presented to the Legislature with the annual report of the Board in January, 1875.

An attempt made in 1875 to exempt New York County from the operations of this law was defeated by the report on "Pauper Children of New York County," which was presented to the Legislature in January, 1876.

The two reports last named are now appended to the remaining undistributed copies of "Homes of Homeless Children" for convenience when referring to the subject of the great reform by which 1,130 children were removed from the almshouses of New York and Kings counties alone, and the degrading system of rearing children in the poorhouses and almshouses of the state was forever set aside.

WM. P. LETCHWORTH,
Ex-Commissioner State Board of Charities.

(Glen Iris), PORTAGE P. O., N. Y.,
JANUARY 28th, 1903.

CONTENTS.

INDEX TO INSTITUTIONS VISITED.

Classified as to Localities.

Page.

Albany 33–58

Albany Orphan Asylum — "The Society for the relief of Orphan and Destitute Children in the city of Albany" 33–40
Western ave., cor. Robin st.

Children's Friend Society, The 40–43
31 Hamilton st.; 16 Canal st.

Child's Hospital 43, 44

House of Shelter, The 44–46
Cor. Wendell and Howard st.

Orphan Home of St. Peter's Church 46, 47
1 Pine street.

St. Vincent's Orphan Asylum Society, in the city of Albany 47

St. Vincent's Female Orphan Asylum 48–53
106 Elm street.

St. Joseph's Industrial School 53–55
261 North Pearl street.

St. Vincent's Male Orphan Asylum 55–58
Western avenue.

Auburn 58–62

Cayuga Asylum for Destitute Children, The.
Owasco street.

Batavia 62–65

New York State Institution for the Blind, The.

Bath 65–68

Davenport Institution for Female Orphan Children, The.
Bath, Steuben county.

Binghamton 68–73

Susquehanna Valley Home and Industrial School for Indigent Children.
Binghamton, Broome county.

Brooklyn 73–121

Brooklyn Children's Aid Society 73–78
61 Poplar st.; 139 Van Brunt st.

Brooklyn Howard Colored Orphan Asylum, The 79, 80
Dean st., near Troy ave.

Brooklyn Industrial School Association and Home for Destitute Children, The 80–86
Butler st., bet. Flatbush and Vanderbilt aves.

Brooklyn Nursery 87–91
66 Prospect pl., bet. Carlton and Vanderbilt aves.

Church Charity Foundation of Long Island, The 91–93
Albany ave., cor. Herkimer st.

Convent and House of the Good Shepherd 93–95
Cor. Atlantic and Rockaway aves.

Convent of the Sisters of Mercy, in Brooklyn 95–98
273 Willoughby av., cor. Classon av.

Industrial School Association of Brooklyn, The, Eastern Dis't.. . 98–102
141 South Third street.

BROOKLYN — (*Continued*): Page.

Orphan Home and Asylum of the Church of the Holy Trinity.. 102, 103
Graham ave., bet. Montrose ave. and Johnson street.

Orphan Asylum Society of the City of Brooklyn 103–105
Herkimer st. and Atlantic ave.

Roman Catholic Orphan Asylum of the City of Brooklyn, County of Kings 106, 107

Roman Catholic Male Orphan Asylum 107, 108
St. Mark's place, betw. Troy and Albany aves.

St. Joseph's Female Orphan Asylum........ .... 108, 109
Cor. Willoughby and Yates aves.

St. Paul's Female Orphan Asylum and Industrial School, 109, 110
Cor. Clinton and Congress sts.

Sheltering Arms Nursery of Long Island, The 110–112
524 Atlantic avenue.

Society for the Aid of Friendless Women and Children, The .. 113–116
20 Concord street.

St. Joseph's Institution for the Improved Instruction of Deaf Mutes in the City of Brooklyn 116, 117
177 Main street.

St. Vincent's Home for Boys.................................. 117, 118
7 Poplar street; 10 Vine street.

Truant Home.. 118–121
Jamaica Plank-road, New Lots.

BUFFALO 121–159

Asylum of Our Lady of Refuge 121–123
Best street.

Buffalo Orphan Asylum, The.................................. 123–126
Virginia street.

Charity Foundation of the Protestant Episcopal Church in the City of Buffalo, The 127–129
Rhode Island st., bet. 6th and 7th streets.

Evangelical Lutheran St. John's Orphan Home, The 129–134
Hickory st., Sulphur Springs.

German Roman Catholic Orphan Asylum of Buffalo, The..... 134–136
221 Batavia street.

Le Couteulx St. Mary's Institution for the Improved Instruction of Deaf Mutes in the City of Buffalo 136–139
125 Edward street.

Society for the Protection of Destitute Roman Catholic Children, at the City of Buffalo, The 140–148
Limestone Hill, town of West Seneca.

St. Joseph's Male Orphan Asylum..... 148–152
Limestone Hill, town of West Seneca.

St. Mary's Asylum for Widows, Foundlings and Infants...... 156–159
126 Edward street.

St. Vincent's Female Orphan Asylum............. 152–156
Cor. Batavia and Ellicott streets.

CANANDAIGUA 159–163

Ontario Orphan Asylum.. 159–162
Main street.

St. Mary's Orphan Asylum 163
Main street.

COOPERSTOWN.. 164–169

Orphan House of the Holy Saviour.
Cooperstown, Otsego county.

Page.

DUNKIRK 169, 170
St. Mary's Orphan Asylum. Buffalo street.

ELMIRA 170–173
Southern Tier Orphan Home.
Cor. Franklin and Fulton streets.

HUDSON 173–175
Hudson Orphan and Relief Association.
Cor. State and North Seventh sts.

LOCKPORT 176, 177
Lockport Home for the Friendless, The.
High street.

MOUNT VERNON 177–180
Wartburg Orphan's Farm School of the Evangelical Lutheran Church, The. Westchester county.

NEWBURGH 180–183
Newburgh Home for the Friendless 180–182
Montgomery street.
St. Patrick's Orphan Asylum 183

NEW YORK 183–382
American Female Guardian Society 183–193
Office, 29 East 29th street.
Association for Befriending Children and Young Girls 193–198
136 Second ave.
Association for the benefit of Colored Orphans in the City of New York 198–202
143d st., bet. 10th av. and Boulev'd.
Asylum of St. Vincent de Paul 202–204
215 West 39th street.
Children's Aid Society 204–230
Office, 19 East 4th street.
Children's Fold, The 231-232
157 East 60th street.
Five Points House of Industry, The 233–236
155 Worth street.
Foundling Asylum of the Sisters of Charity in the City of New York 236–243
68th st., bet. 3d and Lexin'n aves.
Hebrew Ben. Orph. Asyl. Socy. of the City of New York, The 243–248
76th street and 3d avenue.
House of the Good Shepherd 248–250
Foot 89th and 90th sts., East river.
House of Mercy 251–253
Foot of 86th street.
Howard Mission and Home for Little Wanderers 253–256
40 New Bowery.
Industrial School 256
Hart's Island.
Institution of Mercy, The 256–260
House of Mercy 257
35 E. Houston st.
St. Joseph's Industrial School 258–260
81st st., bet. 4th and Madison aves.
Institution for the Improved Instruction of Deaf Mutes 260, 261
1471, '73, '75 Broadway.
Leake and Watts' Orphan House 262–264
10th ave. and 112th street.
New York Catholic Protectory, The 264–275
Office 264
33 Warren street, New York.
Protectory 264–275
Westchester, Westchester county.

NEW YORK — (*Continued*): Page
New York Infant Asylum.. 276–280
Maternity Houses.. 279
24 and 26 Clinton place.
Nursery Home.. 279
Tenth avenue and 61st street.
Flushing Home.. 279
Flushing, L. I.
New York Institution for the Blind.. 280–284
Ninth av., bet. 33d and 34th sts.
New York Institution for the Instruction of the Deaf and Dumb.. 284–288
Washington Heights, betw. 162d and 165th streets.
New York Juvenile Asylum.. 288–301
Asylum.. 288–295
176th st., on Washington Heights.
House of Reception.. 298–301
61 West 13th street.
Western Agency.. 295–298
Normal, near Bloomington, Ill.
New York Juvenile Guardian Society, The.. 301, 302
101 St. Mark's place.
New York Ladies' Home Missionary Society of the M. E. Church.. 302–306
61 Park street.
New York Protestant Episcopal City Mission Society.. 356–358
St. Barnabas' House.. 356–358
304 Mulberry street.
New York Soc. for the Prevention of Cruelty to Children, The 306–308
Office, 860 Broadway.
NewYork Soc. for the Relief of the Ruptured and Crippled, The 308–313
Cor. Lexington ave. and 42d st.
Nursery and Child's Hospital.. 314–320
City Nursery.. 315
Cor. Lexington ave.and 51st st.
Country Branch.. 317
West New Brighton, S. I.
Orphan Asylum Society in the City of New York, The.. 320–325
73d street and 11th ave.
Orphan Home and Asylum of the Protestant Episcopal Church in the City of New York.. 325–328
Cor. 49th st. and Lexington ave.
Roman Catholic Orphan Asylum in the city of New York.. 328–334
Male Orphan Asylum.. 332, 333
5th ave., betw. 51st and 52d sts.
Female Orphan Asylum.. 331, 332
Madison avenue.
Female Orphan Asylum.. 329, 331
Prince street, cor. Mott street.
Boland Farm.. 333, 334
Peekskill.
Sheltering Arms, The.. 334–338
129th cor. Tenth ave.
Shelter for Respectable Girls and Home for Convalescents.. 339–341
Shelter for Respectable Girls, etc.. 339
332 Sixth avenue.
Shelter for Babies.. 340
143 West 20th street.
Society for the Reformation of Juvenile Delinquents.. 341–353
Randall's Island.
Society for the Relief of Half Orphans and Destitute Children in the City of New York.. 354–355
69 West 10th street.
St. Joseph's Orphan Asylum.. 359–361
89th street, cor. Avenue A.

NEW YORK — (*Continued*): Page.

St. Mary's Free Hospital for Children 361–365
407 West 34th street.

St. Stephen's Home for Children 365, 366
145 East 28th street.

St. Vincent's Home for Boys 367–370
53 and 55 Warren street.

St. Vincent de Paul's Industrial School 371–373
343 West 42d street.

School ship "Mercury," The 373–376
Off Hart's Island.

Union Home and School, etc. 376–378
Cor. 11th ave. and 151st street.

Ward's Island 378–379

Wilson Industrial School for Girls 379–381
Cor. Avenue A and 8th street.

Women's Aid Society and Home for Training Young Girls, The, 381–382
41 Seventh avenue.

OSWEGO 382–385

Oswego Orphan Asylum.
Oswego, Oswego county.

PETERBORO 385–390

Madison County Orphan Asylum.
Peterboro, Madison county.

PLATTSBURGH 390

Home for the Friendless of Northern New York.
Plattsburgh, Clinton county.

POUGHKEEPSIE 390–392

Poughkeepsie Orphan House and Home for the Friendless.
Poughkeepsie, Dutchess county.

ROCHESTER 392–432

Church Home of the Prot. Epis. Church, in city of Rochester. 392–395
Mount Hope avenue.

Excelsior Farm and House of Industry for Boys 396–399
River road to Lake Ontario.

House for Idle and Truant Children 399–402
263 North St. Paul street.

Industrial School of Rochester, The 402–405
76 Exchange street.

Rochester Benevolent, Scientific and Industrial School of the Sisters of Mercy 406–407
5 South street.

Rochester Home of Industry 408–410
136 South St. Paul street.

Rochester Orphan Asylum, The 411–415
Hubbell's Park, betw. Greig and Exchange streets.

St. Joseph's German Roman Catholic Orphan Asylum 415–418
Andrew street.

St. Mary's Boys' Orphan Asylum 418–420
Cor. Genesee and West Main sts.

St. Patrick's Female Orphan Asylum 420–422
Cor. Frank and Vought sts.

Western House of Refuge 423–432
Lake avenue.

ROME 432, 433

Central New York Institution for Deaf Mutes.
Rome, Oneida county.

SING SING 434, 435

Home for Christian Care, The.
Sing Sing, Westchester county.

Page.

STATEN ISLAND 435–437
Society for the Relief of Destitute Children of Seamen, The.
West New Brighton, S. I.

ST. JOHNLAND 437–444
Society of St. Johnland.
Smithtown, P. O., Suffolk County.

SYRACUSE 444–464
St. Joseph's Asylum and House of Providence............. 444–446
New York Asylum for Idiots 446–452
Onondaga County Orphan Asylum, The.................. 452–457
East Gensee and Walnut streets.
St. Vincent's Female Orphan Asylum.................... 457–464
Madison street.

TOMKINS' COVE. P. O.................................. 464–471
House of the Good Shepherd, The,
Tomkins' Cove, Rockland County.

TROY 471–483
Day Home, The............. 471–473
Cor. Congress and 7th streets.
St. Vincent's Female Orphan Asylum 473–475
Cor. Washington and 5th streets.
Troy Catholic Male Orphan Asylum 476–478
Cor. Hanover and Bedford streets.
Troy Orphan Asylum, The 478–483
294 Eighth street.

UTICA.. 483–496
House of the Good Shepherd, The........................ 483–485
St. John's Female Orphan Asylum........................ 485–490
60 John street.
St. Vincent's Male Orphan Asylum 490–492
Rutger street.
Utica Orphan Asylum, The......................... 492–496
Pleasant and Genesee streets.

VERSAILLES 496–504
Thomas' Asylum for Orphan and Destitute Indian Children.
Versailles P. O., Cattaraugus Co.

WATERTOWN 505–507
Jefferson County Orphan Asylum.
Watertown, Jefferson Co.

INDEX TO INSTITUTIONS VISITED.

CLASSIFIED AS TO THEIR OBJECTS.

INSTITUTIONS COMPLEX, etc. — (*Continued*):

Page.
Children's Aid Society (Office, 19 East Fourth street, New York) ... 204-230

Industrial Schools:
Cottage Place School, 204 Bleecker street ... 224
East River School, 206 East Fortieth street ... 224
Hudson River School, 350 West Twenty-seventh street ... 224
Avenue B School, 607 East Fourteenth street ... 224
German School, 272 Second street ... 224
Italian School, 156 Leonard street ... 224
Lord School, 135 Greenwich street ... 224
Fifty-third Street School, 340 West 53d street ... 224
Park School, 68th street, near Broadway ... 224
Fifty-second Street School, 52d street, near Eleventh avenue ... 224
Lincoln School, 314 East Thirty-fifth street ... 224
Newsboys' Night School, 9 Duane street ... 224
Girls' Industrial School, 120 West Sixteenth street ... 224
Fourth Ward School, 52 Market street ... 224
Fifth Ward School, 186 Franklin street ... 224
Avenue C School, 304 East Fourth street ... 224
Eleventh Ward School, 709 East Eleventh street ... 224
Thirteenth Ward School, 327 Rivington street ... 224
Fourteenth Ward School, 93 Crosby street ... 224
Sixteenth Ward School, 211 West Eighteenth street ... 224
Water Street School, 14 Dover street ... 224

Lodging Houses:
Newsboys' Lodging House, 9 Duane street ... 207
Girls' Lodging House, 27 St. Mark's place ... 207
Rivington Street Lodging House, 327 Rivington street ... 207
Eleventh Ward Lodging House, 709 East Eleventh street ... 207
Sixteenth Ward Lodging House, 211 West Eighteenth street ... 207
Phelps' Lodging House, 314 East Thirty-fifth street ... 208
Church Home of the Prot. Epis. Church in the City of Rochester ... 392-395
Convent of the Sisters of Mercy (Brooklyn) ... 95-98
Five Points House of Industry, The (New York) ... 233-236
Hebrew Benevolent Society of the City of New York, The ... 243-248

INSTITUTIONS FOR THE CARE OF INFANTS AND FOUNDLINGS.

Foundling Asylum of the Sist. of Char. in City of New York, The ... 236-243
New York Infant Asylum ... 276-280
House of Reception, 24 Clinton place ... 278
Nursery Home, Tenth avenue and Sixty-first street ... 279
Flushing Home (Flushing) ... 280
Nursery and Child's Hospital (New York) ... 314-320
City Nursery, corner Lexington avenue and Fifty-first street ... 315-317
Country Branch, West New Brighton ... 317-319
St. Mary's Asylum for Widows, Foundlings and Infants (Buffalo) ... 156-159

INSTS. FOR THE CARE OF ORPHANS, HALF-ORPHANS AND DESTITUTE CHILDREN.

Association for the Benefit of Colored Orphans in the City of New York ... 198-202
Asylum of St. Vincent de Paul (New York) ... 202-204
Brooklyn Howard Colored Orphan Asylum, The ... 79-80
Buffalo Orphan Asylum, The ... 123-126
Children's Fold, The (New York) ... 231-232
Davenport Institution for Female Orphan Children, The (Bath) ... 65-68
Evangelical Lutheran St. John's Orphan Home, The (Buffalo) ... 129-134
Girls' Department, Hickory street ... 130-132
Boys' Department, Sulphur Springs ... 132-134
Excelsior Farm and House of Industry for Boys (Rochester) ... 396-399
German Roman Catholic Orphan Asylum of Buffalo, The ... 134-136
House of the Good Shepherd, The (Tomkins' Cove, Rockland Co.) ... 464-471
House of the Good Shepherd, The (Utica) ... 483-485
Hudson Orphan and Relief Association (Hudson) ... 173-175
Jefferson County Orphan Asylum (Watertown) ... 505-507
Leake and Watts' Orphan House (New York) ... 262-264
Madison County Orphan Asylum (Peterboro') ... 385-390
Newburgh Home for the Friendless ... 180-182
Onondaga County Orphan Asylum (Syracuse) ... 452-457
Ontario Orphan Asylum (Canandaigua) ... 159-162
Orphan Home and Asylum of the Church of the Holy Trinity (Brooklyn, E. D.) 102-103
Orphan Asylum Society of the City of Brooklyn ... 103-105
Orphan Asylum Society in the City of New York, The ... 320-325
Orphans' Home and Asylum of the P. E. Church in the City of New York ... 325-328
Orphan Home of St. Peter's Church (Albany) ... 46-47
Orphan House of the Holy Saviour (Cooperstown) ... 164-169
Oswego Orphan Asylum, Oswego ... 382-385
Poughkeepsie Orphan House and Home for the Friendless ... 390-392
Rochester Orphan Asylum, The ... 411-415
Roman Catholic Orphan Asylum in the City of New York ... 328-334
Male Orphan Asylum, Fifth avenue, bet. Fifty-first and Fifty-second sts., 332-333
Female Orph. Asylum, Madison ave., bet. Fifty-first and Fifty-second sts., 331-332
Female Orphan Asylum, Prince street, corner of Mott ... 329-331
Boland Farm, Peekskill ... 333-334

INST. FOR THE CARE OF ORPHANS, HALF-ORPHANS, ETC.—(*Continued*). Page.

INSTITUTIONS FOR THE EDUCATION OF THE BLIND.

INSTITUTIONS FOR THE EDUCATION OF THE DEAF AND DUMB.

INSTITUTIONS FOR THE EDUCATION OF IDIOTS.

INSTITUTIONS OF THE CHARACTER OF REFORMATORIES.

NURSERIES FOR INFANTS AND YOUNG CHILDREN.

REPORT.

To the State Board of Charities:

GENTLEMEN — In compliance with the request of the Board, I submit this my report on "Orphan Asylums, Reformatories and other Institutions of the State having the care and custody of Children."

PRELIMINARY.

The history of the orphan asylums of the State, could it be fully written, would not only enlarge our faith in human nature, but strengthen our confidence in the regenerative forces of society. This, however, cannot be done; for the beautiful incidents scattered through all, like sweet-scented flowers in the woodland, are too manifold for description. The prayers for the orphan and homeless, uttered by devout men and women in the silent watches of the night; the days of pleading and plodding with weary feet; the times of dark discouragement and doubt; the monotonous round of patience-trying labor within the asylum itself; the good deeds of the benevolent whose sympathies have bestowed the widow's mite as well as the princely largess or bequest — the first perhaps costing the greater sacrifice — all this and much more can never be told, and is only fully recorded in the Book of Life.

No attempt has been made in this report to give the names of the founders, or most active workers of the asylums. Here and there, more by chance than by method, a few have been noted, and in like manner trivial incidents may have usurped the place of more important items.

It has been my aim throughout to obtain and present the views of as large a number as possible of those whose long experience in the care and reformation of children renders their opinions on the subject valuable; also, in the notes taken, to incorporate largely the language of those identified with asylums and reformatories in order the better to illustrate their workings. It would have been more satisfactory could the views of a still larger number interested in this work, have been included, but in the limited time given this was found to be impracticable.

The attempt has been made to outline, with some care, the system of at least one of each of the different classes of institutions, in the hope that the report, taken as a whole, might give a tolerably correct idea of the manner in which this great work of benevolence is carried on throughout the State. Details, apparently tedious, have been in some instances gone into, but this has seemed unavoidable in order to accomplish satisfactorily the end in view. The whole subject has been treated upon the assumption that whatever affected the present or future well-being of even a single dependent child, was worthy of attention.

Of the institutions named in the report, numbering over one hundred and thirty, all excepting five have been visited in person. In almost every instance minute inquiries have been made, the premises carefully inspected, and, with the assistance of a competent stenographer, full notes taken upon every department.

It has been intended to include in this report mention of all the institutions of the classes treated of in the State. If any have been omitted it has been occasioned either through inadvertence, or inability to reach them in the successive order of visitation.

It is deemed but just to state that these visits have, in every case excepting one unavoidable instance, been made unexpectedly to asylum officials.

The total number of children who were inmates of the institutions enumerated in the report, at the several dates of visitation, was 17,791. Of these, 9,404 were boys, and 8,387 girls; 3,889 were orphans, and 7,610 half orphans; 3,182 had both parents living, and of 3,110, it could not be ascertained whether they had parents living or not. The number of children whose parents were natives of the United States, was 3,337, the number whose parents were natives of other countries, was 10,085. The nativity of the parents of 4,369 could not be ascertained.

The children were distributed as follows:

In Orphan Asylums and institutions of a like character....	12,199
In Institutions for the Blind............................	325
In Institutions for the Deaf and Dumb..................	739
In Institutions of a Reformatory character...............	4,332
In the New York State Asylum for Idiots at Syracuse.....	196
Total.....................................	17,791

The number of children placed out by adoption, by indenture, by returning to parents or guardians, or who were otherwise discharged during the year, will be found in many instances noted in the sketches of the several institutions visited. Owing to the failure of the managers of institutions to make complete returns in all cases, it becomes a matter of regret that the full measure of the work in this direction cannot be given in statistical form.

The total receipts of the Orphan Asylums and other institutions having the care or reformation of children during the fiscal year ending September 30, 1875, approximated	$2,976,152 00
The expenditures	2,689,500 00
The total value of personal estate principally accumulated by bequests, including bonds, stocks and other investments, from which an income is derivable was,	2,542,746 00

The amount of indebtedness upon the real estate was,	$1,113,889 00
Other indebtedness................................	281,935 00
Total..	$1,395,824 00

It will be seen that the receipts have exceeded the expenditures by $286,652. This mainly arises from the income of a very few institutions that are so fortunate as to have become largely endowed. The expenditures of the institutions carrying on this work for children, have generally been about equal to their receipts, and in many cases have considerably exceeded them.

Having completed the work the following thoughts suggest themselves:

Location of Asylums.

It is believed that where the object of the institution will admit, a location outside of populous centers and upon lines of direct communication with cities and towns, is desirable. A district free from malaria, healthful, and having a good soil adapted to garden cultivation and the growing of fruits should be selected. A goodly-sized tract should be purchased, looking to the growth of the institution, as it has been found in many cases that more land was wanted when it could not be obtained. Good land properly tilled under asylum proprietorship has not in any instance depreciated, on the contrary in some places with the encroachments of city growth, its value has increased to a sum that at the outset would have been deemed fabulous. The Western House of Refuge at Rochester, the New York Asylum for Idiots at Syracuse, and the Orphan Asylum Society in the city of New York, may be cited out of numerous instances of this kind. Neighborhood surroundings should be considered as well as the capabilities of the place in an æsthetic point of view, since it is believed that the influence of natural beauty is most happy upon the impressible minds of children. A bountiful supply of good water is of paramount importance, and how it can be made to reach every department of the house should be considered.

Building and Interior.

The plan of the building should be such as to give sunshine to every room in the house at sometime during the day. Courts should not be permitted, as they prevent a free circulation of air, and high parallel wings extending backward from a main building, are not desirable.

Basements, it is found, are generally objected to by superintendents and matrons. They are apt at certain seasons to be damp; are not as cheerful as upper apartments; and not so easily ventilated. It is considered better to have a good dry cellar, and begin with the first floor sufficiently above the ground to admit of the cellar being well lighted and aired. By this arrangement the heating apparatus can be placed entirely out of the way, and good storage place secured. Drain tile should be laid outside, and at the bottom, of the foundation walls, and the walls should be faced upon the outer as well as the inner side. It adds but little to the expense to make the cellar walls "rat proof" by adopting an ingenious device at the base known to builders.

Cellars.—Strong objection has been made in a number of cases, and evidently with good reason, to storing vegetables and substances liable to decay in the main part of the building. It is better to keep them in a cellar apart from the house. Spacious earth cellars are very simply constructed upon a plan adopted at the Western House of Refuge, and elsewhere.

The Laundry should be detached from the main building, or located in a wing, and should be used alone for this purpose or for work connected with it. Complaint has been made that the damp vapor from the wash tubs ascends and affects other parts of the house, and also that soiled garments awaiting the wash are liable, when packed together, to generate unhealthy gases.

Sewage.—A matter of primary moment is the sewage, with a view to the proper disposition of the refuse of the building, to neutralize its noxious character, and prevent the generation of unhealthy gases and their diffusion through the building. The highest authorities should be consulted in order to make available the light which modern science has thrown upon this subject.

Ventilation.— In erecting the walls, regard should be had to securing perfect ventilation. Many asylum officials think it important for every large apartment to have one flue that shall admit of making a small open fire. By this means the air is effectually changed and the chill or dampness taken off in bad weather. This is particularly desirable in apartments used by the sick.

Windows should be numerous, that the light may be abundant in dark weather, and also to aid in ventilation. The sashes should be suspended by means of cords, weights and pulleys.

Halls and stairways.— It is generally recommended that halls and stairway passages be wainscoted a few feet from the floor, and that stairways be so constructed that children may not fall over the balustrade, or that they shall not be hurt in case they do. In two instances it was found that children had broken their limbs by such falls. There are several devices for preventing these accidents. One is by stretching a wire rope through iron braces with loops a little above and back of the rail. Another is by a screen, or by rods, placed a few inches apart, across the openings. In some asylums children are prevented from sliding down the balustrade by inserting short thick wooden pins three-fourths of an inch long, in the rail about 15 inches apart. There should be more than one series of stairways in every asylum building to afford rapid egress in case of fire.

Infirmaries.— It has been found that those asylums are most successful in preserving health that adopt preventive measures against the spread of contagious diseases. In certain institutions noted in this report, it will be seen that the infirmary department is so separated from the rest of the building, that no communication of disease to healthy inmates is possible. Noteworthy examples of this may be found in the Orphan Home and Asylum of the Protestant Episcopal Church, New York, and in the Albany Orphan Asylum. This department is again subdivided into distinct sub-departments. A child being taken ill is at once placed in an apartment termed a quarantine. After the diagnosis of its case has been determined by the physician, it is either transferred to the regular wards for the treatment of contagious diseases, or to the general infirmary. All such apartments should have special reference to securing abundant sunlight. Beautiful models illustrating this feature may be found in the Hospital for Ruptured and Crippled Children, New York, and also in the Foundling Asylum of New York city, under the charge of the Sisters of Charity.

Dining-rooms.— In a few instances it has been found that dining-room tables were furnished quite similar to those in private dwellings, chairs being used instead of wooden benches. In a large number of cases stools take the place of benches. It is believed that the nearer the table conforms to the usages of family life the better will be the results.

Dormitories.— So many hours of a child's life are spent in sleep, that it is unnecessary to emphasize the importance of securing for it during this period, that warmth and comfort which enables nature to accomplish her most beneficial results. In regard to beds the almost universal testimony is in favor of the use of straw for this purpose, with sheets, blankets and other covering according to the season. In many cases a comfortable, or thick blanket, is laid upon the tick and under the sheets, which, no doubt, adds to the comfort of the child. This tick should contain sufficient straw to make a good, thick, elastic bed, care being taken not to pack it too tightly. In some cases a corn-husk mattress is used in addition to the straw bed. Tufted mattresses are objected to for general use, owing to the inconvenience of changing the contents as often as necessary. There is no reason why beds in these institutions should not have abundance of clean straw, frequently changed. It is cheap, and may be used afterward for bedding down stock, as is done at the Roman Catholic Protectory in Westchester county. Here, as well as in some other institutions, the beds were found to be not less than sixteen inches thick. Hair and feather pillows are both in use, the latter being most in favor.

Double bedsteads are almost universally condemned. A diversity of opinion exists as to the use of iron or wooden bedsteads. Iron is more generally used; but some in charge of asylums, who have had long experience, and who have used both wood and iron, are decided in their preference for a bedstead of hard wood. This should be well made, varnished or oiled, having a head and a foot board, particularly the latter, and side boards like the French pattern. It is claimed that in such a bedstead a liberal supply of straw can be used loosely in the tick, and without interfering with the shapely appearance of the bed. Besides, it is claimed, that a bed is more comfortable made up in a bedstead with foot and side boards than otherwise; that it can be tucked in more securely in cold weather and further, that children are not liable to fall out of it. As to the question of wooden bedsteads harboring vermin, the opinion of Sister Tatiana, of the St. Vincent Female Orphan Asylum, of Syracuse, as given in the report of her institution, is quite to the point. In some asylums iron bedsteads have been found with side bars or braces extending from head to foot. Others preferring iron bedsteads recommend a wire network at the sides, and at the head and foot, in order to conform to the French idea. Wooden spring slats are found occasionally in iron bedsteads, so constructed as to be readily lifted out and scalded when desirable. Iron bedsteads with an elastic wire bottom are highly spoken of where they have been tried. They have been long in use in the Nursery and Child's Hospital in New York. These elastic bottoms can be used in an ordinary iron bedstead. They are very desirable for hospital service. If iron bedsteads are used, they should be sufficiently stiff to prevent sagging in the center, which renders the sleeper uncomfortable, and gives the dormitory an unsightly appearance. Bedsteads in use are found to vary from two feet four inches to two feet nine inches in width. Cribs for infants are generally found to be about twenty-seven inches wide. This is the width of those in use at the Sheltering Arms, New York. They stand higher from the floor than ordinary beds. All bedsteads for children should be of ample width.

In some instances dormitories were found to have large windows on three of their sides, high ceilings, and walls hung with pictures and mottoes. A broad strip of carpeting, sometimes of bright color, at others a rag carpet, made in the institution, is laid through the center of the room, and pretty rugs beside each bed to protect little feet when first thrust out of their cozy nests on frosty mornings. Sometimes a little stand with a drawer, having a white napkin upon the top of the stand and decorated with a few toys, prayer-book, etc., has been found beside each bed, while a comfortable varnished chair was also close at hand. All such accessories to a dormitory brighten it, and give a home-like aspect to the room. The Brooklyn School Association and Home for Destitute Children is a notable illustration of this idea. When the weather will permit, dormitory windows should be opened at top and bottom during the day, the blinds thrown apart, and the room flooded with sunshine and fresh air. In some instances sleeping rooms have been found wainscoted and ceiled with wood overhead. But these were not in favor, in consequence of their harboring vermin. A hard finish wall, painted in some soft tint, and capable of being washed, seems to be generally preferred.

Bathing and Wash-rooms for the children should be ample in size and well lighted. The utility, if not the necessity, of having the children wash in running water to prevent inoculation from sore eyes, is generally conceded. The best institutions have almost uniformly adopted this plan. The most popular method is to carry the water along the wall above a sink in a pipe, pierced with small round holes at short intervals. Another way is to place in the center of the room a large circular vat about three feet deep, the bottom set a little below, or upon the floor; if the latter, having a bench about eight inches high around its outer circumference. In the inside of the vat, close to the rim, the water pipe is carried, pierced at convenient spaces. The water in this pipe is tempered by a connection with a hot-water pipe. This arrangement admits of the double use of washing the face in running water and of taking a full bath in the vat when desirable. In some of the asylums, built under the direction of, and managed by the Roman Catholic Sisterhoods, the bath tubs for small children are elevated sufficiently from the floor to admit of the Sisters standing beside them and performing the ablution of the children with less fatigue. This is one of the many interesting features of the St. Vincent Orphan Asylum, Albany. In some asylums the water is admitted to the bath under a lip, according to the French plan, there being no faucets or projections to injure the person. In a large number of the institutions visited, each child had its own towel, with its name or number, or both, upon it, hung on a hook, the hooks being marked to correspond. In some cases each child had likewise a hair brush, a fine and coarse comb, and a tooth brush. Sometimes these were kept in a little drawer, at other times in a little bag hung upon a hook by the towel. This practice would seem to be commendable as serving to inculcate habits of order as well as cleanliness.

School Rooms, if furnished upon the principles now recommended by the various municipal boards of education, will generally be found to embrace all needed requisites. There cannot be too much space allotted to blackboards, and if the floor room will permit, single seats and desks should be used. They are preferable, especially for older pupils, for obvious reasons.

Diet.

It is believed, and the conviction is based upon the experience of those connected with asylums, that a generous diet is essential not only so far as the health of the children is concerned, but that in the end it is true economy. When the diet is not generous, the blood becomes impoverished, the tone of the system is lowered, and when an epidemic assails the little flock, it carries away a far greater number of victims.

The importance of building up strong constitutions in children that they may more readily become self-supporting and productive members of society, is so evident, that every thing having relation to their health is worthy of careful attention. Mrs. Dubois, of the Nursery and Child's Hospital, New York, sensibly remarks upon this point: "Real economy is to give these waifs of humanity a good nourishing diet to form bone and muscle, which can be made available to the country that nourishes them."

Dress.

In a large number of asylums it has been found that great pains has been taken by those in charge to preserve and enforce a high standard of personal cleanliness, which cannot be too highly commended. Under-clothing is frequently changed; the heads of the little ones are, at stated days of the week, combed with a fine-tooth comb; the daily ablutions are thorough; and the weekly bath is given under competent supervision. The children's hands and faces were generally found to be clean, in some instances the faces shining with that peculiar brightness, the result of affectionate care, and the hair of the little girls tastefully done up and secured with combs or bright ribbons. It has been a common custom to dress asylum children uniformly, but this is fast being set aside. The feeling is very strong against it in some quarters. The president of the New York Catholic Protectory at Westchester says that he never "buys two pieces of goods alike." Some object to the custom of dressing children uniformly, as will be seen from the notes of visitation, on the ground that it destroys individuality of character, and weakens independence and self-reliance; others regard it as unkind so to mark a child that when it goes upon the street other children may point it out as a charity subject. Some asylums allow children to sélect material and make up garments for themselves in anticipation of their leaving the institution, and upon leaving furnish them with a trunk and quite an outfit of clothing. The generous provision in this respect made by the Sisters of Mercy in Brooklyn is especially worthy of note. In Watertown also, as we entered the Jefferson County Orphan Asylum, we noticed a little girl who was just leaving with her adopted parents. She was very nicely and comfortably dressed, and had quite an outfit of clothing and toys furnished by the institution, connected with all of which there were, doubtless, pleasant associations. There is something so expressive of genuine sympathy toward a homeless child in such provision for its future comfort and pleasure on the part of asylum managers as to warm the heart toward them and their noble work. By allowing a child to exercise its preferences in regard to dress in some degree, the opportunity comes in to teach it to dress discreetly and in good taste, while making the most of limited means.

Secular and Industrial Training.

A very few asylums have adopted the plan of sending their children to the public schools in the vicinity, the schools being of an excellent character, and the class of children attending them being somewhat higher, socially at least, than the asylum children. Where this plan had been adopted it is found to work quite satisfactorily, and there is no disposition to return to the old practice. Among those in charge of asylums where it has not been tried, there is, however, a wide difference of opinion upon the subject. Some are as strongly opposed to the plan as those who have tried it are in favor of it, believing that association with school children would render the work of discipline more difficult, and teach their children additional bad habits. Others maintain that contact with outside children "brightens them up," and prepares them for coping successfully with the great world, which sooner or later they will be obliged to meet; also, that the asylum should be regarded as the temporary home for the child, and while holding this relation to it, should, as far as possible, exercise the same functions as the parent, imparting to it religious instruction, feeding, clothing and caring for it in sickness; but that the child is more benefited in receiving its secular instruction along with other children at the public schools. It has seemed that in asylums where the children were brought into contact with those from outside, and were instructed with them in the same class rooms, as is sometimes the custom where parochial schools are taught on the premises, they appeared more animated and cheerful than in asylums where they were entirely kept by themselves. This may have been a fancy, but the opinion is, nevertheless, ventured.

While it is believed that all of the asylums having the charge of children aim to impart a thorough knowledge of reading, writing, spelling and arithmetic, some, as will be seen by the notes of visitation, very wisely do not allow this to take the place of industrial training, and so devote about half the time usually set apart for study to this important branch of asylum work. The girls are taught to sew and do general housework, and the boys are drilled in gardening and such occupations as are suited to their years, although of little or no pecuniary advantage to the institution. The classes are changed so that those working in the forenoon will be in school in the afternoon.

It must be admitted that children in asylums and reformatories belong largely to a class whose parents have not been given to habits of industry, and that in order to elevate the children they must have inculcated thorough industrial habits, and be trained to persistency in accomplishing their stated tasks. Such a discipline makes the boy methodical, self-reliant and independent. What is said upon this subject in the report by those who have given it much attention will be found of interest.

Religious and Moral Training.

In these homes for children religious and moral teaching, it is believed, is conscientiously inculcated by those having them in charge. This is gratifying in view of the fact that this class of children having no other homes but the asylum, must look to it for that religious training which it is the duty of the parent to give to his children. This is the more important, inasmuch as the building up of all true character must rest on a religious basis. Unless the child learns its obligations to the Deity to begin with, and is taught the importance of living an upright life, it can hardly be expected to become a good citizen. Enlargement upon a point so universally conceded would seem to be superfluous.

Employment of Domestics.

Too much care cannot be exercised in the selection of all persons that are brought in any way into association with the children. They should not be employed because the wages are within the limits of a fixed rule of economy, but with reference to the influence they are likely to exert upon the children. None but persons of good character, fixed religious principles, and those naturally fond of children, should be engaged about an asylum, for although they may not be, strictly speaking, the companions or instructors of the children, still, from the fact that they come in contact with them from day to day, they become so to a greater or less degree.

In a few institutions it was found that in furtherance of a mistaken economy, mothers having children were employed as domestics. They were willing to work for low wages for the privilege of having their children cheaply boarded in the house. The general testimony, it will be found, is strongly against this practice. Among the reasons urged against it is that, in spite of all precautions, partiality on every possible opportunity is shown by the mother toward her own.

Voluntary Service.

The greater the amount of voluntary service that can be secured in the management of an asylum, the more perfect it would naturally seem must be its work, as that which is done for "our dear Lord's sake," is more likely to be better done than from any other motive. It has been found that even in institutions under the immediate charge of persons receiving fixed salaries, the remuneration in many instances was only a partial compensation, the services being rendered mainly for the love of the peculiar work; also, that a very large amount of gratuitous service was most generally rendered by gentlemen and ladies holding official positions or otherwise interested in the charity, some giving up a great portion of their time to the institution in various necessary services. In a large number of institutions it has been found that a great number of men and women, especially the latter, eminent for their piety, have been found who had given up their lives to the work, in many cases having left homes of luxury and the society of the cultured and refined. The association of such persons with children must have a most salutary effect in the formation of their characters.

Beautiful illustrations of this kind of work are to be found in some of the asylums under the management of Sisterhoods in the Roman Catholic, Episcopal and Lutheran churches, where the personal influence of highly refined and cultivated ladies of pure lives and strong religious faith is brought to bear upon every child. These institutions are arranged so that each Sister has charge of a separate department, the sewing room, dormitory, kitchen, laundry, lavatory, school, etc., each forming one, while over the whole establishment one Sister presides, who is recognized as the head. By this means perfect order and system is maintained in every part of the house. A considerable number of institutions have no paid servants whatever, and a large number have but very few, the work being all done by those in charge, with the assistance of the boys or girls about them. It has been found that members of the medical profession, in accordance with a fundamental principle of charity recognized by the faculty, have rendered valuable gratuitous service to these organizations. Whether this voluntary service in behalf of unfortunate children be rendered within the asylum or outside of it, whether it be given for but a single hour, a day, a month, or for stated periods, as in the Lutheran and in some of the Episcopal Sisterhoods, where ladies pledge their whole time for one or more years to this peculiar work, renewing their pledge at their option, or whether it be a life work, as in the Roman Catholic sisterhoods, these sacrifices are deserving the grateful recognition of all men.

Placing Children in Families.

It has been found that the percentage of children in the orphan asylums of the State, October 1, 1875, who were orphans and at the disposal of asylum managers, was about twenty-seven, while the percentage of those who were either half orphans or had both parents living, and who in a great majority of cases had not been surrendered to the asylums, was seventy-three. The last-named are composed largely of two classes: First, those who belong to respectable families, temporarily broken up by sickness, death or financial embarrassment, and who find a shelter in the asylum till the family can be again reunited. Second, children of unworthy or degraded parents, who are admitted with a view to elevate them and shape their lives to better ends. The number who were actually at the disposal of asylum managers and whom they have power to place in families by adoption, indenture or otherwise is comparatively small. In view of the fact that unworthy parents have the power to withdraw their children at any time and replace them in unhappy associations, the work on the part of the asylum managers is a discouraging one so far as it relates to such; but it is persevered in, and the child retained as long as practicable with a view to perfecting its character, and doing it the utmost good possible. The question suggests itself, however, whether there is not a tendency in some asylums to keep orphan children and those who have been surrendered to them longer than is necessary under their fostering care. The asylum being regarded as but a temporary home, and the establishment of these children in family relations its ultimate aim, should

they not, in all cases where practicable, be put into such relations as possible, care being taken in the selection of homes to see that t efits of previous religious training be not lost? Attachments, i lieved, are apt to grow up between those having charge of childı the children themselves, and separations are reluctantly made. meantime children are waiting for admittance and others are so ible, that with a little effort they might be brought under its sa influence, if the children already in the asylum, who are well pr to go into families, should be put there under an energetic placiı system. When this is done, the asylum may be regarded as a bea instrumentality for rescuing children from homelessness and rei ing them under happy auspices in that divinely ordained instit — the family.

The vast number of neglected and destitute children, that need the helping hand of disinterested benevolence, seem to re that all agencies working for their elevation should be active in efforts to reach this ultimate aim. The grand results that have attained by the Children's Aid Society and the American Fe Guardian Society of New York in the removing of children from associations and placing them in good homes are notable exan of what may be done in this field of labor.

Those having charge of asylums are unanimous in affirming great importance of finding proper homes for children. Applicat are generally denied unless the managers are fully satisfied by pers visitation or otherwise of the disposition and ability of the applic to train and educate the child in a fitting manner. It may be q tioned, however, whether children after being placed in homes looked after and followed up with as kind solicitude as is necessary their welfare. "Out of sight out of mind," is an adage, perhaps inapplicable here. There is no doubt but that periodical inquiı after a child, and, where practicable, visitations of an unobtrusive ch acter at stated periods, would enhance the feeling of responsibility its guardian, and increase the efforts of the child to be thought wort of such attention. If difficulty should arise between the guardian aı the child, the counsel of a third party having some interest in tl matter might prevent wrong-doing on the one side or the other.

The general testimony appears to be that those children turn out tl best who have been placed in farmers' families. The reason of this obvious. The child sits at the farmer's table, and becomes at once member of the family. If a girl, she is not humbled to the positioı of a mere drudge for others, or made to feel that she belongs to aı inferior caste from which she can never hope to rise, but she is set to assist the farmer's wife in the various domestic duties, is permitted to use her needle in the family circle, and to go to town or attend church

with other members of the family. If a boy, he works beside the farmer in the fields, accompanies him to town, and assists him in all his varied concerns. Labor from which he was accustomed to revolt, now becomes to him honorable; men holding the respect of the community he sees are engaged in sturdy toil. Finding himself identified with this class, he strives to make himself a fit associate, and be like those about him. The influence upon him from such surroundings cannot be otherwise than elevating. From the farmer he is constantly learning something to his advantage, both from his successes and his reverses, the latter as valuable to the boy as though the loss was sustained by himself. Whether in the fields, at the market, or in the house, the boy is still learning, and he is taught lessons in economy, on the preservation of property, and on carefulness in bargaining, which must be of great value to him in after-life. To children on a farm is frequently given a pet in the shape of a domestic animal, the responsibility for the care of which has an educating effect. On a farm exigencies are continually arising, sometimes trivial, at other times taxing to the utmost the ingenuity and skill of the farmer and those about him; it may be the breaking down of a loaded wagon, the repairing of a plow, the putting in of a pane of glass, or jobs of domestic carpentering. Even the training of a colt is not without its salutary effect. His judgment is matured, he becomes expert, self-reliant, discreet and cool in times of danger. Daily exercise in the open air brings him a good appetite, sound sleep, and as a consequence, a more even and cheerful disposition, besides greater muscular development and hardihood. Granted these advantages of country life always under good, moral and religious influences, and we may fairly hope that he will develop into a useful and respectable citizen.

Asylum Capacities.

The location of some orphan asylums should be changed, others need to have new buildings constructed, or the old remodeled. Many are not only in debt, but are daily embarrassed to meet current expenditures. It is not improbable that if these difficulties were removed, the accommodations now afforded by the orphan asylums already organized with an energetic system of finding homes for the children, would be sufficient to meet the present wants of the class in whose interests they are established. There are many asylums that have been compelled to contract their work, and decline to receive large numbers of children, sending them back to their degraded homes where their course is inevitably downward. It would seem to be for the interest of the public to come to the rescue of these institutions and sustain them, if for no other than politic considerations. The history of numerous asylums in the State shows that, after a long

period of financial struggle, bequests have accumulated creating handsome endowments, by means of which they have become at length entirely self-supporting, and enabled to relieve the public of a large share of its burden.

REFORMATORIES.

Visitations made to all the juvenile reformatories of the State, give rise to many reflections. It will not be attempted in this report to deal with a subject so extended, nevertheless a few hints are offered. While it is evident that those having charge of this work are accomplishing great results through these institutions that stand as bulwarks against the flood of crime which might, but for them, overflow the land, it is apparent that the principle, at least, upon which some of them are conducted, might be improved. The important results growing out of the work of reforming juvenile delinquents in Germany, within the past quarter of a century, are so great when compared with those achieved in our own country, that they should lead us to scrutinize our systems more closely. It is believed that the gloomy and prison-like character with which some of these institutions are invested, should be set aside. The grated windows of the prison seen from afar, as the boy approaches the reformatory, the high walls of gray stone that surround it, the formidable gate-way at the entrance, through which, as he passes, he hears behind him the clash of bar and bolt, falling upon his ears like the sentence of an irrevocable doom, the passage onward through massive doors that swing heavily as they close behind him, till he finds himself at length in his little room, closed with a grated door and fastened with a massive bar and lock, in what seems to him a felon's cell, must powerfully affect the vivid imagination of the young, no matter how hardened he may be, and tend to break down pride of character and self-respect. The boy under such circumstances must feel that the world has turned its back upon him; that he has lost all; that every man's hand is against him, and that henceforth his hand must be against every man. The shock once over, and the mind of the boy accustomed to the terrible ordeal, what dread has Auburn or Sing Sing for him? It is believed that a large proportion of the boys committed to reformatories do not require these forbidding restraints, and that some different and milder treatment combining in some way the family system should be adopted for a large class of juvenile delinquents now being sent to the houses of refuge. If under this method they be still found incorrigible, they might then be transferred to a more secure place and be put under stricter discipline. It is thought, however, that if the experiment was once tried very few would need to be so transferred. In some institutions it was observed that the heads of departments or principal employés ate at the same time, and in the same refectory as the boys. If this idea, foreshadowing the family system, were carried out in all our reformatories and carried out still further so that those in charge might sit at the same table with the boys, placing themselves in full sympathy with them, joining in their conversations and gaining their confidences, more satisfactory results, it would seem, might be accomplished. This idea has evidently suggested itself to the minds of the Christian Brothers, as we found in asylums under their care that they ate in the same dining-room with the boys and at the same time, though at separate tables. Holding intimate relations with the boys, there is an opportunity to inculcate by the potent force of example many little points of decorum which, though often overlooked, have much to do with the formation of character. The aim of the reformatory should be, not to punish, but to help. If this is correct, that mighty power — the love of God to man, and of man to his fellow — should pervade the whole juvenile reformatory system as it does that of the family; the sentiment, "I am better than thou" should never be felt.

The conviction soon forces itself upon the casual student of juvenile delinquency, that society must extend at once its efforts to preventive measures to arrest crime or suffer deplorably in consequence. It cannot afford to neglect or allow to grow up in ignorance and vice, a class which should be objects of its most sacred care.

In a recent report made to the legislature of Pennsylvania by the Board of Public Charities, the following language is made use of, which is deemed appropriate here: "Vice and misery are not limited to the adult classes who fill our prisons and alms-houses; if they were, the certainty of their extirpation would be but a matter of time. But behind these poor wretches range their children, line after line, from youth to infancy, 'the serried ranks of woe,' with the sign or their heritage of want and guilt upon their faces, pressing forward to take their turn in the prisoners' dock, the poor-house, or the jail cell. To busy ourselves alone with mature and developed crime, and to ignore the breeding mass of embryo vice beneath, from which it is steadily supplied, is to attempt to dam the river at its mouth when it has grown into an irresistible torrent, which, but for a trifling effort, would have 'dried up at the fountain.'"

There can be no doubt but that juvenile crime is on the increase, not only in our own State but elsewhere. The superintendent of the House of Correction, Chicago, has had committed to his keeping during the past year the extraordinary number of 1,335 criminals under twenty-one years of age, being about thirty per cent of the entire number imprisoned. His experience with this class renders his opinions worthy of note. In his report just issued the following language occurs in relation to juvenile crime: "The causes which produce criminals are not checked; juvenile depravity and crime seem on the increase; the idle and vicious youth of our cities are becoming more numerous; the adult lawbreaker more expert and less fearful of the consequences of crime; and the efforts of police authorities to control the dens of the wicked and their habitués, are more easily thwarted than they formerly were. Alms-houses are receptacles for babes who grow up in atmospheres containing only poisonous influences, and prisons are useful only as places for temporary detention, and the surroundings of the homes of thousands of our youth can only generate immorality, and immorality can only lead onward to a criminal life."

It would seem that all legitimate measures in the way of prevention should be exercised against this increase of crime.

If the parent is not able to maintain the child and it comes upon the public for support, the public should see that it has at once the best possible advantages, and that it is placed under wholesome and regenerating influences. As bearing upon this point, the president of the last State convention of the Superintendents of the Poor of this State expressed the following views:

"The idea of placing children under influences that shall prevent them leading that life of pauperism and crime, to which their parents were addicted, is a most important consideration. The project will no doubt meet with great opposition from the community in which they reside. They will think it hard to separate the mother from the child. It is hard; but in cases where the parents have become demoralized, it is not only right, but it is the duty of the overseer to take the children away from such parents, and to place them where they shall receive proper instruction. The children have no chance of ever making themselves self-supporting or of being a credit to society, and the only way they can be saved and brought to lead lives of usefulness is by taking them away from their debased parents. Instead of being a hardship, it is really a benefit to the children, as well as to the parent. We should consider it our duty to separate such families as would, if left together, become an injury to society."

As showing, also, the importance that is attached to giving dependent and neglected children the best possible advantages, we quote the following from the last report of the Board of State Charities of Massachusetts:

"These children ought to know the influence of good homes. Their moral and spiritual natures ought to be encouraged to growth. They deserve something better than the alms-house can give them, a fairer chance to make of themselves worthy and respectable men and women. What individuals can do for them, what the State can do for them, should be done with thankful alacrity, to the end that vice and crime may be decreased; to the end that pauperism and its weighty burdens may be reduced; to the end that these little ones may have such an opportunity for life here and hereafter, as is the right of every human being."

The Superintendent of the New York House of Refuge maintains that, if parents allow their children to grow up in ignorance of legal, moral and religious obligations, and they become depredators upon society, and are sent to a reformatory, the parents, if they are able, should be obliged to pay for their maintenance while there.

On this point the Board of State Commissioners of Michigan, in their report for 1874–5, recommend "that some provision be made by which parents who are abundantly able to do so may be required to pay for the maintenance of their children while kept therein (in the reformatory) * * * that quite a number of persons 'well-to-do' have had sons in the establishment, clothed, boarded and schooled, for a considerable time wholly at the expense of the State."

In carrying on the work of juvenile reformation, it is believed, that an examination of the cottage system as practiced in the Ohio Reform School might lead to modifications in our own system of reform.

The legislation of last winter, relating to pauper and destitute children in poor-houses, recognized the principle of disassociating children from the adult pauper class. The same principle in relation to criminals had been previously adopted, it being illegal to commit children to penitentiaries and prisons, and yet it is believed that in almost all the penitentiaries in the State a considerable number of persons under sixteen years of age will be found. In jails and lock-ups children are also brought into association with criminals, and it is believed great evils have grown out of the practice. In the last very suggestive report of the Prison Association of New York will be found many interesting facts bearing on this subject. During the visitation to Hart's Island, made in October last, boys — mere children — were observed emerging from the hold of the steamer as it lay at the pier, in company with a gang of sixty criminals. It was sad to see this desecration of childhood by such ignoble associations. Public sentiment alone, without any legal enactment, should be sufficient to remedy this evil. At all events there can be no question but that the law should be so rigidly enforced as to bring about an absolute separation of children from adult criminals.

At the congress of the various State Boards of Charities, held last May in Detroit, after a full and interesting discussion bearing directly upon this subject, the following resolution was passed by that body.

"*Resolved,* That this conference recommend that the various State Boards of Charities use their influence to bring about such legislation in their respective States, as shall cause dependent children to be removed from county poor-houses, city alms-houses and common jails, and from all association with adult paupers and criminals, and placed in families, asylums, reformatories or other appropriate institutions."

There has already been much accomplished through a growing intelligence among the people in the way of separating youth from evil associations and surroundings. By the wise action of the legislature last winter just referred to, sustained by the hearty co-operation of the benevolent, there has been removed during the past year from the poor-houses and alms-houses of this State over 1,000 children, and these have been placed in families or asylums, and thus brought under good influences and Christian teachings. So great and intelligent a reform in view of its tremendous consequences, may well be regarded as a cause for congratulation by a whole people.

It seems quite fitting that this important act of the people, which emancipates such an army of little children from the degrading bondage of poor-house life, should be inaugurated upon the first day of the year commemorating the centennial birth of our national liberty.

Industrial Schools.

Distinct from asylums and reformatories is another class of benevolent agencies known as day homes or industrial schools, of which those under the patronage of the American Female Guardian Society, and the Children's Aid Society of New York city, may be cited as prominent. These institutions come to the rescue of families liable to break down through death or sickness of one of the heads, or from other causes. In some cases it was found that the father had either died or deserted the mother. This humane provision was made available to such of these mothers as strove against becoming a public burden. The homes relieved them of their families during the day, and thus enabled them to go out to work. The children are taught such things as are in keeping with their age and sex. They acquire habits of cleanliness, and receive an industrial and moral training. In some instances *kinder-gartens* were found in connection with these institutions, which were well conducted. It is believed that the influence which they exert does not stop with the child, but is carried home with it to the parent.

Another class who are the beneficiaries of these institutions are the children of the very poor, who, owing to their ragged and dirty condition, the irregularity of their attendance, or other causes, do not find their way to public schools. They are received in these schools, washed and clothed, fed and helped along till they are able to seek after a better life. Many of these are prepared for attendance upon the public school, which is one of the aims of these organizations.

It is evident that the beneficial results to society that have grown out of the self-sacrificing work in this direction of a large number of persons, mostly benevolent ladies, is very great, and their labors are worthy of high commendation. A few illustrations of the workings of these industrial schools and day homes are given in the notes of visitation.

A very commendable feature of this work is that of teaching useful trades to young girls, many of whom have been brought up in a shiftless manner, without any knowledge of housekeeping or of any industry whatever. Pleasant rooms, with sewing machines and other facilities for working, are provided, where they may freely come and be taught under competent instructors. In this way numbers of young women are rendered independent and self-supporting, who, but for these agencies, might fall into evil ways.

Differing from these is yet another class of institutions under the charge of Roman Catholic Sisterhoods, generally designated industrial homes, where girls needing industrial training and those too old to remain any longer in asylums, are received, watched over, and kept under a certain degree of restraint until their characters have become fully formed. Meanwhile they are taught useful trades, such as dressmaking, tailoring, etc., which enables them on leaving the institution to earn for themselves a comfortable livelihood. These industrial homes also receive and board at unremunerative rates young girls who are working in shops and stores, and who, without any homes of their own, are exposed to many dangers. Illustrations of the workings of these institutions, which, it is believed, are accomplishing much good, may be found in St. Joseph's Industrial School, New York, St. Joseph's Industrial School, Albany, and the Rochester Home of Industry.

Custodial Care of Idiots.

The need of further provision for the care of idiots has become imperative. The New York State Asylum for Idiots at Syracuse provides for the education of a limited number of teachable idiots. But as this institution was established solely for educational purposes, it does not provide a permanent home or asylum, and therefore does not meet all the requirements. It contains at this time a large number of those who have received all the benefits the institution can confer. They have been educated to the extent of their capabilities, and trained to habits of industry. Those who would have been little better than dumb animals in their neglected condition in the poor-houses, under competent supervision, are now capable of contributing in a great measure to their own support. Having elevated them to this point, it seems unwise to return them to the poor-house, or cast them adrift upon the country. The consequence in either case would be burdensome and hurtful to society. A considerable number of these are females who have attained to womanhood, and who, while fully developed physically, have not sufficient intelligence to protect their persons against the unprincipled of the opposite sex. Numbers of the idiotic and feeble-minded class may now be seen in the poor-houses of the State. Some are about to become mothers of illegitimate children, and these, while promising to be prolific, will never bear any other than illegitimate, and, probably, defective offspring. Some of them are quite young persons. The poor-house system is such that the consequences alluded to are almost inevitable while they remain its inmates, and still more certain if they are turned adrift. In fact, the poor-house is their general asylum, not only during the period of child-birth, but also while nursing their children. The only shelter open to them now is the poor-house. The question presents itself to all thoughtful minds, is this the provision which, from an economic, not to say a humanitarian standpoint, ought to be made for this class?

From the system in operation in older countries for the care of idiots, it has been ascertained that it is possible not only to have institutions providing all reasonable comforts, but which shall at the same time be largely sustained out of the earnings of the inmates; in other words, this class of dependents can be made producers.

The need of further provision by the State for idiots is fully appreciated by those whose relations to this class of persons render them familiar with their wants. At the last State Convention of the Superintendents of the Poor the following resolution was adopted.

"*Resolved,* That in our opinion, the accommodations provided by the State for the care of idiots are inadequate to present and prospective needs, and that the interests of humanity would be promoted by effecting a classification between the teachable and unteachable classes, and that we recommend our committee on legislation, conjointly with the State Board of Charities, to bring this subject to the attention of the legislature."

If those of the class referred to who have already received the benefits of the institution at Syracuse, and who are now held there for humane reasons, could be provided for in a custodial institution such as we have mentioned, their place might be supplied by those who are awaiting admittance.

Family Life.

While the present condition of society renders the existence of public asylums for orphan and destitute children necessary, the opinion is ventured that the true home for the child is the family, and that the ultimate aim of all asylum work should be to establish the child in family relations as soon as possible, and further, that the nearer the asylum system can, in its workings, be made approximate to the family system, the more satisfactory will be the results. In smaller asylums this ideal can be more nearly approached, and in some of these, it was found to be almost reached. In a few, the superintendent and his wife were found assuming the office of father and mother, while the older boys and girls were the elder brothers and sisters of the younger children. All ate at the same table, partook of the same food, the children dressing as comfortably as the heads of the establishment. The employes of the house were selected with special reference to their fitness as associates for children, and the evenings were spent in amusements and devotions, as a family would spend theirs. In those asylums where the Sisters work with the children, and are their constant companions, thus naturally assuming the relation of mothers, where they are the repositories of their confidences and their sympathizers in little trials, the family idea is outlined.

Good Housekeeping.

It is believed that the domestic departments of an asylum must be under the charge of females to be satisfactory. Good housekeeping cannot be maintained without them, and while the presence of the sex refines and subdues the ruder natures of the boys, the effect upon them of good housekeeping is elevating, to say the least. The lad who grows up without it, loses much. Its good effects, even in reformatories, may be seen in Father Hines' institution at Buffalo, where the Sisters of St. Joseph making their home in the St. Joseph's Asylum, upon the opposite side of the street from St. John's Protectory, pass over and assume charge of its domestic affairs in the morning, returning at night. In this way, perfect housekeeping is maintained, and that sweetness and home-like charm which only attends the presence of woman, is secured.

Out-door Employment.

In a few asylums it has been found that the custom prevails of permitting the children to have little flower-beds of their own, which they cultivate during the summer. The children are furnished with seeds in the spring, which they plant. They are instructed how to water and care for the flowers, and preserve the seeds which they yield. Some of these garden plats were quite unique, and will be found described in this report. In other instances the boys are allowed to have little patches of ground in the garden, and are permitted to plant and grow vegetables. A spirit of emulation often attends the work. This employment, so far, at least, as it relates to flowers, not only cultivates a love of the beautiful, but inculcates habits of regularity, and ideas of order and perseverance.

NOTES ON INSTITUTIONS VISITED.

The following sketches or notes on institutions visited are arranged alphabetically, both as to locality and as to the institutions in each city or town.

ALBANY ORPHAN ASYLUM—"THE SOCIETY FOR THE RELIEF OF ORPHAN AND DESTITUTE CHILDREN IN THE CITY OF ALBANY."

Albany.

This organization, generally known as the Albany Orphan Asylum, was incorporated by special act of the Legislature March 30, 1831. The asylum building is situated on Western avenue, corner of Robin street. It overlooks the city park, and is surrounded by patriarchal trees. The lawn is neatly trimmed and intersected with cleanly-kept graveled walks. The grounds present to the eye, on entering them, the appearance of a home of wealth and taste.

The building, which is situated upon a tract containing four and a half acres, is of brick, three stories high above the basement. It is heated by stoves, lighted with gas, and supplied with water from the city. All the rain water is saved, filtered and distributed through the house from tanks in the attic, and is used for drinking and domestic purposes. The bathing facilities are ample. The ceilings are high, and the ventilation is in part effected by wall flues.

The financial affairs of the institution are controlled by a board of eleven managers. At the date of visitation, September 9, it was under the immediate superintendence of Rev. Timothy Fuller, who had held the position for the past ten years, and who had also had much previous experience in the care of children. He is assisted by his son, acting as clerk and steward, and by his wife and daughter, the latter assuming a large share of the responsibility of the domestic affairs. The educational department is under the charge of a lady of experience and culture, aided by a female assistant. The superintendent employs a gardener, two cooks, a laundress, and two seamstresses.

In answer to inquiries, the following information was furnished regarding the institution: "Destitute children of both sexes, without distinction, are received between the ages of three and twelve years, occasionally at two and a half years old. The average age when admitted is about seven years. A large number of the children we have now were sent here by the Overseers of the Poor. They come in a very destitute condition, showing previous neglect. Some of them are partially supported by parents or friends. They generally pay from one dollar to one dollar and a half per week toward their maintenance and care. For the childen sent by the Overseers of the Poor the Board of Supervisors contribute a dollar and a half per week toward the support of each."

The routine of the day, etc., is given as follows: "The children rise at six o'clock. Chapel services take place at half-past six, conducted by the superintendent. Breakfast is had at seven o'clock. After breakfast the chamber-work is done, the children assisting. At half-past eight the bell rings to prepare for school, which commences at nine o'clock. The hour for dinner is twelve, after which the children play until half-past one o'clock, when school commences, and is kept until half-past three. Supper is served at half-past five o'clock, and the children retire at eight in summer, and at half-past seven in winter. Religious exercises are held before retiring.

"On Sunday the children attend the different Protestant churches in the city upon invitations. Sabbath-school is held in the assembly room of the asylum at three o'clock.

"The larger boys aid in the garden during the summer, and the girls are taught to sew and to help in general housework."

In regard to discipline the superintendent says: "With most children nothing more is required beyond depriving them of play. Sometimes we tell a boy to stand aside and put his hands up to his face. Other boys are different. They have been so brought up that something else is required. I deal with them according to my best judgment. In the case of most children we never have had to resort to severe measures. In exceptional cases only we have recourse to corporal punishment."

Regarding the time spent in the institution, and methods of disposing of the children, the superintendent says: "Children stay here a longer or shorter period, according to circumstances; sometimes three or four years; sometimes but a year. The law does not allow their being bound out until they are eight years old. We place them out by adoption, however, whenever an opportunity offers. The children of soldiers stay longer. We have now perhaps six or eight of this class.

"Girls are bound out to remain until they are eighteen. It is stipulated that they shall have a good common-school education, shall be instructed in housekeeping, and shall attend church and Sabbath-school. They are allowed to be taken a month on trial. Parties applying must bring references that are entirely satisfactory as to their ability, character, etc. Farmers taking boys are required to give them a common-school education, instruct them in farming, send them to church and Sabbath-school, and at the age of twenty-one give them two suits of clothes and $100 in money. If at the age of eighteen they prefer to learn a trade, they forfeit the $100.

"Persons taking children are required to report to us every six months. We have a great many applications for children. We always have a large number of applicants' names in advance upon our books. When a child is ready to go out we select from among those who have applied the very best place for the child. I say to the person who comes as an applicant, 'we cannot let you have a child simply because you want one; if we are convinced that you can furnish a good home for the child we will let you have one.' A great many of our children turn out well. Some have turned out badly, but such are mostly those who have gone back to their friends. One or two of our boys have graduated from a medical college. A gentleman from Schoharie county who called here for a boy said that one of our lads had become one of the most prosperous men in that county."

Mr. Fuller says in a note received since the visitation: "Since you were here several children have gone to homes where we know they will be well cared for. One, a bright little girl, has been adopted by a wealthy gentleman residing in one of the western cities, who takes her as his own, having no children, and will give her every advantage, as well as a good Christian home. This little girl is a very encouraging case, as but a few months since from the character of her surroundings her prospects were of the very darkest. I have just learned that two of our girls who were taken by parties living in —— have recently married 'well-to-do' farmers living in the neighborhood of their adopted homes. I have lately met several young men who were once inmates of the asylum. One is doing an extensive business for a leading railroad company. Another holds a position of trust in a large business house in ——, and another is doing a good business in dry-goods in one of the eastern cities. It is very encouraging to meet with such of these as I do frequently, who refer to the time when they had no home but the asylum, and express their gratitude for the care and attention there given them.

"It is customary for such children as can do so, to return here at Christmas time, sometimes spending a few days in visiting, upon which occasion a Christmas tree is provided and presents distributed. This occasion is counted on long before."

It is not known how many children have received the benefits of this institution since its beginning, but the number is large. The number received during the five years from 1870 to 1874 inclusive was 312.

The number of inmates at date of visitation was in excess of convenient accommodations. It was stated that the passage of the law last winter, requiring children to be removed from poor-houses, had created an increased demand upon the institution. The board of managers, composed of energetic men, had asserted, however, with commendable spirit, that "as it had been truly said of the past, that no destitute child had ever been turned away from the doors of the asylum, so it should be declared of the future that none should be refused admittance." Plans were at once prepared for an additional building to be erected in the rear of the asylum, increasing its accommodations from 120 to 200 inmates. At the time of our visit the foundation of this addition was laid, and since then the building has been fully completed.

The boys in the school-room were dressed uniformly in gray cloth pants and linen jackets. Their hair was cut close. The girls were all dressed alike and wore aprons with sleeves. The hair of each was nicely arranged with combs or ribbons. The children were bright in appearance, their manner orderly, and they displayed a spirit of emulation in the school. As we entered the large class-room, the children were singing "Sparkle, sparkle, water pure." As the moral of the rhyme was to inculcate personal cleanliness, they seemed particularly happy in realizing that they were clean themselves.

The teacher said: "Last winter I had a class that could work every example in the higher arithmetic, while some made a good deal of proficiency in grammar, United States history, etc. Children sometimes come here ten and eleven years old, who do not know their letters." It was stated that no aid was received from the Board of Education in sustaining the school.

In the assembly room was a juvenile library of about 200 volumes. In one of the rooms of the house was a large closet completely filled with children's toys.

Miss Fuller says: "We try to inculcate in the children a love of order, and the principle of preserving property. This is a difficult task. All the children are numbered, and their clothes are numbered the same, for which they are held responsible. The clothes are marked to denote whether they are to be used in the school-room, play-room, or elsewhere. We have a thorough system of discipline, and follow it up day by day. We find that if we make a rule, we must adhere to it."

The children marched in to dinner before we left the house. The following grace was said at table, by the children: "For these refreshments and every mercy, O God, we bless and praise Thy holy name, through Jesus Christ our Lord. Amen." The children had for dinner, corned beef, potatoes, green sweet corn, and each a roasted apple. It was stated that pears were sometimes substituted for apples, and that the children have cake for supper twice a week. Syrup is sometimes substituted for butter at this meal. The family partake of their meals at the same hour as the children, in an apartment opening into the dining-room of the latter.

The asylum has separate play-rooms for the boys and girls, each communicating with play yards. The yards are of good size, and near the center of one stands a great tree, the branches of which seemed to stretch protectingly over the children. The central portion of the yard is covered with fine gravel, which was raked very smooth. This yard is inclosed with a board fence. Around its outer limit is a border of rich soil, and this was spaced off into little flower beds. These were filled with flowers; some were fenced with palings about six inches high, made of shingles split and pointed. Several of these little gardens had arbors made of light stuff, over which grew a profusion of morning glories. In the bowers were toy houses and toy garden implements. These little gardens were kept with surprising neatness, and we were assured that no serious differences occurred as to boundary rights. The children were taught to save the seeds that grew in these gardens, and put them in little bags for the next year. Miss Fuller thinks that this employment of the little ones cultivates good taste, industrious habits, method in employment of time, and forethought. The play ground also contained croquet wickets, a little swing and a long shed for shelter in inclement weather.

Regarding the care of the sick, the matron says: "When a child is first taken sick we take it away from the other children, and place it in a room or quarantine by itself, where it is under our immediate care. It is kept here until the physician has determined the nature of its disease, and it is then transferred to a ward or apartment distinct from the common infirmary if contagious. By this method contagious diseases are checked from spreading at the outset." There were no sick children at time of visitation. It was stated that only two had died in the asylum during the past six or seven years.

The dormitories were furnished with double wooden bedsteads. The boys sleep two in a bed. Straw beds and straw bolsters and feather pillows were in use. The straw, it was stated, is changed twice a year, at which time the ticks are washed. A grown person sleeps in each dormitory with the children.

The clothes rooms and dressing rooms were well filled with clothing, which was very tastefully made up. The boys' Sunday suits were cut by a tailor, and thus made to fit them well. They were also given many little things which boys take pride in wearing, such as neckties and paper collars, and the more meritorious boys have white shirts with plaited bosoms to wear when they go to church.

In addition to dresses for every day wear, both in winter and summer, the girls have two other full suits, one for church and one "for out doors." In winter they wear an extra woolen balmoral, and the delicate ones are provided with knit underwear. All the hosiery is made from the same material, the girls assisting in the work. Their dresses were generally attractive in color, especially those for church and holiday wear. The hats were trimmed with pretty ribbons and flowers, and corresponded with their dresses. Most if not all of the girls are supplied with such little accessories to dress as ribbons, gloves, fans and parasols. All the children are furnished with handkerchiefs. They take care of their own clothing.

The girls were allowed to indulge their love for dress to some extent, which Miss Fuller stated she endeavored to temper to their condition in life. She thought in gratifying children in this way when young, and giving them at the same time good advice, their tastes could be educated, and they were less likely to indulge in an excess of finery when first becoming possessed of a little money of their own. Besides, she thinks that dressing the children in well-fitting clothes, and about as well as the children in the middle station of life are dressed, gives them self-respect.

Children on leaving are furnished with one extra complete and nicely-fitting suit, different from those worn in the asylum. That of the boys is made of all-woolen beaver cloth.

In the sewing-room were three sewing-machines. Two women are constantly employed here in doing the lighter sewing of the asylum, the heavier work being sent out of the house.

The children are never left alone. An interesting feature about the asylum was found to be that of a care-taker, in the person of a kindly-disposed elderly gentleman, who is engaged in this duty mainly through love of the children. The evidence of his kindly interest is seen in his face and manner. He watches over them when engaged in their sports, mingling with them in full sympathy with all the simple joys and trials. The superintendent says: "We have learned, after twenty years' experience, that there are many things that must be done in an institution like this that cannot be performed by servants."

About two acres of ground are under cultivation. The superintendent says: "We raise vegetables of all kinds, including potatoes, cabbages, onions, parsnips, tomatoes, squashes, green corn, etc. We have just stored in the cellar one hundred and twenty barrels of potatoes, raised upon less than an acre of land. In addition to vegetables we cultivate raspberries and strawberries, which partially supply the children's wants. Formerly the fruit was sold, but all of it is now used in the institution. We grow a few pears, as well as a good many apples, plums and cherries."

Three cows are kept on the place.

The water-closets are detached from the main building. The drainage was said to be good. The laundry is in a separate building, under which is a large cellar used for storing potatoes and other vegetables. Each bath-room contains three bathing-tubs.

At the date of October 1st there were one hundred and sixty-one boys and girls in the asylum, all from the city of Albany. Forty-five were orphans, one hundred were half-orphans, and sixteen had both parents living. Twenty-one were of native, and one hundred and forty were of foreign parents. Twenty-six were partially supported by parents or friends, one hundred and ten partially by the county, and twenty-five wholly by the institution. The number of children received during the past year was ninety-three; the number discharged, eighty-one. Of the latter nine were indentured, sixty-eight returned to parents or guardians, and one placed out by adoption.

The invested funds of the society amount to $79,963.20; its expenditures during the past year were $17,003.69; of which $1,049.48 was for buildings and improvements, and $3,500 for investment.

The asylum appeared to be doing its work thoroughly, and possesses a home-like character. It is in the immediate charge of a Christian family seemingly of peculiar adaptation to the work, whose various members have each some one of its departments to administer.

Besides the benevolent persons engaged in this work at the present day, and those who in its early history made generous sacrifices for the establishment of the institution, whose names are recorded elsewhere, there are two deserving of special mention here, which occur in the following scrap of history that has been furnished us:

In the spring of 1829 a lady imbued with strong religious feelings, was suffering from illness in the city of Albany. After becoming convalescent her friends came to read to her, and among them a young lady named Miss Eliza Wilcox, a school teacher. Among the books selected for reading was the Memoir of Ann H. Judson. As the two friends read and listened, their spirits were stirred with a desire to labor in the Master's cause, and the question was asked what can we do? Miss Wilcox decided to go to India and engage in missionary work there, and offered her services to this end to the American Baptist Mission to Burmah. They were declined, as none but married ladies at that time were permitted to enter upon the work. Meanwhile the warm heart and active brain of the invalid, whose name was Mrs. Orissa Healy, were devising work in another sphere. Looking upon her own little family of four children, she thought, what will become of them if I am taken away, and turning her thought to others already thus bereft, she said to her friend, "Why should we desire to cross the ocean for mission work while there is plenty around us at our own door?" And in that sick chamber was first conceived the idea of opening a home for orphan and destitute children in Albany. On her recovery she submitted her plans to others, which being approved, a small cottage in the suburbs was rented for the purpose of opening the asylum, a benevolent deacon of the church becoming responsible for the rent.

In the meantime Mrs. Healy's friend had been to New York and visited asylums there for the purpose of acquiring a knowledge of their management. She gave up her school upon her return, and these two ladies entered upon their work. Some simple articles of furniture were supplied, and the day following the opening of the house for children one boy was received — not a very promising subject; the next day a little girl came in. For a week or more these constituted the entire household. In the following April seventy orphan and destitute children had been received into the house. At this period several charitable citizens of Albany joined in an enterprise to secure for the work a property known as Gallup's Hotel. This was used about three years before the present site was secured. During this time these worthy ladies modestly toiled on, one as matron and the other as teacher, for four years without salary or reward of any kind except such as came in the form of blessings from those ready to perish. After Mrs. Healy had established the asylum upon a permanent basis, she removed to Buffalo, where she spent some twelve years in similar philanthropic work. The Albany Orphan Asylum having become somewhat deteriorated in 1845, her services were secured, and she held the position of matron until 1853, when she resigned and removed to New York. This noble lady is since deceased, but the asylum she founded still prospers in its good work, yet her more enduring monument may be seen in the characters she formed.

The Children's Friend Society.

Albany.

The objects of this association are "to gather into schools, vagrant children, who, from the poverty or vice of their parents, are unable to attend the public schools, and such as gain their livelihood by begging or pilfering; to give them ideas of moral and religious duty, to instruct them in the elements of learning, and in the different branches of industry, and thus enable them to obtain an honest and honorable support, and to become useful and respectable members of society. The ages of such children must be within the following limits, viz.: the girls, from four to sixteen; the boys, from four to seven."

Like most charitable work, this was begun by the efforts of a few ladies, to lift from degradation neglected children. A school was opened in Rensselaer street on the first of December, 1856, and the work was there begun. The aspect of things at this early beginning is thus referred to: "Those present, on that piercing winter's morning, can never forget the appearance of those wretched little objects, shivering in their rags, covered with filth, repulsive in looks, and barbarous in manners. Some remember very distinctly the heart-sickening feelings of despair, that irresistibly welled up as they vainly attempted by kindness and persuasion to tame the half-civilized little beings that gathered around them. Some can recall the hopeless, helpless look of one of the ladies, as she said: 'It is utterly vain and useless to attempt the reformation of such creatures.'"

The accommodations in Rensselaer street being found inconvenient, a building on Ferry street was procured and occupied on the 5th of January, 1857. Here again difficulties on the score of proximity to the river, and liability to suffer from the rise of the water presented themselves, and it was deemed necessary to make another change to 48 Philip street, and here the society worked during 1857. The report of what was accomplished that year, despite of financial embarrassments, is thus stated: "The whole number received into the school, during the year, has been 491. The average daily attendance upon the school, 63. The number of meals given, 16,443. The number of pairs of shoes distributed, 197. The number of garments distributed, 435. These, under the direction of the ladies, have all been made by the children. In this connection, we would ask if, setting aside the intellectual and moral advantages, there is any other way equally cheap, pleasant and convenient, by which an equal amount of physical comfort can be bestowed? Nearly 17,000 days of warmth, quiet, order and neatness, and the same number of substantial and abundant meals for poor little neglected suffering children; children who, but for this institution, would have spent just so many days of filth, negligence and exposure to every temptation and absolute want. Nor must we omit to mention another means of doing good through the instrumentality of the school. Twenty-nine girls from 10 to 16 years of age, have been provided with situations as servants in respectable families, and two have been received as permanent members of kind, Christian households."

Still growing, and every change being an advance on the previous one, the society, in May, 1858, removed to a house at 81 Hamilton street, which was purchased and offered to the managers at a rent within their means by a benevolent citizen of Albany.

A good bath-ròom and other conveniences were fitted up in this building, adding to the health and comfort of the inmates.

It is asserted quite truthfully by the ladies engaged in this work, that "there can be no greater charity than to rescue from their abodes of poverty and misery, those poor children whose only heritage is suffering and crime; to withdraw them day after day from the pernicious influences by which they are surrounded; to warm, clothe, and feed the body, to instruct and enlighten the mind; to touch the heart, to point and lead the soul heavenward; to prepare them for a happy and useful life; to fit them for an eternity of blessedness."

In the winter of 1861, the society obtained a grant from the legislature of $1,500, and in 1863, the house on Hamilton street was purchased for $3,500.

The work of the society still continued to prosper, and in January, 1868, another school was opened at 16 Canal street. This building is the property of a gentleman deeply interested in the work, who prepared it for the use of the society, and has generously allowed it to be occupied free of rent.

The society was incorporated February 4, 1860. Its affairs are controlled by a board of lady managers. The immediate charge of its domestic concerns and of the schools are committed to matrons and teachers.

The daily routine of the two schools is stated to be as follows: "The pupils in the principal department are required to study and recite every morning in each of the following branches, spelling, reading, writing, arithmetic and geography. At 12 o'clock the scholars are quietly dismissed to the dining-room, where they receive a good substantial dinner, and are then at liberty to play until 1 o'clock. In the afternoon the girls are assembled in one room, and instructed in that very essential branch for women, needle-work, while the boys have slate and black-board exercises in arithmetic and writing. After a short recess, at 3 o'clock, they are all assembled together and are instructed in catechism, singing, blackboard exercises and arithmetic, or have some other profitable exercise. For good conduct and correct recitations the scholars receive marks, a certain number of which entitles a child to receive a garment, so that after attending the school for some time the children are comfortably clad. Two of the older girls are chosen each week to assist the matron in cleaning the house and preparing the meals, and are thus taught housework in a most thorough manner."

It appears from the report of the Secretary, Miss Russell, that, during the year preceding the last annual report of the society, the total number of children under instruction in the two industrial schools was 323; average attendance, 105; scholars left to enter service, 18; garments made by the children and distributed among them, 269.

The report of the treasurer, Miss Agnes Pruyn, shows that during the year preceding, October 1, 1875, the total expenditures were $2,670.60. The society has an invested fund of $3,400.

The house on Hamilton street is a goodly-sized brick dwelling. It was found at the time of visitation to be in a neatly kept condition. It contains the usual accessories which such an institution is supposed to require, including bath-room, dining-room and school-room. The latter embraces two departments, connected by folding doors, and is furnished with piano, little benches, blackboards, etc. A portrait of Mrs. Samuel Pruyn, the worthy founder of the school, gives increased interest to the room.

Child's Hospital.

Albany.

Among the numerous deserving charities that adorn the city of Albany, the Child's Hospital is so unpretentious that but for the odor of its sweet charity, like the arbutus blossoms hid away among the leaves in the forest, it would be passed by unnoticed.

The hospital is under the charge of Miss Alice Lea, a lady whose work is purely a labor of love, her services being, we were informed, entirely voluntary. An experienced nurse, an assistant, and a cook, are the only employes of the establishment.

Children of all denominations and of both sexes are received. No charge is made for the benefits conferred, the medical attendance, board and lodging being free.

A visitation was made on the 11th of September, at which time the neatness and bright loving atmosphere in which the sufferers were found awakened grateful sentiments toward those engaged in this noble work. The ages of the children appeared to range between nine months and ten years. The beds on which they lay were of the simple iron pattern, each having two mattresses — the under one of straw, the upper one of hair. In some cases a rubber sheet was used over the mattresses. The wards were so full of toys and pictures, and the children seemed so absorbed in them as to have forgotten their sufferings. Some of the cases were quite interesting. One was a little boy from Cohoes, a bright, intelligent child of about five years. He was suffering with a paralyzed leg. His parents belong to the working class. In the girls' ward was a little German girl, seven years old, also suffering from paralysis. She had never walked. The reason assigned was the lack of proper food in the wretched home from which she came. Through careful nursing and nutritious diet she had so far recovered as to be able to put on her clothes. Two little girls were suffering with hip disease ; one could go on crutches ; the other was lying in bed, supported by a frame under her pillow, and playing with a box of block toys. A distressing case was that of a little girl who was suffering from a kick inflicted by her inhuman step-father. For years her knee had been bent across her stomach. She was comfortably supported in bed, and was engaged in playing with toys, her limb being adjusted by a cord and pully contrivance at the foot of the bed. Hopes were entertained of restoring the limb to its normal position. A number of the inmates, we learned, had been injured by lack of food. "Two little boys," the nurse declared, "were so weak when they came that they were unable to sit up in the daytime." We found these playing in the woodshed. A little baby, nine months old, it was said, had been fed excessively with morphine by its depraved mother. "The child was," says the nurse, "the most deplorable object I ever saw. Now she is doing nicely. She gets good beef tea, and bread and milk. She was looked upon as a hopeless case when she came here. Her lower limbs were almost paralyzed."

The upper floor of the house contains the boys' ward, the girls' ward, and the nursery ward, with nurses' room adjoining. On the first floor are the reception room, a spare ward, and the operating room.

Three little boys were in a shed at work with tools, and practicing at carpentering. The youngest, six years old, had an injury of the spine; his brother had a withered leg. Many other cases awakening sympathy were encountered, all of whom were the subjects of tender Christian care. The nurse remarked "that cheerfulness and good food does more for children than doctors and medicine."

Some of the children in the hospitals seemed to have more than ordinary intelligence, and in view of this fact, and that of the utter neglect which they must experience if left at home, and the worse than neglect if left in a poor-house, the existence of such an asylum for their care as the Child's Hospital must be a cause of gratification. It is a charity that must commend itself to the public, and its sphere of usefulness should not be limited for want of liberal support.

The House of Shelter.

Albany.

This institution was organized March 9, 1868, and incorporated January 4, 1869. It was at first located at 49 Hudson street. Subsequently it occupied a building 56 Howard street. December 30, 1872, it removed to the new building which it at present occupies, corner of Wendell and Howard streets. Although not coming strictly within the scope of this report, it is included in view of the work that it has accomplished in rescuing children from courses of infamy. Within the past two years about twenty girls under sixteen years of age have received the benefits of its Christian ministrations.

In regard to its origin it is stated that, for some two years previous, several ladies of the city were impressed with the necessity for such a shelter, and were burdened with its responsibility, until through their earnest and prayerful endeavors, a house was secured and the work begun.

The views by which its founders were governed are stated to be as follows: They believed that "Most humanitarian and benevolent enterprises originate in Christianity: that they are the exponent of Christian love and zeal; that little has ever been accomplished to elevate our race save by the influences of Christ's religion, and the direct or reflex power of the Cross. The establishment of this home for the fallen is regarded as the fruit of a consecration to Christ and His work." In regard to these the managers say, they "have been for long periods members of our sheltered family, most of them born under the shadow of a great woe and a greater wrong. In their helplessness and unconsciousness of their defrauded inheritance, they have appealed very touchingly to our sympathy and watchful care."

The new house of shelter contains twenty-one sleeping rooms, two matron's rooms, two sick rooms, two bath rooms, a large work-room, a laundry, a kitchen, a dining-room and two parlors. This building, with the lot upon which it stands, cost $20,000.

The chief industrial feature of the institution is a laundry in successful operation on the premises.

From the last annual report of the society the following statistics are given in relation to the work of the two preceding years:

Number admitted for the first time	84
Re-admitted	10
Sent to situations in good families	27
At boarding school	1
Married	4
Returned to parents	8
Sent to alms-house hospital	1
Sent to the house of refuge	2
Given over to the justice of police	2
Gone back to their former lives, or lost to our knowledge of them,	27

Present number of inmates in the Shelter:

Adults	20
Infants	5

The total expenditures of the society during the year ending October 1, 1875, were $3,300.

The financial affairs of the Shelter are controlled by a board of gentlemen, managers, and an associate board of ladies direct its internal workings.

It is believed that this eminently Christian work is efficiently carried on, and with good results.

Orphan Home of St. Peter's Church.

Albany.

This is an institution for girls largely supported by St. Peter's Church. Its affairs are administered by a board of lady managers, of which the rector of St. Peter's Church is the president. The asylum is located at No. 1 Pine street, and is under the immediate charge of Mrs. Harriet C. Shanxby, matron. One female assistant is employed. The premises occupied by the Home are owned by the trustees of the Albany Juvenile Retreat, who have given the use of the building for this charitable purpose.

Children are received from three to eight years of age. There were twenty inmates on the day of visitation — September 11th — eight orphans and twelve half-orphans, all except one supported by the asylum. The number of children received during the year was thirteen. The number discharged was nine. Four were returned to parents or guardians and two were placed out to service.

The matron says: "We would rather take full orphans than simply destitute children, but circumstances determine this. When a mother comes whose husband has deserted her and brings her children to us, in such case we take the children. We have a committee charged with the receiving of children. The applications are referred to this committee, and they decide who are to be received. The managers intend hereafter to keep the girls longer, and not put them out so young as they have been doing. Girls going away and coming back again bring with them a great deal that is not good for the Home. It is intended to keep the children until the age of fourteen, and then put them in the families of members of the Protestant Episcopal Church."

Several of the Home girls, the matron says, "are now living in the families of prominent citizens in the city. One has lived six years in a minister's family. They go out mostly as servants, having been previously trained to fill such positions."

The school hours are from ten to half-past twelve. "We teach," the matron says, "all kinds of housework. We change the girls' work every week. We teach the children cooking, but we cannot expect to make them first-class cooks. We bake our own bread."

In regard to discipline the matron remarks: "I am very strict, but I do not punish unless it is necessary. I make the children do their work without any trouble, because they obey me from love."

The house is heated by furnace, lighted with gas and supplied with city water. It was formerly a private mansion, and seems to be tolerably well adapted for its present use. It is arranged as follows: The basement contains kitchen and dining-room, the first floor reception-room and play-room; the second floor matron's room, nursery and bath-room, and the third floor dormitories, etc.

The dining-room was furnished with benches, tables and a little table with baby chairs. The matron dines with the little ones, eating the same food. This was a most gratifying feature of the house, and no doubt accounts for the ease with which discipline is maintained. The school-room is small. The children looked neat and clean, and their clothes were in good repair. The ladies' committee, we were informed, make their garments. One death, and that from whooping-cough, had occurred during the year.

The school on the premises hitherto has been taught in turn by young ladies of the congregation of St. Peter's Church. The managers are now intending to hire a teacher.

The dormitories were furnished with single iron bedsteads and straw beds. The bath-room contained little bags for brushes and combs, one for each girl. The house seemed to be well managed, and the influences to which the children were subjected appeared to be highly beneficial. It is to be regretted that the benefactions of the Home cannot be extended to a larger number. It appears from the last report of the managers that several applications during the year have been denied for want of room. The report of the treasurer, Mrs. John Taylor, shows that the society has no invested funds. Its total expenditures during the past year were $1.270.15.

The St. Vincent's Orphan Asylum Society in the City of Albany.

Albany.

This society was incorporated by special act of the Legislature, chapter 152, Laws of 1849. Under its auspices the following institutions are conducted: St. Vincent's Female Orphan Asylum, 106 Elm street; St. Joseph's Industrial School, 261 North Pearl street; St. Vincent's Male Orphan Asylum, Western avenue.

St. Vincent's Female Orphan Asylum.

Albany.

This institution is located at 106 Elm street, on an elevated site, with pleasant surroundings. The building stands about one hundred feet from the street, and the sloping lawn of green turf is tastefully laid out, with well-kept graveled walks. From the upper windows an extended view is obtained of the beautiful valley of the Hudson.

The building is two stories high, with basement and mansard roof in addition. The main edifice, which is of brick, was formerly a spacious and elegant private residence. To this a large wing has been added in a corresponding style of architecture.

The institution is under the immediate charge of the Roman Catholic Order of the Sisters of Charity, Sister Valentine being the Superior, with seven Sisters to assist her in the work.

This orphan asylum was opened in 1845, in the three-story brick building situated on North Pearl, near Lumber street. It was then intended to accommodate about sixty children.

Sister Lucy Ignatius Guiron, and three other Sisters of Charity, from St. Joseph's House, Emmittsburgh, Maryland, took charge of the institution. After the cholera of 1854 the number of orphans increased so rapidly that it became necessary to build an addition, which was completed in 1855. Since that time about one hundred and twelve orphans have been annually cared for in the institution.

In 1865 the house on Pearl street was taken for an industrial school, and the small children were moved to the large building on the corner of North Ferry street and Broadway, where they remained till 1869, when they took possession of their present home on Elm street.

From the commencement till 1860 the asylum was exclusively supported by voluntary contributions, fairs, and by semi-annual collections of the several parish churches. In 1860 the Board of Supervisors began to allow something toward the support of the children sent from the alms-house, since which time annual appropriations have been made toward the support of such children as become public dependents; at the present time, the sum fixed for such is $6 per month each.

At date of visitation, September 10th, there were one hundred and twenty-nine inmates.

The Sister, in expressing her disapproval of putting children out from asylums at too early an age, said: "Too much seems to be expected of them. We know that they have a great many faults, and that we must bear with them. But the people of the world have so many troubles and cares of their own, that they do not have sufficient patience with them. With my experience, and I have been for the last forty years engaged in this work, having spent ten years here, I find that even in good families there is this same difficulty.

"I am most grateful to God for enabling us to establish our Industrial School. We certainly have saved a great many by this means. Our practice is to keep the girls until they are fourteen, and then send them to the Industrial School to learn sewing, where they remain till they are eighteen or twenty years old. I think the Industrial School is the making of them. A girl needs a mother's care more after twelve years of age than at any other time."

The girls are taught to be saving and economical while in the institution, and this has a good effect on them after leaving. In reference to this the Sister remarks: "Many of our girls after they leave bring us their money to save for them. I put it in the bank in their own name. One of our girls has now over $1,000 in the bank. I say to the girls when they are going away: 'Now mind, look out for a rainy day. The time may come when you will be sick.' A fondness for dress and a desire to be out at night seems to amount almost to a mania among young girls, and I fear will be the ruin of many of them."

The Sister emphasized the importance of the children remaining long enough in the asylum to receive its benefits. She says: "We think it a great charity to take these little children, who have been, as it were, abandoned, and endeavor to make them useful members of society. But if they do not remain long enough to acquire religious principles and to receive the benefits of the moral and industrial training which we give, their short stay does them little good."

The Sister spoke strongly against the influence of factory life on young girls: "So many different kinds of young people come together in factories, and the conversation there indulged in is so very unprofitable, that I think they are bad places for young girls. In such occupations they lose all that feeling of delicacy a young girl ought to have."

In order to exhibit the working of this excellent institution the daily routine is given, as follows:

"The children rise at half-past five in the summer and at six o'clock in the winter. They then wash themselves, comb their hair and gather in the play-room for morning prayers. Breakfast is served about six o'clock in summer and an hour later in winter. After breakfast, housework is in order. The bedsteads are brushed by the larger girls, assisted by the Sisters, while the smaller girls do the sweeping. About seven o'clock the bell rings for all to go to the play-room to have their heads fine-combed. This is done by three of the Sisters, and that none may be overlooked, a little girl stands by and checks off the name of each child from her list as the work is performed. The same system of checking off is practiced in bathing. This combing takes place every day of the week except Sunday. At half-past eight the school-bell rings; the children go to the dressing-room and change their aprons, thence to the school, where they remain till twelve o'clock, at which time there is a recess. Dinner is served at twelve, after which all the older girls are engaged in the kitchen and refectory for a short time. After this, until two, their time is given to recreation. A sewing class is taught from two till five, followed by half an hour's recreation. At half-past five, supper, after which recreation till half-past seven, the hour for night prayers. The children then retire for the night."

In regard to industries the Sister says: "We not only teach sewing in classes, but also teach the larger children to knit. They take a great pride in bringing me stockings which they knit during their hours of recreation. Every child who knits four pairs gets three new pairs the next winter."

The holidays, namely of Christmas and the Feast of the Holy Innocents are observed. On the former occasion, the Sister says: "We have a beautiful Christmas tree. The friends of the institution send in nice presents for the little ones, and we bring out our good things including peaches that have been preserved during the summer."

In the large play-room was a library of about a hundred volumes of juvenile reading matter. Also a glass case containing a great many dolls, and toys, said to be a source of great amusement to the little ones.

The school-room occupied by the children was found to be very pleasant, and was well lighted. The children appeared tidy and clean and dressed uniformly. They receive a plain education. Some specimens of very creditable writing was shown us. The school is sustained without aid from the city school funds.

The clothes rooms were fitted up with drawers and shelves, which were filled with warm, woolen clothing. Each child has two Sunday suits and two every-day suits, also one for midwinter of all wool, green and blue Scotch plaid. A full set of bright plaid cloaks, lined and wadded, is provided for all the girls old enough to go out. The Sister says: "All who take extra care of their dresses get new ones the following year." Their summer bonnets, of pink chambray, were very pretty, as were also their neat, white sun-bonnets. In one of the clothes rooms was a closet, designated as an apron press, containing seven sets of aprons for each child. The same room contained a stocking press. Each child has three pairs of winter stockings. A considerable number of garden hoods were shown us, which, we were informed, had been made by the children out of scraps of muslin. All the garments are made in the house, mostly by the children. They are also taught to fold and put away their own clothes. This is done with great care, as all the folds are of precisely the same width. The clothes rooms were a marvel of order and neatness, and with the large stock of comfortable clothing were suggestive of substantial comfort.

A place is set apart for the shoes of the little ones. They are kept in cases full of pigeon holes. Each hole or box is numbered to correspond with the number and name of the child, and contained a pair of shoes. Each child has two pairs, one for every-day wear and a better pair for Sundays. The Sister says: "The children never bring clothing of any value here. Sometimes we are obliged to burn up every thing that they have on them when they come."

Single iron bedsteads, with straw beds, were found to be in use in the neatly kept dormitories. In regard to beds the Sister says: "We like straw beds the best, because we can change them when desired, which we regularly do every spring and fall. I like the iron bedsteads, because they take up less room and are cleaner." Each dormitory contains a white-curtained bed, and the larger ones two, which are occupied at night by the Sisters. In one of the larger dormitories is a large press for bed clothing.

As an illustration of the scrupulous neatness and economy pervading the asylum, it may be worth while to state that the little girls are taught to save every feather that escapes while handling and brushing the pillows. These feathers are put in a little bag kept for that purpose in one of the closets. The Sister spoke strongly against the custom of letting children sleep together. She had seen much evil result from the practice.

In the infirmary were two little girls sick with consumption. The Sister says, "two died last summer. Only ten have died since we have been here, and these principally with consumption."

The lavatory is arranged for the children to wash in running water. Each child is provided with a little bag for her own comb. The bathrooms in this establishment are of ample size, and so arranged and managed as to accomplish their ends perfectly. All the children are bathed every Saturday. Three Sisters stand at the tubs to supervise the washing and bathing of the children. These tubs are elevated so that they can do their work with less fatigue than otherwise. As the children leave the bath, each one is wrapped in a sheet and passes into the dressing room adjoining. Here they are wiped, rubbed dry and dressed under the superintendence of another Sister.

The laundry is supplied with hot and cold water. The soap used is bought by the Sisters in quantities, and seasoned for economy's sake in a dry loft before using.

A small force of the larger girls are engaged in the kitchen and refectory, and are changed every month. Here they are taught to do housework. A little bread is baked by the girls to teach them how to make it. Under the bread cutter was an aperture in the table, by which all the bread crumbs were saved. These were browned in the oven in a dripping-pan, and used for thickening gravy. The kitchen as well as every department of the house is under the charge of a Sister.

The children at the time of our visit marched into the refectory, an older girl taking a younger one in charge. The larger girls sit opposite the smaller ones and cut their food for them. The children in reverent attitude, said the following grace before partaking of their meal: "In the name of the Father, of the Son and of the Holy Ghost. Bless us O Lord, and these, Thy gifts, which from Thy bounty we receive through Jesus Christ, Our Lord, amen." The tables were covered with enameled cloth. The children had, with their supper, either stewed prunes or apple sauce and tea. After supper the children formed in three crescent lines on the back terrace, the larger girls forming the background. In this position they sang with peculiar sweetness several rhymes, among these were distinguished the following words:

"Singing, cheerily, cheerily, cheerily,
Clapping, merrily, merrily, merrily,
One, two, three, don't you see
Where the orphans ought to be?"

Also,

"See the neat little clock in the corner, it stands,
And points out the time with its two pretty hands."

All the children appeared bright and natural.

The whole number of children in the asylum received from 1870 to 1874, inclusive, was 146. It is not known how many were received since its organization. Of the 129 children, inmates at date of our visit, 100 were orphans, 25 were half orphans, and four had both parents living. All were thought to be of foreign parentage.

Two of the children were partially supported by parents or friends, 100 in part by the county of Albany, and 27 wholly by the institution. During the year ending September 30, 1875, eleven children were returned to parents or guardians, six were transferred to the industrial school, and four were otherwise discharged. The whole number received during the year was 23.

This asylum had a cash fund of $2,000 on October 1, 1875. Its total expenditures during the year were $8,429.24, and its present indebtedness amounts to $55,142.

It is to be regretted, in view of what is being accomplished by this institution, that it should be obliged to carry so heavy a burden of debt. Its management has been described with some minuteness, as it affords a marked illustration of the beautiful results that may be reached through devotion to a single object and by order and perfect system.

St. Joseph's Industrial School,

is located at 261 North Pearl street, in the building formerly occupied by St. Vincent's Female Orphan Asylum, which removed to Broadway in 1865. At this time twelve of the older girls from the asylum remained, and the industrial school was commenced with them. It is supplied with inmates from St. Vincent's Female Orphan Asylum, from which the girls are transferred when about fourteen or fifteen years old.

The building is of brick. It is supplied with city water, heated by furnaces and lighted by gas. It is old, and needs enlargement and repairs to adapt it to its present use.

The institution is under the charge of ten Sisters of the Order of the Sisters of Charity. Sister Bernardine Farrell is superior.

Parochial and select schools are kept in the house, in the teaching of which seven of the Sisters are engaged. There are about 120 children in the select school, and 230 in the parochial.

On the day of visitation, September 9, there were 26 of the larger girls who made their home in the house, and who were being taught fine sewing, embroidery and dress-making. They were all orphans except three.

The work-room is large and well lighted, having windows on three of its sides. The girls were ranged around the room, sitting before neat little work-stands, on each of which a white cloth was spread. There were twenty-three of these stands in all. Behind these, others were running sewing machines. The room was cheery, the lively click of the sewing machines being varied by the song of a canary in his cage. The girls were plainly but neatly dressed, and were quite tidy in appearance.

Some very fine specimens of needle-work were here shown us, all of which were being made to supply orders. A first prize medal was also shown, which had been awarded the institution for ornamental work done by the young ladies, exhibited at the State fair.

The following information was furnished by Sister Bernardine in answer to inquiries: "At the age at which we receive young girls here, they are inclined to be wild, and need further protection. It takes some time to instruct them. We teach them all kinds of plain and fancy sewing, needle-work and embroidery. All are taught to use the sewing machine. As they are sufficiently taught, we get them suitable situations. We can only accommodate twenty-six, and we could have a hundred girls if we had accommodations for them. We need an infirmary very much, having no suitable accommodations for any who may be taken sick.

"About fifty young girls have already received the benefits of the institution, and have turned out well. Some have got married and others have entered Religious Orders. The girls mostly go into families when they leave us. Some go into stores. They have all their own wages when they go out, and, in many instances, they afterward bring their money to us to be saved for them. For such we open a bank account. Formerly, when they left the asylum, every cent they earned they put on their backs; but now they have learned to be economical and save their money. Not a single case has turned out badly, so far as we know, and we think we know all their histories. The girls give satisfaction wherever they live. Ladies seek to employ our girls, and seem to prefer them to any others. They are honest, cheerful and faithful. We endeavor constantly to inculcate these virtues. They have had previous good training at the asylum, and we try to follow it up here."

As a means for looking after the girls after leaving, the Sister said: "The girls have a society called the Children of Mary, and by this means the girls here and those who have left are brought together. There are two of these societies in the house, one for the girls who do not attend school, and another for the school-girls. Another society, called the Society of the Holy Angels, comprises the children in the parish school. Each society has its own president, secretary and treasurer. It is the business of the president to look after the absent ones. The latter society meets every Sunday afternoon at two o'clock, and continues in session until half-past three. From that they go to vespers.

"Our daily routine is as follows: The girls rise at five o'clock in summer, and at half past five in winter. Morning prayers take place at six, after which we have a short meditation. Breakfast is served at half past six. Little duties in housework and recreation occupy the morning till eight o'clock, when the sewing bell rings. The girls sew until 12 o'clock, then have recreation for half an hour, after which they go to dinner. At half-past one the sewing bell again rings, and the girls sew until supper time at six o'clock. After supper, recreation and study take up the time till eight, when the bell rings to retire, and all are in bed before nine o'clock."

No domestics are employed in the institution.

There is an excellent piano in the house, on which the girls during hours of recreation amuse themselves by playing and singing.

An interesting feature of this institution is that of reading at meal times. The head of the table is occupied by the president of the Society of the Children of Mary; another officer of the society occupies the foot. One of the girls is appointed to read while the others are partaking of their meal. Each of the young ladies takes her turn in reading. One of the sisters is always present during breakfast.

The influence under which these young ladies are brought is believed to be very elevating and highly beneficial in its results. The Sisters engaged deserve better accommodations to carry on their work.

St. Vincent Male Orphan Asylum,

Is located on Western avenue, about a mile and a quarter from the city hall. It is a large, plain, four-story, brick building. In front are shade trees, and beds of flowers embellish the grounds. On the city side is an extensive garden with a pleasant vine-covered arbor, a conservatory and an abundance of fruits and flowers. It is under the immediate charge of five of the Roman Catholic Order of the Christian Brothers, of whom Brother Amphian Farrell is superintendent. The force employed by the Brothers to assist in carrying on the work of the asylum consists of a tailor, a baker, a shoemaker, and three female domestics.

The building is lighted by kerosene, and heated by stoves. Its arrangement is as follows: The basement contains kitchen, refectory, store rooms, bake house and lavatory. On the first floor are reception room, sitting room, two class rooms and the chapel. On the second floor are two dormitories, an infirmary and clothes room. The third floor is occupied with a very large dormitory, in the center of which is an open space communicating with the belfry, affording an excellent ventilation. In the belfry is hung the large bell used to arouse the inmates to their daily duties.

There are four acres of land belonging to the institution, three of which are under garden cultivation. The garden supplies cabbages, onions, parsnips, carrots, beets, squashes, tomatoes, etc. Apples are grown to some extent. Pears and plums are raised upon the place, and also raspberries for the children. A small farm is connected with the establishment, the use of which is given by the Bishop. Three farm hands are employed. Eleven milch cows are kept upon the farm which supply the house with milk. Some, besides, is sold in the city. The asylum building is designed to accommodate one hundred inmates. At date of visitation, September 10th, the number of boys was one hundred and eight. Brother Amphian says: "We have more applications for admittance than we can accommodate, and have thirty applications ahead now. Some of these have been standing since December last. We could have five hundred boys in the institution, if we had the means to take care of them."

In answer to further inquiries relating to the asylum and its inmates Brother Amphian says: "The average age of the boys is ten years. They are sent to us by the overseers of the poor. For such children we are paid $1.50 per week toward their support. Collections are made twice a year in the city to meet the additional expenses. The children are admitted upon a recommendation of the priests of the parish to which they belong, which recommendation must be certified to by Mr. Hoxsie, overseer of the poor. This precaution is taken to save us from imposition. A good many are brought to us who do not know their letters. The boys are permitted to remain till they are fourteen years old. On arriving at that age, if they have guardians they are invited to take them, and if they have not, we get places for them. We very seldom put them out before fourteen unless good places open. The guardians can take them at any time. No one is retained against his will. If a lad is a little homesick we try to keep him till he gets over it."

In regard to placing out children the Brother says: "The priests generally send persons here who want children. If the recommendations brought are not satisfactory we make further inquiries ourselves to satisfy us of the fitness of the applicant. The boys are encouraged to correspond with us after they leave here, and to visit us once a quarter. Those who reside in the city come to see us once a month, sometimes oftener. The Brothers encourage this. The children seem to know very little of the world when they go out."

In the school-room the Brothers use the wooden signal peculiar to their order. It has been in use since the time of De La Salle, the founder of the Christian Brothers, more than two hundred years ago. The following explanations of some of the signals were given: One stroke means "Look up;" two strokes, "Mistake;" three strokes, "Repeat the reading." Pointing downward, "Kneel down;" pointing upward, "Stand up," etc.

In regard to their education the Brother says: "We teach them reading, writing, arithmetic, grammar, history and singing. An examination takes place on the first of December, at which time the board of supervisors generally visit us."

"At the close of the school in July we have an exhibition, which includes exercises in singing, dialogues, declamations, etc. To this entertainment the friends of the children are invited. It is generally held out of doors when the weather is pleasant. The attendance was very large last year, larger than we have ever had before. The evening following we generally give the boys a supper. We have a Christmas tree at Christmas, and a Christmas feast for the children. We celebrate the Fourth of July and also keep Thanksgiving day, on which occasion we give the boys an extra good dinner.

"In the way of industries they are taught farming and tailoring, and do a little work about the house. There are six in the kitchen and others in the refectory a part of the day.

"Our daily routine is as follows: The larger boys rise at half-past five, the smaller ones at six o'clock. They have morning prayers in the class rooms. The larger boys stay and recite till breakfast time at seven o'clock. After breakfast they work on the farm, or about the house setting every thing in order. After dinner they go into school at one o'clock and remain, excepting two intervals of recesses, till six o'clock. The smaller boys go into school at half-past eight, attend during the day and are dismissed at half-past three, having had the usual interval for dinner and recesses. Supper takes place at six o'clock, and recreation fills up the evening. The hour for evening prayers for the little boys is half-past seven, and for the larger ones eight o'clock. All are in bed before 8:30.

"We have morning mass at seven o'clock on Sundays and Thursdays. On Sundays we have vespers at 3.30.

"We find a very good way to enforce discipline is, to deprive the boys of recreation, and while others are playing give them something to study. We very seldom find it necessary to inflict corporal punishment."

The asylum chapel is a pleasant, well-lighted room, capable of accommodating about one hundred and twenty persons. The library contains about one hundred and fifty volumes. There are two dining rooms, one each for the larger and smaller boys. The tables are covered with white enameled cloth. At one end of each room was a dais on which was placed a table for the Brothers, who eat at the same time with the boys. In the bath-room were two bathing tubs. Each boy has a basin and towel to himself. All the rain-water is carefully saved in cisterns, and the boys are thus supplied with soft water to wash with. A good well supplies drinking water. There are play-rooms heated by stoves in winter. There were no inmates in the infirmary. Brother Amphian says: "We had some malarial fever last June. The Brothers believed it was caused by the slaughter-houses in the neighborhood." But one boy has died during the last two years. The dormitories were furnished with both wooden and iron single bedsteads. Straw beds were in use. One or more Brothers sleep in each dormitory.

Eight hundred boys have received the benefits of this institution since its foundation. Thirty-nine of the children at date of visitation were orphans, sixty-one were half-orphans and eight had both parents living. Nine were of native parents, and ninety-nine of foreign. Two were partially supported by their parents, and one hundred and six by public authorities. The number of inmates received during the year was twenty-five, the number discharged, twenty-seven. Of the latter four were indentured, twenty-one returned to parents or guardians, one left without permission.

This asylum was founded in the year 1854, under the auspices of the Rt. Rev. J. McCloskey, then Bishop of Albany. It was given in charge of two members of the Order of Christian Brothers, who very shortly after its establishment had under their care forty-three boys. Its work has continued to grow steadily year after year. Its expenditures during the year were $13.219.97, and its present indebtedness amounts to $4,123.15.

The Brothers in charge of the asylum appeared to manifest a deep interest in their work, and are zealously endeavoring to lessen the public burdens growing out of pauperism and crime.

The Cayuga Asylum for Destitute Children,

Auburn,

Was incorporated by an act of the legislature May 10th, 1852. Several months prior to its incorporation a few benevolent ladies of Auburn, desiring to make some provision for homeless and destitute children, rented a small building on James street, gathered in a number of this class and supported them for a time principally by their own labors and contributions. In July, 1853, a lot of about two acres on Owasco street, on which the asylum now stands, was purchased. At the time there was a small wooden building upon it, which, although somewhat larger than the one vacated on James street, was soon found to be insufficient, on account of the rapidly increasing numbers. Encouraged by a legacy of $2,700, made by Dr. Healy of Onondaga, the erection of the main edifice was undertaken in 1857. An appeal was made to the public for aid to carry out this enterprise, which was cheerfully and liberally responded to, and the building was completed the same year. The school building was added in 1865. The main building is of brick, three stories high above the basement, and forty-eight feet front by sixty feet deep. Water from the city supplies every floor. The ceilings are of good height. The dining room, kitchen, laundry and bathing rooms are in the basement. There are three large rooms in the second and third stories occupied as dormitories. Part of three stories are divided into rooms for the matron and her assistants. A nursery, parlor and a large reception room, where the lady managers meet, are on the first floor. Gas is used for light. The matron thinks the use of kerosene dangerous in such institutions. The lamps are liable to be overturned, even with the greatest care, and serious consequences may ensue. Attached to the main building is a brick structure, thirty-eight by forty feet, used for a school room. The school is under the direction of the board of education of the city.

The financial affairs of the asylum are under the control of a board of trustees. The dispensing of its income and the management of its internal and domestic affairs are directed by a board of ladies. In a large number of the towns in Cayuga county societies are organized which work as auxiliaries to the asylum. They are composed of ladies, who sew, knit and otherwise render efficient aid toward supporting the little ones in the asylum. The children are mainly supplied with clothing, and with all their woolen stockings from this source. One of these societies, the Sherwood's Auxiliary society, sent in, during the last season, between forty and fifty entire suits of boys' clothing. The president of each of these societies is entitled to representation in the managing board. The asylum is under the immediate charge of Mrs. J. G. Rogers, matron, who has held this position and discharged its arduous duties about fourteen years. She employs such female assistants as she deems necessary — at present five. A man is employed for out-door duties.

Great need is felt for suitable hospital accommodations. The matron in this connection says: "When any disease comes in, the children are all exposed, there being no suitable place in the house for the care of the sick. I have had as many as sixty children down with the measles at one time." One little boy at the time of our visit was suffering from scarlet fever.

The dormitories are furnished with double bedsteads, some wooden and some iron. The matron would prefer to have the children sleep singly. The school was believed to be quite efficiently conducted. The girls are taught housekeeping and sewing to some extent in the asylum, and those who are old enough attend a church industrial school during the winter months. The little boys weed in the garden. A Sabbath school is held on the premises, and the children are otherwise religiously instructed.

Great pains, it is stated, is taken to find good homes for the children, and especial care is exercised to insure their being morally and religiously instructed in their new situations. There is no committee charged with the especial duty of visiting the children after being placed out. The matron does this as far as practicable, keeping up a correspondence with them. "There is scarcely a day in the week," she says, "but I have a letter from some of the children that have left us." The matron's opinion, founded on experience, in regard to placing children out of asylums before the right kind of a home is obtained, is given as follows: "I do not believe in hurrying children out. They should not leave until a home of the right kind can be found. Many homes that are called good, are places where they get children up at four o'clock in the morning. We require every applicant for children to come well recommended, and to give strong pledges that they will do justly by our children. We take great pains at first, because we do not like to have a child come back. It ruins a child to be returned two or three times. People that do not succeed in managing their own children, will sometimes find a great deal of fault with a child from the asylum." Children are received quite young. One baby in the nursery department was but twelve months old, and fourteen of the children were under two years of age.

On the date of visitation there were ten colored children in the asylum, two girls and eight boys. No prejudice was said to exist on account of color. The matron aims to inculcate among the children a spirit of love. One of the inmates was a little, helpless, half orphan girl, suffering from curvature of the spine, and unable to walk. The matron found great difficulty in taking care of her, and thought she ought to be in an asylum especially devoted to this class. Another of the inmates of the asylum is now being fitted for college, and one who has been an inmate is now a teacher.

The following information was furnished by the matron regarding other former inmates. "A young man, having had the advantages of an education in the higher branches given the advanced scholars in the Asylum by the Board of Education of the city, graduated in the primary and high schools, and was sent by friends of the institution to college, where he led his class each term and won the highest honors in graduating. He is now in the office of a leading and influential law firm in a neighboring state, associated with gentlemen of culture. Another, a true Christian, who gives promise of great usefulness, regards the Asylum as a home and mother to him. A young girl of intellectual ability is nearly through an advanced course of study, and arrangements are made by friends to place her in an Eastern Seminary next year, to fit her for a teacher. Both of the last named are orphans, and but for the Asylum, would have been destitute."

A good sized garden is connected with the institution in which a great variety of vegetables are grown. The place is stocked with a variety of fruit-trees, and a goodly sized lawn in one of the angles is shaded with forest trees. Under these in pleasant summer weather, the children partake frequently of their meals. The play ground is large. A high latticed fence incloses the grounds. The outbuildings are new, and in good repair, and the property bears evidence of being carefully preserved. During the past year some desirable improvements have been made in the sanitary condition of the premises in the way of drainage, and in the building of a new barn with a cellar for the storing of vegetables heretofore kept under the main building. Still a need is felt for play rooms during inclement weather.

During the past year an energetic effort has been made in the way of placing out children with excellent results. By this means the expenses of the society have been lessened, and the children brought under family influence. The number of children in the institution, October 1, 1875, was sixty-five. Of these seven were orphans, fifty-two half-orphans, and six had both parents living. Fifty-seven were of native and eight of foreign parentage. All were from Cayuga County, excepting one each from the counties of Chemung, Seneca and Tompkins. Towards the support of seven of the children, the parents paid a small sum. The number received during the past year was fifty-seven; the number discharged was seventy-two; and the number who died, three.

It is customary for the Board of Supervisors to make an annual appropriation towards aiding the benevolent work carried on by the ladies and gentlemen of the Asylum. The invested funds of the Asylum amount to $5,500. The sum total of its expenditures for the year ending October 1, 1875, was $8,813.42. Its indebtedness was $500.

The whole number of children received in the institution since its organization is one thousand one hundred and fifty-nine.

When it is considered what would have been the consequences to society had the large number of children, that have received the benefits of this institution, been left to grow up in neglect, the important advantages resulting from this worthy charity may be to some extent, though not wholly appreciated.

One very noticeable feature of this work is that it takes with a kindly hand those children who, but for this aid, would be left to pauperism and criminality. For many years past the enlightened public sentiment in this community has rescued all the children from the poor-house, taking them generally from the Town Overseer or the Superintendent of the Poor before going there. Aside from the moral effects growing out of this Christian work, the pecuniary burthens of the Poor Department have been greatly lessened, and the taxpayers of the county are largely indebted to those who have generously sustained the asylum and carried on its work.

Within the year past the society has lost two of its staunch friends, both of whom gave substantial evidence of their interest in generous bequests. One of these, John H. Chedell, was a member of the Board of Trustees at the time of his decease. The following resolutions were adopted by the Board of Trustees December 4th, in relation to the other, its beloved President:

Resolved, That we have heard with sentiments of profound sorrow, the announcement of the death of James S. Seymour, Esq., the President of this Board from its first organization, a period of more than twenty-three years.

Mr. Seymour's long connection with this charity was marked by the same religious earnestness, sincere benevolence, prudent counsel, and systematic liberality which characterized his relations to all worthy undertakings for the glory of God and the good of his fellow-men; the interests of none of which were more constantly in his thoughts or nearer his heart than those of the "Cayuga Asylum for Destitute Children." We feel that it is not too much to say that in his death the asylum has lost its oldest and best friend.

Resolved, That our Secretary furnish a copy of these resolutions to the daily press of the city for publication, and that this board attend the funeral of its revered President in a body.

H. N. LOCKWOOD,
Sec'y Board of Trustees.

THE NEW YORK STATE INSTITUTION FOR THE BLIND.

Batavia.

This institution is located in the village of Batavia, Genesee Co. It was established by an act of the Legislature, April 7, 1865. The village presented to the State fifty acres of desirable land for its site, to which has been added sixteen acres. A considerable extent of ground in front of the institution has been graded and tastefully laid out in graveled walks, forming a beautiful park, where the inmates may promenade in safety. This improvement has greatly enhanced the value of the property. It is located in the outskirts of the village. The site is somewhat elevated, and commands pleasing views of a rich agricultural district. The edifice is a spacious brick structure, and its construction affords a noteworthy example of discretion exercised with official integrity. The Board of Commissioners appointed by the Governor, by and with the consent of the Senate, charged with the duty of erecting the buildings, before proceeding to make contracts, visited in company with an architect other institutions of like character, taking time to gather such information as was desirable from the superintendents in charge. A plan for the building having been carefully prepared and approved by the Governor, Comptroller and Secretary of State, the corner-stone was laid September 6, 1866, and the building was completed July 15, 1868. The expenditure, which included the grading of the grounds about the building, digging of well, the providing of a steam engine, cooking range, etc., as well as the erection of carriage-house and stable, was less by a few hundred dollars than the sum originally contemplated as being necessary to carry out the project. An examination of the building shows it to have been solidly constructed with good materials.

The building is three stories in height above the basement, the latter being constructed of lime-stone quarried on the site. The water-table, quoin-blocks and window dressings are of Lockport stone. The building faces the south, and is composed of four structures, a front and rear, center, and two wings connected by corridors, each fourteen by thirty-two feet, which contain the halls and staircases. The central buildings are fifty by sixty-two feet, and fifty by seventy feet respectively ; the wings are each forty-six by one hundred and six feet ; and the distance from the front to the rear, including portico, is one hundred and eighty-five feet.

The basement contains the laundry, including washing, ironing and drying rooms, bathing rooms and water closets for pupils, besides the rooms for the heating apparatus, coal vaults, cellars, etc. The stories above the basement contain over one hundred rooms, making ample provision for office and reception rooms, public parlors and library ; family rooms for the resident officers and teachers, and dining, school, study and sleeping rooms for one hundred and fifty pupils. The building is heated by steam throughout, and the arrangements for ventilation and bathing are adequate. The rain water from the roof is conducted into two large cisterns, having a capacity of five thousand barrels, from which it is pumped by steam into tanks situated in the attics, and thence distributed by pipes to the different parts of the edifice. In addition to this provision, a well about fifty feet deep, furnishes an inexhaustible supply of excellent water.

The institution at its opening was placed under the charge of the late Dr. A. D. Lord, who had formerly been Superintendent of the Ohio Institution for the Blind, and who was President of the American Association of Instructors of the Blind till his death. To his large experience, adaptability for the work, and his strong sympathies for this class and his excellent moral influence, the success of the institution is mainly attributable. His death was felt to be a serious loss. In the emergency his wife, who had been associated with him in his life labor at all times, as a practical assistant, consented to assume the grave responsibilities lately borne by her husband, and has since discharged them, it is asserted, with ability and to the satisfaction of the Board of Managers and the public.

The most recent visitation was made October 30, at which date, the institution contained one hundred and fifty-three inmates, eighty-six girls and sixty-seven boys. The full course of instruction covers a period of seven years. The district from which pupils are received embraces all the counties in the State, except those of Kings, Queens, New York and Suffolk. During the first month of the past school year, the pupils numbered one hundred and twenty-five, and at its close one hundred and fifty-seven. The total number enrolled since the opening of the institution is two hundred and eighty-two, one hundred and fifty males, and one hundred and thirty-two females. Twenty-six pupils have been discharged during the year. Twelve of these left through illness ; two to follow the broom trade, and one was transferred to the military school, Dayton, Ohio.

The school of the institution was found to be in a flourishing condition. A similar course of instruction is adopted as in the institution in New York. The pupils receive a good English education in grammar, analysis, writing, geography, civil government, natural philosophy, mental philosophy, physiology, history and algebra. About seventy can read and write by the point print system of Superintendent Wait of New York. Three literary societies are held among the pupils. The excelsior lyceum is composed of the older pupils; it sustains a literary paper, and gives public entertainments. The junior societies, made up of the younger pupils, have entertainments among themselves.

Great pains is taken with the musical education of the pupils. There are three vocal classes, the advanced, the intermediate, and the primary. The first of these numbers fifty pupils, and the two latter forty each. One hundred and ten pupils have been taking lessons on the piano, cabinet organ, and melodeon, fifteen on the violin, and a class on the pipe organ has been commenced within the year. Two brass bands have been formed by the pupils, one numbering eleven and the other thirteen members. The junior of these is taught by one of the pupils. The resignation of one of the lady teachers causing a vacancy, an experiment was tried of employing pupils to act in that capacity with very satisfactory results. The experience has proved a practical benefit to the pupils who hope in the future to obtain a livelihood by teaching music. The importance of this kind of training to the pupils is becoming more and more manifest. The late Dr. Lord on this point remarks: " What the educated blind may yet accomplish we cannot foretell; however, it is a fact of no little importance, that at this time and for several years past, the superintendents of some four or five institutions are blind men who were educated as such ; that a number of the most successful teachers of the blind and the seeing are of this class, and that the second purely educational institution in Europe was originated and established, and is still conducted by a graduate of one of our institutions."

Among the industrial features of this institution is the broom shop, where the young men learn a trade, by which they are rendered partially, if not wholly self-supporting. Twenty-four were employed here during the year. Two had already perfected themselves in the trade and left, and six others were expected to leave during the session. The girls are taught bead work, at which one hundred and three were engaged during the year. They are also instructed in both hand and machine sewing, crocheting and fancy work generally.

The health of the inmates was good. There were only four cases of sickness during the year.

From visitations made to this institution from time to time, it is believed that its general affairs are faithfully managed, that the educational interests of the pupils are in the hands of an efficient corps of teachers, and that not only its present work, but past history is creditable to the State.

The Davenport Institution for Female Orphan Children.

Bath.

The situation of this institution is quite picturesque, and its surroundings are peculiarly attractive. It is located upon an elevated terrace of two or three acres in extent, upon one side of the Conhocton Valley, a little apart from the village of Bath. Between the town and the Asylum the Conhocton river flows, bordered by willows and stately elms. In the rear of the building rise abruptly a range of wooded hills covered mostly with evergreens and presenting a belt of dark green foliage in pleasing contrast to the soft grey stone, of which the edifice is constructed. Immediately back of it in the forest is a pleasant play-ground for the children. In front of the Asylum are the rich bottom meadow lands belonging to the institution, down to which the lawn, several hundred feet across, slopes.

The property comprises about sixty acres of land; five of which are in woodland and three in orchard. An abundance of apples, strawberries and grapes are grown.

This Asylum had its origin in the benevolence of the late Col. Ira Davenport of Bath. It is said that the condition of friendless and destitute female orphan children had always awakened his profoundest commiseration, and that the founding of this institution for their protection was the consummation of a long cherished purpose.

He began to erect a building designed for this class in 1861. This institution was incorporated in 1863, and the first orphan received July 19, 1864. The main building was erected during his life, and since his death, a large wing has been added by his executors in accordance with the provisions of his will. The buildings are designed to be fire-proof, and are roofed with slate. Two stone towers vary the outline of their front. A large and commodious barn with stables, hennery and stock yard has been recently built upon the grounds. The whole property is being inclosed by substantial fences. The grounds have been graded, and but little further expenditure is contemplated to complete the institution. When this is accomplished, it is designed to apply the whole of the income to the primary object of the work. As the building will then accommodate one hundred and twenty-five children, its beneficent influence will be still more widely felt throughout the country. The property is unincumbered, and has been liberally endowed by its founder. To the endowment fund, Mr. Charles Davenport, of Allegany county, a brother of the founder, contributed the sum of $30,000. The purpose of the founder and the intention now being carried out is to give a home to orphan and destitute girls, received between five and nine years of age, where they will be educated and fitted for earning a competence for themselves through life.

The institution, on date of visitation, July 28th, contained forty-four inmates. Three of these were orphans, thirty-five were half-orphans, and six had both parents living. Thirty-eight were of native parents and six of foreign. Girls from all parts of the State are eligible for admission, but preference is given to the counties of Steuben and Allegany. They receive a good practical education. To each is imparted a given amount of schooling, and all are required to spend a portion of time in learning to do housework. A school is conducted on the premises. The management of the internal economy of the asylum is committed to the Superintendent, Mr. Elisha Child, whose wife acts as matron. Religious instruction is daily imparted by the Superintendent and his wife. Sunday services are held in the asylum by ministers from Bath, the different denominations alternating.

The by-laws of the institution require that "the children shall be carefully instructed in the principles and duties of the Christian religion, as contained in the Holy Scriptures, and such instruction shall not be confined to the peculiar tenets of any one distinct sect, denomination or church."

The interior of the building is in keeping with its external surroundings; choice engravings and photographs, selected with classic taste, and calculated to have an elevating and refining influence upon the inmates are hung in the halls and various rooms of the house.

The dormitories are large and airy, each being designed to accommodate twelve inmates. They are furnished with iron bedsteads. Connected with each dormitory is a closet fitted up with drawers, shelves and hooks for the wearing apparel of the girls, enabling each girl to have a separate compartment for the care of her own wardrobe. The girls are dressed uniformly, either in blue, check, or brown gingham.

Two sewing machines are kept in use, and the older girls are instructed in machine sewing. The housework is done by the girls, under competent supervision. No domestics are employed, and those acting in the capacity of instructors are selected with reference to their educational advantages and fitness for exerting a good moral influence upon the children.

The building is heated by furnaces, lighted with kerosene and supplied with spring water, which is carried through it as far as the second floor. Fire-proof staircases afford ready egress. The ceilings are high, flues are laid in the walls for purposes of ventilation, and the windows are large.

The laundry is in a wing, separate from the main building. Roots and vegetables are stored in the barn cellar.

The health of the children was remarkably good. The Superintendent says: "We have been in charge of this institution three years and three months, and have not had a single case of sickness requiring us to call a physician. We attribute this to plenty of wholesome and nutritious food, regular habits in diet and exercise, well-ventilated rooms, and clothing adapted to the varying seasons and changes in the weather.

The children are kept in the institution till they can be disposed of in suitable homes. Some are adopted; others enter families as domestics. All necessary precaution is observed in their disposition, and so far, we are informed, the children placed out seem to be well contented themselves, and to give satisfaction to the parties taking them. Although there is no regular system for visiting the children after they leave the institution, it is stated that an endeavor is made to look after their interest, and that in various ways their prosperity and well being is ascertained. Each girl on leaving is furnished with a trunk, two or three dresses, a quantity of underclothing, and two pairs of shoes. Each girl has the privilege of coming back to the institution twice a year, and spending a day with the children. On these occasions they return to it, it is said, as to their own home.

No case of a girl running away is on record, and but two of children who had to be removed. One of these was that of a girl who developed a tendency to insanity. This exhibited itself in a disposition to kill hens, birds, cats or dogs. Dr. Gray, of Utica, was sent for, and pronounced her a fit subject for his asylum, to which she was accordingly transferred. The other was that of a girl who came from a very bad family, with vicious habits already formed. Her influence upon the other inmates being pernicious, she could not be retained in the house. A place in a farmer's family was, we were informed, procured for her, from which she ran away and became so very depraved, that all hope of reforming her in the asylum was given up.

The real estate of the institution, including building, fixtures and furniture, is valued at $142,300, and its invested funds at $155,800.

In the meadow previously referred to, near the banks of the Conhocton, is a little inclosure, surrounding a plain, unpretending obelisk, which marks the resting place of the founder of this beautiful charity, Col. Ira Davenport. Here are also buried the children who have died in the asylum. This simple monument, surrounded, as it eventually must be, with the head-stones of little children, brings a thought of the land of the hereafter, and is typical of the beatific form of this lover of children, surrounded by an angelic little flock of those who in this life had shared his sympathy and care.

Susquehanna Valley Home and Industrial School for Indigent Children.

Binghamton.

The Susquehanna Valley Home and Industrial School for Indigent Children is located about a mile and a half from the city of Binghamton, on the left bank of the Susquehanna. The building stands upon an eminence, the ground sloping away from it riverward and slightly landward. There are forty-five acres belonging to the institution. It lies in a lovely bend of the river, which sweeps in almost a semi-circle around the tract bordered by a growth of native forest trees overhanging the water and fringing it with beauty. Across the river, to the right, upon a still higher eminence, about a mile away, rises the imposing facade of the Inebriate Asylum. The view extends in both directions, up and down the Susquehanna Valley, from the hills where the river is seen to emerge, till it disappears in the opposite direction. Its undulating slopes, covered with the gorgeous drapery of autumn, the city of Binghamton, with its tasteful spires and villas — just far enough away to give a hint of the busy world, without its din — the Chenango Valley, rifted in the distant hills in front, combine to form a landscape that, in diversity of outline and variety of color, is rarely surpassed, and which must have a happy influence on the susceptible minds of children.

The property is a valuable one, and cost $20,000.00. Its purchase reflects credit upon the sagacity of those who secured it for the public use.

The building is of brick, two stories high, with a basement and attic in addition. It is in the form of a parallelogram, fifty by sixty feet, with two-story porches, twelve by twenty-two feet, at each end.

A good-sized substantial brick barn is situated at a safe distance, in case of fire, from the main building.

Adjoining the main edifice there has been recently erected a frame building for a children's play-room. The construction of the main building is such as to effect an entire separation of the sexes, except in the school-room. While at out-door play they intermingle. The building is warmed by steam. Its water supply is derived from a well and from the rain, which is collected in cisterns. Water pipes extend as far as the first floor of the building, to which the water is pumped by hand. The supply, however, is inadequate, and snow water was used last winter. The windows are large, and the sash adjusted by cords, weights and pulleys. The rooms are high and airy. In the basement is a bath room, containing two large bath tubs and a good-sized bathing vat, supplied with hot and cold water. The superintendent states that the inmates are bathed every Saturday.

There are six or eight fire-places in the building, some of which are used sufficiently to afford a fine ventilation. The edifice was built for a private residence, and, on the whole, answers its present purpose very well, though, in some respects, it is inconvenient. The wash-room is in the basement, and the steam and unwholesome odor from the clothes permeates, as it naturally must, other parts of the house. The main halls of the building are twelve feet wide, and are decorated with tasteful mottoes. The school room is large, well-lighted, and cheerful. The dormitories are warmed in cold or damp weather. At the time of last visitation, July 29th, the bedsteads were being changed, and a new set, made of iron, were being put in.

The closets are outside of the building and about sixty feet from it. The drainage of the premises is good. No provision is made for a hospital ward, which is greatly needed.

The Susquehanna Valley Home originated in 1868, in the efforts of the benevolent citizens of Binghamton and the surrounding country; to make better provision for the care of destitute children; particularly for such as were inmates of poor-houses, of which there were then large numbers.

At the time of the first general visitation made to the poor-houses of the State by the Secretary of this Board, Dr. Charles S. Hoyt, soon after its organization, it was found, as appears from the report submitted to the Board, and which was transmitted to the Legislature, March 22, 1869, that the surroundings of the children in such poor-houses of the State, as made a practice of keeping them, was deplorable. In Broome county, the buildings were of wood, old, out of repair, and crowded with inmates. The arrangements for heating and ventilating were imperfect. There were no bath-tubs in the house. In summer, the inmates, when inclined, bathed in the river; and in winter, in their rooms or the wash-house. A proper classification in consequence of the arrangement of the building was impossible. The sexes, it is true, were separate at night, but during the day all classes and ages, including idiots and the insane, freely associated. A large number of adult inmates had been brought to want, in consequence of habits of inebriety, others in consequence of vagrancy, idleness and debauchery; while a few were dependent from sickness and the infirmities of age. Six were negroes of a low type. The whole number of inmates was sixty-eight; twenty-one, or nearly one-third of this number, were children. They were taught in a week-day school, but received no religious instruction beyond the attendance upon service held at the house, and designed more especially for adults.

Subsequent to the visitation to the poor-house, the Secretary held personal conferences with several prominent citizens of Binghamton, and urged upon them the importance of taking measures to secure the proper care and training of these poor children. The fact that the property known as the Susquehanna Valley Seminary building, possessed by the State, could probably be secured as a shelter for the children in this and neighboring counties, until permanent arrangements for their care could be provided, was presented as a fitting opportunity to begin a work on their behalf. This appeal of the Secretary was followed by energetic action on the part of leading residents, including earnest Christian ladies of Broome and the surrounding counties, in which Commissioner Miller co-operated, resulting, finally, in establishing the Susquehanna Valley Home and Industrial School, for Indigent Children. The Home was incorporated March 15, 1869.

The Boards of Supervisors of the counties of Cortland, Delaware, Sullivan and Tioga, took prompt action in the matter, and authorized the Superintendents to send destitute children to the Home as soon as it was ready to receive them. The price agreed upon for maintenance, at the outset, was $1.25 per week. It was subsequently found necessary to increase this sum to $2, and even this amount does not cover all the cost of supporting and clothing the children, and there is still need of aid from the benevolent to sustain the institution. It occupied at first, under lease, the Susquehanna Valley Seminary building, and about four years ago came to use its present property. The legislature in 1874 appropriated $16,000 to the Home "to be paid upon the execution of deed of the property of said corporation to the State." Its indebtedness was thus liquidated.

The school appeared to be efficiently conducted. The children responded promptly in their exercises, and displayed creditable proficiency in history, geography, civil government, astronomy and rudimentary studies. Their singing of the "Bright Forever" and "Home, Dear Home," was in good time and distinct. The teacher stated that her pupils were perfectly familiar with thirty different hymns. Twenty-five out of twenty-nine of the children repeated correctly their last Sabbath school lesson, the Ten Commandments and the Twenty-third Psalm. The Sabbath school, it was stated, was one of the best, if not the best, in the county. Mr. Northrop, the superintendent, has great faith in the good effect of singing on the minds of the children. He says "They learn hymns that have a good moral or religious sentiment, and sing them while at play. Every such hymn learned, is a seed planted which will bring forth its fruit in due time." He thinks the children's choir is as good as any in the city. "We have," he says, "an organ in the school-room, and the school opens with music. During exercises the children have a little practice, and then, again, at close of school. I make it a point to secure teachers who are accomplished in music. We have now one teacher, but the managers have consented to my employing an assistant specially qualified to teach vocal music."

We saw the children while at the dinner table; they appeared to have abundance to eat; the food was well cooked and properly seasoned. The dietary, we were informed, is as follows: Bread and milk for breakfast. For dinner, either meat or fish, with seasonable vegetables, such as squashes, peas, beans, onions, tomatoes, cabbage, turnips, etc.; the meat used is mostly in the form of corned beef. For supper, bread and butter is furnished; sometimes bread and apple sauce, or bread and molasses.

The children's clothing is cut and made up in the house.

The institution is under the direction of a Board of Managers, composed of nine gentlemen. These are aided by a Board of Assistant Managers, composed of ladies and gentlemen residing in Broome, Chenango, Cortland, Delaware, Sullivan, Tioga and Tompkins counties. The various villages and towns in the several counties named being represented in the Board of Assistant Managers.

The Home itself is under the immediate charge of Mr. and Mrs. S. G. Northrop, Superintendent and Matron. The subordinate force consists of a teacher, assistant teacher, sewing woman, baker, cook, chamber girl and farm hand.

The importance of placing dependent children under good influences while young, is thus emphasized by the Superintendent: "I am in favor of having children taken in younger than the rules of the house will now permit. We now receive them between the ages of three and sixteen. I would rather have the first three years of the child's life than the next ten. A little girl, not over three years old, came here some time ago from the County House. She had been associated with pauper women, and it was lamentable to see what she knew at that tender age. She showed all the old pauper ways in her actions. Every thing she said or did savored of the old pauper. She had been with them a little less than three years, and yet it took a long time to get out of her head the snatches of improper songs and other things that she had learned while there.

"I think we should have a nursery. The necessities of the institution demand it. The younger we can get children the better. I think children can be disciplined before they get to be three or even two years old. When a child begins to show spunk, it is old enough to be taught to mind, no matter if its age be only six months. A boy six years of age came here from the the Chenango County Poor-house, where he had been since he was quite young. He was kept with fools and insane people. He could not speak except to say, 'Want to go to fool's part.' He had no manners at table; in fact, he was a perfect savage. He has been here eight months, and shows a marked improvement. He talks, and is at length learning the ways of civilized people. Another from Delaware county, a little girl, came here full of pauper slang. She would have been ruined had she remained in the County House. She has been adopted into a family, has lost her pauper habits, and the family think every thing of her. In rare instances I get children who belong to the incorrigible class. I had one boy an inmate who came to the institution with an unmanageable spirit. Under careful treatment he changed, and became a very bright and useful boy; but unfortunately he developed an irresistible propensity toward thievery. He was convicted several times and forgiven, but at length it became apparent that his influence upon the other children was bad, while the mild home discipline which we here adopt was insufficient for his reform, and I was obliged to have him sent to the Western House of Refuge.

"My discipline is just as varied as are the cases for discipline. It is impossible to lay down any system that will apply equally well in every case. I do not have a great string of rules, I simply say to the children, 'Do what is right, and do not do what is wrong.' I let the children in every case decide whether or not they have lived up to this rule. A complaint comes to me that a certain boy has been doing some wrong act. I call him. 'Have you been doing so and so?' 'Yes, sir; I did not know that you had forbidden it.' I ask, 'What did I tell you not to do?' 'You said I must not do wrong.' 'What did I say you must do?' 'You said I must do right.' I then ask if he thinks what he has done is right, and he answers 'No, sir.' 'Then have I not forbidden it?' I lead them on in this way till they convict themselves. I try to fasten in their minds the principle of *right* and *wrong*, and awaken conscience. I do not punish for the first or second offense, but if it is repeated the third time, I resort to punishment. For punishment I sometimes make them stand upon one foot. When two get to fighting, I supply them with whips and make them flog each other. They do not care to do this, and I find it a pretty effective cure for fighting."

In regard to the disposal of the children, Mr. Northrop remarks: "Children are let out on trial sixty days to parties approved of by the

Board of Managers, after which they are indentured, if satisfactory to both parties. A record is made regarding the disposition of the children, and the ladies scattered throughout the country who compose the Assistant Board of Lady Managers, visit them from time to time, and ascertain and report as to their condition and well-being. The boys do the odds and ends of work around the house, and assist in garden and farm work. The girls learn to do general housework and to sew and knit."

The garden yields all the vegetables used in the institution. Four cows are kept to supply the children with milk.

The number of inmates received during the year was twenty-six; the number discharged, twenty. Of the latter, two left without permission, seven were indentured, and eight returned to parents or guardians. The number of children received from 1870 to 1875 inclusive, was two hundred and fifty-seven. The real estate, including building, fixtures, etc., is valued at $35,700. The expenditures during the past year were $22,582.67. Of this sum, $16,021.29 was paid out for indebtedness upon real estate. The present indebtedness of the institution is $700.

The number of children in this institution October 1, 1875, was sixty. Of these, six were orphans, ten half-orphans, and in forty-four cases nothing was known regarding the parents. Twelve were of foreign parentage, and the parentage of forty-eight was unknown.

The people of Binghamton, as well as those in surrounding counties, who are interested in the work of the Susquehanna Valley Home, are not only benefiting society morally, but are largely reducing the burdens of public taxation, growing out of pauperism and crime. It is a well-established fact that the operation of this institution has considerably reduced the number of inmates in the Broome County poor-house and the poor-houses of several of the adjoining counties, and has broken off a great many hereditary lines of pauperism in families. Its supporters are certainly entitled to the full sympathy of the public.

Brooklyn Children's Aid Society.

Brooklyn.

The following interesting scrap of history is furnished in regard to this Society, which during the past ten years has been carrying on a great work of reform in the city of Brooklyn. We give it substantially in the language of the narrator:

In 1866, the lower wards of the city, notably the Second, Fifth, Sixth and Twelfth, were infested with a growing class of lads, in ages ranging from ten years to twenty, who had been driven by their circumstances in part, and partly by their education, to seek their living by begging and theft. Of course there were many who honestly depended on chance jobs for their living, but without any steady homes, loafing on the street corners in squads by day, and gathering, as the shades of night were falling, in the liquor stores to pass away the evening and arrange for some sort of lodgings which they must seek when they were compelled to leave these haunts. There was but slight chance of these boys ever becoming any thing but confirmed sots and outlaws.

The out-cropping of this increasingly alarming state of affairs at last aroused a number of wealthy citizens to take some steps to protect their property, by abating the nuisance which was assuming proportions almost too vast to be handled by ordinary legal means. Moral restraints are always more efficient than legal. It was, therefore, decided at a meeting held January 13, 1866, at the residence of a prominent citizen of Brooklyn, to perfect an organization whose object should be "the protection, care and shelter of friendless and vagrant youth — furnishing them with food and raiment and lodging; aiding and administering to their wants, providing them with occupation, instructing them in moral and religious truths, and in the rudiments of education, and with such means as the society can properly employ, endeavoring to make them virtuous and useful citizens." The organization of the society was perfected at this meeting.

Almost at the very outset those engaged in this humane enterprise were encouraged by a munificent donation of valuable, improved property on State street, the rents of which now afford a considerable addition to the income of the society. Other citizens, including a large number belonging to a class who give with no stinted hand, contributed liberal sums to the object; in one case, reaching as high as $20,000.

On September 1, 1866, the first lodging house for street boys was opened at 61 Poplar street, and the Society commenced a career of usefulness which has never paused either by night or day. A second lodging house was opened September 1, 1869, in connection with the work in the Sixth and Twelfth wards, at 139 Van Brunt street.

In the first General Superintendent, Mr. William A. Lawrence, the society secured an active and discreet agent, under whose direction its work was successfully inaugurated and conducted to the satisfaction of the Board of Managers. He held this important position up to April 1, 1873."

Both the Poplar and Van Brunt Street houses have been visited, the former at the date of October 16. From the General Superintendent, Mr. R. D. Douglass, the following information relating to the workings of the society were given:

"Our organization comprises lodging-house work, sewing machine school work, industrial school work and special relief work.

"Our lodging-houses are for homeless boys.

"Our sewing machine school is for girls who must earn their own living.

"Our industrial schools are for poor children who are compelled, by circumstances, to gain what little education they may in an irregular and disjointed fashion.

"Our special relief department finds homes in city and country for homeless boys and girls.

"In each lodging-house an evening school for the lodgers is carried on during the winter, also a day school for very young children, who come from the families living in the vicinity of the lodging-houses."

These children are not the inmates of the Homes at night, but are drawn from those families in the neighborhood of the Homes which, from various causes, are unable to send their children to school regularly, or who find it difficult to provide suitable clothing for them. In this department we have made a long stride in advance by the introduction of the Kindergarten System.

With the aid of Miss E. M. Coe, of New York, we have arranged a modification of this system, and adapted it to our own peculiar needs. "Always busy" is the motto of the system, and "always learning something practical." The eager curiosity of childhood is made available, and both the interest and the substantial progress of the children is something we are very proud of.

The evening schools are under the management of superintendents.

"Ever since the Home was opened, it has been our custom to secure the services of several ladies and gentlemen who could give up one evening in each week to the instruction of classes in our evening schools. We have been singularly fortunate in our teachers, several of whom have been with us for many years. This is one of the most powerful influences which we can bring to bear upon these boys. No boy can be in the presence of persons of culture and sympathy without feeling a strong desire to be better and wiser.

"One of our boys was asked to commit some depredations on the property here, and he replied, 'You don't catch me going back on my teacher like that.' The influence of the teacher is very great. Every day we find some fresh encouragement in our work. Ten years ago a class of large boys who were criminals, perfectly reckless of any law, a terror to the police and the community, existed among us. As soon as we opened our house a large number of that class came in. In the course of a month there was a decided change. Now that class, as a class, have gone from the city. They are scattered, and are mostly doing well.

"And if it were not for those causes intemperance, death and disease, which constantly operate to throw children upon their own resources, we should soon be able to reduce the capacity of our lodging-houses and bring our expenses within even a smaller sum than is now required. But there is no cessation of the causes which fill our lodging-houses with unfortunate and homeless children, and there is the ever recurring demand for aid to place them in positions to help themselves.

"The police were rather down on us at first. They thought we would harbor thieves. Now, when any thing happens, they come here first, to look for a boy, and if they find that he has slept here during the night, in nine cases out of ten that fact will clear him.

"In addition to our evening schools we carry on a work for girls in our sewing-machine department. We are running at the rate of about sixty or seventy new girls a month, and are conducting the school to suit those who need our help. We work for every individual who applies to this department for assistance. There is no conversation allowed here, and no opportunity given to make acquaintances. The girls are under constant surveillance while here, and when through with their work, separate. We teach about seven hundred girls in the year. They belong mainly to a class that without our help would go to destruction. We are all the time on the lookout for situations for them in families. We get some hundreds into situations every year of both girls and boys. The girls bring their work, except what is required to begin on — that we furnish. They can make their own dresses, or bring work for their neighbors, or for the little children of the family. We furnish the sewing machine, the room, and a teacher, and then endeavor, in every possible way, to get them employment After having perfected themselves we give them a diploma. We charge a dollar for full instruction on the machine. Not more than one-tenth pay, however. We trust them on the ground that, although nine out of ten of them will never be able to pay, they will feel better to think that they are paying."

In reference to the management of the lodging-houses, Mr. Douglas further says: "We charge our boys ten cents a night. The term *News boys*, means simply a class of street boys. We record them as they come in. We have a bank. We take all the money they wish to save. It is done up in little packages and handed to the superintendent, and if a boy is inclined to save money we invest it and pay him interest at the rate of seven per cent. There is a considerable number of boys that save money now. They have to buy their clothes and their shoes. As a general rule, as soon as they get five or six dollars, they need a pair of shoes. One of our boys has already $1,500, which he earned by blacking boots. He came here a wretched drunkard, and beginning to save was the turning point in his history. As soon as he got $30, he stopped drinking, and he has not drunk from that day to this. We keep him as a lodger here for the sake of continuing this influence over him. He was only fifteen years old when he came, but was just as confirmed a drunkard as if he had been fifty. There is a boy here now saving at the rate of five dollars a month. He is a boot-black. He began to save the 2d of June. He has already $35 invested at seven per cent.

"We give the boys a good substantial meal at night; soup, meat, baked beans or beef stew. We give them a good, comfortable bed. We have three bath-tubs. It is a part of our system to see that personal cleanliness is observed. When a boy comes in, he takes his boots off. We always make them wash their feet before going to bed. We do not allow any profane language to be used in the house. A boy that does not obey the rule in this respect, we consider as giving us notice that he wants to leave. We have a gymnasium for the boys. The school occupies the evening from eight to nine o'clock. On Friday nights we have a lecture, a magic lantern entertainment, or something of the kind. We have a singing school during the week. Sunday night we always have singing. We teach it by note. We have a perfectly competent teacher. She is the teacher in our day school. She has studied music for the last ten years. On Sundays we provide such papers as a boy would be interested in reading; stories, any thing that is not immoral in its tendency. Then we have a library of books to which the boys have access evenings, unless it be during school hours. We expect them to attend school.

"The work is all the time going on in this way. The boys are always under the influence of a lady and gentleman in the house. We consider it a prime point that we have a lady sitting at the desk, and the civilizing effect of that we cannot overestimate. A boy will learn more manners dealing with a lady in five minutes, than he would in dealing with a gentleman for a month.

"Each boy pays ten cents a night, and this includes his breakfast the next morning. We charge an additional sum for bread and meat at lunch — five cents. Some boys pay fifteen instead of ten cents. There is no rule about it. If the Superintendent sees that it would benefit the boy to have him pay fifteen cents instead of ten, he makes him pay the fifteen.

"On Sunday nights we always have religious exercises, but it is strictly non-denominational, for all classes in the city come. There is plenty of ground we can occupy without treading on anybody's corns. Still there is a strong religious influence exerted on the boys all the time. We open school at nine o'clock, A. M., and close at three P. M. The two industrial schools are on the same plan. We give the children a lunch. We always give them bread and syrup, or an additional treat of cake. Our work at Van Brunt street varies only in this, that the number of boys taken in there is not so great as here. There are about 40 newsboy lodgers and 70 children in the school.

"Our system of finding places for the children is this: If a person comes here seeking employment, and wants a place, I enter the name, with other particulars, upon a book. I do the same with persons seeking to employ laborers. I then look my list over, and if I find that there is a likelihood of two parties being suited, I get them together and let them make their own arrangements." In regard to looking after children, when placed out, Mr. Douglas says: "If I do not hear from any child, who is placed out by us, in the course of a year, I write to the parties respecting it. The agreement is that they shall write me. I very rarely get a situation for one child without its leading to the getting of another one for another, and in this way, when I hear from one I usually hear indirectly from three or four others."

The house on Poplar street was carefully inspected. In the workroom were 34 sewing machines. The dining-room was comfortably furnished. The dormitory had double tiers of iron bedsteads, which were provided with husk mattresses. The beds were from two feet one inch to two feet five inches wide. The house throughout was found to be very clean and in order.

It is stated that the number of children brought under the elevating influences of the society, and assisted since its organization, exceeds 16,000, including both girls and boys. Each of these has been in some way practically aided. From the 1st of September, 1866, to November 1, 1875:

5,075 children have been placed in good homes.

8,076 boys have been taken from the streets.

4,792 girls have been taught the use of the sewing machine.

10,869 articles of clothing distributed to children.

341,071 lodgings furnished to street boys.

826,854 meals furnished to the hungry.

$36,325.75 received from boys in part payment for food and shelter.

$1,147.36 received from girls in part payment for instruction on sewing machine.

The whole amount expended by the society, from February 1, 1866, to November 7, 1875, was $227,599.71.

The interest taken in the work by the benevolent citizens of Brooklyn and elsewhere, and the business-like management of its affairs, have kept the society above financial struggles. All its departments are thought to be efficiently conducted, and it is regarded as being unnecessary to commend to public favor a work already so popular, and which has accomplished so large and beneficent results.

The Brooklyn Howard Colored Orphan Asylum.

Brooklyn.

This asylum is located on Dean street, near Troy avenue, Brooklyn. Its object is "to clothe, feed, educate and provide for orphan and homeless colored children." The following is a brief sketch of its history:

"It was formed in the year 1866, under the name of the 'Home for the Children of Freedwomen.' It was designed to relieve those who came north with their children and were unable to obtain situations. The children were declined being received by the Boards of Managers of the New York Asylums, and for several months they were in the house of S. A. Tilman, 104 East Thirteenth street, New York city. There were over twenty children in this gentleman's house for more than six months. Under the advice of Generals O. O. and C. H. Howard and others, the children were at length removed to Brooklyn, and until the organization of The Howard Colored Orphan Asylum, they were maintained by the benevolent and by donations from the Freedmen's Bureau during its existence."

The asylum was incorporated September 7, 1868. It is directed by a Board of Lady Managers with an Advisory Committee of Gentlemen.

On the day of visitation, October 20, it was found to be under the charge of Rev. Wm. F. Johnson, superintendent, assisted by a matron, also by a treasurer and a teacher, all colored. The teacher is compensated by the Board of Education. A seamstress, nurse, cook, laundress and janitor are also employed. The grounds of the asylum comprise four lots, on which are two frame buildings, one of them new. Children are received between the ages of two and twelve, and placed out on arriving at the latter age.

The following particulars regarding the methods of disposing of the children and the workings of the asylum were furnished by Mr. Johnson: "We first find homes for them and then indenture them. We take a good deal of pains to find good homes for the children and look after them constantly. The parties taking the children pay us $5 when they take them and $20 at the end of the year.

"We put this money in a savings bank in Brooklyn, and hold it till the child comes of age. We have at present sixty children under our charge; thirty-two are girls. The capacity of the asylum is for about eighty children. We have never received a dollar from the city or county. We had an appropriation from the State of $1,500, in 1870. Our active managers are mostly of our own color. Two white ladies were admitted into our board during the past year.

"The girls have always been taught to sew, but not as systematically as I would desire. We have prayers and sabbath school, and a preacher when we can get one. The institution is supported by voluntary contributions. We are in debt about $4,000. The new building cost us $2,500."

In the school room is a good sized organ and a library containing about fifty volumes of sabbath-school reading. The children were mostly young. They appeared to be in good health at the time of visitation.. Thirty-four had had the whooping cough during the year. Two deaths had occurred during this period.

On October 1, 1875, the number of children who were orphans was fifteen, half-orphans thirty-eight, who had both parents living, two.

The number of inmates received by this institution, since its organization, is 235. The number received during the year ending October 1, 1875, was fourteen, and the number discharged seven. Of the latter, three were returned to parents or guardians, and one left without permission.

The total expenditures of the Asylum for the year amount to $6,626.16.

This appears to be a meritorious charity, and deserving of a liberal share of public sympathy. The youth coming under its care belong to a class that society cannot afford to neglect, and who are quite susceptible to religious and other elevating influences.

The President of the Board of Trustees makes the following appeal for aid:

"During five years of persistent toil we have overcome much prejudice against our work, vanquished animosities, maintained our credit, and secured the confidence and good will of our fellow citizens. But our pecuniary burdens are greater than we can bear alone. We therefore appeal to the public, in the name of dependent humanity, to bear with us this burdensome debt, and so fulfill the law of Christ. Then shall we have a retreat where the poor and homeless may say, 'Here shall I dwell.'"

The Brooklyn Industrial School Association and Home for Destitute Children,

Brooklyn,

Is situated on Butler street, between Flatbush and Vanderbilt avenues. The Association also sustains four industrial schools in various parts of Brooklyn. It is governed by a Board of Lady Managers, representing all the Protestant churches in the city, and is supported mainly by voluntary contributions and annual fairs.

The Association was organized in April, 1854, and incorporated April 15, 1857, by special act of the Legislature. It first began its work under the name of the Brooklyn Industrial School Association. But the number of destitute children found wandering in the streets uncared for, uneducated and without a home, "touched that instinct of pity existing in every true woman's heart for helpless childhood, touched that measureless capacity for loving and providing for such homeless and friendless little ones as have not had their due share of mother love and home comforts," and the charity became expanded into the Brooklyn Industrial School Association and Home for Destitute Children. The present edifice was erected in 1861–2. It is a brick building with slate roof, in the Gothic style of architecture.

At the time of visitation, October 16, the immediate charge of the institution was in the hands of Mrs. S. B. McCord, Matron, who, in answer to our inquiries, gave us the following information relative to the workings of the institution: "We have always more boys than girls. We take none under two years of age. We take them from two years up to ten, if boys, and if girls a little older. The average age of the children now in the house is about seven years." With reference to the surroundings of children, Mrs. McCord said: "My idea is that the children should be made to feel that this is a home, so that after they have gone away from us they may still look back upon the time spent here as one of the happiest periods of their lives."

We found here a number of children from the nursery of the Kings County Poor-house, who had been generously received by the Board of Managers at the time that institution was broken up. The Matron, in speaking of them, said: "They have given us a good deal of trouble. We have taken, in all, thirty-eight poor-house children, twenty-five of whom come directly from the nursery department. I was thoroughly discouraged when the large boys came. They would not sing, they would not answer, neither would they pay attention to the scripture lesson at night. It was at times very discouraging."

Passing through the house, the eye everywhere encountered indications of good housekeeping and home feeling. Its nursery comprises two sleeping apartments, with a dining-room between, having two little tables about eighteen or twenty inches from the floor. The nursery is furnished with iron cribs. Nurses sleep in each room. One of these, a young Englishwoman, Miss Simpson, in her faithful attendance upon the children who come from the Kings County Poor-house nursery with sore eyes, was so unfortunate as to have caught the disease herself, and, on the day of our visitation, was just recovering the use of one eye, having, we are informed, narrowly escaped total blindness.

In the hospital we found twelve children suffering from ophthalmia. A number of those who came from the Kings County Poor-house nursery were, at the time of their admission, suffering from that disease.

All of these had recovered except two, who were among the twelve. The cure of the Poor-house children, however, was not effected without the inoculation of several of the children of the house with the disease, and at the time of our visit the other ten sufferers belonged to the house. They were, however, all getting better. The room was cheerful and clean. A fire was burning in the grate, to take off the chill and to facilitate ventilation. The walls were brightened with pictures and illuminated cards, all gifts of the Sunday schools of the city.

The children seemed to have every attention, and if cleanliness, comfort and motherly care could restore these little sufferers to health, we felt sure that they would not have long to be numbered with the sick.

The convalescent room of the hospital department was very neat and was, we were informed, furnished by the Sunday schools of Brooklyn. The room is large, with windows on three sides, affording good sun exposure. The walls were hung with illuminated cards and pictures of home life. Beside each bed was a bright colored rug, with some design to please the juvenile fancy worked upon it. Every child here has its own comb, brush, and washing cloth and towel. These, together with the sponge and bowl, are kept at the head of each bed in a little fancy rack, having a pretty picture in the centre. There were in the room fifteen beds. Every thing, apart from its own intrinsic loveliness, had a story which invested it with an individual interest.

Here were memorial gifts, thank-offerings, presents from little ones, tender expressions of affection from the children of the rich toward their less favored sisters, that warmed the heart, as one contemplated them. In reference to these memorials, the corresponding secretary, Mrs. J. Vanderbilt, says:

"Truly 'the children are learning the first two words of the Lord's prayer.'

"There are gifts in this hospital which were purchased as mementoes of little ones whose cribs at home stand empty; others were sent us as thank-offerings for spared life, from the abundant gratitude of anxious mothers' hearts; so that, to those knowing the story, each token of beauty or comfort has the added charm of being some touching memorial gift.

"Six little girls from Annapolis, Maryland, gave, through Miss Meachem, the first gift of ten dollars for the hospital.

"One baby, the only little pet in her home, gives the chairs beside each bed.

"Wise little Carrie furnishes a crib, and desires to have it called 'The Lily of the Valley,' as if sheltering leaves enfolding a pale flower had suggested to her poetic nature the fitness of the emblem."

The dormitories were sweet and clean, and were furnished with single iron bedsteads two feet six inches wide. Straw beds were used. Each bed had two sheets, two blankets and a comfortable. The straw is changed three times a year, and oftener if necessary.

A school is held on the premises under the Department of Public Instruction. The teacher is employed by the Association. The children are carefully instructed at stated times in the Scriptures; family prayers are conducted every day by the matron, and on Sunday afternoon a Sunday school is held on the premises.

The girls, as soon as they are old enough, are taught to sew, and are set to do certain light duties pertaining to housework suited to their years. Twice a week those who are old enough sew with the seamstress. The boys are also trained to make themselves generally useful.

The bath-room is in the basement. A large vat stands in the center of the room, a little elevated. It is about four by six feet, with a six inch inclined shelf at the upper edge. A box of soap is kept on each of the four corners. Crash towels, two feet eight inches long, are kept on numbered hooks. Bathing and washing cloths are also used. In this room is a convenient foot bath. The top is flush with the floor, and when not in use is covered with a lid. It is supplied with hot and cold water. Around the upper margin of the bathing vat is a perforated pipe for the children to wash in running water. Any child having a diseased scalp is kept away from the others. "By watching the children myself," says Mrs. McCord, "we do not have any trouble with that disease. The heads of the children are fine-combed every day, and thoroughly washed every week with carbolic soap."

The children were going to supper as we arrived. After assembling at the table they repeated the following form of grace taught them by the matron: "Our Father which art in Heaven, give us this day our daily bread and bless it to our use for Christ's sake, Amen." The children, after the meal, returned thanks in the following words: "O Lord we thank Thee for this food and for all Thy other gifts, in the name of Jesus Christ, Amen."

The dietary adopted is generous and nutritious, the children being, we were assured, in no way stinted. Their appearance corroborated the assertion, as well as the gleeful testimony of "Frank," a former inmate of the Kings County Poor-house nursery. The surroundings of this boy and his associates, as compared with their condition as seen when in the forbidding precincts of the Kings County Poor-house nursery, awakened the most grateful emotions toward all those who had been instrumental in delivering them from their former degradation.

Mrs. McCord, on being asked if she found any difference in the children now being sent by the Commissioners of Public Charities, from those admitted into the institution at the time of the breaking up of the Kings County Poor-house nursery, said that there was a marked improvement and that they appeared to be the same as other children belonging to the dependent class.

In alluding to the debasing influence of the alms-house on children, Mrs. McCord said: "I had a little boy here from the alms-house who was morally depraved by association with the bad company of the place. He would cry when I talked with him about things he had heard bad men and bad women say when he was in the alms-house. We sent him out west. He has written me a good letter since."

In regard to the disposition of the children, the matron says: "We have applications for our girls every day in the week. Our boys we send west by means of the New York Children's Aid Society. Mr. Brace secures good homes for them. We think he always succeeds well. We do not put any of our girls in the city, but into families on Long Island and other country places. The applicants must bring references from the pastor of the church to which they belong. The mother of the family is required to make the application. We have a cautious committee who see to the placing out of children, and applications must be made at a regular meeting of the Board. We hear from our children frequently after they are placed out.

The subordinate force employed in this institution consists of a teacher, seamstress, two care-takers, a cook, two chamber-maids, three laundresses, a baker, two nurses, and one dining-room woman, all of whom are carefully selected with reference to their fitness for being associates for children, and receive good pay. The inspection made of the Home was very thorough, and the result very satisfactory. The bright, orderly, homelike spirit which pervaded every part of the institution, bespoke the unselfish and constant attention of the ladies engaged in the work.

The number of children in the Home, October 1, 1875, was one hundred and seven. Of these, four were orphans, twenty-four half orphans, and seventy-nine had both parents living. Forty-two were of native, and sixty-five of foreign parentage. The number received during the year was sixty-five; the number discharged, one hundred and thirty-six. Of the latter, four were placed out by adoption, twenty-eight indentured, and sixty-eight returned to parents or guardians.

The amount of its invested funds is $5,000. Its total expenditures during the past fiscal year was $29,482.82. About $8,000 of this was for indebtedness upon real estate.

As further illustrating the aims and workings of the Home, we quote again from the report of the Corresponding Secretary:

"In a healthy plant, growth and expansion are the natural results of life, and no less is growth the normal condition of that charity which has its root in the exigency of the time. As, after industrial schools had been established, the Home was needed for such as had no shelter for the night, even had they been able to attend school during the day, so in time there came to be many in the Home, who, from various causes, were left permanently in care of the Association; and it was necessary that for these good homes should be found. The procuring of such, and placing out children, either by indenture or adoption, form an important — we had almost said the most important — part of the work."

* * * * * * * *

"While our Home has proved itself a happy asylum for the class it was designed to relieve, while we have comfortably clothed, fed and instructed the many little ones intrusted to our care, we should not be acting in accordance with our views, as to the training of our children, did we regard it as a permanent residence for any of them; and we have never hesitated to exchange institution life for a Christian family home whenever circumstances rendered this possible.

We give the following as the number of children who, since the year 1860, have been furnished with homes, and, as far as possible, the results:

Number of children for whom homes have been provided	168
Of these there are doing well	108
Have not given much promise of future usefulness	10
Have improved and are improving	4
Have not been heard from for some years	11
Are reported as either lazy, careless, or untruthful, but not positively bad	10
Have returned to their relatives	13
Have lost trace of	6
Have died	6

Of the eleven reported as not heard from recently, and the six of whom all trace is lost, we would say that most of them are of age, have married and settled in life, and, in moving from place to place, have failed to send us their address. As they are able to help themselves, it has not been necessary that we should continue in communication with them; and it is owing to this that we have lost trace of many.

The industrial schools of the Association referred to are located as follows:

School No. 1. Concord street, opposite the junction of Prince street.
School No. 2. Fourth street, near Smith street.

School No. 3. At the head of Butler street.
School No. 4. No. 602 Warren street.

The following particulars of the schools are taken from the last report of the Corresponding Secretary:

The schools established by this Association recognize those wants of the children which could not possibly be met and provided for in the ward schools, and to this they owe their success.

In regard to the means adopted to dispense the benefits of the schools among the classes needing them, the same lady remarks, "There are other than compulsory laws; in the battle of life, where might is often more potent than right, women have learned by experience that by the strength of love, and the power of gentleness, they can conquer; with these, as the weapons which they can wield to most advantage, they have entered upon this conflict of light against darkness."

Many of the children in School No. 4 are Germans, others are Swedes, and some few are Norwegians, but these have all learned to speak and read English, under the instruction of the present teacher, who is very efficient.

Number of children in attendance during the year.........	706
" " at present on the roll-book	333
" " who can read........................	223
" " who are learning to write............	160
" " who are studying geography	39
" " who are studying arithmetic	71
Number of new garments given out during the year........	2,820
" " shoes	490
" of meals given during the year	40,167

We should feel we had hardly represented the gentle Christ-like spirit which actuates the workers in this worthy charity did we omit to embody the closing paragraph from the last report of the Corresponding Secretary:

"As we look from the windows of the Home into the adjacent public park, we remember that a few years since there were rough sand-hills and stony fields where now we see the beauty of soft, green slopes and fragrant flowers; and we are encouraged to feel that if God will thus reward the work of cultivation in the physical world, He will none the less cause beauty to follow the work of culture undertaken at His command in the hearts of little children."

We finished our visit to this Home, with the impression left upon the mind that it might be truly said of any unfortunate child who had drifted in its homelessness into this sweet haven of rest, that its "lines had fallen in pleasant places."

The Brooklyn Nursery,

Brooklyn:

Is located at 66 Prospect place, between Carlton and Vanderbilt avenues. The Nursery was first incorporated under the general law as the "Flatbush Avenue Industrial School and Nursery." The building occupied, formerly a private mansion, has a large and pleasant yard, shaded with trees in its rear, and is well furnished. The acquisition of this valuable property is largely attributable to a gift from one of the ladies interested in the work.

The affairs of the Nursery are directed by a Board of Lady Managers and an Advisory Committee of Gentlemen. Its immediate charge is committed to a matron. The paid force of the establishment, in addition to the matron, consists of an assistant matron, cook and laundress.

On the day of visitation, October 16, there were twenty-eight inmates of the Nursery. One was an infant, five months old, whose parents had quarreled and separated. Another was a bright little boy who, through an unfortunate circumstance attending his birth, was unable to use his hip joints. His mother was said to be very destitute. The father of one of the children was in the penitentiary; the father of another had left a family of five entirely destitute by his neglect. The history of yet another child was thus given: Its father had deserted his family, leaving the mother with two children unprovided for. The father of one was at sea, and its mother was employed as a wet nurse in a private family. The parents of another were both living, but its father had been sick for a long time, and its mother was out of work. Several additional cases, similar in character, were encountered, all disclosing unhappy phases of social life, and showing the need of such institutions as this for the care of the young.

In the dining room the children were eating their dinner at the time of visitation. The room was furnished with two or three little tables, eighteen inches high, covered with white enamel cloth, little arm chairs and tiny plates and dishes to correspond. Many of the plates were colored and pictured with letters of the alphabet. The little folks seemed to be very happy over their food, which was highly nutritious, and suited to their years.

Many of the children coming under the care of the ladies at the Nursery are surrendered to the institution. "For these babes," the Secretary, Mrs. Aten, says, "the Managers have sought the best of homes, and their desire has been fully realized; for not only has the sunshine of love streamed into the cloudy beginning of the dear babe's life, and the song of 'Home, Sweet Home,' been put into their mouths, but the lonely hearts of the heretofore empty homes have also thankfully basked in this same sunshine, and echoed the new and gladsome song of the babe."

As showing the nature of the work and the circumstances under which it appeals to the sympathies of those engaged in it, we further quote substantially the language used by the Secretary: "Varied are the pictures that stand forth in our experience like living illustrations of heart-joy and sorrow.

"The first we could show represents a day in winter. Bright and cold is the air without. In the open doorway of the Nursery stands a father with a motherless babe of ten months in his strong arms. He bears also in his hands the bundle of little clothing, and the can of milk purchased after the sudden death of the mother. 'What will you have, my good man?' said the cheery voice of the Matron. 'A home for my boy; the mother is taken from me and the babe is left. I know not how to care for him as he needs. I am a stranger in these parts, and know not where to go, but a kind man at the ship told me, when I landed, that good ladies had provided a home and shelter for just such as mine, and so I have brought my boy to you.' A welcome was given the little one, and the sad heart of the father cheered.

"Here is a mother and her babe, the one bearing traces of grief upon her face, the other frolicking in joyous ignorance of all grief. The place which once bore the name of home has been broken up by the intemperance of the father, and nothing remains for the mother but to first find a home for her child, and, if possible, be accepted as nurse under the same roof. When assured such a home awaits both herself and babe, a look of thankful joy takes the place of deep sorrow clouding her countenance.

"A sad, sad picture is that of a father with his little one clinging to him with that trusting love which it is the mother's privilege to receive from her child—but where is the mother? In a darkened cell; brought there by her own wrong-doing, for in hardened recklessness she has drunk herself into a state of utter forgetfulness of the dear child of her bosom, and the care she should give the babe must be sought for at the hands of strangers.

"Again, a mother must leave her babe and busy herself elsewhere to support it, but the consciousness that loving care will be given her child, helps her to bear the separation which must be made for the time.

"In another picture we see the shadows of evening drawing near, the snow is falling fast, and like a mantle is covering the form of a little babe lying on the frozen ground in the court-yard of the Nursery; its cries reach the ears of the inmates, and the deserted babe is soon within the warm shelter of the building. Shall we close our doors and bar our hearts? Oh, no! life still flutters in the little frame, and the eye of Him who numbereth the hairs of our head, sees us as we follow His command. 'Inasmuch as ye have done it unto the least of these little ones, ye have done it unto me.' And chide not the mother too harshly, for the storm of sorrow in her heart may be fiercer and bleaker than the storm which beats upon her innocent babe, and in her despair it is warmed with but one comforting thought — my child is cared for.

"Look once again — three pictures so sweet, touching, and full of meaning. They tell of the mother and father parted from the child they love, called to the home above — the kind friends, tender and true to their charge, bringing the babes to the only temporary home which offers itself. Think you we say, 'Nay, no room, no place!' and turn away? God forbid! The very loneliness of the little ones gives them a passport to our care and protection. The months go by, and one of these little strangers becomes the pet of the Nursery. The others are soon taken to fill happy homes with more joy by their sweet presence, and to be always precious mementoes of a work which, to many of us who toil in this garden of benevolence, seems fragrant with the blossoms of success, gathered from a field of charity God himself hath blessed."

The following information regarding the history and workings of this interesting charity are kindly furnished from the same source: "In the beginning of our work and in the heat of summer, we found ourselves with plenty of work to do, a houseful of little ones, a very slim treasury, a small but earnest band of workers; fortunately, none of the sort to 'give up.' We had numberless applications, and though enabled to assist a great many, the greater number we were forced to refuse. Every year finds our work widening and our working-band re-inforced and strengthened, and we are daily assured that our nursery has proved a shelter and home to many little babes and weary women, an asylum to the heart-broken and homeless ones, and a resting place to the storm-tossed and innocent babe. Many a woman returns to thank us face to face; others write their thanks, and these mothers and the fathers also, we do feel, appreciate the kindnesses extended to them and their little ones through the nursery. We close no doors to the mother, who comes before us with her babe on her bosom, begging us to take her and it into the Home, as we are sure there is enough of *true* womanhood left in her nature to *save* her, when she evinces this desire to maintain and support her child. Many of the little ones have parents who are struggling outside to earn daily bread and support for their children, and we have been surprised to see how many of this class apply to us, as they find it impossible to keep at their employment or labor and care for their infants at the same time,

The parents take pride in being able to pay even the small sums asked for their children's maintenance, and in their weekly visits evince pleasure and satisfaction with their condition. Once in a while, among the many who become members of the household, we find some very hardened characters, but as a whole, the women so conduct themselves as to form a *well ordered* company, and many of them, after being with us for a long while, return to thank us, or if at a distance, write to us of their gratefulness for the kindnesses extended them.

"Since April, 1871, we have had in our nursery over 508 babies and about 215 women. We average about forty children. There have been sixty-four deaths.

"Our household is a changeable one, some of the children remain but a week, others till past the age to be under our charge. Many of the babes, though not sick when admitted, are in a sadly neglected condition and low state, and fail to thrive even with the best of wet-nursing. We have, as before mentioned, had the pleasure of adopting a great number of babes, and as we learn from time to time of the welfare of each of these, we are rejoiced to feel that our nursery was the medium of this mutual happiness.

"We have never received any very large sums except that of Mrs E. T. Pell, mentioned in the fourth annual report. But the sums and donations received have been given with such a willing spirit that they seem very precious to us, and in the aggregate have kept our treasury from being wholly empty. The reception of the appropriation money from the city was warmly welcomed and appreciated.

"I would add that, financially, we have been prospered from year to year, but only through personal and individual efforts on the part of the managers. Our expenses appear and *are* very great, but our household is of that nature requiring the best of food — plenty of milk also for the elder children. The women need this nourishing food or they cannot retain their places as wet-nurses.

"The physicians are *Homœopathists*, and are constant and faithful to their charge."

The number of children received during the year was one hundred and forty-four. The institution has no invested fund. Its total indebtedness in October 1, 1875, was $9,184.33; of this $7,700 was upon real estate. Its total expenditures were $15,571.59, of which $7,693.40 was paid to reduce real estate indebtedness.

A peculiar feature of this work is that it includes a class who, but for this help, would be inmates of the poor-house, and thus sink into dependence and degradation. It rescues from criminality, builds up character, and breaks off the line of hereditary pauperism, and is a remedy applied at the very fountain-source of the evils which undermine society. It is a work, in fact, strictly belonging to the public to do, and is therefore deserving the support of the entire community;

but it is one that cannot be carried on under any public administration of charity, because, to be effectual, it must be inspired and directed by Christian benevolence.

THE CHURCH CHARITY FOUNDATION OF LONG ISLAND.

Brooklyn.

This well-known institution is located on Albany avenue, corner of Herkimer street, in the city of Brooklyn. It was designed to provide a home for indigent persons of both sexes, including married persons too old or enfeebled to maintain themselves; also for orphans and destitute children. It was incorporated March 13, 1851, having been organized the February previous. The Foundation is under the patronage of the Protestant Episcopal Church of Long Island. Its financial affairs are controlled by a Board of Managers, and a Board of Lady Associates take charge of its general concerns. The immediate charge and management of its several departments are committed to the Sisters of St. John, of the Protestant Episcopal Church, called also Deaconesses, seven of whom were engaged at date of October 31. Of their zeal in the work, the lady managers bear the following testimony:

"It is quite proper that we speak, and with warmth too, of our perfect satisfaction in having given the entire internal management of the House to the Deaconesses. The perfect success of the same, and the beautiful spirit evinced under all circumstances, have not only elicited the approbation and commendation of all, but have so completely won our hearts, that words are fulsome. We had long felt the impossibility of carrying on the work as it should be, without such care, and had almost begun to feel it would not come, although we had earnestly sought it, when the providence of God granted us the blessing. While we may not be personal, we may say the very right persons have been given us for their respective positions. We thank God for them. We accept them as His gift, and earnestly pray Him that each one of them may long be spared us."

The Foundation now embraces a home for the aged, a general hospital and an orphan house for boys and girls. The grounds occupied extend from Albany avenue to Atlantic avenue.

Although the home for the aged and the hospital were both visited, with very gratifying results, our attention was particularly directed to the orphan house, which contained, on the date of visitation, seventy-five children. This work is being enlarged by the erection of a new building, which will increase the capacity of the orphan home to 150. This enlargement to the home was greatly needed, as will be seen by the language used in an appeal made by the Board of Lady Associates the early part of last year. The Secretary, Miss P. S. Van Nostrand, says: "We often feel if loving parents, who cannot find it in their hearts to deny their children the smallest gratification, could but see the sad faces of the widows who entreat us to care for their destitute and suffering children, we would be saved from the sinks of misery here and a hereafter we dare not permit ourselves to think of. These children (or some of them) that are turned away will help to make up the lists of vagrants and prisoners in a few years. We cannot safely admit more than seventy-five children, and for the few vacancies there are many applications. How small a sacrifice on the part of each Christian parent would save many a child from degradation. Who has made their children to differ from those knocking at our doors?"

The wing was almost ready for occupation at the time of our visit. A debt was necessarily incurred in its erection, but this disadvantage will doubtless be more than compensated by the increased usefulness of the institution, commending it still more to the liberal support of the public.

In addition to a good secular and religious education, the children are taught habits of industry. A sewing school is held twice a week; the girls are trained in housework, and a few of both sexes learn the business of type-setting, which is conducted on the premises; $2,000 was cleared last year in the printing department. This, however, does not take into account a large amount of voluntary service rendered in carrying on the business.

In the reception-room is a well-filled book-case, purchased out of a sum given to the institution by a benevolent lady as a memorial to her husband.

The sitting-room, or what is called the "social room," is a very pleasant apartment, the tables being covered with crimson cloth. The walls were hung with pictures; flowers filled the air with perfume, and the warbling of canary birds with song. The children appeared to be very happy. "They have not," says the Sister, "the least fear. They come in and say 'such a one took my button,' and 'such a one took my marble.' I could not live here if we had not a home atmosphere."

In the school-room long stems of ivy were trailed on the walls, back of the dais, and pictures were hung around the room. There was an evidence of good taste in the arrangements of this as well as other apartments of the asylum, betokening refining influences, which must exert a beneficial effect upon the children. The room was full of little plants belonging to the children. "They are," says the Sister, "passionately fond of flowers. Everybody has a garden. They plant seeds in them, and are delighted to see them grow. One little boy, the first time he saw a favorite uncle, after being here, wanted to borrow five cents to buy some pumpkin seeds."

The dormitories are furnished with single iron bedsteads, having spring slats. The walls are hung with bright pictures, the frames of which are graced with ivy. A present from the children in the diocese, in the form of a nice seat, stands beside each bed. The rooms are supplied with toys and other objects of childish interest. Ample provision is made for bathing. Each child has its own towel and "ophthalmia is unknown here."

On the 1st of October there were thirteen orphans, fifty-seven half orphans, and two children who had both parents living, in the institution. Two of the children were of native and seventy were of foreign parentage. Eight were partially supported by parents or friends, and sixty-four wholly by the institution.

The invested funds of the Foundation amount to $28,750; its total indebtedness to $31,400. Its total expenditure during the fiscal year ending October 1, 1875, was $29,862.05. Of this, $6,397.65 was expended for buildings and improvements, and $4,844.81 to reduce indebtedness.

The Foundation, besides its ordinary work, publishes a monthly paper called the "Helping Hand." This is intended to find its way into families with a view to elevate and instruct both old and young. It also acts as a medium of communication between the Foundation and its numerous friends.

The efficiency of this institution is doubtless largely attributable to the zeal with which those connected with it are inspired. The beautiful system maintained by the Sisters in the management of its internal affairs is so marked as to give to it something like the sacred character of a home. The beneficial effects growing out of this association of children with persons of cultivation, who are imbued with pure religious sentiment, are so great as to be beyond measurement.

Convent and House of the Good Shepherd.

Brooklyn.

This institution, incorporated December 23, 1868, was founded by a few Sisters belonging to the Order of Our Lady of Charity of the Good Shepherd. The Order was established in 1651. The Mother House, which is at Angers in France, has 120 branches in different parts of the world, where the *Religieuses* labor in reforming the most abandoned of their sex.

The following information, regarding the beginning of the work in Brooklyn, has been kindly furnished:

"The Sisters came to Brooklyn at the solicitation of the Right Reverend John Laughlin, D. D., and some of the principal gentlemen of the place; and, in consideration of the urgency of the case, as no house of refuge existed, to afford a place of protection to those who might wish to reform their lives among the poor unfortunate girls who may be found in such numbers in the streets of every great city, they were induced to enter upon the task without resources, trusting to a generous public to aid in this benevolent project for the general good of society. Dependent entirely upon their own exertion, the life of the Sisters in laying this foundation has been a continual struggle; but they have felt themselves indemnified for their labors by the progress of the penitents, which has been highly satisfactory. Their characters have become elevated and improved; and their habits of idleness have been overcome by the teaching of industries, which will fit them for becoming useful members of society. They usually come utterly ignorant."

The institution is situated on the corner of Atlantic and Rockaway avenues. The building is a brick structure of four stories, standing on a stone basement.

The work in which thirty Sisters are now engaged was begun on Henry street; afterward it was removed to the corner of East New York and Atlantic avenue, and, in the month of July last, the new building was first occupied.

In the workroom for penitents, on the day of visitation, October 18, there were about thirty young girls engaged in making shirts and dresses, and quite a large number of sewing machines were in operation. Perfect order prevailed. About 150 of the Penitent class were in the house. Of another class, called the Preservation, there were about ninety-five inmates under sixteen. It is contemplated having a third class called Magdalens, who take vows to lead a religious life. All entering this Order are first required to take three vows for stated periods to afford time for reflection upon the final step about to be taken, and to afford the Sisters ample time to test their sincerity. After five years of a novitiate they are allowed to make their perpetual vow. The inmates of the institution were partly committed by the magistrates and partly self-committed. The Lady Superior says: "We cannot refuse admittance to any one who comes and shows signs of repentance." Few of the preservation class are under commitment. They are sometimes the children of drunken parents, and often are children who, although having good parents, show inclinations to evil. Those committed by the magistrates must remain their allotted time, and have opportunity to continue in the institution, after its expiration. But children sent there by parents can be removed at any time.

A school is held on the premises, where reading, writing and arithmetic are taught.

Young children are instructed in finishing shirts and in hand sewing, after which they learn to use the machine.

The building is wainscoted throughout, except the dormitories. It is heated by steam, lighted by gas, and well ventilated with flues in the walls. The windows have inside blinds. The building has a capacity for five hundred inmates, and cost between $116,000 and $117,000. The grounds comprise sixty lots, and take up an entire block.

The total number of inmates, both children and adults, received during the year, was three hundred and forty. The number remaining in the institution on October 1, 1875, including both children and adult inmates, was two hundred and fifty-five.

The total expenditures during the year amount to $86,573.86. Of this, $64,787.07 was expended upon real estate, and for reducing indebtedness. The indebtedness of the institution, upon real estate, is $91,000, and for other indebtedness, $6,000. Its cash investments are about $5,000.

It is thought that the Sisters engaged in this peculiar and difficult work are conducting it with great zeal, and that their efforts to reform the class which engages their attention, and to make them useful to society, is attended with satisfactory results. The class coming under their care is, perhaps, the most difficult of any of the offending to deal with, and the experience of those so largely engaged in it as this sisterhood, leads them to think that the most efficacious means of reform lies in the implanting of positive religious convictions.

Convent of the Sisters of Mercy, in Brooklyn.

Brooklyn.

The organization of this institution took place March 18, 1855, and its incorporation March 8, 1865. It is situated on 273 Willoughby avenue, corner of Classon avenue, and is under the charge of Mother Mary Vincent Hare, and thirty-two Sisters of Mercy. Its objects, as set forth in its certificate of incorporation, are:

1st. To establish, maintain and conduct a house of protection, in which young women of good character may be protected and supported until situations may be provided for them.

2d. To visit the sick poor, and to supply them gratuitously with nourishment, clothing and other necessaries.

3d. To give poor girls useful and proper instruction, without charge

4th. To establish and maintain a free school for the general education of female children, and also an industrial school, in which young girls may be taught various branches of industry, without charge.

The following interesting sketch is furnished by one familiar with its early history and struggles: "When we purchased our present property it was in the neighborhood of only a few small frame houses. We defrayed half the expense of grading the hill, which stood in place of the avenue upon which our building now fronts. We purchased eleven lots, and the building was at once contracted for and completed at an expense of $60,000. On the 3d of December, 1862, before it was completed, thirteen Sisters moved in with a handful of furniture, one sewing machine, and $100, which was the sum total of our possessions. The following month we commenced work in our industrial school. Our first work table was of our own manufacture, and composed of three boards placed across two horses left by the workmen on the premises. In March, we borrowed $180 to purchase desks for our own select school, which we were about to open. This succeeded very well, and with the proceeds from it and the use of twenty sewing machines, furnished us on credit, we were enabled to admit into the institution orphan and destitute children, whose number rapidly increased. During this period we were constantly in straitened circumstances, but Divine Providence watched over our struggles, guided us through our difficulties, and, we believe, will yet raise us above the charity of the public, and enable us to discharge fully the works of our vocation. This will not be fully done until our whole time and labor are given to the sick and poor, and to the care of our hospital, which we contemplate building as soon as funds are available. Since the original purchase, eighteen adjoining lots have been added, and it is upon these we hope to erect the hospital, where poor girls, who are without parents or homes (when stricken down by disease), may find a shelter and tender care."

At the date of visitation, October 18, there were in the sewing-room about sixty girls working for the stores. About fifty sewing machines were in operation. The Sister said they were never out of work. The stores kept them constantly employed. Although the compensation was low, yet they were so circumstanced as to be able to work to advantage even with small remuneration. The ages of the children here ranged from ten to seventeen. They appeared neat, having their hair nicely tied back with ribbons. Their dresses were tidy and comfortable, but not uniform. The Sister remarked on this point, "We never dress them alike."

The girls, on leaving, are able to earn from $12 to $14 a week Some of the girls were making cuffs, some hemming skirts and others putting in sleeves and joining them. The girls have each a daily task assigned them. This is regulated by the Sister superintending, and varied according to the capabilities of each. There was manifest, in this department, a pleasing naturalness of manner, indicating a home-like feeling and confidential relations between the children and their superiors.

Another room contained about seventy girls, ranging in age from two and a-half years to twelve. They were seated on benches and engaged in sewing. Two of these little ones showed us, with girlish pride, some of the button-holes they had worked, which were certainly creditable, considering their years. A few of the children in this room were from the Kings County Poor-house. Their clean and comely appearance was in marked contrast to the former condition of children as seen in that institution.

In the day school were about 620 children. On a gallery in one of the class-rooms about 180 little girls were seated, dressed in an array of bright colors, and looking like a parterre of flowers in which scarlet, pink and green were conspicuous. A few of the asylum children were intermingled with the day scholars. The latter seemed to show, in their animated looks and manners, contact with the activities of life, and the association of the asylum children with them was thought by the Sisters to have a happy effect.

Fourteen domestics are employed. The dormitories are furnished with single bedsteads of iron. Hair and straw mattresses are used.

In the infirmary department we found one of the asylum children suffering from sore eyes, which she had contracted from one of those sent from the Kings County Poor-house. Here were also several girls from that institution suffering from ophthalmia.

A very interesting feature about this institution is the thoughtful provision made for the children about to leave. "Each child," says the Sister, "gets her trunk well furnished with under-clothing, a set of toilet articles, and in addition to her stock of plain dresses, a very nice Sunday dress. with a shawl and cloak. The girl who conducts herself properly during her stay with us, gets also a silver medal on leaving."

The children are received at from three to fourteen years of age, and kept till they are eighteen. "By that time," says the Sister, "they are able to take care of themselves and leave the institution with a recommendation that will entitle them to good situations."

The number of children in the institution October 1, who were orphans, was sixty; half-orphans, seventy-seven; who had both parents living, twenty. Eighty-five of these were from the County of Kings; forty from New York, and the remainder from other counties. Twelve were partially supported by parents or friends, nineteen by public authorities, and one hundred and twenty-six by the institution.

The number of children received during the year was forty-two; the number discharged, twenty-four. The total expenditure during the fiscal year ending October 1, 1875, was $27,163.02, about $4,000 of this was for reducing its indebtedness, while for provisions, clothing, fuel and light, $12,120.12 were expended. The total indebtedness is $71,000; of this sum, $57,000 is upon real estate. It has no invested fund.

Quite a large garden is connected with the institution from which the vegetables, excepting potatoes, are supplied. Seven milch cows are kept, which afford a quantity of pure fresh milk.

A pleasant feature of the institution was found to be in its highly cultivated grounds in the rear, within which were abundance of flowering plants, vines, and shady bowers for sitting or promenading. The rear walls of the main edifice and the inner façade of the two wings were covered with a drapery of ivy, the whole soothing the eye, while bringing to the mind a sense of retirement from the world hardly reconcilable with its nearness.

The inspection of the house gave abundant evidence of cleanliness and order throughout. The glass of the windows shone like crystal, and every object upon which the eye rested betokened care. The surroundings and influences to which the children are here subjected, it would seem, must be highly elevating and prove efficacious in forming womanly character.

The Industrial School Association of Brooklyn, Eastern District.

Brooklyn.

This institution is one of the many illustrations of large beneficent results from small beginnings, growing out of woman's faith and Christian zeal. We find the following interesting scrap of history connected with the commencement of this work: A lady, resident of Williamsburgh, who had become deeply impressed with the degraded condition of many of the children of the extremely poor, and regarding their reformation as the most hopeful avenue of charity, personally solicited the sum of $600 for the purpose of organizing a work for the benefit of this class. A meeting was called for those interested in the enterprise, which was held February 20, 1854. An organization was effected, and plans discussed for furthering the objects in view.

The primary object that the benevolent ladies had in view in the founding of the school was "to provide a place where those children whose parents were too poor and degraded to send them to the public school, might be taught to read and write, and be at least partially clothed and fed."

The school was opened on North Second street, Williamsburgh, March 7, 1854, with eleven scholars. It was composed largely at first of colored children. It soon outgrew its original quarters, and was removed to larger rooms. During the first seven years of its existence between seven and eight hundred children were instructed and furnished daily with a good, substantial, warm dinner of bread, soup or meat. Large quantities of clothing were also distributed.

The Association was incorporated March 26, 1860. Its finances are controlled by a Board of Trustees composed of gentlemen. Its general affairs are directed by a Board of Lady Managers, made up of members representing about twenty Protestant churches in the city. Its domestic affairs are in the immediate charge of a matron, and the educational department is under the care of a competent lady teacher.

The Industrial School was carried on as a Day Home for fifteen years. But during the latter part of 1869 the ladies decided to open, in connection with the school, a Home, for the purpose of caring for the children who were without other shelter than station-houses. With this end in view, an appeal was made to the Legislature for aid, resulting in an appropriation of $10,000. By means of this grant, and other funds raised for the purpose, the present building, with seven lots of land, was purchased.

In the winter of 1869, the Home was opened at its present location, 141 South Third street. It is a plain three-story building, having a basement. During the past three years it has been under the care of Mrs. Sanxay, Matron.

"We began," says one of the ladies, "with one boy, whose mother could not support him or herself. She left him with us while she went to a situation. She was never able to do any thing for her son. After caring for him for a time he was committed to our keeping by the Mayor, in compliance with our request. We afterward provided him a home in this State where he still remains, and gives promise of becoming a good citizen." Since this small beginning the Managers have had more applications for admissions than they could accommodate. The Home is not only always full, but is often overcrowded.

The first Directress, Mrs. B. H. Howell, says in regard to the children received: "We take all classes of children between the ages of two and ten years, orphans, half-orphans and the neglected, who are worse off than if they had no parents, in consequence of their habits of vice or intemperance. Some agree to pay a small sum toward the board of their children, which is accepted that they may feel less like dependents. This agreement to pay is, however, rarely fulfilled on the part of the parents."

To guard against infectious diseases every child is examined by the Attending Physician before admission to the institution. On this point it is stated: "A number of our children were affected with 'skin diseases,' and sore eyes or ophthalmia. The doctor gave great attention to their medical treatment, advised the giving of a more generous diet to those suffering from these complaints, and also their separation from the other children. This advice was strictly followed, though in the latter case with extreme difficulty, on account of our limited accommodations. Great care was observed to have the nurses use separate cloths and towels, and clean water in washing the eyes of each child whose eyes were sore. In a comparatively short time the children were entirely cured. At the present time we have not a case of sore or even weak eyes among our one hundred and nineteen children."

The Secretary of the institution, Mrs. S. C. Hanford, in a late report in regard to the school, says: "The children have been thoroughly drilled in the elementary branches of an English education, accompanied by writing, singing and recitation of Scripture, and in all these exercises gratifying progress has been made.

"Many mothers leave their infants in the school-room during the day that they may earn their daily bread. This adds much perplexing care to our teacher, but to refuse such assistance to these mothers is ofttimes to thrust starvation into their homes. Practical instruction is our continued aim and object. The boys attend to the various house errands; the girls assist in the ordinary work. Close attention is paid to their habits and manners. Cleanliness of person is required and obedience enjoined. The sewing committee meet with the girls at the close of each session for instruction in plain sewing. Sixty-five have been taught. Some of them sew very neatly. All are teachable and eager to learn. The girls of the Home made, during the vacation, one dozen large sheets, besides sewing a quantity of carpet rags. They also piece bed-quilts with pieces of muslin, calico, etc., sent in by friends.

The *Teacher's Journal* shows the number of pupils instructed during the year ending October 1, 1875	222
Number of pupils on register at present date	88
Number of pupils dismissed to public schools	34
Number of pupils who have been taught to read	121
Number of pupils who have been taught to write	62
Number of pupils who have been taught to sew	65
Number of pupils provided with situations	40

Of the eighty-eight children who are inmates of the Home or attending the school, twenty-five are supported wholly by the institution, and sixty-three partially by parents or friends. About half the number are of native and half of foreign parents. Twenty-eight are orphans, twenty-two half-orphans and thirty-eight have both parents living.

The Matron furnishes the following statistics relating to the inmates of the Home for the past year:

The number of adults sheltered	7
The number of members of families represented in school provided with situations	28
The number of transient persons provided	34
The number of children received into the "Home"	41
The number of children at present in the "Home"	34
The number returned to parents or friends	22
The number provided with homes	11
The number dismissed to other institutions	1
The number died in the "Home"	1

The Visiting Committee of the Board of Managers reports as follows:

"We have investigated each case referred to us, and have called at the school children's homes. It is in these visits that we witness the destitution and scanty fare, that our deepest sympathy is awakened, and we must rejoice that our Home supplies one comfortable meal each day to these hungered children. At the holidays the children are not forgotten by the good people of the district. At Thanksgiving they enjoy a delicious dinner; Christmas, they have a tree covered with useful gifts, and the parents are invited to partake of the supper with their children."

With regard to placing out children, the Secretary says:

"Faithful efforts are made to place the children surrendered to the Association in thrifty, industrious families in the country, where they receive the child as their own, with the pure desire of benefiting it, of rearing it to a useful life, and a respectable citizenship.

"It is in these families, who have so nobly come forward and reached out their helping hands to comfort the poor, that we recognize the true benevolence, the unmeasurable assistance.

"Our Corresponding Secretary maintains a correspondence with both parents and children, replete with heart-cheering news. Nor do we alone rely upon this method of communication. Many have been visited at their homes, where they are leading useful and happy lives."

During the past six years over forty children have been provided with permanent homes.

In regard to the needs of the Institution, the Secretary further states:

"The usefulness of our Industrial Home and School is sadly limited by reason of the insufficient size of the building at present used. It is crowded to the utmost extent that hygienic considerations will permit. Every nook and corner, from attic to cellar, is put into requisition. Still, we cannot make all our little inmates so comfortable as we desire, and every month we are compelled to refuse many applications from those who are legitimate objects of our charity. Fatherless and motherless children, or children who are worse than orphaned, through the crimes or inhumanity of their parents, have a claim upon the sheltering arms of our Institution, which we realize and admit, and it is with heartfelt sorrow that we ever close our doors upon them. Yet, situated as we now are, we feel that we can make only a slight impression on the great mass of wretchedness, which surges bitterly through the life of a great city. There is a strong undertow of poverty, intemperance and nameless misery, which seizes on the waifs of the slums and the streets, and drifts them forward to the criminal classes, who prey upon society and fill our prisons. We try to rescue the children from its clutch, and we regret that we are able to reach and aid so few."

The institution greatly needs a larger and more commodious building. It has already accumulated a small building fund with that object in view, and when its pressing necessities are more fully understood, it is believed that means will be forthcoming for carrying on without embarrassment its truly benevolent work.

The current expenditure of the Association during the fiscal year ending September 30, 1875, was $4,835.27.

Orphan Home and Asylum of the Church of the Holy Trinity.

Brooklyn, E. D.

This Asylum is situated on Graham avenue, between Montrose avenue and Johnson street, in the Eastern District of Brooklyn. It was founded by the members of the Church of the Holy Trinity in 1860, and incorporated November 23, 1861.

The immediate working of the institution is committed to the Sisters of St. Dominic. Children of both sexes are received and given a religious, moral and industrial education. Secular education is imparted at the parish school.

There were in the institution October 1, 1875, eighty-one children, seventy-two of whom were orphans and nine, half-orphans. Seventy-nine of the children were from the County of Kings. Nine were partially supported by parents or friends.

The work has mainly been sustained through the voluntary donations of the members of the Church of the Holy Trinity, to whom much credit is due for their liberal support as well as to the Sisters for their praiseworthy labors. It is believed that the affairs of the Asylum are well managed, and that it is worthy of public confidence.

The number of children received during the past year was ten, the number discharged, eleven. Four of these were indentured and six returned to parents or guardians. The total expenditure during the fiscal year ending September 30, 1875, was $2,970.10. The invested funds of the Asylum amount to $30,000.

Orphan Asylum Society of the City of Brooklyn.

Brooklyn.

The immediate occasion of the organization of this Asylum, which was incorporated April 15, 1835, was the relief of the large number of children that had been left destitute by the ravages of the cholera in 1832. A voluntary association of ladies was first formed, which continued till its incorporation.

Eight lots of ground were donated by General Robert F. Manly, in August, 1838, on which the first building on Cumberland street, near Myrtle avenue, was erected. Subsequently four other lots were donated by other gentlemen, and an additional building put up, making the capacity of the institution equal to the accommodation of one hundred and thirty children. The funds for the erection of the building in each case were derived from subscriptions of the citizens of Brooklyn.

In 1867 the present property, between Herkimer street and Atlantic avenue, was purchased, and the present commodious edifice was occupied on the 15th of June, 1872. This structure is built of Philadelphia brick, trimmed with Ohio and Connecticut stone, the basement being of blue granite. It stands about one hundred and twenty-four feet from the curb on Atlantic avenue, on which it fronts, and occupies about the center of the plot of forty-four lots, which belong to the Asylum. It is, including the mansard roof, four stories in height. A flight of stone steps leads from the hall into a fine lawn. The grounds are bordered in front and on one side by a neat iron fence, while on the rear side of the building are the play-grounds of the boys and girls, each inclosed by a high board fence.

The institution is under the control of a Board of Lady Managers and an Advisory Board of gentlemen. The immediate charge of the house is committed to a matron, Miss J. R. Davis. There are also in the Asylum an assistant matron, three teachers, two seamstresses, two care-takers, and sixteen domestics.

On the date of visitation, October 20, there were two hundred and seventy-five children in the house, one hundred and twelve of whom were girls, and one hundred and sixty-three boys. The ages ranged between two and fourteen. In the absence of the matron, from the principal of the school, Miss Mary Horton, the following information was obtained: A great many of the children have one parent living, in which case, if part of the child's board is paid, the parent has the right to take it away at any time. A large number of the children are taken by their parents. Sometimes we indenture the children, and we send some West. We have had very good reports from those who have gone there. Some have been adopted, and are doing well. Regarding the time the children stay in the institution, it was stated that it was not intended to keep them after fourteen.

The girls receive two hours instruction every week in hand sewing. The rest of the time is mainly spent in school, which is under the Department of Public Instruction. The school-room, in addition to the usual furniture of such an apartment, contains a piano. A large portion of the space around the wall is well taken up with blackboards. The children are very fond of singing, and receive weekly instruction in vocal music from a gentleman who has given his services gratuitously to the institution in this department for the last twenty years. Moral and religious instruction is carefully imparted, without any attempt at sectarian bias. A Sunday school is held on the premises, and the children attend the various Protestant churches in the city. They have a small library, which is replenished by parties occasionally sending contributions of books. As a stimulus to good conduct, a roll of honor is kept.

The building is well arranged and intended to combine all modern improvements. It is so constructed that, in case of fire, either wing may be shut off from the main by means of heavy iron doors, and the balustrades are protected by iron screen-work, to prevent children from injury by falling over. It is lighted with gas and heated by steam, and has a water supply carried to the various floors of the house.

The dormitories are cleanly kept, and are fine, airy apartments. The bedsteads are single, and of iron, and the beds are amply provided with covering. In both boys' and girls' dressing-rooms are presses about five feet deep, in which their Sunday clothes and other apparel are hung.

The lavatories for both sexes are very complete, being similarly furnished and warmed by steam. Each contains two circular tubs, four feet eight inches wide, with wooden rims. Around the sides of each room are troughs, with perforated pipes running above them the entire length, to enable the children to wash in running water. Each child has its own towel, brush and comb. Great attention is paid to personal cleanliness. Each child's hair is fine-combed twice a week.

The dining-room is furnished with tables and stools. The tables are covered with enameled cloth, and the seats in this apartment are circular and supported by iron pedestals. Bread of a superior quality is used. It is made with hop yeast, and baked in a brick oven.

The Nursery, on the day of visitation, contained thirty little children under five years of age. The play-room adjoins it, and was profusely supplied with toys.

The hospital was without an inmate. This is divided into two departments; one division being for children suffering from contagious diseases, who require to be kept apart; the other for ordinary cases of sickness. All the conveniences of such apartments are here provided.

On October 1, 1875, the number of children in the institution who were orphans was thirty, the number of half-orphans two hundred and twenty-six, and eighteen had both parents living. Fifty-nine were of native parents, and two hundred and fifteen were of foreign parents. One hundred and twenty-six of the children were partially or entirely supported by parents or friends, and one hundred and forty-eight wholly by the institution. They are mostly of respectable parentage. The mothers are working at service, and leave their children here.

The number of children received during the past year was one hundred and forty-six; the number discharged, one hundred and ten. Of this number, one was placed out by adoption, eight were indentured, eighty-six returned to parents and guardians, and eleven sent out of the State.

This long-established institution has accomplished, since its organization, a great amount of good. It cannot be ascertained how many children have received its benefactions, but the number is very large. During the period of its working it has won the confidence of the community, as is evident from its prosperous condition, shown in the expensive structure which has been erected. Its real estate is valued at $200,000.00. Its funded investments are $17,380.00. Its expenditures during last year, were $39,769.06.

It is a pleasant thought, in connection with this asylum, in view of the large field of labor in which it is located, that its present capacity for five hundred inmates enables it to enter upon a still larger work of usefulness than it has hitherto been able to undertake.

Roman Catholic Orphan Asylum in the City of Brooklyn, County of Kings.

Brooklyn.

This asylum was organized as early as 1826, and incorporated May 6, 1834. It now comprises—

1st. The Roman Catholic Male Orphan Asylum, St. Mark's place, between Troy and Albany avenues.

2d. St. Joseph's Female Orphan Asylum, Willoughby avenue, between Yates and Lewis avenues.

3d. St. Paul's Female Orphan Asylum or Industrial School, corner of Clinton and Congress streets.

The affairs of these institutions are directed by the Roman Catholic Orphan Asylum Society in the city of Brooklyn. Its officers are a President, two Vice-Presidents, a Secretary, Assistant Secretary, Treasurer and a Board of Managers, consisting of seven gentlemen. The Bishop of Brooklyn is *ex officio* President of the Society.

Among the numerous objects that command the admiration of the visitor to Brooklyn, there are none that reflect more credit upon her citizens than her large and beautiful asylums for homeless children. Those under the charge of this Society are conspicuous, not only for their magnitude but for their external simplicity, while their interiors are constructed with reference to combining all sanitary improvements.

The work that this Society has accomplished in the way of elevating children during the period of its existence, it is impossible to estimate. It is not known how many children have been sheltered by it since its organization, nor have returns been made to show how many have been received during even the past year, nor how many adopted into families, indentured or otherwise placed out. The work it is doing, however, is unquestionably very large, and worthy of cordial encouragement and support.

In the three institutions named at the date of visitation, there were 1,305 children, 550 boys and 755 girls. There were also fifty-one Sisters, who were devoting their lives to this work, whose services are rendered gratuitously. When it is considered that these children may possibly soon become heads of families, and their children in turn the heads of other families, some conception of the importance of this great work can be formed. If Christian teaching and care have a tendency to diminish crime in the same ratio that neglect has been proven to increase it, as is shown in the case of "Margaret," the mother of criminals, so ably exhibited in the researches of the New York Prison Association, some idea may be formed of the change that is being wrought in society by these earnest workers, and of the extent of the obligation under which they are laying the public in the protection of its best interests.

The Roman Catholic Male Orphan Asylum.

The Asylum edifice is built of dark grey stone, with free-stone mouldings. It is eligibly situated on the corner of Albany avenue and St. Mark's place, and is under the charge of the Roman Catholic Order of the Sisters of St. Joseph, Sister M. Baptista, Superior.

The visitation was made on the 18th of October, at which time the institution contained 550 boys. The establishment generally was clean, well-appointed, and seemed to be managed with thorough system. The dormitories are well ventilated, and have good sun exposure. The boys are provided with comfortable beds, each sleeping alone. The school-room is furnished with all the modern appliances. The boys receive a good English education, and are thoroughly trained into habits of order and personal tidiness.

The bodily wants of the children appeared to be amply provided for, and proper provisions made for their religious, moral, secular and industrial education.

An interesting feature of the Asylum consisted in the sewing department, which is furnished with a considerable number of machines, designed to give the boys instruction in tailoring, who, we were informed, make their own clothes, the cutting out being done by the Sisters.

This institution opened its doors to receive a large number of the children from the Kings County Poor-house at the time its Nursery was broken up. Most of these, it was ascertained, came in tolerably good health. A few had sore eyes. They were, however, very backward in their education, and most of them had to be placed in the lowest grades of the school. They were conspicuous, on the day of visitation, by their seniority in age and larger size, as compared with the other children in the same classes. The Sisters stated that some of them had been very troublesome, rude in their manners, and wanting in respect, but that a manifest improvement had taken place during their short stay in the Asylum. The Sisters felt hopeful in being able to discipline them into good habits by a kind but firm method of treatment.

The reception of these children in this institution relieves society of the charge of a large number of its dependent children, as well as saves these tender natures from the inevitable contamination that awaited them in the poor-house.

The generous manner in which it has opened its doors to receive a large proportion of the children from the Kings County Poor-house Nursery entitles it to the full sympathy of the public who are so largely interested in its work.

On October 1st, the number of children in the institution was five hundred and fifty. Of these, one hundred and fifty-one were orphans, three hundred and twenty-nine, half-orphans, and seventy had both parents living. Forty-six were of native, and five hundred and four of foreign parentage.

St. Joseph's Female Orphan Asylum.

This Asylum is located on an elevated site, on the corner of Willoughby and Yates avenues. It is a four-story building, with mansard roof and a basement. At the head of the establishment is Sister Mary Louise, who, with thirteen other Sisters of the Roman Catholic Order of the Sisters of Charity, carries on the work in behalf of destitute female children.

The Asylum takes children from three years old and upwards. At the age of fourteen or fifteen they are transferred to the Industrial School on Congress street. While here, however, they receive a good, plain English education, and are exercised in industries suited to their years, such as mending and making their own clothes, and assisting in the general work of the house.

At the time of the transfer of the children from the Kings County Poor-house Nursery, this Asylum received within its doors ninety-three little girls. The Sister, being questioned about their condition on arriving, said: "They were not very healthy. They did not come up to the average of other children. A great many had skin diseases; some had sore eyes, and generally, they were very delicate children. There was, it would seem, some mismanagement with regard to their clothing. I found out, from the children, that in some cases they wore each other's clothes in the poor-house nursery. What they wore one day they did not wear the next day."

Regarding the condition of the children that come now from the Commissioners of Charities, the Sister remarks: "Those children that came from the poor-house nursery were not as healthy as those that the Commissioners have since sent."

The children, on the day of visitation, October 18, were mostly in the class-rooms of the institution. These were furnished with the modern appliances of such apartments. In one room were seventy-four children, in another, eighty-two, and in another, forty-eight; while in the school-room in the basement there were about one hundred and eighty. "No child under five years of age is," the Sister informed us, "allowed to attend school."

The dormitories are large airy apartments, with good sun exposure, having windows on three sides. They are furnished with iron bedsteads, single. The beds are of straw. This is packed in ticks and changed as often as the Sisters deem necessary. Great care is taken to preserve cleanliness. Two Sisters sleep in each of the girls' dormitories with a view to better preserve order, and to attend to the inmates if taken sick during the night.

In the infirmary were three children; one suffering from sore eyes; another, consumptive; and the third, slightly indisposed.

An inspection of the work being done in this asylum showed that it was conducted by those feeling a deep interest in the successful accomplishment of its objects.

St. Paul's Female Orphan Asylum or Industrial School,

Is situated on the corner of Clinton and Congress streets, and is in charge of Sister Constantia Hull, assisted by eleven other Sisters of the Roman Catholic Order of Sisters of Charity of Mt. St. Vincent.

This institution is intended to receive girls from the St. Joseph's Female Orphan Asylum, after they have arrived at the age of fourteen or fifteen, and, while giving them a home during what is regarded as a critical period in a young girl's life, to afford them an opportunity of learning a trade which will enable them to become self-supporting. The aims of the institution are shadowed forth in the following statement, made by the Sisters in charge, on the day of visitation, October 18: "We consider this the orphans' home. If their health becomes impaired, instead of going into a hospital, they can come here and feel that they have a home. If, after being placed out, they wish to return, we allow them to come back to us. To those that have no home when sick, we offer shelter. The age for admission is about thirteen years. The girls remain till they are eighteen, and if they are homeless, we keep them as long as they wish to stay. They are taught to do plain sewing, vest-making, dress-making, and all kinds of fancy needlework. They are generally put in what is termed the finishing department first, and then transferred to the machine department. Some having a talent for the work, learn both dress and vest-making. We do private family sewing that requires some amount of taste and skill. We teach the girls how to cut out dresses. We have also a washing and ironing department. If the girls are inclined to be very industrious, after they have performed their allotted tasks, they can work for themselves. When they leave the house we give them a trunk of clothing. It forms a pretty reasonable wardrobe. They can earn, on leaving, from $7 to $14 a week."

The Sister further says regarding their aims: "We have, as yet, no school on the premises, but we intend to commence one next year, giving the children two hours' schooling during the day. Before the establishment of this industrial school, our practice was to place the children out at eleven or twelve years of age. We found, however, that girls at the ages of thirteen, fourteen and fifteen need more care than at any other time."

The house has accommodations for about two hundred and fifty girls. In one workroom were exhibited very elaborate specimens of silk embroidery; in another, a number of young girls were sitting round a large table, all looking tidy, and actively employed; in a third, sixty-four sewing machines were in operation. In the finishing room, seventy-five girls were engaged in completing the work, after it had left the machine. In the dressmaking department were eight girls, who were being instructed, under an experienced lady, in the various branches of this remunerative trade. Attached to the industrial department is also an examining room, where all the work is taken and inspected, before being sent home.

The dormitories of this institution are one hundred and twenty-five feet long, and are furnished with single iron bedsteads, two feet eight inches wide. Two Sisters sleep in each room. The mattresses are of straw, and the pillows of feathers. The Sister says: "We leave the windows partially open during even the coldest weather."

On October 1, 1875, the number of girls in the institution was two hundred and twenty-five. Of these, one hundred and thirty were orphans, ninety-three, half-orphans, and two had both parents living. All with one exception were of foreign parentage; and all, except one, were mainly supported by the institution.

The atmosphere of the house was cheerful; many of the girls were singing at their tasks.

As before stated, one hundred and thirty of the inmates were orphans. These, instead of being left to shift for themselves, were here acquiring habits of industry, and learning useful trades, rendering them capable of earning an honest and independent subsistence; while under the influence of the Sisters, with whom they are brought into intimate and friendly contact, they are forming Christian characters; and when the educational feature of the institution is introduced, as is contemplated, the interest of this class will, doubtless, be still further promoted.

The Sheltering Arms Nursery of Long Island.

Brooklyn.

This institution is located at 524 Atlantic avenue. It was organized by a few benevolent ladies, in April, 1870, but is not yet incorporated. Its objects, as set forth in the report of its President, Mrs. J. A. Paddock, are two-fold. First, "The offering of a home with protection, kindness, care, food, warmth and comfort to little ones, from a month to seven years of age, especially to those who have been deserted by fathers, or who have intemperate mothers, and from whose homes comfort has fled." The secondary object is the helping of the surviving parent of half-orphan children to help themselves.

The institution is controlled by a Board of Lady Managers, and its finances are administered by a Board of Trustees. The immediate charge of the institution is committed to a matron. It occupies what was once a four-story private residence, which has been altered and adapted to its present use. The hall of the Home, as we entered it, on the day of visitation, was jubilant with the noisy prattle of children.

The Matron, Mrs. Christian, stated that the principal work of the ladies was among the day children. "The mothers," she says, "go out to work and bring their children here in the morning. They pay us ten cents, and their children are cared for during the day and returned to them in the evening. A great many of the children are motherless. Parents that can afford it, pay us $1 a week. Some children are supported by different churches or Sabbath schools. We have but one full orphan, and only one of the children really belongs to the institution. This was deserted by its mother. The other is the only child that we can say is an orphan. Some have fathers living; some both fathers and mothers.

"We have forty-six that are permanently with us. The youngest is six weeks old. We have about twenty children that have been brought up in the nursery from infancy.

"The working force of the nursery consists of a matron, care-taker, four hospital and other nurses — night and day nurses being in each dormitory — three wet nurses, a laundress, an assistant laundress, a cook and a woman to take charge of the day children, who are kept separate from the others. The children are taught their letters and singing.

"We have service every Sunday afternoon, and require all the inmates old enough, to attend it. The care-taker, hospital nurse and the principal employes of the institution are members of churches. The managers are particular to have the children under good moral influences. Children are only received by permission of the members of the Investigating Committee. Several of the children are sisters and brothers, or we may have two sisters and a brother. Two-thirds of them are motherless."

The nursery was found to be well kept; the school-room and other parts of the house bore evidence of careful management.

The work of the nursery is very much contracted for want of funds. The Matron says: "We have about fifteen applications a month more than we can take in. We have had to refuse seven this week, all very pressing cases. It is the hardest part of our work to refuse. We had thirty applicants during the months of June, July and August, and it was impossible to admit one of them."

The general health of the inmates appeared to be good, for an institution of its kind, where children are received that have been drugged, ill-fed and sadly neglected. The Matron says: "We have had six deaths this year from the 4th of February. We admit children even if they are in a dying condition. We do not refuse those suffering from any disease, unless it be contagious." In regard to the health of the inmates, the two attending physicians give the following testimony: "A large number of those admitted were in an unhealthy condition, being either exhausted by previous illness or with inherited tendencies to disease. It is to this class of our population that the Sheltering Arms is of the most inestimable value."

The work of the nursery for the past five years is stated to be as follows: "Three hundred and seventy-one have been the recipients of its care by day and night for a longer or shorter period. Seventeen hundred and seven have been taken care of during the day, while their mothers were laboring for their support. During this period sixty-six have died, notwithstanding the care which the institution had bestowed upon them."

The total expenditures during the year were $4,708.08.

The number of inmates October 1, 1875, who were half-orphans, was twenty-eight, and the number who had both parents living, was twenty-two. One was an orphan. All except eight were of native parents.

The work which is here being better done than is possible under any official system, is one which largely belongs to the public to perform, and which gives the institution a strong claim on the sympathy of the people; rescuing, as it does, families from pauperism, children from entering on downward paths, and enabling heads of families to still retain their self-respect and independence by tiding them over difficulties which would otherwise break them down.

It will be seen that since its organization over two thousand children have been brought under its humanizing influences, in whose receptive minds good seed has been sown that may bear promising fruit in after life.

The Society for the Aid of Friendless Women and Children,

Brooklyn,

Was organized by a few Christian ladies in 1869, and incorporated April 28, 1870.

Its objects, as set forth in its certificate of incorporation, are "to aid destitute friendless women and children to help themselves, by providing a temporary home where they may receive proper moral and intellectual culture, until they shall be provided for otherwise. It shall be a prominent object to find them employment and a home where their services are needed, and where they may be surrounded by the best social and moral influences."

The institution is located at 20 Concord street. The building occupied is four stories, including a Mansard attic. Its affairs are controlled by a Board of Lady Managers. The ladies are assisted by an Advisory Board of gentlemen.

At the time of visitation, October 16, the institution was under the immediate charge of a matron.

In reply to inquiries regarding the workings of the Home, the matron, Mrs. Conkling, says: "We receive children while their parents are at work, or while they are in hospitals or jails. Sometimes it happens that a mother is steady and the father a drunkard. Sometimes the father is steady and the mother a drunkard. We generally take orphans and half-orphans for a few days, till they can be placed in other institutions. We receive inmates at all hours up to ten o'clock at night. We take any child or woman that comes to us till their case is investigated. We do not take them if they have any home and can get into any other place. We keep them till better openings offer. On our fourth floor are a few rooms, where young girls in humble circumstances who are learning telegraphy, printing or dress-making in the city, may board at a cheap rate. They frequently have so very low wages that they cannot get board within their means in respectable places elsewhere. If a girl gets but two dollars a week, she cannot keep herself on that."

"We send the children out of the house to Sunday school. Sometimes mothers occupy the rooms here temporarily till their husbands succeed in getting work, or till some relatives take them in, or they have other provision made for them. We never keep children here for years; it is a matter of weeks or months with us. We have thirty in the house at present. We have a nursery, but do not take children under a year old, except when they come with their mothers for a short time.

"Often, just before night, a mother and her family will come in upon us. It's a place that we never can tell exactly how much we may use one week. We are liable, at any time, to have the door-bell rung and see a woman standing at the doorway with her family looking for relief."

The nursery had in it, on the day of visitation, twelve little children, the youngest being two and the oldest five years of age. It is a very pleasant room, furnished with little cribs. A cheerful fire was burning in the grate, and toys were strewn about the room. This apartment is in charge of nurses.

The dormitory, for the larger children, is furnished with single iron bedsteads, straw beds, and kept very neatly and well ventilated.

The hospital department was without an inmate. It is used for any children who may come in afflicted with sore eyes. They are placed here and kept strictly separate from the others. "The children," Mrs. Conkling says, "sometimes come filthy and covered with vermin. Then we have to cleanse them and keep them away in a separate apartment for a week or so, till they are free from them. Each child has a separate towel. Children with eruptions we never allow among the rest. In the month of August alone, we took in fifty-two women and thirty-nine children."

The other rooms of the house were found to be nicely kept. Some were for the use of respectable families who come here for temporary shelter, others for the use of parties in different stations in life. An effort is made to secure for each as much comfort as possible, and to provide for them in such a way that the contrast of their present with their past lives may not suggest any painful reminiscences. To avoid imposition in the distribution of the charity of the Society, the ladies conducting the work say:

"We have a vigorous, daily investigating committee, who endeavor to distinguish between poverty resulting from accident or illness, and that which is the inevitable consequence of vice. There is an amount of this work in our world which seems to be no one's business to attend to. Society does little more than defend itself against encroachments. A part of this work we are doing. We give our means to all applicants, without distinction of sect; in the spirit of the great Hebrew Prophet, 'without money and without price.'"

The ladies further say, in regard to the children coming under their care: "Our Sunday services are not neglected. Our children attend Sunday school, and returning home they, with the older inmates, gather in our chapel, where the voice of prayer and praise and exhortation goes up with earnestness and pathos. These children go from us, from time to time, and are gathered into other institutions, or returned to their own homes, or placed in other homes obtained for them by adoption. The past severe winter has often brought families to our open door. The husband and father unable to find employment, want and hunger came to their wives and little ones, but when work came they were reunited. Never do we advise giving up a home, but rather help them to keep it, which we think is the truer charity." As further illustrating the work being done in this temporary home, we quote from the last annual report of the Secretary, Mrs. J. S. T. Stranahan:

"The improvidence of the class for whom we labor, and the recklessness with which they throw aside a present good for some chimera, is proverbial. A young girl says to me, "I left a good place in the East. I wanted to make a home for my brother; sickness, then death came to him. I have spent all my money, and I don't know what to do. We receive and encourage her; in tears she goes out seeking for work; in joy she soon returns; she has found what she sought, and is passed out into the great army of workers, and we see her no more.

"A Mrs. ——, from the South, came to us bringing letters of reference. Her story was one of difficulties to contend with. She was well educated, with a character not lacking in energy, and we were glad to give her the help she so much needed, which she required only for a short time.

"Mrs. ——, a widow, having lost in a few brief years parents and husband, educated and refined, reduced from ease and comfort, came to New York, leaving two children with a nurse of her family in Providence. The failure of a business left her destitute; through Mr. —— she came to us. Soon a situation was obtained for her as housekeeper, but she must pass through deeper afflictions; as she was leaving us, intelligence came that her children were sick with diphtheria. Almost wild with fear, she left, to find on her arrival, one dead, the other dying. After a time she returned, accepted the situation still open to her, and now, with many thanks to us, says: "What should I have done without your 'Home'"

"One more, a case occurring in our midst. A mother with two lovely children just passing into girlhood, was in great affliction; the husband and father, a broker in Wall Street, was convicted and sent to prison for forgery. In debt for board, she came to us, hoping to find a way out of her difficulties. A firm believer in her husband's innocence, she expects his pardon from the Governor; more than this faint hope, there is nothing before her for five long years. In February she left us to go to some friends in the West.

"These are only a few of the many cases coming under our notice, where penury and refinement are united."

The following statistics are given from the same source in regard to the work accomplished: "Six hundred and twenty-seven women and one hundred and eighty-three children have been received during the year just closed; of these two hundred and ten women have left for service; two hundred and eighty-three to care for themselves. One hundred and eighty children have been taken by their friends or gathered into other homes or permanent institutions. Quite a number of women and children are with us now; these children are asking for a home; these women for work of all kinds. We give them *immediate* relief; they come to us hungry, we feed them; naked and they are sent away clothed.

The number of meals furnished during the year is sixty-two thousand one hundred and seventy-one. Lodgings, twenty thousand six hundred and twenty-four. There have been four cases of diphtheria, two of scarlet fever, and but three deaths."

As showing the spirit with which this energetic band of workers are imbued, we quote the language of one of its officers:

"Looking back eighteen hundred years, we perceive that we belong to a sisterhood notable for pious, benevolent deeds. The first hospital was founded by a woman, Fabiola, and the 'charity planted by her hand' overspread the world, and will alleviate to the end of time the darkest anguish of humanity. We cannot follow, one by one, the links which bind us through successive years to this immortal woman. We know of Paula, of Marcia, of St. Ursula, of St. Augustine's mother; but nowhere, save in the Book of Life, are the names of others, no less lovely, recorded. They worked as we work. Dying, they left their charge to other hands, as we must do at no very distant day!"

The work being done by this Association is of such a nature as to have impressed the community in which it is situated with a sense of its value, and it is gratifying it should be so, as its demands are great, not only upon the corps of laborers engaged, but upon the charitably disposed. The successful rescuing of one family from sinking through business failure, disease or death, from a position of respectability and independence into the ranks of the pauper class, and the saving of the children is of such importance as to heartily commend the work of this society.

St. Joseph's Institution for the Improved Instruction of Deaf-Mutes, in the City of Brooklyn.

Brooklyn.

A society of ladies forming a religious community, under the name of the Order of the Daughters of Mary, manage the affairs of this institution. Five ladies are engaged in the work, Miss Phalen being the first directress. Their services are voluntary, and the Order, we were informed, is self-supporting.

The institution is situated at 177 Main street. It was incorporated and opened in May, 1875, and it had on the day of visitation, October the 20th, 1875, twenty-four pupils, all females.

The art of lip reading and articulation, as well as the sign language, are taught. The course of instruction extends over seven years.

Pupils are received from six years and upward. One in the house at that time was said to be as old as thirty-three; she was a poor person, not able to pay for her board, and was maintained by the institution. The lady in charge said: "I have children under instruction who have never been at school a day." Eleven of the pupils were from the county, an allowance of $300 a year being made for each. Four or five were private pupils, their expenses being defrayed by their parents. A few were educated by authority of the State.

The work of caring for this class of defectives, to whom the melody of human speech is forever denied, and the endeavor to compensate their loss by artificial means, is one eminently worthy of Christian effort. To teach this class requires great tact as well as patience, and seems to come very appropriately within the province of woman.

St. Vincent's Home for Boys.

Brooklyn.

Two private houses, one on 7 Poplar street and the other in its rear on 10 Vine street, are connected by a covered yard and constitute a home for newsboys and others of this class who are being encouraged to earn something on their own account. The institution is under the auspices of the Society of St. Vincent De Paul, and is managed by a Board of Directors.

The house, on the 19th of October, was found to be under the immediate charge of Mr. Michael Dolan, Resident Superintendent. It is fitted up with chapel, gymnasium and school-room, besides the usual accessories of a "newsboys" home. It also possesses a library of entertaining reading matter of some 160 volumes.

The dormitories are furnished with bedsteads of iron, arranged in double tiers. The mattresses are of corn-husks, and the covering was ample for the season. The accommodations of the house are sufficient for 160 boys, and by occupying a floor now vacant, its capacity could be increased to 250. Provision is made for wash and bath-rooms, and each boy has a small closet with lock and key in which to keep his clothing.

If able to do so, boys pay ten cents a day, or seventy cents a week. For this they get breakfast and supper on week days and three meals on Sundays. But although pay is required from those who have money, no boy is excluded for lack of means. The object of charging the boys is stated to be for the purpose of teaching them independence and self-reliance. It is not designed to make the Home a permanent one for the boys, but merely a help toward their attaining something better. They are always at liberty to leave. It was further stated that good reports were heard from the boys who had left the Home, and that many of them go away to work during the summer and earn enough to return and attend school during the winter.

The chapel can accommodate 150 persons. A night school is opened at eight o'clock every night, and remains in session an hour and a half. Reading, writing, spelling, arithmetic and some of the more advanced branches of education are here taught. In connection with the school there is a dramatic club, composed of the boys in the Home, which is intended as a source of innocent and instructive amusement. The friends of the boys are invited annually to one of these entertainments. Careful attention is given to the moral and religious training of the inmates, the aim being to lay the foundation of a good, moral character, which will enable them to grow up useful citizens and worthy members of society. They are also taught vocal music under a qualified teacher. A piano is kept in the house and is used as occasion requires.

The breakfast, it is said, consists of bread, syrup and coffee, sometimes of bread and butter; the dinner or supper, of meat, potatoes and other vegetables, sometimes of stew, with rice or bread pudding.

The house is heated by furnace, and is supplied with water as far as the second floor. The income of the Home is derived from voluntary donations and from the aid given by the various Catholic churches in the city of Brooklyn, and from the payments made by the boys.

An inspection of this institution and an inquiry into its workings left the impression that it was accomplishing much good in the way of arresting neglected youth tending to paths of vice and criminality, and that it is one of the living moral powers in the city.

Truant Home.

Brooklyn.

No opportunity offered to visit this institution, and this report upon it, except the statistical information, was kindly furnished by the Hon. A. A. Low, Commissioner of Kings county.

The bill to incorporate this Home was passed in 1853, but owing to the lack of a suitable location, no steps were taken to carry out the design till 1857. The growth of truancy in the city, and the multiplied instances of children rebelling against parental control, called for some provision to remedy the evil, and to meet this want the Truant Home was established.

The Home first occupied the old Penitentiary building, which was found to be an undesirable location and otherwise unsuited to the purpose. In 1869 the Home was removed to a property known as "Snediker's Hotel," a building on the grounds of the Home, in which it remained until 1870, when the present structure was erected.

It is situated about eight miles from the city hall, on the Jamaica plank-road, in the town of New Lots, near the old Union course. Its grounds cover about eleven acres, eight of which are under garden cultivation, and afford vegetables enough to supply the institution. The premises are inclosed by an ordinary fence.

The building is of brick, eighty by forty, and forty feet high. It has three stories and a deep basement. When the appointments are complete it will have accommodations for one hundred and fifty boys.

The kitchen, dining-room and wash-room are in the basement. The school-rooms are on the first floor; the dormitories on the second and third floors. The building has a portable furnace in the dining-room, which heats the small school-room. This furnace also contributes to the dormitories above. A large furnace in the cellar on a level with the kitchen, and close to it, heats the main school-room and dormitories, which are above each other, and run the whole length of the building. The house is well lighted, having about sixteen windows to every floor. The rooms have the old-fashioned ventilators, and the facilities for ventilating, independent of the windows, are probably imperfect. The school-rooms are separated by a glass partition.

The only water tank is on the third floor, in a closet off the dormitory. This is too small, and the pipes leading from it to the closets are on the north-west side of the building where there is no furnace heat, and consequently freeze up in the winter. The water is pumped into the tank by hand from a well.

One acre of ground in the rear of the building is inclosed with a board fence, fifteen feet high. This play-ground is very muddy at times, and when this is the case, the boys are, it is stated, kept in the house, and have no exercise in the open air.

The laundry is in a shed. One strong woman does all the work, with the assistance of two of the boys. Eight hundred pieces are washed every week, almost without the aid of any modern appliances.

There is an ice-house on the premises, also a small house used for a stable and barn, and for storing products of the farm and garden.

The superintendent's family occupy "Snediker's hotel" which faces the road, but is in the inclosure of the "Home," and belonging to it. The "Home" building stands about fifty feet back and to the left of the hotel. The latter is of wood, three stories high, with as much room as the other house, but the internal arrangements are adapted to its original use.

Children of both sexes, between the ages of five and fourteen, are by law eligible for admission, but as there are no facilities for accommodating girls, only boys are now received. They are committed by the mayor, by magistrates or by justices of the peace. Many are picked up by policemen on the streets, but the majority are sent by parents as insubordinate children.

The school is conducted on the premises under the Municipal Board of Education, the teachers being paid by the city government. The children are instructed in reading, writing, arithmetic, and other studies belonging to the common-school branches. Sunday schools for both Roman Catholic and Protestant children are maintained, but no other religious instruction is said to be given.

Gardening and farming are taught on a limited scale. The strongest and oldest boys are employed, but as the lot is not properly secured, and as the Home has but one watchman, it is unsafe to use many at a time. Six hours are devoted to work.

Since the opening of the Home two thousand three hundred and sixty-four boys have been received. The average attendance is about one hundred. The children are comfortably clad in gray cloth suits, perfectly plain. If parents furnish clothes and wish them to be worn, no objection is made, but very few do, however. Due regard is paid to cleanliness. The boys bathe every Saturday, but the bathing facilities are inadequate. They bathe in large wash-tubs.

No hospital accommodations are provided. The children suffer very little from sickness. Four have died in seven years, three with scarlet fever and one with cholera.

The dining-room is small and almost under ground; the children stand at meals, chairs and benches not being allowed.

The water-closets in the house are out of order in the winter, and those outside are not sufficient. The water freezing in the tank, as it frequently does, makes it necessary to prepare food in the other building. The windows of the dormitories are not properly protected, and as the boys' clothes are taken away at night to prevent escapes, they sometimes tie the sheets together, let themselves down and run away naked.

The financial affairs of the Home are controlled by the Board of Aldermen. It is under the immediate charge of a Superintendent, whose wife acts as Matron. Two teachers, a watchman, a fireman, two women to do general housework, one laundress, two cooks and one seamstress constitute the working force.

The boys are discharged by order of the Mayor, but there is no pains taken to hold them under surveillance afterward. The number of cases reformed is stated to be about ten per cent.

The number of children returned to parents or guardians during the year was one hundred and twenty-three, the number that left without permission eleven. Of those remaining, October 1, eleven were orphans, forty, half orphans and thirty-three had both parents living.

The total expenditures of the institution during the fiscal year ending September 30, 1875, was $23,469.22; of this $4,012.91 was for improvements. The value of its real estate, buildings, fixtures, etc., is $83,600.

Asylum of Our Lady of Refuge.

Buffalo.

This institution, commonly designated as the "House of the Good Shepherd," is situated on Best street. Its buildings are located on a tract of ground three hundred and seventy by three hundred and thirty-four feet, in addition to which is an orchard one hundred and forty-one by six hundred and two feet; the whole being inclosed by a high wooden or plank fence, to prevent intrusion and to guard against the escape of inmates. There are two principal buildings within the inclosure. One is a large three-story stone structure with basement, mainly occupied by the Sisters, the other a large three-story brick building with basement, a little apart from the stone edifice, and appropriated to the inmates.

The objects aimed at by the institution are the reformation of fallen women, and of such idle and vicious girls who may be committed to the custody of the Society for the Protection of Destitute Roman Catholic Children, in accordance with law. By a recent act of the Legislature, a certain class of offending women may be committed to this institution, in the discretion of the magistrate, instead of to the penitentiary. It is also designed to afford a temporary shelter to young girls exposed to temptation, and to aid them in procuring fitting employment. The principal efforts of the institution are directed toward the reclamation of girls who having broken loose from wholesome restraint and entered upon a downward course, are penitent and place themselves voluntarily under its protection.

The institution was founded in 1855, by the Roman Catholic Order of the Sisters of Our Lady of Refuge, and incorporated under the general law January 14, 1866. It is now under the charge of thirty-three Sisters of this Order, of whom Mother Mary, of St. Dominic, is

Lady Superior. They belong to a cloistered Order. There are no paid employes attached to the establishment, except two men engaged in out-door work. At the date of last visitation, August 24, there were one hundred and four inmates, fifty-five of whom where children from seven to fourteen years of age. The Sisters in charge say: "We have some that have passed that age, and remain, because they are not able to provide for themselves. There are three children quite young, that is to say, between four and five years of age. We do not take infants; that is not our work. The youngest should not be below five years, and we should not take these but to accommodate Sisters in other asylums. Those committed here are kept entirely separate from the little children. The unfortunate adult women sent here are separated from the reformatory girls, between the ages of eight and fourteen. We have three classes:

"1st. The preservation class, composed of those who have not erred.

'2d. The consecrated class, composed of girls and women, who make a vow to remain here a certain time, that is to say, a year.

"3d. The penitents, composed of the women sent here by the police.

"After the penitents have served their time out, and they wish to persevere, they are placed among those in the consecrated class. Those committed are sent here for a certain time, some longer, some shorter. They stay that time, in any event, and as long after as they wish. They, however, can never enter our religious Order.

"The industries we carry on are sewing, knitting, coat and vest making. We also take in washing. If we had a place to accommodate them, we could take in a good many more of these poor women, and get employment for them, but we cannot do it for want of room.

"We look after the smaller reformatory children when they leave us, but the larger girls and women we simply return to their friends. We do as much for them as we can. We cannot do as much as we would like. Some, we hear, are doing well. If they behave well while here, we encourage them to communicate with us."

The Sister, on being asked if their work was encouraging, replied: "We are only discouraged in one way, and that is that we have not more room and means to extend it." In regard to the tempers of inmates, the Sister remarked: "The grown women, for a few hours after their arrival, are sometimes stubborn, but generally after a while come and say, 'Well, I will do now what you wish me to.' We discipline them by depriving them of privileges. When they are very bad we let them wear their week-day clothes on Sunday; and for little children we sometimes turn the dress wrong side out. They are usually inclined to obey without punishment, and are pretty docile." The children are kept, the Sister says, till they are about sixteen years of age, and are then either returned to their friends or placed in good situations. Those committed by law must remain till fourteen. The inmates are never allowed to be alone. There is always one of the Sisters with them.

The school-room was found to be small for the number occupying it. The dormitories, also, though neatly kept, were overcrowded. Careful provision was made for the sick in an infirmary department. Among other comforts, hair mattresses were here used. The work-room contained twelve sewing machines. Members of the consecrated class were here at work.

In the laundry were seven of the committed women at work with a Sister, who was also engaged in active labor. No conversation is permitted. A group of girls were also on one of the rear balconies listening to religious reading. It is customary to spend a short time in this way every evening before supper.

Regarding the compensation for the maintenance of inmates, the Sister says: "None of our children are regularly paid for. Sometimes their friends promise to remunerate us, and do so for a week or two and then fail. For the children committed by magistrates from the county of Erie, we receive $1 per week."

A casual visitor to this institution cannot be otherwise than impressed with the patience-trying and laborious work in which this Sisterhood are engaged, and yet it is persevered in with unflagging zeal, and doubtless with much heart-ache. They, as well as all others engaged in like efforts to reform the class committed to their care, are deserving the sympathy and aid of the public.

The Buffalo Orphan Asylum.

Buffalo.

This Asylum, whose object is "to furnish relief and a home for orphan and destitute children," is located on Virginia street, in a pleasant quarter of the city of Buffalo. It was established by the joint action of the various Protestant churches of the city, in 1836, and incorporated April 24, 1837, by a special act of the legislature.

The asylum edifice, which was built in 1850, is of brick, in the Italian style of architecture, and consists of a main with two parallel wings. It is two stories high, with an attic and basement in addition. It is well lighted and has high ceilings. The windows are adjusted by cords, weights and pulleys. It is warmed by coal stoves, lighted by gas and supplied with water from the city works. It is capable of accommodating about one hundred inmates The dining-room, kitchen and laundry are in the basement. An urgent want was felt for play-rooms for boys and girls. The grounds are well inclosed, but its limited space admits of no garden. The institution is supplied very largely with vegetables from the extensive grounds of its president.

Adjoining the Asylum yard is a frame school-house. Here the children of the Asylum are instructed, together with a limited number of children from the neighborhood. The school is under the charge of the Department of Public Instruction of the city.

The financial affairs of the Asylum are controlled by a Board of Trustees. Its internal affairs are managed by a Board of Directresses. It is under the immediate charge of Mrs. Robert McPherson, Matron, who, with the exception of an interval of nine months, has been in charge six years. This lady taught one of the first charity schools in the city of Perth, Scotland. The matron has under her direction a nurse, chambermaid, seamstress, cook, laundress and dining-room girl.

In regard to the kind of helpers selected and the character of the surroundings that children ought to have, Mrs. McPherson says: "We try to have persons of character employed in the institution, and to have all the surroundings of the children neat and clean, such as will tend to elevate their young minds and excite their ambition." Mrs. McPherson, on being asked how she thought this work of caring for children should be carried on to render it most efficient, said: "I think our Protestant asylums do not prosper as well as they might in consequence of not having the right kind of help. We ought to have a Protestant Sisterhood composed of ladies, whose object would be simply to do the work for its own sake. This would insure workers of a refined character."

The children in the Asylum are variously dressed. Great pains is taken to keep them clean. They are required to bathe once a week. Vocal music is taught by the Matron's Sister, and a lady from the city comes on Sundays to teach the children to sing hymns.

In the early part of 1874, when the children from the county poorhouse were transferred to Asylums, twenty-six of the number were placed here. Of these only three on the date of visitation, August 19, remained, the rest having, through the kind solicitude of the managers, been placed in good homes. Up to that time seventy-one children in all had been received from the Superintendent of the Poor.

The inmates appeared to be in good health. No case of sickness occurred the past year; but, during the year preceding our visit, there were three deaths in the institution, the first for a number of years.

Children are taken between the ages of two and twelve years, and placed out as soon as good homes can be found. Mrs. McPherson remarks in reference to the age for receiving children, "the younger they are when they arrive the better. After they are seven years old it is pretty hard to weed out the bad that is in them."

Due attention is paid to industrial and religious training. The children, boys and girls, are taught to sew and knit, and some very excellent specimens of their handiwork were shown in the shape of ornamental pieces of furniture, embroidery, etc.

The matron being a firm believer in the necessity of basing all true reform on Christian teaching, every opportunity that the domestic economy of the house will permit is availed of to inculcate religious sentiments. There is morning and evening worship; grace is said before and after meals, and texts and hymns are committed to memory, and the children asked to repeat them on various occasions in which the sentiment or truth which they embody has a fitting application. The matron says: "I think Biblical knowledge does the children more good than any thing else. I could not accomplish any thing without religious teaching." The evening worship in winter is prolonged, and is generally preceded by some entertainment which the children can enjoy, and which gives them a taste for home-life. Among the amusements the matron encourages the children to entertain themselves, by testing each other's knowledge on subjects which are supposed to be familiar to all. Questions are quickly put and the answers are expected to be prompt. This exercise is often the occasion of much merriment, especially when adults participate in it and a wrong answer happens to be given. The pastime has a tendency not only to stimulate thought, but to make the pupils ready in expression. The ambition of the children is aroused, their desire to excel is awakened, and its effect is seen in the ardent desire to increase their stock of general knowledge. The evening amusements are followed by reading and instruction from the Scriptures — closing with singing and prayer.

In "placing children out," all reasonable precautions are taken to obtain for them suitable homes. More concern is felt for the moral character of the guardians than for their material well being. Children are placed out three months on trial, after which some settlement is effected, either by indenture or adoption if both parties desire it. More difficulty is found in disposing of girls than boys, which is owing, the matron thinks, to a want of Christian charity and patience on the part of those taking them, and to the difficulty of placing them in suitable families. Parties applying for girls, she thinks, "either expect to find one without faults or to procure a girl out of whom they can make a perfect drudge." The asylum has connected with it a visiting committee who look after the children when they leave the institution.

Of the children who have gone out from the asylum, the matron informed us many have attained respectable standing in the world.

Some are in business, some are married and have become happy wives and mothers, and one girl is now in New York city studying music under a professional teacher. The matron makes it a practice to correspond with all the children who leave the asylum. One year we learned she received as many as forty-nine letters.

The house was found to be under good management. The rooms were clean and well aired. The dormitories are furnished with double wooden bedsteads, and are connected with a bath-room. The clothes-rooms of both boys and girls are neatly kept.

In the dining-room were fifty tiny glass vases filled with fragrant flowers. These are regularly supplied by a lady interested in the institution, and are placed upon the children's tables during meals, presenting a bright appearance, and bringing to these little ones a taste of summer delights.

The number of children in the asylum October 12th, was seventy-six; forty-five boys and thirty-one girls. Thirteen of these were orphans, thirty were half orphans, and thirty-three had both parents living. Thirty-two were of foreign parents and forty-four of native. The number received during the year was one hundred and fourteen. The number placed out by adoption was sixteen, the number indentured five, returned to parents or guardians seventy-two, left without permission three, otherwise discharged two.

The sum of its investments was $31,339.51; the disbursement during the year for investment was $3,000; for all other purposes, $7,494.30.

The number of children received in the asylum since its organization is 2,272. The number has been increasing from year to year in the following proportion:

In 1870	it was	46
" 1871	"	62
" 1872	"	62
" 1873	"	74
" 1874	"	109
" 1875	"	113

It will be seen that since 1870 its work has increased over two-fold. It has connected with it a large force of earnest workers, and its affairs are under efficient management. There is no doubt but that besides the elevating moral influence it exerts upon the community, the burdens of taxation are much reduced through its benevolent agency.

The Charity Foundation of the Protestant Episcopal Church in the City of Buffalo.

Buffalo.

This institution occupies what was formerly a spacious family mansion, erected on a large lot on Rhode Island street, between Sixth and Seventh streets. Pleasant shade and ornamental trees surround it, and a lawn embellished with flowers, stretches in front. The porch and windows of the house, at the time of visitation, were tastefully ornamented with flowering plants, the whole presenting a home-like aspect.

The Foundation was incorporated under the general law July 28th, 1858. Its objects, as set forth in its charter, are, "The relief, shelter, support, education, protection and maintenance of indigent, sick or infirm persons, including indigent orphans and half orphan children, and all such children as the Providence of God shall have left in a destitute and unprotected state and condition, giving preference to those who are members of the Protestant Episcopal Church, but admitting to the benefits of this charity all persons who will accept the religious ministration of the Protestant Episcopal Church."

As an exposition of the scope of this work, it is elsewhere stated: "This Foundation rests upon a charter obtained from the Legislature of the State of New York, and covering a wide range of charities. It was the intention of the founders, and has been the intention of those interested in the management ever since, to establish upon this Foundation a complete system of benevolent institutions, so arranged as to be mutually protective, and to enable the Protestant Episcopal Church of the city of Buffalo to carry out the letter and spirit of her Divine Lord's principles of charity. We labor, therefore, in the interests of this Foundation, not simply to build up institutions, but to open homes and houses of refuge, where the church can receive and extend a loving care over such of her children as have been overtaken by misfortune and helplessness."

A Home for Aged and Destitute Females was opened in 1858, on Washington street. For several years a house of moderate dimensions afforded sufficient accommodations for the inmates, but it having been determined in the Spring of 1866 to open an Orphans' Ward, and the number of destitute women claiming protection being greatly on the increase, the building now occupied by the Foundation, on Rhode Island street, near Niagara, was purchased. The financial affairs of the Foundation are controlled by a board of twenty-one managers. The conduct of its internal affairs are intrusted to a board of associate managers, composed of ladies representing the different Protestant Episcopal parishes of the city. It is under the immediate superintendence of a matron. It is required that officials in immediate charge shall be communicants in good standing of the Protestant Episcopal Church.

The building is heated by steam and lighted with gas. Water is distributed in pipes, through the different floors. The children occupy the orphans' ward, a large two-story brick building constructed for the purpose, and standing in the rear of the main. The outlook from the upper windows is quite extensive, taking in Fort Erie, the lake, and Niagara river in the distance. The school in this department is taught by a lady of culture; her salary is paid by the Department of Public Instruction, and the school comes under its direct supervision. The school-room is furnished with blackboards, maps, organ, and modern appliances generally. The children are instructed in drawing, and are taught to sing by note. The smaller children have a kind of an infant school by themselves, in which they are amused by blocks and sundry other contrivances for their entertainment. On the first floor of the main building is the chapel, furnished with an organ and the usual accessories of places of worship. Services are conducted daily, by the chaplain of the institution.

The children were variously dressed, and appeared particularly clean, with their hair neatly combed. On date of visitation, August 25, there were thirty-one children in the institution; nineteen were girls and twelve, boys. The matron, Mrs. Susan Graham, furnished the following information: "The youngest child in the house is four years old; the oldest is a boy of thirteen years. The largest number of children ever in the institution at one time was forty-eight. Children are not retained after fourteen years of age. A correspondence is kept up with the children after they have been put out. A secretary has this matter in charge, and the children are encouraged to write themselves." As an instance of many cases of distress relieved by the charity, the matron related the following: "A poor girl had been in the institution some time; she was taken away by her father to keep house for him. He was a miserable drunkard. The girl at last got sick. We tried to get her back, and succeeded. I never saw a girl more pleased than she was to return. It was a constant expression of gratitude with her. She lived to be sixteen years old and died here."

In regard to industries, the matron remarks: "We teach our girls to sew on the sewing machine. At one time, all the girls' clothes were made by them. All the clothing used is made in the house. The old people do most of the mending and knitting. We made, last year, one hundred yards of rag carpet." Connected with the institution is a fine garden. The matron, in speaking of it, says: "We raise in the garden all the vegetables we use, and have beside sold about one hundred dollars worth already. We are selling some every day, and still have all we need."

The girls' dormitory is a well-lighted, clean room, brightened with illuminated mottoes, which hang over each bed. It is furnished with single, iron bedsteads, with spring slats. The beds are covered with snow-white counterpanes. Adjoining this dormitory is the matron's sleeping apartment. The boys' dormitory is furnished with double bedsteads. The matron's assistant sleeps on this floor. The sick room is also on this floor, but is very little used, no sickness having been in the ward for four years, and no deaths having occurred among the children for five years. The house was found in excellent condition, and reflects credit upon all concerned in its management.

At the date of October 1st, 1875, there were in the Home eight orphans, nineteen half-orphans, and five children who had both parents living. Fourteen of the children were of native and eight were of foreign parentage. Twenty-one came from Erie county, and eleven from other counties. Eight were partially supported by friends, and twenty-four wholly by the institution.

The main building of the institution was erected about forty years ago, and is without any adequate system of ventilation. The material of which it is constructed is stone, and, with the exception of the Orphans' Ward, seems contracted and not entirely adapted to its present use. A scheme is, we are informed, under the consideration of the Board of Managers, for selling the premises at present occupied, and erecting a plain, spacious and commodious edifice, with all modern improvements, on a site owned by the Foundation, on Fourteenth street, near Jersey street.

This lot is elevated, having a dry soil and excellent drainage. It is situated amidst highly improved surroundings, having in its vicinity the city park, upon the beautifying of which large sums have already been expended. The site is an attractive one, and will become still more so when the trees now newly planted shall have attained stately proportions.

The Evangelical Lutheran St. John's Orphan Home.

Buffalo.

This institution originated through the benevolent efforts of the members of the congregation of the German Evangelical Lutheran St. John's Church, stimulated by the zeal of their pastor, the Rev. Christian Volz. It was organized in March, 1864, and incorporated by special act of the Legislature April 14, 1865. Its affairs are managed by a Board of nine Trustees, of whom the Rev. Christian Volz is President. Its work is carried on in two establishments, one in Hickory street, a Home for girls, and another on a large farm at Sulphur Springs, for boys. These will be spoken of separately.

The Home on Hickory street was first instituted. The lot upon which it is situated is eighty by one hundred and twenty-two feet, and there stood upon it at the outset the parsonage of the late Rev. Francis H. Guenther. This man was greatly beloved, and the respect in which his memory was held after his death strengthened the desire to perpetuate his home to the uses of God and charity. The brother of this worthy clergyman, a benevolent citizen of New York city, donated to this object the sum of $2,000, and with this money the parsonage was purchased, and thus secured as an Orphans' Home. The house was immediately enlarged, and opened for the reception of inmates May 9, 1865. During the year nine orphans were admitted, the first two being children of soldiers who died in the late war. During the three following years thirty-one additional children were admitted. In 1868 it was deemed that a separation of the sexes should be made, and a distinct Home established for the boys. Accordingly a very judicious purchase of rich and valuable land, with a large building upon it, formerly a hotel, at Sulphur Springs, was made January 29, 1869, and the boys were transferred there.

In the rear of the house, on Hickory street, was erected a brick edifice, which contains the kitchen, dining rooms, dormitories, bathing and clothes-rooms. It is well constructed, heated by furnace, lighted by gas and ventilated by wall flues. Water is supplied from the city works. The drainage is good. This establishment is under the immediate charge of Sister Louisa A. Adelberg, of the Order of Deaconesses of the Lutheran Church in Germany. Upon application of the President of the Board of Trustees to the Mother House for a Sister, she was dispatched to America to take the charge of the Home. She had been for seventeen years, before coming here, working in hospitals, in children's homes, and other places wherever sent. The name of her Mother House in Germany is Neuendettelsau. It is situated in Bavaria, and was established by Pastor Loehe in 1854. The Order of Deaconesses was instituted by Theodore Fliedner, an eminent German Divine, in Kaiserwerth, on the 13th of October, 1836. Since this time their numbers have rapidly increased, and now they are to be found scattered far and near, tending the sick, training children, and trying to reform the fallen. From Sister Louisa we learned the following particulars regarding the Order and her own labors:

"First, we enter as scholars, then we are novices, and then, if we have done our work well, we are qualified to become Sisters. Some have to wait a long time, some a short time. I have been in America six years. I receive $125.00 a year to buy clothes and for gifts. We do not work for money. When the Sisters are unable to work they can go back to the Mother House, and remain there during their lives: but while away from it they are required to make quarterly reports. All the Sisters are at the disposal of the Mother House, in Germany, and must go wherever they are sent. They comprise ladies from the highest families."

In speaking of the capacity of the institution, the Sister said "We could accommodate altogether fifty inmates, or, if pressed, perhaps, sixty." At the date of visitation there were in the Home thirty girls and four little boys, between three and four years of age. The latter are kept here in consequence of their tender years. The average number of inmates is thirty.

A school is maintained on the premises taught by the Sister. The larger girls spend six hours a day in the school; the smaller, only three. The school-room is on the second floor of the building. It contains neat desks and the usual furniture of a school-room. The children are taught both German and English. The Home possesses a library containing about two hundred volumes.

Religious service is held morning and evening. The catechism of the Lutheran church is taught, also the History of the Bible. A Sunday school is held in the Home, and the children attend Divine service in the Lutheran St. John's Church on the opposite side of the street. A serious defect in the institution is the lack of sufficient play-ground. Good sense is displayed by the Sister in her methods of discipline. The usual penalty enforced for disobedience of rules, is that of limiting recreation to the boundaries of the house. Only in rare cases is it necessary to inflict corporal punishment, and then only for grave offenses.

At the time of visitation it was observed that one little girl, an invalid, was kept in a cot, while the other girls were sitting around her cheerfully working, and at the same time entertaining her with their girlish chat. Thus, while the little sufferer's wants were fully looked to, she was enabled to share the sympathy of her playmates and make one of their number. The children are taught to sew and knit as well as to do house-work. Three sewing and one or two knitting-machines are in use, and the children are taught to sew and knit both by hand and on the machines. All the clothing is made on the premises. The children wear woolen stockings in the winter, and have a very large supply of clothing. Besides doing the work of the house, the girls earned $100 last year by working for the stores. This was earned in part by the knitting-machines. Yarn is furnished and the girls knit it into stockings at a given price per pair.

Each girl, when old enough to do so, makes her own bed. There are forty-one iron bedsteads in use. The beds are protected on the sides with a strap or brace, thus allowing the use of a liberal quantity of straw. This is changed in the bed-ticks twice a year. Every two weeks there is an entire change of bed-linen, but the change is made in parts. Woolen blankets are used. The sick-room is nicely carpeted.

In the clothes-room two shelves and four hooks are allowed for each child, with her name and number affixed. Many of the little girls, true to maternal instincts, had here preserved with care, their dolls and doll-bedsteads.

On the second floor is a large bath-room. Connected with this is a room for shoes, each girl having a compartment for herself. The children bathe once a week, or oftener, if necessary; but more frequently in summer than in winter. The girls rise in summer at half-past five, and in winter at half-past six. The smaller girls retire at seven, while the larger are permitted to stay up until nine. Sister Louisa says: "We have no servants in this house. Our large girls must do the house-work."

The basement contains the laundry and vegetable cellar. In the laundry, on the day of visitation, were eight girls, aged from twelve to fifteen years, doing the washing of the house. The bread, which is excellent, is baked on the premises in a brick oven ; and the children are taught to make it. The vegetables used in the Asylum come from the farm at Sulphur Springs. The farm also supplies milk, from which all the butter used in the Home is made by the girls. It was thought that the children could be maintained for $75 a year each.

Our visit to the Home was unexpected, and yet the Sister received us as though it were a day for reception. The children's hair was very neatly combed, and their faces were clean and bright. Their dresses were tidy and in perfect order. The windows of the house were transparent, the floors well scrubbed, and the clothes and closets in perfect order. In fact, order and cleanliness reigned supreme, and everybody was cheerful and happy. The good lady in charge, who had given up her life to this noble work, had no other associates in the discharge of her multifarious duties, including the care of an invalid and several small children, than the little loving hearts about her. It was evident, however, that she was overtasked and needed one or more assistants.

The department for boys at Sulphur Springs, about four miles southerly from the city, is under the immediate charge of Mr. John Muller, Superintendent, or House Father, assisted by his wife, the House Mother, or Matron. A lady assistant and two of the girls from Hickory street were temporarily helping her with the general housework. A farmer is also employed. The building occupied is a frame structure, three stories high and forty by sixty feet, having a porch extending along its front. In the rear of the main building there has been recently constructed a frame addition, three stories high, twenty-four by forty-four feet. The building is surrounded with pleasant shade trees. It was dedicated to its present use October 11, 1868, and the boys were transferred from the Home on Hickory street in Buffalo, January 29, 1869. Twenty acres of land were first secured with the building, since which, additional purchases have been made, making in all one hundred and five acres, comprising garden, meadows, orchard and woodland. Between twenty and thirty acres of land are unsubdued. Two acres were planted in carrots, one and a half in onions, two in cabbages and eight in potatoes. Oats, rye and corn are also grown. Eight cows are kept.

At the date of visitation, August 24, there were thirty-six boys in this department of the Home, between the ages of two and fifteen. Two of the children were from the poor-house; one was suffering from curvature of the spine. They were aged respectively five and twelve years, and possessed of average intelligence. The county pays $1 a week each for their maintenance. Another boy aged sixteen years has but one arm. In addition to the thirty-six inmates, there were ten boys in the city learning trades, who were partially supported by the institution, and who are regarded as belonging to it. They return when sick, and report to the Pastor in the city every Sunday on their behavior during the week. All the boys are said to have turned out well. One of them is now earning $3 a day. Five boys, half-orphans, were reported to have run away from the institution. In regard to boys leaving, the President remarks: "Boys having relatives living are sometimes discontented, and want to be away, but those having no other home are glad to stay, and generally turn out the best. We do not know of one of our boys who has turned out badly. We never have had one in jail."

The chapel is a small separate frame building, and is used for school purposes on week days. It contains an organ. A Sabbath school is held here every Sunday afternoon. Morning and evening prayers are conducted; grace is said before and after meals. Six hours a day are spent in school, but no school is kept during the months of July and August. German and English are both taught.

The accommodations of the house are ample for even a greater number of inmates than it contains. The rooms are large, ceilings high, and the sashes of the windows hung with cord and pulley. The dormitories are furnished with single iron bedsteads. One disadvantage under which the institution labors is that the cellar is damp and often flooded with water, owing to the construction of a dam near by which causes the creek to overflow. This was constructed against the wishes of the managers by an outside party. The cellar is used for storing coal. Rain water is saved in cisterns. The boys are reported as being healthy, only one having died during the year. The institution is crippled for want of funds, and many needed improvements have in consequence to be deferred.

In regard to the aims of the managers, we have the following information: "Our object is to give a Christian education to children. It is a home for orphan, half-orphan and destitute children." In regard to the ages for receiving children the President says: "We take children here at every age. We have had even infants. We keep them till they are eighteen years old. Girls after leaving us generally go into families to do housework. Some get married."

In regard to the system of looking after children, the President says: "We had a system for looking after the children that had been put out, but could not carry it into effect. It was this: Each child had what we call a judgment-book, and every week this was submitted for inspection. It was found to be impracticable, for the reason that the masters and mistresses would not take the trouble to write it up."

At the date of October 1, 1875, there were, in both the Hickory street and Sulphur Springs departments, forty-two orphans and thirty half orphans. Six were of native and sixty-six of foreign parentage. They were mostly from Erie county. Three were partially supported by friends, four by the institution, and sixty-five in part by Erie county. During the year sixteen inmates were received; three were returned to parents or guardians, six left without permission, and eight were otherwise discharged.

The total indebtedness of the institution was $11,000. Its expenditures during the year were $8,495.54, of this $1,684.92 was paid out for needed improvements.

The Lutheran Church deserves great credit for originating this charity and for the sacrifices that have been made to establish it. The conception of a home for boys away from the city, where they may devote themselves to agricultural pursuits, is a good one, and it is to be regretted that the property is so heavily incumbered with debt. It would seem that this burden should be lifted off by the charitably disposed, and the institution be thus enabled to go on more freely with its beneficent work.

The German Roman Catholic Orphan Asylum of Buffalo.

Buffalo.

This institution was formerly located at 221 Batavia street. During the past year a spacious and commodious brick edifice has been erected on Best street, to which the children, forty-three in number, were transferred on June 1, 1875. The present building is a quadrangular structure, with a front tower and rear projection. Its plan contemplates the addition of parallel wings at each end of the main, with gables facing outward. It will accommodate at present about one hundred inmates and over three hundred when completed. Its location is high and airy. The lot upon which it stands adjoins the city park, and contains seventeen acres. It was formerly used as a cemetery. The selection of the site, and the building itself, reflect great credit upon its benevolent projectors and those who have worked so zealously for its establishment.

This Asylum was first established in 1852, and placed, December 8, under the charge of the Roman Catholic Order of the Sisters de Notre Dâme. Its financial affairs are controlled by a Board of Trustees.

The Asylum grew out of the following conditions: The severe cholera season of 1849 threw a large number of orphans upon the charity of the members of St. Mary's Church for support. These were at first cared for in families of the congregation, and for several years afterward, when it was found that some permanent provision must be made for this constantly increasing class. On August 6, 1856, the Orphan Asylum was incorporated under the general law. The institution is now under the immediate care of five Sisters of the Order of St. Francis, Sister Mary Gabriella being Sister Superior. Orphan, half-orphan and destitute children of all ages, up to ten years, are admitted.

At date of visitation, August 24, there were in the house sixty-three children; twenty-four girls and thirty-nine boys. The youngest child in the Asylum was one and a half, and the oldest, a girl, fourteen years old. A school is maintained on the premises, and is taught by one of the Sisters. Early hours are kept, the children rising at six in the morning and retiring at half-past seven o'clock at night. The parents of a few of the children pay $1.50 per week toward their support. Children, as soon as they are ready to leave, are discharged by adoption into families, or apprenticed to farmers or tradesmen.

The dormitories are furnished with single, iron bedsteads, each bed having a side-strap of iron, which keeps the straw bed in its place, and strengthens the frame. The asylum possesses ample bathing facilities, and the children are required to bathe once a week. It is customary to cut the boys' hair short. In one of the rooms in the basement, a little company of girls was observed ironing, under the supervision of a Sister, and in another, a band of little boys was piling up wood, with a manifest ambition to do their work well.

From Sister Mary Clara, who was in charge on the day of visitation, the following information was obtained: "We train the girls to do housework, and the boys to work in the garden. We have a man hired to do out-door work, but keep no paid girls. We do all the work ourselves, with the help of the children. We discipline them by keeping them from recreation, or making them sit away from the others at the table. Sometimes we have to resort to corporal punishment. It is difficult in all cases to make the children mind, because so many of them come from homes where they have not received proper training. We have received children eleven and twelve years old, that did not know their *a b c*. I did not think, before entering upon this work, that there was so much to do. Parents, when they are not able to manage their children, sometimes bring them to us and ask us to take them, saying, 'I cannot manage this child.'"

A large number of the German people, of Buffalo, have made considerable sacrifices toward this charitable enterprise, and considering the valuable site the corporation has acquired, the commodious buildings erected upon it, the number of children that are now receiving moral, religious and industrial training under its auspices, the establishment of the asylum upon a more permanent basis may justly be regarded as a cause for congratulation by all interested in the welfare of homeless children.

Le Couteulx St. Mary's Institution for the Improved Instruction of Deaf Mutes in the City of Buffalo.

Buffalo.

This institution is located at 125 Edward street, corner of Morgan street, in a healthy quarter of the city. The following incidents are connected with its history. In 1839 Lewis Le Couteulx deeded a lot containing about one acre of land for the use of a Deaf and Dumb Asylum. In 1849 the heirs of this gentleman confirmed to the Right Rev. Bishop Timon the original benefaction. Having no means to erect a suitable edifice, the Bishop purchased several small frame houses in the neighborhood, and caused them to be moved on the lot in the spring of 1856. Three Sisters of St. Joseph assumed the charge of the new Asylum, and immediately opened a day school for its support, and to enable them to prepare it for the reception of mutes. In October, 1857, the instruction of the deaf and dumb commenced with four female pupils who lived in the house, and a few day pupils, whose homes were in the vicinity. The institution at this time struggled against financial embarrassments, and but for the active benevolence of Bishop Timon the work, we are assured, would have been abandoned. Those at first in charge received their knowledge of the sign language from a graduate of the Deaf and Dumb Asylum of Caen, France. Difficulties of a pecuniary nature again arising, the work was suspended for about two years. In the meantime Sister Mary Ann Burke, a member of the Community of the Sisterhood of St. Joseph, was sent to the popular institution under the charge of the late A. B. Hutton, at Philadelphia, to acquire an acquaintance with the mode of teaching deaf mutes which the institutions of the United States had adopted, and preparations for resuming the work were made. A four-story building, twenty-eight by thirty-four, with basement, was completed, affording a spacious dormitory, sitting-room, refectory, kitchen, etc., and the frame houses were converted into class rooms. In 1862 the instruction of the deaf and dumb was resumed, and has been successfully carried on to the present time.

The Asylum realized the most sanguine expectations of its founders in the rapid progress of the pupils. It is stated that, with but few exceptions, all had shown a desire for improvement, and many left capable of performing the duties incident to the practical business of life. The success of the enterprise was so encouraging, and the number of children seeking admittance so large, that the managers were induced, in 1867, to put up an additional wing. Subsequent additions and improvements have also been made, till, at the present time, the edifice has a front extension of one hundred and eighty-eight feet.

The building is lighted by gas, heated by furnaces, and supplied with city water. A Board of Trustees or Directors has the general management of the Asylum, and the Community of the Sisters of St. Joseph the immediate charge, Mother Mary Ann Burke, the Superior of the Community, being at its head. Fifteen Sisters, at the time of visitation, August 26, were engaged in the work, one or more having charge of each department. The Sisters have worked with commendable zeal in the interests of the institution, having spared no sacrifice for the cause, even contributing from their own means to its support, and to their devotion its success is largely attributable. The most recent visitation, of which several have been made, was that of August 26, 1875. The number of inmates at that time was seventy-eight, forty boys and thirty-eight girls. The average age was about thirteen years. The demands upon the institution are so greatly in excess of its accommodations, that a further addition has become an obvious necessity. Mother Mary Ann remarks: "We find ourselves in great need of room. During the past year the accommodations were somewhat enlarged by changes in the interior, but still they are insufficient for present requirements. We have found it necessary to increase the force in all departments. We take children from the county and from other sources. We now receive for county children $300 a year. We take children from six years of age upward. Deaf mutes are supported for five years. Any specially talented receive aid for a longer period."

How far the dispositions of this class of defectives differ from those of other people is a matter of some importance, and the remarks of those who have had experience will be read with interest. On this point Mother Mary Ann remarks: "Deaf mutes are very sensitive, but this is in a great measure owing to their misunderstanding the intention of others. I tell them they must not judge from appearances, that it does not necessarily follow that there is want of interest in them if they are passed by without notice, as the person's mind may be occupied with something else. I do not think they are naturally more passionate than other children, nor are they more given to vice. I discipline them as I would ordinary children, by depriving them of little things in which they take pleasure. Severe punishment is never necessary. Many of them are self-willed, on account of their parents not knowing how to manage them. Instruction is the best means of curing them of this. You can appeal to their sense of honor. Should they get into violent fits of temper, we wait till this is over, and then tell them that they have no excuse for such manifestations. It is a daily work to endeavor to teach them to govern their temper.

"The studies pursued are the acquisition of language by means of writing, speaking and signs, general history, geography, grammar, mental and practical arithmetic, composition, penmanship and drawing. We teach the Visible Speech Method which was introduced by Professor A. S. Bell, of London. One of the Sisters and myself went to Boston and spent several months there learning his system. In the latter part of 1873 it was introduced here, and it is now a general study for all the classes. I think for the greater number of deaf mutes it is of little value, but for those who have lost their hearing through sickness, and can spend the time to acquire it thoroughly, it is a great benefit. It has nothing to do with mental culture. It serves to keep up the voice of those who have lost their hearing from four years of age upwards; but for those who have never spoken it requires a great deal of time to acquire it. They can be taught to say some words, but many deaf mutes do not seem to have any voice, and their efforts to speak are labored. In teaching it we draw a picture on the board, showing the vocal organs that are used in pronouncing each consonant and in pronouncing each vowel, then for any consonant the position of the vocal organ that is used in uttering it is adopted, and the same plan is followed in the case of vowels. The characters or alphabet in this method form thus a series of pictures. The eye becomes accustomed to these, and a mute who is practised in this system can, by watching a person's mouth while speaking, tell what he is saying although he cannot hear a word; and by recollecting how to place his vocal organs, can himself talk back, though still not hearing any sound." This is the theory, but Mother Mary Ann thinks "that by writing and signs alone can conversation be sustained. The best speaker of this method that I ever knew of," she says, "was here once, and we could not converse together without the signs. I asked him if on going to church he could understand what was said, and he told me he could not. No schools that I have ever visited could do without the sign language."

The whole establishment was found to be in excellent order, and the system of housekeeping very thorough. It possesses ample bathing accommodations. The dormitories are furnished with iron bedsteads; snow white counterpanes cover the beds, each pillow having over it a neat white tidy. All sleep singly except the very little ones. The beds, it was said, are all taken apart once a week in summer, and once a month in winter and thoroughly cleaned. It is aimed to give each inmate a separate compartment for clothes.

The institution possesses a garden about three miles from the city, from which it obtains a full supply of vegetables.

The health of the inmates was good; one death had occurred during the year. The school hours are from nine till twelve, and from half-past one till four. The children work or play the remainder of the day. Dressmaking and tailoring are taught. "Many of those who have left us are doing," the Mother says, "remarkably well. The boys become good tradesmen and the girls good dressmakers. Children coming here have every thing to learn, and hence they require to be kept at school longer. The teaching of industrious habits we regard as all important. Especially is it important to teach them self-control." Twenty to thirty boys, on the date of our last visit, were engaged in making cane seats, others were learning to make coats. Four sewing machines were in use.

At the date of October 1, 1875, there were in the institution eighty pupils, six of native and seventy-four of foreign parentage. Sixteen were supported partially by friends, twenty-two by counties, thirty-four by the State, and eight wholly by the institution. The total amount of its indebtedness was $10,687.

It is manifest that the Sisters engaged in this work take pride in the progress made by their pupils, that they devote themselves to the peculiar work with assiduity, and have spared no trouble to acquaint themselves fully with the most improved methods of instruction. The orderly and respectful demeanor of the children indicated the wholesome moral influence under which they were being trained; while the industries taught, apart from their disciplinary worth, must be of great value to both sexes in after-life.

The Society for the Protection of Destitute Roman Catholic Children, at the City of Buffalo.

Buffalo.

The history of the benevolent work which culminated in the establishment of this society, to partially outline which an attempt has been made in sketching the early struggles and financial embarrassments of the St. Joseph's Boys' Orphan Asylum (and continued in the notice of the St. John's Protectory), would, if fully written, form a most interesting chapter in the growth of charitable enterprise.

"The object of this society is to take charge of and provide for the support, education and training of such idle, truant, vicious or homeless children of both sexes, under the age of fourteen, as may be intrusted by their friends to its protection; and the children of Roman Catholic parents, between seven and fourteen years of age, who may be committed to its custody, by the order or judgment of any magistrate of the Sixth, Seventh and Eighth Judicial Districts, together with those of like parentage and age in county poor-houses, and transferred upon the order of superintendents of the poor. It was organized on the 12th of January, 1864, and incorporated on the 25th of April of the same year, by a special act of the Legislature."

The affairs of the society are controlled by a Board of Managers of whom the Rt. Rev. Stephen Vincent Ryan is president. The boys coming under its jurisdiction are sent to its establishment, generally designated as the St. John's Protectory, located at Limestone Hill, in the town of West Seneca; and the girls to the House of the Good Shepherd on Best street, under the charge of the Sisters of Our Lady of Refuge.

The St. John's Protectory may be regarded in one sense as having grown out of the St. Joseph's Male Orphan Asylum, and is a part of the large system of charity under Roman Catholic direction at Limestone Hill. From a conversation with the Superintendent, the Rev. Father Hines, on the day of our visitation, we obtained the following particulars regarding its history:

"Bishop Timon coming to the conclusion that, in addition to the children properly belonging to the institution, we had a class of boys in the St. Joseph's Orphan Asylum who were fit subjects for a reformatory, and as this class was increasing and likely to exert an undesirable influence upon the others, he proposed, in 1862, to establish the St. John's Protectory. He said he would give me his diocese to collect money in. A number of liberal donations were made to us by individuals, and the State allowed us a grant of $3,000. The Society for the Protection of Roman Catholic Children was incorporated in

1864, and such boys as were suitable subjects for the reformatory were transferred from St. Joseph's Orphan Asylum to the Protectory.

"The erection of the building now in use was begun in 1865 and completed in 1866. I was very much afraid to enter upon this work, but the Bishop assisted and encouraged me. We made the brick for the building ourselves. The edifice is fifty by sixty feet, three full stories high, with attic and stone basement. It was opened on the 14th of October, 1866. Since then another building of fifty by sixty feet has been added. In the spring of 1867, we commenced to build a chair factory. The idea of a chair factory was suggested by Mr. Patrick Barry, of Rochester. I was on a visit there and he took me to the House of Refuge. It seemed to me that it was a light and proper work for boys. Our shop was of brick, two stories high, one hundred feet long by thirty-two feet wide. In the rear stood a small engine and boiler-room. We had it going only about a year when it burned down, and every thing in it was destroyed. This was disheartening; but our managers and friends held a meeting and decided to build again immediately. We tried to save all we could of the old building, put a new roof on a part of it, and went to work and erected another building at right angles, in the rear of the present, two stories high, of brick, eighty feet long by forty-two feet wide. We had our works in operation in January, 1869. Since that time we have been quite successful. Just previous to Bishop Timon's death we raised some funds upon a mortgage, but it has never been paid off."

In regard to the disposal of children, Father Hines said: "If a farmer comes along and we think him a suitable man, and he wants a boy, we let him have one. I never force a boy away. I ask him if he desires to go. Where we find that a boy wants to go, and that a man wants to take him, he is pretty sure to succeed. We work off the boys as fast as we can advantageously. If we did not, it would soon take three houses like this to contain them. We work off forty or fifty some years. Farmers like boys of some size. They do not want to take very little fellows. They are given out under the direction of the Board of Managers. Their meetings are held quarterly. Applications for children are then presented. It is a part of my duty to receive applications, and inform myself as to the character of the applicant, and as to how he lives. Each case is considered. We generally bind the boys until they are eighteen or nineteen, and do not lose sight of them until they are at least eighteen years old. The party taking the boy agrees to give him at least two suits of clothes, and not less than four months' schooling every year. I am required by the Board of Managers to ascertain how he gets along. We assume the responsibility of seeing whether the boy is dealt justly with or not. If I hear that something is wrong about a boy I write to the Pastor of the place to find out about it. Applicants for boys must come recommended by letters from the priests in their parish. The Bishop requires priests to have a special care over every boy. If there is any thing wrong the priest writes to me about it. A few weeks ago I got a letter from a priest in a distant town, telling me that a certain man was not treating his boy rightly. I wrote to the man telling him I wanted to know why it was that he was not treating his boy well. The boy I found was unruly; the man whipped him. He was a hot-tempered man. Perhaps he overdid it. They were out drawing hay, and the boy left the horses to go after a swarm of bees. The horses ran away and smashed every thing, and the man was angry and whipped the boy. I had a talk with them both, and they arranged matters. I heard from them since that they were doing well. I had a boy down on Grand Island. They neglected him, and never sent him to school or to church, and he had no Sundays, but had to work all the time. I wrote to the man and said, if he did not give up the boy I would sue him. I took the boy and gave him to another man. The excuse they gave for not sending him to school or church was, that the snow was too deep; but it was not too deep to go into the woods to draw wood. Some of the boys are returned to their parents.

"If a boy cannot obey here he will not obey outside. Even parents are refused in our Board to have their boys back unless they are fit to go. Recently certain parties complained because their boy was not returned. A petition was presented signed by prominent men to have the boy released. I found the boy's record was bad, and I found that there were no better facilities in his home for taking care of him than before. The question was put to the Board, and they decided to keep him. The Managers say any boy guilty of petty larceny should not be released in less than six months. To let such a boy loose in a month is to bring him back worse than he was at first."

In regard to discipline, Father Hines remarks: "The conduct of the boys is marked. Each boy is told when a mark has been made against him. The best boys are allowed white bowls and spoons, and knives and forks in the refectory." In the refectory the tables are classified, and as the boys improve they are promoted from one table to another. Father Hines remarks on this point: "No matter how small the punishment is, if it will effect the purpose, I use it. If I stand at the window and see a boy boisterous, I send for him. I say, 'now rest yourself on this cistern.' It is just these little ways that we use. In other cases I keep them in the school-room during recreation. If there is any thing hard to be done I send an offender to do it. Sometimes the Sisters may slap some of them on the hand. A bad boy is put in the dormitory, or he stays in bed all day. Lying in bed may be pleasureable at first, but it soon becomes painful. If a boy complains that he is punished unjustly, I investigate his case. I always give him the benefit of the doubt whenever one exists. If you put a boy down absolutely, it is bad. It is better to make him feel that you have some confidence in him.

"A good many of our boys, now men, work in the city of Buffalo. I had eight or nine, with their wives and children, come to see me recently. They all had homes of their own. Some belonged to the Orphan Asylum and some to the Protectory. We have sent a number of boys west. About three years ago this past summer, one of these boys married a farmer's daughter in good circumstances, and the husband and wife have been here to visit me. Several of the boys have gone into the printing business; two of them are in Chicago comfortably off. There are three of our boys holding official positions in the city; two of them are masters of vessels on the lakes. I have lost sight of a number that have married."

Father Hines was asked in case of a stubborn boy coming to the Protectory, how he would treat him. He said: "Well he comes in, stalks around and says, 'I hain't going to stay here.' He is told to sit down. 'I don't want to sit down!' We let him have his own way and let him stand up if he wants to. By and by the boys come in; his appearance generally amuses them and they laugh at him. When he sees the other boys all sitting down, then he sits down too. He is asked, 'What is your name?' He will hold his head down and mutter something. 'Don't you think you would feel better if you had a wash?' 'I don't want a wash!' A Sister will come and try to take off his coat; 'Let's alone!' They will let him alone. In the afternoon or evening he will say, 'I want to go out.' He will go out and walk back again. By and by it is supper time. He will start up and want to go to supper. He will be put back again. Then the Sister says, 'You must wash; you are dirty and cannot go down in that state.' 'I am as clean as the rest of them!' The next thing, he gets his supper alone; a cup of tea or bread and milk. He washes at last. They have a terror of water and soap. Soon it is bed-time. He has a place given him in the dormitory. He is told to say his prayers. 'I will say no prayers!' 'Bless yourself! did you ever bless yourself?' 'I used to once.' He will kneel down and mutter something. The boys say their prayers and go to bed. He will straggle around, sure to be the last. He is told, 'There's your place, go to bed!' He will want to tumble in just as he is. A Brother will come along and make him take off his clothes and go to bed properly. So ends the first day. In the morning he is sure to be up in time. The Sisters won't let him down to breakfast. They say, 'When you get your hair cut.' He don't want his hair cut. A Sister comes around him and begins to cut it quietly. He commences to cry. She says, 'Don't cry! I will fix it up nicely. Then I want you to come to the wash-room, and I will give you a good wash. You cannot have your breakfast until you are clean.' After a little he submits, and by noon he is in better spirits. When such boys have a good crying spell, they are sure to come round pretty soon. He wants to do something. He is sent to help carry wood up from the yard. He is glad to do this. Soon he wants to sit by the Sisters and talks with them. He steals gradually over by their side and begins: 'I saw a boy that was here before.' 'Did you? What is he doing?' 'He is living with such a man.' 'How did you come to get here?' 'I used to be out nights and got with such a boy, and took beer.' So he goes on and tells his whole story to the Sisters. In this way we work upon him, and he will open his whole heart to us. We try to reason with him: 'How good God has been to give you eyes to see and ears to hear, but instead of bestowing these in the service of God, you use them against him.' After a while the boy will submit.

"After four, five or six months he is wanted perhaps by his friends, perhaps by some one else. I ascertain what his record is, and also try to ascertain who it is that wants him. I can tell pretty soon what the home of the father and mother is when I see them. Sometimes I am satisfied to judge from their appearance, without going any further. My report of the boy, made up from his record, may run thus: 'Johnny has been in the institution so long. We find he did not avail himself of the advantages he has had. His standing is such that we think it is better to retain him in the institution. If we should restore him to his parents we fear he would fall back again.' This is given to the Board of Managers, who we find are generally satisfied to act in accordance with this decision. On the other hand, we might often find the boy fit to go out, but the party applying not being suitable, we refuse him the boy. It may be, perhaps, because it is evident he wants him only for some servile purpose. We mean to look after the boy's interest and keep him till the right opportunity presents itself."

In regard to the employment of time at the institution, and other matters, Father Hines says:

"The daily routine is as follows:

5.30 A. M.	There is morning prayer.
6 "	Study and recitation.
7.30 "	Breakfast and various duties, read and spell.
8 "	First division go to work in chair factory.
9 "	Second division, small boys, go to work in cane room.
12 M.	Dinner and recreation.
1 P. M.	Study and recreation, writing, geography and catechism.

2.30	P. M.	Work in chair factory and cane room.
4.30	"	Second division leaves off work.
5.30	"	First division leaves off work.
5.40	"	Supper and recitation.
6.30	"	Study and recitation
8.30	"	Night prayer and retire.

Our Sunday exercises are:

6	A. M.	Morning mass.
9	"	Religious reading.
11	"	Catechism instruction.
2	P. M.	Miscellaneous reading.
4	"	Catechism instruction.
7	"	Lecture.

Several of the Sisters are engaged in teaching in the school-rooms. From the beginning of the institution to January, 1868, the schools were taught by the Brothers, when, at the suggestion of the judge of Erie county, *ex officio*, a member of the Board of Managers, the idea of securing the Sisters to teach in their stead was adopted. He thought that "if they could teach as well as they could keep house, it would result in good schools and clever scholars." Two Sisters were accordingly engaged for that purpose, and the change has been attended with very satisfactory results.

During the year 1875, four hours a day have been devoted to the school. The Superintendent says: "It appears to work well so far, in securing closer application to lessons and good recitations by the scholars. Those who are strong and well advanced in their studies labor five hours a day, while those who are backward are required to work but three hours daily.

"The Sisters endeavor to make the boys do every thing in a systematic way. We endeavor to inculcate the following ideas: They must honor the school-room, because there the noblest part of their being, their mental life, is brought into exercise. They must honor the Church still more, because it is the house of God. We also inculcate the idea of the preservation of property. I now and then have a long talk with the boys about it. I say to them, 'you are bound to take care of the property of this house; if you do not take care of this property now, you will not take care of your own by and by.' When a boy gets a new pair of shoes it is recorded, and when he wears them out he has to account for them. The same way with his dress, and thus a check is kept upon him which tends to make him careful. The boys make their own beds, under the superintendence of the Sisters. They have to wash their dormitories. The Sisters teach some of the boys to cook. There is one Sister in the kitchen for that purpose.

"We have eighteen milch cows. We buy our butter. We do not use very much tea or coffee.

"We have two or three colored children in this house, and two in the other, St. Joseph's Asylum, across the street. There was a colored child at the Poor-house, and when the various asylum people were there to get the children, nobody wanted to take him. I said, 'I will take the little fellow.' There was a little prejudice against him, among the boys here, but as soon as they found that the Sisters would fix him up and comb down his curly hair, it soon passed away.

"The parents of the majority are foreigners, Irish, English, Polish and German. One boy here lost his leg by an accident on the cars. About one-eighth of the children here have parents who contribute something toward their support. I think it costs about $1.60 per week to keep them. We have more applicants for admission than we can accommodate."

Additions have been made to the original purchase of land at Limestone Hill, increasing the farm to about three hundred acres. Fifteen acres of this tract have been appropriated to the uses of the Protectory. The soil is a sandy loam lying upon an elevated ridge, about a mile from the shore of Lake Erie. About one hundred and twenty acres are in meadow land and a hundred acres in pasture. The remainder is in woodland excepting some twelve acres under garden cultivation, in which potatoes, cabbages and early potatoes are mostly grown There is an orchard of about three acres of grafted fruit on the place. It does not, however, supply all the apples needed, as it is subject to lawless depredations.

The buildings are heated by steam, lighted with kerosene and ventilated by fire-places. Drinking water is supplied from good wells. Four or five cisterns are in use for preserving the rain water. It is intended to put tanks under the roofs and distribute soft water in pipes throughout the building. The drainage is imperfect; the bathing facilities are insufficient, but a building is now being constructed ample for the purpose. The children bathe twice a week, some once a day for a time. There are some children that have to be kept, for a time, away by themselves, being covered with vermin when they come in. The water-closets are detached. The washing and ironing are done in a separate building. The boys sleep singly on straw beds and on French bedsteads. One of the Brothers sleeps in each of the dormitory rooms. The dormitories are also classified, the good boys getting the best. The beds have white counterpanes. All the boys' clothing, including shoes and stockings, are made on the premises.

The vegetables are mainly stored in a basement under the barn.

In the work-shops is a thirty horse-power engine, and a large steam boiler. One of the boys runs the engine and has done so for two years past. The work-shop is a perfect hive of industry. From sixty to seventy boys were caning seats, the smallest being seven years old. Two circular saws are running, attended by experienced adults. There are, also, among other machinery, two turning and three hand lathes. The work in the factory is done by boys with the exception of about five experienced instructors and workmen. Carved and well-made chairs of a variety of patterns, manufactured in the shop, were shown. The boys are not worked long enough in one position to have it become irksome; but as soon as a boy gets tired he is relieved by another. Thus the machinery is run uninterruptedly. All of the workmen are required to be of good character and habits. The institution, in addition to the Superintendent who is also treasurer, has three Brothers of the Order of the Holy Youth and Infancy of Jesus, and twelve Sisters of the Order of St. Joseph, of whom Mother Philip is Superior, engaged in its work. The Brothers receive, in addition to their simple clothing, $30 a year. There is only one farm hand on the place. There were one hundred and forty-three children in the Protectory at date of visitation.

A chapel for the use of the inmates has recently been constructed near the Reformatory, to which they have access without going upon the street. It is of brick, plain architecture and tasteful in its interior and exterior decorations. The windows are of stained glass, the gift of different individuals, each window bearing the name of the giver. It is designed to accommodate five hundred and forty persons, and has been built at a considerable sacrifice on the part of those directly interested. It has long been a cherished project of the Superintendent.

The friends of this institution are considering the project of erecting some memorial to the late Right Rev. Bishop Timon, and subscriptions have already been made for this purpose. In view of the practical benevolence characteristic of the life of this distinguished prelate, it has been deemed that some expenditure which should perpetuate the good work he was so largely instrumental in inaugurating would be most fitting. It is therefore proposed, in case the means can be raised, to erect here a tasteful brick building, suitably adapted to carry on the shoe-making business, and to dedicate it as a memorial. It is estimated that the carrying out of this project would cost about $12,000. It is hoped that this commendable undertaking will be successful.

The number of children that have come under the charge of "The Society for the Protection of Destitute Roman Catholic Children at the city of Buffalo," since its organization, is seven hundred and thirty-eight. The number of boys received during the past year was one hundred and three; the number of boys discharged during the year was ninety-five. Of these nine were adopted, six indentured, fifty-five returned to parents or guardians, seven left without permission, ten transferred to other institutions, five sent out of the State and three otherwise discharged. The number remaining October 1, 1875, was one hundred and thirty-nine. Twenty-eight of these were orphans, forty-one half-orphans and seventy had both parents living. Eighty-eight were of native and fifty-one of foreign parents.

The total expenditure for the year ending October 1, 1875, was $18,616.08. Its indebtedness at that date amounted to $16,505.

It is difficult to estimate either the pecuniary saving or moral benefit to Erie county, and a large district in Western New York, wrought through the agency of this Society. The class upon whom it is asked to exercise its benevolence is an unpromising one, and yet it is believed that its efforts in the way of juvenile reformation are highly successful. In this view it would seem that the work should receive the substantial encouragement of the public in whose interest it is being carried on, and that a more liberal compensation for maintenance of the children than is now paid by the county should be allowed. The sum fixed, one dollar a week *per capita*, falls far short of the actual cost of their support.

St. Joseph's Male Orphan Asylum,

Buffalo,

Is situated in the town of West Seneca, on the opposite side of the highway from the St. John's Protectory. The grounds about it are elevated and command a fine view of Lake Erie, the harbor, and the city of Buffalo. It is but a short distance from railroad stations, two leading lines of which connect it with the city.

This asylum was organized in August, 1849, and incorporated on the 2d of August, 1851. Prior to its establishment, an attempt had been made to provide a home for orphan and destitute boys at Lancaster, in Erie county. In 1849 this was broken up, and the children, forty-seven in number, were brought to Buffalo, under the charge of Father Early, and provided for on Best street in one of the buildings now occupied by the Sisters of Our Lady of Charity. In 1856 the children were transferred to Limestone Hill, where, for a time, they were under the care of a band of five Sisters and three Brothers. The Sisters belonged to the Order of the Holy Cross, and came from South Bend, Indiana. They were not, however, fully sustained in their good work. In 1857 the Right Rev. Bishop Timon, who, in addition to his large benevolence, possessed the rare faculty of just discrimination of character, selected from among his seminarians in St. Joseph's College, a young man then in his third year of Theology, and ordained him priest, placing him over the St. Joseph's Asylum, which was then newly organized at Limestone Hill.

One hundred and five acres of land had been purchased at Limestone Hill for a cemetery. A part of this was set off for the Asylum, and Father Hines came here, as had been previously arranged by the Bishop, on the 7th of May, 1857, and assumed charge. There were then but sixty-eight boys at this place, and the building in use was a frame one. The following named Sisters of the Order of St. Joseph were delegated to assist in the work which was then undertaken: Sister Veronica, Sister Anastasia and Sister Petronella, the last-named since deceased. These Sisters entered upon their self-denying labors, receiving then, as is customary now, no pay, except an allowance of $25 per annum for clothing, etc.

It is thought that a clearer idea of the work that has been done here in the past may be obtained by giving, in a connected form, the answers to the numerous questions asked Father Hines on the day of our visitation.

"The day we came here we did not have any thing but corn meal in the house. Sister Petronella went out to try and buy something. She went down to Martin's Corners, near here, but did not know the way back. While seeking for the road she met Bishop Timon in his buggy, and he said: 'My child, where are you going?' she replied: 'Bishop, we have nothing to eat and I am looking for something to purchase.' He got out of his buggy and put the Sister, with a little orphan boy that was with her, into it, and taking her basket directed her to drive home and he would soon follow. The Sister again lost her way, but the Bishop brought us the basket with something for the children and ourselves to eat.

"We commenced our work here in a small wooden building, twelve by eighteen feet, and lived in it six months. It was erected in front of the square wooden building that was here when I came. The little boys used to sleep over my head, and when they were disorderly I could touch the ceiling with my hand, and call them to order. The bishop next allowed me to go through the diocese and solicit money for the work. It took me a year to get around. I went about from church to church, and presented the condition and claims of the orphans to the congregation, and received the offerings of the charitable, coming home every week to pay the men. We soon set to work to erect a building, which is now the right wing of St. Joseph's Male Orphan Ayslum, across the street. I noticed a man from Buffalo, drawing clay from our farm, and learned from him that he used it in making flower-pots. It occurred to me, that we might make our own brick out of the same material. We got some rude apparatus, and hired two men who were brick-makers, to manage the work; the boys assisted.

Of course we did not make the very best brick, and some laughed at them, but they made a very good asylum. I cared very little what was said. I tried to do what was for the best. The boys carried the brick away, drew sand and wood with a yoke of cattle, and did every thing else they could do. We quarried our stone near by. The building was three stories high, and forty by fifty, on the ground, and was occupied on the 1st day of November, 1857. It accommodated eighty children. This was the number we had at that time. They were principally orphans, on account of the cholera of 1856 and 1857. During that time, I think the people were more charitable than they are now. I think great public calamities tend to make them so. In those days I performed a great many funeral services. At every service the people gave something for the benefit of the orphans. In the summer of 1859, we were crowded with children, and at the suggestion of Bishop Timon, I made up my mind that I would go through the diocese again and beg. Rochester and Buffalo were then in the same diocese. Each priest gave me a Sunday in his church. I began on the 19th of June, and use to address the people morning and afternoon, and receive their offerings. Bishop Timon gave me $2,000, and we set to work again making brick for another building on the premises. At the same time we quarried stone for the foundation. It was inclosed in the fall of 1859. It is sixty by seventy feet, on the ground, and forms the main portion of St. Joseph's Asylum. Preparations were made to have this work prosecuted vigorously during the winter, and we did all the work we could in the spring of 1860, and had it plastered and were occupying it in July of the same year. During this time, I made my little circuit to get money to pay the hands off, and went along that way. We introduced shoemaking here, and put up a large frame building north of this, forty by fifty feet, two stories high.

"In April, 1860, we employed a foreman and commenced the shoe business. We had at that time plenty of hemlock bark on our land, and we thought it a good plan to tan a little leather. We got a lot of tubs, set them up, and hired a tanner to come out from the city. We gave him three or four boys to help him, and so we began to tan a little. We were encouraged to put up a small frame building the following fall in connection with this enterprise, which did us good service. We tanned all our calf skins. It succeeded well. A year ago last November, our supply of tan-bark was exhausted, and its scarcity in this vicinity made it unadvisable to continue the business any longer. The work, while it lasted, was carried on solely by the orphan children. There were also a great many little boys, too young for this business, who made themselves useful in various ways; some in taking care of the cows, of which we had, in 1860, '61 and '62, about sixty. At this time we had a man who took our farm products daily to the city.

"After a while one of the boys grew up and attended to it for three years. He is now a wealthy man. His successor is working with us yet, and, by saving his money, has now about $1,000. One of our boys married the daughter of a very respectable man in this neighborhood, and is doing well.

"Our place filled up rapidly during the war, and we went into gardening. We had a large garden, where we cultivated onions, tomatoes, etc. We put the boys to work at hoeing and weeding, so we worked along for some time.

"In 1866, Bishop Timon transferred a number of boys, who properly belonged to the reformatory class, to the St. John's Protectory, and thus this Asylum has since been enabled to devote its energies to the class that are more particularly the objects of its benevolence."

The financial affairs are controlled by a Board of Gentlemen, and Father Hines is still its Superintendent. He is assisted by nine members of the Roman Catholic Order of the Sisters of St. Joseph, of whom Mother Veronica is Superioress. This lady has shared in all the trials incident to the early struggles of the institution, and has labored throughout with a steadfast devotion to the poor children's cause. In an unpretending way her laborious and monotonous round of work goes quietly on, and though the world may be none the wiser, it is certainly much the better for it.

Connected with the institution is a farm of about three hundred acres, which gives employment to a considerable number of the inmates during the summer.

Shoemaking is still carried on to some extent. All boys of a suitable age are engaged in some useful work when not in school. Sufficient time is allowed for recreation. A school is taught in the institution by the Sisters. The boys are not kept long in the Asylum, but are placed out when homes can be found for them in good families.

The building contains large school-rooms, spacious dormitories, a chapel, and other necessary rooms, including those for washing and bathing.

The boys are taught to sing. They acquitted themselves very creditably in this accomplishment on the occasion of our visit.

The Sisters who are occupied in the St. John's Protectory during the day unite with the Sisters in the Asylum for evening prayers, and make their homes here at night.

This Asylum has, since its organization, cared for 1,027 boys. The inmates on October 1, 1875, numbered 118. The number received during the year was fifty, and the number discharged, thirty-five. Of these, seven were adopted, three were indentured, fifteen returned to parents or guardians, and seven transferred to other institutions, or otherwise discharged.

For children committed by the superintendent of the poor, the county allows one dollar a week. But this it is stated falls far short of the cost of maintaining them.

The total indebtedness of the Asylum was $8,000. Its expenditures during the fiscal year ending October 1, 1875, were $9,652.03.

Some repairs are needed, and improvements might be effected that would bring the Asylum into a higher condition of efficiency. In view of the large amount of voluntary service tendered, and the good work that is being accomplished, it would seem that it should be well sustained.

St. Vincent's Female Orphan Asylum,

Buffalo,

Is situated on the corner of Batavia and Ellicott streets. It is under the management of the Roman Catholic Order of the Sisters of Charity. The sole and absolute title to the property is vested in this community. The Asylum owes its origin to the late Right Reverend Bishop Timon, whose zeal inspired others, and whose personal efforts as well as means contributed largely to sustain it during its subsequent struggles. Twelve Sisters are at present engaged in carrying on its work, Sister Robertina Lenahan being Sister Servant, which office she has filled since 1854. No hired domestics are employed.

The institution was incorporated January 29, 1849. Two brick structures, about twenty-two by seventy-two, and fifty by ninety-five feet, respectively, are at present occupied, with a capacity for about one hundred and twenty-five children. The last-named structure was formerly St. Patrick's Church. The buildings are warmed by both hot air and stoves, lighted by gas, and ventilated by the windows.

The latest visitation was made August 26th. There were then one hundred and twenty-four inmates. The children were out for the day upon an excursion. Sister Robertina kindly furnished the following information regarding the growth and present condition of the Asylum : "The institution commenced in June, 1848. The Buffalo Hospital of the Sisters of Charity and this house were commenced the same year, under the charge of the Sisters of Charity. The institution began with three Sisters, viz : Sisters Anne De Sales, Anacaria and Mary Clare. The inmates increased in number daily. The cholera broke out in 1849, and the poor people required some place for their children. They were brought in here and were obliged to sleep on the floor. The rooms were small. This building was not erected then. They had a two-story cottage back of the present edifice, facing on Batavia street. They also kept a day school, but it was discontinued in July, 1868. Bishop Timon died in April, 1867, and the following vacation we discontinued the day school. The number of orphan and destitute children was so great as to demand our entire care. The old church, called St. Patrick's, was given to us in 1855.

"We are very much crowded now. About one hundred and twenty-five is all that we can accommodate, and many are awaiting admission at the present time that we cannot take in for want of room. We need yard room very much. Our location is very unpleasant. The children's play ground is entirely too small. We have bought a place on Main street. The lot is not yet clear, only $6,000 having been paid upon it. Our location here was formerly very healthy, but during the last three years we have noticed our children do not enjoy as good health. We have had eight deaths during the past year, four with scarlet fever and three with consumption. Our children generally range from five years old upwards. We seldom receive them under five, because the Infant Asylum is intended for that class. We take orphans, half-orphans and destitute children. Several at the present time have both parents living, but they would be just as well off without them. We take all classes that apply, without distinction of religion or social status. We desire to keep them long enough to make them useful young women, but if they have parents or friends who wish to take them, we let them go. It takes some time to train them to domestic duties. Again, it is very hard to get them instructed; some are so very dull that it is very difficult even to teach them to read. I do not wish to keep them any longer than is necessary to fit them for work in families.

"We never bind children out, but place them in proper hands so far as we can ascertain. If a child is not contented, or the parties are not satisfied with her, we take her back. If a young girl wishes to go to live out, or to learn any employment or trade, we provide for her. Most of them go to service; a few of them get married. We require parties taking our girls to treat them as their own children, and, if they stay long enough, till they wish to settle in life, to give them something; but it is very seldom they remain that time. We require reports to be made of their condition from time to time. The girls write to us very often, and thus we keep up a correspondence with them, while those living around the city the Sisters see. We have a society formed among our children while in the house. The girls retain their membership after they pass out of the institution, and are required to attend its meetings every Sunday if possible. It is a meeting for young girls. One Sunday we may have thirty or forty, the next not so many. The members are obliged to look after each other, and report to the Sister in charge. One reports why another is absent, and if she is sick, we go to see her. This is one means for looking after our girls. Our children generally turn out well. Some have gone astray, and come back again like the prodigal son. As a general thing, however, we have very little trouble with them. In the last twenty years I think there has not been more than four that have not done right. It is very encouraging, because young girls nowadays are very hard to manage."

In one of the rooms of the Asylum is a photographic group of girls. These, Sister Robertina says, "had been at one time either in the house or were members of the Parish school and of this Society. Some of them are now Sisters of Charity, working in hospitals and asylums scattered from New York to New Orleans. We have one girl who was married last year, and who is doing well. She had been in the house eighteen years. When we have a picnic of those in the house, the former inmates, once girls, come and march out with them. Even when they are married they come here to visit, bringing with them their children.

"We aim to make our girls useful members of society. We teach them to respect themselves and that then others will respect them. We try to raise their thoughts above this low don't-care way of girls. We try to instil in their minds the principle that they must work and be independent. We say to them on leaving, 'If you conduct yourself properly you need never want a home.'

"We try to influence our children by kindness, mingled with firmness. For punishment, we put them to bed for half a day. If they are disobedient on Saturday, we do not let them out to church on Sunday. Not to let them out with others is the most effectual kind of punishment. They are accustomed to harsh treatment in their own homes, they do not mind that; but this method is new to them. If they are rude we make them stay up stairs in silence. We very seldom have occasion to use any corporal punishment.

"In regard to education, we teach them reading, writing, geography, arithmetic, grammar and history. We use the same text-books as are used in the public schools. The school department pays the salary of three teachers.

"The girls are taught all kinds of house-work, cooking, washing, ironing, baking, and plain as well as machine-sewing. Dress-making is also taught. All of the girls, as they are growing up, learn to use the sewing-machine, and those who have a taste for embroidery are instructed in it by one of the Sisters. We had a class in knitting, but found it too confining for the little ones, and the time of the larger girls is too important for this employment. The children make all their own clothing. They do their own dress-making and mending, and also make rag carpets. Each makes her own bed and does all her own work. The larger girls have little ones to help them. From about eight years old they commence to do some work. We change every week so that each girl learns to do all kinds of work. All the house-work is done by eight o'clock in the morning. Sister Genevieve has had charge of this department for sixteen years. We bake some bread every day, but buy most of our bread. We give the children the same food as we have ourselves; soup, meat and vegetables, with bread and butter, every day. When we have plenty of milk, we give the children bread and milk. We have the milk from six cows. It is brought in twice a day. The children, every day at three o'clock, have a lunch, of either apples and crackers or cake, or something of the kind."

The dormitories are heated by registers in each extremity. Seventy-six wooden bedsteads are in a room which is forty by eighty feet. Beds for the Sisters, inclosed with neat white curtains, are in each corner of the room. Another dormitory for the little ones has twenty bedsteads in it, mostly wooden. The Sisters say: "We find very little trouble in keeping our beds clean. We clean one row every day, and every bedstead in the house once a week." Straw beds and feather pillows are used. The dormitories are kept with the utmost neatness, order and cleanliness. The counterpanes of the beds were folded back and looking down the long range, the folds formed a perfect line. The windows were down and the sunshine was pouring into the room on all sides, the fresh air from the open windows affording good ventilation.

The infirmary had in it one little sick child, about two years old. The house is so crowded that even the infirmary has to be converted into a general sleeping-room at night.

At the date of October 1, 1875, the number of children in the institution, who were orphans, was twenty-nine; half-orphans, seventy-four, and who had both parents living, eighteen. One hundred and two of these came from Erie county, and nineteen from other counties. Twenty-one were of native and one hundred of foreign parentage. Seventeen were in part supported by friends, seventy-nine partially by counties, and twenty-five wholly by the asylum. The whole number received during the year was eighty-five. The number discharged by adoption was ten; the number placed out was seven; the number returned to parents was fifty-two. One left without permission, three were transferred to other institutions, and nine died.

The total expenditure for the fiscal year ending October 1, 1875, amounted to $10,574.97. The indebtedness of the institution, on the 1st October, was $19,000. It has no invested funds.

Little comment upon this useful charity is needed. Its work speaks for itself. Since its organization one thousand one hundred and eighty-seven children have been received into the Asylum and brought under its refining and elevating influences. It is greatly to be regretted that it should have to carry so large a burden of debt, and its field of usefulness be thus circumscribed.

St. Mary's Asylum for Widows, Foundlings and Infants.

Buffalo.

This institution is located at 126 Edward street, in a healthy part of the city, upon a lot with about one hundred and twenty feet frontage. The building is a plain brick structure, consisting of a main with two wings, standing thirty-four feet from the street, and having a neatly kept lawn in front. The land upon which it is located was donated by Louis Le Couteulx, Esq., a philanthropic citizen of Buffalo, in 1852.

The Asylum was incorporated January 13, 1852. The necessities out of which it originated are stated as follows: "Before its establishment, poor lying-in women and infants, orphans and foundlings, were obliged to be taken to the hospital of the Sisters of Charity in the city, as they could not all be received in the Orphan Asylum for larger children. It was painful to the Sisters in charge of the hospital to refuse admittance to this class of patients and children. They saw the necessity of opening a separate institution for them. Owing to the breaking out of the cholera in 1854, the hospital of the Sisters of Charity was crowded with patients afflicted with that disease. As the effects were serious on the lying-in patients, it was determined by those whose sympathies were aroused to make other immediate provision for them. Three frame cottages were put upon the Le Couteulx lot, and this class of sufferers were at once transferred there. Previous to this time foundlings were frequently picked up dying or dead on the door-steps, along the streets, in alleys and by-ways; but since the hospital was opened such cases rarely occur."

In 1855, the first wing of the Asylum was erected, having three stories. The central building has four stories, and was built in 1858. An additional wing has since been erected. Under the same roof, but forming a distinct department, is St. Mary's Lying-in Hospital. The whole is under the charge of the Roman Catholic Order of the Sisters of Charity, of which Sister Mary Elizabeth Sinnott is Sister Servant. She is assisted by eight other Sisters. Sister Elizabeth has been in this Asylum six years, and during the war was in the military hospitals, assisting in taking care of the soldiers.

At the date of visitation, the 20th of August, there were about ninety children as inmates. About half of this number were between the ages of three and five years, and the remainder were mainly infants. The children, we were informed, are adopted whenever a good opportunity presents, but if remaining at the age of five, the girls are transferred to St. Vincent's Female Orphan Asylum in Buffalo, and the boys to St. Joseph's Male Orphan Asylum at Limestone Hill. Children of delicate constitutions are retained till six years old.

In regard to instruction the Sister in charge says: "The children are so young that about all we can teach them is, who made them, and the Lord's Prayer."

The institution keeps six cows for the use of the children. The milk of one cow is reserved for such infants as are being weaned. It is brought to the Asylum in a separate can night and morning.

The Infants' Asylum is divided into two departments, one for the nursing children, the other for older children. These are on different floors. The department for the nursing children communicates with the Lying-in Hospital, enabling mothers to come in at stated hours to nurse the children; but there is no communication between the older children and the Lying-in Hospital or with the infants. The mothers are as far as possible induced to remain to nurse the children. Each mother who is able must nurse two children, her own and one other.

Sister Elizabeth says: "It is found impracticable to provide as many nurses as desirable." There were about twenty at the date of visitation, and it was found necessary to keep from ten to fifteen children on cows' milk. "They are," says the Sister, "fed with the spoon, as we find it preferable to bottle feeding." In speaking of some of the cases cared for, the Sister said: "It is not long since we had to take in three women with their young children, who came from the city, their husbands abused them so. They had infants in their arms and had, we ascertained, other children sheltered in neighbors' houses. One woman had been going around from house to house, the husband having taken almost every article of clothing from her, and threatening to take her life. One of the others had two children and a baby nine months old. Her husband abused her shamefully. He is almost a savage. He came here to try to get her. The poor thing told me that she had not had a month's peace since her marriage till she came here. 'Unfortunate women' who come here are only received once. We tell them when they are in the house that they never will be received again."

In regard to the health of the children the Sister remarks: "A great many of the children die; they live in proportion as we can procure nurses for them. The Sisters are constantly on the watch to see that the nurses take the same care of the little ones they nurse as of their own. No money can buy their attention to the children, and they will neglect them unless you have a person there to look after them. We go in at all hours of the day and night to examine the children, and see that they are not neglected. We require mothers to provide for their children as far as they are able. If a child is nursed for only two weeks and then weaned, it generally lives but two months.

"We have had to beg hard to get funds to improve the building. We have walked often twelve miles a day, collecting money from among the poor to help us in this work."

Our last visitation was made toward evening, when the children were preparing for bed. On entering we found twenty-one little children on their knees, saying, with upraised hands brought together, their simple, childish prayers.

The bathing facilities are ample; closets large and commodious were found on each floor, and in unexceptionable condition. Each child has its towel, which is hung on a separate hook in the bath-room. Under each of these is a little drawer containing a fine and a coarse comb. The children appeared well clothed and clean, and the dormitories, sitting-room, play-room and kitchen were found to be neat and orderly. In the rear of the building is a yard, planked in the center, for the purpose of affording the children air and exercise without dampening their feet. It contains a fine large shade tree with seats around it, and also a swing.

In the rear of the Infants' Asylum and Lying-in Hopsital, is a large brick building recently erected for a laundry. It is conveniently arranged and constructed on modern principles, having good light and ventilation. The lower floor, twenty-five by fifty feet, is divided into washing and drying-rooms. The upper floor is the ironing department, a dumb waiter communicating with it and the lower floor.

The perfect order and scrupulous cleanliness, manifested not only in this building but in every department of the Infant Asylum and the grounds about it, are deemed worthy of special note.

The number of children inmates on October 1, 1875, was eighty-six. Of these forty-two were orphans, thirty-eight half-orphans, and six had both parents living. Thirty-six were of native and fifty of foreign parentage. Seventy-six came from the county of Erie and ten from other counties. The number discharged during the year, by adoption, was nine; the number returned to parents or guardians, forty-three; the number transferred to other institutions, fourteen, and the number who died was ninety-five.

The total receipts for the year ending October 1, 1875, were $15,519.75. Its total expenditures were $17,233.32, of which $5,134.09 was for improvements. The amount of its present indebtedness is $1,300.

As bearing upon the work of the asylum, we quote from the report of the medical attendant of the institution, J. S. Smith, M. D. "The number of infants and children admitted into the asylum, from January 1, 1862, to November 1, 1875, was 1,209. The number of infants born in the hospital was 905, making a total of 2,114. Of these 1,080 have died, and 1,034 have either been adopted into families, transferred to other institutions when old enough to be educated, or remain yet in the institution. A large proportion of the infants attempted to be raised by hand have died, although receiving every possible care and attention that the means of the Sisters would allow as to food, ventilation, cleanliness, etc. It is very gratifying to state, however, that with better facilities and larger experience a greater proportion of infants are now being raised.

"For the children of two years old and upwards, the percentage of mortality has not been as great as in the city at large. During a recent epidemic of scarlet fever, only two deaths occurred in sixty-two cases. These results could only be attained through nurses possessing experience and willing to sacrifice their own ease and comfort to the welfare of the sick and suffering under their care.

* * * * * * * *

"It gives me great pleasure," the doctor continues, "to testify to the cheerful perseverance and judicious management manifested by the Sisters in fulfilling the arduous duties they have taken upon themselves."

Ontario Orphan Asylum.

Canandaigua.

This Asylum stands on Main street, in the northern suburbs of Canandaigua, surrounded by a beautiful grove of forest trees. Its situation is healthful and pleasant.

The history of the Asylum is in part related as follows: "In 1862, the children left to public charity were generally placed in the poorhouse, and fathers, who enlisted during the war, had no other prospect than this for their children, if left orphans and poor. In this state of things, the necessity of an asylum for children became apparent, and the benevolently disposed came forward and subscribed pretty liberally toward that object. A small legacy was also received. A building was purchased for $5,000, one-fifth of the amount being paid down. The work was materially aided by a State appropriation of $2,500. The services of a matron and a teacher were secured, and the institution opened its doors for the reception of inmates. It soon had twenty children under its care. People in all parts of the country became interested in the work, and so popular did it become, that in 1868, the Board of Supervisors of Yates county made arrangements to send their dependent children to the asylum, thus removing this unfortunate class from the poor-house.

The edifice is a three-story brick building, having a basement and mansard roof. It is capable of accommodating seventy inmates, or, with the mansard attic fitted up, about one hundred. A wide veranda is attached to its front.

A Board of Lady Managers form the governing body of the Asylum. Each town sending children to the Asylum is represented in this Board. They are aided by a Board of Gentlemen, Trustees. The Asylum is under the immediate charge of a matron, assisted by two nurses, a cook and a laundress. A farm hand is also employed.

At the time of our visitation, July 9th, a pleasing impression was made upon our minds as we entered the house by the voices of the children in one of the rooms singing "Safe in the arms of Jesus," and by the flowers that freshened and brightened the hall. The school and reception rooms are on opposite sides of the hall; the dining, bath, washing and ironing rooms, kitchen and store rooms in the basement, while the upper floors are used for dormitories.

In the reception room is a small marble tablet bearing the following inscription :

"In memory of Miss Betsy Chapin, a friend of the orphan, 1867."

The school-room is a pleasant, well ventilated apartment, enlivened with suitable engravings, and furnished in keeping with modern improvements. The names of forty children were on the roll. The usual English branches are taught, the object system being used as far as practicable. The children are instructed in drawing. One of the scholars, a little boy only nine years old, had taken quite a fancy to this kind of work. Specimens of birds and various other objects which he had sketched without lines of measurement, were shown, exhibiting considerable proficiency for one of his age. The school hours are from nine to twelve in the forenoon, and from two to half-past four in the afternoon. Younger pupils are not kept in as long as the older.

The dormitories are large, with high ceilings. The window sashes are hung in modern style. The floors were clean, and the beds apparently receive due attention. The bedsteads are wooden and of the French pattern. The children sleep two in a bed. The matron, however, would prefer to have them sleep separately.

The boys and girls occupy the same dining room. One table is better furnished than the other, having a white linen cloth, and here those children who behave best, and are examples in cleanliness and tidiness, are allowed to sit. In fair summer weather the children take supper out of doors.

Fifty-one children have been received from county poor-houses during the past year. Seventeen of these were girls. Three girls and six boys were colored. The ages of the children varied from three to twelve years, the larger number being between five and eight.

Thirty of the children were sick with the whooping cough, and one little girl, a new comer, while disobeying the rules of the Asylum had fallen over the balustrade and broken her arm, thus adding another to the sick-list.

About eighteen of the children had fathers or mothers contributing to their support. The sum paid was about fifty cents a week for each. This, however, is but a small part of the expenses, which average two dollars a week, pèr capita.

On October 1, 1875, there were in the Asylum forty-seven children. Of these six were orphans, thirty-five half-orphans, and six had both parents living.

In reference to the children, the Matron, Mrs. Anna S. Biegler, remarks: "Our aim is to teach them self-respect, to correct the idea which many of them have on coming here, that no matter what they do, they will be cared for all the same. We want them to learn to work, to attend school, and as soon as they are able to support themselves to go out into the world and work. I notice a great difference in the children who come here. Those who have previously been at the poor-house are by far the worst, and I attribute it to the demoralizing association of poor-house life." The Matron's opinion about the importance of selecting proper persons to have charge of the children, is thus expressed: "We do not approve of employing any but first-class, Christian nurses; they watch over the morals of the children. I believe in beginning the work of Christian education with children, as soon as they are able to understand, and by the time they are twelve years old, the effect of a good training will show itself. Our greatest difficulty is in eradicating tendencies to untruthfulness, which seem to be innate in many of the children. Not unfrequently, when uttering falsehoods, they will look at you so innocently and ingenuously with their bright eyes, that it is almost impossible to believe they are telling untruths, and it is often a very perplexing matter to know how to deal with them. It is next to impossible at first to get them to acknowledge their wrong doings."

The custom observed in placing out children is thus described: "Children that have parents are not placed out without their full approval, and this is often the occasion of much embarrassment. The mother does not wish to part with her children, and clings to the hope of being able to provide for them. Those at the disposal of the asylum are taken six weeks on trial, after which, if the parties are mutually satisfied, indentures are drawn. Only one case has been returned to the asylum since its foundation. Parties taking children are required to make reports regularly. The asylum has a Children's Committee ; its Chairman, Mrs. Callister, has visited every child who had been placed out during the past year."

The lot on which the asylum stands, comprises four acres of excellent land, a portion of which is planted with choice fruit trees. The place yields apples, cherries, raspberries and currants, and the garden, potatoes, carrots, turnips, onions and other vegetables. The yield of apples last season was fifty barrels. A number of domestic fowls are kept, and also four cows, which supply the institution with milk.

The drainage of the building is poor, and needs attention. The bath-room accommodations would seem to be too contracted. The washing and store rooms might be advantageously separated from the main building. Some improvements, it is thought, might still be effected on the grounds which, while they would add to their artistic appearance, would at the same time render them more in keeping with the spirit of this noble charity. When the bequest of $45,000 of the late Mr. Post, of the town of Seneca, becomes available, it is expected that some changes will be effected which will enlarge the usefulness of the asylum.

A marked feature in the administration of this asylum is the promptness with which children are placed in families, the care taken in selecting for them suitable homes, and the regularity with which they are visited after such homes for them are found. By this means the dependent children are absorbed into the healthy portion of the community, thereby greatly reducing pauperism in this and the adjoining counties.

This asylum for many years was sustained almost entirely by the benevolent efforts of the ladies connected with it, and by voluntary contributions. Its management has been such as to gain for it the confidence of the people, and it is probable that the time is not far distant when it will become self-sustaining and the county be entirely relieved of any pecuniary burden growing out of the care of its dependent children. In addition to the bequest before alluded to, we are informed that another has been made by a gentleman who, once an orphan child himself, realized in his own experience the needs and benefits of orphan asylums. He has left to this charity his entire fortune which becomes available upon the death of his wife.

At the present time, however, it is asserted by the President, Mrs. Dr. Cooke, that the asylum is greatly in need of funds to carry on its work. Its total expenditure during the fiscal year ending October 1. 1875, was $4,484.57, while its invested fund, from which an income is derivable, is only $5,800. This should be borne in mind, and in view of the thorough work it is doing for the public, it should be liberally supported.

St. Mary's Orphan Asylum.

Canandaigua.

The St. Mary's Orphan Asylum was established in 1854, and incorporated under the general law, October 6, 1855. It formerly occupied a plain two-story frame dwelling on Saltonstall street. About two years ago it was removed to the spacious mansion and grounds of the late General John A. Granger.

The object of the institution is "for the care, support and instruction of orphans and other children who may need such care or instruction." It is under the immediate care and charge of five Sisters of the Roman Catholic Order of St. Joseph, of whom Sister Mary Paul is Superioress. There are other Sisters of this Order connected with the institution who are engaged in teaching two parish schools, one for girls and another for boys. The former is kept in the asylum building, and the latter in another part of the town. There were no hired assistants connected with the institution.

The building is lighted by gas and well supplied throughout with water. The school-room is furnished with modern appliances. The dormitories and house generally were found, on the day of visitation, July 9, to be scrupulously neat and clean and well ventilated. The garden supplies but few vegetables. A portion of the fruit used is grown upon the place.

It is intended to take children at all ages under fourteen years. They receive a good education in the Asylum, and "when the Sisters have confidence that they are perfectly trained and fit to go, they are placed out, but not before the ages of fourteen or fifteen years." They have the privilege of coming to the Asylum once a month and spending a Sabbath with the Sisters.

At the date of visitation, October 1 1875, there were seventeen children in the Asylum. Thirteen of these were orphans and four were half-orphans. Three of the children had native parents and fourteen had foreign parents.

The number of children cared for by the Asylum, since its organization, was 203. The number admitted during 1875 was five, and the number discharged, six.

The expenditures during the fiscal year ending October 1, 1875, were $1,968.75. Its indebtedness was $3,400.

The Asylum is sustained by voluntary contributions. The Sisters appeared to be zealous in their work, and the influence to which the children are subjected is believed to be highly elevating.

Orphan House of the Holy Saviour.

Cooperstown.

In a spacious family dwelling-house, by the shore of the beautiful lake of Otsego, are gathered, from the county poor-house and desolate homes, a band of twenty-eight little children. Most of these, on their arrival here, presented all the traits of children whose early years had been neglected. Some had become soured and apathetic; some perverse and morose; the natures of others had, by the corrupting influences of pauper and criminal associations, been corroded into forbidding angularities. But under this hospitable roof a beneficent change has been wrought in these susceptible natures. They have been brought to feel the warmth of true love and the benign workings of Christian teaching.

The Orphan House is situated on the borders of the quiet village of Cooperstown, opposite the village cemetery and Mount Vision, commanding a view of the bold and picturesque scenery which surrounds it, and which has been rendered familiar, alike to visitor and stranger, by the pen of America's great novelist.

The necessities out of which the institution originated may be stated as follows: In 1869, and the few years previous, it had been painfully evident to those interested in orphan and destitute children that an Orphan house and Industrial school for the relief of this class in Otsego and adjacent counties, was greatly needed. Miss Susan Fennimore Cooper used the following language in describing the condition of the poor children at that period: "Until now the poor-houses have been their only resource, and they have been exposed to the constant evil examples of the older paupers, too many of whom are men and women of the very worst characters and habits. They are scantily fed, clothed and sheltered, with schooling for less than half the year, usually from three to five months. These are the benefits they receive. On the other hand, they are not taught the great lesson of work. They have no moral or religious teaching beyond one hour on Sunday, when they are possibly, though not necessarily, taught by volunteer instructors from the neighborhood."

The importance of this work was brought to the attention of the benevolent of Cooperstown and elsewhere, and through the untiring zeal of Miss Cooper a beginning was made in this large field, which is even now but partially occupied. The Orphan House of the Holy Saviour, having for its object to provide a home and industrial school for orphan, half-orphan and destitute children, was incorporated by special act of the Legislature in 1870. It is under the patronage of the Protestant Episcopal Church of the Diocese of Albany, and the special guardianship of Miss Susan Fennimore Cooper, who devotes to it a great part of her time, and who has made for it large personal sacrifices. Its immediate charge is assigned to Mrs. E. M. Stanton, who resides at the home, and who is assisted by her daughter. Both are ladies of culture and well adapted for this important work.

At the date of visitation, July 30th, the following interesting snatches of history were ascertained from the teacher, of six children who had been taken from the county poor-house, and who were brought at our desire under our special observation:

1. A little boy "from a very low family. His father died of dissipation. The child has been in the home a year; is one of our most obedient boys. He ranks among those who take the best care of their clothes."

2. A little girl. "Her father is not known. Her mother was so profane that they could hardly endure her in the county house. This little girl is very promising, very affectionate, sings any thing, and learns rapidly."

3. A little boy. "He was brought to the Home on a pillow. The physician had given him up. He was covered with scrofulous eruptions and obliged to eat his meals in a dark corner. We commenced giving him baths, and very little medicine, but gave him nourishing diet. Now he is a bright boy with clear eyes and an intelligent countenance. He learns rapidly, is a close observer, and although near-sighted sees much quicker than many who have the full use of their eyes."

4. A little girl, sister to No. 1. "She is a delicate child, not so promising as her brother."

5. A little girl. "She is one of the most obedient children in the house. She will not recognize any of her relatives, which is something very unusual."

6. A little colored girl, called by the teacher, "Sunshine under a cloud," from her very pleasant disposition.

The average age of the children in the house was about eight years. Six of them were under three years old.

The following information regarding the institution, was obtained from Miss Cooper:

"We would gladly take all the children from the county-house to our institution, had we room for them. Our house can only accommodate thirty children. We have no building of our own, as yet. We took six children from the county-house last winter, and shall probably have room for two or three more this year. We agreed to take from the supervisors all that we had room for, but we shall not have over three other vacancies this year. We rent the house which we occupy, with its garden, for which we pay $350 a year.

"The children have three hours of schooling every morning. In the afternoon, the girls sew and do housework, while the older of the boys work in the garden, under an old man who has charge of it. We have a paid woman in the kitchen, also a woman who comes to wash two days in the week. We find all that is needed for thirty children. We keep them till the age of fifteen, if desirable, and then place them in good homes."

Miss Cooper, on being asked whether she thought it better to place the children in families as soon as possible, or to keep them in the asylum till they were of a certain age, said: "I think both courses ought to be adopted. The utmost care should be taken, as regards the families into which they are placed. There are very many private families where there is very little home-like character, and there are public institutions that have a great deal. It is better to keep children longer in such institutions than to place them in families where they will not be properly treated.

"In our institution we teach the children to consider themselves as brothers and sisters, and try to make them feel at home with us. We are very particular about their morals.

"Our institution is for orphans, half-orphans and destitute children. If they are half-orphans, we try to cultivate affection for the remaining parent, teaching them that it is their duty to help such in times of need, and especially during sickness and old age. We teach them to pray for their parents, and constantly inculcate the general principle that they must do what they can for their parents, even when they are bad. We are not unnecessarily strict with our children in every little minutia. I think this is one cause of the difficulty in England. They establish most admirably arranged asylums and orphan homes, but they are exceedingly strict in all matters of detail, and when the children leave the institutions and return to their own families, where every thing is loose and lax, there is a reaction which proves disastrous to the children.

"When children leave us we endeavor to get them situations in respectable families. In some cases where we have children of uncommon promise, we ask them to be left with us, and we take the whole charge of them for a time. The great object we have in view is the formation of character and industrial habits. These are the two things that we look to most of all. We have now two or three bright children who will probably become teachers, and we keep that in view in their education. Some will learn trades. Others will go out into families to do housework. In some cases families wish to adopt them, and we consent to it if we see they are suitable parties. Every afternoon the girls sew, and we hope that every girl who leaves the home at the age of fourteen, will be able to make her own clothes, at least. They also learn to knit. They, of course, make their own beds, sweep, wash, iron and make bread. We had some excellent bread baked by a girl of fourteen, which was exhibited at our last examination. When we have a new and larger building, we shall probably have a trade taught on the premises."

In regard to discipline Miss Cooper says: "Our system is to blend firmness and kindness together, and when this principle is acted on faithfully it is pretty sure to succeed. We have always found it so, and we have had some quite wild ones to manage. I had a specimen in a little boy about six years old. The lady who sent him to me said he had been in her house six weeks and had not minded her once. We bore with him at first. If you said 'Charlie, you must not do that,' he would go straightway and do it. I would call him, 'come here, Charlie,' he would walk right away. 'Charlie, keep your seat,' he would stand up immediately. He was a very troublesome child, and was looked upon as a regular 'black sheep.' After he had been at the Home for about two months, he seemed all of a sudden to change. The change seemed to come upon him almost miraculously. It worked so well that at the end of three or four months he was like the other children, and is now one of the best boys I have—the most obedient. I think there is a great deal in the atmosphere of the house, and as I have said, in the blending of kindness with firmness. We never had one who has not come round by this method."

On being asked if she thought all children could be reformed, Miss Cooper said: "I believe that any child under fifteen years of age can, with proper Christian influences, be reformed. I have had a girl at our Orphan Home who came from a very bad family. I shrank very much from taking her on that account. She was badly spoken of as regards honesty, and I almost trembled to take her on account of her influence on the other children. She is now doing exceedingly well, and her name is read out at every examination as one of the most trustworthy and honest of our girls. We have a practice of reading before the Trustees, at our yearly examination, the names of the best worker, the best bread maker, the best sewer, etc. The matron marks for family life, and the school teacher for school life, and these marks, good and bad, are all read before the Trustees at the end of the year."

In regard to the aim held in view in educating the children, Miss Cooper says: "We endeavor to give our children an industrial education. We deem this very important. We do not think it necessary to teach Latin, Greek, French and German to all. We aim to give them a plain, practical, English education, good so far as it goes. But if there are any bright children, who have capacity to go on, we afford them every opportunity to do so."

The children looked bright and happy and were particularly clean and neat in their personal appearance. An air of contentment was manifest in their demeanor, and they seemed to be on the alert to obey through a seeming regard, if not love, toward those caring for them.

The appointments of the house throughout were orderly, and an air of sweetness and purity, such as is peculiarly characteristic of a Christian home, seemed to pervade it. The floors were clean. Snow-white counterpanes covered the beds. The house was thoroughly ventilated, and throughout the rooms were distributed illuminated cards with mottoes, which not only appealed to the æsthetic nature, but inculcated order and moral sentiments. A retrospective thought of the former wretchedness of the little ones here congregated forced upon the mind the blessedness of that Providence that had brought them under such elevating and refining influences, and an earnest hope was awakened that the little company of children, seen the day previous amidst the degrading associations of the county poor-house, might soon, through the exercise of a wise benevolence, be permitted to share similar advantages.

The number of children in the institution, October 1, 1875, was twenty-eight. Of these five were orphans, twenty half-orphans, and three had both parents living. Twenty-three were of native and five of foreign parentage. During the past year twenty-two children had been received and thirteen discharged. The expenditures for the year amounted to $2,895.59.

A great need seemed to be felt for a larger building. "We are compelled," says Miss Cooper, "to refuse to take between fifty and a hundred children a year. So many families have been deserted by their fathers that we have always a number of applicants whose parents are still living. Husbands desert their wives, leaving them with four and five children. The women come to me and say, 'We cannot struggle under this burden. We do not want to send our children to the poor-house. Can you not take one or two of our children? We are willing to work.' But we are obliged to turn them away for want of room."

It is proposed to erect a new building as soon as means can be provided for this purpose. A tract of land containing 15 acres eligibly situated near the village, has been secured and paid for. A plan has been drawn for a building to cost $15,000, which will accommodate eighty children. The same design may be enlarged so as to comfortably provide for one hundred and twenty. The project of erecting a suitable asylum building is a heartfelt desire on the part of Miss Cooper and those co-operating with her.

It was gratifying to see the daughter of one of America's greatest writers in the very spot which had given birth to numerous productions of her father's gifted pen, engaged in so noble a work for the outcasts of society, thus sanctifying by her self-denying Christian life the place which the genius of her father had immortalized. It was sad, however, to reflect, that while there existed a large and urgent field of labor in her immediate vicinity, this lady should be restricted in her beneficent work merely from lack of funds. It is believed, however, when what is now stated becomes more generally known, that out of a grateful sentiment felt toward the father by those who have enjoyed the rare intellectual treats from his labors, the means will be forthcoming to erect in the village of Cooperstown a tasteful and commodious edifice, where the daughter may be permitted to carry on her self-sacrificing work in an enlarged field of usefulness.

St. Mary's Orphan Asylum.

Dunkirk.

This Asylum is located on Buffalo street, Dunkirk. Its object is "to provide a home for orphan and destitute children." The inmates are exclusively girls. It was organized in 1857, and incorporated January 11, 1858. The building at present occupied is a frame edifice of two and a half stories, measuring forty by seventy feet. It was formerly a private residence, purchased in 1864. In the rear of the main building is a two-story frame structure, the upper part of which is used for a children's dormitory, and the lower for kitchen and wash rooms. The lot upon which the building stands is one hundred and twenty by sixty feet.

The institution is under the immediate superintendence of Sister Anastasia Donovan, a lady of large experience, nineteen years of her life having been devoted to the care and instruction of children. She was one of the first of the Sisters who undertook the task of teaching the boys in St. Joseph's Orphan Asylum, at Limestone Hill, near Buffalo. She is assisted in her work by three other Sisters, all belonging to the Roman Catholic Order of the Sisters of St. Joseph. There are seven others of this Order, connected with the Asylum, who are engaged in teaching two parish schools in the town; one composed largely of children having American parents, and the other of children of German parentage.

The average daily attendance in the two schools is about four hundred and fifty. The Board of Education makes the Asylum a small allowance for the instruction rendered the Asylum children, of which, at the date of visitation, July 15, there were fifteen, ranging in ages from six to fourteen years. The Asylum is supported mainly by donations and voluntary contributions. A small income is also derived from the sale of needlework, which the Sisters engage in after school hours. Sister Anastasia says: "We are very particular to see that children are placed in good families, when they leave us, and not to lose sight of them after they are placed there."

The children are taught to sew, and the larger girls "alternate weekly in the kitchen to learn housekeeping." At the time of visitation a few of the older girls, who had evinced a musical talent, were being instructed, by one of the Sisters, on the piano.

The institution is apparently managed with rigid economy. A careful inspection showed its scrupulous neatness and order. The furniture in use is somewhat out of repair. But the Sisters contemplating building a new asylum, have been carefully husbanding their resources for that purpose. A lot of sixty acres of land, about a mile south of the present asylum, has already been purchased, where it is intended to erect a new edifice. It is an eligible site, possessing good soil. From this property all the fruit, vegetables, butter and milk used at the asylum is supplied. The farm cost $6,000 and is free from incumbrance — $5,000 having been very discreetly saved by the Sisters toward the new building. In the expectation of receiving about $10,000 out of a bequest made by H. J. Miner, Esq., a former resident of Dunkirk, it is contemplated to commence next spring the erection of a plain, commodious, brick building, on the farm, as a home for orphan and destitute children.

The large number of people in humble circumstances residing here, afford a wide range for the exercise of benevolence, and this field is likely to be still further extended owing to the recent depression of certain local manufacturing interests.

Southern Tier Orphan Home.

Elmira.

The early history of this institution may be thus stated. During the late war the city of Elmira having been designated as a military depot, a great number of soldiers' wives and children were gathered there, some of them in very destitute circumstances. While every effort was being put forth for the care of soldiers in the field, no adequate provision was made for their wives or children, who, like themselves, were equally sufferers by the war. For the protection of this class an association was organized, October 12, 1864, under the name of the Elmira Ladies' Relief Association. A suitable building was provided and contributions solicited which were readily forthcoming. Women were provided with work, and the sick and children cared for, in addition to ministering to the soldiers in the hospital. In January, 1866, a small piece of land, with a house upon it, was purchased, a matron with her assistants was secured, and the house thrown open to children. It was soon filled to its utmost capacity. The charity was liberally sustained by the people of Elmira and the surrounding country. Entertainments of various kinds were given to raise funds for its support, and furniture and other necessaries were cheerfully donated. A large number of benevolent ladies of Elmira identified themselves with the work, and have continued to be the warm friends of the institution. The original building was enlarged from time to time, and was a means of affording care and relief to multitudes of suffering women and children.

After the close of the war the number of soldiers' children decreased, but it was found that there were large numbers of children equally destitute, who belonged to another class. To meet this necessity it was decided to change the existing organization so as to widen its sphere of usefulness. It was accordingly re-organized, the name being changed to that of the Southern Tier Orphan Home, and incorporated, February 14, 1868, under the provisions of the general act. In 1868, an addition of about three-quarters of an acre of land was made to the previous purchase, making the lot now owned by the Home about two acres.

The Home is situated on the corner of Franklin and Fulton streets. Its field of labor has been so rapidly extending that an attempt has been made to raise an edifice of suitable dimensions to meet the increased demand. At the date of visitation July 28, a large and commodious brick edifice, three stories high, with basement, having a ground floor of one hundred by fifty-four feet, was being erected in the rear of the present frame Asylum building, which it is intended hereafter to remove. The new structure was ready for a slate roof, but in consequence of lack of funds, the managers thought it would be necessary either to suspend work or to mortgage the property for $10,000 to complete the design, and render the building fit for habitation. It is to be heated by furnaces and ventilated by flues in the walls. The ceilings are high, halls wide, and windows large. The edifice, as a whole, promises to be well adapted to its uses and capable of meeting all present demands.

The institution is managed by a Board of Ladies, numbering eleven. It is under the immediate charge of Mr. Duncan, Superintendent, assisted by his wife as Matron. The teacher, Miss Mary S. Preston, is employed by the Department of Public Instruction of the city of Elmira. This lady acts as Corresponding Secretary, and devotes a large share of her leisure gratuitously to the interests of the institution. The school is in a separate building. Children of neighboring families are admitted, and are taught with the Asylum children. They are instructed in the ordinary branches of an English education, and great attention is paid to religious and moral training. Children are taken at all ages, and disposed of as soon as possible. Great pains is taken to ascertain the suitability of applicants for children, and none are allowed to leave the institution unless to parties whose characters are thoroughly well ascertained.

While in the Home the children are taught to do such work as is compatible with their early years. The boys chop wood, work in the garden, and the girls render such aid as they can in the house. They appeared to be as well cared for as their incommodious premises would admit of. Very early hours are kept. The children retire at half-past seven in the evening. The larger rise at five in the morning, and the smaller at six. The Superintendent, availing himself of his army experience, is trying the experiment of a military system in the establishment. The boys are detailed in squads to perform the work of each day, having an orderly at their head. A drum calls the routine of each day's duties. A breach of rule subjects the offender to a court-martial, made up from among the boys.

Two of the children of the Home, aged eleven and twelve years respectively, were simple-minded. One of these, it was said, had been placed out a short time previous to our visit, and had come back saying, "The man would not mind me."

The Supervisors have been in the habit of voting an annual sum toward the support of the institution. This year their appropriation amounted to $1,000, and a supply of flour for the house.

On October 1, 1875, there were forty-seven children inmates, eight of whom were orphans and thirty-two half-orphans. The counties of Allegany, Broome, Chemung, Steuben and Tioga were represented. Six of the children were partially supported by friends. Two cows are kept to supply the inmates with milk. The garden is cultivated as far as possible, but it is very stony. The present Superintendent has planted thirty-two young apple trees and twenty vines. They are not thriving. A great deal of the fruit used is donated.

It appears that 649 children have been received by this institution since its organization, and that during the past year 64 children were received and 62 discharged. Of the latter, 20 were placed out by adoption, and 29 returned to parents or guardians.

So great a work, aside from its humane character, unquestionably greatly lessens the burdens growing out of pauperism and crime, and gives the institution a strong claim for liberal support upon the people of the whole district benefited.

The total expenditures during the fiscal year ending October 1, 1875, were $15,431.88; of this $12,355.16 were expended for buildings and improvements.

The present building is entirely insufficient for the requirements.

It is inconvenient, and the work is being carried on at a great disadvantage. It is to be hoped that the situation will be appreciated, and that this worthy and needed charity will be liberally sustained by the people. A lady deeply interested in this work remarks: "When the people of these counties generally comprehend the magnitude of the work, and understand that the doors are open to the homeless, friendless ones throughout their borders; that here they may be fed, clothed, instructed and loved, that here the influence of a happy, Christian home may surround them, until opportunities are offered to place them in private families where they may find permanent homes and gladden many a household that has never known the sunshine of childhood, or that has been darkened by the shadow of death, then without doubt the contributions from adjoining counties will correspond with the increasing demands of the institution. These children must be supported by the public or suffer. Is it not better to provide a home adapted to their wants, than to leave them to privation, crime and ruin, or to crowd them into the county houses, where, under existing circumstances, it is impossible to give them the attention necessary? Is it not sad to have to say to any shivering applicant, 'no room for any more?'"

Hudson Orphan and Relief Association,

Hudson.

At the time this institution was established the population of Hudson was about seven thousand. "The necessity of an asylum, where poor neglected children could have a comfortable home, became apparent to the mind of a benevolent lady, Mrs. Robert McKinstry, who spent the greater part of her time in looking after and ameliorating the condition of the poor. She became so impressed with the importance of having such an institution, that she rented a part of a small house for the purpose in 1843, hired a woman to take charge of it, and took eight children from poverty and distress to a comfortable home, without knowing at the time whether any one, besides her husband, would be willing to assist in defraying the expenses. She succeeded, however, in interesting other parties, and a few ladies became associated with her in the enterprise. At first, they went from house to house soliciting second-hand clothing and food, and, in this way, the Asylum was mainly supported, and annual subscriptions obtained. After a time, a lot of ground was promised by Mr. Hammond, the father of Mrs. McKinstry, if an amount of money could be raised sufficient to erect a building, and, after unwearied efforts, this was accomplished in 1847. The institution has been in successful operation since that time, and has been the means of saving hundreds of children that might otherwise have become outcasts. Mrs. Robert McKinstry was chosen first directress in the Board of Managers, and held that office until, in 1862, death deprived this institution of its best and earliest friend to whom it was indebted for its very existence."

The Asylum is located on the corner of State and North Seventh streets. It is managed by a board of five trustees and a Board of Lady Managers. The building is of brick, two stories in height, with basement and attic. The Matron, Miss Elizabeth Jones, has been in the institution sixteen years. One woman is employed for cooking and general housekeeping, and another for washing and cleaning.

At the date of visitation, September 11, there were twenty girls and thirty boys in the institution. The average for last year was about fifty-six. Between twenty-five and thirty were from the county-house. The county pays the same price for the maintenance of these children as it would cost to keep them at the county-house. It varies at different times. Last year the price fixed was about $1.50 per week; the year previous it was $1.75.

"We try," says the matron, "to make the institution a home for the children." A school was formerly held on the premises; now the children attend the public school, and the school-room is used for a play-room. Children are received from three to ten years old. "We do not," says the matron, "like to take children over ten years old. We do not refuse them, however, but we find it difficult to control such. We keep the children till they are twelve, unless adopted before that age. They may be adopted at any age; but we do not bind them out in any case till they are twelve years old. Homes are found for them mostly among farmers."

In regard to visiting the children after being placed out, the matron says: "A Committee of the Board generally manages to go around once a year, and find out how they are getting on. We either hear from them or see them once a year."

In the way of industrial training, the matron says: "Our boys chop wood, carry water, and work in the garden. Nine of them are quite large boys. The girls are taught to sew. They take care of their rooms and wash dishes. The children's clothes are cut, but are not all made in the house."

On the day of visitation, nine of the children were on the sick-list; but it was stated that they were generally healthy. None had died during the past year, and but one during the past seven years. The matron further remarks, as bearing upon the treatment of children, "They do not come very clean. We usually have to use the bath-tub the first thing. We discipline them by keeping them in the house.

About the greatest punishment that can be inflicted upon them is to make them sit by themselves."

The dining-room for children is in the basement. Crockery plates, knives and forks are used at table. The children are provided with nutritious food.

The institution possesses a library of three hundred volumes, presented, as shown by the inscription plate, by Alice B. Haven, 23d of August, 1863; also an organ, on which some of the girls take music lessons. "Ladies come in at different times to sing with the children." The features of family life are preserved in this institution as far as possible. The matron says: "At the morning and evening prayers the practice is for the children to read from the Scriptures, each reading a verse. They learn verses from the Bible every day. On Sundays, Sabbath school is taught in the house by ladies from different churches." The holidays are duly observed, and entertainments for the children at such times are provided. "Our children," says the matron, "as a general thing, turn out well. We have one boy now who wants to study for the ministry. Quite a number of the older children marry. We have one who lives in town."

The number of children in the institution, October 1, 1875, was fifty-one. Of these, sixteen were orphans, twenty-three half-orphans and twelve had both parents living. Thirty-nine were of native and twelve of foreign parentage. Three of the number were partially supported by parents or friends, thirty-three partially by counties, and fifteen wholly by the institution. The number received during the past year was nineteen, the number discharged, twenty-four. Of the latter, one was placed out by adoption, eight by indenture, twelve were returned to parents or guardians, and three transferred to other institutions.

The current expenditures of the institution during the past year were, $6,339.50. It has an invested fund of $52,850, and no indebtedness.

The whole number of children received into this institution, since its organization, was seven hundred and seventy-five.

This charity, blessed as it was in its beginning, by the self-sacrificing labors of its founders, and fostered since by the benevolent who have interested themselves in its work, appears to enjoy the confidence of the people of the county and surrounding country, and, while doing a very humane work, is evidently one of the essential safeguards to society in the district in which it is located.

The Lockport Home for the Friendless.

Lockport.

The Lockport Home for the Friendless originated in a society known as the "Ladies' Relief Society and Home for the Friendless," which was organized in 1865. During the six years preceding October, 1871, the society had received from donations, concerts, etc., about $1,250 in cash. Of this sum, $600 was invested in a permanent fund, the balance having been disbursed. The society, in addition, had material remaining valued at $116.

On the 8th of February, 1871, The Lockport Home for the Friendless was incorporated, and the means and materials of the former society were transferred to the use of the new organization. Subsequently, the Board of Supervisors appropriated to this corporation the sum of $3,473.47, upon condition that a like sum be raised by voluntary contributions, and that an asylum or home be at once established. The sum required to be raised was promptly subscribed by the citizens of Lockport and Niagara county. In December, 1871, the trustees of the Home purchased a commodious private residence on High street, attached to which are two and a half acres of ground stocked with apple, pear and other fruit trees. The location is elevated and the surroundings are pleasant. The building stands a little apart from the street, has a goodly-sized grassy lawn in front, with abundance of shade. It is a two-story, frame structure, with a wing extending rearward. The building is heated by furnaces, lighted by kerosene, and supplied with rain and well water.

The financial interests of the Home are controlled by a board of nine trustees. Its internal affairs are managed by a board of directresses, numbering twenty-five. The domestic and other concerns of the Home devolve upon the matron. It is required that she shall be a "professed believer in the doctrines of the Bible, and competent to give religious instruction to the children. She shall abstain from all sectarian teaching."

There were in the Home four adult females at the date of visitation, August 23, and thirteen half-orphan children. One of the adult inmates, who assists in the work of the house, is a female, aged thirty-five, the mother of two of the children. Children are received from the age of two to nine years. One dollar a week was paid by parents or friends toward the board of five of the children. One of the adult inmates, who was about fifty years of age, did not seem to be a fit person for the companionship of children. It was stated of her that she was "somewhat out of her mind." She was excited at the time of visitation. The matron says "her mind has never developed any since she was seven years old. She gets out of patience at times and uses bad language. I never allow her to get very bad, however. We have to watch her closely, but she breaks out occasionally."

Seven is the largest number of children that have been beneficiaries of the institution at any one time, until the past summer.

The financial affairs of the Home seem prudently managed. Its total expenditures for the year ending October 1, 1875, were $1,108.93. It has an invested fund of $600.

Niagara county presents a large field for charitable work. The amount disbursed for public relief here is very large, and it is believed that a building, such as the Home now occupies, might posssbly be filled with indigent old ladies, but undoubtedly could be fully occupied with destitute children. This being the case, the question naturally occurs whether it would not be better to classify the inmates in separate establishments and devote the asylum at present in use to the care of children solely. At the date of November 5, 1874, there were twenty-seven children in the Niagara County Poor-house, showing that a large number of this unfortunate class are thrown upon the public in this county. An examination of these children revealed the fact that all of them, save one, were proper subjects for asylum care. It would seem that if county officials were relieved of the burdensome task of procuring homes for children, and that such children as it was proper to place in families, were at once committed to asylums by the Superintendent of the Poor, a great amount of good might be accomplished by the benevolent interested in such work, by clothing and preparing the children for families, finding good homes for them and by subsequently looking to them after homes have been found. There is a field for benevolent work in behalf of children in Niagara county, and it would, no doubt, be gratifying to the public, as also the charitably disposed, who have already made considerable sacrifices in this direction, if the large number of influential persons who carry on the work of the Home of the Friendless, should direct their benevolent efforts to this grand object.

The Wartburg Orphans' Farm School of the Evangelical Lutheran Church,

Mt. Vernon,

Is located in Westchester county, on a farm of one hundred and twenty acres, with a suitable building for the accommodation of about seventy children. It is under the patronage of the Lutheran Church, and affords a beautiful illustration of the family system in orphan asylum life.

The institution was visited October 26th, and from the Resident Director, Rev. George Charles Holls, the following information in regard to its origin, work, etc., was obtained: "The property was purchased from the Five Points House of Industry for $32,000, and the building now in use cost an additional $54,000. Previous to the time of its purchase, Dr. Lewis, a Lutheran clergyman, in passing through the streets of New York, saw so many destitute children there that he thought an institution for their care was greatly needed. Soon after, he met Mr. Peter Möller, who was at the time contemplating erecting a memorial to his son, at a cost of $30,000. The claims of orphans being set before him, his sympathies became aroused in their behalf, and he proposed to pay for a part of the building of this house if we would raise money enough to buy the farm. This was agreed to, and in about two weeks the sum of $25,000 was collected in the city of New York. The property was subsequently secured, and I was called here to assume charge, which I did in September, 1866, taking with me five children from the institution at Zelienople, to form a nucleus. There was then an old house on the place which we occupied for four years. We entered our present building in 1870. Of the $54,000 expended on its erection Mr. Peter Möller contributed $30,000. The remainder was subscribed by his brother, Mr. William Möller, and Mr. John C. Roebling.

"Since 1870 we have received eighty-eight children. Of these twenty-eight have been discharged, and but one has died during the whole time. The institution is for full orphans."

The spirit of this Asylum may be understood from the following remarks of Mr. Holls: "We want to give these children a home. They are orphans, and have no other. We receive them here and keep the boys till they are of age, or old enough to learn trades; the girls till they are eighteen years old, and have become fully acquainted with housekeeping. A number of our boys are now out learning trades. If they get out of employment, or get sick at any time, they can return here to their home. This is their home at all times, till they can get a home of their own. *They are received here at my table. They eat the same food. There is no special preparation made for the so-called 'officers' table.' We don't know such a name here. We are a family. We have no domestics at all.*"

The institution is managed by the Director, whose wife acts as matron. The work of the house is all done by the children. The clothing is made on the premises. The mending and washing are also done here. Nothing is sent out.

In the kitchen, on the day of visitation, we found the wife of the

Director engaged in domestic duties, with six young girls around her doing other branches of the family work. The children seemed to be quite happy and natural in their manner.

The secular, moral and religious education of the children is carefully attended to, a school being held on the premises. In the evening the family get together and spend it in reading Bible stories, the Lutheran catechism, etc. The birthday of every child in the house is kept, and all the regular holidays, national and religious.

The children have a garden of their own, divided up into beds. Seeds are given them to plant, and they attend to them during summer, and preserve the seeds in the fall. They are required to keep their gardens clean. Sometimes two go into partnership, and keep a patch together.

About ten acres are laid out in walks and flower beds, and planted with shade trees and evergreens. In the extensive garden, grapes, raspberries, blackberries, apples, pears and corn are produced. A rustic summer-house, the work of the boys, adds an attractive feature to the place. The rising nature of the ground affords a fine view in every direction. The location of the Asylum edifice is picturesque, and the lawn surrounding it has been improved with taste, and in such a way as to preserve its natural beauties.

The building is constructed so as to secure a perfect separation of the sexes. The dormitories are furnished with iron bedsteads. The mattresses are of corn husks. The whole house is well kept, and every want of the children seems to be anticipated.

"It costs," said Mr. Holls, "$6,000 a year only to support the institution, which is about $100 per capita. We never have received a cent from the city or State, nor have we ever asked for any aid from public sources."

Mr. Holls, in speaking of what he deemed to be the proper treatment of juvenile delinquents, said: "I consider that the system of the Houses of Refuge in this country is wrong. If you treat a boy who is a delinquent as a criminal, he will be a criminal in the course of time. We received in the *Rauhe-Haus*, in Hamburg, with which I was connected, the class of children which you have here in the Houses of Refuge, and even a worse class. I have had children under my care who had been repeatedly committed; boys of about twelve years of age. I have had a girl of eleven years who had set fire to six houses; a boy who tried to burn three or four villages. Well, we received those characters, not to lock them up anywhere in a cell, but to say to them we are your friends. We know all about you. We know your whole life, but we won't speak to you about this except you want to talk to us yourself about it. We will forget every thing. Here, now, you have a chance to begin an entirely new life. If you want to run away, there is no lock on the doors, you can run away, but if you wish to begin a new life here we will assist you. You have but to come under our rules and regulations and the way to reform is open to you, and then we treat them just as we treat our children, and have them sit down with us at the same table. I have seen the worst children melt with tears under such treatment, and begin a new life."

The opinion of Mr. Holls upon the question of Juvenile Reform is carefully noted, being deemed of value, coming as it does from one who had been a pupil of Dr. Immanuel Wichern, of Hamburg, a man whose labors in the reformation of children have been as remarkable for their successfulness as for the novelty of the system they inaugurated, and whose *Rauhe-Haus* at Horn and Brotherhood of St. John, have wrought such changes in the criminal classes of Germany as may well engross the attention of all interested in the subject.

Fliedner, the founder of the German Order of Deaconesses, visited this country in 1849, and four Deaconesses accompanied him to establish an Infirmary at Pittsburg, Pa., for the care of the German emigrants. Many of these dying left their families unprovided for, and the first Lutheran orphan asylum in this country was established in 1851 for these children, Mr. Holls assuming charge.

Newburgh Home for the Friendless.

Newburgh.

This institution was incorporated April 7, 1862. It is stated that it had its origin in an association auxiliary to the American Female Guardian Society of New York, and went into operation in the autumn of 1861, gathering in destitute children and collecting money to care for them. Subsequently a disposition on the part of the ladies engaged to concentrate their entire energies upon the neglected children of Newburgh, and to work independently, manifested itself, and meeting with general approval the society, under the name of the Union Female Guardian Society, was organized and set vigorously to work. An industrial school was opened for such children as were prevented by poverty from attending the public schools of the city. During the first winter of the industrial school, which opened with thirty-three pupils, it is stated that "the managers alternately performed the duties of Matron in preparing the morning toilet of the children and serving their dinner, the most of whom came to the school-room literally clothed in rags, and had no regular food, excepting the one meal per day furnished at the rooms."

The press of children into the school-room rendered the task of the

Receiving Committee extremely difficult. The ladies, referring to this period, say: "At the end of the first month one-third of the original number was rejected; on the ground of our being wholly dependent upon the charities of a generous public, it was our duty to confine our labors to the very poorest objects, and not to experiment too largely in the infancy of our undertaking. It was painful, indeed, to read the countenances of these suffering little ones as we went through the ranks to select those who must be discharged; and to hear the cries and entreaties of those who were told they must leave, would melt an adamantine heart. One little girl said, 'Then we'll have to live in the road!' Of those that remained, the glistening eyes and trembling voices, as they exclaimed, 'I thought you were going to send *me!*' showed their appreciation of the friendly care bestowed, and they have since repaid, a thousand fold, the patient toil of their teacher, and those who otherwise had the oversight of them last winter can scarcely realize that they are the same children.

"During the year six thousand three hundred and eighty-eight meals were given in the school, and twelve orphan and half-orphan children were thrown upon the society for support. Nine of these were motherless, and three were the children of volunteers. It became evident that if provision was to be made for even the orphans of the soldiers of our own vicinity, more enlarged accommodations must be provided. In 1865 the Home family numbered sixty-eight. Forty-two of these were the children of soldiers; twenty-four had fathers who had given their lives for their country, one of them dying in Libby Prison. Others were worse than orphaned, being in the possession of unnatural guardians, from whom vice had eradicated every parental motive, principle and sentiment. In March, 1864, a more suitable building was purchased, at a cost of $7,750. Before the following November, $5,310 of this was subscribed by twenty of the citizens of Newburgh."

In 1865, in consequence of the increase in the number of the permanent Home family, it was deemed expedient to discontinue the day school.

The visitation was made October 28th, when the Home was under the charge of Mrs. Isabella Thistle, Matron. A teacher, seamstress, laundress, chambermaid and cook were also employed.

The location on Montgomery street is quite elevated. The building is of brick, two stories in height, having a porch in front, facing the river, supported by four large doric columns.

The number of children on the day of visitation was forty-three. Eleven of these were quite young girls. The children are educated and taught to be industrious, and as soon as a good opportunity occurs they are placed in families, the families of farmers being most generally preferred.

The Matron, in speaking of the children, said: "Our children have always turned out well. I do not think it is a good thing to keep children here very long, but while here my idea is to make them industrious from the first. They are brought up in idle habits. Both boys and girls are idly inclined. I teach them to do their own work as much as possible. If necessary, I have them do it several times over to make them do it perfectly. It is better for them. I teach both boys and girls to sew. We hear from the children who have left the Home, through others, and occasionally the children are brought to see us.

The dormitories are furnished with iron bedsteads, single, two feet six inches wide. Straw beds are used. Bath rooms and night closets are conveniently arranged.

The children are variously dressed, and appeared to be well cared for. Their moral and religious training is made a matter of the highest moment, which was shown by the answers given to questions put them by the Matron on the day of visitation.

The number of children received into this institution since its oganization is three hundred and eighty-three; the number in the institution October 1, 1875, who were orphans, six; the number who were half-orphans, twenty-three; who had both parents living, fourteen. Forty-one were of native and two of foreign parentage. Sixteen of the children were partially supported by parents or friends, and twenty-six wholly by the institution. The number of children received during the past year was twenty-three; the number discharged, twenty-five. Of the latter, fourteen were returned to parents or guardians, and nine were placed out by adoption.

The total expenditures of the Home during the fiscal year ending September 30, 1875, were $5,275.66; of which $1,098.21 were for improvements. The total indebtedness was $1,588.21. It has an invested fund of about $6,000.

This institution has grown steadily in public favor; beginning in a small but well-directed effort, it has demonstrated its utility by the valuable results it has accomplished. It is gratifying to state that its present condition appears prosperous, and that its affairs are administered with great prudence. It is managed by a Board of Ladies, representing the various Protestant churches in the city.

St. Patrick's Orphan Asylum.

Newburgh.

This Asylum was founded and incorporated in 1868. It is under the charge of the Roman Catholic Order of the Sisters of Charity of Mt. St. Vincent, Sister Paulina being the Sister Servant. The Asylum is pleasantly located on an elevated site within the city of Newburgh. At the date of October 1, 1875, it contained seven orphan children, who were supported by voluntary contributions.

At the time of our visitation, October 28, the funeral of one of the inmates was about to take place, and inquiries in regard to the workings of the institution were in consequence deferred.

No report is at hand showing the financial condition of the Asylum.

American Female Guardian Society.

New York.

The early history of this society may be regarded as a protest of Christian mothers against the moral blight which then seemed to be effacing from poor and neglected children the Divine image. It is replete with interest, and for this reason is given at some length.

"In 1834, a band of women whose hearts were moved by revelations of sin, sorrow and moral ruin existing among the young in the city, organized an association, afterward incorporated, whose aim was to prevent crime, diminish the victims of the spoiler, and save the perishing. The place first occupied by this association, in 1835, was under the old Tract House, in Nassau street. It removed thence, in 1839, to rooms in the chapel of the old brick church, corner of Nassau and Beekman streets, which for several years were used for a publishing office, and the various purposes of the society. For several years the homes of sundry managers became the temporary shelter for the homeless till more permanent provision could be otherwise made. The number of these protégées annually increased, till at length a 'Home for the Friendless' became a manifest necessity.

"Many anxious efforts were made to secure this Home, and many discouragements caused these faithful mothers to despair. During 1847, the work of collecting funds was prosecuted, and in March, 1848, five lots on Thirtieth street were purchased, and on the 9th of December following the Home was completed.

"The society had, up to the year 1849, passed under the name of the 'American Female Moral Reform and Guardian Society,' but by an act passed April 6, 1849, its name was changed to the 'American

Female Guardian Society,' its present title. Among the names of its corporators were many distinguished for their benevolence.

"Presently the labors of the association began to be more and more turned to the children. The conviction was strengthened by constant observation that the class which furnishes much of the material for the hecatombs of the outcast and the lawless that fill our prisons with victims and wring human hearts with sorrow, is found among the children of the street, trained in miscalled homes, and doomed early to wear the brand of the pauper; and, furthermore, that there is a point in each young life where, if withdrawn from moral pitfalls into the sunlight of Christian nurture, the child may thus be saved for this life and the next.

"It was felt that further legislation was needed to enable the society to extend its sphere of usefulness in directions where it was urgently needed, and at its Anniversary meeting in 1849, the following resolution was passed:

"*Resolved,* That the condition of thousands of children in our large towns and cities, without friends or homes, who are growing up ignorant and vicious, and thus becoming fit subjects for the prison or the gallows, calls loudly upon us as philanthropists, as Christians, and as Christian mothers, to devise some plan and unite our earnest efforts in its accomplishment for restraining, educating and preparing for usefulness this whole class of poor, forlorn ones in obedience to the blessed precept, 'As ye would that men should do to you, do ye even so to them.'

"A petition was prepared and submitted to the legislature, praying for legislation to provide for the care and instruction of idle and truant children, which resulted in the passage of a law for that purpose, April 12, 1853.

"In 1857, June 3, a building, called Home Chapel, was opened for the society, at which date it was stated 7,000 beneficiaries had found shelter in the Home, besides the great number of mendicant girls who had been fed, clothed and instructed in a large industrial school opened by the society."

The society has thus contined to grow till, on the date of visitation, October 8, 1875, it had in successful operation, besides the Home, ten industrial schools. To use the words of its corresponding secretary, "The society has continued to care for the children from infancy to adult years, and now, in looking over a quarter of a century, can contemplate the change in the condition of hundreds with great satisfaction. Once friendless and homeless, they have now many friends, fill positions of respectability and usefulness, are returning the benefactions received in similar care for others; in short, have become a blessing and not a curse to society."

House of Reception.

The house on Twenty-ninth street, besides the office of the society, school-room and chapel on the lower floors, contains also a shelter for young girls and a nursery for the infants given over to the society. The shelter, which is on the third floor of the house, is to afford, at a very cheap rate ($2 per week), a comfortable Christian home to girls who are, during the day, at work in shops, stores and printing offices, and to maintain them while they are out of employment. These are unable to defray their expenses in respectable boarding-houses, and would be exposed to vicious influences in the places to which their limited means would give them access.

An air of comfort pervaded this department of the house. The sitting-room was well furnished with a bright carpet, tables, chairs, comfortable lounges, a settee and an organ. Its walls were hung with pictures of an elevating character. The room also contained a library of suitable reading. The bed-rooms were very neat and clean, and the dining-room and kitchen, connected with this department, were furnished with all necessary appurtenances.

The nursery is on the fourth floor, and is supplied with all needed comforts for infants. It is, however, regarded as but a temporary shelter for the little ones till they are adopted into families, and this is done as soon as possible. It has rarely more than fifteen or twenty inmates at a time.

The school in this house had an attendance of 148 on the day of visitation, October 8; but the number on the list was about 210. The children came from poor families in the neighborhood. They get bread at noon, and the girls are taught to sew in the afternoon. The room was furnished with modern appliances for school work, and contained a library of about 100 volumes, also an organ. On the walls were scriptural texts.

House on Thirtieth Street.

This is a spacious building, over thirty years old, containing in the basement the dining-room, kitchen, play-room, etc. On the first floor the parlor, committee-room, children's nursery, etc.; on the second floor the sewing-room, girls' play-room, dormitory and private rooms; and on the third floor the boys' dormitory, and rooms for the employés. The nursery is a pleasant apartment. It contained twelve iron cribs and four small iron bedsteads. The number of children present was fifteen. The ages of the inmates of this department, we were told, range generally from four to ten years.

The children wash in running water, and take a full bath every week.

The house is under the charge of an efficient matron, and was found to be very cleanly and orderly kept. This lady informed us that the children come in a very neglected condition. "We have," she says, "some so bad that we must destroy every thing they have on. We usually give them a good bath, and then dress them in our clothing."

Very little can be done in the way of industries, owing to the ages of the children, and the aim of the society to get them into the natural life of the child, that is to say, the family, as soon as possible, but those who are old enough are taught sewing.

As a means of setting the work of the society before the public, and as an instrument for getting homes for children, the society publishes a semi-monthly periodical, entitled the "Advocate and Family Guardian." This has been edited by the corresponding secretary, Mrs. J. S. Bennett, for the past twenty years, who has likewise been actively engaged in the work of the society for the past forty years. From a conversation with this lady, regarding the scope of its labors, we derived the following: "The society has aided in clothing hundreds and thousands of children gathered from the streets, who were below the level of the public schools. We take such into our schools, lead them along and as soon as they can read, graduate them into our public schools.

"We aim to help the poor parents, by keeping the children, and giving a foretaste of a better life. The little hymns the children learn at our schools they sing at home. They also draw books from the school library, and take them home to read. And we distribute a children's paper among them and tracts of an interesting, though non-sectarian character, all of which find their way to the parents.

"In distributing our aid, we endeavor to do it wisely, to assist none but worthy applicants.

"We employ visitors, who go to the homes of the poor and ascertain the character of those applying for relief. We report the names of unworthy cases to the Bureau of Charity.

"We have a committee of ladies divided among our twelve industrial schools. They visit the families of the children attending them, and take a special interest in the schools. These schools have many interesting features in the personal histories of the children attending them. Only Saturday I was asked to go and see a young girl, whose father and mother are now in the Tombs, awaiting their trial for murder. She belonged to a low, miserable family, given to drinking, and living in a tenement house. The little girl had attended one of our schools, and looked to us for protection. We took her and placed her in a good family, where she is safe and allowed to go to school, and we are going to ask the judge to commit her to us, in order that we may be able to protect her.

"We have constant applications from worthy families for children of different ages. But we are very particular to get good homes for the children before we let them go, and we have our visitor make a personal visitation of the family, unless we are fully satisfied otherwise that the home is a desirable one. We then let the children go three months on trial, after which, if satisfactory, we indenture them. Infants and little girls we get adopted. They come in one day and go out the next. This house is made a kind of protectory for children that are in trouble till we can find better homes for them.

"We have a visitor whose duty it is to visit them at their homes after they are placed out. Parties also volunteer to do this work for us. Perhaps a lady on Long Island will say to us, 'give me the names of the children in this locality and I will visit them.' This relieves our visitor, and so we keep ourselves informed about all our children. We keep a register which gives the history of every child that passes through our hands, so far as we can get at it. We find the best homes for children among the well-to-do farmers. We do not believe in children being brought up in idleness, but I think they ought to be dealt with reasonably and taught the value of their opportunities, and the way opened, so that they may become something when they reach manhood or womanhood."

Mrs. Bennett, on being asked what success had attended the work, said: "While there are drawbacks, and discouragements, and trials in the work, still the pleasure of seeing the larger proportion of the children doing well pays for all the labor and trials connected with it. There are some of both sexes who do not do well, but a majority have a record that is creditable entirely to their families, their foster-parents, and to the great work of Christian benevolence that has provided for them.

"Children that were here twenty years ago, and who are now men and women, come back to report to us. Their friends come to us and inquire after them. The mother treasures in her heart the same love for her child, and it is a consolation to her, after years of separation, to be able to come here and know that it is doing well, and perhaps see its portrait. One mother, a paralyzed woman, sent to us for the record of her child the day he became of age. We forwarded it to her, and we learned that the poor woman set out to find her child, and did find him at last.

"Wednesday a young man came to inquire about his three brothers. He had not seen them for twenty-three years. I took the name and turned to their histories. One had learned a trade, another was a clerk, and the third held an official position. The young man went away, promising to return and give me an account of his visits."

On the walls of the secretary's room were hung in frames the photographs of a large number of children. These, we were informed, were the portraits of some of the children who had been helped into good homes by the society. They were taken by their new guardians and sent to the society. These simple pictures of faces, rendered pleasant by the love which had elevated and made them purer, were of more interest than the rarest works of art, and were a fitting embellishment to the office of these earnest workers for poor children.

The records made of the children, on the books in the office, are very complete, beginning with its earliest work and tracing the history of each individual to maturity. These have been systematically kept and show the conscientious manner in which they have been uniformly written up through a long series of years. It is deemed of sufficient interest to insert a few specimens taken at random from the books.

"M. S. F., born in New York. October, 1847; M. M. F., born in New York. February, 1850; T. W. F., born in New York.

"February, 1852. The above family, a brother and two sisters, were brought to the Home by the bereaved father, who was unable to provide for them.

"May, 1856. Legally surrendered; father deceased a few months later. The brother was soon adopted by a worthy family. Details of his history up to manhood are exceedingly good.

"M. S. F. taken by a family in New York State.

"July, 1856. * * * Legal papers executed.

"January, 1857. Heard from favorably. Was attending school and making commendable improvement.

"1858. Visited by secretary; regarded very kindly. Has faults that cause some solicitude.

"1860. * * * The foster-mother writes: M. S. plays well; has several music scholars; has also acquired a good trade, and is efficient and self-reliant.

"* * * 1869. Foster-mother writes again: 'On Thursday eve last, our daughter was united in marriage to a worthy young man in our village.' * * *

"October, 1875. The venerable foster-mother writes: 'Our beloved M. and her little family reside near us. She proves a truly worthy wife and mother; is a consistent member of the church, and is filling a sphere of usefulness in all her relations. The dark antecedents of her history are now far in the background.'"

The younger sister has a record similar to the foregoing: Was followed by faithful supervision up to womanhood; is now pleasantly settled in life and well rewards the care bestowed upon her training and education. The brother and sisters, since reaching their majority, have corresponded and enjoyed satisfactory interviews.

"S. P. J., 1855. Born in New York. Left homeless and friendless; was committed with a brother and sister to the American Female Guardian Society, in accordance with its charter.

"January 15th. Placed in the family of ——, on trial for three months; very worthy parties, and highly recommended.

"May 1st. Favorably reported, and adoption papers requested and forwarded.

"October. Good account received per letter.

"April. Good account received per letter.

"October. Good account received per letter.

* * * * * * * *

"August, 1866. Letter received asking permission to return the child, to which the Executive Committee gave consent.

"October. Letter received saying that improvement was apparent, and the foster-parents proposed to keep her longer, as they hoped she would yet become a good girl.

"March. A good report received.

"September, 1868. A letter indicating marked improvement and encouragement received from foster-mother; also one from S. P. J. very creditable to herself and satisfactory to her friends.

"* * * June. Again a favorable report from parties visiting the child, who sent a generous donation to the 'Home,' in token of her 'grateful remembrance.'

"February, 1869. Letter received from S. showing commendable improvement; also a letter from the foster-mother full of interest and very satisfactory.

* * * * * * * *

"October, 1872. The adopted daughter visited the Home, appearing exceedingly well, now a young lady of culture and education, of whom any parents might be proud.

"April, 1875. A letter received from S. P. J.'s foster-parents saying that she is now settled in life happily, and now wishes herself to adopt a child from the Home.

"E., M., G. and C. Whole family of children, aged respectively eleven, six, four and two years.

"July 12, '47. Brought to the Home (July 1) from the bedside of a sick and dying mother, who was a very worthy woman, and who died of starvation, their wants not being made known. The father, who was sick at the same time, recovered, but became very intemperate. When sober he was a fond father.

"The boys G. and C., aged four and two years, were well adopted (1848), visited from time to time, and through the years of childhood and youth had always a good record, and the same was true of both the sisters. The desire of the father to see them was very strong, and he was at length promised 'on condition that he would sign the pledge and keep it sacredly for a full year, being in the meantime industrious and provident, he should then have an interview with his children in their respective homes.' To this he assented, met the conditions named, and at the close of the year was permitted to visit each of his children, and wept for joy to find them so well situated. From that time until his death he continued strictly temperate. He united with a Christian church, and at the time of his decease had accumulated quite a little sum to be divided among his children. Each member of this family attained their majority with an excellent record of well-doing, and have since filled positions of usefulness in life."

In addition to its other work, the society sustains the following industrial schools:

Industrial School No. 1, 29 East Twenty-ninth street.

Industrial School (Rose Memorial) No. 2, 418 West Forty-first street.

Industrial School No. 3, Twenty-fifth street, corner Eighth avenue.

Industrial School No. 4, 15 Tompkins street, near Broome.

Industrial School No. 5, 244 West Thirty-third street.

Industrial School No. 6, corner of Broadway and Fifty-fifth street.

Industrial School No. 7, Seventy-sixth street, between Second and Third avenues.

Industrial School No. 8, 161 Tenth avenue.

Industrial School No. 9, 335 East Sixtieth street.

Industrial School No. 10, 438 East Houston street.

Industrial School No. 11, Fifty-second street and Tenth avenue.

The notes of visitations made to a few of these schools are given with a view to affording a clearer understanding of their character and work.

The Rose Memorial School; or, Industrial School No 2.

This school was organized in the year 1857, by a small committee of ladies, with seventeen mendicant children and a devoted teacher. It met, for the first few months, at the Mission Sunday-school rooms of Rev. Dr. Hatfield's church. The number of children gathered from crowded alleys, garrets and cellars soon increased, and the work to be done assumed dimensions beyond the capacity of the small committee to compass, and the school was therefore transferred to the Managers of the Home for the Friendless, and has for more than eleven years past proved an agency for good, exceeding their most sanguine expectations. For more than ten years the Home Managers have hired and occupied rooms for this school in the rear of the German church on West Fortieth street. These rooms became at length much dilapidated, and, owing to unhealthy sanitary surroundings, entirely unfit for permanent occupation.

Every practicable effort made to secure a better location for the school proved abortive, and the prospect of success seemed hopeless. About this time, Messrs. Chauncey and Henry Rose, hearing of the dilemma, gave to the Home a special donation of $10,000 toward the erection of the present building, and subsequently added the sum of $5,000.

Thus encouraged, two lots of ground, 25 by 100 feet each, were purchased, and the present edifice was erected, with special reference to all the wants of the school, present and prospective. The expense incurred for the lots was $5,000, the cost of the building something over $22,000.

Besides the large audience room, which will seat some 400, and serve also for a chapel on the Sabbath, there are two large class-rooms, an infant school-room with gallery, two large play and clothes' rooms janitor's rooms, closets and bath-rooms; also convenient yard room, surrounded with a high fence, which for the time, it is asserted, is quite necessary for the protection of its windows, and the safety of teachers and pupils.

The visitation was made on the 7th of October, 1875, and the immediate charge was then in the hands of Mrs. Elizabeth Smith. The average daily attendance was stated to be about 400, though there were on the register about 700 names.

From Mrs. Smith we obtained the following particulars relative to the workings of the school: "The children do not attend regularly. They come and go. They are a very changeable population. Our attendance is smaller now than it has been for the three previous years. We require our larger scholars to leave for the public schools. Besides giving books and instruction free, we give bread every day to about fifty, and clothing as they need it.

"We teach the ordinary branches, reading and spelling, with and without defining. We teach addition, subtraction, multiplication and division tables. The children do not remain with us over fourteen years of age. They are then generally obliged to go to the factories. They come in from three to fourteen years. The average age of our children is about nine. We have seven teachers."

Industrial School No. 3

Is situated on the corner of Twenty-fifth street and Eighth avenue. The entrance is on Twenty-fifth street. It occupies an upper floor of the house. The visitation was made on October 7th.

The school was found to be in charge of Miss F. A. Rowland, with a lady assistant.

The following particulars regarding the school were obtained: There were then in the school one hundred and ten children, and the attendance was increasing every day. It promised to be much larger than last year. "The school hours," says the Principal, "are from nine till five o'clock. We take children at any age from two to sixteen years. Sometimes we have older girls. We have a little one only eighteen months old. The larger number range from eight to ten. We receive any body that comes. But they are mostly very poor children, whose parents cannot support them at home. They buy their own clothing with tickets that they earn at school, and they get a lunch of bread at noon. We teach the common branches, the four rules of arithmetic, and other studies that are in keeping. We open school by the children repeating the Lord's Prayer and reciting a psalm in concert."

The school was regarded as being in a flourishing condition. The Principal says: "I can see a great improvement in the scholars, both mentally and physically. They sometimes come in dirty, when we send them to wash their faces. We require them to observe personal cleanliness." The school possesses an organ, also a library belonging to the Sunday-school connected with the work.

Industrial School No. 5

Was visited October 7th. The Principal was, we were informed, at home ill. Fifty-seven children were in attendance, their ages ranging from four years up to ten or twelve. From the lady in charge we received the following information: "School is opened at nine o'clock by the teacher reading a chapter from the Bible, and the children reciting the Lord's Prayer.

"The children use Sander's First Reader and Third Reader. A few read Parley's History. We teach arithmetic and the common branches. We do not write on copy books but on slates. We teach sewing from Thanksgiving on to about March. The sewing class is formed by the ladies. They settle their own time for coming. They come once a week and sew from one till three. The children make dresses and patchwork. The ladies provide the materials. We have a Thanksgiving dinner. A committee of five or six ladies raise money among the friends of the school, and the money left over is used for buying material to make dresses. We are commencing to get a library. One of the ladies sent sixteen volumes yesterday."

The school-room was furnished with patent desks, which we ascertained were presented to the school by the Twenty-ninth Street Presbyterian Church. A concert was given by them for the purpose of raising the money.

The school occupies the first floor of the house; the basement is used by the janitor; the upper part is rented to a family. The building is owned by the Society.

It will be seen, from what has been already accomplished by the large and earnest force of workers of this organization, that it is one of the great moral powers opposing itself to stupendous evils, which, but for such barriers, would soon undermine society. Its work has been conducted with so much system, the placing out of children has been looked to with so much care, and the records of them through long periods of years have been so faithfully kept, as to serve in these respects as a good example, for others engaged in like efforts, to make the world better.

Association for Befriending Children and Young Girls.

New York.

This institution was organized and incorporated in 1870. It grew out of the work of a mission school, which began in 1869, and was held semi-weekly, for the purpose of imparting to children growing up in vice and depravity, some knowledge of religion. "The school opened at ten, and the children were kept at work sewing, and taught hymns, prayers and catechism till twelve o'clock, when they were provided with a good dinner. Girls of a larger class, 'long ago lost,' beginning to make their appearance at the school, and implore for help, the necessity of enlarging the work in some way became apparent. And thus there grew the idea of a home where these forlorn and abject children of the streets would be welcome, and where also the girl, scarce a woman in years, but old in the knowledge of sin and consequent suffering, might hide her shame, and where both should come voluntarily."

The House of the Association for Befriending Children was opened at No. 316 West Fourteenth street, on the Feast of the Annunciation, 1870. It had accommodations for forty-five persons. Every bed was filled the first night, and many had to go away unprovided for. In May, 1871, the Association removed to 247 East Thirteenth street, and the name was changed to its present title. Here it remained till 1874, when, in the month of May, it again removed to 136 Second avenue, its present commodious premises. This building has been raised two stories, and otherwise altered to meet the needs of the work, and contains the usual modern appliances for the health and comfort of about 100 inmates.

The premises were carefully inspected October 6, on which occasion we were furnished by the President, Mrs. Mary C. D. Starr, with the following information regarding the aims and workings of the institution:

"The object is reformation. We do not propose to receive people, except such as require reformation; but there are none too depraved or too unfortunate for us to admit, whatever their vice may have been, whether intemperance or an abandoned life. Children are not received under twelve years, nor adults over twenty-five. Our rules are not so fixed in regard to the older women; but they are in regard to children under twelve, because for children of that age commitment would be necessary. We receive them on their own application. The only thing that we require to know is, that they are unfortunate and that they need what the institution proposes to give to them. We do every thing that is necessary for them. We clothe them, feed them, give them secular instruction and also religious and industrial training. They pay nothing. They give nothing. The only thing that is required of them is, that they shall be willing to remain six months, because to do the work well that we propose, requires time.

"On admission, applicants are placed in some one of the various departments of the house, and we find out, after a while, what they have the best capacity for, and they are placed at that and trained thoroughly in that department. If for laundry work, they are taught to perform that in the very best manner. Others are placed in the machine-room and learn to do all kinds of sewing. Then again others are taught household work. So we train them for laundresses, seamstresses, cooks, waitresses, nurses, chambermaids, whatever they have most fitness for. Those especially, that have sewing every day, are also taught household work. Then, of course, their religious education goes on at the same time.

"We receive all grades. We never ask whether they are Protestant or Catholic. Then, after they have remained as long as we consider desirable, at least six months, they are supplied with employment. We place them in families. We never send them out alone, so that there is no interval between being here and in a place of security. We require every lady employer to bring references as to character, and to come here and take the girl with her. When the girls come here, some of them know just as little as it is possible for a person to know to live. When they go from here they get high wages, because they have been trained.

"If they conform to all our rules, this house is their home. When they leave a place, they can always come back. If they are out of health, they may come here and get well. If they have been worked hard, they can come here and rest. We want to make the circle of work complete. We want to obviate any necessity for them to go back to old associations.

"Many girls have not one being in the world to whom it is safe for them to speak. Of course we have all grades here. We have girls who are educated, and even some women who are accomplished. We have had them all the way down to the lowest stratum of society. Those who have been of a better class have, in many instances, been separated from their friends. Of others, the fathers and mothers are their worst enemies. We say to them 'you are always welcome to come here.' I am constantly in correspondence with them when they are away. Almost every day I have a letter from some one of them.

"Our great aim is to follow up this work after they leave us. The most important part is watching over them afterward. We have a society formed here in the house, of which those who aspire to a better life become members. The rules of this society are, that its members shall come here to a meeting once a month, on the second Sunday in the month, when we have religious services and a reunion. I can tell by their appearance how they are getting on. I can tell by their dress. There is an opportunity then to say a word to them, and advise them. None but those in the house meet at these reunions.

"Every one finds her level here. The educated naturally seek the society of the educated. They are, if possible, restored to their families. The chief thing for us to know is where they are and what they are doing. The institution is supported mainly by private charity. We earn a great deal by our own labor. As soon as a girl is morally and industrially fitted to go, we send her out to work.

"The rule of the house is very strict in regard to conversation on the past life. Of course religious influence is the first, last and middle of every thing, and the obligation not to speak of the past is very strong, and generally adhered to. Every girl is told when she comes in that girls have come here for different reasons. We tell them 'nobody will ever know why you came in unless you tell them. No one will ever know your history except myself. We want you, when you go away from here, to lead a different life.' This is the very strongest argument that can be used.

"Under the influences here, you will see them acquiring a spirit of self-respect. It grows beautifully, and sometimes those that have led the most unfortunate lives are the most sensitive. My intention is to raise *the woman.* No amount of outward reformation is going to avail any thing if you do not raise the woman's idea of her own dignity *as a woman.*

"Our work could be extended with more means. It is very necessary to have a boarding-house where these girls, going out to work by the day, could come back at night and be safe. And yet, with this work, we are always crowded. We never have room. Some one comes in and there is no place to put her. Then the question is, 'Who can go out?' The ages of those in the house vary from twelve to twenty-five. The average is from sixteen to twenty. That is the most hopeful period. Over twenty, there is very little that can be done in the way of reform.

"Nearly all the reformatories for this class are obliged to use punishment. The most extreme punishment that is used here is bread and water for breakfast or tea. We certainly have the most lawless people under our care. We have people for whom prison or police have no terrors. Of course it is very much more laborious where we use but moral suasion and moral force, but it is the only effectual way.

"There are four ladies, beside myself, engaged in this work. They give up all their time to it. They are ladies of culture, and are in charge of different departments of the house. There is no compensation. Their circumstances are such that they have no home-ties. I have always superintended personally. I am so situated that I can spend a certain number of hours here every day. Some of our girls, who have been with us many years, are placed in positions of responsibility as monitors. But it is only a lady of character that can have any influence over the girls we wish to reform. Each girl costs us $50 for her clothing, maintenance, etc.

"We have no paid servants. Our labor all comes from the inmates. There is only one paid person in the house, and that is the head laundress. The laundry has from ten to twelve hands employed. It is not as large as it should be. If it were, we could add greatly to our income. We make $150 a month by it at present."

In the basement of the house are the kitchen and the girls' lavatory. The first floor contains chapel, parlor, offices for the reception of inmates, and private rooms; the second floor machine room, with twenty-five sewing machines, community room, and class room. The third and fourth floors are entirely devoted to dormitories. The fifth floor is the recreation room, fifty-five feet long, in which there are a piano and other means of entertainment. On the basement floor is a bath-room supplied with hot and cold water. Mrs. Starr further says:

"Every girl in the house has her own bed, her own towel, soap, brush, tooth brush and comb, and it is capital punishment if they do not use them. Each has her bath every week. It is not left to her own choice. A person in the bath-room keeps a list of every one in the house, and sends for them in regular order, from the oldest to the youngest. Every article of clothing is changed weekly, including bed-clothes, and every floor in the house is washed. Some of the rooms are scrubbed every day, and none of them less often than three times a week. All sleep on single iron bedsteads. Every bedstead is washed once a week. I do not think iron bedsteads are cleanly. Leaving undone any of the precautions we take for one month would fill the house with ophthalmia and other troubles.

"When a girl comes in she at once receives a bath, using carbolic soap. If her hair is in very bad condition, and it is indispensable, it is cut, but we always give them a chance to save their hair. If necessary, as sometimes happens, they receive a bath every day after they come in for several weeks. Every article of clothing on them is changed, and whatever they bring with them is washed before it is used.

"The beds are of straw. They are supplied with fresh straw every three months, and the ticks are washed. The straw is taken out of the house and new put in. The result is that we never have any illness except those that come in with diseased and broken-down constitutions. We use a great deal of farinaceous food."

In the chapel is an organ which is played by Mrs. Starr during service. A very good choir is formed of the girls. The dormitories are neat, clean apartments, with tinted walls and counterpanes of snowy whiteness. On one side is a shelf with white bowls, and above each a compartment for towels, brush and comb. When not in use a wooden screen hung on weights shuts down over it, so that it appears part of the wall. Strips of carpet are laid through the center of the floors. Each of the dormitories is named after its patron saint, among whom were conspicuous St. Ann, St. Vincent de Paul, St. Joseph, St. Elizabeth and St. Catharine.

The clothes room had the appearance of great neatness and order; curtains were hung before the shelves. Some of the inmates who have been reformed, it was stated, consecrate themselves to do the work of the house. They wear a black habit, and a black cross attached to a scarlet braid. They have adopted the name of the "Sodality of the Precious Blood of Our Lord." They bind themselves to a life of reparation and missionary work for one year. At the expiration of that time they are allowed to renew their vows. Their labor, supervised as it is by cultured ladies, may perhaps account for the beautiful order and freshness of every part of the establishment.

The work being done in this institution is of a peculiar nature. It appears to be thoroughly done, and those engaged in it are not only well qualified for its performance by their social advantages, but from the earnest missionary spirit which actuates them.

The whole house bore evidence of being kept in the very highest condition of cleanliness and order. In addition to the industrial training, the moral influence and religious teaching of the house must prove of great advantage to every inmate. The impression was made upon the mind that the work being carried on by these earnest Christian ladies has proved remarkably successful, and is deserving of liberal support.

At the date of visitation a little over one-half of the inmates were orphans, and a large number were half-orphans. All except one were of foreign parentage.

The whole number of persons received during the past year was 225.

The number that were placed out or returned to parents or guardians was 236.

The current expenses for the fiscal year ending September 30, 1875, were $6,321.17.

The total indebtedness of the institution is $36,926.92, of which $25,000 is upon real estate. The association has no invested fund.

Association for the Benefit of Colored Orphans in the City of New York.

New York.

The history of this charity, which was incorporated in 1838, is given as follows:

"In the autumn of 1836, a few persons, feeling that humanity and justice demanded that something should be done to elevate and improve the condition of colored orphans in New York city and State, enlisted themselves in their behalf, and the sum of $2,000 was obtained mostly by small subscriptions. A society was formed, and, near the close of the year 1836, twenty-two lady managers were elected, and five gentlemen were chosen as an advisory committee. The managers tried in vain, for three months, to hire a suitable house on account of existing prejudice against color. As the only alternative, a purchase was decided upon, and a cottage house, situated on Twelfth street near Sixth avenue, was obtained for $9,000. The Trustees of Lindley Murray's Charitable Fund subscribed $1,000, which was added to the amount already given. After the purchase of the house, not a dollar remained to furnish it, or provide for the orphans. Recourse was speedily had to the garrets of the managers for rejected articles of furniture, and, by additional contributions, the cottage was soon supplied with requisites. The promise of $500 from the Manumission Society, toward education, authorized the formation of a school for the neighboring children. Forty scholars were soon found in attendance, whom the managers themselves instructed by turns. Owing to limited resources, the utmost caution was used in the admission of orphans, and interested friends furnished supplies from their table. One little girl of four years was at first admitted, others soon followed, and, at the close of the financial year, seven months from the opening of the house, the managers found themselves with a family of twenty-three children, the current expenses for that time being only $234.03. About this time the managers received a donation of $6,000 from the estate of William Turpin. During the year 1839, donations were received to the amount of $10,000 for the purpose of purchasing lots and erecting a new building, better adapted to the accommodation of children. Some small children were boarded with good families in the country. This year, for the first time, $425.93 was received from the Commissioners of the Public School Fund for the purposes of education. It has been continued to the present time. The institution, during its early history, was mainly supported by donations. It received much timely aid from the Manumission Society and the Lindley Murray Fund. In June, 1842, the city corporation made the Association an appropriation of twenty lots of ground lying on Fifth avenue, between Forty-third and Forty-fourth streets, and on this site the managers erected a plain substantial brick building capable of accommodating one hundred and fifty children, and, in May, 1843, the children were moved to the new Asylum.

"In 1848 the Association received a legacy of $5,000 from the estate of John Horseburgh, who had given a like sum at sundry times during his life, also an appropriation, for the first time, from the Legislature of $335.53, and an allowance from the city of a certain sum per week for each child supported from the city.

"In July, 1863, the asylum was assailed by a mob, pillaged and burnt to the ground. The children were taken quietly and safely out, and in a few days were temporarily provided for at Blackwell's Island.

"The following October the family was moved to a residence in Carmansville, rented for the purpose. The next year Chauncey Rose donated $20,000 to the Association, and a claim upon the city for the destruction of the asylum buildings by the mob was allowed, amounting to $73,000. It was not deemed advisable to rebuild upon the old site on Fifth avenue and Forty-third street, and the land was disposed of for $170,000, and these amounts were reserved for the purchase of land and the erection of new buildings. Donations were received from John Haven, $5,000, and Chauncey Rose, $1,000, both of which were added to the building fund. During the year of 1866, forty-five lots were purchased, situated on Tenth avenue and One Hundred and Forty-third street, at a cost of $45,000, upon which the present building was erected. It was ready for occupation in May, 1868."

The institution, at date of visitation, October 22, was under charge of a Superintendent, Mr. O. K. Hutchinson. There were about 270 children in the asylum, two-thirds of whom were boys. The edifice is a two-story brick structure, with a mansard roof and basement, having improved grounds about it. A fine view of the Hudson is obtained from the premises. The halls of the building are wide and the stairways quite roomy. The balustrades are made of black walnut. The doors are of natural wood, varnished. The ceilings are high and the windows large. Separate yards, furnished with swings, are provided for both boys and girls.

Mr. Hutchinson informed us that half-orphans, full orphans and destitute children were admitted.

The following are rules and regulations in force:

Children may be admitted between the ages of two and ten.

Children should not be indentured under twelve years of age.

Homes in the country must be invariably provided, unless there offers a good opportunity of apprenticing a boy to a trade.

Persons taking children must produce good testimonials of character, circumstances, etc.; a note from a minister is required, certifying that they are members of some religious denomination.

A boy is entitled, at the expiration of his term of indenture to $100, which sum his master should pay by yearly installments into the hands of the treasurer, to be by her placed in trust for the child. But should he leave his place before the expiration of his time, or so conduct himself that he becomes an unworthy object, this sum, or such as shall have accrued, shall revert to the institution. This rule applies equally to boys and girls.

It is requested that the person to whom a child is indentured shall communicate with the Board as to his welfare, before the expiration of two months.

Six months' schooling is required for the first two years of a child's apprenticeship.

Three months' trial will be allowed. If, at the expiration of that time, the child is insubordinate, he may be returned. After that the Board does not hold itself in any way responsible.

A child placed in the institution by a surviving parent or guardian, with the intention of withdrawing when at the age of twelve, shall be charged 75 cents per week.

No parent shall be allowed to withdraw a child whose board has not been paid, or who cannot offer security for its future payment. This should be clearly understood when the child is entered.

No child shall be transferred without the knowledge and approbation of the Indenturing Committee.

The institution is supported by donations, subscriptions and income from investments. The Commissioners of Public Charities and Correction pay ten cents a day for destitute colored children belonging to the city. About one hundred and eighty children are at present paid for at that rate.

Mr. Hutchinson says: "We get a portion of the School money, and also a portion of the Excise money. The children are visited after they are placed out, but this is not systematically done. Parties taking children pay us a certain sum; for a little girl it is $50. It is paid annually, and when we get that money we hear from the children. The money is put in a bank, in the name of the treasurer, for the child.

Each child has a bank-book, held by the treasurer. The child has this money when it is of age. The children are too young to be taught any regular industries in the asylum. We teach the older boys to work upon the grounds. The girls are taught to sew, in school. One afternoon in the week, and during the summer vacation, we have a class in sewing. They also assist in the housework. We get along with just as little servants' help as we can. The asylum is built with reference to classification. We have very little trouble with that matter. The boys and girls meet together in the same school-room and dining-room.

"The working force consists of a superintendent, matron, six teachers and fifteen or sixteen servants. About twelve of these are females. The force includes an engineer, baker, and a man who takes care of the boys. We have forty-five city lots. The building was opened seventeen years last May. It cost $130,000, all told; the grounds alone cost $40,000. The building is heated by steam, mainly. The ventilation is effected by means of wall flues.

"A book of records is kept, in which are entered the names of all the children indentured, the day of indenture, the residence of parties taking them, an account of the receipts from each, and a report of conduct."

Fire-proof doors divide the building, and a fire-proof stairway affords egress in case of need. The school-room is a large and well-lighted apartment, which is used also for a chapel. It has a bay window on one side. Outside of the bay window is a broad porch, from which a view of the Hudson is obtained. Vocal music is taught. A piano is used in accompaniment.

The dormitories are furnished with iron bedsteads, single, straw beds and feather pillows. The beds are two feet eight inches wide, and seemed very comfortable. The children dress almost, but not altogether uniformly.

In the clothing-room we found a large supply of woolen garments, prepared for winter. The underwear of both girls and boys is, we were informed, made by charitable societies in the city. The dining-room is a spacious apartment, and is furnished with tables and stools, the latter being fastened in their positions.

The bread used in the asylum is baked on the premises, in a brick oven; hop yeast being used. The kitchen was very clean. In the lavatory is a large circular vat, about twelve feet in diameter, with a lead pipe running around the inside rim. The children wash in running water. Each one has his own towel, which is changed twice a week.

The nursery department is a pleasant room, well-lighted. It is furnished with little tables and little benches. The children here, at the time of our visit, were from two to five years of age. About twenty of them, in charge of a young colored woman, were in this department. The children belonging here being small, sleep two in a bed. A fire was burning on the hearth, and flowers brightened the room. The nursery leads out upon a little balcony, where the children are enabled to play in safety.

The Superintendent says, "Nine children died in the institution during the year. Colored children are constitutionally weak, and are afflicted with lung and scrofulous complaints. We cannot make them healthy children."

The institution appears to be well managed, and its affairs are in a prosperous condition. It is doing an important work. The number of children that have received its benefactions since its organization is 2,150. During the past year seventy-seven children were admitted and ninety discharged. Of the latter, thirty-one were indentured, fifty-seven returned to parents or guardians, and two transferred to other institutions. On the 1st October, 1875, there were, remaining in the institution, eighty orphans and one hundred and fifty-two half-orphans. The total expenditures for the fiscal year ending September 30, 1875, were $34,836. The value of its invested fund is $168,912.65.

Asylum of St. Vincent De Paul.

New York.

This Asylum was founded through the benevolence of a Mrs. Crooks, and has been sustained by the ladies of the Roman Catholic Church on Twenty-third street, in the interests of destitute children of French parentage, but its benefactions are not confined wholly to this class. Its affairs are directed by a Board of Lady Managers, and its finances are controlled by a Board of Gentleman Trustees. Its immediate charge and workings are intrusted to the Sisters of the Religious Order of the Marianites of the Holy Cross. Fourteen Sisters are engaged in the work, Sister Mary of the Archangels being at the head of the establishment. No domestics are employed, the work being done by the Sisters with the assistance of the older girls.

The Asylum was visited October 20, in company with Commissioner Hoguet, at which time there were one hundred and twenty-five children in the institution, forty-seven of whom were boys. Children are received as young as four years and are kept, if boys, till twelve, and if girls, till they are eighteen years of age, provided their guardians consent. The best disposition possible is made of the children, when they are ready to leave. The Sister says: "Girls are always wanted, but boys are hard to dispose of."

The children, while in the asylum, are instructed in both the French and English languages, and the girls are taught to sew, wash, iron and cook. Sewing is taken in for the purpose of helping to support the institution, and also to enable the industrial education of the children to be carried on with greater efficiency.

Of the children in the institution on the day of visitation, forty-three were paid for by ladies of the church of St. Vincent de Paul, who constitute themselves guardians of a certain number. Others were more or less paid for by their parents; the balance were entirely supported by the institution. The parents of some of the children pay toward their support, we were informed, sometimes $6, sometimes $5 a month, but more frequently nothing.

On visiting the sewing department we found thirty-five large girls employed. They were variously dressed. Very creditable specimens of their work, which is all done for private families, were on exhibition. The boys and girls are kept strictly apart, even to attending separate schools and eating in separate dining rooms.

The chapel is capable of accommodating about two hundred and fifty. It is neatly fitted up with seats of natural wood, having black walnut moldings. The dormitories are furnished with single iron bedsteads and straw mattresses. Washing arrangements are in connection with the dormitories, and the inmates wash in running water.

The dining rooms are furnished with tables and benches. The laundry is well arranged. On the day of visitation six little girls were here ironing along with the Sisters. The building is constructed with high ceilings. It has wall flue ventilation, transom head-lights over the doors, and is heated by steam and lighted with gas. The window sashes are hung according to the modern plan, with cords, weights and pulleys. The children were apparently quite healthy.

The number of children inmates on October 1st, 1875, was one hundred and twenty-three, twenty-one of whom were orphans, and one hundred and two half-orphans. All were of foreign parentage. One hundred and eleven were entirely or partially supported by friends, and twelve wholly by the institution.

This institution is mainly supported, as has been stated, by the members of the Roman Catholic Church on Twenty-third street, the custom being for particular members to sustain certain children. This feature, it is thought, insures a personal interest in the protégés on the part of their benefactors. The management of the Asylum is marked with great economy. The total expenditures for the month of September for the support of the entire household, as shown by the account books, were:

For the sustenance of fifteen Sisters......................	$116 16
For the sustenance of one hundred and twenty-three children,	423 00
Total..	$539 16

This, it will be seen, has been less than $4.00 a month, per capita, including the support of the Sisters.

The demeanor of the Sisters was such as it would seem must naturally win the confidence and respect of the children, and the atmosphere of the house was cheerful and home-like.

Children's Aid Society.

New York.

The history, development and beneficent operations of this Society have been already well illustrated in the work prepared by its devoted Secretary, Mr. Charles L. Brace, entitled "The Dangerous Classes." This work is so complete an elucidation of the objects and purposes of the Society, that little, if any thing, can be added. The work of the Society from the first, has been conducted with the munificent spirit characteristic of its leading supporters, and its operations have been upon so grand a scale as to stamp its impress upon the age to which it belongs.

The results of visitations made to several of the many institutions of the Society, showing them in their every day aspect, and a few statistics gathered from its last report, may be interesting. The statistics are given at some length, for the reason that the work of the year is regarded as somewhat larger than ever before, and seems still more satisfactory.

The Association was formed in 1853, and incorporated January 1st, 1855, under the general law. An office was opened on Amity street, and a beginning made, to check the growth of the "dangerous classes" which infested New York. "The different parts of the city where the lovely form of childhood was being changed into aspects as revolting to the sight as they were harrowing to the feelings, became more fully known, and the extent of the work inaugurated soon appeared appallingly evident." The laborers, however, pushed forward the undertaking, expanded it to meet every new exigency, till at length we find it working in six Lodging Houses for boys and girls, in one of which alone over one hundred thousand homeless boys have been sheltered, fed and instructed; in twenty-one day industrial schools, and in thirteen night schools, where during each year over ten thousand destitute children "too poor and too busy on the streets to attend the public schools, have been instructed, and partly fed and clothed. The great work of the Society, however, has been the placing of homeless children in good country homes."

In the last twenty-three years nearly forty thousand have been so placed out. Of these, Mr. Brace says: "We follow the fortunes of vast numbers of them, and, so far as we can trace, not more than five per cent turn out badly; *i. e.*, commit criminal offense, or become chargeable on the public. The whole West, where these children have been sent, are satisfied with the work, and the demand for them is far beyond what we can supply. Many of these thus sent out have now accumulated property, and occupy positions of trust and responsibility."

If the figures are even approximately correct, as given by the Prison Association of New York, in its thirtieth annual report, from the researches conducted by Dr. Harris and Mr. Dugdale, as the penalty of neglecting one homeless child, "Margaret," in Ulster county, the amount saved the country by placing forty thousand destitute children under wholesome family influences in one branch of the work alone, in twenty-three years, can hardly be conceived. In regard to this economic feature of the work, the Secretary of the Society, in his last annual report, says:

"If each vagrant, homeless, and unprotected child saved by the Children's Aid Society during the past year, and placed in a good country home, be reckoned as a pecuniary saving to the community of at least $1,500, then will the saving to this city from our emigration operations alone, during the past year, amount to at least several millions of dollars. But when it is considered that from each of the little vagrant girls thus saved there might have come forth a long line of paupers and criminals, the immense gain to the future of our community from these labors of charity may be feebly estimated; and still higher, if we recall that each of these little abandoned street children is an heir of immortality, and one of "the little ones of Christ," for whom He lived and died, we may still better judge of the momentous importance of these humble labors of charity."

The emigration feature of the work is thus stated:

"During the time of the greatest distress last winter, and as special funds were afforded, many extremely destitute families were sent to places of work in the West and South. Not one, so far as we know, has failed to be self-supporting. A vast correspondence is still kept up with these children by Mr. Macy and the clerks in the office, and the history of each little waif, with his own name, is carefully recorded on our books. Names are never changed without informing us, and that only in cases where a child is adopted by its employer, in order to inherit his property and become a member of his family."

In our visit to the office of the Society on Fourth street, October 26, we noticed about eighteen or twenty little fellows from twelve years old upwards, who were being prepared to go west; others, we were informed, were expected in to make up a company of about thirty. Upon inquiry of the Assistant Secretary, Mr. J. Macy, the following particulars were given concerning them: One group was a German family of five children, accompanied by the father; another was a family of three children, with both father and mother; a third was a family of two children, with father and mother; a fourth was a father and mother with two boys; a fifth was a family consisting of father and mother and three children; a sixth was a mother with four children. There was also a widow who came from Dacotah in a condition of abject poverty, going to her mother in New England; a young man, aged nineteen, going to friends in Springfield, Ill.; and a man and wife, with four children, going to Minneapolis. These, it was stated, were found in a condition of the most abject poverty. Among the number was an honest-faced English lad, eleven years old, who was being sent, upon application, to a gentleman with whom it was thought he would have unusual advantages. Three boys were going to Indiana, to their father, who is now able to take care of them. Three others, whose father was intemperate, and whose mother had died, were going to Missouri. They had previously obtained their living by begging from house to house. Friends had interested themselves in them, and they were surrendered to the Society. The faces of the older parties bore traces of privation and sorrow. All were comfortably attired, a number of the garments worn being new. The company appeared clean, and a rejuvenation seemed to have taken place through the brightening influence of the new hopes arising out of the opening future. A particular inquiry into the history of these families left the impression that, if left to follow the natural course of circumstances in the city, they would probably pauperize. It was stated that it was unusual for so many adults to be included in these parties sent out to the care of the western agent. The Society proposed taking these families under its keeping till they were, so to speak, set once more on their feet and started anew on the road to self-support. The work of the Society in this department, during the past year, is thus stated by its Secretary:

There have been provided with homes and employment during the year:

Boys	1,853
Girls	1,552
Men	263
Women	358
Total	4,026
Last year	3,985
Excess for 1875	41

The following Schedule shows the number sent to each State during each month, together with the nationality and parentage.

Where sent.		Month.		Nationality.		Parentage.	
New York	241	1874.		American born,	1,509	Parents living	841
New Jersey	118	November	259	Irish	921	Father living	425
Ohio	268	December	223	German	965	Mother living	780
Indiana	262			English	229	Orphans	1,126
Illinois	397	1875.		Scotch	77	Unknown	233
Iowa	331	January	225	French	41		
Wisconsin	305	February	255	Swedes	124	Total	3,405
Michigan	260	March	426	Italian	1	Men	263
Minnesota	114	April	404	Poles	114	Women	358
Nebraska	106	May	377	Bohemian	37		
Missouri	251	June	373	Swiss	2	Total	4,026
Kentucky	11	July	329	Danes	5		
Virginia	20	August	620	Spanish	1		
Delaware	46	September	326				
Maryland	13	October	209	Total	4,026		
Kansas	60						
Connecticut	34	Total	4,026				
Massachusetts	21						
Rhode Island	15						
South Carolina	56						
Vermont	1						
Nevada	18						
Canada	14						
California	17						
Colorado	29						
North Carolina	31						
Tennessee	42						
Louisiana	4						
Pennsylvania	35						
Texas	10						
New Hampshire,	2						
England	5						
To sea	8						
Ret'd to friends,	156						
City	651						
Other institu'ns,	79						
Total	4,026						

Total sent since 1853	40,389

The following are the names of the Lodging Houses conducted under the auspices of this Society:

Newsboys' Lodging House, 9 Duane street.

Girls' Lodging House, 27 St. Mark's Place.

Rivington Street Lodging House, 327 Rivington street.

Eleventh Ward Lodging House, 709 East Eleventh street.

Sixteenth Ward Lodging House, 211 West Eighteenth street.

Phelps' Lodging House, 314 East Thirty-fifth street.

A few of these were visited, and the notes taken will, it is thought, be a fair exhibit of their workings as a whole.

The Newsboys' Lodging House (*corner of Duane and New Chamber Streets*).

This institution is a six-story brick building, with an attic in addition. It is a new and stately edifice, with buff-colored stone moldings, and was first occupied in March, 1874. The first floor is fitted up for stores, and designed to be rented.

A visitation and careful inspection was made October 4th. It is under the immediate charge of Mr. and Mrs. Charles O'Conor, who have been in the work for the past eighteen years. The following information was given by Mr. O'Conor in the course of our conversation:

"We commenced in the old 'Sun' building, on the corner of Fulton and Nassau streets, in the year 1854. We had about forty boys there. It was conducted on the same general principles as it is now. Since then a large number of boys have gone out from us and done well. There is hardly a day that I do not meet boys that have been successful in life, who were once with us. They come up and talk with me, and express gratitude for what I have done for them.

"Our first boys are to be found in all professions in life. I have had boys here who are now ministers, whom I placed out. One of these had been in the House of Refuge before coming here. I met him after the war. He said, 'You do not know me, Mr. O'Conor. I am a different boy now from what I was.' He knew that I took him out West and placed him on a farm. He was sent to school and got a religious turn, and became a good boy.

"The last time I was out West I met several of my boys. One would come and tap me on the shoulder and ask me if I knew him. 'I am the editor of that paper over there.' Another, 'I keep the largest bakery in the city.'

"Numbers of our boys that have succeeded West send to me for others to come and live with them. Only two months ago one that we had sent West when a boy, got married to an only daughter of a very respectable family, a highly educated young lady, and has thus become connected with a good family. Another lad has got one of the largest wholesale groceries in the town. There is a great field out West for boys. A great deal depends upon the family into which the boy enters. Our agents are very particular, and will not allow a boy to enter an improper family. He visits all the families where boys are placed. Our office keeps a printed form that they send to the employer once in three months, with the request that he send the information about the boy's conduct, etc., and then a record is made of that.

"A great many of the boys that come to us are orphans. A large number of the boys have dissipated parents. In almost all cases their destitution proceeds from the dissipation of the parents or guardians. Many of their parents are at Blackwell's Island, every now and then. Parents make a resolution to be good, and break it before the end of the week. The mothers are usually strong, healthy women, and go off with other men.

"We know what every boy is doing, and no boy who is able to support himself elsewhere is kept here. We have a bank and encourage the boys to save their earnings. This place is only to help boys who are trying to help themselves. I have a personal interview with every boy that comes in. I find out who he is, what is his home, where he came from, and if he has any parents living. We can generally tell from his appearance whether he has run away from home or not. If we suspect that a boy has parents living, and he is non-committal, we generally get another boy to sleep with him and he will generally get out of him his whole history before morning. We then send a message to his family, and hold the boy till we hear from them. In this way we send a great many boys home who have been led to New York by reading the yellow-covered books. They come from Chicago, Philadelphia and all over, thinking that they will make their fortune here.

"Each boy on coming has to register his name, age, parentage, where born, if he can read and write, if he is an orphan, half-orphan, and if he has any money. If he has only six cents he is asked to pay for his lodging. If he has nothing, he gets his two meals and lodging free. His underclothing is washed free of charge once a week. A great many boys never had any change till then. We help them to a shirt where we know they cannot earn one for themselves. We make it a principle to make the boys feel that they must help themselves all they can. No matter how shiftless a boy is, he can generally manage to make enough to support himself. He is not so negligent that he will go without food.

"We tell the boy, on his arrival, nothing else except the rules of the house, until we find that he has no home. Then we suggest that he go West and get employment with a respectable employer. I advise the boys myself. I advise them to be honest, industrious and, before all things, to keep from chewing tobacco. The first thing I did, when I took charge of this institution, was to take away all spittoons from the house. They all thought I was crazy; but I have had no need for them since. If a boy comes in here and persists in chewing tobacco, I turn him out. I tell the boys that, if they want to get employment, they must keep themselves clean.

"Boys generally come here in a very bad condition. Their heads are often like a rotten apple. We have sometimes to burn all their clothes and put ointment on their heads. But in a few days the change is so great that we would hardly know them. The boys are sometimes in the habit of sleeping out for months before they come here.

"They are encouraged to deposit each month's savings in a savings bank. We have a number with deposits in the savings bank. Some of them must buy clothing with their savings; others will have to divide it with their poor parents."

Routine of the day.—"The boys rise a little after five, wash and dress, and fix matters up till a quarter past six, when they have breakfast. Each boy has a ticket, which he presents to the engineer at the door of the breakfast-room. He then passes on and takes his place at the table, eats his breakfast and goes. The boys come and go. They don't all eat at the same time and finish together.

"After breakfast the boys scatter through the city, and don't put in an appearance till six o'clock in the evening. In winter they come at half-past four. We don't allow them to hang around the premises.

"When the boys return in the evening, each one takes off his hat and goes and registers himself and pays six cents for a meal and six cents for his lodging. Some of them have a good deal of spirit, and would not take a free meal, and if they have no money they get credit. Frequently boys pay in advance. After registering, they each get a ticket and a key which is numbered, the number corresponding with the number on some clothes' closet in the house, where the boy puts all his clothes except pants and shirt, goes and washes and gets ready for supper, which is served at seven o'clock. At half-past seven he goes to school. Two teachers are employed and about one hundred and twenty boys attend. The school is over by a quarter to nine o'clock. The boys then prepare for bed. The school is closed by all the boys repeating the Lord's Prayer. Every Friday evening the boys sing hymns and rehearse the Sunday-school lesson.

"Sunday evenings we usually have gentlemen from the city come and talk with the boys. Some of them interest the boys a good deal; others don't succeed so well. The criticism of the boys, after the speakers are gone, is usually very sharp and amusing. Horace Greeley used to come and urge the boys to go West, and tell them how to farm and save money, and above all things to steer clear of city life and politics; and William Cullen Bryant would also come and talk to them."

Dining room.—The boys sit on benches. No table-cloths are used. The tables are made up of horses with boards placed on them. The legs of the horses are hinged and so constructed as to be closed up when set aside, thus occupying but small space. The tables are two feet eight inches wide, and the two ends of each are fitted together by an iron socket in one and a pivot in the other. Crockery plates, bowls, knives and forks are used. The boys, we are told, 'seldom break any thing. Whatever breakage occurs is done by the domestics.' The dining room can seat about five hundred.

Audience room.—This is a large room, occupying the whole of one floor. It is furnished with patent seats, folding back, and has large windows on three sides. At one end is a raised dais, with an iron rail in front, also a piano. The walls on three sides of the room are fitted up with "cupboards." They are used for the boys' clothing. There are two hundred and fifty in all. The largest sizes are intended for boys who have Sunday clothing. The locks on each are different; each key opening but one lock.

At the other end of the room, opposite the raised dais, is a recording desk, with an iron railing around it, where each boy is registered. It also contains a key-board, with keys numbered to correspond with the clothes cupboards. At the registering desk is a "savings bank." This consists of a table perforated with one hundred and ten holes, each hole numbered consecutively from one to one hundred and ten. The holes are just large enough to drop in a silver half dollar. It contains a drawer running both ways, with three differently constructed locks. The drawer has an iron bottom, and different little compartments under each number. A cover, formed of two pieces hinged on each end, lapping over the table and meeting in the center where they are locked, is now used for greater security. The boys used to "fish out" the fractional currency with crooked wires.

"The boys," the Superintendent says, "are fined for infringement of rules. A boy is fined ten cents if he takes his key out in the street. He must leave it at the registering desk every time he goes out. They are expected to be in by nine o'clock. If any are out later than nine, there is a fine of one cent between nine and ten, five cents between ten and eleven, seven cents between eleven and twelve. We are more particular about the fine than the lodging money. The boy cannot get his lodging without paying the fine. It makes the boys resolve not to go out the next day. When they stay out after hours they are generally at places of amusement, where they ought not to be, and for that reason we are particular about the fines."

In this room were several mottoes, among which were the following:

"Boys having homes not received here."

"Boys desiring homes in the country should apply to the Superintendent."

"Boys' underclothing washed every Friday, free of charge."

"The use of tobacco is strictly forbidden."

The audience room is also used as a school-room. Reading, writing, arithmetic and geography are taught. "It is surprising," says the

Superintendent, "to see how smart some of them are. Many of them are very apt scholars."

Bath-rooms.— Bath and wash-rooms have troughs running around three sides of the room, affording accommodations for fifty boys to wash at a time. Tin basins are used. On the fourth side are six bath-rooms, two tubs in each. One end of the room is partitioned off for the water-closets, with accommodations for eleven boys. The boys use soap in washing. Here are also a considerable number of foot-baths.

Drying Room.— "It was found," says the Superintendent, "that many boys would come in drenched with rain, and their clothes used to be put away wet. In the morning, of course, they were still wet, and had to be put on in that state. This room was put up to meet that difficulty. Now, if a boy comes in with his clothes wet, they can be dried here in five minutes. Drying clothes by steam has also a tendency to destroy vermin and other impurities that may exist in the clothes."

Dormitories.— Dormitory number one contains one hundred and thirty-four beds. Iron bedsteads are used, arranged in double tiers. Each bedstead is two feet one inch wide, and five feet ten inches long. The upper bed stands three feet ten inches from the floor. The lower one stands one foot five inches. Each bed has a straw mattress, husk pillows, a pair of sheets, a "comfortable," wadded with cotton, and an outside spread or counterpane; and, in cold weather, an additional comfortable was said to be used. The beds were clean, and well aired. "During the cold weather the room is kept at a moderate temperature." The Superintendent would prefer not to have the boys sleep one above an other. "A man stops with the boys till eleven o'clock at night. Very few boys come in after that hour. They never raise a row. They sleep soundly and quietly during the night."

The dormitories are so divided into sections that any particular boy can be found at once, if inquired for. Dormitory number two is furnished the same as number one. Dormitory number three is a smaller room, furnished with beds, five feet two inches by two feet seven inches. These beds the Superintendent prefers to the others. The boys occupying them are charged ten cents. "We charge more for these," says the Superintendent, "to prevent jealousy."

The gymnasium is furnished with horizontal bars, boxing gloves, swinging ropes and various other kinds of apparatus for exercising

The result of the visit was very gratifying.

The year's work of this institution is thus stated by the Superintendent in the recent annual report:

"Our savings bank has been used by 1,311 boys (an increase of 39), who have saved $3,206.15.

"During the year we have had 9,286 different boys with us, being an increase of 373. They have paid $8,105.64. Our receipts from the boys this year are $1,938.11 more than last year, being an increase of 31½ per cent.

"During the year 527 boys have been placed in good homes. There have been restored 973 lost and truant boys to relatives and friends. Parents often wish us to learn about lost children.

"We have averaged 238 lodgers nightly, being an increase of 44 over last year, an increase of 20 per cent. We have, during the year, furnished 91,253 meals, an increase of 18,586, or nearly 26 per cent; 86,880 lodgings, an increase of 16,199, or about 23 per cent.

"Since our establishment we have furnished 10,000 boys with permanent homes and employment. It will be seen that we have thus placed in situations ten per cent of all boys coming under our care."

The Girls' Lodging House, 27 St. Mark's Place.

This establishment, which has been in operation for thirteen years, was visited October 6, and found to be under the immediate charge of Mrs. E. S. Harley, matron. The institution embraces a lodging house for girls, a training department for domestic servants, a sewing machine school and a dressmaking department. The following information, relative to its inmates and workings, was furnished by the matron:

"We take girls between the ages of nine and twenty-five years. We do not take them any younger than we can get situations for; but if a child is given up to us, we will take it at any age. We get homes for the children who come to us. We do not keep them here. We sent eighty-eight to situations last month and eighty-seven this month. They went mostly to the neighboring country. About nine or ten of these went West. I was just answering a letter from one of the girls who went out West with the last company as you came. I have never had but one sent back. I have been in the work for twenty years. We do not take married women or widows. The rule of the house is 'under eighteen,' but I cannot keep strictly to that rule, so many girls come in who say they are eighteen when I know they are over that. They need shelter just as much as the others. If they behave well we keep them. If they want to go out at night and won't obey the rules, why we won't allow them to remain. In our dressmaking department we give the girls instruction free of charge for six months. We then find places for them. They have all done remarkably well. The children under my care I place out myself. We have constant applications here for girls. It is very seldom that we have them placed under our care by parents.

"The object of the institution is to take charge of such as wish the shelter, and to guide, guard and keep them from going astray. I believe that it has saved a great many girls. On coming here I ask them some questions. I usually ask them, 'Have you any father or mother? Where did you stay last night?' I try to get their history as near as I can. A great many of them are girls out of situations. They pay six cents a night for lodging, six cents for their meals, or $1.50 for a week's board. Their supper is six cents, and dinner is six cents. If they have no money they come in, and we say, 'If you are willing to submit to the rules, and to work around the house till I can get a situation for you, you can stay.' The Society thinks it well to fix this nominal sum for the girls to pay. We have, I suppose, about eight or nine girls in the house who are working for their board. We teach sewing on the machine. We have twenty-four machines in the house. Outside girls who choose to come and learn to operate the sewing machine can do so. They pay nothing for that. They bring their own work. We give them the instruction free. We also teach housework. Some of our girls are in the kitchen learning to cook. Some are in the dormitories making beds and doing various kinds of work. We had thirty-two here last night. We had, for the three months previous, over one hundred. The last two months the number has been lower. About fifteen hundred were inmates of the house last year. A great many of them only stay a night. Since last November eight hundred and eighty-one girls have received instruction upon the sewing machine gratuitously.

Religious Instruction.—"We have services Sunday morning and evening through the winter. They are held from eleven to twelve in the morning, and from eight to nine in the evening. We have prayers every evening, with the reading of the scriptures. The girls go to bed early. They are all in bed at a quarter to nine o'clock. The girls stay a very little while, and we cannot look for any very great change; but I know some of them have improved wonderfully. They feel that there is somebody to take an interest in them."

An interesting feature of this house is the girls' sitting room. This is a pleasant apartment, illuminated with pictures of home life; it contains a piano for the evening entertainment of the inmates. It is also used during the religious services.

The dormitories are furnished with single iron bedsteads. They were very clean. Straw is used in the ticks. Each bed has a blanket and comfortable and white spread, and in winter two comfortables. White tidies were laid on the pillows, giving the beds a neat appearance. The straw in the ticks is changed in the spring and fall. The walls of the dormitories were nicely tinted.

One of the rooms of the house is for sewing classes. The Matron says: "Several ladies come here and teach the girls sewing. It is a separate department, and has been very successful."

The working force consists of the Matron, house-keeper, dress-maker and machine sewing teacher, each attending to her own department.

The dining room tables are covered with white cloths. Crockery ware, knives and forks are used. The girls get simple but nutritious food.

The house is heated by furnaces, and lighted with gas.

Some of the cases rescued by this institution, during the year, are thus described:

"A few weeks since a girl of sixteen came in, with a sad face and sweet voice; her story was, that she had a drunken mother and step-father, and after living a life of drudgery for months, with some one who failed to pay her for her labor, she went home to her mother, who took a trunk strap and beat her unmercifully, because she brought her no money. This woman can earn from $40 to $50 a month as cook, in hotels, but she spends every cent of it for drink."

"Another, a sewing-girl of nineteen, said she had had no employment for weeks, had begged something to eat after her money gave out, and slept wherever she felt safe, or sat under stoops all night, sometimes, rather than go to station-houses where there were so many dirty people. Had never heard of this place till a lady directed her here."

"Yesterday, a dear little bright-faced orphan girl of sixteen, in whom the whole household was interested, went to a good home in the country, who came to us a short time since, having been turned on the streets to look out for herself. The frequency with which mere children are thus treated is almost incredible. Not long since, three came here in one week. One was a gentle, little blue-eyed girl, who had been forsaken by her mother when only six months old, but had been well taken care of for several years by a kind woman, who afterwards died. She then went to live with a family who beat and abused her, and at last turned her out, when she wandered about the streets till taken by some children into an industrial school, from which the teachers sent her here. . Another of thirteen, came of her own accord. The person with whom she had been living, not requiring her services any longer, sent her heartlessly into the street. This was a very interesting girl, and the lady who has adopted her, writes that she is very proud of her little daughter."

"The third girl was older than the other two, being nearly fifteen, and her story, told in an artless manner, with many tears and convulsive sobs, impressed us as the saddest of its kind we had ever heard. She was a German orphan girl, of respectable parentage, had been living at service, and had committed some trifling fault, for which she was sent away. For three successive days and nights, till a late hour, she had the *streets for a home,* wandering up and down, accosted often by bad men and women, from whom she would run, and when too frightened to stay out any longer, would take shelter in the station-house, from which she was sent here. This girl had been in one of our industrial schools for some time, and showed the value of good influence upon her. We found her perfectly innocent and inoffensive, and she was sent to a comfortable home in the west."

The statistics of the Girls' Lodging House, for year ending November 1, 1875, are:

Number of lodgers	1,327
Number of lodgings furnished	11,703
Number of lodgings paid for	5,044
Number of meals provided	27,542
Number of meals paid for	10,097
Number of girls sent to situations	807
Number of girls found employment	42
Number of girls sent to friends	51
Number of girls sent to other institutions	46
Number of girls sent West	46
Number of girls sent to hospital	18
Number of girls sent to Europe	5
Number of girls learning to operate sewing machines	939
Number of girls found employment on sewing machines	589

Expenses, less construction account	$5,127 47
Less receipts from inmates	2,206 89
Actual expenses for the year	$2,920 58

The Rivington Street Lodging House.

While all the Lodging Houses of the Children's Aid Society have a characteristic attraction for the visitor by reason of the work which they are doing for the well-being of children, and by reason of their being the depositories of many interesting biographies, this feature of the Rivington street house is concealed under the mantle of the gentler aspects of the charity found in its flower mission.

The Lodging House occupies numbers 325 and 327 Rivington street, near the East river. The first floor is taken up with both dining-room and school-room. Arrangements are adequate to seating fifty-eight at the dining tables. The apartment communicates by a side door with the Superintendent's house and the kitchen department, where hot meals are prepared for the children. The dormitories are on the third and fourth floors, and are furnished with iron bedsteads, arranged in double tiers, and well supplied with comfortable and clean bedding. On the second floor are bath-rooms supplied with hot and cold water, and also a gymnasium. Of this feature the Superintendent, Mr. George Calder, says: "For this valuable auxiliary to the Lodging House we are indebted to Mrs. Wm. E. Dodge, Jr., who not only furnished a complete set of gymnastic apparatus, but with characteristic generosity defrayed the expenses of a gymnasium building. It was opened in August last, is a great success, is exceedingly popular, and has done more than any thing else to attract our boys from the evil associations of the street at night."

Connected with the Lodging House is a dispensary department containing a medicine case well supplied with medicine for sick children, in reference to which, and the work connected therewith, the Superintendent says: "During the past year we have relieved, in one way or another, from the Sick Children's Fund, nine hundred and thirty-six different families, containing two thousand three hundred and eighteen children. The aggregate number of visits made by our physicians to the homes of sick children or their parents, is thirteen hundred and fifty-seven, while nine hundred and fifty additional cases were treated at the doctors' offices, the latter mostly gratuitously, excepting in surgical and other cases occupying considerable time. We have paid the entire funeral expenses of eleven children, and assisted in that of fifteen others."

The most attractive part of the house is the second floor. Here is a large school-room, where at night a school is held, taught by three lady teachers, of whom Miss Anna Johnson is principal. In regard to the school the Superintendent states: "The street boy's education has been sadly neglected. Many of them have been obliged to 'paddle their own canoe,' as they say, from the time they were able to gather a few cents worth of junk, or pick up a pail of coal upon the street, and so they have had no opportunity to acquire an education, excepting at the night schools of our Lodging Houses. It is a rule with us that every boy must attend night school unless he is legitimately employed elsewhere, and to satisfy us on that point we require certificates from their employers. The principal school-room, in addition to the usual school-room furniture, contains several other features of interest. There is a large library of reading matter, the character of the books comprising which may be inferred from a remark made by one of the older boys, who said, with some show of satisfaction:

"They are books you can read; none of your dry stuff." A refreshing sight in this room is a good-sized aquarium, supplied with marine plants, among which large gold fish were lazily disporting. The glassy surface of the water was shattered into tiny dimples by the falling spray from a little fountain. From this room a glimpse of the conservatory, into which it opens by a wide doorway, is obtained. The camelias, tropical and other plants which it contained, could not only be seen from the school-room, but the odorous blossoms permeated it with a delicate perfume. The young man in charge stated that the conservatory had been added to the lodging-house by Mr. Howard Potter. Connected with the conservatory is a propagating department, in which slips are propagated, and little plants potted and given to the children of the schools to take to their homes. This department includes a little garden, in which the slips are grown after being started in the hot-bed. These slips of fragrant geraniums, etc., are given as rewards among the children of the industrial schools, and are taken by them to their homes. Bouquets of flowers are also sent from the conservatory to brighten the homes of the poor, and to the bedsides of the sick. The Superintendent says: "Nowhere does a flower look more beautiful than in the hands of a poor sick child." When the squalid poverty that invests the homes of many of these children is considered, and the depressing influence of nearly every object that surrounds them, the advent of one of these little plants from the Flower Mission is not unlikely to be regarded as a type of something purer and better, the incentive to reach which may then for the first time find lodgment in the soul.

Religious services for the boys are held on Sundays, regarding which the Superintendent remarks: "The street boys, as a rule, do not attend a regular place of worship, and these Sunday evening meetings afford the only opportunity they have of acquiring an elementary knowledge of religious truth. The large attendance and deep interest always manifested by our boys in these simple services are very remarkable, and refute the common notion that they are either averse to religion or disposed to ridicule it. The meetings are held from November until May, and are conducted alternately by Mr. Howard Potter and Mr. Henry E. Hawley. These gentlemen have long been friends of this lodging-house, and have taken a deep interest in the welfare of the boys, and their faithful counsels have led many a poor waif to pursue a higher course of life."

Like the other Lodging Houses, this has also a savings bank. It is stated by the authority last named "that the boys of this Lodging House have always been liberal patrons of the 'savings bank.' It is amusing, as well as interesting, to see the pompous and self-important air with which some of these boys drop their pennies in the 'bank.' Some of them save only thirty or forty cents a month, and yet this, with the interest, is sufficient to buy them a pair of second-hand shoes in Baxter street. Others will save several dollars, with which they generally purchase clothing or 'stock.'

"During the past year we have had two hundred and eighty-five depositors, whose aggregate savings amount to $771.29."

The following, selected from the Superintendent's report, will further elucidate the work:

"When a poor boy enters the Rivington Street Lodging House he discovers — it may be for the first time in his life — that in this great busy city there is some one who takes an interest in *him*. In every appointment of the house he recognizes a provision for his especial benefit. He is confronted with a code of 'rules,' the observance of which completely upsets his old habits and introduces him to a higher social life. As he takes his seat in the reception room, his eye is arrested by such mottoes as the following: 'Shall there be a God to swear by and none to pray to?' 'Boys who are in trouble, or in want of homes and employment, will find the Superintendent willing to help them.' 'The wise boys put their pennies in the savings bank, and get five per cent a month interest.' And again: 'A boy's best friend is a good education; come regularly to evening school.' The first of these mottoes, in the form of an illuminated scroll, was placed over an archway at the suggestion and expense of our excellent friend, Mr. Howard Potter. It is in the front of the room, where every boy can see it, and its silent influence has done much to check the habit of swearing, so common among the street boys."

The following statistical information is derived from the same source:

Ages.

Aged 6	2
Aged 7	15
Aged 8	31
Aged 9	40
Aged 10	50
Aged 11	92
Aged 12	99
Aged 13	153
Aged 14	220
Aged 15	242
Aged 16	320
Aged 17	160
Aged 18	79
Total number of boys provided for during the year	1,503

Nativity.

Born in United States	1,225
Born in Ireland	97
Born in Germany	66
Born in England	57
Born in Scotland	17
Born in Canada	14
Born in Italy	12
Born in France	7
Born in Austria	3
Born in India	2
Born at sea	2
Unknown	1
Total	1,503

Parentage.

Number of orphans	1,182
Number of half-orphans	219
Number with parents living	102
Total	1,503

Education.

Number able to read and write	1,184
Number able to read only	193
Number unable to read or write	126
Total	1,503

Occupations.

Newsboys	209
Bootblacks	174
Peddlers	92
Errand boys	80
Cigarmakers	66
Laborers	49
Printers	41
Canal boys	37
Wood bundlers	30
Baggage smashers	29
Cart drivers	25
Boxmakers	25
Bookbinders	25
Oyster openers	24

Book folders	22
Bowling alleys	22
Sailors	21
Waiters	20
Tinsmiths	19
Brass finishers	18
Tailors	18
Brushmakers	18
Clerks	18
Coal pickers	16
Bakers	16
Barbers	15
Actors	15
Bell boys	15
Telegraph messengers	14
Paper collars	14
Wire workers	14
Butchers	13
Oyster saloons	13
Hoisting-horses	13
Foundry boys	13
Bill distributors	13
Hatters	12
Heating rivets	12
Varnishers	11
Soapmakers	11
Bill posters	11
Masons	11
Umbrellas	10
Coopers	10
Machinists	10
Type breakers	10
Cooks	10
Other occupations	80
No occupation	39
Total	1,503

It will, of course, be understood that the majority of these boys are *learning* the trades placed opposite their numbers.

Number of boys provided with permanent homes in the West	104
Number of boys provided with homes and employment in the city and suburbs	78

Number of boys restored to friends	63
Amount saved during the year by 285 depositors in the Savings Bank of the Lodging House	$771 29
Average attendance at night school........	70
Average number of nightly lodgers	95

Lodgings and Meals.

Total number of lodgings furnished..................	34,753
Total number of lodgings paid	31,485
Total number of lodgings, free	3,268
Total number of meals furnished	56,903
Total number of meals paid..........................	52,370
Total number of meals, free	4,533

Expenses and Receipts.

Total expense	$10,003 12
Deduct improvements and repairs....................	1,052 82
Net expenses of Institution	$8,950 30
Deduct receipts for lodgings, meals, rents, etc.........	4,125 12
Net cost, including partial rent, but not interest on capital	$4,825 18

This Lodging House has been in operation for eight years. It commenced with five lodgers. It now averages ninety-five nightly. During the past year it has provided for fifteen hundred and three boys.

We have gone at some length into details, regarding this establishment, because of its possessing some peculiar features, and because it is a good illustration of not only what is aimed at, but what is being actually accomplished by the benevolent workers in this field. The Lodging House is located in one of the most wretched quarters of the city, where the door-ways of its dwellings are haunted by the gaunt figures of want and disease. This house, kept with scrupulous cleanliness and order, with its sweet air and all its pleasant accessories of flowers and books, stands ever open to the neglected, wayward or unfortunate. Its elevated moral teachings and educational advantages must inspire many a forlorn little being, permitted to enjoy its privileges, with high aspirations and manly hopes.

In regard to the Lodging House branch of the work of the Children's Aid Society, the following table, from the Secretary's last report, will be found interesting:

Tabular Statement since organization.

YEAR.	Number of boys.	Number of lodgings.	Number of meals.	Returned to friends.	Expenses.	Paid by boys.	Number of boys using bank.	Amount saved by them.
1854 to 1855	408	6,872	......	......	$1,199 76	$397 56	......	....
1855 to 1856	374	7,599	......	......	1,431 82	391 26	16	$643 58
1856 to 1857	387	5,157	......	......	1,762 56	262 56	116	270 70
1857 to 1858	800	8,026	11,923	......	1,925 03	298 03	......	....
1858 to 1859	3,000	14,000	13,114	......	2,199 34	807 15	......	....
1859 to 1860	4,500	19,747	13,341	100	2,113 56	955 44	23	110 10
1860 to 1861	4,000	27,390	16,873	247	3,420 57	1,036 98	230	1,259 77
1861 to 1862	3,875	32,954	19,809	......	2,736 08	1,138 88	388	1,376 59
1862 to 1863	3,000	29,409	20,000	396	3,402 82	1,102 33	347	1,315 10
1863 to 1864	6,325	36,572	25,506	437	5,758 16	1,559 10	405	2,080 06
1864 to 1865	6,793	42,446	30,137	576	7,159 95	1,944 22	499	2,505 92
1865 to 1866	7,256	43,797	32,867	633	10,058 13	2,127 44	599	2,486 43
1866 to 1867	8,192	49,519	33,633	719	10,847 79	2,718 79	542	2,121 76
1867 to 1868	8,599	51,740	35,617	819	12,094 00	3,177 69	703	2,203 45
1868 to 1869	8,944	53,610	54,092	896	23,333 45	3,644 49	796	2,057 76
1869 9 months	7,383	39,077	33,207	642	13,445 24	3,180 85	659	1,688 22
1869 to 1870	8,655	55,565	56,128	713	15,102 11	4,214 42	1,107	2,433 60
1870 to 1871	8,835	53,005	53,214	1,100	14,898 03	3,349 77	1,065	2,588 31
1871 to 1872	8,757	57,661	57,740	723	15,479 65	4,313 93	1,029	2,644 43
1872 to 1873	7,568	57,719	58,202	635	16,085 28	4,382 79	1,235	2,406 49
1873 to 1874	8,913	70,681	72,567	912	16,470 61	6,167 53	1,272	3,330 86
1874 to 1875	9,286	86,880	91,253	973	20,640 06	8,105 64	1,311	3,206 15
Total	125,850	849,426	729,223	10,521	$201,564 00	$55,276 85	12,342	$36,729 28

The Society at present maintains the following industrial schools:

Name and location.	No. on rolls.	Average att'nd'ce.
Cottage Place School, 204 Bleecker street	466	149
East River School, 206 East Fortieth street	517	225
Hudson River School, 350 West Twenty-seventh street.	247	138
Avenue B School, 607 East Fourteenth street	227	105
German School, 272 Second street	536	185
Italian School, 156 Leonard street	825	342
Lord School, 135 Greenwich street	440	100
Fifty-third Street School, 340 West Fifty-third street.	705	313
Park School, Sixty-eighth street, near Broadway	905	304
Fifty-second Street School, Fifty-second street, near Eleventh avenue	625	230
Lincoln School, 314 East Thirty-fifth street	271	88
Newsboys' Night School, 9 Duane street	368	94
Girls' Industrial School, 120 West Sixteenth street	294	93
Fourth Ward School, 52 Market street	479	88
Fifth Ward School, 186 Franklin street	413	93
Avenue C School, 304 East Fourth street	578	186
Eleventh Ward School, 709 East Eleventh street	834	240
Thirteenth Ward School, 327 Rivington street	516	196
Fourteenth Ward School, 93 Crosby street	631	218
Sixteenth Ward School, 211 West Eighteenth street	384	127
Water Street School, 14 Dover street	96	45
Total this year	10,357	3,559
Last year	10,288	3,556
Increase this year	69	3

The cost of maintaining the schools of the society for last year was as follows, viz.:

Rent of rooms	$12,032 26
Salaries of superintendent and eighty-three teachers	41,046 01
Food, clothing, fuel, etc	23,634 75
Expense on account of thirteen evening schools	3,688 72
Total	$80,401 74

Several of these schools were visited, and the following notes taken

The Hudson River Industrial School

Is under the charge of Miss L. Noble, an efficient lady, who has been thirteen years a teacher, and ten years devoted to this work, in which she is evidently deeply interested. The school is divided into three departments, infant, middle and graduating classes. The rooms were furnished with large patent benches and abundance of black-boards.

The attendance on the day of visitation, October 7th, was one hundred and ten, which was considered small. The largest daily attendance during the past year was said to be one hundred and forty-five. The ages of the children range from three years up to seventeen. In regard to the school and its workings, Miss Noble gave us the following information:

"The children go from us into the grammar department of the Public Schools. They stay with us on the average about two years. Their attendance is irregular. They stay two weeks and are gone two weeks. When they are not working, our old scholars come back to us. I try to teach them as much in a small space of time as possible, and slide the different grades of the school into one. I have four grades. I cannot classify them properly. My grade runs from about the fourth to the first. I have a grammar class, a class in fractions, a class that have gone through geography, and then a class that are beginning it. I use the object system of teaching. The usual routine is to call the children to order, sing one or two hymns, read a lesson from the Bible, and then the children recite the Lord's Prayer. This forms our opening exercises. Then we proceed with the work of the day. We have arithmetic classes, reading classes, spelling classes, both written and oral, geography lessons, and three times a week we have composition and letter writing. In the afternoon the sewing teacher takes a class. The infant class take lessons in sewing every afternoon except Friday. The larger children sew every other day. They make all their own clothing. In this way we clothe the children. The effect of this is to make them capable women. The secret of so much poverty is that the mothers have never been taught to work. Mothers do not know how to sew. We are obliged to make even the jackets that we give them!

"By observation and strictness we keep the children clean. Every morning I examine the condition of their faces and hands, and once a month I examine their heads. We have a washing room down stairs. We did have a bathing room, but found it rather detrimental to us. My class and the second class are very proud of their appearance. If a boy is particularly clean I call the attention of the other boys to it. A great deal of public spirit may be created in a school if you begin right. You can put a great deal of public spirit into your school if you let the children think that they can do right. I have boys that swear fearfully down town, but they are very careful not to use any profane language before me. We have very little fighting to trouble us. We have found that a very difficult matter to overcome, but now we get along very nicely. Every Friday afternoon the teachers report to me children who have come to school every day during the week with clean hands. The children come from some of the most filthy homes, and we reach mothers through the children. The janitress teaches them how to sweep floors and scrub. She goes along with them and tells them the reason why every thing should be done in a particular manner.

"We give a warm dinner every day to the children. This is a donation from a wealthy lady, the late Mrs. James J. Jones. It is a life memorial for that purpose. She died a year ago last August. She has provided this dinner for the children for eight years. She was in the habit of coming in here every week to see the children, and, if any of them did not look just right, she used to tell me to get a pair of shoes, a garment, or something else, for the child.

"We have a Board of Lady Managers connected with the school who take a great deal of interest in it. Many of them belong to wealthy families. We don't give out clothes very promiscuously. The children must earn them. We found when we pursued that plan that the children go to another school a week and get clothes, and then come to us, get the same here, stay awhile, and go away again.

"We keep Christmas by having a Christmas tree and a good dinner. We also give a good dinner at Thanksgiving. In summer we have an ice cream festival."

The school contains a good circulating library. This was begun by Mrs. Jones, who gave to it the first contribution of books, consisting of one hundred volumes. It is called Mrs. Jones' library, out of compliment to that lamented lady.

Miss Noble, in speaking on the point of visiting her scholars, said: "My children follow me more than I follow them. They meet me in the streets and speak to me, or say something that I have taught them before."

Our visit was entirely unlooked for, but the working of the school was most gratifying. The teacher seemed to possess the respect, as well as the affection, of the whole school, and the influence of her cheerful disposition seemed to brighten the faces of the children like a stream of sunshine.

The Italian School

Is under the charge of the Children's Aid Society and an Italian sub-committee, composed of Mrs. E. P. Fabbri, Prof. V. Botta, Messrs. G. Albinola, E. G. Fabbri and O. Fabbricotti.

The following is a brief sketch of its history as furnished by the Secretary of the Children's Aid Society: "Twenty years ago large numbers of poor Italian children, engaged as street musicians, newsboys, boot-blacks and the like, were found to be growing up utterly without education or moral discipline. They were either the children of those who were driven from Italy during the revolution of 1848 and 1849, or of poor people who came hither to better their condition. They were packed and crowded in tenement houses in the neighborhood of the Five Points. In a small upper room would be found frequently several families, men, women, children, dogs and monkeys, all crowded together, and the place filled with an almost unbearable odor. In the midst of all this confusion and dirt the women might often be seen rolling the agreeable preparation of maccaroni for their families. The Italians seemed at that time the dirtiest population in the city, and the children the most unbefriended. The experiment of an industrial and common school, entirely devoted to their interests, was tried for their improvement in 1855, and placed under the charge of Signor A. E. Cerqua, an Italian gentleman who was then an exile from Italy for political reasons, but who has since been made 'Chevalier of the Order of the Crown.'

"The greatest difficulties to be overcome were the greed of the parents to get all possible earnings from their children, without regard to their education, and the existence among them of a species of serfdom, whereby a child in Italy could be apprenticed to an association and sent by it roaming over the world with some hard and cruel master. This 'padroni' business was the means of degrading a great number of little children every year.

"But this, through the efforts of the Children's Aid Society and the assistance of the Italian Consul-General Chevalier De Luca, has been broken up by act of the Italian Parliament and similar acts passed in this country.

"Mr. Cerqua opened his school with an attendance of only thirty, in a room kindly furnished gratuitously by the Rev. Mr. Pease, of the Five Points Mission. In this room, and others generously loaned in the locality, the school continued its patient efforts at reform and education during a number of years. But few of the children had any knowledge at first of English. They acquired the language, however, with reasonable readiness, and since that time, under the methods of phonetic instruction introduced by the Society, they have learned English with remarkable rapidity. The study, however, in which Italian children are most successful is arithmetic. As year by year passed by, the school, under the constant exertions of Mr. Cerqua, began gradually to attain greater size and solidity. The prejudices of the bigoted were overcome, the ignorant began to see the advantages of learning, and the Italian population gradually felt that the school belonged to them and was designed for their benefit. Nothing, however, could have sustained it through many depressions of business, if the American public had not come forward generously with their subscriptions, and carried it on during the various panics and the civil war. The children soon began to show the natural mental improvement which would result from such faithful instruction. When the school was opened, only two in the whole colony had any knowledge of writing, and these two had to perform all the writing and reading of English or Italian letters for their more ignorant compatriots, receiving, in each instance, from 25 to 50 cents for the service. Now, out of the thousands of children who have been in the school, only the youngest are unable to write, while the copy-books of the school show as good work as those of any industrial school of the Children's Aid Society, and the graduates of the school, both young men and women, can write as correct and business-like letters as any of their class in the city.

"In 1864, Mr. Fabbri conceived the idea of forming a building fund for this school, opening it with $95. This sum he gradually increased by his own liberal donations and those of his friends. Subsequently he became Trustee of the Children's Aid Society, and a considerable addition to the fund was made by the friends of that Society. When, at length, the amount had reached the sum of $22,000, Mr. Fabbri consented to purchase lots and to erect a suitable building with this money, provided the Society would take upon itself the balance of the expense, to an amount not exceeding $30,000."

The new building was opened and occupied on April 27, 1875. Our first visitation was made October 12. The house is a four-story structure in highly ornamental style of architecture. The first story is of free stone, the remainder of brick. The interior finish of the building is substantial and elaborate. The rails of the balustrades are of carved oak.

Evening school is held on the premises from four to six and from seven to nine o'clock, and during the winter the attendance is between three and four hundred.

The house contains a nicely furnished reading room, with a library and newspapers. This contained the portraits of a son of the king of Italy, and of "Margarita de Savoja," which were presented to the institution by the Italian consul. It also contained a painting of George Washington.

The school is still under the superintendence of Mr. A. E. Cerqua, who teaches English to a class of adults. The principal of the school is Mrs. E. T. Alleyn. She is assisted by three other ladies.

The first floor of the house contains several class-rooms and the reading room. The school-rooms were brightened with mottoes in excellent taste. The furniture and accessories of the house are in keeping with modern improvements. The second floor is a counterpart of the first, and contains the music room. This room, as we were informed, was furnished by the Society. The young men who wish to learn music pay for their teacher. They study here and become accomplished enough to make music a source of living. One little company of them, instead of spending their leisure time in the evenings in drinking shops and gambling saloons, have devoted themselves to the scientific study of music, and under the instruction of Prof. Conterno, have formed a competent band of musicians.

On the third floor is the class room for the little ones, also a large assembly room, with an organ, where festivals are held. The walls and ceilings are tinted, producing a pleasing effect. On this floor is also a sewing room for girls, with two sewing machines. The children, we were informed, are supplied with clothes and presents on Christmas.

In the basement are the washing apartments for both girls and boys, several bathing tubs and a large washing room, with combs, towels and soap. Our first visit was made by daylight, and the house was then empty. We could only note its excellent appointments and the neat condition in which every thing was kept. On October 25th we visited it at night.

Descending into the comfortable bath-room, we found in one room four boys busy combing their hair after bathing; and, peeping into the bath rooms, we found six boys luxuriating in the water, two being in each tub. On the other side of the hall we were informed, the girls were bathing and washing under the charge of a lady. About one-fifth of the scholars are sent down to bathe at one time, and when these are through, others take their places, and so on till all get a bath. These children had been out during the day working in various ways for a livelihood.

We found about three hundred pupils in the school, in addition to a class of about thirty-five adults who came to learn English.

The first or primary class of the children are taught by Leigh's phonetic system. They learn numeration only to hundreds and the addition tables. There were boys between fifteen and sixteen years old in this class. It contained thirty-two girls and forty boys.

In the second class the children combine sounds, begin with primary lessons in writing and learn numeration to thousands, the addition table and multiplication table.

The third class use the first and second readers, and learn numeration to millions.

The fourth class use the second and third readers, and study geography and writing. The principal informed us that formerly two-thirds of the school were girls, but now it is the reverse.

An attempt is made to teach industries. The principal says: "During the afternoon there is a session from four to six, when we teach a sewing-machine class. We have only two sewing machines, but I wish we had twenty-two."

In regard to the character of the children, she remarks: "The children are very tractable. Their parents as a class never drink. I have visited among them and never found one drunk. They live in horrid places. The homes are wretched in the extreme; but those who are every day working keep their homes very nice."

In the school-room we noticed ten mottoes worked on perforated board. These were all neatly done, and were, we were informed, the work of the girls.

The teacher said: "It is impossible to imagine the amount of good that is done by these schools. As a class, the children who attend cannot go to the public schools, because of their inability to be present, perhaps, more than three days in the week, and many of them are too poor to dress to go at all. A great many, even if they went, could not stay all day."

The success of the enterprise has been so great in reforming the class for whom it was intended, that it is said that "so far as is known, out of the children numbering about five thousand who have been in the school, hardly three individuals have ever been arrested, and not one, so far as is known, for stealing."

The Cottage Place School

Was visited October 12, at which date it enrolled one hundred and eighty scholars, both sexes being admitted. It occupied three rooms on the second floor of the house, each room having a separate class.

The children receive a common school education, and are provided with a meal during the day. In addition to the day school, there is a reading room opened every night at eight o'clock. The school possesses a piano and a library.

This neighborhood is one of great wretchedness, and the boys, as might be expected, are of the worst kind. The following fully describes the situation:

"Most of our boys, this winter, have been truly hard cases, rough materials, daily exposed to most corrupting examples, and we have had many anxious fears about them; some days the teacher has been so tried and discouraged that she felt she could not labor with them longer; then would come the suggestion that they were the proper subjects for our care and sympathy."

The Children's Fold.

New York.

This institution was organized in 1867, and grew out of the personal ministry of the Rev. Edward Cowley, its President. Its object is to support and educate those children who are found by means of the Episcopal mission, especially at Blackwell's, Ward's and Randall's islands. The children of sick emigrants, just landed upon our shores, are alike received. Children were at first boarded with different parties in the city. In May, 1867, limited apartments for their care were hired, and they were brought together and supported mainly by a ladies' association, attached to the institution. This association bore the burden of supporting fourteen children, defraying the expenses of rent, fuel, lights, servants' wages, food, clothing and undertaking the personal supervision and the whole responsibility of the Home till 1871, when the Society became incorporated and a Board of Trustees was formed. The Home, in February, 1869, was removed to 1119 Second avenue, and on the 1st of May, 1871, it was again removed to 437 East Fifty-eighth street, and, in 1875, it changed its location once more, for its present commodious apartments on 157 East Sixtieth street. The Fold is governed by a Board of Trustees, of whom Rev. Edward Cowley is President, and the Right Rev. Horatio Potter, D. D., LL. D., is Visitor.

The number of inmates at the date of visitation, October 9, was fifty-three, the sexes being about equally divided. The house was under the charge of Rev. Mr. Cowley, assisted by his wife. It bore evidence of being well kept, and being under the immediate eye of a Christian lady, it partook largely of the informal character of a well-ordered home. The dormitories were well furnished, and the house appeared to possess all needed accessories for the preservation of health, while the children's appearance was a sufficient evidence of good cheer. We are indebted to Mrs. Cowley for the following information, relative to the aims and workings of the Fold:

"Its benefactions are confined to no particular church, orphans, half-orphans and destitute children generally being admitted. Boys are not received over nine years old nor under three. The children are supplied from various sources. Three of those at present in the house belong to a woman whose husband deserted her. One of the girls is an orphan whose father was employed in the American Express Company, but died, leaving no provision for his family. Our children often come from families who have suffered a great deal before letting their wants be known. A family of children was brought here some time ago by the mother, whose husband was unkind to her. Some of our children have both parents living, and are worse off than if they had no parents. We take children for a longer or shorter time. We give them a good religious education. We have morning and evening prayers. Every Saturday is devoted to preparing for Sunday. All the children know their catechism. They learn the collect for every Sunday in the year. They have good secular instruction as well. The oldest children attend the public schools. The children measure themselves by other children. Fourteen of the children were on the roll of honor in the public schools last week. They have to be extra good to get there. They learn their lessons at home in the evening, and recite them before going to the public school. If they are not old enough to bring their books home with them, I make them learn tables or spell. The children are taught music every week. We have a teacher who comes from New Jersey."

The children sang for us very sweetly, "Glory to Thee who safe has kept," and repeated in a manner showing perfect familiarity with it, the Duty Toward Your Neighbor, in the catechism of the Protestant Episcopal Church.

In answer to inquiries about the industrial feature of the house, Mrs. Cowley said: "That is *the* feature. The children do the work of the house; they know how to make up rooms, to sweep and dust. It is the ambition of the youngest ones to be able to wash. As they get old enough they learn to wash, cook and sew. They learn to set table properly, and are able to set a table in any respectable family. We do not bake our own bread, because we have not got the conveniences for that, but they can make muffins, gingerbread, etc. Every Saturday during the winter the girls have a sewing class. The older ones make their own clothes, and are taught to use the sewing machine." In regard to placing out children Mrs. Cowley says: "If the girls are surrendered to us, we keep them till they are able to take care of themselves. Boys are put out at an early age."

The average age of the children in the Fold on the day of visitation was about eight years.

This institution, though small, appears to be doing a very thorough and satisfactory work. Its strong characteristic is that of a family home, with a lady and gentleman of refinement at its head. While its industrial feature is marked, moral and religious principles are faithfully inculcated.

The bringing of such influences to bear on destitute children must be regarded as the highest kind of benevolence, and the good people conducting the Fold are certainly deserving of the thanks of the public for their devotion to the children's cause. No financial statement or other statistics relating to its work the past year, has been furnished.

The Five Points House of Industry.

New York.

The character of the field in which this work is carried on is so well known as to scarcely need a repetition here. Its population at one time was made up mainly of the most wicked and abandoned of the people. Prostitution and intemperance were fearfully prevalent, and dens of thieves were on every hand. The spot well deserved its notoriety. The Rev. Lewis M. Pease commenced laboring here about 1850 as a missionary, and the Five Points House of Industry originated from his labors. For the first two or three years Mr. Pease carried on the mission alone, after which he resigned its direction to a body of corporators consisting of thirty gentlemen. From this Board nine Trustees were elected. The Rev. Mr. Pease was the first Superintendent, and remained in that office till 1858.

The Five Points House of Industry is devoted mainly to the preservation of children from suffering and crime. They are received, cleansed, clothed, fed, taught, and furnished with labor as early as practicable, or sent to a home in the country. Assistance is also rendered to adults, as far as it can be done without encouraging a dependence upon charity, and efforts are made to reform and procure employment for such as are willing to labor.

The inmates on the day of visitation, October 4th, numbered two hundred and ninety-three. Of these one hundred and forty-nine were boys, one hundred and six girls, and thirty-eight women. The day school for that day had three hundred and forty children in attendance. This included both children residing in the house and those from outside. From the Superintendent, Mr. Wm. F. Barnard, the following information was obtained regarding the scope of the charity: "Three classes are kept in the house.

"1st. Those who are given to us by their parents, or others who have the right to commit.

"2d. Children whose parents are unable to provide for them for the present. It very frequently happens that a mother may come to us with several children on her hands, where some misfortune has overtaken her. She is obliged to break up house for a time, hoping in a few weeks to be able to provide for them herself. She asks us to take them in till she is able to care for them.

"3d. Boarders. These children come in this way: A mother or a father with children on their hands are not able to stay at home to take care of them. They must go out and earn their living. They cannot afford to pay for their board in families. We take them and charge according to their ability to pay.

"The ages of the children vary from two and a half up to fourteen years. We receive none before they are weaned. The average age of those given up to us is about six. The average age of the children in the house is eight. Those given up to us we keep here for a while. We do not dispose of them at first. We usually wait a few months to see if the child shows any special aptitude for one thing more than another. Then having ascertained what this is, if we possibly can we put the child where its talent will be developed. In regard to the other children, if we find their parents neglect them we procure places for them ourselves.

"The women in the house belong to a class who are addicted to drink. Perhaps some of them may be classed under the head of fallen women. They are homeless and friendless, and want employment. They are willing to come in here and do our work for their board, with the understanding that we find them employment. We thus open here a kind of intelligence office. They have nothing whatever to do with the children, and do not come in contact with them.

"The industrial education of the children is well attended to. The boys are instructed in sewing, type-setting and telegraphy. This latter is taught gratuitously by a lady.

In the shoe shop a man is employed to make and repair shoes. The Superintendent says: "He also teaches the boys to repair shoes. We depend for our supply on donations of second-hand shoes. They are repaired in the house by the boys and this man." These, after being repaired or remade, were said to be more durable than new shoes.

"The girls are taught sewing, and it is contemplated giving them lessons in cooking. This industrial training is taught systematically, and, yet, is not allowed to interfere with their regular school exercises.

"In placing children out, we do not bind them. Our present plan is to make the parties, taking children, sign a paper, agreeing to feed and clothe them, and provide for their religious and secular education, giving them an outfit and a sum of money when they become of age. We hear frequently from the children placed out. But we have no visiting committee."

The institution occupies two large brick buildings, one of them comparatively new, in which are located the school rooms, children's dormitory and play-room and the nursery, while in the other are the apartments for the women, the hospital, dining room, etc.

The dormitories were clean, furnished with iron bedsteads and straw beds. No pillows are used. The bed clothing was abundant. The rooms are ventilated by wall flues. The nursery is furnished with iron cribs.

The sewing room is about twenty-five by forty, and at the time of visitation contained about thirty little girls busily plying their needles and thread. At the end of this room were little play-houses fitted up in the shape of booths, with tapestry curtain entrances, full of toys. While visiting this room the little girls sang "Never alone is the Christian." The room contained four sewing machines.

The school room occupies the whole of one of the floors of the new building, and is divided by glass sliding doors to form class rooms for the separate grades. The room is furnished with patent desks and other suitable appliances for school purposes. It also contains a piano.

The bath-room is provided with a large tub about twelve feet by two and a half. The children wash in running water. The towels were found to be on rollers, and were said to be changed every day.

In the dining room the children stand at meals. Both crockery and tinware are used, also knives and forks.

There were forty-seven inmates of the hospital on the day of visitation, only eleven of whom were confined to their beds. Seven had typhoid fever. Most of the diseases are of a scrofulous character. The hospital is kept clean, its walls are brightened with illuminated cards, and unlike the children's dormitories, its beds are provided with pillows.

The buildings are heated by stoves and furnaces, lighted with gas, and supplied with water from the city. Careful provision is made in the event of fire. On the several floors are fire extinguishers, and a fire-proof stair-case communicates with each story of the building.

The prevalence of typhoid fever in this institution naturally leads to the question of its ventilation, and the examination of this feature in the construction of this building is believed to be a subject worthy the consideration of the benevolent supporters of this large charity. The play-yard, it was observed, is surrounded on three sides by the high walls of buildings, and on the fourth is also partially inclosed. Thus it would seem that the foul gases accumulating have no means of escape, but remain in the inclosure as at the bottom of a well. It may be found that there is an insufficient current of pure air circulating in the play-yard, or possibly lack of sun exposure to insure health. The yard, on the day of visitation, contained a large number of children, and seemed to be too contracted.

The institution possesses a spacious chapel, where religious services are regularly held, and where an effort is made to christianize and elevate the degraded mass around its doors. The work being done by the House of Industry is very extended, and requires a liberal support to meet its daily needs. Since its organization nearly twenty thousand persons have been relieved through its instrumentality, and seven hundred and ninety-four were admitted during the past year. The number of orphan children in the institution October 1, 1875, was seven, the number of half-orphans seventy-three, and the number having both parents living, one hundred and seventy-one. The nativity of the parents could not be ascertained. They were, it was stated, "mostly all foreign." Sixty-six were partially supported by friends, and one hundred and eighty-five wholly by the institution. During the year fourteen children were adopted, two hundred and seventy-six were returned to parents or guardians, and fourteen died.

The invested funds of the Society amount to $52,000. Its total indebtedness is $48,573.09. Its expenditures during the fiscal year ending September 30, 1875, were $69,608.33, of which about $35,000 was paid to liquidate indebtedness.

The Foundling Asylum of the Sisters of Charity in the City of New York,

New York,

Is situated on Sixty-eighth street, between Third and Lexington avenues. The building, of brick and stone, is imposing in appearance and intended to embody in its construction all the latest improvements. "In the center of the lot, and facing on Sixty-eighth street, is the administrative building, ninety-nine feet wide by sixty feet deep, and five stories high, exclusive of the basement. In the basement of this building are the kitchen for the community, dining rooms and offices. The main story contains the chief offices, reception rooms and parlors for visitors, the community room, and an apartment for the resident physician. In the second story are the apartments for the Sisters, and the sewing and linen rooms; the third, fourth and fifth stories will contain dormitories, and the upper floor an infirmary.

"On each side of the main building, and parallel therewith, will be the ward buildings, with large pavilions at each end, making the total length of each one hundred and sixty-four feet. One of these buildings is now completed; it is three stories in height, exclusive of the basement. They are placed a sufficient distance apart from each other to allow an ample free circulation of air and a full play of the sun's rays around them; to aid which, the corridors connecting these several buildings with each other, above the basement story, consist of open arched passages extending but one story in height. The ward-rooms are each thirty by ninety feet. The south pavilion contains, on each story, one room for the Sister in charge of the adjoining ward, a linen store-room, two private rooms, and a closet and bath-room. The north pavilion likewise contains, on each story, a children's wash-room, a small kitchen, a room for steam drying of linen, and a closet and bath-room for nurses. In the basement story, under the ward buildings, are the offices for the physicians, dispensaries, waiting rooms, nurses' and sewing rooms, small kitchens, store-rooms and closets.

"The heights of the several stories, in the center and ward buildings, are as follows: Basement, ten feet six inches; first story, fifteen feet six inches; second story, fourteen feet six inches; third, fourth and fifth stories, fourteen feet high.

"At the center of the lot on Sixty-ninth street, there is a two-story building, thirty-one feet deep and ninety feet front, to be connected by corridors with the several ward buildings. In the first story are placed the laundry, a steam drying room, an ironry and a large kitchen for the general purposes of the establishment. In the basement cellar are an ice-vault, store-rooms, engineer's rooms and coal-bins. The west side of the second story of this building contains sleeping apartments for laundresses and servants, and the entire eastern side is devoted to the purposes of a quarantine. Thus this portion of the establishment is completely isolated from the children's wards. The mortuary receiving vault is in a portion of the cellar under the north end of the chapel building."

The buildings are heated by steam and lighted by gas. The institution is under the charge of the Roman Catholic Order of the Sisters of Charity of Mt. St. Vincent.

The primary object of the institution is to prevent infanticide. Those identified with the work assert that "there is no class of suffering humanity whose cry for help and life is so sad and touching as the foundling's. Scarcely has the unfortunate inhaled the vital air, unaware of all of life except its first necessities and sufferings, before its disposal becomes a grievous question with the attendants upon its birth."

The work was begun on Twelfth street, in a private dwelling-house, Oct. 11, 1869, the institution having been incorporated on the 9th of October of the same year. It is stated that "many and almost insuperable difficulties necessarily attended the beginning of such an undertaking; the wants to be supplied were numerous and varied, and many voices were raised to oppose, and even to condemn, the whole work as a real evil under the guise of an imaginary good."

The first month of its existence twenty-eight little unfortunates were admitted, which the Sisters considered "abundant proof not only that vice was prevalent, and that such an asylum for the waif sorely needed, but also that the opening of the asylum had nothing whatever to do with the existence of the waif or the sin of its parents."

On the day of visitation the following interesting scrap of history was obtained from Sister M. Irene then in charge: "We began work about six years ago, without a cent, in a dwelling-house on Twelfth street, our principal object being to prevent infanticide and save the reputation of the women. Since that small beginning we have received over six thousand children and over one hundred mothers. The three Sisters who began the work with me were Sister Teresa Vincent, Sister Ann Aloisius and Sister Frances Liguori. They all continue in it except one. We remained on Twelfth street one year, and then rented a house on Washington Square, paying $7,000 a year rent. We remained there three years. In the meantime we obtained this lot of ground from the city on lease for ninety-nine years, at a nominal rent. By an act of the Legislature the city was authorized to grant us $100,000, provided we could procure a similar amount by private subscriptions. We collected it in about a month. At one single fair we realized $71,000. The rest was derived from private subscriptions. The sum of $320,000 has been expended on the property, buildings, etc. We left Washington Square and came to our new building Feb. 1, 1873. We had about fifty children then. We commenced this work with two cups and saucers. The first morning we had to beg our breakfasts. We slept on straw on the floor the first year, rolling the mattresses up during the day." Since that time about a million of dollars have been expended by the Sisters, and they now have what is said to be one of the best buildings in the city.

On the date of visitation, October 9, there were five hundred children, and about one hundred nurses in the institution. In addition, about one thousand children were being boarded out, at the expense of the asylum. These children are brought, at frequent intervals, by those having them in charge, to the Sisters, to be examined as to their health, etc. On the Wednesday preceding our visit, one thousand children were thus brought to the asylum, and, after passing inspection, were taken back to the homes in which they were being nursed.

"A great many of the children in the asylum," Sister Irene said, "are between the ages of two and five, the oldest child is about six years. Our first plan was to take the children and keep them; now we return them to their mothers, who sometimes come and claim their children. There is no child that cannot, from its first arrival, be traced. We have returned hundreds to their parents."

The children we found to be generally intelligent, and remarkably tidy in their personal appearance. The little girls had their hair neatly tied, and wore plaid dresses and check blouses with colored sashes around their waists. Among the number were two colored children; one of these, a little girl, had a red bow in her hair, and looked particularly bright. The Sister informed us that they had forty-eight colored children, who were being boarded out and nursed.

Nursery No. 1 contains sixteen iron cribs and sixteen iron bedsteads. Each of the cribs accommodates two infants; the larger beds, which stand one beside each crib, are for the nurses. The cribs have straw mattresses and husk beds, double blankets and white covering, the whole being protected with white mosquito nets.

The bathing room is furnished with French tubs, and was very neat and clean. There are no projections about the bath-tubs to injure a child's person, in the process of bathing. The water is let in under a lip.

A drop for soiled clothes extends throughout the building, and a dumb-waiter from the kitchen communicates with every floor. The floors above Nursery No. 1 are counterparts of this. On the upper floor, a room with immense windows, and having good sun exposure, is used for cases of pneumonia. "During the year 1874," says Sister Irene, "in the month of January, an epidemic broke out of purulent ophthalmia. One of the Sisters who attended the children lost one of her eyes, and came very near losing her life, in consequence of being inoculated with this disease."

In the play-room were a flock of children, boys and girls, dressed very neatly, and a lady entertaining them by playing an organ. Their average age was about five years, and there were in all about one hundred and thirty. The children wear shoes and stockings. Their diet is generous, consisting of bread and butter for breakfast, roast beef for dinner, and bread and milk for supper. They have, it was stated, an abundant supply of milk. All wear flannel drawers.

In the kitchen are two large copper boilers; one of a capacity of twenty-five gallons for milk, and another of thirty gallons for bread and milk. The meats are chopped with a machine. The school room is a pleasant, well-lighted, airy apartment, and contains a piano. It is intended to adopt here the *kindergarten* system of instruction.

Connected with the institution is also a bakery.

In the building designated as the quarantine were, in one room, six little ones afflicted with whooping cough, and, in another, fourteen. Another department is called the Syphilitic Ward. This exhibited a sad sight; six little children, all bearing the woful marks of the sins of their parents. The quarantine department is under the charge of two Sisters. A very large percentage of the children, we were informed, are of foreign parentage.

Pursuant to chapter 644 of the Laws of 1874, the city allows thirty-eight cents a day per capita for the children supported. Their names, date of admission, etc., are duly registered on arrival, and if they are put out to nurse, the name of the nurse, with other particulars, is entered on the register. A separate account is kept for each child that is placed out to nurse. The records and accounts are kept with admirable neatness by Sister Maria.

The rule is absolute, never to take more than one child from the same mother.

The condition of the little foundlings on arrival is said to be quite deplorable. Those engaged in the work say: "The only wonder is that any can be saved, when we consider how difficult it is to rear a child, even with all its mother's care; yet the poor little outcast, it would seem, is expected to live through neglect and ill-treatment, which children of a year's growth could scarcely survive. Language would fail to describe the condition of many who are left in the crib—to be cared for a little time and then to be buried. No human skill could restore such little ones, yet they often linger for days, sometimes for weeks, with just enough of vitality to breathe."

As further illustrating the work of the Sisters, we quote the following from their last annual report:

"The reception crib is no longer exposed. This is done to avoid imposition; for, strange though it may appear, many mothers, in order to save the expense and time of nursing their legitimate children, have been known to abandon them for a time to the asylum through the medium of the crib. This was a fraud upon the asylum and the city treasury, but it cannot, under the present system, be practiced any longer. Only illegitimate children, who are exposed to destruction, through the shame or poverty of their mothers, are now received. These, too, must be born within the limits of our own city. No information is required or sought as to names or family, etc.

"Children of wet nurses are never received. This exclusion is based alike upon duty, morality and controlling economy. The asylum needs this class of nurses; the mother who wishes to leave her child has always the opportunity of nursing it there. If she will not, but abandons her child, she exhibits a heartlessness which we feel ourselves obliged to rebuke and oppose. Besides, the reception, nursing and maintaining of the offspring of a mother who declines to perform her maternal duty toward it, preferring to her own infant a stranger's child, would be an inexcusable waste of the contributions of our friends and the public at large.

"As far as practicable, it is our aim and effort to induce the mother to remain to nurse and care for her offspring. Thus affectionate endearments between mother and child necessarily follow, and sunshine is poured upon the hearts of both. This, in fact, has become a very considerable, although a secondary object of the institution. The vast amount of good effected even in this way is greatly encouraging, and of itself stimulates to renewed and more zealous endeavors. Employment is also given to many poor women as in-door nurses. A double purpose is thus subserved. The maternal instinct is thus kept alive in many a heart that would otherwise be dead to that sweet and salutary affection which both softens and elevates a woman's nature; and many poor women, who might otherwise be outcasts from society, are enabled to earn an honest livelihood without any exposure of their unhappy fall. In this new outgrowth from the original and more immediate object of the Foundling Asylum, the hapless unwedded mother sees the institution expand from a mere ark of safety to her child into a protector and savior of herself. Thereby she is screened from the mocks and scorns of a heartless world, saved from destruction, and restored to home and virtue. There are instances in which women married form the exception above mentioned, and are afforded shelter for themselves and their legitimate offspring; but this only occurs when circumstances and actual necessity oblige them to such a course. No outward distinction, however, is at any time made. Thus the wedded mother is saved from humiliation, and the unwedded from the mortification calculated to dispirit her. Nor can the visitor distinguish the one from the other.

"It must always be kept in view, however, that the main object of the asylum is to prevent the unnatural and dreadful crime of infanticide, to preserve to God and society lives which would otherwise be sacrificed to cloak the unfortunate mother's shame, or to relieve her of a burden she felt she could not bear. To save these innocent victims from the merciless hands of selfish and cruel parents, to secure to them at worst a natural death, and if they outlive the period of infancy, to put them in the way of being brought up virtuously, is, in a vast city like New York, a work of crying necessity, which ought to enlist the sympathies of every philanthropic heart.

"The nursing of children outside of the asylum entails a heavy expense upon the institution, but it cannot at present possibly be escaped. Nevertheless it is a great benefit to many of the poor people of our city. It gives employment to nearly a thousand women, and many families have been kept together by means of this resource. For, although the sum allowed for each child is small, amounting to only $10 per month, yet this may pay the rent, and thus secure a roof for the family, which is in itself a great charity and a social benefit. So eager, indeed, are the many for this employment, that an average of twenty or thirty daily present themselves for nurslings. Of this number of applicants only those are employed who present a certificate of good health from a physician, and another of good character from some known and reliable person. No question whatever of religion arises to determine the choice, but whoever appears likely to make the best nurse receives the preference. Yet, the good of the foundlings being our primary object, still another precaution against deception and neglect is taken.

"The services of the gentlemen of the Conference of St. Vincent de Paul, who had kindly offered to assume the supervision of these nurses, were gratefully accepted. They make their visits at times when they suppose they are least expected, and they send in their report monthly to the asylum, giving the conditions of the children, and their reasons why the nurses should be continued or discharged. Thus they are, in a private way, organizing an efficient detective force. To these gentlemen we are thus indebted for information which has led to a great reform in our outside nursing, resulting in marked improvement in the condition of the children. The detective detailed to the asylum is also employed in continued surveillance of these nurses."

The number of persons received during the past year was 898. The total number discharged was 619. Twenty-five children were placed out by adoption, 181 returned to parents or guardians, four transferred to other institutions, three were otherwise discharged and 406 died. The average number of inmates during the year was 1,356. The number remaining, October 1, 1875, were: Boys, 690; girls, 780; total, 1,470.

The total expenditures during the fiscal year ending September 30, 1875, were $305,107.05, of which $114,515.20 was paid to reduce its indebtedness. Its total indebtedness was $25,873.01. Its invested fund was $5,000.

Among the numerous model charities of New York, there are, perhaps, none that excel in order, system and condition of cleanliness the Foundling Asylum of the Sisters of Charity; while the executive ability displayed in the management of all its internal affairs commands admiration.

The following statistics are extracted from the last report of the medical attendant, Dr. Reynolds:

"During our fourth year, from October 1, 1872, to October 1, 1873, there were left at the Asylum 1,125 infants, of whom 26 were black. From October 1, 1873, to October 1, 1874, there were received 589 infants, of which number 94 were discharged and 193 died.

"At the beginning of our fifth year, October 1, 1873, we had 1,136 infants belonging to the Asylum, and during the year we received 589 infants, giving us 1,725 infants to account for. During this year 213 infants were discharged and 321 died, leaving 1,191 foundlings, October 1, 1874.

"We have been unable during the past year, 1873–4, to keep as full and as accurate statistics of our infants as during former years, on account of the confusion consequent upon moving the records, children and hospital furniture from Washington square into our new asylum, and the arranging and fitting up of the differents wards. We must also crave a little kind indulgence for some slight irregularities in our records, incident to increasing our medical staff at the beginning of the year 1874.

"But by referring to the following table for 1872–3, the condition in which the 1,125 infants which were left during that year will be seen, as also the number that survived and the causes of death in those that died:

Whole number, from October 1, 1872, to October 1, 1873.	Black.	Twins.	Condition upon entrance.					Living.	Discharged.	Died.	Diseases which caused death.								
			Good.	Poor.	Dying.	Premature.	Syphilitic.				Intestinal.	Pulmonary.	Broncho-intestinal.	Prematurity.	Syphilis.	Inanition.	Erysipelas.	Convulsions.	Various.*
1,125	26	25	400	531	59	91	44	470	56	599	364	48	30	68	34	1	3	8	43

* Marasmus, 26; Tuberculosis, 3; Chronic Hydrocephalus, 3; Tubercular Meningitis, 3; General Struma, 2; Spasm of Glottis, 2; Diphtheritic Croup, 2; Catarrhal Laryngitis, 1; Membranous Croup, 1.

"As above shown, only 400, or 35 per cent, were in a healthy condition upon entrance; while of the remaining 725, or 64 per cent, feeble and diseased, almost five per cent were dying, eight per cent premature, four per cent syphilitic. Deducting the dying, premature and syphilitic, our mortality was almost 36 per cent. As in former years, premature infants were left, weighing from one and a half to four pounds. These infants were, in many cases unavoidably, in other cases carelessly or designedly, exposed to cold on their way to the Asylum; and this exposure, added to the previous improper, or even total want of, nourishment, afforded very little chance of saving any of them.

"We can but repeat in closing what we have already said, and which seems now especially pertinent, that the success attendant upon our efforts is mainly due to the conscientious, constant and intelligent watchfulness of the Sisters of Charity, in whose charge the New York Foundling Asylum has been placed."

The Hebrew Benevolent Orphan Asylum Society of the City of New York.

New York.

This society was organized April 8, 1822. The following incident is connected with its early beginning: In the spring of the year 1820, a Jew, who had been brought, in a critical condition, to the City Hospital, expressed a wish to see some of his co-religionists before his death. He had been a soldier in the American war of Independence, and was without money or friends. The fact becoming known, a few gentlemen visited him and collected some money for his support. Shortly afterward the soldier died, leaving about $300 in the hands of these gentlemen for their disposal. The question as to the best disposition of this money occasioned much deliberation and conference. It was at length decided to form a benevolent society, to whose members assistance could be given in time of need.

"In 1847, the society having perceived the necessity and felt the want of a refuge for poor Israelites that were stricken down by sickness, submitted to the Hebrew Benevolent Society and to the several Jewish congregations of New York, a proposition to unite for the erection of a hospital and for the use or investment of its general fund and a certain portion of its yearly receipts. The Hebrew Benevolent Society promptly joined in the proposal. A meeting of deputies was convened, but several of the larger congregations declining to co-operate, the project failed. The money voted for the object by the German Benevolent Society was kept apart and augmented steadily. In February, 1859, the opinion having become general that the cause of charity would be better served and greater good be effected by a consolidation, negotiations were entered into between the Hebrew Benevolent Society and the German Hebrew Benevolent Society, with this object in view.

"The German Hebrew Benevolent Society having, by a unanimous and final vote of its members, declared that 'the hospital fund now belonging to the German Hebrew Benevolent Society shall be appropriated to the establishment of an Orphan Asylum and Home for Aged and Indigent Jews,' and having settled by conference all minor matters relating to a union, the respective societies met in the month of April, 1859, when their consolidation was completed. The two societies united under the name of the Hebrew Benevolent Society of the City of New York. In April, 1860, the house No. 1 Lamartine Place was rented by the Society, and made a provisional home for orphans. In October, 1860, a grant of property was procured from the city authorities, and funds for the erection of the present Asylum were received by way of collections and donations from the different Jewish congregations and from individual co-religionists. The building was commenced in 1862. On September 30, 1863, the corner-stone of the new Asylum was laid, and the edifice dedicated to its present use November 5, 1863. In 1869, a frame building on Seventy-sixth street was appropriated for the teaching of shoemaking, and, on the 10th of June, 1870, type-setting and printing were introduced."

The institution is located on Seventy-sixth street and Third avenue.

It is governed by a Board of Directors, and is under the immediate superintendence of Rev. Jacob Cohen.

A visitation was made October 12. The building consists of a main and two wings, and is a substantial brick edifice. Its interior is enriched by tasteful embellishments. The halls are broad, and by means of stained glass in the windows, the light is softened within. The entire house is warmed by steam, and supplied with water from the city.

Orphans, half-orphans and destitute children are received. The children attend the public schools, but, in addition, there is a school on the premises for supplementing their education with Hebrew and German. Music is also a feature in the educational system. A band of musicians is made up from lads in the house, who have a taste in that direction.

In the reception room is kept, with great care, a book called the "Book of Life," in which those desiring to do so may subscribe to the objects of the Society. It is thus designated, as the names inscribed therein are supposed never to be lost. The contributing of a certain sum entitles the subscriber to a page, for private use, where the memorial of relatives and friends, who have died, may be inscribed. A form of prayer is read on the Day of Atonement, and all the names that are inscribed in this book are then read in connection with the prayer.

The dormitories are furnished with single iron bedsteads. White fibre and moss mattresses are used. The boys' beds are two feet four inches wide, and those in the girls' dormitory are two feet six. Each inmate is furnished with a comb and brush, and also a tooth brush, which are required to be kept in their proper places.

The bath-rooms are supplied with hot and cold water. The wash-bowls are set in marble slabs. The water-closets adjoin these rooms.

The clothing of the children, we were informed, is made by an auxiliary sewing society, composed of ladies of the Jewish congregation. The Superintendent, in speaking on the subject of clothing, said: "We have to thank the auxiliary sewing society for dressing our children. They are not by any means stingy." The wardrobes for both boys and girls were well furnished and orderly kept. Each boy had a box, with his number on it, for his clothes.

The hospital room is furnished with four single, iron bedsteads. It had no inmates at the time of inspection.

The kitchen was found to be well kept and, with its brightly polished tin and copper-ware, was an attractive feature in the institution. In the children's dining-room the tables were covered with marbled, enameled cloth. Crockery plates and tin bowls are also used. Both boys and girls eat in the same dining-room. The following is the usual dietary: For breakfast, bread, butter and coffee, and sometimes cake. White bread is given on Saturdays and Sundays, and brown bread on other days. For dinner, they have soup, meat, potatoes and other vegetables, in their season. A lunch is given in the afternoon. For supper, bread, butter and tea, and sometimes potatoes and cheese are supplied. The children were about partaking of their evening meal as we entered the room. The following blessing was asked before eating: "Blessed be Thou, Eternal God, King of the universe, who bringeth forth food from the earth." Thanks are returned after meals.

In connection with the institution is an industrial school, where the boys, who are old enough, learn printing or shoemaking. They enter at the age of fourteen, and remain until they are eighteen. The Superintendent says: "They are taught such trades as they are adapted to, some becoming printers, others shoemakers; while those who have a taste for study are sent to college. We never lose sight of those that have once been inmates here; we keep their deposits for them till they are twenty-one years of age. As they must have some incentive to work, they are paid for their services, some more and some less; but whatever sum it may be, it is kept for them."

The industrial school building is about thirty feet wide and seventy feet long, and stands directly in the rear of the asylum proper. The basement contains the engine and boiler, which supply the power for the printing department. Over this are the dining-room and store-room. On the next floor is the printing office; over this is the shoe-maker's shop, and a room in which an evening school is held. On the next floor is the dormitory, for this department.

The industrial department is under the charge of Mr. S. Arnheim, assisted by Mr. W. H. Rice. The latter gentleman is foreman of the shoe shop, while the printing department is under the immediate charge of the former. This department employs also a music teacher for the band, a proof-reader and an engineer. Particular pains are taken that no boy goes into the world before he has his trade properly learned. "Our object," says Mr. Arnheim, "is to teach them their trades thoroughly. A boy will come to me with some task hour after hour till he has done it to my satisfaction. I show them the necessity of turning out good work if they mean to get a living. I take a boy step by step till I have made him a workman, and given him a good trade. Some of our boys earn from $8 to $16 per week after they leave us. I have a boy that will go out in January, and he will be able to earn $14 a week. At present we have plenty of work on hand." In the printing department the boys were engaged on a piece of work requiring some ingenuity and mechanical skill, which was being prepared for exhibition at the coming Centennial. Some neat specimens of illuminated and other styles of printing were shown us, the work of the inmates.

On the day of visitation there were in the institution fifty-five girls and one hundred and twenty-two boys, also thirty apprentices in the industrial school.

The working force of the entire establishment was as follows: Superintendent, Assistant Superintendent, Matron, Governess, two teachers, fireman, nurse, four seamstresses, cook and three kitchen girls, four chambermaids, five laundresses and two persons to do the cleaning, etc., of the industrial school. These are all paid.

The children are all of Jewish parentage; no fully grown girls are kept in the house. At the age of thirteen they are transferred to a House of Reception, where also the very little children are kept, there being no room for them in this house. The House of Reception is situated on Eighty-sixth street. The number of inmates there on the 1st of October was thirty-nine girls and twenty boys.

"We have," says the Superintendent, "also seven boys and three girls boarding out, for whom we have no room in the house. Formerly, we had a great many children boarding out. It was found difficult to oversee them all, and to meet the difficulty the House of Reception was organized. It is called the House of Reception because small children are first taken there and afterward brought here, at five years of age. The older girls learn sewing and dressmaking and all kinds of ladies' work. They have a teacher and a matron, with three domestics."

Great pains are taken to find suitable homes for the children in families. On this point the Superintendent remarks: "Whenever we find a family willing to undertake the responsibility of supervising their moral welfare, we place them there. Four of our boys are attending the New York City College. One is at present in the Sophomore class, the others are in the Freshmen class."

The institution has a circulating library for the children, containing about four hundred volumes.

The children, we were informed, bathe once a week in the winter, and almost every day in summer.

The Ladies' Sewing Society meets at the institution from November till April, every Wednesday, from ten to four o'clock. The ladies come from seventy to one hundred in number. They take upon themselves the task of clothing the orphans.

No report is at hand showing the financial condition of the Society. The number of children who have received the benefit of the institution since its organization is five hundred and sixty-five. The number in the institution October 1, 1875, was two hundred and sixty-four.

Of these fifty-four were orphans, nine half-orphans, and one had both parents living. All were of foreign parents except one.

The thoroughness of the work that is here being done, and the zeal actuating its workers, is thought to be worthy of commendation. It is but just to say that so faithful have the Hebrew people been in providing for their own poor that the cases that find their way into county poor-houses are extremely rare. In fact, in the recent examination into the causes of pauperism and crime, conducted by this Board, there was found in all the poor-houses of the State but one Jewish inmate.

House of the Good Shepherd.

New York.

This institution is situated at the foot of Eighty-ninth and Ninetieth streets, East River, on a plot of ground containing about thirty-nine city lots.

It consists of two main buildings connected by a high brick wall, with seven adjacent cottages. One hundred and twenty-five feet east from these is the chapel and convent building, erected in 1861, which, with the addition of a building eighty by fifty feet, for Magdalens, built in 1870, presents a frontage on the river side of two hundred feet.

A building measuring fifty by ninety feet, and five stories high, was erected for the voluntary penitents in 1864, and another of equal size, contiguous to it, to serve as a House of Detention, was completed in 1869. The two houses form an edifice of fifty by one hundred and eighty feet, and extend from Eighty-sixth to Ninetieth streets. This institution, we were informed, 'was founded at the request of the late Most Reverend John Hughes, his Vicar-General, the Very Reverend D. Storrs, and some charitable ladies, who undertook to restrain young girls from leading bad lives, and to give them a home where they could be taught their duty to God and society, till reformed and restored to their families, or provided with honest employment.'

The work was begun on Fourteenth street on the 2d of October, 1857, by five *Religieuses* of the Order of Our Lady of Charity of the Good Shepherd, one penitent being then received. It was incorporated November 1, 1858. In January, 1860, the institution was removed to its present retired location, at which time the number of penitents reached seventy-five.

The visitation was made October 20th, in company with Commissioner Hoguet.

The institution, under the charge of Mother Magdalena, then contained four classes of inmates.

1. Magdalens, or penitents who have been converted and are lead-

ing the life of *Religieuses* under the rule of the third order of St. Teresa.

2. Penitent women and girls who have been received in order to be converted.

3. The Preservation Class, composed of children who are in danger of falling, and mostly those of bad parents.

4. Those girls within the ages of fourteen and twenty-one committed by magistrates.

Many of the inmates have been victims of misfortune or treachery. These have, in a great many cases, been committed to the institution by the magistrates and the city makes an allowance for the maintenance of such at the rate of $110 a year, per capita.

A school is taught on the premises for such as need instruction in reading, writing and arithmetic. Ample provision is also made for their industrial training, shirt and dress making, laundry work and all kinds of domestic employment being conducted in the institution.

"More than one hundred and twenty-five of the four hundred and fifty inmates of this year were," the Sister says, "under sixteen." "A great many of these young girls come here sick. A great many tell us that they have been drugged, and while in that helpless condition have been taken advantage of. A girl was brought here the other day in boy's clothes, alive with vermin. We had to cut off all her hair. The poor child had a pretty face and it was sad to see her. Some of those who come are very bright girls; others have not much intelligence. But as a general thing the greater number are smart girls. They come here without having been taught any industry. They do not generally know how to sew, but belong to the class who go to parties, attend balls and spend their time looking in at shop windows." At the date of October 1, there were eighty-five girls in the institution under sixteen years of age.

As to the success of this work of reform, the Sister thinks that at least one-half of those that go out from the institution do well and are restored to society.

Every inmate is registered. The date of admission, name, age, birth place, birth places of parents, social, physical and mental condition, and cause of commitment are noted. The younger children are kept entirely separate from the older inmates.

The discipline is of a mild and conciliatory nature. The Sisters call them children, and they in turn address the Sisters as mothers. "It must," says the Sister, "be a very gross offense that makes us lock any of them up.

Inmates when reformed are either restored to their friends, or secured situations where they are thought to be safe. Stores are not popular with the Sisters for the disposal of their girls, owing to the temptations that arise from the loose class of persons frequently moving about them. "Ladies," they say, "are glad to receive the inmates. Some go as nursery maids, some as house maids. When we place them with ladies, we hear from them. If the ladies find that they cannot do their duty by them, they bring them back to us. In stores they get from $6 to $8 per week, but if a lady gives them $2 for family service they are as well off, for they get their board, and generally their clothes in addition.

A large part of the labor of the house is employed in the laundry. Washing is taken in, and an income of $1,000 a month is derived from this source during ten months in the year.

In connection with this institution is a farm of eighty-five acres, situated at Peekskill. The soil is somewhat rocky, but, nevertheless, well adapted to the purpose contemplated in its purchase. One thousand fruit trees have been already planted upon it. It is proposed to build here a suitable edifice for the magdalens and the children of the preservation class. The plan has already been drawn, and is very elaborate. The grounds will be laid out in lawns, roadways, graveled walks, etc., and will form a delightfully retired spot for the work to which it is to be dedicated.

This property was purchased out of a legacy left by a New York lady. It cost $55,000.

The Mother House of this Order of Sisters is at Angers in France. In connection with the Order there is a class of *Religieuses* called Magdalens, with a Sister of the Good Shepherd as Superioress.

The whole number of persons received in the institution during the past year was 373. The whole number of inmates, children and adults, on October 1, 1875, was 440. Of these 85 were under 16 years of age. Of native parentage there were 102, and of foreign parentage, 338.

The total expenditures of the house during the fiscal year ending September 30, 1875, were $80,428.28. Of this, $12,415 was paid to reduce liabilities. Its present indebtedness rests upon its real estate, and amounts to $45,000.

Since the commencement of their work in New York, these good Sisters have exerted their reforming and elevating influence on nearly five thousand young girls and women, preserving the chastity of many in peril, and inducing others to turn from lives of idleness and profligacy to ways of industry and virtue. The saving to society, effected through their work, can hardly be overstated. How many wounded hearts have been healed, and how many bereaved families gladdened by the return of their lost ones, will never be known.

House of Mercy.

New York.

This institution, having for its object the reformation of wayward girls and young women, occupies what was once an old family mansion, to which extensive additions have been made. It is beautifully situated on the banks of the Hudson, at the foot of Eighty-sixth street. The grounds are inclosed with high fences and walls, and are tastefully embellished with flowers and shrubbery. An air of peaceful seclusion pervades the place, quite in keeping with the gentle spirit of its work. Upon entering the house the eye encounters many quaint pieces of furniture, family heirlooms of the Sisters; and the æsthetic sense is gratified by the refining atmosphere which pervades the establishment.

For the past twelve years the work has been carried on by the Order of the Sisters of St. Mary of the Protestant Episcopal Church. Seven of these ladies were engaged at the date of visitation, October 22, 1875. The founder of this institution, Mrs. Wm. Richmond, wife of the Rector of St. Michael's Church, Broadway and One Hundredth street, it is said, visited the prisons and hospitals of the city, selected the most encouraging cases, and brought them to a house which she had provided for their reception, soliciting means from the benevolent for their support. The Rev. William Richmond acted as Chaplain of the institution until his death, in 1858. In 1863, the trustees placed it under the charge of the Sisters of Mercy. The institution was incorporated February 23, 1855.

At the time of our visit there were seventy-six inmates. Their average age was about seventeen; the youngest was twelve years old.

"A portion of the inmates are committed by the courts; others voluntarily surrender themselves, and a few are received upon the application of parents or friends. They are admitted for indefinite periods; but are retained, as far as practicable, until their habits are fully assured. Upon leaving the institution, if without protectors, they are placed in families, and none are discharged unless to go to good situations."

They are divided into three classes: the probationers, or first class, the middle class and the honor class. These classes dress differently, eat at separate tables, and have each its own peculiar privileges.

The chapel is fifty feet long, and terminates in an apsis. It has carved oak seats and stained glass windows imported from England. The altar and reredos in the chancel are of carved stone, and are supported by polished marble pillars; while the floor is laid with encaustic tiles. At the west end are two concealed galleries, one for visitors, the other in communication with the infirmary for the accommodation of the sick, who are here enabled to sit in invalid chairs and listen to the service. Its font belonged originally to old St. Michael's Church, and two of its memorial windows keep ever fresh the memories of its founder, Mrs. William Richmond, and one of its early workers, Sister Jane Haight.

The infirmary is furnished with single iron bedsteads, double pillows and hair mattresses. The room was, at the time of our visit, full of sunlight. It is ventilated by flues in the walls, and has a very bright and cheerful appearance. A large iron balcony for the use of the inmates projects from the infirmary, from which a fine view of the Hudson is obtained. Adjoining the infirmary is a Sister's room, conveniently situated, to enable her to supervise the sick during the night.

The dormitory is in the dormer attic, and extends the full length of the wing. The beds are arranged on each side, and are covered with counterpanes of snowy whiteness, and made up with the utmost neatness. The furniture of the room included a stand for books, etc., with a drawer, beside each bed. The walls were pleasantly tinted, and at the side of each dormer window were hung in rustic frames pictures of home life. At the end of the dormitory were hung two prominent mottoes, "Thou God seest me," and "The eyes of the Lord are in every place." A Sister's room adjoins this.

The linen room is fitted up with cupboards. Each cupboard is divided into compartments and numbered. The clothing they contain is correspondingly numbered. The Sister informed us that the clothing of the inmates is cut out and made in the institution.

The house throughout was found to be kept in a high degree of efficiency.

The Sisters make industry a prominent feature of the institution. No domestics are employed, and in addition to the regular work of the house a large laundry business for outside parties is done by the inmates, and yet pains is taken to avoid arousing their antagonism by assigning them labor for which they have neither taste nor inclination. "We allot to them," says the Sister, "such tasks as are in keeping with their strength and preferences. One may have an aversion to sewing, another to washing or ironing. We endeavor to bear this in mind, and so adjust all the work of the house that the establishment may present the salient features of a well-ordered family. The dispositions of the girls vary. Some on their arrival are very unmanageable, but as soon as they learn that our rules are made in a spirit of kindness, they yield obedience quite cheerfully. With some it is best to reason, with others a more decisive mode of dealing is necessary. Our severest penalty, however, is bread and water for dinner."

The Sisters are well aware of the important aid rendered in the elevation of the moral character by a cheerful mind and a healthy physique. Frequent out-door exercise is taken, the girls are encouraged in the culture of flowers. Every attempt is made to divert their thoughts from contemplating their past lives, and incentives are offered them to aim after something higher and nobler. Yet the Sisters do not hastily conclude that an instant relinquishment of old ways, or a satisfactory conformity to the rules of the institution, is sufficient proof of a permanent change in any inmate, but prefer to base their judgment on the matured revelations of time. On this point the Sister remarks: "If, after leaving the institution, they continue steadfast in an upright course for three or four years, we begin to think it is reformation. Still we always hope they are benefited by their sojourn with us, even when their future deportment is a source of disappointment."

The discipline of the house is of a mild character, and its reformatory work aims rather at the conversion of the heart of the fallen one than at correcting her faults, by an iron rule of retribution. The work of these Sisters is one of faith; and they are content to toil on in the path of duty, to maintain the dignity of their sex, by seeking the salvation of its fallen members; sometimes seeing the fruit of their earnest efforts, at other times unable to trace it; but at all times willing to leave results to their Lord and Master, in whose name they have undertaken the work.

Howard Mission and Home for Little Wanderers.

New York.

The particulars of the establishment and workings of this institution may be gleaned from the following short outline of its history, furnished by one of its officers:

"The organization of the Howard Mission, in May, 1861, was the expression of a desire, on the part of its projectors, to render a helping hand in the work of benefiting the needy and poor in the city of New York.

"The Mission is located in the Fourth Ward, and surrounded by a region which had a population of nearly three hundred thousand inhabitants to the square mile, and where there was an average of two dwelling-houses to one grog-shop, dance-house or other establishment for the propagation of wretchedness. This region swarmed with children of the poor. A very large portion of the parents were intemperate, ignorant and vicious, having no comfortable home, nor the disposition to exert themselves in order to obtain one. The wants of such a population were truly appalling, and no humane person could pass through this part of the city without a feeling of profound sadness and pity. To ameliorate this wretched condition of the people here, was the object of the Mission.

"The principal work is with the children. We try to benefit them in two ways.

"1st. When their parents or guardians can be persuaded to give the Mission legal control of them, they are taken under our immediate care, prepared for and transferred to good comfortable homes, where they receive a proper secular and Christian education, are trained up to lives of usefulness, fitted for the various responsibilities of citizenship, and thus enabled to become honorable members of society.

"2d. We gather into day and Sunday-schools all the children we can reach, whose parents will not surrender them to the Mission, or consent to their being sent away. All this work brings us in contact with the parents, secures their confidence, and makes us acquainted with their condition and wants. We endeavor to improve these opportunities. Experienced missionaries visit constantly among the homes of the children, discover where there is real want, and give relief. The inception and organization of the Howard Mission is to be credited to Rev. William C. Van Meter, who commenced operations on the New Bowery near Chatham square, in May, 1861, without a dollar in the treasury, relying solely on the voluntary contributions of the public. The cash receipts from the beginning increased every year, till in 1871 they reached $50,000 for that year.

"Financial depression subsequently diminished the income, but the Mission has managed to struggle along, and has, since its organization, been the means of permanently benefiting twenty thousand children and adults. The Mission Chapel is about one hundred feet long and sixty-five feet wide. It is built of hard brick, with stone copings and slate roof. It is heated by steam. The main audience room occupies one entire floor, and is capable of accommodating one thousand persons. A speaker's platform is at one end, and an elevated gallery at the other, arranged to seat two hundred and fifty children."

Adjoining this chapel is the home building, where the missionaries reside, and where children are sheltered and cared for until they are placed in permanent family homes.

The Superintendent, Mr. William D. Clegg, on the day of visitation, stated that the work of the Mission was a union movement, in which all the Protestant churches were interested, and that it saved society from bearing heavy burdens. He says: "We help families over hard places that, but for us and this timely aid, would become burdens to the tax payers. Were they obliged to go to 'the Island' (Randall's Island), they would become hopelessly paupers. These families, that we have helped, often come to me, and slip a half dollar into my hand for the purpose of helping others in distress, a proof that the way in which we give aid, so far from developing a spirit of public dependence, makes it the ambition of its recipients to endeavor to help others. Even the children taught in our Sunday-school catch the same spirit, and come to us with their pennies to assist other poor children to advantages similar to those which they have enjoyed.

"Children that come to us from Randall's Island seem to be broken in spirit, and do not seem to possess the life and animation of other children."

During our visitation a little girl was about to be returned to her mother. She was a bright, promising child, and dressed very prettily, with a jaunty hat and feather and bright worsted leggins. She had a white fur muff and a little carpet-bag in her hand. She sang very sweetly, for our entertainment, a childish song. Her winning ways had endeared her to those in the home, and she had become quite a pet. She was now being taken by one of the ladies to be returned to her mother, who insisted upon this disposition of her child. The circumstances were such as to create the most unhappy forebodings as to the child's future. This case is noted as it illustrates one of the discouraging features of asylum work generally.

On October 1, 1875, there were fourteen children who had found a home in the Mission, one a full orphan of native parentage, and thirteen half-orphans, of foreign parentage. Besides these there were connected with the Mission, it was asserted, thirteen hundred other children and eight hundred families, to whom relief is in one way or another afforded.

The good effects of the Mission, in rescuing people from the rash acts to which the despair of poverty would prompt them, are illustrated in the following incident, clipped from the quarterly issue of the Little Wanderer's Friend, published by this Mission:

"The other day a woman and her child were discharged from the hospital. They were in rags, penniless, and without shelter. Disheartened and discouraged the woman resolved to commit suicide and take her child with her. Reaching the Grand street ferry, the little girl asked her mother what she was going to do. 'We shall starve here, my child. Let us jump into the river, and it will soon all be over.' 'No, no,' said the little girl, 'let us go to Howard Mission. When I went to school there, poor people were fed and had clothes given to them.' Led by the child, the pair tramped their weary way from the foot of Grand street to the New Bowery. The doors were closed, but the child knew the private entrance. Both were made welcome, were fed and clothed. Work was secured for the woman, and she is now happy and cheerful, and earning a competent support for herself and child."

Industrial School.

Hart's Island.

The Industrial School on Hart's Island is now but a temporary place of reception for boys committed to the school ship "Mercury."

There were but nine boys on the Island on the day of visitation, October 25. They were under the charge of Mr. Dunphy, a gentleman of experience, who resides here, having charge of a large force from Blackwell's Island, engaged in making improvements.

A painful spectacle came under our observation on the day of visitation. While standing on the dock, the steamboat arrived with supplies. It brought up sixty convicts from Blackwell's Island. In company with this gang of prisoners, closely packed in the forward part of the steamboat, were eleven boys, mostly mere children; some of them showing in their appearance great neglect and destitution. Before we left the Island, however, these little fellows had changed their clothes, and were transferred to the school ship "Mercury," wearing only pants and shirts. This association with hardened offenders was painful to behold. In contrast to this dark picture was another incident which tended to brighten the day. A large number of ladies and gentlemen had come from New York, and taken about two hundred of the boys from the school ship to Hart's Island. Here the boys were sumptuously feasted, the tables being bountifully supplied with delicacies, and brightened with flowers brought by the ladies and gentlemen from the city. The boys were not only entertained with the good things in the way of feasting, but with what was far better, kind words and wise counsels; the festival culminating in the ceremony of receiving the boys into the church by the rite of confirmation. Such kindly attentions from ladies and gentlemen holding respectable positions in society, must not only encourage these boys to pursue a different life, but strengthen their self-respect.

The Institution of Mercy.

New York.

The general object of this institution, which was founded and is managed by the Roman Catholic Order of the Sisters of Mercy, is for the service of the poor, the sick and the ignorant. Besides the St.

Catharine's Convent, in which a large number of the Sisters reside, it comprises,

1. The "House of Mercy," which, with the convent, occupies Nos. 35, 37, 39, 41 and 43 East Houston street; and

2. The St. Joseph's Industrial School, located on Eighty-first street, between Fourth and Madison avenues.

We are kindly furnished with the following particulars of the objects, history and workings of the institution: "The Sisters of Mercy visit, relieve and instruct the poor, the sick and the ignorant in their poor homes and in the hospitals and prisons. The number of such visits made by them in New York city averages, annually, about eleven hundred. In many cases whole families are instructed and relieved at each visit. But the special object of the institution is the care and protection of young women of good character, and with these, their daily intercourse with the poor brings them into constant contact. The knowledge thus obtained of their need of moral, industrial and economical training, and of the ghastly evils to which destitute and unprotected young women are exposed, led to the establishment of a 'House of Mercy,' where such persons might be properly trained and cared for until employment could be procured for them.

"The House of Mercy was first established in New York city, in November, 1848, and forms one of the most important features of the Institution of Mercy, which was incorporated under the provisions of the general act. The building is of brick, in plain Romanesque style of architecture, and is capable of accommodating one hundred and twenty persons.

"When the institution was first organized, only a few young women could be accommodated, and these resided in a portion of what is now the 'Convent' or residence of the Sisters; but in 1848 the Sisters, encouraged by the aid and approbation of the late Archbishop Hughes, who first induced them to come to the city, undertook the erection of the present House of Mercy, adjoining the Convent. By order of the Archbishop, each pastor in the city collected from his congregation the sum of $500 to aid in the erection of the building, and many donations and subscriptions were made by other friends of the institution; but no grant was applied for, either to the city or State, as the Sisters of Mercy did not then feel that they had established any claim on the sympathies of the public. In November, 1849, the house was ready for the admission of inmates, and afforded conveniences of the plainest kind for the performance of the work in which they were to be employed.

"Much of the time and care of the Sisters is taken up in the industrial training of the young women under their protection. Such as are strong and accustomed to manual labor are employed in the laundry, and instructed in the best methods of performing the work done there, while those who are less robust or more refined — for sometimes persons delicately nurtured are sick and need the protection of the institution — are taught the different kinds of needlework, and the use of the sewing machine.

"A select intelligence office is conducted by the Sisters, by means of which suitable situations are procured for the girls, great care being taken to place them in respectable families. If their conduct has been satisfactory, and they return with recommendations from their employers, they are again supplied with situations by the institution. The Sisters make it a matter of duty to induce these young women to make good use of their money, and to secure for themselves a little independence by putting a portion of their earnings in the bank, from month to month; a plan which they have found productive of excellent results, both as regards society at large, and the comfort and character of the individuals themselves."

At the time of visitation, October 9th, the house contained about thirty-three children. The officers of the institution consist of a President, Treasurer, Secretary, and a Board of Trustees, all of whom are elected from among the Sisters. The present presiding officer is Mother Catherine Seton.

St. Joseph's Industrial School.

"For a long time the Sisters had been convinced, that no work nor service rendered society was more productive of good results than the establishment of industrial institutes, for the protection and moral and educational training of female children. In addition to this experience, came that acquired in the military hospitals during the late war, where they saw the heart of many a brave soldier rent with anguish at the prospect of leaving his little ones without house or friend. While these disastrous years lasted, the Sisters exerted themselves in every possible way to comfort widows and save orphans, then every day created, and thus were prompted to attempt the establishment of this Industrial School. The financial struggles were arduous; it was made necessary to meet the first appropriation of $25,000, by an equivalent sum collected among friends, in the short space of five months. This amount cleared the ground and put up part of the brick work of the building.

"The following year another appropriation of $30,000 was made, but with the same provision that an equivalent sum should be raised. Nothing daunted, the Sisters again appealed to friends, with like success. The latter sum finished the brick work, roofed in the building and partially plastered the walls. Then came another standstill, when the Sisters enlisted the sympathies of friends, laid before them the state of their finances and the necessity of completing the work already begun. In response to this appeal, they received the sum of $50,000, without the conditions accompanying former donations. Previous to the receipt of the $50,000, in order to save from injury the work so near completion, it was deemed prudent to execute a mortgage of $30,000 on the building known as the Convent of Mercy, situated on the corner of Houston and Mulberry streets (then entirely free from debt) for this worthy object. The treasurer must now meet the interest on this sum from the industry of inmates or the charity of friends.

"The building was commenced in the spring of 1867. The grounds were leased to the Institution of Mercy, by the corporation of the city of New York, for ninety-nine years. The building is of brick, with cut stone trimmings, in modern Gothic architecture. It is four stories high with basement and attic. The school was opened September 24, 1869, twenty-four of the children from the Houston street institution being transferred there."

At the time of visitation, October 9, the school was found to be in charge of Sister Agnes Muldoon. Fifteen other sisters were associated with her in the work. Girls, we were informed, "are received from the age of three to fifteen, and kept till they are competent to earn their own support." "We teach them," says the Sister, "housekeeping, family sewing, knitting, machine and laundry work, and when they are ready to leave, we place them where we think they will be most likely to succeed, and watch over them afterward.

On the day of visitation the number of children in the institution was one hundred and fifty. The capacity of the building, however, could, it was thought, by slight alterations, be increased to make accommodations for about two hundred more. The want of means deters the sisters from enlarging their work, although there is further and continued demand upon their benevolence.

In one room were fourteen little girls doing very creditable crochet work. The sewing room contains thirty-six sewing machines. In this room we found twenty-nine girls making shirts for stores. The girls were singing in concert while at work. Three Sisters were among them, each attending to some one department of the industries. The Sister said: "We do not think any thing of making seventy or eighty dozen shirts in a week." As to the earnings of the girls, she said "A girl well trained can earn $9 or $10 a week. The last two that left us get $10 a week."

The dormitories are furnished with single iron bedsteads. A Sister sleeps in each room.

The institution contains a large school-room and an infirmary. The latter had only one inmate.

The dining-room is furnished with the usual appurtenances of such an apartment, except that no table-cloths are used, either by the Sisters or the children. In regard to the comfort of the children, the Sister remarks: "We lay it on our consciences to make them as comfortable as we can."

The spacious brick building is heated by steam, and is well drained and ventilated. Ample arrangements are made for bathing, and each girl has her own towel and toilet box.

The health of the children appeared to be good. But one death had occurred during the past year, that of a little girl three years old.

The institution employs an engineer, and also three women to bake. The children assist in baking, and thus gain experience in that important branch of domestic economy.

The house contains a spacious chapel, in which the children sit on each side, facing the altar. The Sisters sit in the central aisle in stalls. These are arranged in two rows on each side of the aisle, facing each other. At the end of each row, and facing the altar, are larger stalls for the Sisters Superior. On the right of the central altar is a sepulchre of the Saviour, which is a memorial presented by a lady whose son died while studying for the priesthood.

The entire number of young girls received and cared for by the Institution of Mercy, during the twenty-seven years of its existence, is stated to be eleven thousand three hundred and eighty-seven. Besides these, large numbers have received out-door relief. The imprisoned, the sick and the dying have likewise shared the ministrations and mercies of these good Sisters, who have well earned the beautiful designation of their order.

The total expenditures of the Institution of Mercy during the fiscal year ending September 30, 1875, were $18,323.17. Of this $3,500 was for interest on indebtedness. Its total indebtedness is $54,135.18.

Institution for the Improved Instruction of Deaf Mutes.

New York.

This institution is located at Nos. 1471, 1473 and 1475 Broadway at the intersection of Broadway and Seventh avenue. It was organized on the 28th of February, 1867, and incorporated on the 12th of April, 1870. It commenced its work at 134 West Twenty-seventh street. In 1868, its location was changed to 330 East Fourteenth street, and subsequently to its present quarters on Broadway. It occupies three private houses, in which slight alterations have been made, so as to adapt them to the purposes for which they are now used. The first of these is used by the principal and officers of the house; the second by the girls, and the third by the boys. It appears from the financial statement that the sum of $7,800 was paid for the rent of these houses in 1874.

The institution is controlled by a Board of Trustees, and is under the immediate charge of David Greenberger, principal, assisted by eight lady teachers. Its domestic affairs are intrusted to a matron and an assistant matron. One male and eight female domestics are engaged. A clerk is also employed.

Pupils of both sexes are received, from seven years old upward. Admissions are made during the month of September only. The price fixed for the maintenance and instruction of each pupil is $300 per year. Clothing is not included.

On the day of visitation, October 7, 1875, there were ninety-two pupils — fifty boys and forty-two girls.

The system of instruction is the German, lip reading without the aid of artificial signs. The opportunity was not favorable for forming an opinion upon the merits of the system adopted, or the proficiency made by the pupils.

The class rooms were pleasant and well furnished, and the house generally possessed all the modern conveniences for health and comfort. Boys and girls are together at meals and in the class room. At other times a separation of the sexes is effected.

October 1, 1875, there were in the institution ninety-two pupils. Of this number three were orphans, twenty-one half-orphans, and sixty-eight had both parents living.

Thirty-four of the children were of native and fifty-eight of foreign parentage. They were principally from New York city. Nine of them were supported by friends, forty-eight by counties, thirty-four by the State and one by the institution.

The number of pupils received during the year was thirteen; the number discharged to parents or guardians, twelve. The total expenditures of the institution, during the fiscal year ending September 30, 1875, were $36,214.39, and of this $8,000 was invested. Its total receipts were $37,991.95, from the following sources:

From the State	$18,585 66
From appropriations of Boards of Supervisors...........	7,061 01
From individuals for the support of inmates............	4,975 00
By donations and voluntary contributions..............	250 00
From interest and dividends on investments............	700 00
From all other sources..............................	6,420 28

The value of its personal estate, including bonds, stocks and other investments, is set down at $18,000.

Leake and Watts' Orphan House.

New York.

The property of the asylum consisted, originally, of twenty acres of land eligibly situated at Bloomingdale, now One Hundred and Tenth street. The corner-stone of the Orphan House was laid on the 28th of April, 1838, and it was completed in November, 1843. The original cost of the land and building, it is stated, was $80,000; but so valuable has the property become, that, within a few years, four acres were sold for the sum of $130,000. The edifice consists of a large central building with two wings. The front entrance is approached by a broad flight of granite steps. The porticos, in front and rear, are supported by six stately Grecian columns. The building is quite imposing in its general aspect. The basement is of granite, with three upper stories of brick. The eastern wing is allotted to the boys and the western to the girls. A wide veranda, protected by a massive balustrade, is attached to each story. Outside stairways, or fire-escapes, afford means of egress in case of fire. In the rear, and connected with the main building by a covered passage-way, is a one-story building, in which are the kitchen and the dining room. This is a recent addition.

The affairs of this corporation are controlled by a Board of Seven Trustees, consisting of "the Mayor, the Recorder, the Rector of Trinity Church, the Wardens of the said church, the oldest minister of the Dutch Church, and the oldest minister of the Presbyterian Church." The Orphan House is under the immediate charge of a superintendent, Mr. William H. Guest, who is assisted by his wife as matron.

At the date of visitation, October 22, there were one hundred and fifty children in the house, twenty-nine of native and one hundred and twenty-one of foreign parentage. From Mrs. Guest, in the absence of the Superintendent, we obtained the following information: "Boys and girls, without distinction of country or religion, are received if legitimate and full orphans. We have a capacity for accommodating three hundred. Children are not received under three nor over twelve years of age. We place them out at fourteen. If they have friends able to take care of them, they are then given over to their charge. If not, they are bound out. The boys are bound out till the age of twenty-one; after which time, according to agreement, each boy is entitled to $100, a suit of clothes and a Bible, from his employer. During his time of service it is stipulated that he shall spend a given time at school. The girls are bound out till the age of eighteen, when they are to receive $25, a Bible and a new suit of clothes. We have a regular form of indenture. The boys we find do best on farms. They are there more like members of the family. We very seldom get boys to learn trades. We send many of the children to Long Island. As a general thing they do very well. We do not approve of making them servants."

In the boys' dormitory, formerly the chapel, is a tablet bearing the following inscription:

"John and George Leake and John Watts, founders of this institution for the reception, education and maintenance of helpless orphan children. The liberal endowment and practical benefit of this charity furnish their elegy."

The bedsteads are three feet eight inches wide, each intended to accommodate two children. The beds are of straw, and are very thick. The girls' dormitory is similarly furnished. The dining room is commodious. The boys and girls eat together. The children sit on stools with backs, the seats of which rest upon iron pedestals and turn upon pivots. The dietary is substantially as follows: For breakfast, weak coffee with milk and bread. For dinner, meat four days in the week; coffee and bread one day, rice and molasses another; bread, butter and coffee on Sunday. For supper, bread and milk, the latter being warm. No cooking is done on Sunday. The floors of this and other rooms were very white, being frequently scoured with soap and sand. The infirmary is in the attic, and occupies two rooms with all needed conveniences. The building throughout is heated by steam, lighted with kerosene, and well supplied with water, which is forced to every floor.

One death had occurred during the past year, but the health of the inmates was said to be generally good. They were all dressed alike, and well clad. In winter, flannel is worn by both sexes, also woolen stockings, while for the mild spring and summer weather thick cotton is substituted. The boys have their hair cut short. The secular and religious education of the inmates is carefully guarded. A school is maintained on the premises, in which five teachers are employed. Daily morning and evening prayers are conducted. The children say grace at meals, and attend four religious services on Sunday. The institution possesses a library of seven hundred volumes, selected especially for children.

The institution has a large garden devoted to the raising of vegetables. An extensive hennery is also kept. The play-grounds are very large, and contain a pavilion.

The children in the school room presented a cleanly and bright appearance. The boys and girls were in separate rooms. In the girls' room was a piano, also a cabinet of minerals. Illuminated texts decorated the walls.

A marked feature of this institution is the pains taken to provide the children with comfortable clothing, bedding, etc., adapted to the various seasons. The house is very cleanly kept, and the children are believed to be under excellent influences.

This long established and worthy charity has given shelter to a large number of orphan children, thereby entirely relieving the public of the burden of their support. At the date of October 1st, 1875, the number of inmates was one hundred and fifty, all of whom were being supported wholly by the Asylum. While much remains to be done in the field in which this institution is situated, it has, nevertheless, already accomplished a great work, and its founders will ever be held in grateful remembrance for their philanthropy and munificence.

The number of children received in the institution, during the year ending November 1, 1875, was thirty-six, and the number discharged twenty-three; of the latter, six were indentured, fourteen surrendered to guardians or relatives, two eloped and one died. Its total income from investments, for the year ending December 31, 1875, was $30,914.20. This corporation is possessed of the following property:

Real estate, valued at $300,000. This is productive of no income, and is subject to taxation. The value of its personal estate, including bonds, mortgages and stocks at par, and balance of cash on hand is $443,278.52. Its only indebtedness is $22,700, being for unpaid taxes, etc. It receives nothing from the State or city, excepting an appropriation toward the salaries of teachers which, during the year, was $1,272.18.

In view of the large personal estate of this asylum, from which an income is derivable, as also of the fact that its accommodations are adequate for double the number of children inmates, the question suggests itself whether a greater number of orphan children could not be permitted to partake of the solid comforts and share the elevating influences of the asylum. The opportunity of aiding this class, in New York city, is very great, and it is thought that if those who are sharing the benefits of this asylum were placed in good families as soon as properly prepared to become members thereof, without waiting till they have attained a fixed age, and their places occupied by those greatly needing the benefactions of this noble charity, its sphere of usefulness might be still more enlarged.

The New York Catholic Protectory.

Office, 33 Warren street,

New York.

The object of this society is "to provide for the education and support of such idle, truant, vicious, or homeless children of both sexes, from seven to fourteen years, as may be properly surrendered to its protection, or committed to its custody by the order of any magistrate of New York, or by the Commissioners of Public Charities and Correction." In addition to the class of children sent to the Protectory under commitment, the officers are allowed to take children who may be intrusted to them by their parents.

The origin of the society is thus stated: "The Roman Catholic citizens of New York had long felt the need of an institution where poor and vicious children, having Roman Catholic parents, might be cared for and educated in accordance with their own faith. The organizations then existing were not, on religious grounds, considered as proper asylums for this class. It was, therefore, decided, in 1862, that an appeal should be made to the Legislature for a special act authorizing the establishment of a society of benevolent gentlemen who should work without pay or emolument, to whom would be granted the power to provide for and control such of the poor children of the Roman Catholic faith as were heretofore committed to other institutions. In accordance with this purpose a charter was obtained April 14th, 1863, incorporating the 'Society for the Protection of Destitute Roman Catholic children in the city of New York.' This name was, by act of the Legislature, in 1871, changed to its present title. The first meeting of the society at which a board of managers was elected was held May 1, 1863.

"The asylums for the care and custody of the children were first located in two comparatively small buildings in Thirty-sixth and Thirty-seventh streets, and for three years the society struggled against difficulties of the most trying character; inadequate accommodations, want of pecuniary means (during nearly one whole year the daily wants being supplied by cash advances from some of the managers), and malignant diseases, all seeming at one period to combine against and seriously threaten the very existence of this institution.

"The ever confiding faith of its devoted first president, Dr. L. Silliman Ives, in the protection of Divine Providence over such a good work, aided by the untiring zeal of the Christian Brothers and the Sisters of Charity, who had been selected to take charge of the educational and disciplinary branches of the asylum, as well as the generous assistance of the citizens of New York, overcame gradually all impediments. The managers hired, soon after, larger premises on Eighty-sixth street, near the East river, for the girls, and also two houses in the same street, near Fifth avenue, for the boys. The working of the institution was continued on these premises until the spring of 1867, when a farm was purchased in Westchester county for the permanent location of the institution, and in addition to the buildings already on the grounds, a large brick building was erected, as well as a commodious frame one, affording, in the aggregate, excellent accommodations for the separate and yet compact management of both male and female departments. The State Legislature showed its appreciation of the efforts made, by granting it fixed pecuniary aid, and thus placed it on a nearer basis of equality with similar establishments of the city of New York. The generous and sympathetic response of the citizens of New York, as shown by the successful result of the great fair in 1867, to raise a sum of money to be specially devoted to the making of better provisions for the poor girls in charge of the society, was another powerful encouragement. This confidence was an additional incentive to more energetic efforts, if possible, on the part of the managers. It enabled them to prosecute their undertaking on a scale commensurate with the unfortunately growing requirements of this crowded metropolis."

The city office and receiving house of the Protectory is at 33 Warren street, corner of Church, where a large stock of shoes and other work made in the institution is offered for sale. A van plies daily between the office and the Protectory, conveying inmates and material back and forth. The Protectory is located in the town of Westchester, in Westchester county, eleven miles from the City Hall in New York. Its post-office is Westchester. The institution may be reached by a short ride upon the Harlem Railroad, leaving the train at Tremont station. A ride of about two miles from the depot brings one to the extensive group of large buildings which comprise the Protectory establishment. Prominent among these, and first arresting the attention, is the boys' department, an imposing brick structure, four stories high, with basement and mansard roof, having a central tower containing a fine tower clock. The architectural design of the tower, as well as of the entire building, is quite elaborate, the whole presenting a stately appearance. The edifice is situated in the midst of extensive grounds, which are being improved. The site is an eligible one, the land in front gently sloping away from the main building. The soil is desirable for agricultural purposes, and the location is healthful.

A visitation with Commissioner Hoguet was made to this institution October 15, on which occasion the boys' department was found to be under the care of Brother Teliow, assisted by thirty of the Roman Catholic Order of Christian Brothers, and the girls' department under the charge of Sister Helena, with twenty-two other Sisters of Charity of Mt. St. Vincent associated with her in the work.

Although it will be difficult to convey to the reader, in the short space allotted to it in this report, an adequate idea of the system and arrangement of this immense establishment, yet a brief sketch of its noteworthy features which came under our observation will be attempted. The various parts of the institution were visited in the following order, beginning with the

Boys' department.— There were here at the date of visitation about thirteen hundred and forty boys. In the large printing room there were between seventy and eighty, under the supervision of a foreman, himself once an inmate, but now a superior workman. In this room are three steam-power presses. Stereotyping is carried on to an extent enabling the establishment to make all the castings used in its printing. About fifty-five boys were setting type, whose ages averaged about fourteen, and twenty little fellows were folding paper, none of whom were older than eleven years. There were also ten, between fourteen and eighteen years of age, working at the presses.

In the tailoring department were about thirty boys sitting cross-legged on a platform, like tailors, and very busy at work; others were operating sewing machines, in all about sixty boys. The boys make every thing they wear, and in addition do a great deal of work for employers.

In the room appropriated to the boys' clothing are cases containing fourteen hundred small compartments, one of which is allotted to each boy. These are numbered, and the clothes that are in them are also numbered to correspond. The garments are of a warm woolen material, and of various colors. The President remarked: "I will not permit the boys to wear uniform clothes. I never buy two pieces of cloth alike."

In the shoemaking department there were nearly four hundred boys, ranging in ages from eleven to seventeen years. There are two shops in this department, one for making nailed and the other for making sewed shoes. The work is done largely by machinery. The boys wrought with alacrity, and seemed cheerful and attentive to their duties. The Brother says: "They have stated hours for labor and for education, and a given space of time for recreation. They have certain tasks to do, and when these are done they can go and play."

It is gratifying to state that the system of letting out the services of the boys to contractors at a fixed price per day is not in practice here. On this point the President of the Protectory remarks: "The boys do not work on contracts. We make a shoe and sell it for as much as we can. We are training boys to be shoemakers. We are working this institution for the benefit of the State. We are taking the raw material and trying to make out of it self-sustaining men. If in the process we can save a few dollars so much the better, but that is not our primary aim. We have conducted this department for years without making a shilling. Last year we made money; this year we lose."

About two hundred boys were employed in the cane-seating department, their ages varying from nine to eleven years. The work here seemed to be well done, and the boys' movements were brisk and orderly.

In a room in the basement were found about four hundred boys engaged, some in blocking out soles, and all working with a will.

The laundry contains four steam washing machines. The washing for the institution is all done by the boys, under the supervision of one of the Brothers and an assistant.

In the cabinet making department the boys were engaged in making bureaus, chests of drawers, wash-stands, etc. Many creditable specimens of their handiwork were there for inspection. Attached to the establishment is a blacksmith's shop, a wheelwright's shop, a horse-shoeing and a wagon-making department, and a machine shop, in which the machinery is repaired. The iron bedsteads used in the establishment are also made here. Bedsteads are likewise made to supply outside orders.

In the box-making department the boxes for packing shoes are made. All the carpentry about the institution, the Brother says, is done by the boys, and two buildings have been put up by them. In addition to the trades taught in all the departments named, the boys are instructed in gardening and farming. About seventy-eight were engaged in this kind of work.

A good working Fire Company has been organized among the boys, which is equipped with engine and hose cart. The Company does good service, not only in the institution, but in the neighborhood, having laid residents in the vicinity under obligations to them in several instances by putting out their fires, and thus saving their houses.

There is also a fine Cornet Band, composed of the boys who have a talent for music. This was organized by one of the Brothers. They wear a blne uniform. This band, the Brother informed us, attend the Jerome Park races regularly, and get thirty dollars a day for their services.

One of the large yards containing swings, etc., for the boys' recreation, was at the time of our visit filled with juveniles, who were here allowed to pursue their sports, and to indulge their boisterous propensities, to their hearts' content. The Brother said: "We have three hundred boys unemployed, simply because there is no money to put up workshops for them."

The steam engine in use on the premises is from forty to fifty horse power. The steam from several large steam boilers heats the building, and affords steam for cooking. A spring supplies the house with water, which is gathered in a reservoir, and carried through the building in pipes.

Thirty-five cows are kept on the place. All their milk is used in the institution, bnt even this, we were informed, is insufficient for the inmates. All the vegetables used are raised in the extensive gardens of the Protectory, except a full supply of potatoes. The lands of the institution cover one hundred and forty-seven acres. One hundred and thirty-five acres are under cultivation, twenty acres being laid out in garden.

The domestic part of the house is on the same large plan as the industrial. The kitchen, with its huge caldrons and polished boilers for coffee and tea, and with its other appurtenances, is on a scale commensurate with the requirements for feeding fifteen hundred mouths at a single meal, and is suggestive of the hospitality of baronial times.

The refectory is capable of accommodating eleven hundred boys at a sitting. In addition to these, a considerable number of the foremen sit here on a dais at one end of the room, and eat with them. A smaller refectory for the little boys could seat about three hundred. A Brother sat at one end, and the clerks and foremen of departments at the other. The boys were well supplied with a meat stew, bread, turnips, potatoes and apples. Before eating, the form of grace usual in Roman Catholic Asylums was repeated, and after the meal thanks were in like manner returned.

Beeves are butchered on the place to supply meat for the table. A very large and well-constructed slaughter-house, furnished with all the necessary conveniences for butchering the animals required for the sustenance of the children, has been erected during the year.

The dietary is as follows:

For ordinary days: Breakfast — Coffee, bread, butter and meat.

Dinner — Soup, meat, vegetables, bread and fruit in its season.

Supper — Bread, butter, tea and dessert.

For Fridays: Breakfast — Coffee, bread, butter and cakes.

Dinner — Soup, fish, potatoes, bread and coffee.

Supper — Bread, butter, tea and biscuits.

In the Junior Department meat is served but once a day; and as a substitute gruel of Indian or oaten meal, rice, etc., is given in the morning.

The dormitories are very large, containing about three hundred and fifty beds each, and are all similarly furnished. They are lighted on four sides. The windows are large and mullioned. In an alcove off each room, and separated from it by curtains, are beds for three of the Brothers. The boys' bedsteads are of iron, single, two feet four inches wide, having head and foot rails. Straw beds are used, the straw being changed every three months; the pillows are some of husks, some of sponge and some of hair. The beds were square and regularly made; they were very thick, the depth of straw in the ticks being fully fourteen inches. The Brother remarked on this point: "It pays us to buy straw to make decent beds for the boys. As soon as it becomes broken and inelastic we send it off and use it in the stables." Each bed had two sheets, two blankets and a coverlet. The covering is increased as the weather becomes colder. The rooms are lighted by gas. A spacious gas-house, with all its necessary dependencies, retorts, iron receivers, tank, store-house for coal, and full complement of service pipes for all buildings of the institution, has been constructed.

Night closets adjoin each dormitory.

The chapel is of old Saxon-Gothic architecture, and has a capacity for seating fifteen hundred. It contains a large central altar, a confessional at each end, a gallery and a piano. The piano when used is accompanied by music upon stringed instruments.

The infirmary is on the same floor as the chapel. There was here one inmate, suffering from consumption; another from pneumonia; and a third from a swollen foot. This department is in charge of a Brother, and contains twenty beds. In connection with it is an apothecary shop. A large gas jet is kept burning in a flue in the center of the infirmary, for the purpose of ventilation.

The halls of the Protectory are ten feet wide, and extend through the whole length of the building. In addition to the central staircase are four other flights of stairs, rendering easy egress from the building in case of fire. Each floor has a water-pipe and a number of leather buckets ready for use in case of fire.

The library contains about one thousand volumes, embracing a great variety of reading matter, including a collection of the Rev. Jeremiah Kinsella, and another of the Rev. Dr. L. Silliman Ives. The reading room is furnished with tables and comfortable chairs, and contains three large library cases with fifteen hundred volumes. Conveniently situated is a separate building, forming a department where the large boys amuse themselves with dominoes and other innocent games.

The lavatory arrangements are very complete. The boys wash in running water. Each has his own towel.

The school is divided into four class-rooms, each containing about sixty boys. The primary classes are given practice in calisthenics. One of these classes presented a lively sight, as we were passing through the room, the little boys singing, meanwhile, a simple song in which we distinguished the words:

> "Hold your right hand up!
> Hold your left hand up!
> See the blacksmith strike," etc.

The programme of studies in the male department comprises spelling, reading, writing, grammar, history and arithmetic, which are taught in every class, so that boys of every age and condition of advancement receive continued instruction in these branches during their whole residence at the Protectory. Such boys as are sufficiently advanced in these fundamental studies, are also instructed in composition, practical and intellectual arithmetic, algebra, book-keeping, geometry, and mensuration.

There is also attached to the senior division a class in phonography, and another in music. The smaller boys have seven hours of study and class exercises every week-day. The larger boys have two hours instruction in the forenoon, and nearly three hours in the evening, the middle of each day being spent in the various industrial departments.

An interesting feature of the institution is what is termed the "bank-book system." The boys are encouraged to save their money. Some, we were told, have already $400 or $500 to their credit, and others again have scarcely any thing. The more advanced boys are paid a percentage out of their earnings. It is put to their credit, and from this fund they purchase their own clothes. In this way independence and self-reliance are being inculcated, and the boys are learning how to adapt means to ends and laying the foundation for habits which come into play in the honorable acquisition of property.

Discipline is maintained by a mild form of punishment, such as detention from play, that of a corporal character being seldom resorted to. The Brother said: "The cases that we cannot manage are very few. I do not think we have many really incorrigibly bad boys in the house, and yet ninety-five per cent are regularly committed to us. Some have stolen, others have tried to fire buildings, have been guilty of vagrancy, have gone into bad places, or done something else to bring them here. During the preceding year we have had but three cases that we had to place elsewhere, by recommitment of magistrate."

In reference to the principles of reform by which his associates and himself are guided, Brother Teliow says: "Money will never sustain reformatory enterprises. It may help to prepare the remedy for a social evil, but can never apply it. True reformation must be found in plans conceived and directed by the heart as well as the brain. We have worked upon the principle, that thorough reform is consequent only upon a complete change of habits and associations. And we have been most scrupulous in causing youths, during their term of pupilage, to lose sight entirely of their past errors and the odium incident to them, and, if possible, to forget their present dependence. They must be impressed with the idea that they are not eating the eleemosynary bread of the workhouse, as it always tends to paralyze their manly aspirations.

"Our religious view is positive. The aim of our instruction and discipline is to send forth our children with minds freed from the distraction of commingled doctrines and fortified against temptation by a well-defined faith, an abiding hope, a never-failing charity. My assistants are animated solely by religious motives. We work in harmony for the same end and with the same principle prompting and directing us."

Girls' Department.— The spacious and tasteful edifice, formerly occupied by the girls, was burned down and its contents destroyed, July 25, 1872, causing much inconvenience to the institution. This building had been erected at a cost of about $165,000, mainly from the proceeds of a single fair. In the interval, between its destruction and the partial completion of the new building, temporary structures on the grounds were improvised. These were still in partial use on the day of visitation.

A new engine and boiler house is in progress of construction for the female department, and the managers are making arrangements for the introduction of steam power into a part of the temporary wooden buildings, which are being converted into a large workshop, in which the business of silk-winding will be conducted, under a contract recently entered into by the managers with well-known silk manufacturers.

A commodious edifice, combining modern improvements, is now being built, the west wing of which is occupied by the girls. The unfinished part of the building is intended for dormitories, chapel, kitchen, store-rooms and dining rooms. The dormitory apartments are planned with high ceilings, supported by iron columns. Flues are in the walls for ventilation, and transom head-lights over the doors. A suitable apartment for invalids or convalescents, so especially needed in the event of an epidemic, or the outbreak of a contagious disease, is one of the features of the new structure.

The chapel is designed to seat one thousand persons. Its tinted walls, varnished wood-work, and stained glass windows, render the apartment quite attractive. The altar is lighted from above with gothic windows on each side. The marble altar, costing $2,000, was purchased out of a legacy left by a benevolent gentleman.

A wing for this main building, corresponding with the west wing already completed and occupied, is in contemplation. The number of girls on the day of visitation was six hundred and one, their ages ranging between seven and sixteen years. They were dressed neatly and differently, the Sisters preferring variety in color and material as a matter of taste. The girls' hair was mostly tied up with ribbons, and their faces looked clean and bright.

Care is taken in the arrangements for ablutions. Each inmate has her own towel. This is numbered with her own number. Every girl in the house, Sister Helena informed us, has a number, and this number is on her clothes, her books, and every thing allotted to her, and each is held responsible for her own. In this way an opportunity is more readily afforded for observing and rewarding those who show the most neatness in the care of what belongs to them.

The school comprises ten classes of about fifty each in the primary departments, and sixty or seventy in the classes of the older pupils. The rooms are furnished with patent desks and all modern appliances. The personal cleanliness of the inmates was marked. The Sister says: "The mornings and evenings are devoted to the school, and the afternoons to work. Young children of either sex are not expected to work. Their day is divided between the school and the play-ground. Special pains is taken to give young girls ample out-door recreation. About three hundred and seven girls, comprising all of the junior classes, are kept in school five hours per day. Those girls who are engaged in the industrial departments during part of the day, are kept in school two hours in the morning, and those employed in house labor are kept in school two and one-half hours in the afternoon."

In one of the classes we found about sixty-eight girls engaged in finishing off shirts. In the "operating room" there were sixty-two machines, all worked by girls, who are paid according to their capacity. The following figures will better explain the extent of the industrial features of this department: About ninety-six girls are engaged at shoe-fitting, about one hundred and seventy-six in plain sewing, and about twenty-five in house-work.

The average annual cost for the maintenance of each girl is stated to be $115.31. Regarding the value of the labor, it is said that "$5,000 in cash has been paid into the treasury in 1875, from the proceeds of their labor in 1874; and the inventories of the female industrial department just made show profits of nearly $14,000 for the year just closed." It is further asserted that "a continuance of results such as these, together with a total cessation of building, would, in the course of a few years, materially decrease the share of the present floating debt justly chargeable to the female division of the Protectory."

The room intended for school purposes is now used as a dormitory. It is furnished with single iron bedsteads, two feet three inches wide. The beds are of straw and very thick.

The house was found to be very clean and tidily kept and the order prevalent throughout in all the housekeeping as well as industrial departments, it would seem, must have a beneficial effect upon the children, many of whom, before coming here, were brought up in the utmost neglect, and left to habits of heedlessness. The demeanor of the Sisters appeared to be that of earnest women, engaged in a work undertaken as a duty, investing them with a dignity that seemed to inspire respect among the children.

The whole number of children, both boys and girls, in the Protectory at the date of October 1, 1875, was 1,944. Of these, 538 were orphans, 1,021 half-orphans, and 365 had both parents living. There were of native parentage, 147, and of foreign parentage, 1,797. Of the entire number, fifty-three were partially supported by parents or friends. The number of children transferred from Randall's Island Nursery and the county poor-house of Westchester at the time the system of rearing children in these institutions was broken up, was 108. The whole number of children received during the year was 941; the number discharged, 839. Of the latter, 84 were indentured, 643 returned to parents or guardians, 79 left without permission, 19 were transferred to other institutions, and 14 died.

A new feature relating to the disposition of the children in the Protectory is thus outlined by its Rector: "We hope soon to have agencies established throughout the State, by means of which the institution can be relieved, its objects extended, and the State in general benefited. Through these agencies, it is the intention to locate boys in self-sustaining positions with farmers and mechanics, thus making room for others in the Protectory, and benefiting the community by furnishing well-tutored and reliable youths to mechanical, agricultural and general commercial pursuits."

The total expenditures of the society during the fiscal year ending September 30, 1875, were $288,991.31. Of this, $127,756.67 was for buildings and improvements. The total indebtedness is $317,224.48. The value of its personal estate, including bonds, stocks and other investments, is $176,050.83.

A per capita allowance of $110 has been received from the City Treasurer for the last eight years. This is stated to be at least $20 per child less than the cost of maintenance.

"The additions made to the permanent improvements of the Protectory during the year just closed have been very large, and the greater part of their cost constitutes the increased indebtedness of the institution, which is now $87,176.45 more than it was on October 1st, 1874.

* * * * * * * *

"The cost of annual expenses has been increased this year by the depreciation of values in some of the industrial departments, viz.:

"The shoe manufactory, instead of showing, as in former years, a profit, shows a loss of nearly $8,000, and the printing shop shows a decline of over $2,000 in its account for the year ending September 30, 1875."

During the year 1875 the Protectory met with a great loss in the death of its distinguished President, Dr. Henry James Anderson. The extent of this bereavement, and the estimation in which he was held by those associated with him in the work, may be in some measure comprehended by quoting the language of his successor, the Hon. Henry L. Hoguet, which is as follows:

"During twelve consecutive years, was the Protectory the object of Dr. Anderson's every-day laborious attention and solicitude. This ripe scholar, this distinguished mathematician, this learned linguist, this ex-professor of the first seat of learning in the State, did not consider it beneath his capacity to perform the dull routine work incident to the business requirements of the Protectory.

"He attended daily at the office, not only supervising the administration of its affairs, but with a patience and self-abnegation never to be forgotten, he entered into the minutest details of its workings, discharging himself a large part of the clerical duties, writing most of its correspondence, attending personally to litigious cases in court, in which his legal acquirements and high moral reputation were of great value to the Protectory.

"Oftentimes has this great, good man himself conveyed the wretched-looking objects of his solicitude from the courts to the Institution, happy in having rescued these waifs from the misery, sin or crime to which they had till then been exposed. All of these services were rendered with a quiet, patient, unobtrusive, but persistent tenacity of purpose, the source of which must have been a heart brimful of Christian benevolence."

The Protectory is under the direction of an energetic Board of Managers, and the Christian Brothers and the Sisters of Charity are zealous in their good work.

During the first year of the existence of the Society for the Protection of Destitute Roman Catholic Children, the institution provided for three hundred and twenty-three children; and during the succeeding six years, for three thousand three hundred and fifty-three. The whole number that have received its benefits up to the present time, is nine thousand seven hundred and twelve.

The reformatory work of this Society is of such magnitude, and its beneficent results are so apparent and generally recognized, that special allusion to them seems superfluous. As an Asylum, at once reforming and elevating for thousands of poor Roman Catholic children, who through lack of proper home training and poverty are in the direct path leading to misery for themselves and hurtfulness to others, this institution must be regarded as an indispensable aid and safeguard to society. So multitudinous are the benefits growing out of its work, that those engaged in it are certainly deserving that heartfelt commendation due to all those who are earnestly laboring to elevate unfortunate children.

New York Infant Asylum.

New York.

The New York Infant Asylum was founded in accordance with the provisions of a charter granted by the Legislature in 1865, and at that time it was recognized as one of the institutions by which Christian efforts were being made to prevent infanticiding, suiciding and moral abandonment among homeless and despairing young women, and to repress at the same time certain of the most inevitable causes of pauperism and wretchedness. We have been kindly furnished with the following information by those familiar with its history and deeply interested in its workings:

"At first, that is in 1865–66, the founders believed that the work would be chiefly that of a 'foundling asylum.' It was organized as a foundling house, receiving only abandoned infants. A large mansion in the suburbs was soon filled with foundlings, but the experiment proved that its plan and policy had been unwisely chosen. It was acknowledged that less than twenty per cent of the infants would survive to their first birthday anniversary.

"It was clearly seen that inducements and ample means would need to be supplied to persuade mothers to accept the duty to nourish and care for their infants, or the endeavor to save such infants to live and be reasonably worth rearing must be abandoned. The latter alternative was accepted.

"In 1871 public sentiment and the prolonged study of the subject induced the managers to re-organize, and they adopted a new policy, and sought out adequate methods to attain the greatest benefits which a reception house and refuge for homeless infants could afford. The re-organization of the work was effected by agencies which Christian ladies and physicians devised.

"The institution is under non-sectarian control, but it is governed by a Board of Lady Managers, representing all the Protestant denominations of the city, and by a like constituted Board of gentlemen, acting as Trustees."

It is stated that the mothers of the children whom this asylum seeks to save, represent every grade of society and every degree of intelligence, and that in most cases the mothers are the victims of seduction under the promise of marriage; that these young mothers possess the affection that would lead them to care for their babes, if they could do so and preserve their respectability. On this point the physicians assert:

"It is an altogether mistaken opinion that the mothers of the illegitimate have little natural affection for their offspring; on the contrary, they part with their children with the most marked evidence of intense sorrow. Whenever placed under such circumstances that they can nurse their children, they refuse to part with them, and will follow them into almost any institution which affords shelter and protection. The attendants upon institutions which have a reception basket, where the mother may deposit her child, unknown, but not unseen, relate daily instances of the most intense grief manifested by the mother as she is about to turn away forever from her babe; in many instances she returns repeatedly and fondles it before finally leaving. In general these foundlings have upon their person some token by which they may hereafter be recognized. Such facts prove that these mothers are at this period extremely susceptible, and may be rescued from an impending life of shame if placed with their children under the home-like discipline of a well-ordered charity. Thus not only would the life of the child be saved, but the mother would also be saved. They prove also that the crime of abandonment and infanticide is perpetrated only under the most aggravated state of mental and moral disturbance.

"The evils avoided by the New York Infant Asylum are these:

"First. All temptations and errors by which a mother would resolve upon the abandonment of her infant, because of the provisions of the asylum.

"Second. All inducements to the mother to seek any vocation which should result in the sin of forsaking her infant when newly born, either by offering herself in the market of wet-nursing, or seeking equivocal or sinful modes of life, because of shame or despair.

"Third. The asylumizing of children after they become mature enough to be adopted as foster children for family culture and a home life.

"Gradually the plans of the institution have taken shape so as to secure the objects here mentioned. These objects have been obtained as follows:

"Distribution and classification, by obtaining for use a place of reception which has a spacious Maternity House.

"Two Nursery Houses in salubrious, rural neighborhoods, one in Flushing comprising eight acres of open grounds, and one on Tenth avenue and Sixty-first street, in the city, comprising nearly ten city lots on the heights near the Central Park.

"Secondly. By securing a basis of material aid precisely equivalent to the certified minimum or average expenditure of the City Alms Department for pauper infants, and cases in Infants' Hospital Maternity Wards, week by week, or day by day, for the last preceding year. The Commissioners of Public Charities annually certify this rate of per diem cost of their pauper nurslings, and the city gives a corresponding amount of aid to infants in this asylum.

"The institution is now so organized that its methods of mercy and care reach out the hand of succor to the homeless mother and infant, and to the friendless and cruelly forsaken young woman on the eve of her greatest want, when woe and terror make such silent acts of mercy the plainest duty of Christian charity. These timely and prudent acts of charity produce an undying impression upon every beneficiary, and they are designed alike to save the soul from despair and the recipients from the touch and doom of pauperism. As respects the infants themselves, no other method of care could save them from the fatal results of neglect and disease, and of ultimate pauperism or the worse alternative of vicious courses of life.

"The terrible desperation and bewildering alarm and dread which may be about to tempt the young mother to destroy herself, or in some way destroy her newly-born babe, or worse, to plunge into the moral oblivion by the horrid alternative of sin, are superseded and wholly prevented. It is a silent, natural and certain way of saving lives that need not be lost, and saving from woes worse than death or pauperism.

"Silently, prudently and with most careful instruction each mother, who is reached by the methods of this institution, is taught her duties and helped onward to her best destiny, while every infant, which cannot be well and most wisely provided for by mother and kinsfolks, is adopted into a family of real foster-parents. Each beneficiary infant or mother is as gently as possible brought into the sanctuary of a fixed and good home, to be surrounded and filled by natural affections and ennobling hopes.

"The statistics of the New York Infant Asylum from the date of its new organization on the commencement of its present existence, are concisely summarized as follows:

The total number of infants left by unknown persons, *i. e.*, actual foundlings	100
Total number of infants born in the asylum, maternity houses, 24 and 26 Clinton place, was	309
Total number of mothers admitted to the asylum with living infants	400
Total number of infants, not foundlings, admitted without mothers,	133
Grand total of infants (admitted to and born in asylum) from December, 1871, to November 30, 1875, was	942
Whole number of deaths in the above total	178

"Percentage of deaths to the total number of infants in four years, 18 per cent. (The per cent of deaths in foundling houses generally, the world over, in five years periods of their history is from 85 to 94 per cent of total number of infants admitted.)

"Total number of infants (weaned children) adopted out by the adoption committee was forty-five.

"The annual report for 1875 shows that the inmates of the asylum in its three branches, on the 30th of November, 1875, were distributed and classified as follows:

"In the maternity houses, at Nos. 24 and 26 Clinton place, Eighth street, in the city of New York —

Mothers and women in waiting	41
Infants	32
Total	73

"In the Nursery Home on Tenth avenue, Sixty-first street —

Women	52
Infants	74
Total	126

"In the Flushing Home —

Women	27
Infants	56
Total	83

"Total number of salaried employés in the three branches of the asylum, November 30, 1875, was six.

"Though only four years in progress, the plan of the asylum in regard to the admission, the distribution, the adopting and otherwise placing in separate and permanent homes, all the infants it cares for, works well. Thus far not a complaint or ascertained wrong has occurred in the forty-five cases of adopted infants, though the process of adoption was inaugurated three years ago.

"Besides these adopted infants whose escape from dishonor, want and pauperism seemed to depend on such fortunate adoption into families of true foster-parents, a still greater number of the infants have been taken by mothers and friends who have shown their competence and fitness to assume such permanent care and education of them. This class of cases is an evidence of the moral worthiness of a large number of the young mothers.

"The presence of this unpretending refuge in this great city in which thirty-five thousand infants are born each year, with destinies of happiness and virtue, or with fearful possibilities or certainties of misery and vicious and shameful ways of life awaiting each individual thus added to the population, may seem only as a drop and a ripple in the great flood of human life. Nevertheless this is a useful part in the total scheme of beneficent efforts to which the thoughts and labors of the benevolent are contributing."

The total number of persons received during the last year was four hundred and fourteen; the total number discharged was three hundred and fifty-four. Of the latter, twelve were placed out by adoption, one hundred and two returned to parents or guardians, one hundred and ninety-seven were otherwise discharged, and forty-three died.

The total expenditures of the Society during its fiscal year amounted to $56,238.47; of this $8,109.01 was expended for buildings and improvements, and $25,347.50 paid upon indebtedness on real estate. The total indebtedness of the institution amounts to $16,000, and the value of its personal estate is estimated at about $40,000, including its cash balance.

A large number of earnest workers are engaged in this field. Included in its medical staff are names distinguished alike for their philanthropy and scientific knowledge; while among its lady managers are persons of widely-known benevolence.

New York Institution for the Blind.

New York.

"The first organized instruction for the blind in this country was begun under the auspices of this institution, March 15, 1832. Since that time, however, the subject has grown in significance, until there are now no less than thirty-two American institutions devoted to this work."

The location of this educational institution is on Ninth avenue, between Thirty-third and Thirty-fourth streets, in the city of New York. It was incorporated by an act of the Legislature, passed April 1, 1831. Its property is vested in the Association, and its affairs are controlled by a Board of twenty Managers.

The main edifice is a substantial structure, built of Sing Sing marble, to which a mansard attic has been recently added. A three-story brick building has also been erected in the rear. The whole is planned so as to secure a perfect separation of the sexes. The Superintendent of the Institution, Mr. W. B. Wait, expressed himself as opposed to buildings with L-shaped wings for asylum purposes, on the ground that they shut out the sun and induce fevers. He would have buildings so constructed, that while securing the needed separation of the sexes, they would permit the sun to shine into every room in the house at some hour of the day. The site of the building, with reference to its convenience for receiving a water supply, he thought an important consideration, and stated that fully one barrel of water per day, for regular consumption, must be secured for each inmate, beside a reserve, in case of fire.

The number of inmates, on the day of visitation, was eighty-three boys and eighty-six girls. They are admitted between the ages of twelve and twenty-five years, and receive in the Institution a good practical education in the English branches, music and some branch of industry.

In regard to the peculiarities of blind children, Mr. Wait remarks: "Blind children have no peculiar characteristics in consequence of being blind, but their defect becomes the occasion of many. If, however, they are instructed in time, this, as a natural result, would be prevented. We do every thing we can to lead them to think they are not different from other children. We do not allow our teachers to talk to them as if they were different."

The education of the blind being a work of some difficulty, special provision must be made to meet their peculiar wants. The school is furnished with dissected maps, which, when put together, show the physicial features of the countries by elevations and depressions. Globes, both terrestrial and celestial, are made on the same plan. For reading books, several kinds are adopted, some in the Boston type and some in the Glasgow type. The library embraces Bible history, novels, some selections from Shakspeare, Dickens, and Hawthorne. Most of the printing for the blind is in the Boston type. Mr. Wait, the Superintendent of this Institution, has invented a new system, which can be written as well as printed. By means of this the blind can write letters, compositions, music, or take notes in class. It is called the New York Point System. Points are substituted for lines. A certain number of points represent the letter A and a certain number each of the other letters of the alphabet, and thus any word can be written by combining these points.

In speaking of its capabilities, Mr. Wait says: "It enables the pupil to record his own thoughts and to express the thoughts of others. It enables him to produce something of his own. He becomes his own amanuensis and has thus facilities for recording and re-arranging his ideas on any subject. It gives him a power, of which he was before unconscious. The system is a complete one and is capable of expressing all shades of thought. Instead of depending on others to teach him his lesson, the pupil can learn it himself.

"The boys are taught to make mattresses under the instruction of a blind man, himself once a pupil in the institution.

"Many of our pupils go out with the means of self-support. One of our girls belonged to a family of nine children. Her father was a poor, laboring man. She saved, while with us, enough money to buy herself a sewing machine. She has gone home, and now does all the sewing for the family as well as some for others. This she could not do by hand. This girl became blind in her early youth from small-pox, but is very intelligent. Instead of becoming dependent herself upon her family, she has become, so to speak, its main-stay, through the benefits bestowed upon her by means of this institution. Besides the peculiar advantages in this respect, she carries, it is thought, to her home the elevating influence of the institution which the wise foresight of the State has provided."

Considerable attention is given to music. There are seventeen pianos for the use of the pupils who are taking lessons. There is one in each of thirteen rooms, and in two other rooms there are two each. Music is taught both by teachers and advanced pupils. The latter instruct beginners and thus gain practice in the art of teaching. The superintendent says: "We have as fine a choir as is to be found in the city. They sing the Alleluiah Chorus, the best opera choruses, madrigals and the vocal music of the best authors." As we entered the assembly room, a primary class were receiving a lesson in music. The girls were on one side of the room and the boys on the other. There were in all about forty-five pupils. The teacher sat before a grand piano and played, while the children sang from memory. This room can accommodate four or five hundred. It contains an organ with twenty-one stops running through the entire key-board, and three manuals of keys. All the advanced scholars, whom it is thought may be benefited by the accomplishment, are taught to play. On the walls of the room are several mottoes, prominent among which is, "Light is Risen," the motto of the institution.

Three rooms are devoted to piano tuning; each was occupied, at the time of visitation, by one pupil, all under the supervision of one teacher, who is himself blind.

One of the rooms in the house was set apart for the younger girls. This was nicely carpeted and had a pleasant out-look. It was fitted up with closets for clothing. Each inmate has a drawer and a closet, used for clothing, and each knows her own. The superintendent says: "Occasionally we get one who is not exactly strict in observing the rights of property, but it gives us no trouble" A play-house is on the table. Another room of a similar character is used for the little boys. The children, it seems, appreciate bright and cheerful surroundings.

The dormitories are furnished with single iron bedsteads, two feet eight and a half inches wide. Hair mattresses on the top of straw mattresses are used. The ventilation is by the windows, the sashes being adjusted by cords, weights and pulleys.

The dining room is sixty by fifty feet, and is embellished with illuminated mottoes. The girls occupy one side, the boys the other, while the teachers and officers sit at the central tables. They are indulged in the privilege of conversation to a limited degree. The tables at which the smaller children sit are covered with white enameled cloth, but the tables for the larger children are furnished like those of an ordinary family.

"This system of having teachers, officers and pupils eat together in the same dining room, and at the same time, has," says the Superintendent, "been inaugurated in order that all distinction between the blind and the seeing may be obliterated, that there may be no recognition of the blind as a class. The moral effect of this it is difficult to measure. The influence is rather of a social nature, refining and elevating. The blind are received here for the purpose of being educated. They have their faculties and, in the abstract, are equal to other men, only differing from them in the fact that they have been deprived of this one sense. It would be manifestly unjust to emphasize their misfortune by making a distinction at meal time. In 1863, I began to inform myself as to how the distinction heretofore observed as to the classification between the blind and the seeing affected the blind. I found them to be quite sensitive on the subject. This existed to such a degree that I was induced to make a change. At the proper time I called the teachers together and laid the matter before them, as something which they might indorse — which they might say they were glad of. They co-operated cordially with me, and I was thus enabled to make a change in our whole system in this respect, which, although attended with some difficulties at the outset, has been productive of very satisfactory results, and works quite harmoniously."

All the inmates appeared neatly clothed. The girls especially, it would seem, evince a disposition to ornament their hair, and are very fond of all kinds of personal embellishments. The material used for clothing is of good quality and varied. The Superintendent says: "We have a tailor in the house, who measures the boys so as to secure a good fit for each. I take great pains to have them becomingly attired. Our reasons for doing so are these: First, a blind person is quickly noticed. If there is any thing peculiar in their garments it attracts attention, and this makes their misfortune all the more apparent. Second, they appreciate neatness and even color. A blind person is seldom found who has not at some time seen, and retains a recollection of color. It is difficult to account for it. But this impression, possessed by every person who has once seen a color, whatever it may be, is never lost. He may have lost his sight before three years of age, but still it is remembered. The blind are conscious of the pleasure seeing-people have in looking upon diverse colors, and so when our children get a new dress they are particular to ask what is its color, and derive particular satisfaction in being able to converse understandingly about it."

The infirmary department is well situated, and a nurse is specially employed for the work. The health of the children is carefully guarded, and every little indisposition of which they may complain, is treated at once, and thus more serious ailments are escaped.

The building is lighted with gas. It is heated by steam pipes, and provided with fire-proof stairways. Its drainage is good, and the water supply is from the city. The closet accommodations, part of which are without, and part within doors, are quite extensive and very ingeniously arranged.

The girls are taught to sew, knit and crochet, also the use of the sewing and knitting machines, on which they become fairly expert. A great many thread the needle as quickly and as surely with the teeth and tongue as persons having sight. Their fancy work includes many varieties, such as tidies, baskets, knitting work and bead work. As we were leaving the room allotted to this work, the girls were briskly promenading, arm in arm, and chatting in the hall.

An interesting feature of this institution consists in the savings bank system by which inmates may, while pursuing their education, accumulate a little capital to start with when leaving. Mr. Wait explains this feature as follows: "We compensate our pupils for the work which they perform while with us, giving each a proportion of their earnings — a third, a half, and in the last year the whole. Whatever they can earn while at school in this way is placed to their credit and accumulated in the savings bank. We have some seventy accounts at present, and they range all the way from five to one hundred dollars. When they leave, this serves as a capital with which to begin life."

The establishment in all its departments was found to be in good order. It is believed to be under efficient and highly intelligent management. The capacity of the institution is for about two hundred, but its funds do not admit of a greater number of inmates than one hundred and fifty.

The current expenditures during the fiscal year ending September 30, 1875, were $52,460.18. The average weekly cost of support was $5.83 per capita. The funds and investments of the institution amount to $19,000.

New York Institution for the Instruction of the Deaf and Dumb.

New York.

The grounds occupied by this institution comprise about twenty-six acres, and are located upon the banks of the Hudson river at

Washington Heights, between One Hundred and Sixty-second and One Hundred and Sixty-fifth streets. The entrance to the grounds is at the corner of Tenth avenue and One Hundred and Sixty-second street, about nine miles from the City Hall.

The institution was established by an association of benevolent gentlemen of the city of New York. Its affairs are controlled by a Board of Directors, selected by its life members. They serve without compensation. The title to the property is vested in the association. At present the institution is divided into two departments — the administrative and the educational. The former is under the charge of Wm. Porter, M. D., designated as the Superintendent and Physician, and the latter under the charge of Isaac Lewis Peet, A. M., LL. D., as Principal.

At the time the first steps toward founding this institution were taken, in 1816, there was not a school in America, for the deaf and dumb, and not more than twenty-five in Europe. More than sixty deaf-mutes were found in New York city, belonging to the very poor classes, for whose education no provision existed. A society was accordingly formed, and an act of incorporation obtained, dated April 15, 1817, and in May, 1818, the school was opened with four pupils. The system recommended by Dr. Watson, of England, was first tried for two years. This included the teaching of articulation, but the results were so unsatisfactory, that it became necessary to abandon it. Methods borrowed chiefly from the published works of the celebrated French teacher, Sicard, were next adopted with some success, till in February, 1831, Dr. Harvey P. Peet became Principal. He remained in that office thirty-six years, inaugurating the methods of tuition which have contributed so largely to the success of the institution. He was succeeded by his son, Isaac Lewis Peet, who still discharges the duties of that important position.

The school was first opened in one of the public buildings of the city. In 1829 it removed to the buildings on Fiftieth street, afterward occupied by Columbia college. In 1856 it removed to its present, beautiful and highly favorable site, known as Fanwood on Washington Heights.

At the date of visitation, October 22, the basis of the system of instruction was found to be the language of gestures, or what is called the Sign Language. For very young children, a method devised by Dr. Peet, called Language Lessons, is used. This holds the same relation to deaf-mutes that the Kindergarten system does to young children who have their hearing.

From Dr. Peet, in answer to inquiries, the following views were obtained, regarding the sign language and the visible speech method, sometimes called the "Improved System of Instruction for Deaf-mutes":

"The conclusion that I have come to, after many years' experience, is, that it is impossible, with congenital deaf-mutes, to prevent them thinking in the way of what may be called the sign language. They have no ideas that are not of a pictorial character. Their thought is nothing but a series of images. Their efforts to converse are nothing more nor less than the reproduction of these images. Even those who profess to dispense with the sign language altogether, cannot prevent the pupils conversing through that medium. It is only in the school-room that the attention of the deaf-mutes is turned to the other mode of expressing their thoughts.

"We do not use signs in the earlier exercises of the school, but in all explanations of abstract terms and difficult sentences, in all testing of their ability to give to thought expression in language, we use the sign language. In the early part of the course, however, we prefer to use a system of object teaching, in connection with the instruction of deaf-mutes, in order to give as many as we can the ability to express ideas by means of written language and by articulate speech.

"Articulation is nothing more than one of the forms of expressing in language the thought required. It is a means of expressing ideas. In almost all the schools there are persons who have lost their hearing at five or six years of age, without losing the ability to speak, if it was cultivated. In these cases it is obviously a duty to keep their speech, and require them to read the lips. Then there is a class of deaf persons, deaf from birth, who yet have a partial hearing. This advantage can be used to a great extent, if vocal intonation is given, and yet if they did not go to an instructor of the deaf and dumb they would learn no language. For such, articulation is desirable. But the class of congenital deaf mutes have never heard any sound; and it is, in my opinion, simply a question of economy, whether or not it is desirable to teach them articulation. It is only an approximation to speech. It is not really speech. It is no doubt a great comfort to their friends, who can accustom themselves to this kind of speech, but it is disagreeable to people generally. It makes their misfortune apparent. The cases of successful teaching of articulation among congenital deaf mutes are not very many. I think there is a great deal of time lost in teaching them the system. As an honest man, I do not favor it. In our institution we combine every thing which we think will be of any advantage to the pupil. We use Prof. A. G. Bell's system. There is no question of its value. The symbols in this system represent all the sounds made by the lips. We require the pupil to translate from a page of reading matter into these symbols. If he has done it correctly he will approximate the articulation of these words. Then we have deaf mutes who watch a speaker's lips, and put what he says into symbols. This exercise calls precise attention to what the speaker is doing. We study every thing which we think will advance the interests of the deaf mutes. We do not wish to waste property or time by futile efforts. Our great aim is to teach them the English language; to enable them to communicate with the outside world. We make every thing yield to that. We spend a great deal of time on arithmetic, geography and book-keeping. The higher classes get a very good academic and scientific education in physics, chemistry and physiology. The higher mathematics are also taught, as well as grammar, rhetoric and logic. We do not attempt to teach foreign languages.

"Our pupils study natural history. We have a large cabinet used for illustrations, and our proximity to Central Park affords us unusual facilities for making this study interesting as well as of practical value to the scholars. I think our deaf mutes get a very good, sensible education."

The boys are instructed in some branch of mechanical industry, such as tailoring, shoemaking, and cabinet-making. This work is so arranged as not to interfere with their schooling. The school is divided into two departments. The first division go to school at 8 A. M. and remain till 12 M. The second division spend this time in the workshops, and attend school in the afternoon, while the first division take their place in the workshops. Thus one-half of the school is in the workshops and one-half at their studies. The girls learn to sweep, wash dishes, sew and do general housework.

Great care is said to be exercised to preserve the health of the inmates. Regarding the health and dispositions of deaf-mutes generally, the steward, Mr. Brainerd, remarks: "These children do not give any more trouble than others, but they are not so healthy. They usually come having a weakness somewhere, especially those that have become deaf through disease. So far as their dispositions are concerned, it depends very largely on the early training they have received. They are brought up, for the most part, on the street among other children who take advantage of their affliction. They say, 'there goes the dummy,' and hoot him. He gets, after a while, so that he feels that he must fight his way along. I have known persons to speak of some particular child as having a fearful disposition. But when you come to look into it, you will find that it is occasioned by the way in which he has been treated. Further than that I do not see any bad disposition in deaf-mutes."

The dormitories were furnished with both iron and wooden bedsteads, varying in width from two feet six inches to two feet eight inches. In the dining-room the furniture consists of tables and stools; crockery plates, and knives and forks are used at meals. The building is heated by steam, lighted by gas and ventilated by fan ventilation. It has a capacity of about five hundred and fifty pupils.

Wooden pins are inserted at intervals in the rails of the balustrades, and the open spaces are protected by rods laid across to prevent accidents to inmates who may chance to fall over. Water buckets are in the halls for use in case of fire.

The grounds about the institution are well laid out in pleasant walks and planted with shrubbery. They are so extensive that ample space is secured for the recreation of inmates. The garden is large and supplies all the vegetables needed.

The average number of inmates during the past year was five hundred and fifteen. The average weekly cost of support is $5.50. The amount of current expenses, less clothing, for eleven months, from October 1, 1874, to September 1, 1875, is $147,502.33. The total expenditures, including extraordinary expenditures during the same period, were $160,767.41. Its receipts are as follows:

From general appropriations	$95,761 63
From counties, towns and cities	34,889 49
From individuals for the support of inmates	1,540 88
From interests and dividends on investments	5,498 62
From all other sources	23,468 72

The institution has invested funds to the amount of $116,000.

The lateness of the hour at which the visit was made prevented a thorough inspection of the premises, but the impression made upon the mind was that the institution is maintained in a high condition of efficiency, and that its management is in every way creditable, not only to those directing its affairs, but to the State.

New York Juvenile Asylum.

New York.

The New York Juvenile Asylum, incorporated June 30th, 1851, has for its objects "the receiving and taking charge of such truant, disobedient, friendless and neglected children of both sexes, between the ages of seven and fourteen years, as may be committed by competent authority, or voluntarily intrusted to its custody; the providing for their support, and the affording them the means of moral, intellectual and industrial education."

The following rules regarding the admission and discharge of children are observed:

"I. Truant and disobedient children, and such as require discipline for any cause, between seven and fourteen years of age, belonging to the city of New York, are admitted into this Asylum.

"II. An order from a Police Magistrate, or a *surrender* from parents or guardians, is required as the condition of admission.

"III. Children having no friends to care for them, or whose friends choose to give them up wholly to the care of the Asylum, are provided with homes in the country.

"IV. When parents or friends desire to *surrender* children, it is only necessary to bring them to the House of Reception and sign the proper form of surrender.

"*No uniform time* can be fixed for the attainment of these ends, as every thing depends on the character of the child, and its home training."

The institution is controlled by a Board of Directors, serving without compensation. The immediate charge is given to a Superintendent and physician, assisted by a suitable corps of officers and teachers.

The Asylum is located on One Hundred and Seventy-sixth street, at the upper end of Manhattan Island, on Washington Heights, near High Bridge. The location is one of the finest on the island, commanding a view of the Hudson River and Palisades for many miles, the Harlem River and Long Island Sound, and the whole country for miles around, dotted with cities and villages, and elegant country seats.

The Asylum grounds contain about twenty acres, extending from Tenth avenue to Broadway, and are inclosed by a substantial stone wall and picket fence. On the part adjoining Tenth avenue is a fine oak grove of four acres, and a new double cottage for the use of employés. Twelve acres are used for farm and garden purposes. The buildings and yards occupy the remaining four acres, which form an eminence near the central part of the grounds, and are inclosed on three sides by a brick wall eight feet high. A ground plan of the buildings, showing their extent and the uses to which they are severally devoted, is here given. The Asylum is easily reached by the Hudson River Railroad, taking the cars at Thirtieth street and Ninth avenue, and stopping at Fort Washington Depot.

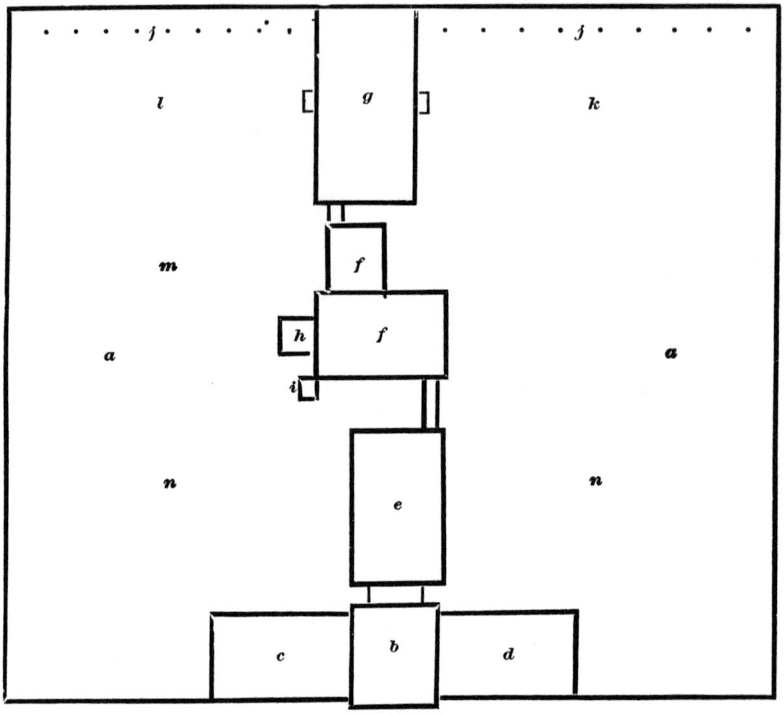

PLAN OF BUILDINGS.

a a. Inclosure wall of brick, 400 feet rear, 585 feet deep, and 8 feet high.

b. Center front building, 50x60, containing the Superintendent's and officers' apartments and ward on fourth floor.

c. West wing, 45x75, containing the girls' apartments in the basement and on first floor, and boys' wards on second and third floors.

d. East wing, 45x75, containing a cellar, basement-kitchen, storeroom and temperance room, and boys' wards on first, second and third floors.

e. North wing, 44x83, containing the children's dining room in basement, chapel on first floor, teachers' rooms on second floor, and hospital on third.

f f. School building, 40x66, and wing, 26x35, containing a cellar, a laundry, kitchen and bakery on first floor, four school-rooms on the second floor, and four on the third.

g. Gymnasium building, 42x108, containing a cellar, a bath-room and a gymnasium on first floor, shoe shop, tailor shop and sewing room on second floor, and wards on third floor.

h. Engine house, 24x27, with three boilers.

i. Engine chimney.

j j. Sheds in boys' yards, 200 and 150 feet long and 14 wide.

k. Boys' play-ground, first division.

l. Boys' play-ground, second division.

m. Girls' yard.

n n. Flower-beds, grass-plats, shrubs and trees.

The dormitories are forty-five by sixty feet, each containing seventy-two iron bedsteads. These are narrow, some being two feet and some two feet two inches wide. Straw mattresses, cotton sheets and pillow slips, and woolen blankets are in use. The rooms are ventilated both day and night by opening the windows.

The children wash in running water, and bathe every Wednesday and Saturday afternoons.

The tables in the dining rooms are furnished with crockery ware; the children sit on stools at the table.

A school is held on the premises, where the children are instructed in the ordinary branches of an English education. There are eight grades, each under competent teachers. The annual visitation and examination of the schools was made by the city school superintendent in September. Special instruction is given the children in vocal music.

The industrial department is an important auxiliary in the work of this institution, and is considered of primary importance to the children, who are soon to be thrown upon their own resources. Of this department the Superintendent, Mr. E. M. Carpenter, says:

"We endeavor to educate the hands as well as the heads and hearts of the children; not, however, by a rigorous exaction of as much work as unwilling hands can be forced to accomplish in a specified time, but rather as the children of a well-ordered family are taught to make themselves useful in door and out, each cheerfully and industriously engaged in performing the allotted labor or duty. Under the direction of persons properly qualified, the children make and mend all the children's clothing and shoes, bake the bread, do the kitchen, dining room and house work, and all the work of the garden and farm."

Thirty-eight girls work in the sewing department, in two divisions, alternating forenoon and afternoon, so that each may be able to attend school. Thirty-two are in the mending department, also in two divisions, for the same reason. Fifty-six boys work in the tailor shop, twenty-six in the shoe shop, three in the bakery and a few on the farm; their work, like that of the girls, being so arranged that their schooling goes on regularly at the same time. Some of the boys are organized into a brass band, having a full set of silver cornet instruments, drums, etc., and under the direction of the foreman of the shop, who is also a musician, they are drilled from one to two hours daily in band music, playing by note. The first band, organized four years ago, were all discharged within two years, and a second band formed, but eleven of whom remain. They play very finely. A third band of twenty-six members has recently been organized.

The chapel or assembly room is capable of seating five or six hundred children. The speaker's desk occupies an elevated platform at one end. The teachers, during Sabbath exercises, are seated at the left, facing the children. The organ is upon the right. Upon the wall over the organ is a tablet, upon which is inscribed:

"Tell the boys of the New York Juvenile Asylum that they must follow truth, justice and humanity if they wish to become useful and honorable men."

"ABRAHAM LINCOLN."

"*September*, 1860."

This message was sent to the boys by Mr. Lincoln upon his being invited on a certain occasion to visit the asylum.

Children are kept, on an average, about one and a-half years, when they are returned to their friends, if they have any. If they have none, they are sent to the Western Agency.

About one-fourth of the discharged children are sent west, and the others are returned to their parents or placed in families in this State.

The discipline and system of management adopted by the Superintendent, as well as his views on the general subject of the reformation of juvenile delinquents were sought, and the following ideas elicited:

"I call a conduct roll at the close of each week. For ordinary misconduct a child receives one or more misconduct marks. Five such marks received during the week, lower the standard from first grade, good conduct, to second grade. Five more the week following will lower it to third grade. And five more the week after, to the fourth or lowest grade, and the child is then deprived of play for one week. Any in the fourth grade may reach first grade by ascending a step each week.

"Where, in the experience and judgment of the Superintendent or principal teacher, corporal punishment would have the desired effect, it is administered by them. Cases that are supposed to require it are referred to them. Cases of serious misdemeanor are always referred to myself.

"I aim at good family discipline. Consequently, in cases of misconduct the child's attention is directed to himself as guilty of wrong-doing, care being taken not to divert his attention to some formal rule, as if the effect of the misconduct consisted chiefly in being degraded on the roll-book, or in the misfortune of being deprived of the privilege of wearing a badge on his coat collar, or something of that kind.

"The great lever which is used here, in maintaining good discipline and securing the reformation of the children, is not a well-wrought roll system, or badge of honor system, or any other device that directs the attention of the children chiefly to outward conduct, while in the institution; but it is this rather: I seek to show them themselves, their habits, their course of life and the result, if unchanged; to show them the steps to be taken in changing their course, and the assistance we can render them here. This is done not in a set, formal way, but by familiar talks with the children, when they are assembled in chapel or school, and by personal conversation with them, giving special attention to the boys who exert a controlling influence. I educate my officers and teachers to the same ideas. The result is the establishment of a public sentiment among the children, that is for good. Such is the basis of good family government, and we make it the basis of our discipline here. I know of no other method that is truly reformatory in its character and influence.

"The children here try to do right, because it is right, not because they get paid for it by certain privileges and immediate advantages. Our conduct roll is simply auxiliary.

"Our children are assembled morning and evening, for the reading of the scriptures, singing and prayer. The chapel services on Sabbath forenoon are conducted by myself. We have no sectarian teaching. In the afternoon we have a Sabbath-school, the children being assembled in their several class-rooms, and taught by their teachers, who use the International Series of Sunday-school Lessons.

"Home is the proper place for a child, but as homes are not always what they should be, and as they are often broken up, and for that and other reasons, children become truant and disobedient and need restraint, institutions beoome a necessity. But the assembling of a great many children in one family compels the adoption of rules for the maintenance of order, etc., which are necessitated by the circumstance of numbers. Children in an institution, therefore, whether there be twenty or five hundred, must of necessity, by reason of numbers, be subjected to rules and deprivations, not necessary in a family. But the conduct of the child necessitated the institution, and the institution necessitated the discipline, at least that part of it which, like school discipline, becomes necessary simply by reason of numbers. These disadvantages, however, are more than compensated by the advantages which accrue. Nevertheless, children should not be subjected to such rules, day and night, and deprived of family privileges longer than may be necessary to lay a permanent foundation for a different course of life in future. I have seen so many instances of the ill-effects of institution discipline and restraints, when continued through a course of years, that I am thoroughly convinced there is almost as much danger from detaining children too long in an institution, as from a too short detention, and the effect of the latter is almost invariably pernicious.

"If institutions like the Juvenile Asylum, which receives children in the early stages of delinquency, were multiplied, I think there would not be any need of multiplying Houses of Refuge.

"A more complete classification of delinquent youth is very important. Instead of having the classification made in one institution, with the idea of making promotions, as in the Irish system, I would prefer entirely separate institutions. For example, when the judges commit boys to us that are hardened and better fitted for the Refuge, we request that they be committed there, which is generally done. Stubborn children in Orphan and other Asylums are committed to us.

"The special object of a reformatory should be to lay the foundation for a permanent change for the better in the character and habits of its inmates or wards. If this object is not attained, then the management is a failure, and the money expended for the support of the institution is, in part at least, virtually thrown away, no matter how economical the management of its finances, or how excellent the discipline may appear to be. Such at least are the views on which my management of an institution is based. According to my observation, the most serious mistake in the management of reformatories lies generally in the discipline. To maintain order in a family of four or five hundred bad boys, especially when they are assembled in one room, as a dining room or chapel, and to guard against the constant practice of lying, profanity and pilfering, and other habits which have become to them almost second nature, is so difficult a task, that to accomplish it successfully is thought by many to be the all-important object, as if the special object of a reformatory was simply to maintain order and secure obedience to a series of rules and regulations.

"Hence the problem with many disciplinarians has been, 'How can I secure order and discipline?' Some have felt that it could be secured only by severity, corporal punishment being chiefly relied on. Others have devised various methods, all based on an appeal to pride and selfishness. A boy sees on the one hand high walls and the difficulty of escape; on the other hand he learns that strict obedience and conformity to rules will secure his one desire, release. He chooses the latter, and the result is a suppression of bad habits, not a change in them, not a permanent reformation. My method has been this: to establish a sound public sentiment for good among the children as the basis of discipline and of reformation, and this I do by plain, familiar talks to the children from time to time when they are assembled, usually in chapel before retiring for the night, and by personal conversation with the hardest and most influential among them; I hold up their past lives before them, their habits, and what these would lead to; I contrast them with obedient boys and good habits, and I impress it upon their minds that it is possible for them to change for the better, and that this is the special object of this institution. The right and justice of all requirements are presented to them, and the general result is cheerful obedience. In this way I awaken their hopes and secure their confidence."

An interesting feature of the Juvenile Asylum is that of a temperance society formed among the boys. For this purpose they have a room of their own tastefully fitted up with appropriate pictures, mottoes, charts, black-boards, library, organ, etc. Under the superintendence of one of the asylum officers the boys choose their own officers and conduct their meetings on each Friday evening. They are regularly instructed by the superintending officer in physiology and other subjects bearing upon the subject of temperance. The members of the temperance society, numbering usually about eighty, sign a pledge not to use tobacco or liquor, nor to indulge in profane language. The general influence of the society upon the children is good, and it is asserted by the asylum officials "that the boys who become members of it, with few exceptions, will hold to their pledge through life."

The boys and girls are encouraged to cultivate plants and flowers; certain of them having spaces of ground allotted to them for this purpose.

On October 1, 1875, there were in the institution five hundred and thirty-eight inmates, twenty of whom were partially or entirely supported by friends, and five hundred and eighteen were supported by the cities. One hundred and sixty-four were of native and three hundred and seventy-four of foreign parentage.

Forty were orphans, two hundred and seventy-nine half-orphans, and two hundred and nineteen had both parents living.

The number of children received during the year ending September 30, 1875, was six hundred and eighteen; the number discharged, six hundred and forty-two. Of the latter number, two were placed out by indenture, four hundred and eighty-five returned to parents or guardians, one left without permission and one died. One hundred and fifty-three were transferred to the western agency.

The total expenditures during the fiscal year ending September 30, 1875, were $85,500.67. The value of its invested funds, from which an income is derivable, is about $5,000.

The original cost of the land purchased at Washington Heights was $1,800 per acre. Its present value is set down at about $15,000 per acre, and the total valuation of buildings and appurtenances is now estimated at from $120,000 to $150,000.

The Western Agency.

A large dwelling, with an acre of land, has recently been purchased at Normal, near Bloomington, Ill., which is occupied by the Western Agent, Mr. E. Wright.

"Children are sent from the Asylum to the Agency at favorable seasons of the year, in companies of from 20 to 40. These companies are not usually brought to the Agency Home and distributed from there, but taken directly to some point where the fact and date of their coming have for several weeks previous been advertised. From among the applicants gathered to meet them, those who have been selected are permitted to take the children upon trial for a period of two weeks.

"If all parties are suited, the child will then be apprenticed until of age — boys until 21, girls until 18. The articles of indenture provide: (1) that the child shall be cared for both in sickness and in health, with proper medical treatment, food and clothing; (2) instructed in some trade; (3) sent to school four months in each year; (4) trained in moral and religious precepts and habits; (5) paid a specified sum of money at the end of the term of apprenticeship.

"Provision is also made for relief in case of dissatisfaction or difficulties which cannot be otherwise adjusted."

Mr. Wright, in his report dated December 31, 1875, gives the following interesting information regarding the work in this department:

"Wards of this year. — There have been received from the Asylum, 153 children — 124 boys and 29 girls — sent out in six companies:

February 22	23 boys,	3 girls.	Total, 26
April 26	21 "	7 "	" 28
June 7	23 "	5 "	" 28
Sept. 6	32 "	7 "	" 39
Oct. 18	11 "	7 "	" 18
Nov. 29	14 "	— "	" 14

"Their average age was 12⅗ years.

"There were committed for destitution, 79; for disobedience, 21; for truancy, 36; for pilfering, 7; for vagrancy, 10.

"Twenty-five per cent (37 children) were full orphans, fifty-five per cent (85 children) were half-orphans; father dead, 45; mother dead, 40; and twenty per cent (31 children) had both parents living.

"Their parentage was: Irish, 62; American, 37; German, 35; English, 12; Scotch, 3; French, Swiss, Italian and Cuban one each.

"They have been placed on trial in 227 houses; 98 have been placed once, 33 twice, 12 three times, 5 four times, and 1 seven times, and four absconded before placing; 118 have been indentured, 3 are working for wages, 3 have been returned to the Asylum, 2 are at the House, 8 have absconded, and 19 are still on trial. Ten of those indentured have since been removed, of whom six have been re-indentured and 4 are still on trial.

"The whole number of visits made on account of these children is 256, and the number of removals since the first placing is 79.

"*Wards of former years.* — The number of wards of this class reported by the Agency to the General Office is 505, of whom 141 have been visited, and the others have been reported to the Agency by employers, 12 orally and 352 by letter. Sixty of these wards have been removed and replaced, of whom 21 have since been indentured, 14 are working for wages, 18 are still on trial, 2 have been sent to New York, 2 are at the Agency, 3 have absconded. 10 placed last year have been indentured. Seven indentures have been canceled by order o. the committee in the case of boys sufficiently advanced in age and skill to make their way without further aid from the Agency. The whole number of visits made on account of these wards is 233, and the whole number of removals is 78.

"*Field work.* — The labor performed in this branch of work has been bestowed upon the wards of this and former years in about equal proportions. The first placing has been attended with almost no trouble beyond that of thoroughly advertising the coming of the several companies, and of selecting from among the many applicants those most worthy to be intrusted with apprentices. Much pains has been taken to awaken a general interest in the work, and on every occasion the companies have been greeted on their arrival by a large concourse of citizens ready to offer them homes. It is probable that no better method than this of securing good homes could be devised. The sight of a company of children thus situated moves many to apply for them, purely out of sympathy and kindly feeling, who have no expectation of any pecuniary benefit, and who would not go to an institution in quest of them, as many do, when actuated by selfish motives.

"The children in all cases have been placed on trial for a period of two weeks, and sixty-four per cent have been indentured at the expiration of the first trial. The remaining thirty-six per cent have been re-placed from one to seven times. Of this latter number thirteen per cent have subsequently been indentured, and the remainder, except the few who have been otherwise disposed of, are still on trial.

"Children who become a public charge may be classified as (1) destitute, (2) demoralized, (3) criminal, (4) defective. With the first class an apprenticing agency can deal successfully, and with the second it can deal satisfactorily, after their wayward and vicious propensities have been cured by skillful treatment in a reformatory. It is chiefly with these two classes that this agency has to deal, and its success is mainly attributable to the thorough preparation for apprenticing which they receive at the Asylum before they are committed to its charge. ***As a rule, private families cannot manage demoralized children, and it is better economy to detain them for a while in efficient training schools than to consign them to an apprenticing agency, with their evil habits and propensities uncured.***

"The latter two classes, comprising those who have become fully developed criminals, and those who are diseased, deformed, feeble minded, deaf mutes and blind, families will seldom consent to receive and maintain, and they must needs be cared for in public establishments. * * * * * * *

"In addition to the present corps of laborers which is occupied with the unavoidable work, there is needed an agent for general visitation. This line of work has been prosecuted only to a very limited extent, but its importance can hardly be overstated. * * *

"Inquiry is often made as to what proportion of agency wards do well. Fifty per cent may be said to do well throughout their minority and afterward, though many do not remain in their first homes, nor in any homes as apprentices through their full terms. A large proportion of the remainder are occasionally somewhat troublesome, and a portion of them become so insubordinate and wayward as to cause solicitude for their future. But even of the troublesome ones a large proportion ultimately become prosperous and reputable, and it is believed that ninety per cent of all the wards may be included in the number of those who, in the long run, do fairly well. This opinion is based upon abundant data, and is not a mere random guess."

The House of Reception for this Asylum is located at 61 West Thirteenth street, in the city of New York. The office of the institution is here, where all the children are received and discharged, and the meetings of the committees and the Board of Managers are held. It consists of a four-story brick building, seventy-five feet front, with wing and basement, and is fully equipped for the permanent accommodation of one hundred and thirty children. It is under the care of Mr. E. D. Carpenter, Superintendent. The object of the house is to afford a temporary stopping place for the children committed to the Asylum. From here they are transferred to Washington Heights. All children voluntarily surrendered to the institution are first brought here. Commitments are also received here, and the particulars relative to the cause of arrest, the personal character and history of the child, as far as practicable, are ascertained and recorded. While in the house the habits of the children are carefully studied and their instruction provided for. The time of detention here is twenty days, during which the child may be removed, but at the expiration of that period the surrender or commitment becomes final, and the child is in the full custody of the institution.

In the room of the Board of Directors are two large frames, "containing," the Superintendent says, "the photographs of about ninety children that have been sent West years ago, and who now are men of property, occupying good positions there. We have records of all of them." There was also a portrait of the venerable President of the

Society, Mr. A. R. Wetmore. This gentleman is, we were informed, "now eighty years old, and yet he visits here on all holidays, and comes regularly every Sunday afternoon and reads stories to the children."

In the small dormitories were found single iron bedsteads two feet six inches wide. Husk beds and husk pillows were used. The larger dormitory contained one hundred and twenty single iron bedsteads. It was well-lighted, having windows on three sides, well-ventilated and had a fresh, sweet atmosphere. On the window-sills were placed boards at an angle of forty-five degrees. Back of this the window is raised about five or six inches. In this way a current of air is admitted without striking the heads of the boys. Night closets are attached to the apartment. There were also buckets of water in the dormitory and upper halls, for use in case of fire. A separate stairway in the building is designed for a fire-escape.

"The number of inmates," the Superintendent says, "fluctuates very much. We have been recently accommodating over one hundred and thirty, our capacity is but for one hundred and twenty. We have, however, a vacant dormitory, which is used when the number is larger."

In the school rooms we found thirty-six boys dressed in suits of grey, with hair cut tolerably close, and averaging in age about eight years. Among them were two colored boys. In another room for the larger children there were about fifty-two boys under instruction. Their average age was about eleven years. This room is used also as a chapel. It was furnished with patent desks and chairs, and also contained an organ. The school is under the supervision of the Department of Public Instruction.

The dining room has a seating capacity for one hundred and twenty children. White table cloths are used, also stools instead of benches. It is a pleasant room. The legs of the stools are set in a plank, and so adjusted that, by removing the plank, the whole range of stools can be simultaneously set aside. The boys are taught to seat themselves at the table in an orderly manner. They repeat, in concert, the following form of grace: "We thank Thee, our Heavenly Father, for these gifts of Thy Providence and for the expression of Thy goodness, and may these mercies lead us to Thyself through Jesus Christ Our Lord. Amen."

The tables are furnished with crockery plates, knives, forks and spoons.

The following is the usual dietary, as given us by the Superintendent: Bread and milk for breakfast and supper; and for dinner, meat, potatoes and other vegetables.

In wet weather the boys congregate in a large play-room, provided for that purpose, with yards adjoining.

The bath-room contains a large circular vat, eleven and a half feet in diameter, made of brick and cement, with a stone coping, three feet deep on the inside, and two feet three inches from the floor on the outside. A two-inch pipe is carried around the inner rim, filled with small perforations, about thirteen inches apart, enabling the boys to gather around and wash in running water. It is supplied with hot and cold water. Towels on rollers are used, instead of a separate one for each lad. The water closets are in the yards.

A camera obscura has been provided for the entertainment of the children on winter evenings.

Only boys are kept here. "Formerly," says the Superintendent, "we kept girls, but now we send them up to Washington Heights immediately upon their arrival."

The institution employs an agent to visit in their homes the children after they are discharged. "The agent in the city," the Superintendent remarks, "goes to see that the children have suitable homes, and by calling upon them afterward he finds that it has a very salutary influence. Thinking he may come around, they are more apt to show obedience. The very fact of his visiting has an influence on them. He writes up reports of his visits in the record book every night. The agent's time is spent continually in visiting. Children are discharged this week, for instance; he will wait for a couple of weeks, and then go around and call at all the different places. He is often obliged to go repeatedly to the same place. The parents frequently say to him, 'my boy is inclined to be a little wild, and I think if you would call around it would be well.'

"He sometimes finds that the parents cannot care for their children, and a little conversation induces them to send them to homes in Illinois. He does not often continue his visits after the space of a year and a half or two years. He can determine in that time whether there is a necessity for it."

Since the organization of the New York Juvenile Asylum seventeen thousand seven hundred and twenty-two children have been brought under its reformatory influences. It has accomplished, without question, a vast amount of good during the period of its existence, and it is believed that if institutions directed and controlled by benevolent individuals, without compensation, aided by the public authorities, and supervised by the State, were multiplied, society would be greatly benefited thereby. This institution originated out of the philanthropic spirit of its founders, and the work it has successfully accomplished may be owing, in a great degree, to the continued exercise of the same spirit directing all its affairs, and the securing, for the discharge of its varied duties, not only efficient but humane officers It is not, even with the per capita allowance made by the city for its inmates, self-supporting. The sum of $10,715 was realized last year by donations and voluntary contributions.

The New York Juvenile Guardian Society.

New York.

This organization should not be confounded with the New York Juvenile Asylum, nor the American Female Guardian Society, both of which institutions are of a widely different character, though having titles somewhat similar.

The Society formerly maintained a school in one of the upper rooms of 207 Bowery. This was found, on October 12th, to have been given up.

The Society still keeps in session a school at No. 101 St. Mark's Place. The school occupies the first floor over the basement of what was formerly a private dwelling-house. Some other parts of the house are rented to poor families. About one hundred and thirty children of both sexes were in attendance, some of these being taught, in the front part of the house, by the principal, a gentleman, and the remainder in the back part, by a lady. The average age of the children was about eight years.

The principal, Mr. Eugene Eshman, at the date of visitation, October 12, made the following statement: "The school is opened and closed with singing, reading the Bible and repeating the Lord's Prayer. We teach the common branches. German is also taught. Most of the children are German. Nothing is given now to the children in the way of food. I was not here last winter, and can only speak from hearsay as to what is given to the children in winter, but I hear they get a warm substantial meal. We are not distributing any thing now, but if a boy comes here and says he is very poor, and wants shoes, I go down to Mr. Robertson, the secretary, and try to get something for him."

The lady teacher complained of the room being cold, and the children suffering in consequence. She said she had thirty-two boys and twenty-seven girls, that no fuel had been sent in, and that they could have no fire in consequence; that the attendance was falling off; that some of the children had taken cold, and were at home sick, and that others the mothers objected to send, lest they should catch cold.

The books used by the children were very much soiled and worn. There was a lack of black-board space, and a general appearance of neglect in all the appointments of the school; there was, however, a piano on the principal's platform. The day was raw and cold, requiring the use of overcoats, and fires were in general use elsewhere. The rooms were cold and cheerless, and the children appeared to be pinched and suffering, their condition exciting our pity.

Both the lady and gentleman teachers seemed kindly disposed and intelligent, but, it appeared, they had not been long engaged, and knew little of the Society or its affairs.

No report from this institution has been rendered for the past year regarding its financial condition, or as to the number of children that have come under its care.

New York Ladies' Home Missionary Society of the Methodist Episcopal Church.

New York.

A very important branch of the work of this Society is that known as the Five Points Mission at 61 Park street, which is mainly devoted to the elevation of children, and to it our attention in this report will be solely directed.

The Mission at 61 Park street, generally known as the "Five Points," was organized in 1850, and is the eighth mission inaugurated by the New York Ladies' Home Missionary Society in the neglected and destitute portions of the city. Before securing its present site the work was carried on in a hired room, formerly a liquor store, at the corner of Cross and Little Water streets.

When the advisability of securing more commodious accommodations became apparent, and the Society had resolved to change, its Advisory Committee undertook to ascertain what suitable locations for their mission were available, and report the results of their inquiry. Various places were named by these gentlemen, but before any selection was made one of the ladies, Mrs. J. A. Wright, whose errands of mercy among the residents of that ward made her familiar with the entire locality, proposed the purchase of the old brewery, very much to the surprise and even to the amusement of the gentlemen. This lady it would seem, however, had a clearer perception of the needs of the work than any of the others present at the meeting, and by urging and pleading she at length succeeded in winning over to her view all the members, and steps were taken to carry out her suggestion.

The following sketch of the history of the Mission is given by one familiar with the subject: "The locality known as the Five Points, as it existed twenty-six years ago, has been often described, and is well known to have been the most God-forsaken place ever existing in a

Christian land. It was here that a band of Christian ladies inaugurated the great reformatory work which has proved to be such a triumphant success. They entered upon the hazardous enterprise in the name of the Holy Trinity, accompanied by a missionary appointed from the New York Conference of Methodist Ministers and an Advisory Committee of judicious business men. In the month of May, 1850, they hired a house on the corner of Park and Little Water streets, and opened a Sunday-school of about seventy scholars, who were rude and disorderly in the extreme. In the after part of the same day they held a public service for the benefit of the older population. From that date the Mission has braved every difficulty and gone on successfully in the midst of nameless trials and hindrances."

The notorious Old Brewery building was purchased in 1851, cleared and occupied. In 1853 it was taken down, and the present edifice erected. The main building is one hundred feet front and four stories high, above a well-ventilated basement. In the central portion of the building is an excellent chapel, extending throughout the whole length of two stories, the ceiling of which is supported by iron columns. Two floors above the chapel are fitted up with separate rooms for poor families. The rear building is devoted wholly to school purposes. It is one hundred feet front by one hundred and forty-six deep, and admirably adapted to the uses for which it was built.

The Mission is under the patronage of the Methodist Episcopal Church, and is governed by a Board of Lady Managers. It is under the immediate charge of Rev. C. S. Brown, Superintendent. A lady visitor, a clerk, a financial secretary and several teachers form the corps of workers. No domestics are employed. A janitor is hired to take charge of the premises. From November till May an industrial school is in operation, which is largely attended, and necessitates additional teachers.

On the day of visitation, October 12, there were in the house fifty children and twenty adult inmates. There were also in attendance upon the day-school over four hundred children, and upon the Sabbath-school over five hundred. The children in the day-school are given bread daily, and supplied from time to time with clothing, as they need it. The clothing is made by a number of ladies, who meet in the house regularly for the purpose of sewing for the children.

On the day of visitation ten of these ladies were thus engaged. Two of these, Mrs. Wm. B. Skidmore and Mrs. Wm. Ryer, whom we had the pleasure of meeting in the office, have been connected with the Mission twenty-six and twenty-five years, respectively.

"These ladies," says the Superintendent, "with others equally devoted to the work, give their hearts to it, and are wholly intent on doing good to the children under our care. They bear their own expenses, even to the lunch provided for them on the days they are here. * * * Mrs. J. A. Wright has also been engaged in this work from its inception, and in all these years, save when absent with her husband, has manifested the deepest interest in the welfare of the un fortunate in this locality."

Various religious services are held on the premises to aid in the furtherance of the work. There is preaching morning and evening on Sunday, a lecture on Tuesday evening, and, from time to time, other religious exercises.

Regarding the adult inmates of the house the Superintendent says: "We have accommodations for seventeen families, whom we receive and shelter during some period of temporary embarrassment. They are usually composed of a widow and her dependent children, a mother deserted by her husband, or similar cases of distress. One of the families lately relieved was that of a business man on Broadway, who, in consequence of loss of sight, was reduced to poverty. These families have rooms free of rent, and are assisted in other ways till they are again able to acquire an independence.

"We have a lady visitor, Miss Elliot, who is indefatigable in her work among poor families. She has been connected with the Society for thirteen years. The school is under the supervision of the Department of Public Instruction."

The principal school room is twenty-seven feet long, furnished with patent desks. Mottoes are on the walls. A piano is placed on a dais in front of the teacher's desk. Good specimens of the children's writing were framed and hung upon the wall as an example to stimulate others. This room is also used as an assembly room, and such exercises as the children have in concert are held here. The school is divided into six grades, all taught by separate teachers. In the infants' department were about one hundred children. The room is fitted up with a gallery.

A good deal of singing is combined with their instruction, which requires the use of a piano, with which the department is furnished. In the next grade were seventy-five children. Among these were observable many Italian faces.

At a given signal the children came together into the assembly room, marching in from their various classes, with their hands behind them, in charge of their teachers, keeping time with the piano, on which a march was being played by the principal, Mrs. Van Aken.

The children, on being seated, sang, in good time and with much spirit, "Hold the Fort." Then a little girl read a composition on "Robin Red Breast," after which they all sang the anthem, "Come unto Me all ye that labor and are heavy laden, and I will give you rest." Calisthenic exercises were then engaged in. The teacher played a lively piece, and a little girl, an adept in the exercises, stood on a chair, and led the others. The exercises were performed with such expertness and exactness as to gratify one's sense of order, while the novelty of their movements, at one time, in the undulatory motion of innumerable hands, resembled the fluttering of leaves. These exercises, while developing the physique of the children, were inspiriting, and evidently a source of entertainment.

"Some of the best scholars," the Superintendent says, "make their home in the house, and attend the ward schools. The teachers have all been connected with the Mission for long periods. Mrs. G. Van Aken, the principal, has been engaged in the school for eighteen years; Miss Schaffer, the First Assistant, thirteen years; Miss Thompson, ten; Miss Osborne, eight; and Miss McEvoy, in charge of the infant department, has been a long time in the Mission."

In the reading room the tables were covered with green enameled cloth, and the room, with its furniture, appeared to be in perfect order. "Six years ago last May," the Librarian says, "the reading room was opened."

This is for the use of young men who wish to avail themselves of its privileges in the evening. Upon a later occasion it was visited at about nine o'clock at night, when it was found to be well lighted. A number of young men were seated in plain but comfortable chairs, absorbed in reading.

This room is in the basement. The windows of the apartment, looking out upon the street, are protected by iron work to prevent injury from the mischievously disposed. The statement must be made with regret, that, notwithstanding the purely benevolent intentions of this work, it had not found entire favor with the lower type of humanity in the neighborhood, as in the entrance-way were seen evidences of missiles of an offensive character, that had been thrown recently within, much to the annoyance of the librarian, an elderly gentleman. As we passed in and out a policeman was standing at the door. He was stationed there as a precautionary measure by the captain of the police. The librarian stated that the interruptions of late years were comparatively few.

The chapel is an apartment with side galleries, and is capable of seating five or six hundred persons. It is furnished with a piano. In addition to the other religious exercises is a large bible class, which has been in operation some time. Its first members are now grown men and women.

The aim of this society is sufficiently indicated by its name. It is to brighten the homes of the poor and ennoble their inmates; to elevate families in the natural way, by making them retrace the steps taken in their progress downward to wretchedness and dependence.

"We try," says Mrs. Wm. Ryer, "to inculcate the home spirit among the children. We try to keep families together and elevate them, and really the families are reached through the children." Aside from the christianizing influences of the work, not only upon the inmates and upon the homes from which they come, the burdens of pauperism are greatly lessened by helping families over difficulties at times, which, but for this aid, would break them down and render them charges upon the public.

The total expenditures of the society during the fiscal year ending September 30, 1875, were $17,000.84. The amount of invested funds from which an income is derivable, is $1,000. Its financial statement shows no indebtedness. The Superintendent says, "notwithstanding the pressure of the times, we have been greatly favored during the past year, and our work was probably never more hopeful than at the present time."

The New York Society for the Prevention of Cruelty to Children.

New York.

This society was incorporated by an act of the Legislature, passed April 21, 1875. Its objects, as stated by its President, John D. Wright, are substantially as follows:

"To enforce, by lawful means and with energy, the laws now existing for the protection of children, and to secure the prompt conviction and punishment of every violator of those laws, not vindictively, not to gain public applause, but to convince those who cruelly ill-treat and shamefully neglect little children, that the time is passed when this can be done in this State with impunity." After enumerating a large number of asylums and institutions devoted to the care and reformation of children, the President further states that "these organizations, which it is the aim of the society to aid, assume the care and control of the inmates only after they have been legally placed in their custody. It is not within their province to seek out and to rescue from the dens and slums of the city those little unfortunates whose childish lives are rendered miserable by the constant abuse and cruelties practiced on them by the human brutes who happen to possess the custody or control of them. This work the Society for the Prevention of Cruelty to Children undertakes and proposes to carry out.

"Ample laws have been passed by the Legislature of this State for the protection of, and prevention of cruelty to, little children. The trouble seems to be that it is nobody's business to enforce them. The societies and institutions referred to have as much as—nay, more than they can attend to, in providing for those intrusted to their care. The police and prosecuting officers of the people are necessarily engrossed in securing the conviction and punishment of offenders of a graver legal stripe; and although ready to aid in enforcing the laws referred to when duly called on so to do, can hardly be expected to seek out and prosecute those who claim the right to ill-treat children over whom they have no apparent legal control.

"Hence the child-beaters live in comparative security. Hence the children, hardened by brutality and cruelty, grow up to be men and women scarcely less hardened than their tyrants. The men swell the ranks of the 'dangerous classes' which imperil the public peace and security, and the women are lost, body and soul, often before they are women in age and maturity."

The office of the society is located at 860 Broadway.

The Secretary, Mr. E. Fellows Jenkins, during a visit to the office, October 7, furnished the following information in regard to the operations of the society:

"We have agents about the city to look after poor children in the streets. In cases where we find children are hired to beg, we arrest the parties who hire them out. This is frequently done by Italian organ-grinders, of whom we arrested quite a number during the past month. The society in all its transactions in reference to children, brings them before the court having jurisdiction in the matter. If a complaint is made to us of any child being ill-used, we send an officer to investigate the case and see what can be done. If the child is very badly abused, we cause it to be taken away and put into an asylum or otherwise properly provided for. Children abandoned in the streets are likewise disposed of. We also give advice and information to all parties asking for it, relating to children, and a great many come to us for this purpose. When there is any offense committed against the child, like that of inducing a young girl to go into a house of ill-fame, we follow the case through to the end. We have caused many children to be sent to Randall's Island,* but we do not like to send them there."

During the short time the Society has been in existence it has done a large amount of humane work, a record of which will be found in its first annual report just issued. Seventy-two children have been disposed of at the instance of the Society, as follows:

Homes found or situations obtained for	8
Stolen or lost children returned to parents	11
Sent to the Association for befriending Children and Young Girls	1
Sent to Commissioners of Charities and Correction	31
Sent to N. Y. Roman Catholic Protectory	11

* This statement was made before the Randall's Island Nursery was broken up.

Sent to N. Y. Infant Asylum	1
Sent to N. Y. Juvenile Asylum	3
Sent to Roman Catholic Orphan Asylum	3
Sent to St. Vincent's Home for Boys	2
Sent to Women's Aid Society and Home for Friendless Girls	1
Total	72

The receipts of the Society have been from donations and dues of members, $5,800; from other sources, $198.24. The expenditures thus far have amounted to $5,077.13.

The New York Society for the Relief of the Ruptured and Crippled.

New York.

The following report on this institution is kindly furnished by Commissioner Roosevelt, whose opportunities for frequent visitation give to it special value:

"The suggestion of this special form of organized charity was due to James Knight, M. D., of New York. In the winter of 1842, through his efforts, the first public clinics for cripples were held in the medical schools of this city, at which a large number were gratuitously treated. The relief thus obtained was, however, very limited, as no adequate provision was made for the free supply of suitable surgical appliances for the indigent patients, or for their proper diet or nursing. Deeply impressed with the existing necessity of an institution for the special treatment and cure of this large class of sufferers, Dr. Knight persistently and earnestly appealed to his fellow citizens on their behalf, but without any marked success until April, 1862. At a meeting of the Board of Managers of the Association for the Relief of the Poor, held on that day, Dr. Knight appeared and presented orally and in writing the arguments and facts establishing the importance of this special organized relief. His appeal was successful, and steps were immediately taken to secure an organization for this object. In 1863, the dwelling-house of Dr. Knight, provided at his own expense with twenty-eight beds, and a workshop with all the implements required for the manufacture of surgical appliances for the patients, was hired by the Board of Managers for three years at a nominal rent. At the expiration of this time, the premises were purchased by the Society at a cost much less than the market value, and its operations were continued in this building until the completion of the new hospital building, corner of Lexington avenue and Forty-second street, in 1870. From the beginning, Dr. Knight superintended the institution as Resident Physician and Surgeon, residing in the house until it was sold for five thousand dollars more than the original cost; Mrs. Knight managing the domestic concerns of the establishment, and their daughter, most of the time, teaching the children without compensation. The late Mr. Jonathan Sturges, then Treasurer, in a paper on the progress of the institution, writes: "Dr. Knight has paid into the treasury every year from fees received from those able to pay, more than his salary, and has been instrumental in raising large sums for the purposes of the Society.

"In the spring of 1867, five full lots were purchased on the corner of Lexington avenue and Forty-second street, and in June, 1868, the plans of the present hospital building were approved. Voluntary contributions to the amount of $332,417 were made to pay for the cost of the new building; when it was completed and furnished there remained a surplus, which was invested for the support of the hospital. The hospital was completed and ready for the reception of patients in May, 1870. It occupies a lot of ground 125 by 100 feet, on the north-west corner of Lexington avenue and Forty-second street. The ground plan consists of a central parallelogram of 115 by 45 feet, to which are attached semi-circular wings of 22 feet radius at three angles of the central portion — two facing the south on Forty-second street, and one at the north-east angle on Lexington avenue. On the north-west angle is a rectangular wing 32 by 22 feet. In the central portion, rear of the building, is a space of equal dimensions to the north-west wing. Each ward occupies an entire floor, and has ample windows on all sides, and the projections at the angles of the building, in which are the nurses' rooms, bathing rooms, etc., are so rounded as not to cut off the sunshine from the windows of the wards.

"A fire-proof staircase, communicating with every floor, is placed in a tower on the north side of the building. In the same tower is an elevator, by which the patients can be carried up to the wards, and from the wards to a play-room on the top of the building. This play-room is so constructed as to be open in summer, inclosed in winter, open to the sun on all sides, and yet shaded from it overhead. It is always dry, of an even temperature, airy and cheerful, and affords a beneficial change from the confinement of the lower wards. It is claimed that in this respect and in the ventilation of the wards, this hospital is equal, if not superior, to any other existing building for such uses.

"The structure is of brick, with hollow walls, which aid in heating and ventilation. It is warmed by steam throughout, has four ample fire-places in each ward, and all the modern improvements and conveniences. The basement has a reception room for patients, retiring room, etc., besides kitchen, bakery, laundry, store-rooms, heaters, and a steam engine used for working the elevator and for various other domestic purposes. The first floor affords suitable rooms for twenty private patients, and apartments for the resident physician. The second and third floors are occupied by wards, which have accommodations for two hundred patients, and the fourth by the play-room above described.

"The certificate of incorporation of the society sets forth its object as follows, viz.:

'That the particular business and object of such society shall be to supply skillfully constructed surgico-mechanical appliances, and the treatment of in and out-door patients requiring trusses and spring supports, also bandages, lace stockings and other suitable apparatus for the relief and care of cripples, both adults and children, and, so far as possible, to make these benefits available to the poorest in the community.'

"All manner of curable cripples are treated in the institution.. The required surgical appliances and apparatus, all manufactured on the premises, of the best materials, and in the least expensive manner, are gratuitously supplied to those unable to pay for the same. Healthful nourishment, perfect ventilation, personal cleanliness and amusement are principally relied upon as curative means, and these in a few days start new life in the most helpless cases. Medicines are administered when necessary. Surgical operations are limited mainly to the subcutaneous division of tendons for the relief of contorted limbs. Amusing exercises, adapted to promote physical energy or to relieve contractions and stiffened joints, are included in the system of treatment. The play-room on the top of the building is furnished with swings, in which the patients move by their own exertions, thus exercising their bodies and arms when deprived of the use of their lower limbs. A variety of gymnastic exercises or appliances are made available for the healthful recreation of the patients, under the direction of a professional gymnast.

"The following is an annual summary of the patients received and treated since the opening of the institution.

Number of patients treated from	May, 1863,	to	May, 1864	828
" " " "	1864,	"	1865	965
" " " "	1865,	"	1866	1,489
" " " "	1866,	"	1867	1,684
" " " "	1867,	"	1868	2,006
" " " "	1868,	"	1869	2,285
" " " "	1869,	"	1870	2,507
" " " "	1870,	"	1871	2,721
" " " "	1871,	"	1872	3,306
" " " "	1872,	"	1873	4,023
" " "	1873,	"	1874	4,634
" " "	1874,	"	1875	5,023
				31,471

Analysis and description of cases in regard to sex.

	'63.	'64.	'65.	'66.	'67.	'68.	'69.	'70.	'71.	'72.	'73.	'74
Males	529	524	840	971	1,108	1,315	1,515	1,615	1,881	2,310	2,707	2,858
Females	299	441	649	713	898	970	992	1,106	1,425	1,713	1,927	2,165
												31,471

Age of patients.

	'63.	'64.	'65.	'66.	'67.	'68.	'69.	'70.	'71.	'72.	'73.	'74.
Over 21 years....	432	465	730	811	910	1,116	1,326	1,411	1,750	2,216	2,606	2,788
Between 14 and 21 years.......	62	84	109	100	142	159	179	163	208	250	289	325
Under 14 years..	334	416	650	773	954	1,010	1,002	1,147	1,348	1,557	1,739	1,910
												31,471

Out and In-patients relieved.

	'63.	'64.	'65.	'66.	'67.	'68.	'69.	'70.	'71.	'72.	'73.	'74
Out-patients	688	787	1,305	1,373	1,602	1,830	2,032	2,019	2,547	3,151	3,738	4,077
In-patients.. ...	30	32	32	35	25	26	26	72	99	127	104	115
Out-patients (continued)....	84	104	124	234	322	362	376	464	468	511	531	565
In-patients (continued)..... ...	20	26	21	24	26	26	26	107	125	163	174	177
Incurable	6	16	7	18	31	41	47	59	67	71	87	89
												31,471

"The city of New York pays at the rate of $150.00 per annum for each indigent child in the hospital, which sum is quite inadequate to defray the expenses of even the *in-door* department of the institution. The balance of the outlay and the maintenance of the *out-door* or dispensary department, including the professional treatment of more than five thousand patients annually, and the supplying of these with the various surgical appliances necessary for their relief, are met by private contributions and the amount received from paying patients. Of the latter class but thirteen, at the date of October, 1875, paid; six of these, in full for board and surgical treatment, the remaining seven paying a trifling amount."

The number of children inmates, October 1, 1875, was one hundred and sixty-five. One hundred and twenty of these were of foreign parents, and forty-five of native. Eighteen of the number were orphans, and fifty-nine half-orphans.

The expenditures of the hospital during the fiscal year ending September 30, 1875, amounted to $42,289. It has invested funds to the amount of $129,000.

Dr. Knight, whose long experience and humane sympathies toward this suffering class render any thing emanating from him of special value, says:

"It is with feelings of gratitude to Divine favor, that we have been permitted so long to assist in the labors that have assuaged the sufferings of so vast a number of the indigent afflicted and others, that have availed themselves of our professional service, in all to the number of 31,471, during the past twelve years.

This is truly gratifying. But alas ! a review of the past and of those associated in these beneficent labors, reminds us that we have to mourn the loss of one-fourth of the original Board of Managers, and our first President, who have been called home to their heavenly rest; two within the past year, of whom it may be truly said : 'And their good works do follow them.' They assisted most successfully in the establishing of what may now be considered one of the most extensive and most needed charities known of in this or any other country. With their assistance has been elaborated, by experience (there being no precedent), a most extensive and complete system, to the actual surprise of the public; demanding their support, as the most effectual and economical means of relieving suffering humanity from bodily infirmity and compulsory pauperism; who if not relieved tend to a consequent tax for their support, and in many instances during their lives—thus burdening the community at large, not only for the support of helpless crippled children, but of many children possessing their physical powers who are deprived of the support and care of their parents, from disenabling ailments relievable by surgico-mechanical appliances, that they are unable to purchase. Of these means of relief, there have been supplied 11,722 trusses, 3,655 laced stockings, 1,663 supporting belts, 2,383 braces for lateral curvatures and caries of spine, 1,311 clubfoot shoes, 1,067 springs for knock-knees and bow-legs, 1,311 steel supports for incurable paralyzed limbs, enabling, in many instances, the unfortunate helpless cripple to earn a living. This is an extraordinary amount of relief rendered by this institution during the past twelve years. These aids to labor were not furnished the poor previous to the organization of this Society, and their use continued by repair, all free of charge. The county had to take charge of the afflicted paralyzed children, and of parents until temporarily relieved by rest in the Charity Hospital—the latter persons being often detained several months, during which period their children were left to lead a vagrant life, sweeping crosswalks, obtaining food at the Missions, in many instances becoming vicious paupers, and finally a charge on our reformatories or prisons as a protection to the public. This pitiable condition of the unfortunate cripple and of children deprived of parental care, is now alleviated by giving timely relief to adults and children at a comparatively very moderate expense, attainable at the Hospital for the Relief of the Ruptured and Crippled. The city and county fail to give this relief from any other source. Application is made from all parts of this State for surgical treatment, but it being impossible for this institution to supply the demand of the indigent cripples from this and other States, we have the painful duty of answering their letters with a refusal to render them the much needed relief. What greater boon can be conferred upon the industrious poor than to restore to them physical ability to labor and support their dependent families in respectability. A few dollars from individual or private charity, or a stay in the alms-house for several months, will not excite their pride and energy to maintain, or attempt to obtain a respectable position in the community. Their pride is seriously compromised when unavoidably reduced to that unfortunate condition of depending upon the industry of others for support.

From the following statement of a few cases of extraordinary cures made, an idea may be entertained of the amount of relief that is afforded to the indigent in the indoor department:

"F—— W——, male, ten years of age, was admitted May 29, 1874, for the relief of club-foot of eight years' duration. Discharged July 10, 1874, walking with foot squarely on the floor. Cure complete.

"R—— G——, male, twelve years of age, suffering from white swelling of knee joint, came under hospital treatment July 6, 1874. Discharged cured, July 17, 1874, having been under our treatment less than six weeks.

"B—— G——, female, four years of age, came under treatment July 6, 1874, for white swelling in the acute stage. The knee was very much increased in size, and the pain was so great that the child was unable to stand. Within less than six months she was restored the use of her limb. The joint is natural in size, motion good, and general health fair. Now walks with an almost imperceptible limp.

"M—— T——, female, aged eight years, was admitted July 21, 1874, for hip disease — second stage. Completely restored to the use of her limb, and discharged cured, December 10, 1874.

"C—— B——, female, aged nine years, entered August 26, 1874. Ailment, club-foot of seven years' duration. Discharged cured, October 9, 1874.

"C—— H——, female, nine years of age, admitted June 30, 1874, for disease of spinal cord, producing a most pitiable deformity of lower extremities. Suffered greatly, and could not even straighten her limbs. Cured in three months, and discharged October 18, 1874.

"D—— W——, male, twelve years of age, came under treatment May 12, 1874, for white swelling of knee joint, of several months' standing. By the end of July following, discharged cured.

"L—— S——, female, aged eleven years, came under treatment for white swelling of ankle joint of two years' standing, August 6, 1873. The case was unusually tedious, but in less than eight months she was completely restored, and discharged May 15, 1874, walking with perfect ease.

"M—— L——, male, aged nine years, was admitted November 2, 1874, for the relief of hip disease. Relieved, and discharged cured January 26, 1875.

"N—— O'K——, female, eight years of age, for several years paralyzed from caries of the spine, was admitted September 24, 1874. In less than three months restored to the use of her limbs.

"A—— H——, female, thirteen years of age, entered hospital March 2, 1874, for the relief of white swelling of both knees, two years' standing. Discharged cured, August 18, 1874.

"F—— J——, male, eleven years of age, came under treatment December 6, 1874, for disease of spinal cord with inability to stand. Completely restored in less than two months, and now walks and runs with perfect ease.

"M—— K——, female, aged eight years, entered hospital August 27, 1872, suffering from hip disease — second stage. Tumor, simulating abscess, had formed and the prospects for recovery were poor. After a long course of treatment the tumor disappeared, motion in joint returned, and the child was discharged October 15, 1874, walking freely, and with no sign of disease remaining.

"J—— B——, male, thirteen years of age, was admitted October 30, 1873, suffering from paralysis of lower extremities, produced by a fall through a hatch way, fracturing spinal column about the middle. Completely restored to the use of his limbs, and discharged June 12, 1874."

Nursery and Child's Hospital.

New York.

The field of charity covered by the Nursery and Child's Hospital is very extensive.

Its objects are "the maintenance and care of the children of wet-nurses, and the daily charge of infants whose parents labor away from home, and also the care of lying-in women and foundlings. The institution was organized and incorporated on the 19th of April, 1854. Its sources of income are thus stated by the First Directress, Mrs. Cornelius Du Bois: "The board of some of the children; the subscriptions and donations; the Charity Ball and the per capita allowance the law allows us, enable us to provide liberally, but not extravagantly, for our inmates."

The circumstance which led to its establishment illustrates so aptly the necessity for its existence, and the warm Christian charity to which its inception is due, that it is considered not out of place to relate it here, although to many it is doubtless familiar.

"On the 5th of February, 1854, two ladies of this city were conversing about the great suffering among the poor; one of them, who had long been a manager of the Marion Street Lying-in Asylum, spoke of the miseries of infants, of their neglect, and of the suffering mothers, whose poverty forced them to give the nourishment intended for their own infants to the children of the rich. She told the following story: 'A well known monthly nurse called to see a lady whom she had attended, and while looking at her infant was surprised to find its wet-nurse in tears. On expressing her wonder that one surrounded with every comfort should grieve, the poor nurse replied: "It is just that which makes me cry, for see what a good bed, good meals, and comfortable fire I have got, while my own dear child may be starving or freezing." On being asked why she did not see to it, she replied: "I have promised the lady with whom I live never to do so as long as I am nursing her child, and I have extra wages on that account." Extreme poverty had induced her to make this promise. The nurse, a good woman, volunteered to go and see her child, and hastily taking the address, went at night-time to a small, dirty basement room, where she found a sick woman lying on a miserable bed, who, on being asked for "the baby," said, "My baby died yesterday, of small-pox." "And where is the nurse's baby?" asked the visitor. "Oh, if it's that you want, here it is," and the woman, leaning over, drew from under her bed a basket of soiled clothes, among which lay the child, whose mother might well weep for its utter wretchedness, neglect and danger. The visitor stripped every rag from its little squalid body, and wrapped it in her own shawl, took it to her own home, bathed and dressed it, sent for a physician, and had it vaccinated that same night, and by the blessing of God the child was saved from the loathsome disease to which it had been exposed, and from that death which was most certainly at hand.'"

"To this child the present Nursery and Child's Hospital owes its origin and success, for this story was told to one who had been blessed with many children of her own, who had known the care they required, even when in good health, who had watched the sick beds, and closed the eyes of many who had been taken to happier homes; and this sad story awakened in that true woman's bosom a chord which can never cease to vibrate, while the infant needs a home, or there are sick children who claim her care and sympathy."

The Nursery and Child's Hospital, founded by Mrs. Du Bois, is at the corner of Lexington avenue and Fifty-first street, and was intended to prevent the frightful mortality among infants, particularly among the children of wet-nurses. The idea that the children of the poor were sacrificed for those of the wealthy classes, was so repugnant to the maternal instincts of one who had lost four out of ten of her own dear ones, though surrounded with every comfort and care, that she desired to provide, for the poor little neglected children, a shelter, where at least they should not suffer from want. The effort was made, and, it is asserted, so great has been its success, that the mortality among this class of children has been diminished from between eighty-six and ninety, to between ten and fifteen per cent.

The city Nursery, at the corner of Lexington avenue and Fifty-first street, is a large building, having beds for three hundred and sixty inmates, and hospitable accessories. No children over four years of age are left in the city, but are transferred to the Country Branch. In the city Nursery there is a large Lying-in Asylum, which is always full. If a woman applies for care during her confinement, and has other children unprovided for, the whole family is transferred to the Country Branch Nursery and Lying-in Asylum; also all who are not expecting confinement within two weeks of admission. "This enables the married woman to extend her maternal care to her family, till her hour of illness. It also provides a shelter for the erring, where they can be under proper religious influences, and preserved from the desperate resources formerly so common, to hide their shame by suicide, abortion or infanticide. They are required to bring evidence of former good character, and when they have been long enough in the institution to entitle them to a good recommendation, places are provided for them, and their infants are kept."

The following particulars, regarding the history and workings of the institution, were obtained from a lady long identified with the work.

"In February, 1854, three weeks after the first idea of a Nursery was conceived, $10,000 was collected by personal exertions. On the first of May following, the house in St. Mark's place was opened, and so great was the demand for places that every bed was full in less than a week. Overcrowding was the result. It seemed impossible to refuse miserable, starved and drugged infants, though it was evident nothing could save them. Still they died in a comfortable home, and for a time that seemed to be our best encouragement. But as we learned the economy of charity, we began to save lives, and now we have learned by many instructive lessons that infant mortality among the poor with us is not necessarily larger than in ordinary private families among all classes.

"We hope to improve still more, and rejoice in being able by our dearly bought experience to encourage others in all parts of our country who constantly appeal to us for our rules and results. From Canada to Florida, nurseries have been commenced, taking the New York Nursery and Child's Hospital for their guide, and in Calcutta one is flourishing bearing our name and following our footsteps.

"Wet nurses obtain high wages, and their babies are received by us on payment of $10 a month for board. Mothers are expected to pay as far as able for our care of their children, but there are so many willing to take them in private families, that we generally have the destitute who would otherwise go to the alms-house. We try to keep families together instead of separating them, as they do at alms-houses.

"The mothers are required to work, and are glad to do so if allowed to keep their children with them. This saves many mothers from pauperism."

At the date of visitation, October 9, we found fifteen children in the lying-in ward of the City Branch, corner of Lexington avenue and Fifty-first street, and one hundred and eighty-three in the nursery department. These children, we were informed, are at the age of four removed to Staten Island, to what is called the Country Branch of the Nursery and Child's Hospital at West New Brighton.

The medical department of the institution is under the care of the Resident Physician, Dr. Beckwith, to whom we are indebted for the following information: "The house is under the charge of a Matron. In the lying-in ward are three nurses. The children's ward has two divisions, the larger one attended by three nurses and the smaller one by two. Thirty-eight domestics are employed, including cooks, laundresses, ironers, etc. We have fifty women, each nursing two children. Of these, six or eight are usually paid, but the remuneration is small. The women who nurse two children have generally one of their own, and nurse another with it. Then we have thirty other women who nurse their own children and take care of others. They have just enough milk to nurse their own children. Every woman is obliged to nurse her own child while she remains in the institution. If she wishes to leave it here to board, she pays for it, but she has to wait till we get a wet nurse to take her place. We have no bottle feeding. I think it is better to partially nurse them. If they get sick, they can give them nothing else.

"The city allows $10 a month for such children as have no friends able to pay for them. Children are taken in at any time. Applications for admittance are generally made at the Hospital. But unmarried women are taken only for their first child, and they have to bring references from some one who knows them. Married women come and go at any time. Quite a number of married women come in now, too poor to stay at home."

The Nursery department was found to be very pleasant and well lighted, having windows on three sides, and flue ventilation to some extent. The beds and cribs are arranged around the room so that a bed for the mother and a crib, capable of accommodating two infants, are placed side by side. The cribs, two feet by six, were protected by mosquito nets over an iron frame. The iron bedsteads for the mothers were three feet wide. Hair and straw mattresses were used. The Doctor thinks children should not be weaned till they are fourteen months old.

The "waiting room" is a large apartment, furnished with iron bedsteads. While awaiting confinement, the women utilize their time by sewing, but their labor is not of much value.

The ward for the women who have just been confined is furnished with single iron bedsteads of good width. Wire-woven mattress bedsteads are used. These beds, the Doctor says, have been used for three and a half years constantly, and have not "sagged." They cost $16.50. The mattress can be fitted to any iron frame bedstead.

Most of the children born in the institution, the Doctor thinks, are the children of the "unfortunate" class. The dietary furnished is of a very nutritious character.

In the children's department we were greeted by a flock of little children quite happy, and crying out for candy. A number of little hands were held forth to receive the contents of our pockets in such a manner as gave birth to the suspicion that there was some good soul a frequent visitor, more thoughtful than ourselves.

The room was furnished with little tables and chairs, and was very clean, and the children showed good care.

The children of Protestant parents are baptized in the institution as occasion offers, and the children of Catholic parents are permitted at all times to be taken out and baptized in accordance with the faith of their church.

The chapel of the institution contains a reading desk, organ, etc. Services are held here every Sunday afternoon and Thursday evening.

The walls of the house are painted in a soft tint. The heating is effected by furnaces. The water supply from the city is abundant. The bathing arrangements are ample. The house seemed nearly filled to its capacity.

The Country Branch, is located in Middletown, three miles from the post-office at West New Brighton, on a highly elevated site, commanding a view of the Kills, Newark bay and the country around. It includes forty-eight acres of ground, on which are a large and commodious house, used as a Lying-in Asylum and Hospital for Children, another large house with a capacity for one hundred inmates and fourteen cottages, each capable of sheltering from twelve to thirty-six inmates. These are arranged in such a manner that all are under surveillance of the matron and two lady physicians. Each cottage has its head, who reports instantly any change observed in the health of the inmates.

Quarantine arrangements are easily made by means of these separate cottages. If, in the Lying-in Asylum in the city, puerperal fever appears, the waiting women are transferred to the Country Branch. This prevents the disease from spreading, but the original idea of the Nursery on Staten Island was to give change of air to children with cholera infantum and kindred diseases. The terrible mortality among infants, and the means to prevent it, have always been subjects of deep interest to the philanthropist.

Each year, in the Nursery and Child's Hospital, the mortality has been steadily decreasing, but the havoc of cholera infantum it seemed impossible to arrest till the experiment was made of sending the infants, who appeared incurable, across the bay to a small hospital, hastily improvised for their reception on Staten Island. Here, under the daily supervision of Mrs. Du Bois, many recovered who had been admitted in an apparently dying condition. The success of this experiment led to the purchasing, in 1870, of the present beautiful and commodious country hospital, which was immediately filled with delicate and sickly children. The cottages subsequently built are two stories high, and so arranged that the upper story can be entirely disconnected from the lower by staircase and separate entrance. Fenestrals are so placed that no dampness can accumulate underneath. One long window is so situated on each side of each ward, that the floors may be flushed with fresh air when needed. Open fire-places and transoms over every door furnish good ventilation. Radiating stoves are used in very cold weather. Various disinfectants, necessary for sewers and out-houses, are freely used. and a thorough system of deep tile drainage adds to the sanitary condition of the place.

A small and tasteful building near the gate is called the dispensary, and is in charge of Dr. Helen M. Betts, assistant lady physician. It is intended to accommodate outside patients. Poor people, in addition to those in the nursery, are supplied with medicine from here gratuitously, but those who are able to pay are charged.

A school is held on the premises and two others in the village. There are several boarding-houses in the village, in which about one hundred and twenty children are boarded, and are under the supervision of the nursery. No child, over five years of age, is kept at the nursery.

In the ward for the sick, in the main building, were six inmates. Two lady nurses, from Bellevue Training School, were acquiring experience in their profession here under the superintendence of Dr. E. E. Judson, the resident lady physician of the nursery.

The cottages were at first found to be cold in winter, but by means of plastering, this defect was remedied and they were with greater ease kept free from vermin. They are frame buildings, lined with pine, with black walnut moldings, and although cheaply and strongly constructed, they are, nevertheless, very tasteful.

The water supply is procured from a spring. A steam engine forces it to every building. Ample provision is made for bathing.

One of the cottages is used for a chapel, where services are held morning and evening.

Another of the cottages, inclosed with sash, is designated the Sanitarium, affording a play-room fully large enough for one hundred children.

In connection with the institution is a large garden, supplying all the vegetables.

The total expenditures of the Nursery and Child's Hospital, during the fiscal year ending September 30, 1875, amounted to $118,851.19, of which sum nearly $23,000 were for buildings and improvements. Its invested fund was set down at $6,000, and its total indebtedness at $13,203.88.

The following are some of the views of Mrs. Du Bois, the results of her large experience in this work, which are recorded for general information.

Mrs. Du Bois believes that, as a rule, infants who are wet-nursed should be in an institution, because there the ventilation is better attended to, the earliest indication of disease noticed more quickly, the food given more regularly and of a better and more nourishing kind than in families, but at three years of age children are better off in private families if watched by visiting agents. Many families will care for the children faithfully without watching, but as a rule it is necessary for every cottager to feel that some one takes an interest in the children. No child should ever be in an alms-house. Physical and moral degradation ensues. The children of drunkards should not be allowed to remain with their parents. Much vice would be saved if mothers knew they would be separated from their children if they did not reform and take better care of them. The law on this point is now very defective.

"Children at three years should be taught by the *Kindergarten* system enough to amuse their minds and keep their bodies exercised.

For infants under eight months, wet-nurses are indispensable; if not to be obtained, then the former rule does not apply, but they should be placed singly in private families, to be bottle or spoon-fed. Institutions cannot save many bottle-fed babies, though every year the result of present efforts in that direction is more encouraging.

"The Nursery is so full that we are glad to have good places at the West found for children, as they get old enough, by the Children's Aid Society. The Home for the Friendless takes many very young children, who are adopted, and great care is taken to place them in Christian families well known to the managers. But as long as they remain with us they are well taught and made useful on the farm or in the house.

"We have one hundred and fifty children boarded out in families on Staten Island, and at present there are two hundred on our grounds and in cottages. Our number of women and children in the city and country institutions varies from seven hundred and fifty to eight hundred. While it is necessary to have a nursery in New York as a receiving house and as a refuge for those whose parents are obliged to be near the city, it is all-important that children should as soon as possible be transferred to the pure air of the country and given the fresh cows' milk so easily procured there."

Although an efficient force of wise workers are engaged in this institution, its growth and success must be attributed mainly to the large comprehension and executive capacity of its first directress, Mrs. Cornelius Du Bois. The time will come when its management must be committed to other hands. It having been demonstrated by her, however, what may be accomplished in this direction, it is believed that this great charity rests upon so sure a foundation that its work will go on, an enduring monument to a most noble character.

The Orphan Asylum Society in the City of New York.

New York.

A very brief outline of the history of this old and well established charity can only be given, it being too lengthy to be fully detailed here. "Prior to March, 1806," says one of the officers of the Orphan Asylum, "when the Society was organized, the Society for the Relief of Widows with Small Children was the only existing charitable organization for the care of children in New York. A few of the destitute orphans of those widows were collected by Mrs. Isabella Graham, and to provide a permanent home for these, 'The Orphan Asylum Society in the City of New York' was established. The first house used for this purpose was hired in Rasin street, Greenwich, and during the first six months twelve orphan children found there a home, a suitable man and his wife taking charge and instructing them. In January, 1807, the First Directress, Mrs. Sarah Hoffman, with the consent of the Board of Trustees, drafted the plan of a constitution, and the Legislature granted the petition for its incorporation. The first annual meeting was held at the City Hotel, April 2, 1807, on which occasion twenty orphans, then inmates of the Asylum, were presented to the friends who had shown an interest in them. On July 7, 1807, was laid the corner-stone of the first asylum building to be erected on four lots of ground in Greenwich village; thence the children were removed to their present home in 1839–40, the number amounting to one hundred and sixty-five. The Society had at first to struggle through many years of debt and dependence on the liberality of its friends; afterward, however, subscribers increased, legacies were founded, and the nucleus of an income was formed. Mrs. Isabella Graham and her daughter, Mrs. Bethune, Mrs. Sarah Hoffman and Mrs. Elizabeth Hamilton, were among the first projectors of this good work."

The asylum building is a three-story brick structure, with two wings, and has a capacity for two hundred and twenty-five children. The main building was erected in 1836, and the wings in 1855, but during 1874 the whole was remodeled, painted and frescoed. The building is heated by steam, lighted by gas, and supplied with water from the city. It has good sewerage. The ventilation is by flues in the walls. The window sash, containing lozenge-shaped panes, are hung with cord, weights and pulleys.

The institution is located on Seventy-third street and Eleventh avenue. It faces the Hudson river. A belt of the City Riverside Park intervenes between it and the bank.

It is governed by a Board of Lady Managers, who have associated with them an advisory Board of Gentlemen. The immediate charge is committed to a superintendent. The force associated with him includes each a matron for both boys' and girls' departments; a gentleman teacher, with an assistant; two lady teachers; a lady in charge of the nursery; a "sick-nurse"; a housekeeper, engineer, and six or eight domestics.

There were in the institution, at the date of visitation, October 11, one hundred and eighty-four inmates, of whom sixty-nine were girls.

The following information was obtained from the Superintendent in charge, Mr. George E. Dunlap:

Children of both sexes, orphans, half-orphans and destitute children generally are received, without regard to their religion. They are admitted at all ages up to ten, but not before they are weaned, a nursery being in the Asylum for the younger children. They remain till the age of fourteen, when they are placed out by indenture. The children apprenticed are not lost sight of, but are visited or written to at least once a year.

The schools are in the wings of the building, the boys occupying one, and the girls the other. They are furnished with patent seats, and the usual school appliances. The children receive a common English education, and are trained to industrious habits. They are carefully instructed in religious truths.

In the dining room the boys occupy one side and the girls the other. The children sit on stools. Table cloths, crockery ware, knives, forks and spoons are used.

It is designed that every inmate shall have a towel, brush and comb. The latter are kept in a large cupboard divided into compartments. Each compartment contains a hair-brush, comb and tooth-brush. The arrangements for both boys and girls in this respect are the same.

Each of the two bath rooms is furnished with twelve bath tubs. The boys' hair is cut tolerably close. On two of the floors in each wing are lavatories with eight wash-bowls. The children wash in running water. Night closets are in the hall connected with the sleeping rooms.

In regard to the character of the employes the Superintendent says: "Women that have children in the house are not employed as domestics."

In the dormitories are single iron bedsteads, straw beds and feather pillows. The bedsteads are two feet three inches wide.

At the end of each wing is a stairway approached from within and without, giving egress from each floor of the wing, and access to a room one story higher than the wing, used for infirmary purposes when needed, and affording complete isolation from all the other inmates.

The location, commanding as it does, a full view of the grand scenery of the Hudson, is delightful. The grounds are being improved. A great elm tree stands near the door of the main entrance to the Asylum, on the easterly side, and its huge bole is a favorite rendezvous for the children.

The early history of this charity shows that it was not exempt from the financial trials to which many similar institutions are now subjected, but it persevered amid discouragements, and its work made its silent impression on the mind of the benevolent man of business pursuing his daily routine, and the fruits are seen in the liberal bequests that have been made to it from time to time. It is now a wealthy corporation. The value of its real estate is set down at $600,000, its invested funds at $199,000. Its expenditures during the last year were $71,661, of which $31,961 was for improvements upon buildings.

The number of children that have been inmates of this Asylum since its beginning is two thousand one hundred and twenty-three. The number in the institution October 1, 1875, was one hundred and eighty-five. Of these ninety-three were orphans, seventy-nine half-orphans, two had both parents living, and of eleven it was uncertain whether they had parents living or not. Forty-five were of native parentage, and one hundred and twenty of foreign. The parentage of twenty was unknown. The whole number of children received during the year was sixty, and the number discharged thirty. Of these fifteen were placed out by indenture, eleven were returned to parents or guardians, one was transferred to another institution, and three died. The number of the boys October 1, was one hundred and sixteen, girls sixty-nine.

The spirit with which the successful workers of this Society were imbued, is illustrated in the text prefacing a copy of their constitution.

"Among the afflicted of our suffering race none makes a stronger or more impressive appeal to humanity than the destitute orphan. Crime has not been the cause of its misery — and future usefulness may yet be the result of its protection. The reverse is often the case of more aged objects.

"God himself has marked the fatherless as the peculiar subjects of His divine compassion. 'A father of the fatherless is God in his holy habitation.' 'When my father and my mother forsake me, then the Lord will take me up.' To be the blessed instrument of divine Providence in making good the promise of God, is a privilege equally desirable and honorable to the benevolent heart."

An interesting feature of this institution is the place that has been set apart for the purposes of prayer and praise. The walls of the old yet beautiful chapel, hallowed by interesting associations of the past, are eloquent with the generous deeds of noble natures that long since have rested from their labors. The visitor's eye is here arrested by numerous memorial tablets and records of legacies, which the trustees of the institution have here placed "in grateful remembrance." These inscriptions, seen in the golden sunset light of an autumn evening, are given at some pains, for like illuminated manuscripts of the olden time, they tell of the Asylum's history and its work:

"Sacred to the memory of Mrs. Isabella Graham, who died 27th July, 1811, and of Mrs. Sarah Hoffman, who died 29th July, 1821. They were both founders of this institution. To their prayer of faith and wisdom in directing its affairs, the society is indebted for much of the success that has attended it. They were lovely in their lives, and during many years they traveled together the walks of charity. 'When the ear heard them, it blessed them, and they caused the widow's heart to sing for joy.' They now rest from their labors, partakers of the blessedness of those that die in the Lord. 'Their works do follow them.'"

"Sacred to the memory of Mrs. Joanna Bethune, who was one of the originators of the plan of this institution, and the last survivor of its founders. For fifty years she gave to her beloved orphans the best energies of her mind and heart; her prayers and efforts never wearied nor flagged; and it was only at the advanced age of 87 years that she withdrew from active co-operation in their behalf. She died July 28, 1860, aged 92 years."

"Sacred to the memory of Elizabeth Hamilton, widow of Gen. Alexander Hamilton. She was one of the founders of this institution, and during 43 years watched over its interests with untiring devotion. She presided as its first directress for 27 years, and only resigned that office on her removal to Washington city, where she died, November 9, 1854, at the advanced age of 97 years."

"In grateful remembrance of Mrs. Sarah Startin, one of the founders of this institution, for many years its Treasurer, and, while she lived, a most liberal contributor. She bequeathed a legacy of $100."

"In grateful remembrance of Charles Leroux, the first testator who remembered this institution, and in 1811 bequeathed a legacy of $250."

"This tablet is erected in grateful remembrance of Philip Jacobs, who died 1818, and bequeathed to this institution property of a large amount. Considerable expense was incurred in defending suits brought by other claimants, and not until the year 1832 was his intention fulfilled, and the society put in possession of real estate valued at $75,000, the rents of which only are expended. Thus, while the legacies of other benevolent individuals have been necessarily employed in supporting the institution, for Philip Jacobs was reserved the honor of establishing a permanent fund. An Israelite by birth and education, the despised Nazarene became his Saviour, and dying in the faith of Jesus he bequeathed his property to feed His lambs."

"In memory of Thomas Dickson, to whom, for 54 years, this asylum was a home. Though deaf and dumb, he cheerfully bore his cross, and by patient effort became a worthy, useful employee of this institution; and as a token of his love, bequeathed to it the earnings of his life, amounting to $3,612."

"Sacred to the memory of Capt. Henry McKavitt. He was reared in this institution, graduated at West Point, and died in the service of his country at the battle of Monterey, September, 1846. He bequeathed all his property to this asylum. Also of Elizabeth Davis, who was reared in this institution, and in 1857 bequeathed to it her all, amounting to $57."

"This tablet is erected in grateful remembrance of James P. Van Horne, whose life-long interest in this asylum was followed by a generous bequest of $35,000. Also, of Mary E. C. Van Horne, his wife, who, after 44 years of untiring labor as a trustee, at her death bequeathed to this institution $20,000."

These marble tablets record the following legacies:

Mrs. Sarah B. Loftus, $1,400; Mrs. McKenzie, $1,400; Robert Hodge, "one of the first benefactors of this institution," $2,875; Jacob Sherred, "a liberal contributor to this institution while he lived," $5,000; James Thomson, $5,000; Miss Pyne, $500; Thomas Tom, $250; Mrs. Mary McCrea, $250; Mrs. Walmsley, $250; James R. Smith, $250; Mrs. McAdam, $250; Mrs. James McEvers, $250; Mrs. Douglas, $250; Mrs. Wilkes, $250; Thomas Allen, $4,000; John Murray, $200; Mrs. Judith Bruce, $100; Mrs. Ann B. Pollock, $100; Mrs. Clarkson, $100; Mrs. Mary Perkins, $100; Mrs. C. Depeyster, $50; John Stanford, $30; Joseph Barbee, "a soldier of Tampa Bay, who left all his property, amounting to $57"; John Van Blarcom, $500; Joseph Watkins, $500; Edmund Seaman, $500; Daniel McCormick, $500; Rachel Vanderbeck, $500; "Doctor John Austin, late of Demerara," $500; Alexander S. Glass, $300; Mrs. Charlotte Ablin, $388; Samuel Milligan, $125; A. Craig, $25; Mrs. Stansbury, $750; Colonel Rutgers, $1,000; "Mrs. Doctor Pendleton, one of the first subscribers and patronesses of this institution," $5,000; Captain Miles Burke, $15,000; Miss Mary Ludlow, "long a subscriber to this institution," $2,500; John Johnston, $1,000; Mr. Tinkney, $800; Miss Sarah Penny, $500; Mrs. Lyell, "of Freehold, N. J.," $500; James McBride, $500; Miss Mary Walton, $300; Mrs. Sarah Wagstaff, $250; Miss Frances Ludlow, $200; Mrs. Jane Ann Ferris, $200; Miss Eleanor Coffee, $150; Mrs. Mary Parkinson, "of Poughkeepsie," $100; Mrs. James Boggs, $100; John H. Keyser, $100; Mrs. Louisa S. Trevor, $1,000; Mr. Lispenard Stewart, $300; Miss Esther Allee, $200; Mrs. Elizabeth B. Stewart, $300; Mrs. Elizabeth Rutgers, $500; Mr. Charles O'Neil, $1,000; Mr. William Forgay, $1,000; Miss Mary Hassell, $2,543; Mrs. Martha Ritchie, $1,000; Miss Jane Hyslop, $500; Mrs. Mary A. Varnum, $5,000; Mrs. Augusta Bibby, $1,000; Mr. Caleb Swan, $500; Miss Elizabeth Demilt, $3,000; Miss Margaret A. Prall, $3,000; Miss Eliza Chapman, $3,000· William Howel, $1,500; John Vernon, $1,500; Samuel S. Howland, $1,500; Mrs. Harriet Howel, $1,500; Gardiner Howland, $1,000; John Morrison, $1,000; Mrs. Jane Clarkson, $5,000; John Horsburg, $5,000: Mrs. Sarah Skates, $4,050; Thomas F. Thompson, $4,000; John Noble, $2,000; John Grey, $2,000; James Murray, $9,303; Miss Elizabeth Gelston, $1,000; Mrs. Matilda Parsons, $500; Mr. Peter G. Arcularius, $1,000; Mr. S. V. Sickles, $12,729; Miss Rosamond Miller, $1,000; Mrs. Henry Andrew, $500; Mrs. Ann Wood, $500; Miss Eliza Fogan, $21; Mr. Thomas Riley, $5,639; Miss Cornelia Bingham, $400; Mr. Thomas Egleston, $2,000; Mrs. Sarah A. Riley, $100; Mr. W. E. Saunders, $500; Mr. Robert C. Goodhue, $1,000; Mrs. Ann Currie, $500; Mr. Pelatiah Perit, $1,000; Madame Martelle, $4,500; Mr. William Willis, $100; Mr. William Kinch, $500; Miss Julia Camman, $280; Madame Jumel, $5,000; Mr. James B. Murray, $1,000; donation from Messrs. Chauncey and Henry Rose, "from estate of the late John Rose," $16,000.

Orphans' Home and Asylum of the Protestant Episcopal Church in the City of New York.

New York.

Those familiar with the growth of this large charity state the following particulars in regard to its history: "The institution originated in 1851, in an effort on the part of some Christian ladies to fulfill the dying request of a father, that his children might be brought up under the care and training of the Protestant Episcopal Church, into which they had been baptized in infancy. As no church home then existed in the city, a room was hired in Renwick street, and a person engaged to take care of the children, at the expense of these ladies and other members of St. Paul's Chapel in New York. Under the care of the late Rt. Rev. Bishop Wainwright, Rev. John K. Hobart, D. D., and subsequently of the late Rev. Dr. Hanks, the undertaking grew into an Orphan Home of the Protestant Episcopal Church. After two years it was removed to Hammond street, the number of inmates increasing gradually from two to sixty. In 1857 two small houses in Thirty-ninth street were hired, and immediate efforts were made to obtain funds for the erection of a suitable building, which was not accomplished till 1861. The institution was incorporated in 1859

The means of support, from the beginning up to the present time, have been church collections, annual subscriptions, voluntary donations, and a payment on the part of some of the children's friends, of seventy-five cents a week. Legacies are devoted to the creation of a permanent fund."

The Home is situated on the south-west corner of Forty-ninth street and Lexington avenue, in the city of New York. It is governed by a Board of Lady Managers, representing nearly all the Protestant Episcopal churches in the city, and an advisory committee, composed of four clergymen and four laymen, the Bishop of the Diocese being President. The immediate charge of the asylum is committed to a matron. There are also employed by the institution three resident teachers, a nurse, a cook, a laundress, a seamstress and a fireman. Both girls and boys are received, not younger than three, and not older than eight years.

The asylum edifice is a large three story brick structure, with mansard roof A wing, two stories high, was èrected in 1867, the upper part of which is used as an infirmary. The main building is one hundred feet by fifty, and on the upper floors on each side are the dormitories for boys and girls, matron's room, and rooms for the nurse and teachers. The next story contains school, dining and committee rooms, also a parlor. The basement is used for children's dining room, play-room, kitchen and laundry. The house is heated by two furnaces, and stoves are also used in the school-rooms. Careful provision has been made for the ventilating and sunning of the rooms.

On the day of visitation, October 8th, the Asylum was found to be in charge of Mrs. Jane Inglee, Matron, to whom we are indebted for the following information:

"We receive orphans and half-orphans. If full orphans, we take them older than eight years. None of the children are supported by the city, and there are but few even partially supported by parents. When we place children out, we never lose sight of them, till they are of age. We have a committee of ladies to visit them. Those that are placed out by their parents are at their disposal. We do not send children to the West, nor any farther than we can look after them. We do not bind out any children. We place a child out, allowing a person to take it on trial for three months. We had one case, where they became dissatisfied with the child, and we took it back. I have been connected with the institution from the first — twenty-two years ago. The children turn out well. We have some who are now married, and settled very well. We have some in New York in business — two on Wall street, and one a clergyman in the Protestant Episcopal Church. We teach the children household work, to sweep, dust, sew, wash and cook. We have a sewing room, and the children go up every day for an hour, and are instructed in sewing; even the smaller ones are taught in the sewing room."

One of the large rooms in the house is set apart for the use of the ladies, who meet every Friday to sew for the children. The house is furnished throughout with inside blinds. The school department is divided by means of folding doors into two rooms. The girls are taught in one room, and the boys in the other.

The girls' dormitory is a pleasant room, and was found to be very clean. It can be well aired, and exposed to the sun, having windows on three sides. It is furnished with single iron bedsteads, two feet seven inches wide. The beds were well supplied with clothing. The children sleep without pillows.

The washing room connected with this dormitory is fitted up with twelve marble-top wash stands, and two bath tubs. Water closets adjoin it.

The infirmary department is a very interesting feature of the institution. It is complete in itself, and shut off from the rest of the house. The clothing, crockery and other appurtenances belonging to this department are kept entirely separate. In the convalescent room there were three beds, a little rocking chair, and smaller chairs. Beside each bed was a little table having a drawer. The sick room is furnished with all the conveniences of such an apartment. By means of a dumb waiter it is brought into communication with the kitchen below.

The Matron says: "We had one death during the past year, the only one which has occurred in eight years."

The upper dormitory, for girls, is a room furnished similarly to the one first visited. The nursery accommodates thirty-two beds. The boys' dormitory is furnished likewise with iron bedsteads.

In the dining room the children stand while eating, the boys at one side, the girls at the other. This room contains a high chair for the Matron or teacher to overlook the children while at their meals. In this apartment we found four little girls washing dishes, and one sweeping. The Matron stated that no benches or chairs were used except for the very little ones.

Adjoining the dining room is the boys' play-room, used in stormy weather, and on the opposite side is the play room for girls. On the day of visitation there were in the Asylum one hundred and thirty-eight children, sixty-three of whom were boys. The institution was found to be managed with great prudence, and it is believed to be accomplishing a good work. The arrangements for caring for the sick are very humane, and, as has been seen, are attended with very gratifying results. The provision for the health and comfort of the inmates was so generous, and the appointments of the institution generally were so complete, that the absence of seats for the children in the dining room, and of pillows upon the beds, was more noticeable than it would have been otherwise.

Since its organization about eight hundred children have shared the benefactions of this charity. No returns are at hand embodying statistical information relating to the work of the past year.

Roman Catholic Orphan Asylum in the City of New York.

New York.

This charity ranks among the first of its class in importance in the city of New York. Under its sheltering aegis, and that of the societies out of which it grew, numberless orphan and destitute children have been protected from the adverse storms of life. It has always included in its working force, aside from the gentlemen comprising its Board of Managers, a large number of *Religieuses,* who have devoted themselves to the furtherance of its objects, and who at the present time are giving the best portion of their lives to its labors. It is impossible to arrive at any correct estimate of the total number of children that have been received by it since its organization, and who through its agencies have been fitted for respectable and useful positions in society; but the number is very large, as will be seen from the fact that the number admitted during the five years preceding and including 1874, was one thousand one hundred and seventy-nine.

The Roman Catholic Orphan Asylum was organized in 1817, and incorporated by an act of the Legislature in April of the same year, under the name of the "Roman Catholic Benevolent Society." Its location was the same as that of the present Asylum, on Prince street, and the children were under the care of the Sisters of Charity. At the date of April 13, 1852, the above society was reorganized and "The Roman Catholic Orphan Asylum in the city of New York," was incorporated for the purpose of consolidating under one management the several societies having the care of children that were then being conducted under Roman Catholic auspices.

Those most familiar with the institution state the following regarding its early history: "The societies which have preceded ours were set on foot under the pressure of scanty means and difficulties of all kinds, and had little time for chronicling passing events. Consequently there are but meagre records of their histories. Cornelius Heney, who gave the building on the corner of Mott and Prince streets, and the site of the same, is the earliest and most noted benefactor of the institution."

The corporate powers of the institution are exercised by a Board of twenty-five Managers, twenty-four of whom are elected by ballot of the members. One-third of the number are chosen yearly. "Any person contributing the sum of $3 annually shall be a member of said corporation. The Most Rev. Archbishop or Ordinary of the Diocese of New York shall be President of the Society."

"The objects of this Society are to provide for destitute and unprotected orphan and half-orphan children of both sexes, and to educate them in the Roman Catholic faith." A committee have charge of the admission of the children into the Asylum, and the binding of them out at a proper age. They are governed by the following rules: "No child shall be received by them under the age of four or over nine years. When children are bound out, it shall be done according to law, and the committee shall in every case be satisfied not only that the master or mistress will treat them kindly, but that they shall be brought up as Catholics, and they shall in all cases give preference to the admission of full orphans. They shall meet twice a month."

The Asylum has also a visiting committee of five members, who meet monthly, and whose duty it is to visit, or see that they are visited, from time to time, all male and female orphans and half-orphans, bound out in the city by the Society, for the purpose of protecting and advising them.

This corporation controls and directs the affairs of the following institutions: The Female Orphan Asylum, Prince street, corner of Mott; The Male Orphan Asylum, Fifth avenue, between Fifty-first and Fifty-second streets; The Female Orphan Asylum, Madison avenue, between Fifty-first and Fifty-second streets; The Boland Farm, Peekskill.

The total number of inmates under the care of the Society, during the past year, was twelve hundred and nine. The number received during the year ending October 1, 1875, was two hundred and seventy; the number discharged, two hundred and thirty-three. Of the latter seven were placed out by adoption, and twenty-two by indenture. One hundred and thirty-four were returned to parents or guardians. Four left without permission, ten were sent out of the State, thirty-five were otherwise discharged, and twenty-one died.

The total expenditures of the Society for the fiscal year ending September 30, 1875, amounted to $94,975.22, of which nearly $4,000 was for buildings and improvements. The personal estate and investments are valued at $3,895, and the indebtedness is set down at $45,000.

Female Orphan Asylum, Prince street,

Is a large plain brick edifice, erected in 1825, to which additions have been made at various periods. It is under the immediate charge of thirteen Sisters of Charity of the Order of Mt. St. Vincent, Sister Mary Frances being the Sister Servant.

On the day of visitation, October 12th, there were two hundred and two children as inmates, varying in ages from three to fourteen years. A school is kept on the premises, under the supervision of the Department of Public Instruction, and an Industrial School, where those old enough to sew are trained in machine and hand sewing. Work is taken in from the shops.

In the Industrial School, or sewing department, there were over one hundred children, averaging twelve years of age, seated on three rows of comfortable seats, each seat accommodating three girls. Three girls were at work on sewing machines. The rest were engaged in finishing shirts. The room is large and well lighted, having windows on each side, and is brightened with pictures. It is under the charge of two Sisters. The Sisters say: "The children are taught the English branches of education, four hours every day, and spend from one and a half to two hours in the sewing department." The room contains a piano, which is occasionally played by a Sister for the entertainment of the girls.

The girls, we were informed, are kept till they are sixteen, and then suitable places in families are found for them.

In the Asylum is a chapel, capable of accommodating two hundred and thirty persons; also, a neat library, of two hundred volumes, for the use of the children. The school-room, "for little ones," contains children from three to thirteen years old. They appeared healthy and were free from diseases of the eye or skin.

The infirmary is a very pleasant room, and has a strip of carpet through its center. The beds looked very neat, but were unoccupied, none of the children being sick at the time.

The dormitories are furnished with single iron bedsteads, straw beds, feather pillows, and good warm bed covering.

In the dining room we found the table supplied with good bread, butter, and tea for the evening meal. The Sister gave us the following as the usual dietary: "For breakfast, bread, butter, and coffee, meat being added for the larger girls. For dinner, bread, meat and vegetables, varying according to the season. For supper, bread, butter, and tea. Fruits are furnished abundantly in their season, and the invalids have meat three times a day. A portion of the supplies used in the asylum come from the Boland farm at Peekskill. All the national holidays are observed with due honors. "At Thanksgiving," the Sister says, "the children have roast turkey and other good things, and Christmas generally lasts for a week."

The children are variously dressed. When attending funerals, however, they all wear black, with white aprons.

The house is well ventilated, and is lighted by gas. It was found to be very clean, and bore evidence of excellent house-keeping.

Of the two hundred and two inmates at the date of October 1st, ninety-seven were orphans, and one hundred and five half-orphans. Six were of native, and one hundred and ninety-six of foreign parents. All were from the city of New York.

Female Orphan Asylum, Madison Avenue.

This is the largest, the most commodious, and, in architectural appearance, the most imposing of the three asylums under the direction of the Roman Catholic Orphan Asylum Society. The building was begun in 1867, and opened in 1868. It was planned to embrace another wing, and to accommodate between six and seven hundred girls.

The asylum is under the charge of the Religious Order already referred to, Sister Clotilda being the Sister Servant. She is assisted in her work by seventeen Sisters of her Order. Seventeen domestics are employed in the washing and cooking departments.

The building is heated with hot air, lighted by gas, and supplied with city water. A fire-escape stairway communicates with each floor in the rear of the building. Great pains have been taken in the plan and construction of the asylum to combine all needed requisites, and the edifice reflects great credit upon its benevolent projectors.

At the date of visitation, October 8th, the Sister Servant stated the following in relation to children coming under her charge: "We receive children from four to nine years old, and keep them till they are fourteen, unless withdrawn by their friends before that age. We adopt many, and place out others in families. It is not usual for us to indenture. The children are visited after they are placed out. We may drop in upon them at any time, and if we find they are ill-treated they are withdrawn."

The Sister spoke quite feelingly of the children that had come to them from the Nurseries on Randall's Island, remarking that they had all the ways and manners of the pauper class, and that she did not see why a child must be degraded simply because it was poor. The following remarks of the Sister Servant illustrate, in some degree, the generous zeal actuating them in the important work in which they are engaged: "I do not think it is well to make children feel that they are dependent. It depresses the spirits. On the contrary, we should try to elevate them. If they behave well, and make good use of their opportunities, they have as good prospects before them as any other children."

The children are instructed in the ordinary branches of an English education. They are also taught plain sewing, and receive singing lessons twice a week from a professor of music, while those who have special musical talent are afforded every opportunity to develop it.

During our visit the children sang several hymns in a manner reflecting credit not only upon themselves, but upon their teacher. The music books are said to be the same as those used in Vassar College.

We found the children distributed in four class rooms, each containing about sixty pupils, under the charge of a Sister. They were variously dressed, and appeared cleanly. The schools were furnished with patent seats and the modern appliances of school rooms.

The dormitories are large and airy, with high ceilings supported by iron pillars. The large mullioned windows have inside blinds. Each dormitory has four lines of beds. The bedsteads are iron, single, two feet three inches wide, and four feet ten inches long, each having a railing on which to hang the clothes at night. Feather pillows and straw mattresses are used. Each bed had two sheets, a blanket, a coverlet, and in cold weather a comfortable was said to be added. The beds were all covered with blue check spreads, and so made up as to present a very neat appearance. A large room, measuring one hundred and forty-two by thirty-eight feet, contained one hundred and forty-one beds. At each end of the room are night closets and lavatories. The children wash in running water. Two Sisters sleep in each dormitory.

In the infirmary we found one little child sick. In speaking of the health of the children, the Sister said: "Last year we had scarlet fever and diphtheria. Eight of the children died of the former, and two of the latter disease. Two also died of consumption. We had only three deaths during the years 1872 and 1873." In this department there were double pillows on each bed, and little rocking chairs in the room.

The refectory is a very large apartment furnished with the usual accessories. Crockery mugs and dishes, knives and forks and spoons are used. The cooking and laundry work are done by steam.

Three sewing machines were in use on the premises.

The number of children in the institution October 1st, was five hundred and four. One hundred and sixty-nine of these were orphans, and three hundred and thirty-five half-orphans. Fifty were of native, and four hundred and fifty-four of foreign parentage. All were from New York.

The house throughout was neat and orderly, and the children were evidently under high moral and religious influences.

Male Orphan Asylum, Fifth Avenue.

The building occupied by the male orphans, consisting of a main and two wings, was completed in 1851, and the children were removed into it in November of that year. It is a spacious brick structure, and with its grounds occupies two-fifths of a block facing Fifth avenue, between Fifty-first and Fifty-second streets. The main building is about sixty by thirty feet, and has balconies fifteen feet wide in both front and rear. The north wing is used for cooking, washing, etc. An exhibition room is on its first floor. The south wing on the first floor contains the chapel, and the upper stories of both wings are used for dormitories. The school rooms are in the main building. The Asylum stands a little back from the street, the grounds in front being terraced and tastefully planted with flowers and shrubbery. It was designed originally to accommodate four hundred and fifty children.

The Asylum is under the charge of the Sisters of Charity of Mt. St. Vincent, of whom Sister Ann Borromeo is the Sister Servant. A call was made at the Asylum, October 8th, but owing to the lateness of the hour it was not convenient to make a full inspection of the premises. There were on the day of visitation, altogether, twenty-five Sisters engaged in the work, nine of whom were teachers. Eleven or twelve female domestics are employed.

At the date referred to, there were in the Asylum five hundred and seventeen boys, one hundred and ninety-nine of whom were orphans, and three hundred and eighteen half-orphans. All were from the city of New York. One hundred and seventy of the boys were of native, and three hundred and forty-seven of foreign, parentage.

The boys, while in the Asylum, receive a plain English education, and, so far as their tender years will allow, are disciplined to habits of industry.

Boland Farm, Peekskill.

This valuable property, consisting of two hundred and forty acres of land, was purchased about five years ago for $50,000, out of a legacy left by Mr. William Boland, a citizen of New York. The amount of the bequest was $50,000, but, by judicious handling on the part of those to whom this sacred trust was confided, this sum, with the interest accruing thereon, has amounted to nearly $100,000. The gift was made to this corporation for the general purpose of protecting orphan and half-orphan children. The intentions of this benevolent gentleman are certainly well carried out in this humane project of establishing an industrial home for boys in the country.

The farm lies just outside of Peekskill in a northerly direction. It is intended mainly as a home for boys who are not otherwise disposed of after they have remained their allotted time in the Asylum.

A farmer is at present employed to work the farm. Accommodations have been provided for a few Sisters of Charity of Mt. St. Vincent, who look after the domestic concerns of the house, and are the guardians of the boys while there. This arrangement, however, is but temporary, it being the intention of the managers to place the institution in the charge of the Christian Brothers. A building is soon to be erected. The plans are already drawn, and the workmen were, at the date of October 8th, making excavations preparatory to laying the foundations. The size of the building will be forty by one hundred feet. It is planned for three stories.

At last reports there were eighteen or twenty boys at the farm.

The business and financial affairs of the farm are directed by a committee of five members of the Managing Board of the Roman Catholic Orphan Asylum, who keep an account of its products, and charge the different Asylums respectively, with what is sent to them.

The Sheltering Arms.

New York.

The Sheltering Arms was first opened on the 6th of October, 1864, in the house of its President, the Rev. Thomas T. Peters, D. D., on the corner of One Hundredth street and Broadway, who generously donated its use to the institution for ten years. Preparations were made to admit forty children, and, on the first night, every bed was engaged, and the house was full. The work continued to grow till an addition to the building became a manifest necessity. Exertions were accordingly made to procure subscriptions, and, in 1866, the desirable addition was complete, thus increasing the capacity of the institution, so as to accommodate ninety children.

With a view of extending the work still further, land was purchased at Manhattanville, and a series of cottages erected, planned on the model of the *Rauhe Haus* in Hamburg. To these it was subsequently removed. In explaining this system, the President remarks:

"It is our hope by this new system of distribution to break up in some degree the institution feeling, and make a nearer approach to the family relation. In order to accomplish this object, we propose placing at the head of each cottage a lady to stand in the relation of mother to the children, and in that capacity to have the superintendence and control of the occupants of her cottage out of school hours. Under this direction the inmates of the cottages for the larger children, divided into companies of ten each, will be expected to do the work in the dormitory and keep in order the play-room and bath-room of the family."

The internal arrangements were under the care of the Religious Order of the Sisters of St. Mary, from the commencement of the institution, till 1870. Upon their resignation the President paid the following fitting tribute of appreciation to their gentle services in the good work:

"Our patrons are already aware that during the past year we have lost from the Institution, after five and one-half years of quiet and prosperity, its kind and constant friends, the 'Sisters of St. Mary.' Their devotion and self-denial, their readiness to carry out, in relation to the children, the wishes of the Trustees, had endeared them to all connected with 'The Sheltering Arms.' Thanks cannot repay them for all that they have been to us. Without their aid we should hardly have ventured to open our doors at the first; and throughout these years of rapid growth they have modified and in a large degree directed the development of the institution. We shall ever remember with gratitude and pleasure this long term of faithful and unsalaried service."

This institution is situated at One Hundred and Twenty-ninth street, corner of Tenth avenue, within the former precincts of Manhattanville, and is under the patronage of the Protestant Episcopal Church. The building comprises five sections or cottages—a central, thirty-six by forty feet, used for offices, parlor and private apartments for those in charge, and two lateral wings, one for each sex, each wing being forty by fifty feet, and containing two dwelling-houses or cottages for the children. Each cottage has its own dormitory, dining room and play-room for children. The cottages are named after the parties who built them. One of them is called the "Ladies' Association Cottage," being built by a number of ladies who formed an organization to support the Nursery. They paid $5,000 for the cottage. Another is named after Mrs. Peter Cooper. Two other cottages are named after "Mr. John D. Wolfe and Major Montgomery." These gentlemen, it is said, gave the money to complete them. The architecture of the building is attractive, and the interior appointments plain, but tasteful, the walls being mostly tinted and the moldings shaded. Two of the cottages have large porches, with glass windows, where the children play during the winter. In one of these was a pleasing portrait of the lady who built it. On the walls of the play-room were bright pictures, subjects of home life, with autumn leaves twined gracefully over the frames.

In the dining room were tables to seat thirty-five children. Chairs and stools of wood-color were in use. Inside blinds, and wainscoting of pine about five feet from the floor, were also pleasing features of this department. On the wall of the dining room, in a conspicuous position, was a motto, presented by Mr. Bergh, as follows: "I promise to protect dumb animals, and may God in His Mercy protect me."

The division walls of the cottages on each side of the main do not extend above the first story, consequently the dormitory floors in the second and third stories of each two adjoining cottages form one large room. The large room on the second story is used for one cottage, and that on the third story for the other, thus securing better light and ventilation than would be possible were the cottages divided on the second and third floors. The dormitories are furnished with single iron bedsteads, twenty-nine inches wide, having high head and foot pieces. Mattresses and husk pillows are used. A considerable number of the beds have little cards bearing the names of those who support the occupants. One hundred and thirty-eight dollars a year maintains a child. One card read, "Supported by Miss Sophie Furness." Several read, "Supported by a gentleman." Grace church supports one bed. Other beds are supported by churches, and others again by ladies and gentlemen, and some are supported by officers of the institution.

On a lot near the Shelter is a small brick building used for an infirmary. It is furnished with ten beds. A competent and faithful nurse is always resident. "Thither at a moment's notice may be transferred any sick child, without delaying a day or even hours until a nurse can be procured from without. A nurse thus hired for the occasion would be probably a stranger to the children, and that at a time when they most need a familiar hand."

The girls are taught to sew in classes under the superintendence of a lady instructor.

The sewing room is over the main cottage. It contains two sewing machines. The Mother of the house sleeps in a little room adjoining the dormitory.

While our sympathies were out-flowing toward the homeless, they were directed in another channel by the following inscription upon one of the little cribs in the nursery: "In memory of little Alice." A silent blessing went out from the heart toward those bereaved, who, rather than bury their love in the grave of their lost one, had bestowed it upon a living object whose very helplessness had established a claim for pity. There are two beds in the nursery that are thus endowed, one in the sum of $2,000 and the other in the sum of $1,000.

The Nursery also contains a baby play-house, profusely stocked with toys. In the dining room, connected with the nursery, the tables are low, and the chairs in keeping; some of the little chairs having arms.

The institution possesses a melodeon, which is used on Sundays in the Sunday School.

A love of flowers is cultivated in the children, and many of them are permitted to have little garden patches of their own.

Each cottage has a door opening into the general play-ground, in which is an open shed, twelve or thirteen feet wide, with seats at the back, used for play during the winter and in stormy weather. In the play-yard was a little wooden play-house which the children had constructed. It was of two stories, displayed considerable ingenuity in its plan, and was a source of great delight to the children.

The school is conducted in a separate building. About one hundred of the children attend. It is divided into primary and advanced departments. The school-rooms were brightened with flowers. One contained a good organ, and with this as an accompaniment the children sang "Rain upon the Roses."

The children wash in running water, and each have separate towels, tooth brushes and looking glasses. The latter, it was stated, they had kept for two years, without breaking. The children are subjected to family influences. They are invited into the parlor every evening to sing to piano accompaniment. "We cannot," says the lady in charge, Miss Sarah Seton Richmond, "carry out the family system fully. The institution gives one person thirty to take care of, whereas, the number ought to be only ten or fifteen. If you want to give the children the best chance, I think, ten or fifteen in a cottage is enough. One person cannot study the characters of thirty children, and it is important for the person having charge to know the disposition of each child. Children often come to-day, stay a week and then go. But we have about fifty children who have been with us five years."

A library of about four hundred volumes belongs to the institution. The portrait of Dr. Peters,* the founder of the charity, is in the parlor; and one, of the founder of each cottage, is placed in one of the play-rooms of the several houses.

The number of children in the institution, October 1, 1875, was one hundred and thirty-three — sixty-three boys and seventy girls. Of these, three were orphans, ninety half-orphans, and forty had both parents living. Forty-seven were of native, and eighty-six of foreign, parentage. Fifty-eight were partially supported by parents or friends, and seventy-five wholly by the institution. The number of children received during the year was ninety-three; the number discharged, ninety-three. Of the latter, eighty-six were returned to parents or guardians, four transferred to other institutions, and three were otherwise discharged.

The total expenditures during the fiscal year ending September 30, 1875, were $25,093.14. The invested fund of the institution amounts to $3,500.

Notwithstanding the number aided in this institution, the field of work could be greatly extended with additional means. On this point, Dr. Peters, in a recent report, says:

"During its ten years of activity the Sheltering Arms has received six hundred and fifteen children. Of these there were admitted during the year ending May 1, 1874, seventy-one, selected out of three hundred and eighty-five applicants. In pain and grief the larger portion of the remaining three hundred and fourteen were refused or postponed. For a few, perhaps twenty, we were able to obtain places in other charitable homes. A larger number, possibly seventy or even one hundred, would not be reckoned among those especially needing our care. Of the rest we can only say sorrowfully that, yearning to welcome, we were obliged to deny.

"To know what these refusals mean, one must pass days beneath our roof, listen to the sad tale of the deserted wife; and to the piteous story of the father, whose home is broken up by his wife's sickness. With that loved companion at the hospital, himself at board, his scanty income suffices now to provide for only a child or two in some inexpensive way and place. But what shall be done with those other sons and daughters for whom he cannot pay, and for whom no house of relative or friend stands open? Even to these we must say no! Day after day, for long, sad months, this is the only possible answer. Throughout the whole year three or four each week have been reluctantly dismissed, while we longed for the power to do, and mourned the necessity which closed our doors upon the stricken and the hopeless."

An interesting feature in this institution is the attempt made to engraft the family upon the orphan asylum system. This has proved so successful in Germany, in the work first inaugurated by Dr. Wichern, the philanthropist, that its introduction in this and similar institutions in our State will be watched with great interest.

Aside from the novelty of the system here adopted, the conception of the building is ingenious and would seem to be worthy the attention of those contemplating changes in their system of work, or in the construction of their institutions. Those advocating this system assert, "second to the religious benefit we place the social advantages of the cottage system.

"With one hundred and forty or more children in one mass, the individuality is gone. Could we reduce our households to twenty, we should be better pleased than now. But even with thirty or thirty-five inhabitants, the cottage, if rather a populous home, is still a home. After evening prayers, in each family by itself, the younger members being sent up to bed, the older children play the games presented to them, or gather around the table, cheerful with its neat cloth and pillar light and picture papers and piled up books, and there, with the Mother of the Family, read or draw, or otherwise pleasantly and usefully pass the social hour.

"This cottage system engenders, too, a little salutary rivalry both among children and patrons, to have each cottage and family more orderly and perfect than its neighbor. The children have always had in each dormitory distinct cupboards, with ample room for their clothes. Now, in addition, through the thoughtful provision of kind friends, the Wolfe Cottage has, on the play-room floor, a closet with a shelf for each boy, where are kept his books, drawing materials and little treasures."

SHELTER FOR RESPECTABLE GIRLS AND HOME FOR CONVALESCENTS.
New York.

The Shelter is under the charge of the Order of the Sisters of the Holy Communion of the Protestant Episcopal Church, Sister Catharine being Treasurer and Secretary. This Sisterhood formerly had charge of St. Luke's Hospital. The Sisters are required to engage for the term of three years, with liberty of renewal. Those entering the Order are required to pass a novitiate of six months.

The institution is situated at 332 Sixth avenue, New York. It was founded in 1871, and has for its objects "to provide a shelter for unemployed Protestant girls, and a home for those requiring rest before employment again."

Six Sisters are engaged in this work, including also the teaching of a parish school, the conducting of an Old Ladies' Home, and the managing of a Shelter for Babies. The home for the Sisterhood is situated at 328 Sixth avenue, where they also maintain a dispensary for the poor of the neighborhood. The Home for Aged Women and the Parish School are at 300 Sixth avenue, and the Shelter for Babies is at 143 West Twentieth street.

The Shelter for Respectable Girls and Home for Convalescents, is, the Sister informed us, intended for Protestants of every denomination. The great object aimed at is to keep girls from getting into trouble, when they find themselves without means and strangers in the city. Such are received into the Shelter, boarded two weeks for nothing, and secured suitable situations. The Shelter is not intended to be an intelligence office. Its main objects are two-fold: "First, to afford a temporary home, where patients discharged from the hospital before they are strong enough to work, and who have no home to which they can go, may remain till they are able to take situations. Second, to offer a shelter to girls who, while seeking situations, have no home or relations to whom to go for protection, and who would otherwise be obliged to seek lodgings in some tenement house already overcrowded, and where they are sometimes exposed to wickedness and temptation of which they before had no idea."

All the work of the house is done by the inmates, also a great deal of sewing for the other institutions under the care of the Sisters. The girls are expected to give one-half of the day to the service of the house, the other half to their own work. They can go out during the day if necessary, but all must be in the house by six o'clock. The sum of $2 a week is charged each inmate who is able to pay. The house was nicely furnished, and seemed to possess all the requirements of a comfortable home.

The personal histories of those who receive the benefits of this

Shelter are very interesting. Sometimes it is that of a young English girl found in the city without home, friends or money; at other times, that of a delicate young woman discharged from the hospital half cured, with no place to go to; and then again, a blooming maiden, innocent of the snares of city life, is about to enter the service of a party apparently respectable, but who really only seeks her for the vilest purposes. A case illustrating the timely aid of the Shelter to persons in the perilous circumstances last mentioned, is thus given by the Sister: "Two sisters sought the protection of the Shelter in August. They were the daughters of a physician, whose continued ill health rendered it impossible for him to support a large family. These two, being the oldest children, felt that they must leave home to seek employment in the city to relieve their father. They brought a little money with them, which was, however, soon exhausted. They lived in one of the many cheap boarding-houses, and vainly sought for employment. They were subjected to numerous insults, both in advertising and in answering advertisements, and finally came to us, their money all gone, and they almost in despair. In a few days they engaged to go to situations in our immediate neighborhood, and it was only by the timely visit of one of the Sisters to make some further inquiries of the person who had engaged them, that they were prevented from going to this house, which would have proved their ruin, and from which their youth and beauty would have made it almost impossible for them to escape. A good home was soon after obtained for them in a responsible family, where they gave perfect satisfaction." This branch of the Sisters' work is a very important one. The results attained are substantial, and it is believed the money expended in its support has been used with great prudence and advantage.

The Babies' Shelter is in a private house. At the time of inspection the double parlor was converted into a nursery. Here were little arm-chairs, with and without rockers, rocking-horses, etc. There were also little tables in use twenty inches high, and easy chairs for the babies. The children were under the charge of a Sister, who seemed to watch over them with a mother's tenderness, directing their little pastimes, settling their childish differences, and permeating all with her own gentle, refining character. They were clothed in bright-colored dresses, and white aprons with sleeves. "Nearly all of them," the Sister says, "have mothers, but no fathers. We have a few that we do not get paid for. The mothers of all pay if they possibly can." The children sleep in pretty iron cribs, and at night are cared for by a nurse who sleeps in the same room. Every thing in this house was arranged in good taste, and with due regard to convenience. The rooms were large, airy and liberally stocked with toys. In the rear is a piazza, where the little ones can get fresh air.

Two classes of children are kept. First, "day children," or those who only remain during the day while their mothers are out at work; and, second, "house children," who remain day and night. The cleanly and happy appearance of the children was very gratifying, and the loving care bestowed upon them by these good Sisters commands grateful recognition. The importance of investing childhood with bright surroundings, is seen not only in its effect upon the future well-being of the child, but indirectly upon that of society itself. Thus, this self-denying work of the Sisters assumes a character that is far-reaching in its results.

Society for the Reformation of Juvenile Delinquents (New York House of Refuge).

New York.

This institution is situated on Randall's Island, fronting the Harlem river. The walks approaching it are graveled, and shade trees, a fountain and other attractive objects adorn the grounds in front.

"The buildings are of brick, in the Italian style. The two principal structures front the river, and form a façade nearly a thousand feet in length. The line of their fronts is exactly parallel with the city avenues. The larger of the two buildings is for the accommodation of the boys' department, the other for that of the girls. Other buildings are located in the rear of these, and are inclosed by a stone wall twenty feet high. A division of like height separates the grounds of the boys' department from that of the girls, and in each department, walls separate the inmates into two divisions.

"The boys' house is nearly six hundred feet long. The dome-surmounted portions are devoted to the use of the officers; the central mass also contains the chapel; while the extreme portions contain the hospitals and lavatories." The portion between the center and end buildings is appropriated to dormitory purposes, and contains six hundred and thirty-six solidly constructed cells, five feet wide, seven feet long and seven feet high. "In the rear is the school and dining hall building, seventy by one hundred and thirty-eight feet. A central brick wall divides the building in each story into two equal parts, one for each division. The lower story is appropriated to dining rooms and the upper story to school-rooms. In the rear of the school building are the kitchen and bakery, occupying a space twenty-five by ninety feet. The work-shops are at the northerly and southerly extremities of the yard, and are each thirty by one hundred feet, and three stories high.

"The girls' house is two hundred and fifty feet long, the central portion of which contains the apartments of the matron, assistants and female teachers, while the wings contain two hundred and fifty dormitories for the inmates. In the rear, connected by two corridors or covered halls, is a building for school-rooms and dining halls, the hospitals, sewing rooms and lavatories being at each end, with the laundry in the rear.

"The whole establishment is supplied with Croton water, brought across the Harlem river in a three and one-quarter inch lead pipe. Tanks are in the attics of the principal buildings, and a reservoir of one hundred feet diameter, located beyond the inclosure, affords a reserve for extraordinary occasions, as well as a plentiful supply of ice in the winter."

The institution is over fifty years old, having been organized March 29, 1824, and opened for practical work January 1, 1825. It was located on Twenty-third street, New York, till October 31, 1854, when its present eligible quarters were entered upon. The property covers thirty-seven and a half acres of land. The institution is under the superintendency of Mr. Israel C. Jones.

Its affairs are controlled by a Board of Managers, elected by the stockholders, and serving without compensation. The title to the property is vested in the association. Children of both sexes are received, the admission of boys being restricted to the eastern counties, while girls are admitted from all parts of the State.

As we entered the hall, on the day of our visit, October 12th, a boy, who had just been brought in, was undergoing the usual examination upon admittance. He was about sixteen years of age, a vigorous youth, with a sharp face, indicative more of cunning than of intelligence. He spoke German, and, consequently, the examination was conducted by means of an interpreter. The boy, on being questioned, told the following story. He came to America from Hamburg, on a steamer. His father was a dealer in horses and cattle. The boy had been in the city eight weeks, and had stolen a watch worth ten dollars, for which he was arrested. His own account of the transaction is as follows: "I got a situation with a poultry dealer; I carried the poultry around the town; I worked for a German Jew; he would not pay me, and I stole his watch." The boy had no friends in the city, and, according to his own confession, could neither read nor write. He evidently belonged to the criminal class, and the circumstances would warrant the suspicion that he had been sent out of his native country for his country's good.

An examination of the house was made in company with the Superintendent. The cells, in which the boys are locked at night, are furnished with iron bedsteads, two feet three inches wide. Straw beds are used. Each bed has two sheets and two blankets. Additional bedding is added when needed.

In the bath-room are two large iron vats, with pipes running under the inner rim, pierced with holes to enable the boys to wash in running water. The towels are hung on rollers about the room. The floor is of stone.

In the dining room the tables are each set for twelve, and were furnished with the ordinary table furniture, excepting table cloths. Two boys at each table act as monitors, one sitting at each end of the table. The meal, on the day of visitation, consisted of soup and bread and butter. The boys sat on chairs. Five boys acted as waiters. If a boy's plate needed replenishing, the monitor at the head of his table held up his hand, and he was waited upon. Three hundred and five boys were in the dining room in charge of two officers.

The school rooms are large, well-lighted apartments, furnished with all modern improvements.

The printing, we were informed, is a branch of industry introduced last spring. In this department were four small rotary presses, worked either by hand or by power; also three large presses. The labor of the lads is contracted for at thirty-five cents per day. In the composing room about eighty boys were employed. Occasionally the boys work after their allotted tasks are performed, for which they are paid, and allowed all they earn. There is, in connection with this department, a stereotyping and electrotyping branch.

In the wire department were a large number of boys, engaged in working wire into various shapes for toasters, rat-traps, etc., etc.; also one hundred and twenty-five small boys, employed upon a hoop-skirt contract, and a hundred upon another article of ladies' wear. In another department there were one hundred and twenty-five boys employed upon a stocking contract.

In the schools the following branches are taught: reading, writing, arithmetic, geography, etc. It is stated by the President of the Board of Managers, Mr. Edgar Ketchum, in the fifty-first Annual Report of the Society, that "the apprehension of the inmates is generally quick, and their advancement from ignorance to knowledge rapid. * * * * The poor children who are brought to us have many of them been grossly neglected, and are very illiterate, and find here their first regular and careful instruction." The principal of the school, Mr. E. H. Hallock, it is thought, wisely believes in the importance of exercising the element of human sympathy in the labors of himself and associates. He says, in his last report on the school: "Sympathy is one of the latent forces of our being. We cannot philosophize upon it, yet all confess its power. It sometimes flashes along every line of the soul, conquering minds when every other device has failed. Our life here is full of illustrations of this fact. There are minds, however, that sympathy, in common with all other efforts, fails to reach. They are found among the older boys. One thing, it seems to me, is established beyond question. A boy's chance for reformation begins to wane at fifteen years of age, and at seventeen his case is almost hopeless. I pause in this writing, while I hold in contemplation the eight hundred souls before me with all their necessities and wants. Each has a separate nature with special personal powers which he cannot alienate, and which we cannot take from him; poisoned, perhaps, at the fountain, tarnished by voluntary alliance with evil, yet possessing numerous inherent and wondrous qualities that live even though the soul descends to the deepest infamy. Each one is struggling on toward the judgment with such interests about him that, were he to be reformed in heart and life, it would cause a thrill of emotion in all the realms of heaven, for there is joy in the presence of angels over one sinner that repenteth."

In the girls' department the dormitories, dining-rooms, bath-rooms and school-rooms are similar to those of the boys' department. The girls do all the domestic work of their own department, make their own and the boys' clothing, and attend to the laundry work. The sewing machines of this department are run by power.

In reference to the girls' department, the Secretary of the Ladies' Committee connected with the institution, Mrs. Martha S. Ferris, in her report, says: "The number of girls has increased in the past six months from one hundred and nineteen to one hundred and thirty-six. Some of these wayward ones are brought to us from dens of iniquity; others are creatures of circumstances over which they have no control, but all need to be brought to the Saviour of the world, whose blood alone can cleanse each heart from every stain of sin. We seek not only the reformation and elevation of these, by change of heart and moral suasion, but we aim at making them useful members of the community, by having them taught the simple English branches and domestic duties."

The chapel is a large room with a dais at one end, upon which is the lectern, and a gallery at the other end where the girls sit, the relative position of the sexes being such as to prevent the one being seen by the other. The chapel is furnished with an organ. Sabbath services are held regularly here, and clergymen of all Christian denominations are, from time to time, welcomed to the pulpit to preach to the inmates, the only limitation being that nothing sectarian shall be taught. The Scripture lessons by the American Sunday School Union are adopted in the Sabbath School. On Wednesday evening there is a lecture by the Chaplain, which both officers and children attend. The Chaplain, Rev. Geo. A. Smyth, in his last report expresses the following opinion: "The success of the work of reformation depends more upon the individual qualifications of the persons engaged in it, the wisdom and enthusiasm with which it is prosecuted, than upon any particular system of reform or peculiar machinery applied."

As evidence of what is being accomplished here in the way of reformation, we further quote from the same source: "The seed sown in these youthful hearts — often very barren soil — by sermons, lecture-lessons, personal conversations, daily devotions, kindly admonitions, we are not permitted to see ripen except in comparatively few cases; for when a boy has given evidence of reformation he is dismissed on the first opportunity that offers him a proper home and legitimate employment. But from time to time we do see that the seed cast upon the water is not lost.

"The well-to-do farmer comes to cheer the boys and express his gratitude to the House where he was an inmate more than forty years ago. The lad that went from the Refuge on a whaling voyage turns up many years after, master and owner of his vessel. A promising law firm, two hours ride from this Island, is composed of two of our graduates, who afterward took their diplomas from the best college of their State. The hero of Melville's South Sea fiction 'Omoo and Typee,' was once a boy of the Refuge, and is still living. He is now a worthy member of the Episcopal church in a New Jersey city. With his rector he lately dined at the house.

"A list of the faithful, efficient officers in the house, taken from the boys and girls for the last fifty years, would make a roll of honor alike creditable to the Institution and its wards. Alas! all do not turn out well, but if twelve thousand of the sixteen thousand who have come under the care of the Refuge are saved from a life of vice and set forth on a life of virtue, as the records show, then it is worth while 'to labor and to wait' for even greater success.

"When we think of the many others whom these twelve thousand might have corrupted had they gone on in their criminal career, of the sorrow to their friends, suffering to themselves, and the evils entailed upon the State, we cannot easily over-estimate the wisdom and economy that seek to check crime and pauperism in their early stages."

In regard to the importance of preventive measures for arresting crime, the Chaplain says: "Some one has said it would be wise economy for the State to board every criminal at the Fifth Avenue Hotel if that would put a stop to crime. Be that as it may, no one will doubt that if crime and pauperism can be prevented, the remedy must be applied to the children, and the earlier the better. It would be a great step gained in advance if the measures adopted were such as would reach the child before the child reaches the Reformatory.

"The most effectual preventive would begin at the nursery. Cruelty to animals is bad, but cruelty to infants is monstrous, and the humane law that steps in to shield the brute should not be less humane in stepping in to save the boy. Were Mr. Bergh to stand by while some untoward teamster beat and cut his horse, and then come with bandages for the poor animal, he might be esteemed kind, but would certainly be thought careless; and when the community stand by and see a child battered and bruised into a criminal on the street, and come along only to poultice the wounds it might have prevented, it is a day too late with its remedy. The child, if ever healed, will be scarred through life, the stigma of crime will be upon him, the poison of crime will be in him."

The institution contains extensive libraries. In the main library, used by the employés, there are fifteen hundred volumes. In the cases for the boys and girls there are two thousand five hundred and eighty-four volumes. The entire collection numbers four thousand and eighty-six works. Additions are made from time to time of such select works as may prove entertaining to the young, and assist in the work of education and reform. During the past year there have been distributed one hundred and twenty-five copies of the Youth's Companion and forty-four copies of the Christian Weekly, which have been given to the boys of the first division. The following opinion is expressed by the Librarian, Luther L. Feek: "The benefit derived from the library by the inmates has been commensurate with the advantages it has offered; and its good effect, in nearly all cases, is seen in their intellectual development and moral bearing."

The office of the institution is placed in telegraphic communication with every department of the house, enabling the Superintendent to direct all its workings without leaving the office.

The discipline of the house was thus explained by Mr. Jones: "The most effective means of discipline is the keeping of grades and badges. Of these we have four classes, and weekly changes are made either in the way of promotion or degradation, according to the merit or demerit of the boy. We never omit this. I have been here nearly twenty-four years, and this has never been once omitted. We have but two rules for the boys to keep. These have been in force without amendment for forty-nine years. The first is, '*Tell no lies,*' the second, '*Always do the best you can.*' Every boy on entering the house is taught these two rules. He is made to repeat them over, and has their meaning explained to him. His subsequent conduct is pronounced good or bad, according as it conforms to or deviates from these two rules. There are two conditions upon which a boy can obtain a dismissal from the institution. First, he must have advanced to the third grade in school, be able to read and write and understand the first elements in geography and arithmetic. Second, he must have credit for six consecutive weeks in the first grade, wearing the first badge. The shortest time in which any boy could be discharged from the institution is three or four months. The average length of time is about a year. No boy is discharged unless he has as good a prospect for advancement as he has here. We never turn a boy adrift. We expect to advance his interest. If he has friends, he is restored to them. If not, we find a home for him. There are people all over the country wanting boys. They usually apply here in the spring of the year. We investigate their claim, and require a certificate from their clergyman, or from some respectable man in their neighborhood, recommending them as suitable parties to be intrusted with the care of a boy. The lad is then called aside and is told that such a man wants him, that he expects him to do such and such things, and that he will have certain privileges; for instance, to be one of the family, eat at his table and sit in the same room in the evening. He is asked how he would like to go. If he is willing, articles of indenture are signed for three or four years. For the larger boys it is three years. A report is required from the man twice a year, and it is expressly stipulated that the boy must have free access to his own correspondence. The larger number of the boys, however, have friends to whom they are intrusted.

"Every two weeks a committee of the Board of Managers meet. There is nothing left to go hap-hazard. There are from forty to one hundred persons here every two weeks to press applications for the discharge of children. For instance a party comes and says, 'I want to apply for the discharge of John Smith.' His badge and scholarship being found satisfactory, the committee inquire about the character of the home to which the boy is going. The address of the applicant is taken down, his circumstances and his ability to take care of the boy are considered, and then the case is decided. If, on investigation, it appears that the boy would not be bettered by the change, they do not make it.

"Delinquency," the Superintendent thinks, "grows like a crop of potatoes. If fathers and mothers would perform all their duties to their children, require them to attend Sunday-school and church, give them fun and frolic, all that they want of it; such children would never be in the House of Refuge. But after a boy has been allowed for sixteen or seventeen years to run to the bad, it is not an easy matter to reform him."

Careful records of the history of each inmate are kept as long as any trace of them can be found. Among these are many interesting biographies.

The long experience of the Superintendent renders his views valuable. We quote from his last report on the necessity for systematic labor:

"The experience of the past year satisfies (if there was doubt before) that systematic labor is necessary as a means to the reformation of juvenile delinquents. The happiest, the most contented and the most hopeful among the boys, were those who were fortunate enough to be chosen for the shops. It is further evident that the form of labor that enlists the mind as well as the hands, is productive of the best reformatory results. Especially is this observed among the boys employed at printing. Not only do they show interest in their work here, but they are hopeful because they see the opportunity, when they are discharged, for earning an honest living, an important matter to them and to the community.

"Idleness has been the bane of these children. Sixty-two per cent of those received during the year were habitual idlers. Of those reported as having regular employment, very few were engaged in learning any trade or followed any systematic form of labor. Through idleness their habits became perverted and their moral and mental sensibilities blunted. Under no control, they found their way into the streets to mingle with others idle and bad as themselves. To reform such and to train them into industrious and virtuous citizens by mere precept, without the practical aid of a regular and systematic form of labor, would be quite as difficult as to attempt to teach them mathematics without the aid of figures, or geography without the aid of the globe and map.

"Another point of the highest importance is, that with a regular form of labor (and mechanical is preferable), the boy has the opportunity to earn something for himself to have when he is discharged. The knowledge that he is participating in the profits of his labor makes work not a drudgery but a pleasure, and induces patience and hope, thus preparing the mind in the best possible way to receive instruction."

The Superintendent gives it as his opinion, based upon statistics gathered with some pains, that juvenile delinquency has been on the increase during the last fifty years in proportion to the increase of the population, in the ratio of *thirteen to one*, and that the difficulty of finding proper places for the children, after they leave the house, is also much greater than formerly. On this point he says:

"The first thirty years the demand for boys' help on the farms in this and the adjacent States, and on whaling voyages, was sufficient to take all that were suitable for these occupations. Occasionally a boy was apprenticed to learn some mechanical trade.

"These several occupations took up about 86 per cent of the inmates of the Refuge during the above period, the annual average number being then about 250 boys and girls. The next ten years, 1855 to 1865, the number of commitments increased, and the annual average was about 350. The places offering were for about 60 per cent of the whole number.

"The last ten years, 1865 to 1875, the number of commitments nearly doubled those of the preceding decade, and only about 26 per cent could be placed at any of these occupations. Thus it is seen that only about one-quarter was apprenticed during the last ten years, and there is no probability that the opportunity to find places out of the city will be any better in the future. Probably about 50 per cent of the boys and girls sent here these later years (the class as a whole is of a higher grade than formerly), can safely be returned to their homes. This class is made up of those who have fair homes, but who, from carelessness or thoughtlessness of their parents, have been allowed too great freedom at night, and who unfortunately have been drawn aside by wild companions. A few months' detention and discipline generally serve to correct their habits, and, what is more important, brings forcibly to the parents' mind the necessity of guarding their children, and so save them from greater evils.

"This leaves about 25 per cent without places."

The following table shows the disposition made of the Children sent out during the past year:

	White boys.	White girls.	Color'd boys.	Color'd girls.	Total.
Discharged to friends	432	37	12	5	486
Discharged to hire	27	7	1	1	36
Discharged by *habeas corpus*	2	....	....	....	2
Indentured to farming	58	....	10	....	68
Indentured to housewifery	....	32	....	7	39
Indentured to servant	2	....	....	....	2
Indentured to clerk	1	....	....	....	1
Transferred to alms-house	1	1	....	1	3
Transferred to authorities for criminal prosecution	3	...	....	....	3
Transferred to penitentiary under act of 1873	1	....	....	....	1
Escaped	5	....	....	....	5
Died	3	1	1	....	5
Total	535	78	24	14	651

Since the opening of the Institution, January 1, 1825, the whole number of children under its care has been 16,430.

Boys	13,091
Girls	3,339
Total	16,430

The 1st of January, 1875, the number of inmates was as follows:

White boys	**641**
White girls	**96**

Colored boys	36	
Colored girls	16	
		789

Were received during 1875:

White boys	588	
White girls	101	
Colored boys	40	
Colored girls	13	
		742
Total in the House during 1875		1,531

The following table will show the parentage of the inmates received during the past year:

American	99
German	72
African	44
English	21
French	8
Italian	2
Polish	2
Irish	344
Jewish	3
Scotch	7
Spanish	1
Mixed	34
Indian	1
Total	638

The following table shows the offenses of the children committed to the institution during the last ten years:

YEAR.	Whole number committed.	Committed for petty thieving, vagrancy, disorderly conduct.	Per cent, nearly.	Committed for Grand larceny, burglary, arson, etc.	Per cent, nearly.	Committed for crimes against the person.	Per cent, nearly.
In 1866	750	655	87	83	11	12	2
1867	682	631	92	42	7	9	1
1868	603	553	92	43	7	7	1
1869	452	418	92	26	6	8	2
1870	406	359	89	44	10	3	1
1871	552	495	90	41	8	16	2
1872	407	371	91	31	8	5	1
1873	484	402	83	73	15	9	2
1874	636	557	88	70	11	9	1
1875	638	568	89	62	9	8	1
Total	5,606	5,019	90	515	9	76	1

The total expenditures during the past year were $113,328.95. The earnings of the boys amounted to $21,684.24.

In reference to the causes of juvenile delinquency, the Superintendent has taken great pains during the past year by means of home examinations to ascertain as to the antecedents of the children, which has resulted in securing much valuable information on the subject. The following facts were elicited:

1st. Character and condition of homes:

Resided in private houses	67
Resided in tenement houses and shanties	417
Homes comfortably furnished	250
Homes not comfortably furnished	214

2d. Social condition of the family:

Fathers living	327
Mothers living	401
Fathers dead	175
Mothers dead	101
Parents separated	35
Stép-fathers	43
Step-mothers	37
Temperate fathers and step-fathers	221
Temperate mothers and step-mothers	335
Intemperate fathers and step-fathers	139
Intemperate mothers and step-mothers	79
Parents having property other than household furniture	77
Parents having no property other than household furniture	401

3d. Habits and antecedents of the children before their commitment here:

Attended school regularly	134
Attended school irregularly, or not at all	373
Were habitually employed	162
Were habitually idle	312
Were truants from home and school	312
Were under arrest previous to being sent here	221
Had been inmates of other institutions	168

It is shown, among other things, "that poverty is closely connected with juvenile delinquency, and that intemperance is intimately connected with poverty. In eighty-three per cent of the homes visited it was found that the parents possessed no other property than their scanty furniture. Many of the homes were uncomfortably furnished; while in the best there were few attractions to induce the boy or girl to be contented in them. Far the greater number were in tenement houses. These houses were occupied by many families having numerous children, and the rooms were usually untidy, and in some cases filthy. From ten to twenty families under one roof were frequently found. One house was occupied by thirty-two families, having in the aggre gate ninety-six children. In some cases the officer found the parents so much under the influence of drink as to be unable to give intelligent answers to his questions.

"Is it any wonder that the children find greater attractions in the streets than in such homes? It is well, in considering the causes of crime, to give large attention to the influences in and surrounding these homes, that it may be ascertained to what extent they contribute to this great evil, and to inquire if, through legislation or otherwise, these hurtful influences and conditions surrounding these unfortunate children may not be corrected. It is universally acknowledged by parents that bad companions caused their children to go astray, and there is much truth in the statement; but they fail to see that the misfortune came to their children by their neglect."

The following valuable tables, showing the admissions and discharges, and other statistics during each decade, from 1825 to 1875, are taken from the fifty-first annual report of the Society:

	1st decade. 1825 to 1835.		2d decade. 1835 to 1845.		3d decade. 1845 to 1855.		4th decade. 1855 to 1865.		5th decade. 1865 to 1875.	
	Whole number committed, 1,678.	Per cent.	Whole number committed, 1,858.	Per cent.	Whole number committed, 3,101.	Per cent.	Whole number committed, 3,490.	Per cent.	Whole number committed, 5,664.	Per cent.
Males	1,261	75	1,304	70	2,508	81	2,709	78	4,763	84
Females	417	25	554	30	593	19	781	22	901	16
Native parents	740	44	643	34½	674	22	498	14	771	13 6–10
Foreign parents	938	56	1,215	65½	2,427	78	2,992	86	4,893	86 4–10
Could read	1,090	65	1,047	56	1,691	54½	745	21½	1,136	20
Could not read	598	35	811	44	1,410	45½	2,745	78½	4,528	80
Criminal	904	54	882	47½	1,866	60	2,145	62	3,212	57
Vagrant & truant	774	46	976	52½	1,235	40	1,345	38	2,452	43
Were returned	249	15	311	16½	583	19	547	15½	653	11
Under ten years of age	130	8	98	5	95	3	69	2	224	4
From ten to fourteen years	693	41	735	39½	1,151	37	1,196	34	1,787	31
From fourteen to sixteen years	591	35	723	39	1,294	43	1,439	41	2,106	37
Sixteen years and more	264	16	302	16½	561	18	786	23	1,547	28
Were indentured	1,160	70	1,523	82	2,486	80	1,905	55	1,217	26
Were discharged	195	11	186	10	409	13½	1,349	39	3,571	72½
Were enlisted	254	15	72	4	141	4½	185	5	3	....
Escaped	45	2½	57	3	33	1	24	½	25	½
Died	24	1½	20	1	32	1	27	½	59	1
RESULTS.										
Favorable	792	47	702	37	1,189	38½	988	29	*568	12
Unfavorable	273	17	198	10½	616	20	819	9	206	4
Unknown	589	36	938	52½	1,264	41½	2,156	62	4,101	84

* 4,875 discharged.

Showing statistics of those heard from favorably during the five decades.

	1st decade. 1825 to 1835.		2d decade. 1835 to 1845.		3d decade. 1845 to 1855.		4th decade. 1855 to 1865.		5th decade. 1865 to 1875.	
	Whole number, 792.	Per cent.	Whole number, 702.	Per cent.	Whole number, 1,189.	Per cent.	Whole number, 988.	Per cent.	Whole number.	Per cent.
Males	579	74	450	64	919	77	716	72½	...	....
Females	213	25	252	36	270	23	272	27½	....	....
Native parents	335	42	231	33	286	24	165	17	....	....
Foreign parents	457	58	471	67	903	76	823	83	....	....
Could read	535	67	406	58	628	53	193	20	....	....
Could not read	257	32	296	42	561	47	795	80	....	....
Criminal	419	53	299	42	658	55	628	63½	....	....
Vagrant and truant	373	47	403		531	45	360	36½	....	....
Under ten years of age	57	7	42	58 6	52	4½	44	4½	...	...
From ten to fourteen years	339	42½	296	42	509	43	365	36½	....	....
From fourteen to sixteen years	274	34½	275	39	458	38½	375	38	....	...
Sixteen years and more	124	16	89	13	170	14	204	21	....	....
Were indentured	634	81	656	93½	1,024	86	703	74	....	....
Were discharged	49	6	24	3½	119	10	189	19	....	....
Were enlisted	109	13	22	3	46	4	66	7	....	....

As having reference to the results which have been achieved by this society and the importance of its work, we quote from a letter of Ex-Governor Horatio Seymour, read before the society at its fiftieth anniversary, June 2, 1875:

"It has been my painful duty to act upon thousands of prayers for pardon, and to study with care the sources and history of crime. Beyond most men, I have had opportunities for seeing the great value of the work of 'The Society for the Reformation of Juvenile Delinquents.' I will not dwell upon its direct charities. It has, beyond these, a wide influence in teaching our people and their legislators the causes and courses of wrong-doing. It is among youthful offenders, where the earliest influences which shape character are most clearly seen, that the great truth that crime is the outgrowth of social condition, is exhibited in the clearest light, and that the public as well as the offender is involved in its guilt. There never was an indictment found against a man which was not, in some degree, an indictment of the community in which he lived. Criminals are representative men."

Society for the Relief of Half-Orphan and Destitute Children in the City of New York.

New York.

The following report on this interesting charity has been kindly furnished by Commissioner Roosevelt:

"This Society was organized December 16th, 1835, a day long to be remembered, for on the following night, the fire commenced which destroyed a large portion of the lower part of the city, and which, for many years, was spoken of as the 'great fire.' The consequent gloom and depression throughout the city almost compelled those who had commenced the undertaking to relinquish it. Fortunately they were enabled to persevere.

"At that time there were two orphan asylums in the city. One supported by Protestants, admitted only children who had lost both parents; the other, under the charge of Roman Catholics, was open to those who had lost either or both. There was no Protestant institution in the United States which provided for the care of children having parents living. The necessities of this class were brought prominently before Mrs. Wm. A. Tomlinson, who originated the plan of this institution, which was designed to provide for the care of children who had lost one parent, and by this relief to enable the surviving parent to work more advantageously, and contribute weekly a small sum for their board. A basement room was hired in White street, and the Asylum thus opened received four children. In May the number of children had increased to fifty-nine, and a house was hired in Twelfth street. In April, 1837, the Society was incorporated under the name of 'The Society for the Relief of Half-Orphan and Destitute Children in the City of New York.'

"Mr. James Bowman was one of its earliest and most liberal friends. Through his means in 1839 the Society was enabled to purchase a house covering two lots of ground in Tenth street, and known as the Nicholson house. The children were taken to this building in May of the same year. The number of inmates continued to increase, and at the end of three years the building in Tenth street proved too small and inconvenient. Four liberal donations of five thousand dollars each, enabled the Trustees to purchase two lots on Sixth street, adjoining, in the rear, the property in Tenth street. Here a building was put up, to which the Asylum was removed in 1842. The Tenth street building was occupied partly as a nursery and partly rented. Fifteen years later it was again found necessary to enlarge the accommodations, and the Asylum was removed in May, 1857, to the building which it now occupies, No. 69 West Tenth street. This building stands on the site of the original Tenth street house and two adjoining lots, which were purchased in 1854. The Asylum is comfortable and commodious, and though not including all the improvements found in more recent buildings, is well adapted to its purpose. It is ninety-five feet front by fifty-seven deep, and four stories in height. There is an inclosure in the rear ninety-one by sixty-six, which is flagged and used as a play-ground. In the basement is a play-room fifty by sixty feet, besides laundry, drying, bath and furnace rooms. On the first floor are kitchen, dining, sewing, matron's, and committee rooms and pantries. On the second floor are school rooms and nursery. On the third and fourth, sleeping rooms and infirmary. Two hundred children can be accommodated in it. During some years two hundred and thirty or more have been received, but experience has shown that so large a number is undesirable, and of late has not been necessary, as the number of institutions for the care of children has greatly increased.

"It is forty years since the Asylum was opened, and it may well be considered one of the established institutions of the city. There are no incumbrances on the property, which is held by a Board of Trustees. The internal affairs of the Asylum are superintended by a Board of Ladies.

"The current expenses are met from the payment of board by the parents, annual subscriptions, donations, occasional legacies, rents from the Sixth Avenue building, and the proportion of the public school fund. There are now one hundred and ninety-four children in the Asylum. Since the opening of the Asylum three thousand four hundred and sixty-three children of various nationalities, grades and religion, have been received, cared for and instructed. The cost of each child, including all expenses, averaged in 1875 a little less than seventy-five dollars. On Sunday the children attend morning service at the Church of the Strangers, Rev. Dr. Deems, where the inmates have been attendants for over thirty years. In the afternoon a Sunday-school is held at the asylum, which is superintended and taught by volunteer teachers from different churches."

The total number of children received during the past year was sixty-four, and the total number discharged one hundred and two. Of the latter, one was placed out by adoption, eighty-three were returned to parents or guardians, two left without permission, two were transferred to other institutions, nine were sent out of the State, four were otherwise discharged, and one died.

The total expenditures during the year were $23,285.25. The value of its personal estate and invested funds is set down at $27,000.

St. Barnabas' House.

New York.

The St. Barnabas' House is located at 304 Mulberry street. Its object is to afford a home for homeless women and children who are taken in at any time of the day or night, unless intoxicated or known to be fallen women.

The institution was established in 1863, by Mrs. William Richmond, of New York, who for over two years conducted its affairs without public aid. In 1865 its management was transferred to the Protestant Episcopal City Mission Society, which has since directed its operations. The financial affairs of the institution are controlled by a committee of gentlemen. Its internal and domestic concerns are managed by the Sisterhood of the Good Shepherd, whose services are voluntary. Five Sisters were engaged in the work on the day of visitation, October 12, Sister Ellen being in charge of the house. A housekeeper, a dining-room girl, a cook, a laundress and a doorkeeper are employed; also two nurses for the day nursery. Sister Ellen gave us the following information regarding the work: "Our domestics are generally women who desire to reform. They come into the house as the other women, desiring employment. We receive them, make a home for them while they remain with us, and procure for them suitable places. The rest of the work is done by those who are waiting for places. Our rule is, that all who are admitted are expected to work. They usually comply with the requisition, and we notice that the women seem to be elevated by the influence to which they are subjected while with us. To take them in we require no references whatever, except to inquire whether they ought to be at the midnight mission. We do not mix the innocent with the guilty. If they come back to us after we have found places for them, we require satisfactory letters from their late employers. It gives them a chance, if they do well, to get on. A great many have been coming and going for five, six and even seven years, who find here a home again, where they are safe and where they can be provided with situations."

In addition to the class of women spoken of, the house, on the day of visitation, had under its shelter seventeen children, whom the Sister called "house children." They are not given over to the institution. The parents are at liberty to remove them at any time. Although unable to provide for them, they are unwilling to surrender them to the institution. Children are not usually taken in under four years of age.

In connection with the house is a Day Nursery for the care of little children whose mothers during the day are away from home. They are admitted at seven in the morning and kept till seven in the evening, during which time they receive their dinner and supper.

The house children are taught to do all kinds of work, sweep, dust, make beds and help to take care of others. The boys at eight years old are transferred to the "Sheltering Arms," on One Hundred and Twenty-ninth street and Tenth avenue. Of the day children, all that are old enough learn to sew. This work is done at regular hours, in classes. They are lost sight of when parents take them away.

Only Protestants are taken as "house children," but children of all religious denominations are eligible to the Day Nursery. The children are kept entirely apart from the women.

The institution also extends its charitable work to providing a dinner for numbers of poor families, who bring vessels daily to receive and carry it home. The Sister says they have as many as twenty-five such families each day to relieve. Any person coming hungry may get a warm meal, but after that, is visited by the Sisters. One Sister gives up her whole time to visiting.

On the premises is a chapel capable of accommodating about one hundred and fifty persons.

A sewing school for outside children is taught in the house by ladies of the Protestant Episcopal Church, independent of the work of the Sisters. One day they meet the children, and another day the mothers, to teach them sewing.

The house contains a spacious reading-room, under the control of an association of gentlemen. This room is furnished with large tables, writing desks, and comfortable chairs. The walls are brightened with pictures; the room contained nine files of newspapers and a library of about four hundred volumes. The Atlantic, Harper's, Scribner's and Appleton's magazines are sent in regularly as donations.

The play-room for the children is a cheerful apartment, with windows on two sides. In it was a child's toy-house, well filled with toys. Twenty little children were found in the school-room, which was also a very neat apartment, with its furniture suited to the youthful character of the pupils. The children sang for our entertainment, with childish sweetness, "Little Drops of Water." In an upper room we found a number of the small children sitting around a long table, playing with pictures and dolls; a rocking-horse was also provided for those possessing equestrian proclivities. In this room were the day children, under the care of one of the Sisters. There was here a number of little cribs, in which the children could take a nap during the day, two being occupied at the time of our visit. The floors were well scrubbed, and the entire room was in a condition of extreme neatness. The children were clean. The "day children," although returning to their wretched hovels at night, seemed as though they had been brought up in homes of comfort. While expressing our surprise at the fact, the Sister said, "The most of our time is spent in making them tidy."

The dormitory for the "house children" is furnished with single iron bedsteads, two feet four inches wide, straw beds, husk mattresses, and hair pillows. The room was hung with steel engravings, many of them being, we were informed, Christmas presents, which added to the interest of the apartment.

A Sister sleeps in a room adjoining the children's, so as to be at hand if any should need her presence during the night. Each child has its own towel. The school for the "house children" was adorned with pictures, which were chosen with excellent taste. It also contained a library for the children.

The sleeping apartments for the women we found to be very clean. "The accommodations are not," the Sister says, "sufficient for the work that is being done." The house is an old one. The lot, however, is sufficiently roomy to admit of larger and more commodious buildings.

The total number of persons received in the house during the past year was 1,687, and the number discharged, 1,690. It is stated that the number of inmates received gives but a faint idea of the number assisted. This will be made somewhat apparent by the statement that 118,411 meals were furnished during the year. There are from thirty-five to forty families who send to the house daily and receive one or two meals in baskets or pails. These are people truly worthy, whom the Sisters visit regularly, and assist to what is most needed.

The total expenditures of the institution during the fiscal year ending September 30, 1875, were $11,358.79. Its total indebtedness was $17,000. It has no invested funds. There is so little work procurable, and so many out of employment, that the admissions to the house are unusually large, and the efficient working of this worthy and prudently managed charity calls for more means to enable it to cover the field which so urgently needs its benefactions.

Ladies wishing to enter the Order of the Sisters are required to make a visit to the institution of a month's duration. Then, if their desire remains unchanged, they are invited to prolong their visit five months more, during which time they discharge all the duties of the Sisters, and are subject to the same rules, with the exception of wearing a habit. If they are satisfied with the work, and are deemed suitable for the life of a *Religieuse*, a further period of eighteen months is necessary before they are admitted, thus making the period of their novitiate cover two full years. There is no vow taken, but they are expected to devote their lives to the work, unless peculiar circumstances arise making it in accordance with their duty to withdraw. There is another class of ladies who come for stated periods of six months as visitors, who do not contemplate joining the Sisterhood. These take the place of Sisters, enabling them to rest and recruit their health, and prove a very grateful source of assistance.

St. Joseph's Orphan Asylum.

New York.

This Asylum has for its object the maintenance of orphan, half-orphan, homeless and neglected children, especially those of German origin. It was organized in 1858, and incorporated April 15th, 1859, by special act of the Legislature.

The particulars of its history are thus stated: "In the years 1848 and 1849, the Missionary Fathers of the Most Holy Redeemer, who visited the different hospitals and poor-houses in the city of New York and vicinity were often called upon to take charge of orphan children, especially those of newly arrived emigrants, or children whose parents were sick and unable to support them. The Missionary Fathers at first arranged for the care of these children in a private family living in a tenement house in Thompson street, their expenses being paid by the churches of the Most Holy Redeemer and St. Alphonsus, but their number kept increasing so fast that other provision became a necessity. In 1857 the Rev. Joseph Helmpraecht commenced to organize a society for the support of the orphan children, and was so successful, that with the assistance of the congregations of the two churches already named, he was enabled to purchase the ground where the St. Joseph's Asylum is now located. A charter was then secured from the Legislature, a building erected costing $36,000, and orphans, half-orphans, and children whose parents were, for various reasons, unable to give them a home, were admitted. The Asylum at its completion was given over to the management of the Sisters of the Order de Notre Dame, who have since that time had its care."

The institution was visited October 9th. Its location is on Eighty-ninth street, corner of Avenue A, near the East river. The tract of ground belonging to the Asylum contains about twenty-eight lots. The building is of brick, plain but substantial, with a tin roof. In the basement are the kitchen, dining rooms and laundry. In the first story, two school rooms, two parlors, the chapel and private rooms. In the second story are two large general sitting rooms for the children, the bathing rooms and the sleeping rooms for the Sisters and waiters. The third and fourth stories contain the sleeping rooms for the children. This building was erected in 1860. A plain, two-story, frame building is also on the grounds, which contains twenty rooms, of which three are used for small children, two for patients, and one for a work-room. The basement is used for wash-house and bakery.

On the day of visitation the Asylum was in charge of Sister Hyacintha, assisted by fourteen others, Sisters of the same Order. The number of children then sharing the benefits of the institution was stated to be about two hundred. They are admitted from two years old upward. Both boys and girls receive a good practical education in English and German, and are trained to habits of industry. The boys are exercised principally in out-door work, and the girls in housekeeping; they are also taught both hand and machine sewing. Particular attention is given to singing, and a very good choir is formed from among the children. At the age of fourteen the boys are put out to learn trades, and continue to be the wards of the Asylum till their trades are learned and they are started in life.

The dormitories are furnished with single, iron bedsteads, and with clean and comfortable beds. The day of our visit being Saturday, the Sunday clothes of the children were being orderly arranged, in this department, for the morrow.

The stairways are protected by a wire screen above the rail of the balustrades, so arranged that the little ones cannot fall over.

The bathing accommodations are ample and well regulated.

In the dining-room the boys are separated from the girls by a partition, sufficiently high to serve the purpose of a screen. Crockery-ware and knives and forks are used. The larger children have napkins at meals, the smaller, bibs.

The house in the yard, apart from the main building for the smaller children, is called the "Babies' house."

On our entering, the children sang in German, "Praised be the Lord Jesus," which we were informed is their usual custom of greeting strangers.

The grounds about the building are neatly kept. The boys are trained to garden culture.

Six milch cows, belonging to the establishment, afford a good supply of milk for the children. The dignity of labor was here vindicated by one of the Sisters, whom we found with a little flock of delighted children about her, milking the cows. Our visit, as usual, was unexpected. The table was prepared for the evening meal, and was bountifully spread. The diet is a very generous one. In addition to their regular meals, at four o'clock every day the children all get a slice of bread, made luscious to the childish palate, by the addition of a little molasses.

The house was bright and cheerful and the children seemed well cared for. It was evidently a home of plenty, and there was a naturalness in the demeanor of all those about it that gave it a homelike atmosphere.

On October 1, 1875, the number of children who were orphans was seventy-eight; half-orphans, one hundred and six; and the number who had both parents living was twenty. One hundred and eighty-six of the children were of native, and eighteen of foreign, parentage. The children were mainly from the county of New York. Forty of the children were wholly or partially supported by friends, and one hundred and sixty-four by the institution.

Since its commencement the Asylum has provided for thirteen hundred and fifty-five children.

The number of children received during the past year was seventy-nine; the number discharged, sixty-nine. Of the latter, six were adopted, eight indentured, forty-four returned to parents or guardians, one left without permission, four were transferred to other institutions, and six died.

The total expenditures during the fiscal year ending September 30, 1875, were $16,829.41. The value of its personal estate and invested funds was $17,400.

The results of the inspection were very satisfactory. Whether considered as to the condition of the house, the children or the property, the institution is in a prosperous state, while a prominent idea of plain wholesome comfort, so characteristic of the German people, is too marked to escape notice.

St. Mary's Free Hospital for Children.

New York.

This Hospital was begun in 1870, on a small scale, and has since continued to grow steadily till it has become recognized as one of the indispensable and beautiful charities of New York city. Its present location is at 407 West Thirty-fourth street. As soon as funds for the purpose can be secured, it is intended to build an edifice specially adapted to its use, which shall enable it to extend its sphere of beneficence. It is in the charge of the Sisterhood of St. Mary, an Order of Sisters of the Protestant Episcopal Church. The objects of this Order are "the care of the sick and needy, the orphan and the fallen, and the education of the young."

The visitation was made October 7, at which date there were twenty-five patients under its care. The Hospital is in charge of three Sisters, assisted by two postulants. Their work is entirely gratuitous. A training school for young girls is maintained in connection with the hospital. Certain household duties devolve upon the pupils, thereby relieving the Sisters, who are enabled to give themselves entirely to the work of attending upon the little sufferers. No domestics are employed in the establishment.

The benefits of the hospital are bestowed free of charge. It is devoted solely to the caring for and nursing of the children of the poor, who are received between the ages of two and fourteen years, and sometimes, in special cases, younger. They are sent to the hospital by the physicians, who frequently find at the dispensaries children that need more careful nursing than can be bestowed upon them at their own homes to insure recovery. Ladies visiting among the poor occasionally meet such cases, and direct them to the Hospital, where they are received without regard to faith, color or nationality. This is the only general hospital in the city for children suffering with acute diseases. No children with contagious diseases are admitted.

The ward for little boys, in the front room on the second floor, is furnished with single, iron bedsteads. Between the beds were little tables, covered with white fancy tidies, on which a profusion of toys were spread, and in the center of the room a low table, also full of toys, with baby chairs surrounding it, where those able to be up, sit and amuse themselves. The beds are two feet four inches wide, and four feet ten inches long. They are high, standing five feet seven inches from the floor, for the convenience of the attendants. A strip of bright carpet was spread through the center of the apartment. Pictures hung on the walls, and toys representing a great variety of domestic animals were on the mantel-piece. Boxes including every conceivable variety of attractive toys were about the room. A little library was here, well stocked with books of fairy tales and other children's stories. Contrivances for holding toys, and which also do duty as dining-tables for such little sufferers as are confined to their beds, were among the hospital appliances. On the wall, at the head of each bed, is a ticket case, as is usual, with the name of the patient and the date of admission; its number is also on the register.

Some of the mattresses are of straw and husks, and others are of hair. Each child is provided with its own towel, wash cloth, brush and comb. "We have been," says Sister Catharine, "providentially preserved from the spread of any contagious disease. We had one case of scarlatina, but we prevented it from spreading to the other children. We have a room for cases that need to be isolated."

One of the patients was a little boy nine years old, who was suffering from hip disease. The Sister said: "He was brought here more than a year ago, upon pillows, and was then unable to stand up. His case was considered hopeless. Now he walks up and down stairs. He came from a German family, in which there were seven other children."

The Hospital possesses a valuable case of surgical instruments, presented to the institution by the Guild of St. Hildreth. This Guild is composed of young ladies from St. Mary's School, in Forty-sixth street.

There is a ventilating shaft between the front and rear wards. The dispensary of the Hospital is on the second floor. The appurtenances of each bed, including its wash cloth, towels, etc., are all numbered to correspond with the beds to which they belong. Between the wards are closets, used for the children's wardrobes.

The ward for little girls in the rear room is furnished neatly and carpeted. Toys, pictures, a library, and a little canary bird, singing cheerily, are some of its attractions. The ward for younger children is on the first floor, and extends the whole length of the house. It was originally a double parlor. Over the mantel-piece was a large Calvary Cross, with the motto, "Nearer, my God, to Thee." Seven cribs for quite young children were in the ward. Six of the children were amusing themselves in bed with toys on trays as we entered.

One of the leading features in this nursery is its cheerful bright aspect and its bewildering display of toys. Four little children in baby chairs surrounded a low table, and were amusing themselves with their playthings. One was building a brick house, another throwing one down, and each seemingly happy in its own work, whether constructive or destructive. Among them was a little girl about four years old, who was born in the West Indies. She arrived on the 26th of March, suffering with hip-joint disease. She was "getting on very nicely," and would, it was thought, recover. A little child, not able to stand, was playing on the floor. A case of club foot, we were informed, had been discharged on the day of visitation. It had been successfully treated and entirely cured.

"It is not intended," the Sister says, "to take chronic incurables. This is a hospital, and not a home for them." Cases which elicited pity met us at every turn. A little boy, sitting in a rocking-chair, had disease of the elbow joints. The dead bone, we were informed, was to be removed. Other and similar cases were awaiting operation. The Sister informed us that generally when the children are admitted they are in such a wretched condition of health that it is necessary to keep them awhile to get them into a proper condition to be operated upon. They are fed on a very nourishing diet.

The carpet in the center of each ward is taken up frequently and the floors purified. The walls are "hard finished," and admit of washing at stated intervals. The wards have fire-places in which fires are kindled, as occasion requires, to change and purify the air. The house is warmed by furnaces.

It is customary, when the doctor is dressing a wound, to surround the bed with a screen to prevent the sensibilities of the other children being disturbed. When a child is very ill or dying, the screen is also used, that the circumstance may not depress the spirits of the others.

The Sister who has charge of the dressing is, we were informed, thoroughly trained and competent to instruct the postulants that work under her.

In the center of one of the wards is a large doll-house, in which the children have a miniature hospital, where dolls' legs and arms are bandaged in a serio-comic, pains-taking manner by juvenile surgeons.

The various ingenious expedients resorted to by the Sisters to divert the minds of the little sufferers from themselves, showed the depth of interest that was taken in their welfare. This interest was manifest throughout every ward, in the toys and numerous other objects to engage the youthful fancy. The children able to sit up are dressed in bright-colored garments. The hospital is kept with the most scrupulous neatness, and an air of cheerfulness pervades every part. The work being done here is one that is undeniably lessening public burdens. The humane efforts of the physicians, whose services are gratuitous, and the faithful and self-denying labor of the Sisters cannot fail to command universal sympathy.

It may not be inappropriate here to quote the language of another, recorded after visiting this interesting institution:

"Plain and simply furnished as it is, I felt, while walking through its apartments, that I was treading upon holy ground. I knew it was a house in which my blessed Master delighted to dwell. I knew it was a work, above all others, which He smiled upon. I felt that He was walking among those little beds.

"The hospital requires many things yet to fit it up as it should be. It has neither lands nor endowment.

"In what more appropriate or beautiful manner could parents who have means and desire in some way to honor the memory of a loved and departed child do so than by endowing a bed to its memory in St. Mary's Hospital? Let us carve our monuments to the memory of our loved and departed ones upon living, suffering hearts, rather than upon cold, lifeless marble."

The managers, in their last report, state that during the last two years the work has increased so constantly that a much larger house is a positive necessity, and deem that the time has come when a building of suitable size and accommodations should be undertaken for an institution which, as an efficient agency for relieving human suffering, has already fulfilled the most sanguine hopes of its founders.

The present building is in no wise commensurate with the opportunities for doing good which are afforded by the accumulating demands of the sick poor.

The benefactions of this institution are not confined to the city of New York. At the date of visitation there were in the hospital children from the counties of Columbia, Richmond, Sullivan and Westchester. During the year ending September 30, 1875, the number of patients received into the institution was seventy-five, and the number discharged sixty-nine. Of these, forty-five had recovered, eight had been improved, seven unimproved, and nine had died.

The total expenditure during the fiscal year ending September 30, 1875, was $7,204.97.

St. Stephen's Home for Children.

New York.

This Home was organized May 1, 1868, with the object of affording a shelter to needy and destitute children. It is located at 145 East Twenty-eighth street. The work was begun on Second avenue, with a small number of children. Several changes were made previous to the occupation of the present house.

The Home is under the charge of the Sisters of Charity, and supported mainly by collections in St. Stephen's Parish Church. Seven Sisters carry on the work, Sister Frances Xavier being Superior. No domestics are employed.

Children of both sexes are received between the ages of two and thirteen years. They are clothed, fed and instructed, and afterward returned to their friends, or good homes are procured for them.

On the date of visitation, October 7th, there were one hundred and thirty-one children in the house, of which forty-two were boys and eighty-nine, girls.

The number of children received since its organization is six hundred and forty-six, the number received during the past year was seventy-five, and the number discharged fifty-one. Of the latter, four were indentured, forty-one returned to parents or guardians, five transferred to other institutions, and one had died.

The number of orphans in the institution, on the day of visitation, was sixty-five; of half-orphans, fifty-two; of children having both parents living, fourteen. Forty-three were of native parentage, and eighty-eight of foreign. Nineteen were partially supported by parents or friends, and one hundred and twelve by the institution.

The house was very crowded. Beds have to be made in the class-rooms at night to accommodate all the inmates, but the Sister says: "The health of the children is remarkably good." One death occurred during the past year from diphtheria — a child of about eighteen months.

In regard to the disposal of the children, the Sister says: "Quite a number of the small children have been placed out by adoption, and they do very well. We rarely bind out a child. We prefer to put it in a family, watch over it, and, if it is not well treated, take it back again. We see that they have good homes. Some we send to the

Industrial School on Forty-second street. Others we place with dress-makers. We always place them with reliable and responsible persons—with persons that will exert a good influence over them. Not one-tenth of the children belong to this parish. There are a few whose parents or relatives pay something toward their board, and a good many whose parents agree to pay, but do not. We keep them till they are fourteen years old. A father, for instance, places his children here, the mother having died. As soon as one of his girls gets so as to be able to keep house she goes back to her father, and keeps house for him, and the family is reunited."

The industrial education of the children is well attended to. All are instructed according to their capacities. Some learn music, others are taught to sew on the machine. "Two," Sister Frances says, "have developed remarkable talent for music. Kind friends have sent them to a boarding school. Another, a boy, has been sent to a college in Canada. We have two boys attending college in Sixteenth street. One is a very bright boy, and it would be a pity not to give him assistance. Two of our boys are in Stewart's, and are liked very well."

The school room was clean and furnished with patent seats and desks. The children sang very sweetly "Roses underneath the Snow." Their average age is eight years. The boys had clean faces and hair neatly combed. The parlor was furnished with both an organ and a piano. A melodeon was also in the house.

The dormitories were clean and furnished with single iron bedsteads, straw beds and feather pillows. The house has good ventilation.

The yard is small, flagged, and has the usual provisions for the recreation of children, including a swing. The walls on each side covered with morning glory, *wistaria* and Virginia creeper, betokened tasteful care, while within the establishment were traces of refinement, the influence of which seemed to be evident in the appearance and demeanor of the children.

Sister Frances has been engaged in the children's work since 1851. Two of the Sisters visit Bellevue Hospital daily, others visit the sick poor of the parish.

The Sisters are zealous in their good work, and the influences brought to bear upon the children are believed to be highly elevating. The house is evidently too small for the field of labor surrounding it, and the institution is deserving of liberal aid, with a view to increasing its benefactions.

St. Vincent's Home for Boys.

New York.

This institution, partaking largely of the character of a news-boys' home or lodging house, is situated at 53 and 55 Warren street. It was incorporated in 1871, and was formerly called St. Vincent's Lodging House for Boys. It began in 53 Warren street, May, 1870, occupying part of the building, and subsequently grew so as to need the addition of the upper part of the adjoining store. On the day of visitation, October 6th, the Home occupied four floors of 53 Warren street, and the third, fourth and fifth floors of No. 55. At present, its needs are so great as to require still larger accommodations for the numerous class whom it seeks to benefit.

The Home is under the auspices of the Society of St. Vincent de Paul, and is in the immediate charge of the Rev. John C. Drumgoole.

The dormitories of the Home are furnished with double tiers of iron beds, one over the other. The dining room, having a seating capacity of two hundred, is fitted up with tables and benches, and has ample provision otherwise for the hungry appetites to be satisfied after a day's exposure in the open air. The usual dietary, as given in the words of Father Drumgoole, is as follows:

"For breakfast, bread, butter and coffee, as much as they want. Little extras are also furnished to such as pay the small charge which is intended only to cover the cost, and many avail themselves of the opportunity to add meat, cake, or eggs to this repast. For dinner—which is not so well patronized as the other meals, owing to the boys being at work in different parts of the city—soup of a good quality, as we can testify, or meat and bread, together with coffee. For supper, tea, molasses and bread, and any little extra that may be paid for. It will be seen that the bill of fare does not rival Delmonico's, but to the boys it is superb. Besides there is a great argument in its favor, as will be seen by reference to the prices that are charged: Breakfast, five cents; supper, five cents; lodging, five cents, and washing free."

The boys wash their hands and faces in running water, and wash their feet every night in a trough constructed for the purpose. The wash-room is supplied with looking glasses and other conveniences.

The Home contains a gymnasium, chapel and school room, and the boys are taught the common branches of an English education. Their clothes are kept in little boxes, which are a part of the fixtures of a large room.

The aims and spirit of this charity, it is deemed, cannot be better expressed than in the language made use of by Father Drumgoole on the day of visitation:

"The object of the Home is to care for little children. To bring them up and do for them what a humble parent will do for his children, help them till they are able to help themselves. We give them an opportunity to cultivate a spirit of self-reliance and honest industry, and prepare the boy to take his place in society as an upright, honest, industrious and self-supporting man.

"We take in any one, black or white. My idea is to keep a boy till he is able to earn $6 a week. Then, I think he is fitted to pay his way in a respectable boarding-house, and he will have to graduate from here.

"I have a great many boys for whom I have got situations. They come to me to confession. Some of the worst cases that had ever been in this city, were with me, and have turned out as good citizens as we have. Some of the boys who had been almost a terror to the city, are now holding respectable situations, and would not go back to their former life for any consideration.

"Of course, with Catholic children, the Sacraments of the Church have a great effect. They are taught that they must live well and be faithful to all their relations, to God and their neighbor.

"We keep for them whatever money they get. Some of the little fellows have saved as much as $70 or $80. I encourage them to save their money. I do not have a savings bank in the house, but I have about twenty boys in the house that have bank books. I have about one hundred and eighty to one hundred and ninety inmates. In a few weeks we expect to have about two hundred and forty or two hundred and fifty. Last winter we had that number, and some days more. I was obliged to have some of them sleep on the benches in the cold weather. Had I means, I have no doubt I could have thousands of children around me of that class.

"I think it is really our fault that they are not better. Their condition is owing to our own neglect. The little fellows are very easily controlled and brought under religious influence.

"I have over fifty children here under nine years of age. I get attached to them. The boys are healthy, fine little fellows. They are well inclined, and I am trying to do something for them in the way of covering them. All they want is kind words and kind acts, to bring them up and make them an honor to the country. It is our fault, not theirs, if they do not turn out well.

"The very mention of the name of their parents to these little fellows, often makes them grow pale with fear. I find that there is one great thing that they possess when prepared for the Sacrament, and that is, a horror of the state from which they have been rescued.

"Sunday mornings I lecture to them. All the boys that have no homes I look upon as my congregation. I say to them they ought to be very thankful that God has sent a priest here to care for them; that if they were princes and had private chaplains they could not be much better off, and that I want them to tell all the little homeless boys, especially all the 'hard cases,' to come, that they are part of my congregation and I am their chaplain. The boys one day met a street lad down town whom they thought was a hard case. They said to him that he ought to go to Father Drumgoole. The boy said 'no; he would not be willing to let me in.' 'Yes he will,' said the boys; 'he told us the other day that he wanted all the hard cases to come — that he was their chaplain.' The boys brought him in and came to me and said, 'here, Father, is a hard case.' The boy said, 'Father, if you take me in hand, I'll try to be a good boy, but if it is a hard case you want, you never could scare up a harder one than I am.' It appears that this boy was a regular 'Fagin,' and had under his training, for pickpockets, over twenty boys. He now holds a very responsible position in the city of New York, and he has said to me 'Father, I would rather die than go back to that state.'

"I tell the boys that they ought to take great pride in the fact that they are American citizens. If they are only faithful to God they must be faithful citizens.

"When the little fellows get under the influence of religion, it is extraordinary how it restrains them from wrong-doing. A little boy came to me one time and said, 'Father, I was down to the market and I saw a gentleman with his pocket-book hanging out of his pocket, and I was so tempted to steal it, but I thought of what you told me on Sunday about hell, and I did not take it.' Another will come and say, 'I was down town yesterday and a market-woman went away and asked me to take care of her little money-box, and while she was away I was going to make a drive at it, but just then I recollected what you told us, and did not. Father, I kept my hands off and I staid there, and when the woman came back, she gave me ten cents for taking care of the box.'

"If I had the means I would not be afraid to undertake to turn out one thousand reformed children every year, that cannot be reached in any other way. I have little theatricals for the boys to amuse themselves with during the winter evenings. Lord Rosberry, an English gentleman who came here to see me, and took a great interest in the work, seemed quite pleased with this feature of it. He said, 'You have the theater to capture the little fellows' bodies, and then you have your chapel to capture their souls.' We get a great many children from poor widows who have four or five children on their hands. I have known them to have as many as eight, and no way to support them but by going out to work. They leave home about seven o'clock in the morning. The oldest of the family, nine or ten years of age.

has to stay at home to take care of the younger ones. They run about all day, learn bad habits and imbibe bad morals. I want a place for these poor women's children, where they may remain till their mothers come for them in the evening, where I may have the assistance of the Sisters, who can take charge of them. Then we will be able to bring up a superior class of children. Protestants even now come here and say, 'I want one of your boys.'"

Routine of the day.—"The boys are called at six o'clock. They assemble in the room down stairs. I meet them shortly after six, and we have a little instruction for five minutes on the principal mysteries of religion. I have to give it in small doses. After that we have morning prayers. Then they have breakfast, and are out of the house by seven o'clock, except my little orphans. They all attend to whatever little business they have. I tell them I do not want any beggars around me. The boys come in at five o'clock, and the great majority of them are in bed by nine. I have fifty orphans now. Some of them will make very bright young men. Some of the boys now attending the Commercial College began at my evening school."

The whole number of boys that have been admitted to this institution during the year ending September 30, 1875, was 2,415. The total expenditures during the same period were $12,995.

The visit made to the St. Vincent's Home for Boys left the impression upon the mind that a great amount of good was here being accomplished. The vast number of idle boys that are growing up in the streets of New York, and swelling from year to year the ranks of the "dangerous classes," seem to require the fullest possible exercise of every existing benevolent agency, the efforts of which are directed toward their elevation. Father Drumgoole is endeavoring to benefit this class in his own way, and, it is believed, with very successful results. He regards it as indispensable that those neglected boys should be brought under strong, moral influences, and thinks that little can be effected in the way of real reform without implanting in the youthful mind positive religious convictions. He is laboring to this end; is thoroughly in earnest, and exhibits a devotion to his work worthy of emphatic commendation. It is to be hoped that this worthy laborer in the Master's field will soon have better facilities furnished him to widen the scope of the institution under his immediate charge. While there is a single boy left to grow up in neglect in the streets of New York, it is neither for the interest of the municipal authorities, nor her merchant princes, to spare money or means to provide in the best possible manner for his proper training or reformation.

St. Vincent de Paul's Industrial School.

New York.

The object in organizing the St. Vincent de Paul's Industrial School was to afford young girls of limited means an opportunity for learning useful trades under Christian influences, thereby saving them from the dangers to which they would be exposed while acquiring a remunerative means of subsistence in large city establishments.

Girls are received from the age of twelve upwards, and in addition to their industrial training, receive daily two hours of English tuition. Their religious and moral edification is held to be of paramount importance, and every incentive to successful application is employed by the Sisters in the effort to send forth from the institution a class of young women possessed of the means of maintaining a position of respectability and usefulness in society.

Plain sewing, embroidery, dress and cloak making, the use of the different sewing machines now in vogue, and domestic economy are all taught.

A charge of $135 per annum is made for those who can afford it; a lesser amount is accepted from others, while a large number of worthy girls, who can pay absolutely nothing, are received gratuitously and share the benefits of the institution equally with the rest; the inmates not knowing who are subjects of charity and who pay.

The small sum of $135 a year for all their expenses, washing, stationery, etc., included, makes the work a charity even to those who pay, but the Sisters have in mind the imparting of its benefits to poor young girls free of all charge whatever, as soon as their means will admit.

The institution is located at 343 West Forty-second street, in the city of New York. The building, erected in 1865, is a plain, substantial brick edifice, covering an area of 100 feet by 70 feet, and is 60 feet high. There is a fine cellar, an over-ground or English basement, and four clear stories, besides the attic story. The basement contains spacious refectories, sculleries and kitchen. The first story proper, a chapel, two parlors, a large assembly room for the community, an office, and a number of fine class-rooms. The second story, a large study hall, music rooms, class-rooms, etc. The third story, sewing rooms, infirmaries, clothes rooms, etc. The fourth and fifth stories, a series of dormitories. Should any contagious disease appear among the pupils, perfect isolation can be secured in a comfortable well-lighted attic room. The institution can accommodate two hundred pupils. The entire building is heated by hot-air furnaces, and the ventilation is excellent. The toilet room is provided with baths, and there are also bathing accommodations attached to the infirmaries and other parts of the building.

The work was begun in 1856, in two dwelling-houses located on Seventh street, between First and Second avenues. Five Sisters were placed in charge, and the school rapidly increased from two to thirty; but the large rent and the incompetency of the pupils for the work procurable, caused much embarrassment. In 1857, it was resolved to purchase four lots, and to erect on two of them a suitable building. The corner-stone of the same was laid March, 1858, and in September of that year the school was removed to its present location. Its increasing numbers soon necessitated an addition, which was finished in 1865.

A visitation to this institution was made October 20, in company with Commissioner Hoguet. Twenty-five Sisters of the Roman Catholic Order of the Sisters of Charity of Mt. St. Vincent, were then engaged in the work, Sister Mary Beata being in charge. Ten domestics are employed.

The work rooms were conducted with system and regularity. About sixty sewing machines were in use. One class of girls was making clothing and cloaks, and another was engaged on fine and fancy sewing. Nearly all were working for the shops. The Sister informed us that they are taught not only to make but to cut out the garments.

The dormitories were neat; the beds were well made up. This work is done by the girls, each attending to her own bed. Feather pillows are used, and both hair and straw mattresses; the several beds having one of each. The bedsteads are single, and of iron. Their average width is about two feet five inches.

The rest of the house was equally precise and orderly in its appointments, and among other features of interest are a pleasant chapel, recreation rooms and a well-selected library.

On October 1, 1875, the number of girls in the institution who were orphans, was fifty-one; the number of half-orphans, seventy-three; and the number of children who had both parents living, was twenty-two. Twenty-four were of native parentage, and one hundred and twenty-two of foreign. The children were principally from the county of New York, a few from Kings, and nine from the State of New Jersey.

It is thought by many, that much of the misery and many of the social disorders that afflict society are clearly traceable to the lack of industrious habits in young women, whether they remain single or enter the marriage relation. The training necessary to the formation of these habits, unless received under high moral influences, is likely to be attended with danger. Many young persons, while debarred from all such industrial training in their poverty-stricken homes, cannot obtain it elsewhere, unless under circumstances likely to destroy true womanly delicacy. To obviate this, institutions like that of the industrial schools of these good Sisters have grown into existence, and it would seem they should be welcomed as an additional safeguard thrown about those who need protection.

The School Ship "Mercury."

New York.

The School Ship "Mercury" was visited on October 22d, at which date it was anchored off Hart's Island. It is a full-rigged ship of eleven hundred and fifty-six tons burden, and was under the command of Captain Frank F. Gregory, U. S. N.

This ship was purchased by the city of New York at a cost of $35,000, July 1, 1869, and placed under the charge of the Commissioners of Public Charities and Correction. After undergoing repairs in the dry dock, on the 3d day of July she was removed to Hart's Island, where such internal alterations were made as would adapt her to the uses contemplated in her purchase. Quarters were provided for some three hundred boys, together with her complement of officers and seamen.

On the first of September the ship being reported ready for the reception of the boys, fifty were sent on board from Hart's Island, and the ship duly put in commission.

It is intended to be a reform school for boys who are unmanageable at home, and for others guilty of petty delinquencies. These are in part committed by the magistrates, but mostly by the Commissioners of Public Charities and Correction. No definite length of time for their detention is fixed. They are frequently held at the option of their parents or guardians.

From the Captain on board we obtained the following information relative to the ship and its workings:

"The officers of the ship consist of First, Second and Third Officers, Instructor, Surgeon and, when in port, two Chaplains. Boys are received at all ages between twelve and twenty-one. There is no regular time for keeping them. I have shipped twenty-three boys into the navy, but I cannot tell how many have entered the merchant service from the ship. None have entered this year. We are constantly meeting boys that have been on the ship, who are now in the merchant service. The boys that do well on the ship and obey its rules, almost invariably go into the merchant service. The fact is recognized that these boys make as good sailors as any others. My opinion is that the discipline of the ship is valuable to the boys, and that many of the lads that are now sent to the workhouse should be sent here. We have had boys here this last year, some of whom had been sent up to the workhouse for trivial offenses that can be cured here, but cannot be cured there. I have seen little boys in the penitentiary that fairly made my heart bleed. We had but three boys, out of three hundred on this ship, sent for misdemeanor. When the school-ship was first organized, they sent boys here for serious offenses, and the ship got a bad name. Now, the class of boys we have are very different. They are those whom parents cannot well manage at home, and they send them here for discipline. All that is necessary to make the school-ship a success is for the judges to practice a little discrimination in the class of boys they send here. I can generally tell the character of every boy that comes on board the ship, by looking into his face. Orphan boys, or even boys who are not orphans, that have been picked up for such little offenses as swimming around the docks, should be sent here instead of to the workhouse.

"Sending a boy to the penitentiary is certain moral death to him. Very few come out of it who are not ruined. It is not the prisons that we want multiplied, but the reformatories."

A register is kept on board entitled "Record of admission, progress, discharge and subsequent history of the pupils of the School-ship Mercury." The register is designed to show the particulars of their commitment, whether or not board is paid, their progress in seamanship and scholarship, whether discharged, deserted or transferred; also their subsequent history.

The captain says: "The subsequent history of these boys is very hard to get at." Very little of it appears upon the records.

"The boys are called at 5:30 A. M. The first thing in order is the washing of the decks, then the washing of themselves. Breakfast is partaken of at 7:30. After breakfast the brass work is polished and the ship generally is cleaned. At 9, a general muster to the drum beat takes place. The boys are then examined and reported to the captain. At 9:30 A. M. one watch goes down to school; the other remains on deck. The watch that goes below in the forenoon must be on deck in the afternoon, and this alternation goes on the year through.

"At sea," says the captain, "in our winter cruises, we have regular classes in navigation. But all must have passed decimal fractions before they can enter it. Some of the boys take hold of it very quickly, but no one gets up as high as a mate. A man must have experience before he can be a mate.

"Our instruction is of a practical nature. We give them sufficient knowledge of navigation to enable them to rise to be mates of ships if they improve their opportunities. We have school every day except Saturday and prayers every evening. Each boy, before retiring, is compelled to kneel and repeat his prayers, whatever they may be, according to his own creed.

"We can accommodate, comfortably, two hundred and sixty-five boys. We have had on the ship three hundred and ten, but that is too many; it is more than any one man can do to look after so large a number."

At the time of our visit, one of the lads was in irons, having been so placed in consequence of an assault with a knife upon one of the subordinate officers.

In regard to discipline, the captain says: "One of the greatest helps toward maintaining discipline is, that every one that comes here, before he is fifteen minutes on board, will be posted by the older boys as to what he has got to do. Sometimes we resort to corporal punishment; but very rarely. Since the first of last November, we have punished two. Some of them got drunk in the West Indies, and I disciplined them for example's sake.

"One of the hardest punishments that we have is to make the boys that have misbehaved during the day stand in a line and not allow them to talk to one another while the others are at play. I like it better than any other kind of punishment. Another aid to discipline is promotion on deck. If a boy behaves himself well and makes progress in seamanship, he is made a petty officer.

"Fourteen of the boys who were transferred from the ship to the United States Navy had," the captain said, "just returned from a three years' cruise in the Mediterranean. They did first rate. Some of them have between two and three, and some four hundred dollars saved. Now the great problem is what to do with these boys. They have got no friends, and if they do not rejoin the navy, I do not know what will become of them. A good many who are sent to sea never make sailors."

The captain, on being asked about the conduct of the boys at sea, said: "We have been in storms and they did very well. Off the coast of Madeira we had a severe gale, which blew away our main-topsail. There was not enough left to make a shirt. We had a continuance of the storm for twelve days, culminating on Christmas night, in 1870, but the boys did their duty. We did not get on, of course, as well as with a regular crew of sailors. That would be impossible.

"Our winter voyages are the best thing for the boys. They know there is no such thing as getting away from the ship, and they try to make the best of it, and behave very well. Last winter we had a very prosperous time. We were off the coast of South America. The people on shore were very kind to us. The old planters invited the boys ashore, took them to their homes, and loaded them down with sugar cane."

On the day of visitation, October 22d, there were about two hundred boys on board. The ship was found to be under thorough discipline, and in a condition of cleanliness and order highly creditable to its officers. The boys appeared to be in good health.

It is asserted that it is pretty well understood by the truant boys in New York that a commitment to the School-ship is by no means an event to be desired, and the contingency is held over them by many parents having disobedient children, as a help to family discipline. On the steamer that returned us from the ship,—it being one of the days on which parents were permitted to visit their children,—were a large number of parents of boys who had been committed, as well as some of the boys who had been released from durance. A conversation with several of these parents developed the fact that they were satisfied that their children had been benefited by a detention on the ship. A subsequent conversation was had with one of the boys, whose views were based upon actual experience. The lad was of bright appearance, about fifteen years of age. He said that he thought it was a bad place for boys, because "they learn to use bad language, and to chew tobacco. Tobacco that costs ten cents in the city you have to pay sixty cents for on ship. Besides," said George with some emphasis, "if you don't mind what you are about you get the rope's end."

The cursory examination of the School, as well as the lack of definite knowledge of the subsequent history of the boys that had been on board, prevents the reaching of any satisfactory conclusions as to the merit or demerit of the system as a means of juvenile reformation.

[Since writing the foregoing report, information has been obtained from official sources to the effect that the School-ship Mercury was put out of commission on the 31st December, 1875, no appropriation having been made on her account. In regard to the boys, those who had relatives and friends were given over to them; those having none were sent to institutions or discharged, being able to provide for themselves.]

The Union Home and School for the Education and Maintenance of the Children of our Volunteers who are left Unprovided for.

New York.

The history of this charity is thus given by its late Secretary, Mrs. David Hoyt: "The Union Home and School was established immediately after the fall of Fort Sumter. A property on Fifty-eighth street was purchased by its managers. Toward this purchase the State contributed $7,000. This locality, after the laying out of the circle by the Central Park Commissioners, being considered too valuable for an institution, building materials being very expensive, and the house not large enough to accommodate the ever-increasing number of applicants, the managers, whilst looking out for another site, bought twelve acres of ground and a large frame building at Deposit, Delaware county, keeping the house on Fifty-eighth street as a reception house. The place at Deposit they occupied only a year, finding it difficult to keep it under such strict supervision as they wished. Unwilling to trust their little charges to hirelings, they bought, when offered to them, the mansion formerly rented by the Colored Orphan Asylum on Eleventh avenue. They met with many difficulties. Another institution of the same nature was started in opposition a year afterward, and the two became confounded in the public mind. During the war adventurers like the notorious Col. ——, took up ostensibly the cause of the soldiers' orphans, and went about with a small company in uniform, collected a great deal of money, but were discovered to be impostors. This made the task the ladies had undertaken the more difficult. But right always prospers in the end, and the Union Home and School bravely fought its way through 'good report and evil report,' contending for justice, merely obliging strict monthly accounts to be made of expenses, and quarterly statements to be submitted to its Advisory Committee. Keeping rigidly out of debt, it has by plain figures and statements silenced its interested adversaries. The institution removed in 1868 to One Hundred and Fifty-first street, having, with money raised by the sale of their six lots of land in Fifty-eighth street, bought the 'Field Mansion' with ten lots of ground on Eleventh avenue, corner of One Hundred and Fifty-first street, its present location."

This institution was organized May 22, 1861, and incorporated April 22, 1862. Its charter was amended March 30, 1866. It is situated on One Hundred and Fifty-first street and Eleventh avenue, in the city of New York.

On date of visitation, October 22, we found about one hundred and seventy children within its doors. About sixty of these were girls. The average age of the boys, we were informed, was eleven, and that of the girls about the same. The number of inmates received during the year ending October 1, 1875, was seventy-four; the number returned to parents or guardians was seventy-one. One was transferred to another institution and one died. Children are received quite young, but not over fourteen years of age. None but the children of soldiers are admitted. Some of them have both father and mother living who are too poor to support them. "We do not," says the matron, Mrs. E. B. Hull, "propose to keep them over sixteen years of age. They are then either placed in the hands of their friends, or we find homes for them. The girls are taught to do housework and to sew on the machine. Our girls are smart in that way and make all their own clothing. The boys are taught telegraphy." About fourteen were pursuing this study under an instructor on the day of our visit. Two of the boys were then said to be good operators.

The dormitories are furnished with double wooden bedsteads. The dining room tables are provided with benches.

The force of the establishment consists of a matron, two ladies in the sewing room, a cook, two laundresses, a nurse, a person to take care of the boys, who also acts as band-master, and a chambermaid. The girls and boys wash in running water. They dress variously.

The institution is governed by a Board of Lady Managers, aided by an Advisory Board of Gentlemen.

The lateness of the hour upon which the visitation was made prevented a full examination of the premises.

The work of caring for the orphan and destitute children of those who have served the country by the imperiling of their lives in its defense, is an object so well worthy the consideration of the benevolent, as to need no special comment here.

The value of the real estate of the institution, including buildings, fixtures and all appurtenances, is estimated at $110,000; value of its invested funds, $5,573.48; its total indebtedness, $47,500, of which $45,000 is upon its real estate.

Its total expenditures during the year ending September 30, 1875, were $24,865.14. Of this there was expended for interest, $3,150; for salaries of officers, wages and labor, $7,781.73; for provisions and supplies, clothing, fuel and lights, medicines and medical supplies, $19,863.58; for buildings and improvements, and ordinary repairs, $2,502.35; for all other purposes, $2,499.21.

The receipts during the same period were: From appropriations by Board of Supervisors, $23,579.65; from donations and voluntary contributions, $963.82; from all other sources, $1,060.73.

Ward's Island.

New York.

Ward's Island was visited October 13, 1875. One of the buildings for the care of the emigrant classes is set apart exclusively for children, and is under the immediate charge of a matron. Children were also found in other departments on the Island. The entire number cared for on the day of visitation was one hundred and fifty-four. Sixty-four of these were in the hospital, where the emigrant women are confined; twenty-four were in the male department; one was in the insane department, and sixty-five were in the nursery. Forty-nine of the nursery children were between the ages of four and eight.

The children appear to be well cared for. The system adopted is such that they are kept no longer than is requisite to find good homes for them, when they are placed out by the Commissioners of Emigration. While on the Island, however, such as are able attend school.

Wilson Industrial School for Girls.

New York.

This institution is situated at 125 St. Mark's Place, corner of Avenue A, in the city of New York. It was incorporated February, 1854. Its object is to give to a class of children, whose parents are too poor to send them to the public schools, instruction in the elementary branches of an English education, and in sewing. The following information, regarding its history, etc., has been kindly furnished:

"The school was commenced in 1853, in a hired room, in an upper story, on Avenue D, between Eighth and Ninth streets, through the efforts of Mrs. James P. Wilson, who became its first directress, and served the society most efficiently until her removal from the city. Its prominent projectors included a number of other benevolent ladies deeply interested in the work. All that section of the city east of Tompkins Square was then called Mackerelville, and was inhabited by a population of the most degraded character. The manifest vice and degradation of the girls connected with these families, many of whom passed their time in the streets as beggars, rag-pickers, etc., seemed to show the necessity of making some effort to Christianize and civilize them.

"This was and continues to be only a day industrial school, the girls returning to their homes at night. The number at first was limited by the lack of accommodations, but has steadily increased, till this year four hundred and eighteen names have been on the books, with an average attendance of two hundred, all of whom are provided with a dinner five days in the week."

At the time of visitation, October 6, the institution was found to be in charge of Miss Emily Huntington. The edifice is a plain brick structure, four stories in height, and fifty by ninety feet. It was purchased in 1869 by the Board of Managers. The basement and fourth story are rented for manufacturing purposes, though the room is needed and could be put to good use in the prosecution of the work if means permitted. A portion of the ground floor is used for a chapel the remainder is occupied by a nursery, the missionary's room and store rooms. On the second floor are the managers' room, teachers' dining room, dining room for the children, kitchen and sleeping rooms for the matron and teachers. On the third floor are the school-room and work-room, night refuge and other sleeping apartments. The bath-rooms, etc., are in the basement.

The departments of work in the institution comprise:

First. A day school, open from 9 A. M. to 3 P. M., where two hundred girls are, in the morning, instructed in elementary English branches, and, after a hearty dinner, are taught sewing by hand, while making their own garments, which they earn by a system of credit marks, thus preserving them from the pauperizing influence of indiscriminate gratuitous distribution.

Miss Huntington remarks: "The idea is to teach these children whatever they most need to enable them to support themselves. They are very poor. We do not propose to take in any that can support themselves, or that are able to attend the public school. The children received are from a class that cannot afford to attend the public schools. They must be earning their support somewhere. Many of them have nothing except what they get here. We do not *give* them any thing. They must earn it all. They are credited with all they do, and as soon as they earn a garment, and need it, we furnish them with one.

Second. Industrial classes. These are composed of girls from twelve to twenty years of age, who are instructed in dressmaking, family sewing, and the use of sewing and button-hole machines.

Third. Household classes in which the pupils receive instruction in domestic duties. Miss Huntington makes housewifery a school study, and imparts instruction by a system which she has elaborated with much care. Charts containing drawings of the usual articles needed in a home are used. The children learn their names and uses and are examined as to their proficiency by the matron. With this theoretical instruction and the opportunity of carrying it into practice, which is afforded in the institution, it is thought a great deal is accomplished toward rendering these little girls capable, as they become older, of self-support and of performing valuable service.

Fourth. A night refuge affording comfortable lodging and meals to poor but respectable girls. In the dispensing of this relief, it is found great discrimination needs to be exercised.

Fifth. A mission church organized on the union plan, in 1867 (an outgrowth of the day and Sabbath schools), with its pastor and bible reader, its Sabbath morning and evening services, and Thursday evening prayer meeting.

Sixth. A Sabbath school, organized in connection with the day school, in 1853, and now numbering two hundred and fifty scholars, and open at 2 P. M.

Seventh. A mothers' meeting held for the benefit and instruction of the mothers of the scholars, every Wednesday, at 1 o'clock P. M., from November to May.

"This institution relies wholly for support on voluntary contributions. Its annual expenditures, with strict economy, amount to $9,000. Located in the western boundary of the Eleventh ward, which contains a population of 64,230 souls, and embracing in one organization so many branches of Christian labor, its usefulness is only limited by the condition of its treasury.

"It is designed by the managers, as soon as means are provided, to erect on a vacant lot which they own, adjoining the Mission House, a suitable chapel, which will enable them to use the room now occupied by the church as a reading room, much needed for the young men in that neighborhood."

A marked feature in this institution is the pains taken to inculcate a knowledge of housekeeping by a systematic plan of instruction under the personal supervision of the Matron, who is strongly imbued with the importance of this branch of education for young girls, and who has given the subject much thought. Her views are compiled in book form, and are about being published in a series of simple rules adapted to the comprehension of children. Those immediately connected with the school seem to be quite earnest in their efforts, and are accomplishing good results. It is believed that the charity is deserving of liberal support.

The property is a valuable one, but not productive of any revenue.

THE WOMEN'S AID SOCIETY AND HOME FOR TRAINING YOUNG GIRLS.

New York.

The object of this Society is to afford a temporary home for poor and friendless girls, and to impart to them such industrial training of a domestic character as will fit them for situations with which the institution provides them. The rule of the house is, that applicants for admission may remain one month and must take situations approved of by the Matron. This institution is situated at 41 Seventh avenue, at the corner of West Thirteenth street, in a private house. It is governed by a Board of Lady Managers, who have associated with them an Advisory Committee of gentlemen. It has been organized since 1866, and was incorporated in 1870. At the date of visitation, October 11, the institution was found to be in charge of Mrs. R. B. Pierson, Matron, who furnished the following information relative to the aims and work of the society: "This house is for respectable girls only, and for such as are eligible for situations. Its purpose is to save and protect young girls. They generally come in a deplorable condition, ill-clad, hungry, and greatly needing the use of the bath tub. Their ages range from eight to twenty years. Policemen frequently bring them to the house. Expressmen often direct them here. They occasionally find a girl on the streets out of a situation, who does not know where to go. Sometimes the city missionaries, or the ladies of the institution, send such poor girls here. They come here, and by doing so are saved from going to the cheap lodging houses or to restaurants. In addition to this regular work, the house procures situations for many respectable women, who have an aversion to the regular intelligence office, and who are too old to come in here as inmates."

The house has a capacity for sixteen inmates, which is about the average number. They are coming and going constantly. An effort is made to improve the girls intellectually while in the institution, and pains is taken to surround them with elevating Christian influences. The result of the inspection was satisfactory, and the institution is believed to be a source of amelioration to the multifarious distresses incident to all large cities.

Oswego Orphan Asylum.

Oswego.

The Oswego Orphan Asylum is located in the outskirts of the city of Oswego, about one mile southerly from its center, on a highly elevated piece of ground, from which is obtained a commanding view of the city, harbor and lake.

The edifice is a well-constructed, three-story brick building, measuring sixty-five by fifty feet on the ground floor, and is capable of accommodating between seventy-five and one hundred inmates.

The grounds are well inclosed and contain eight acres of land, which cost $2,000. The lawn in front of the Asylum is shaded with forest trees. About one and a half acres in the rear are appropriated to garden cultivation, and the remainder to pasture and meadow.

The object of the institution is the support and education of orphans and destitute children. It had its origin in the desire of the benevolent citizens of Oswego to promote the welfare of homeless and neglected children. It is stated that about twenty-five years ago "two gentlemen of Oswego, feeling that something must be done for the destitute children of the place, set themselves earnestly to work to devise ways and means for meeting the emergency. Obstacles, seemingly insurmountable, at first presented themselves; but it was remembered that those children whom orphanage had cast upon the mercies of Christian charity had been, in most cases, distributed among the families of the poor and ignorant, who hold only that relation to them which money can buy. There were no loving attentions — money does not buy them — the desire in the heart of every little one, deeper and stronger than that for food, to be loved and cherished and brooded over with motherly tenderness, was never gratified. They were fed, to be sure, as the animal is fed, and for much the same reason. Neglect, and oftentimes downright cruelty characterized their treatment. The noiseless cry of suffering had often gone up from those wretched places, and its silent voice was heard again pleading for help. The emergency of the case urged the matter to be presented to the people, and the charitably disposed readily responded to the call. A small dwelling-house was at first rented and seven children were at once gathered in. This building was occupied from 1852, till the completion of the present spacious edifice in 1856, soon after which the number of children had increased to seventy-four. About this time the managers, with commendable spirit, turned their attention to the unfortunate children in the county poor-house. The authorities had no way but to group the homeless children under their charge in that public receptacle for hardened want, poverty and crime."

This zeal on the part of the managers was met with a corresponding liberality by the Board of Supervisors, and an arrangement was brought about for transferring the children from the county poor-house to the homelike influence and surroundings of the asylum. The spirit manifested by the people of this county in caring for their homeless children is worthy of note. At the date of August 6th, 1875, there was but one child, a young infant, in the county house, and but one child that had passed the limit of three years of age, temporarily sojourning in the Oswego city alms-house. The people of this county deserve great credit for the enlightened and benevolent theory they have put in practice, of looking after homeless children while they are young and susceptible of moral and religious training.

Since the organization of the Oswego Orphan Asylum nearly a thousand children have been the recipients of its benefactions. Many have grown to maturity, and it is asserted "are scattered over the country; some in business life, respectable citizens; some in private homes, secured by the managers, and some lie on the battle fields in the South."

The property of the institution is controlled by a Board consisting of ten Trustees, Gentlemen, and an equal number of Lady Directors. The institution is under the immediate charge of a matron.

On the day of visitation, August 6th, there were fifty-two inmates, thirty-four boys and eighteen girls. Three of these were colored. The children are not dressed uniformly, except on Sundays. They are received at all ages between two and eight years, and are disposed of as soon as good homes for them can be found. They all appeared healthy, and it was stated that for a year and a half there had been no occasion to call in a physician.

The children receive intellectual, industrial and religious education. compatible with their years. Four hours and a half a day are spent in school, and the boys make themselves useful in carrying water, wood, coal, and doing all the odds and ends of work about the asylum, while the girls render aid in the general house-work. Sewing is taught in school one afternoon in the week. On Sundays all the children attend service in some one of the Protestant churches in the city.

The children come from the city and the adjacent country. Such as are charges upon the county are committed by the Overseers of the Poor, the county paying $1.50 per week toward their maintenance. Some children are placed in the asylum by widowed mothers, who either pay the entire cost of their support, or such a portion of it as they are able to defray. Six months' trial is allowed in placing out children, and, if both parties are satisfied, the child is adopted or indentured. The younger children are generally adopted. The children are looked after when placed out, and although there is no regular visiting committee, they are heard from in various ways. On this point the matron, Mrs. Julia Wilcox, in reply to our questions, remarked: "We learn about them by making inquiries from the neighbors and from the children themselves. But whether they feel at liberty in all cases to write the truth about themselves or not I cannot say. I think a visiting committee is important."

The dormitories are large, well ventilated, and furnished with double bedsteads of iron, straw beds, snow white counterpanes, and an abundance of blankets and sheets. The windows are double, and the sashes hung with cords, weights and pulleys.

The wearing apparel of the children is made in the house, two seamstresses being engaged for the purpose.

The school room is large and cheerful, furnished with maps, charts, neat desks and chairs. Its furniture, as well as the library of between two and three hundred volumes, was presented by the children of the public schools.

Both boys and girls bathe once a week, each sex having its own bath-room. They wash their faces and comb their hair before going into school, and wash their feet at night.

The elevated location of the asylum renders it difficult to secure an abundant supply of water, and almost the entire dependence is on the rain water, which is saved in a large cistern.

The building is heated by furnaces and stoves, and is well ventilated throughout. The hired assistants sleep on the same floor with the children, and "are the best that the means of the Asylum will admit of employing." The Matron says she has "no necessity to keep any room in the house under lock and key."

The garden supplies potatoes, beans, sweet corn, onions, squashes, cucumbers, etc., for the institution.

On October 1, 1875, there were in the institution fifty-seven children — three orphans, thirty half-orphans, and twenty-four with both parents living. Six of these children came from Fulton county, and fifty-one from Oswego. Ten were partially or wholly supported by friends, thirty-eight by counties, cities, etc., and nine wholly by the institution.

The number of children received since its organization was nine hundred and twenty-eight. The number received during the past year was fifty; the number discharged, forty-one. Of the latter fifteen were placed out by adoption, and twenty-four returned to parents or guardians. One left without permission, and one was transferred to another institution.

The total expenditures during the fiscal year ending September 30, 1875, were $3,178.91. Its total indebtedness is set down at $971.07. The value of its personal estate, including bonds, stocks and other investments, from which an income is derivable, is stated to be $23,386.73.

In view of the earnest workers among the prominent supporters of this charity, the amount of good it has already done to the county, and the results it may yet achieve in the way of saving dependent children, and the consequent reduction of pauperism, it is greatly to be hoped that its sphere of usefulness may not be curtailed for lack of liberal encouragement.

Madison County Orphan Asylum.

Peterboro.

But a short distance from the old homestead of the late Gerrit Smith, stands the orphan asylum which he founded, and in which, when at home, he was accustomed to spend a part of each day during the summer, and a part of one day each week during the winter. The old Academy building at Peterboro was donated by him, with ten acres of land, for this worthy object. It is a three-story frame structure, resting on a high basement of masonry, and is situated in the midst of a lawn, partly shaded with forest trees, forming an extensive play ground. The building stands opposite the village park.

The affairs of the Asylum are directed by the County Superintendents of the Poor. Its finances are controlled by a Board of five Trustees.

On the day of visitation, September 15th, the Asylum was under the immediate charge of Mr. C. L. Blakeman. He was assisted by his wife, acting as Matron, a lady teacher and two female assistants.

The house is heated by stoves, and lighted, in the children's department, by candles, and in the family part by kerosene. A bountiful supply of water is secured from a spring on the place, and from the rain which is saved. It is not, however, distributed in pipes throughout the building. The ventilation is effected by the windows, which are hung in the old style, with barrel bolts.

In the rear of the main is a frame building which was being finished, the lower part of which is designed for a school, and the upper part for a boys' play-room. The closets are detached, and are some little distance in the rear. An ice house is being constructed.

The basement of the Asylum contains cellar, kitchen, store room and bath rooms for boys and girls; the first floor, reception room, dining room, pantry, family rooms of the Superintendent and girls' play room; the second floor, Superintendent's office, boys' dormitory, girls' dormitory, clothes closets, etc. The third floor is at present used for the school room. It is intended, however, to convert it into a dormitory for the boys.

At the date of visitation there were thirty-one children in the Asylum, only three of whom were girls. "We had," says Mr. Blakeman, "forty children all last winter, but we have been quite successful in putting them out. Our average is thirty-five. With some slight alterations in the rooms we could accommodate some seventy or eighty." The children were all from Madison county. No others, we understand, are admitted. The youngest, on the day of visitation, was three years old.

The health of the children was good. On this point Mr. Blakeman remarks: "They enjoy pretty good health. We have never lost a child since we started. Our doctor's bill does not usually exceed five dollars a year. Last winter, however, a boy broke his leg, which increased the expenses of medical attendance to fifteen dollars. We have had such diseases as measles and mumps, but did not find it necessary to call a physician."

The children bathe every Saturday, and their under clothing is changed every week. The condition in which they come to the house is thus described: "They come in bad shape, nearly all of them. Our custom is to give them at once a good cleaning, and cut the boys' hair short."

While in the Asylum the children receive a good common school education, and are taught to be regular and industrious in their habits. Their religious instruction is carefully attended to. Family worship, with the reading of the Scriptures, is observed every day, and on Sundays the children attend the Sabbath-school of the village church.

The Sabbath-school is held before church service. Any child who wishes to remain for service can do so, but there is no compulsion. The younger children, not able to go to Sabbath-school, are taught in a class at home by Mr. Blakeman.

In regard to the disposal of the children, Mr. Blakeman further says: "Children are kept till they are fifteen years old, unless homes are found for them before that time. We make quite an effort to get them into homes. We have put out seventeen since last November; some into excellent families. Some families it is hard to find out about. We do not let them go, however, without a good recommendation from the best people of the village where the families applying for them reside. They go mostly to farmers. One has gone to a blacksmith. They are to remain till the age of twenty-one, when they are to have a certain amount of money. We make inquiries as far as possible, and take pains to find out about them, especially if we hear that any thing is wrong."

In the reception room is a fine steel engraving of the late Gerrit Smith, also a glass case containing a library of one hundred and sixty odd volumes, presented about a year ago by the Oneida Aid Society. The walls are hung with pictures presented by the people of Cazenovia. The Madison County Bible Society has presented the institution with twenty-five Bibles, bound in Morocco, with large clasps and ribbon book-marks. One is to be given to each child on leaving. The Society further proposes to furnish others as needed.

The dining room was a neatly kept apartment, having painted floors, and was furnished with tables and stools of stained wood. Its walls were embellished with illuminated texts. Crockery ware, spoons, knives, forks and napkins are used by the children at meals. The children were about to partake of their evening meal as we entered this room. The food was wholesome and abundant. Before eating, the following verses, composed by a lady of Peterboro, which are intended to teach the children, among other things, table decorum, were repeated, as is their usual custom:

"In silence all of us must meet,
And fold our hands before we eat,
And lift our hearts to God above
In praise for all His wondrous love.
Our mouths with food we must not crowd,
Nor while we're eating speak aloud;
Must turn our heads to cough or sneeze,
And when we ask, say 'if you please.'
With care our napkins we must fold,
And must not go till we are told;
And when the bell tells us to go,
We must go quietly and slow."

The dietary is generous. The children have plenty of bread and milk and vegetables throughout the season. An abundant supply of apples for the institution is procured through the custom which prevails of allowing the boys to pick apples on shares for the neighboring farmers.

The kitchen was orderly. In the store-room every thing appeared to be well cared for.

The large dormitories were clean, and furnished with double bedsteads of iron. The beds were of straw, and hair pillows and white counterpanes were used. The bed linen, we were informed, is changed as often as necessary. The provision for ventilating this department was inadequate.

Singing is a feature in the education of the children, and on the day of our visit we were favored by request with a favorite hymn of the late Gerrit Smith, which the children were in the habit of singing for him during his visits to the Asylum, and which, when his ear was no longer attuned to their sweet music, they sang once more as they gathered around his remains on the day of his funeral. This, entitled "Scatter Seeds of Kindness," we give:

"Let us gather up the sunbeams
Lying all around our path;
Let us keep the wheat and roses
Casting out the thorns and chaff;
Let us find the sweetest comfort
In the blessings of to-day,
With a patient hand removing
All the briars from the way.

CHORUS.

Then scatter seeds of kindness,
Then scatter seeds of kindness,
Then scatter seeds of kindness,
For our reaping by-and-by.

Strange, we never prize the music
Till the sweet-voiced bird has flown!
Strange, that we should slight the violets
Till the lovely flowers are gone!
Strange, that summer skies and sunshine
Never seem one-half so fair,
As when winter's snowy pinions
Shake the white down in the air!

If we knew the baby fingers,
Pressed against the window pane,
Would be cold and stiff to-morrow—
Never trouble us again—

Would the bright eyes of our darling
Catch the frown upon our brow?
Would the print of rosy fingers
Vex us then as they do now?

Ah! those little ice-cold fingers,
How they point our memories back
To the hasty words and actions
Strewn along our backward track!
How those little hands remind us,
As in snowy grace they lie,
Not to scatter thorns — but roses —
For our reaping by-and-by."

The children have ample recreation. They play base ball, foot ball, croquet and many other games. The opportunities for exercise in the open air are abundant and are eagerly availed of by the boys whose fertile fancies are never at a loss to add new features of pleasure to their pastimes; while the light garden labors of summer, the autumn season with its apple pickings and nut gatherings enable the managers to so combine industry with sport as to make the out-door life of the boys something like a prolonged holiday.

The 4th of July, Christmas and New Year are duly observed. At Christmas there is a tree and a school exhibition, at which time singing and recitations by the children take place, and are a source of enjoyment to them. Much interest is taken in these festivities by the numerous friends of the Asylum.

The garden of the institution covers two acres, in which are raised potatoes, sweet corn, beets, carrots, turnips, squashes, tomatoes, etc.

On October 1st, 1875, there were in the Asylum thirty-five children. Of these nine were orphans, twenty-four half-orphans and two had both parents living. Twenty-six were of native, and nine were of foreign parentage. There were discharged during the year fourteen children by adoption and one by indenture. In addition to these, seven were returned to parents or guardians. The total expenditures during the fiscal year ending September 30, 1875, were $3,291.63.

Madison county has made great advances on the alms-house system in providing such a home for its dependent children, and it was gratifying to see them humanely cared for, and an energetic system in practice for restoring them to the privileges of family life. It is well established that the further the care of dependent children is removed from official management, under party control, and intrusted to the private benevolence of the people, particularly ladies, the more elevating and refining are the influences which come into play and which are indispensable in making the children self-supporting and respectable members of society.

The ladies of the surrounding country have already proved themselves valuable auxiliaries in carrying on the work of the asylum, and it is thought that their services might be rendered still more effectual by investing them with some responsibility in the management of its affairs.

Home for the Friendless of Northern New York.

Plattsburgh.

This institution has but recently entered upon its career of usefulness, having been organized March 16, 1874, and incorporated the following May. It originated in the desire of a few benevolent individuals in Clinton county to make more humane provision for destitute children and for a certain class of aged females, than the county house afforded. The enterprise met the prompt approval of the Board of Supervisors of the county, who directed, by resolution passed December 12, 1874, that children henceforth becoming a public charge should be placed under the care of this charity and maintained at the expense of the towns whence they came, until suitable places in families are procured, instead of being subjected to the influences of the county house associations.

A house was purchased by the Society last November, for the uses of the institution. The business affairs of the Home are directed by a Board of Managers. Its domestic affairs are under the immediate charge of a Matron, Mrs. Atkinson. It is supported mainly by voluntary contributions.

At the date of October 1, 1875, the Home contained six children. Its expenses during the year amounted to $526.01.

The president of the Board of Managers, Mrs. M. K. Platt, says: "Our association, though young and weak, has not been without its salutary influences in this community, and it is most surely growing in interest."

The history of other institutions in the State shows that from even such small beginnings great good has come, and it is to be hoped that the benevolent ladies and others interested in this charitable enterprise, will eventually find their most sanguine expectations realized.

Poughkeepsie Orphan House and Home for the Friendless.

Poughkeepsie.

This Home was the outgrowth of an organization incorporated as the Poughkeepsie Female Guardian Society. In prosecuting their work the ladies of this society found many children in need of temporary homes. It was with the view of meeting this necessity that the building now occupied was erected and opened to the public, February 22, 1857. Since that time many children have through its agency been provided with good homes, and some are now worthy members of society, with homes of their own. It was incorporated in April, 1852.

The Asylum is governed by a Board of Lady Managers, representing the various Protestant denominations of the city. Its object is to provide a home for destitute and friendless children of both sexes, until they can be committed to the guardianship of foster parents or worthy families, who will train them to respectability and usefulness.

The Asylum edifice stands about fifty feet from the street, having a lawn space in its front. It is a two-story brick structure, with a basement. It is warmed by furnaces, and supplied with water from the city, which is carried to the bath rooms in pipes. Ventilation is effected by the windows, and the house is lighted by kerosene.

Two visitations were made to the institution, one of them in company with Commissioner Eastman.

At the date of the last visitation, October 28, it was in charge of a Matron. She employs a seamstress, care-taker, nurse, cook and laundress. The number of inmates varies from forty-five to fifty. Mrs. J. M. Farrar, the Matron, furnishes the following information relative to the workings of the institution: "There is difficulty in disposing of the boys, but the girls are placed out with comparative ease. The children all come from Dutchess county.

"We could accommodate seventy, by putting two in a bed. But I should prefer to have none but single beds in the house.

"The children go out to Sunday-school, and the greatest punishment I can inflict is to keep one at home. I think the more these children associate with others the better it is for them. It brightens up their ideas, and the Asylum does not seem to them so like a prison as when they stay in one house all the time. It wakes them up."

The Matron expressed herself as decidedly in favor of sending Asylum children to the public schools. She says: "Allowing children to go to the public schools might at first occasion trouble and annoyance, but after the first year, I have no doubt it would be better for them. I judge of this from the good resulting from their attending Sunday-school elsewhere. I judge also by what my own feelings would be if I were shut up in a house for ten months.

"I do not approve of keeping children in an institution a very long time. I have seen the evil effects of this plan before I came here. The children that were put out after a reasonable residence in an institution, I have found did better than those who were kept for four or five years longer. Boys grow accustomed to being constantly watched, but when they are put on a farm where they work for themselves, they do much better."

Children are put out by indenture after a trial. References are required from the parties who take them, and a careful correspondence is maintained with the children after they are provided with homes to insure their being well treated.

A school is held on the premises under the supervision of the Department of Public Instruction. The Department pays the teacher's salary.

The number of children received into the institution since its organization was eight hundred and sixty-nine; the number received during the past year, twenty-nine, and the number discharged, thirty-two, Of the latter one was placed out by adoption, four by indenture, twenty-one were returned to parents or guardians, and six were sent out of the State. On the date, October 1, 1875, there were remaining in the institution forty-two children. Of these seventeen were orphans, thirteen were half-orphans, and twelve had both parents living. Ten of the children were of native and thirty-two of foreign parentage.

The total expenditures during the fiscal year were $5,447.29. The value of its personal estate, including bonds, stocks and other indebtedness, is set down at $40,000.

The house showed evidence of good management. The children were clean and bright, and their intellectual, industrial and religious education seemed to be faithfully attended to.

Church Home of the Protestant Episcopal Church in the City of Rochester.

Rochester.

The Home is located on Mount Hope avenue, amidst healthful and pleasant surroundings. The lot is about one hundred by two hundred feet. The main building stands about a hundred feet from the street. A grass plat, flower beds, ornamental shrubbery and graveled walks set off its approach in front. The building is constructed of reddish sandstone, and is in the gothic style of architecture. It is two stories high, exclusive of basement and a mansard attic, with a frontage of seventy and a depth of forty feet.

The kitchen, laundry and dining room are in the basement. The first floor has a wide hall and contains a parlor, matron's room and seven rooms for old ladies. On the second floor are the chapel and about six rooms for old ladies, also a nursery. On the third floor are the dormitories for the children. An old building in the rear, where the work commenced, is also used to some extent for a sleeping apartment and a play-room.

An air of extreme cleanliness pervades the house. The walls are tinted, and its varied appointments arranged with exquisite taste.

The ceilings are high. The windows are hung in modern style, and are finished with inside blinds. Water from the city is conveyed to the middle floor; gas fixtures are in the several apartments; and steam radiators heat the entire building.

The dormitories are neat and airy, and furnished with wooden bedsteads of the French pattern. The nurse's room is between the boys' and girls' dormitories, and communicates with both. It is a rule of the house that the doors opening into the dormitories shall be left open at night, in order that she may hear if any thing is wrong.

Each child is provided with a little place for its clothing, and, as an incentive to order and tidiness in the care of their apparel, the ladies distribute prizes to the meritorious candidates. Three hundred credit marks entitle one to a prize. The marking is done by the nurse, who gives a credit mark to every child whose clothes are found in their proper place, and a bad mark to those who keep them disorderly.

The lavatory is a large room, eighteen by twenty feet, fitted up with basins and hooks. Each child old enough to use them, has a towel, tooth brush, comb and brush. The bath-room is in the basement. The children bathe once a week.

On the day of our unexpected visit we were so fortunate as to find the Board of Lady Managers holding one of their regular meetings at the Home. To Mrs. D. M. Dewey, the President, and the other ladies present, we are indebted for much of the information relative to the aims and workings of the institution.

The work of the Home is dual in its character. First, in sheltering, educating and elevating poor and needy children, of whom there were on the day of visitation thirty-five, twenty-seven boys and eight girls. Second, in offering a quiet retreat to friendless but deserving members of the Protestant Episcopal Church, where in their declining years they may have their wants cared for, and enjoy the consolations of religion. Fifteen inmates of this class were provided for at the time of our visit.

"We take," the ladies say, "the children of families where the mother is sick and the father obliged to be out at work. Many of our children are motherless. Men by the death of their wives are often left with a family of children on their hands, and our Home comes to their relief. About six of the children have been adopted by the Home. We call them our own. The others are mostly boarders. We generally charge one dollar per week. Sometimes more is paid. We take children without regard to the religious faith of their parents, but we place them under the Christian influences of our own church. We aim to do the largest amount of good possible to all classes of children. Our house is full. We feel that we are accomplishing a great deal of good.

"When we take children we pledge ourselves to keep them till we shall find for them homes where they will be well taken care of in families belonging to the Protestant Episcopal Church."

A school, under a competent teacher, is conducted on the premises, where the children receive an education suited to their tender years. One of the boys, we were informed, was so far advanced as to be looking forward to entering De Vaux College.

Great care is taken in the selection of all who come in contact with the children, and none but members of the Protestant Episcopal Church are chosen to fill the principal offices. The nurses, we were informed, are of the better class, and the Matron is expected to be a lady of education.

Each child, the ladies say, is washed and undressed below stairs, and when they are ready to say their prayers they come up to their dormitories. Here they find their prayer books in little bags hung at the heads of their beds, opening which they kneel down by their bedsides, and repeat their prayers in unison. The ladies say it is a pretty sight. They use the Prayers for Children framed by the late Bishop Lee. These are compiled in a little volume in large type, short and very simple. The prayers are for the following occasions: For morning and evening of each day of the week, for all the festival days of the Episcopal Church, for a birthday, prayer for sickness and recovery, and for absent parents; thanksgiving for a safe return, prayers for a sick parent, brother or sister; prayer after death of a parent, brother or sister, companion or school-mate, minister or Sunday-school teacher; prayer for a disobedient child, for a child who has told an untruth, and prayer for a very young child.

The same volume also contains a few simple morning and evening hymns, the Lord's Prayer in rhyme, and others equally simple and beautiful.

On the first and the third Friday in every month parents and guardians are permitted to visit their children in the Home.

The rooms for the old ladies appeared very comfortable and cosy. They are furnished by different parties; two were shown, one furnished by Mrs. Hiram Sibley, of Rochester, the other by Mrs. Henry Anstice. The chapel is a neat little apartment, appropriately furnished for religious worship.

The health of the children was good. The ladies said: "None of the children have sore eyes. We place any such at once under medical treatment. If children are sickly on coming here, they soon get strong and healthy. We give them plenty of milk."

Care is taken to have some responsible person always with the children. On this point the ladies say: "The children are never left alone. The nurse is always with them, unless they are in school. They are not allowed to leave the school-room till the nurse comes for them."

Of the thirty-two inmates of the Home, October 1, 1875, four were orphans, twenty-two half-orphans, and six had both parents living. Five were of native parents, and twenty-seven of foreign. Twenty were partially supported by parents or friends, six by public authorities, and six wholly by the institution. Twenty-seven were from the county of Monroe, three from the county of Wayne, and one each from Steuben and Yates. The number of children received during the year was ten, the number discharged, fifteen. Of the latter, three were placed out at service, ten returned to parents or friends, and two died.

The total expenditures during the fiscal year ending September 30, 1875, were $4,478.51. Its total indebtedness, being upon the real estate, was $3,000.

The work of this institution, though comparatively limited, is so satisfactory, and the influences to which the children are subject so refining and elevating, as to make one wish that its capacity were largely increased to admit to a share in its benefactions the many neglected and homeless children still uncared for.

"This institution originated in a desire of the members of the Protestant Episcopal Church to provide an asylum for the destitute, especially for those of their own faith. At the time of its organization the various charitable institutions of the city were pretty generally filled, and a need seemed to be felt for greater provision for the unfortunate. In 1868, Mr. George R. Clark and Mr. George E. Mumford purchased a house and lot on Mount Hope avenue, at a cost of $5,300, and donated it to the Association, which had then been organized." It was soon found that this building was too small to meet the demands upon the Association, and an appeal made to the various Episcopal Churches resulted in very liberal contributions, enabling the Board of Trustees to erect the present appropriate and commodious edifice, at a cost of about $22,000, leaving it ready for occupation in 1869, incumbered with but a small debt. The finances of the institution are intrusted to a Board of Trustees, and a Board of Lady Managers direct and control its work. The immediate charge of the Home is committed to a matron.

Excelsior Farm and House of Industry for Boys.

Rochester.

Excelsior Farm is located about three and a half miles from the city post-office, on the river road to Lake Ontario, and on the west bank of the Genesee river. The situation is salubrious and the surroundings are delightful.

The farm consists of about forty-two acres of choice land, stocked with a great abundance of fruit trees and vines, and peculiarly adapted to fruit raising and gardening.

The main building consists of what was formerly a spacious farm-house, having a lawn frontage with ornamental shrubbery, shade trees and flowers, the lawn being intersected by a graveled walk. There are spacious barns and out-buildings upon the place. The whole seems embowered among fruit trees and vines, which give it an air of plenty. To the farm-house has recently been added a frame addition for the accommodation of the lads who make this retreat their summer home. It is contemplated to erect further buildings adapted to the needs of this promising charity. The institution is under the management of five Sisters of the Roman Catholic Order of St. Joseph, Sister Gertrude being Superior. A gardener is employed to direct the agricultural labor of the boys, and an engineer is engaged in the canning department.

The average number of boys during the summer is thirty. At the date of visitation, September 2d, the summer's work had begun to slacken, and the majority had returned to St. Mary's Asylum in town, leaving but fourteen in the house. The Sister in charge says: "The boys here are those that have grown up with us in the St. Mary's Orphan Asylum. They came out here for the summer, and will return to the asylum, after the work here is finished, to attend school during the winter. Their ages range mostly from fourteen to eighteen. We keep them until they are eighteen, and then if they wish to learn a trade the Bishop gives them an opportunity. We have recently sent two boys from here to be taught trades. We have never had any trouble with the boys, nor have any ever run away. We keep up an evening school, which lasts from seven to nine. We commence our work here in April and break up in November. Three Sisters remain during the winter. We raise on the place a great many tomatoes for canning, also peas, beans and corn. Our vineyard contains about eight acres, and we expect to sell a great many grapes this year. We produced last year about eighty barrels of apples and fifty bushels of peaches. We had this year ten acres in tomatoes, five in sweet corn ten in peas, four in beans, and four in potatoes."

The Sisters have acquired an enviable reputation for canning fruit, and this has led to a large demand for their productions in this line. The process of canning is a delicate one, requiring the exercise of great care. The tomatoes are first scalded in a large pan, and then peeled. This is done rapidly by the boys, who use short knives adapted to the purpose. The tomatoes are packed in cans containing about sixteen large tomatoes each, and then boiled for a short time in a large caldron. The cans are then taken out to cool, and afterward labeled. The canning is done in a large building, which contains a cylinder flue engine boiler, for generating the steam, vessels for scalding the fruit, large tables for peeling it, and other necessary apparatus. The boys, under the supervision of the Sisters, have become very expert at this business, and have been known to put up three hundred and thirty-five cans in two hours and twenty minutes. The price at which the cans are marketed at wholesale seems incredibly low.

Scrupulous order and system pervaded the establishment, not only in the fruit-canning department, but elsewhere. The orchard, vineyard and extensive gardens were well kept and clean, no weeds having been left to go to seed. The out-door work appeared to be all well done, and done in season. The boys were mostly at work in the garden, and were closely applying themselves to their labor.

This institution has not yet been incorporated, its originators preferring to wait until what was begun as an experiment should prove successful beyond fear of failure.

In its conception and early growth, it is a beautiful feature of the charities of the city of Rochester. The bringing of destitute boys out from the city, giving them a taste of out-door life, and teaching them to be industrious in a way that they seem to enjoy and under conditions quite nearly approaching to family life, in association with the pure and refined, who are devoting their lives to their welfare, it would seem, cannot but work most beneficial results, both morally and physically. It is not to be wondered at that the Sisters should testify that they have never had any trouble with the boys, and that none had ever run away.

As further illustrating the aims and objects of Excelsior Farm, the following statement from its founder, the Right Rev. Bernard J. McQuaid, will be found interesting:

"Experience taught me, some time ago, that there was a radical defect in our system of asylums for orphans. These children are necessarily treated with great tenderness in such institutions, and at a very early age are placed among strangers, who for the most part have no consideration for their loneliness and the peculiar way in which they were brought up, and they too often become disheartened and feel that the world is against them.

"Many of those who take children from the orphan asylums regard them as mere money-making machines, to be used while they pay, and to be cast off when they cease to pay. The fact that boys taken out of the asylum in the spring, by farmers, were returned to the asylum in the winter, after eight months of hard work, compelled us to look for a remedy.

"It is not advisable to keep children too long in an institution, treading the same track, year in and year out, nor is it good policy to keep boys in such places, under females, past twelve or thirteen years of age. Under such gentle treatment, with little physical work, boys become effeminate and disinclined to apply themselves steadily to manual labor. Furthermore, in this country it is almost impossible to place boys as apprentices to trades until they are seventeen or eighteen years of age. To tide them over the exceedingly trying years from thirteen to eighteen is the difficult problem we have to work at.

"With these considerations in view, and feeling that to guard orphan children in great kindness until thirteen years old, and then cast them off to go to perdition, for the most part, was not worthy of humane and Christian people, I began the experiment of Excelsior Farm. We intend hereafter to place on this farm only boys that have passed through the orphan asylum, and who are old enough to leave it. These boys will remain on the farm the entire year. We propose to make this their home until they are seventeen or eighteen, when we shall secure them the trade they choose. Besides these boys, many of the younger children spend from two to three months on the farm, engaged in work suitable to their age and strength. This change breaks up the monotony and routine of asylum life, develops self reliance, shows them that they can do something toward their own support, and is conducive to health and physical development. I have taken the farm on my own responsibility, have advanced all moneys needed to carry it on, without asking any aid from civic authorities or individuals, and I am confident that before long, Excelsior Farm will return the moneys loaned, pay for the farm, besides supporting the institution. We are careful to let the boys know they are paying their own way, and are not objects of charity.

"The farm was bought in the spring of 1873. All attention was given at first to raising of vegetables for the Rochester market, not knowing that Rochester is a poor market for vegetables, as almost every one has his own garden, and the rich country around the city so gluts the market that gardening on our scale would not pay. We consequently lost money but gained experience. Our attention was then called to the packing of fruits and vegetables. Having no capital to spare and risk, we began packing tomatoes as an experiment. This was successful and profitable. The present year we have packed peas, beans, sweet corn and tomatoes. Our calculations are that the farm will pay expenses, the interest on the purchase of the place, and return at least $1,000 of the money loaned. Next year it is proposed to double our work, and extend it to fruits and pickles. The only persons hired are the gardener and one man in the packing factory. I need not say that without the services of the Sisters of St. Joseph who watch over the boys and care for all their domestic needs, it would not be possible to do the work."

House for Idle and Truant Children.

Rochester.

This institution, located at No. 263 North St. Paul street, stands on a tract of land containing between six and seven acres, three of which are under garden cultivation. The building is a tasteful, two-story brick structure, with a mansard roof. The outlook from the rear is upon the high and precipitous banks of the Genesee. A little to the right stands a quadrangular frame building two stories in height, where the work of the House was begun.

The following sketch of the early history of the institution will throw some light upon its origin and aims:

"On one occasion two street loafers, in one of our public streets, got into a quarrel, when one of them, in the heat of passion, plunged a knife into the heart of his antagonist. The murderer and his victim were each about twelve years of age. This event led to the formation of a 'Juvenile Reform Society,' under whose auspices a school was opened for the reformation and care of this class of children. The same Society took the initiatory steps to have a law enacted to provide for such delinquents, which resulted in the passage of the truant act, passed April 12, 1853, and in the organization, the spring following, of the 'Home for Truants,' under the provisions of said act. The number of children at its first organization did not exceed twenty, but the exact number is not now known. It was, in the beginning, under the temporary supervision of a person appointed by the Common Council. The first Superintendent appointed by the Board of Managers was the late Samuel Chipman, who resigned his position in 1856, and was succeeded by the Rev. Timothy Fuller, who resigned in 1866."

The institution is managed by a Board of nine gentlemen, appointed by the Common Council of the city of Rochester — three being appointed each year. The working force consists of a superintendent, a matron, a teacher and four assistants. Its income is derived mainly from a municipal tax.

The House is arranged as follows: In the basement are a visiting room for the use of parents who come to see their children, family dining room, washing room, kitchen, and dining room for children. On the first floor are reception rooms, superintendent's apartments and sewing room. On the second floor are the family sleeping apartments, girls' dormitory, and bath room ; also the hospital. The third floor is used for boys' dormitory. "The attic," the Superintendent, Mr. Elisha Bryant, says, "is used as a dormitory for boys upon their arrival. The best boys occupy the best rooms." He further states: "One-third of the children are sent here for truancy, vagrancy and very slight misdemeanors. Very few are orphans. Many of them have drunken parents. As soon as we can find suitable homes for the children, and can recommend them, we let them go. We claim under the law that while our children are supported by public charity, we have the control of them.

"Children sent here are generally committed by the Police Justice. At first it was expected that they could be committed by the Poormaster ; but almost the entire number are now sent here by the Police Justice. We have about three committed by the Superintendent of the Poor, who pays for them $1.00 per week.

"We take children from three to sixteen years of age, but I think this is not a proper place for any under five years old. The children are generally healthy. We had two deaths in March from scarlet fever."

In regard to the methods of placing children out, the Superintendent says: "Children are mostly indentured. Some are out, by permission of the Board of Managers, on trial. We have no committee for looking after children put out, except the discharging committee."

In regard to religious education he remarks: "We try to avoid sectarianism as much as possible. A Sunday-school is held on the premises at three o'clock every Sunday afternoon, in which we use the International Sunday-school paper. The inmates repeat the Lord's Prayer every night and morning."

The average age of the children at the date of visitation, September 8, was about nine years.

The Superintendent says: "My opinion is that the institution is better adapted to boys than girls. We want a certain number of girls to do sewing and kitchen work, but that is all."

The kitchen is well furnished, and has a good range. In the dining room are long tables covered with white cloths. There are stools for the children to sit upon. The dormitories are furnished with single wooden bedsteads of the French pattern. The beds have white counterpanes ; sheets and pillow cases are changed once a week. The window sashes are hung with cords, weights and pulleys. Transom lights are over the doors.

In the rear building on the first floor, were a number of boys engaged in making cane seats for chairs. "Some of the boys," the foreman in charge says, "are not seven years old. One of this age can cane seats as well as the older ones. I can teach a boy to do this kind of work in two days; there is a great difference in the boys; some learn more quickly than others. The average time taken to learn, however, is about four days. The boys are assigned their daily tasks, and can leave the shop when these are completed. They generally work three hours, and have five hours' schooling."

The school is held in the second story of this building. The room is a pleasant one, and furnished with modern improvements. The teacher, Mrs. M. H. Wilson, exhibited some of the pupils, who acquitted themselves very creditably in singing, drawing, reading, writing and general information. One of the boys, fourteen years old, drew a plan of the school-room on the blackboard, and answered very intelligently numerous close questions thereupon. The teacher says of him: "He came in March last, and was rather backward for one of his age." Another little boy, fifteen years old, drew a ship and appeared to be quite as familiar with every part as any sailor. The teacher remarks of him; "He has been here seven years, and did not know the alphabet when he came." A third boy drew rapidly a map of the State, showing the railways, canals and rivers intersecting it. The teacher, who seemed to have the confidence of the children, as well as some knowledge of their antecedents, says: "Most of the children have intemperate parents, and they very often speak to me of their troubles.".

Two little boys, four and a half and six years old, and two little girls, eleven and nine years old, formed one family group. "They have a step-mother. Their father is intemperate, and is in the work-house." Two boys, one four and the other six years, and a little girl, eleven years old, formed another family group. "Their mother having been abused by her intemperate husband, deserted the family." Two boys, ten and thirteen years, formed yet another. "Their father tried to burn their mother to death. He was arrested and put in jail, and the children think he is now dead. The mother visited them once or twice, and the children are very home-sick." One of the lads in the school, who had lost the use of one eye, was said to be remarkably studious. The school was found to be in charge of an efficient and earnest lady teacher, and is worthy of special note. The children were well advanced in their studies, and the influences under which they are brought in the school-room is believed to be highly elevating.

It may be regarded as doubtful whether as strict a separation of the sexes is maintained in the institution as desirable. A particular inquiry into the methods of discipline left the impression upon the mind that it was not such as to reach the best results. Leaving out of consideration the educational department, it must be said regretfully that the visit was not on the whole satisfactory, and the grand object, the reformation of the inmates, was not as fully reached, under the system adopted, as it should be. This subject is deemed to be of sufficient importance to be worthy the careful consideration of the managers.

An institution having its avowed objects, it would seem, is much needed in the district in which it is located. The suggestion is ventured, whether the house might not be advantaged by calling to its aid a force of benevolent ladies, and permitting them to exercise some direction in its affairs.

No returns have been made showing the number of children received and discharged during the past year. The whole number received since its organization has been about nine hundred. There were in the Home at the date of October 1, 1875, fourteen orphan children, fifty-two half-orphans, and twenty-seven having both parents living. Fifty-seven were of native, and thirty-six of foreign parentage.

It is stated by the Treasurer, that "Our expenditures, from April 1 to December 1, 1875, were about $6,000." The real estate and buildings are valued at $45,000; personal property at $1,877.50.

The Industrial School of Rochester,

Rochester,

Was organized in December, 1856, through the zealous efforts of a few Christian ladies. Its objects are, "to gather into the School vagrant and destitute children who, from the poverty or vice of their parents, are unable to attend the public school, and who obtain a precarious livelihood by begging or pilfering; to give them ideas of moral and religious duty; to instruct them in the elements of learning, and in different branches of industry, and enable them to obtain an honest and honorable support, and to become useful members of society."

The great end this organization had in view was to prevent street begging by poor children, and to benefit their physical condition by furnishing them daily a warm, nutritious and abundant meal, and giving them shelter and instruction during the day; also to supply them with clothing when their own was insufficient. Those interested in the institution claim that the prevention of street begging has been largely accomplished, and that the improvement in the moral and physical condition of the children after a short attendance at the school is marked; that the healthy, clean, well-ventilated rooms are in such marked contrast to the wretched, unsavory hovels whence most of the children come, that the very atmosphere invigorates.

The School is located at 76 Exchange street, in a central portion of the city. The building occupied stands upon a lot having about one hundred feet frontage. It is a spacious brick edifice, and well arranged for its purposes.

The financial interests of the institution are under the control of a board of gentlemen, and its general management is directed by a board of ladies chosen from the different Protestant churches of the city. Its immediate charge is in the hands of a Matron, who is assisted by two nurses and two female domestics. Two lady teachers in the school room are compensated by the Board of Education.

At the date of visitation there were thirty children making their home in the house, and about sixty attending the day school and receiving a mid-day meal. Eight of the regular inmates were girls. The children's ages range from eight months up to fifteen years. Four of them are under two years. From the Matron in charge, Miss Sarah Wheeler, the following information was obtained:

"Our children that live in the house are of the lowest and poorest class. All are half-orphans except three or four, who have fathers that have deserted their mothers. The mothers work in laundries, and in hotel kitchens. They put their children here and pay a dollar a week for their care. They are mostly German children. We could accommodate about fifty inmates. We have also a day school, with an average attendance of ninety-five; during the winter it is larger. We have a Visiting Committee who determine what children shall be admitted to the School. When children are brought or come here to the house, the Chairman of this Visiting Committee is notified, and the families are visited to see if the applicants are fit subjects for the School. If it is found that the parents are able to send them to the public school they are not admitted here.

"In addition to the visiting committee, there is a children's committee, to see to the children that are brought into the house to board. Some of these are partially boarded by the poormaster. Others stay and work for their board; others again are paid for by their friends, in which case the friends are at liberty to remove them at any time. We keep them, however, as long as we can, as we think that if they are here only a little while it will do them good.

"Some of the mothers bring their children here as early as six o'clock in the morning. If little ones, they are placed in the nursery and stay there till the parents return for them in the evening. While here they need constant supervision.

"The school is under the Department of Public Instruction. The common branches of an English education are taught. Every Wednesday afternoon a committee of ladies attend and form a sewing school among the girls. The girls are entitled to whatever they make. The boys do all kinds of work; clean, sweep, dust, make fires, chop wood, and clean the cellars. The girls make the beds and assist in general housework."

The house is commodious. The basement is used for washing and store-rooms. On the first floor are the parlor, reception room, nursery and bath-room. The nursery is furnished with nine cribs, five of them being on rockers; also with twelve little baby chairs. The walls are hung with pictures, and the room is airy and well lighted.

Back of the parlor is the children's sitting room; a large, nicely furnished room, used also by the Matron. It contains a library of two or three hundred volumes, in a handsome case. In the rear of the main structure is the boys' bath-room and children's dining room.

Over the nursery is a large dormitory for girls, furnished with double bedsteads. The ladies' sewing room is also on this floor. It contains two sewing machines.

The school-room is large and will seat comfortably about one hundred children. It is furnished with the usual school apparatus, and contains a good organ.

The boys' dormitory is on the floor above that of the girls. It is a well-ventilated apartment, furnished with double bedsteads of iron.

A fair specimen of the homes from which most of the little children come, and of the evil influences from which the Industrial School seeks to save them, is thus described by one of the teachers who went to ascertain the cause of the absence from school of two of her scholars in whom she took a deep interest: "A man, the father, lay stretched upon the floor, drunk, and at the further end of the room sat the mother of the boys, a woman of delicate appearance, absolutely cowering with shame before the visitors. Poor thing! she had known better days, but step by step the family had gone down into that sad desolation through the vice that changes man into a demon. This mother had veiled her sorrow from human ken as long as possible; had borne up for her children's sake, till in despair, she stretched out her arms for aid, and sent her boys thither."

The manner in which this institution comes to the aid of little children, inspiring them with hope even under the most discouraging circumstances, is aptly illustrated by the career of two little Sisters who have been inmates at intervals during the past year. The mother is addicted to fits of intemperance. When in these moods, the children are in the habit of drifting to the school. They generally come looking pinched, dejected and sad, but soon, through the influence of the other children, they brighten up and become as happy as the rest. As soon as the mother recovers she comes to the school and demands her children and takes them away till her next intemperate fit comes on when they are back again, with the usual dejected and sad look. The father, it appears, has deserted the family. By last accounts these little children were in school, dreading the approach of their mother to take them away. "They are bright as well as fair, quick and intelligent, and learn rapidly. It were a pity that aught so lovely should be blighted or spoiled."

The work of the ladies' sewing committee is thus stated in a late report of the society:

"Eighty-four new garments have been made for our children in the past year; six hundred and fifteen garments have been repaired, and six hundred and forty have been distributed. In addition to this, one hundred and fifty-two pairs of shoes and fifty-nine hats have been given out. Seventy-five bundles of clothing have been donated, together with a large box of clothing from the Baptist Church at Nunda. The expenses connected with our work department have been for the year, $462.08."

On October 1st, 1875, there were in the institution one hundred and eight children, of whom two were orphans, forty-six were half-orphans, and sixty had both parents living. Seven were of native parentage, and one hundred and one were of foreign. They were all from Monroe county. Eighty-eight were partially supported by parents or friends, ten by counties, towns or cities, and ten by the institution.

The total expenditures of the institution during the year ending September 30, 1875, were $3,941.32. It has an invested fund of $10,000.

The health of the children on the day of visitation was good, but during the year several deaths had occurred among the young infants whom the maternal instincts of the ladies had induced them to take in and try to save from perishing, and although their success was not encouraging, yet they felt that this helpless class could not be discarded. An asylum, or some charity, for the special care of infants in the city of Rochester would seem, at the present time, to be greatly needed.

The earnest spirit which pervades this charity, and the noble work it is accomplishing, find a fitting expression in the modest statement of its devoted President, Mrs. George F. Danforth. She says: "We have struggled on with our institution with many inconveniences, by dint of strictest economy, doing the utmost with the means intrusted to our disposal. We feel that we have done the city good, and the State too, by turning many little boys and girls, who had never heard the voice of prayer, into God-fearing children."

Rochester Benevolent, Scientific and Industrial School of the Sisters of Mercy.

Rochester.

This institution was incorporated May 21, 1857. It is situated at No. 5 South street. The building in use was formerly a private residence, to which another story has been added. In 1871, an adjoining house was purchased and connected with the first. The establishment is heated by a furnace, lighted with gas and supplied with city water.

The institution is under the charge of the Roman Catholic Order of the Sisters of Mercy. Mother Camillus, the Superior, is assisted by seven others of the Order in carrying on the work. In answer to inquiries made during the visitation, September 2, the following information was furnished by the Mother Superior, who has been twelve years in charge. She says: "We do not get any help from public authorities toward the support of these children. We have opened a select school in the house, and teach the children of the city, who pay from three to five dollars a quarter. Three dollars extra is charged for French and ten dollars for music. We have now twenty-eight girls in the industrial school. We commenced with three or four. Young girls who have no one to protect them are exposed to great danger. Our object is to keep them from the temptation to which they are exposed in the shops, to educate them and teach them trades, and when we send them out, we hope that they will be able to protect themselves and earn their own living.

"We take any children who are brought to us, either by the priest or by respectable people who desire to place them with us. Dying mothers sometimes ask us to take their destitute children. We could do more work if we had more means and a larger building. We are often obliged to refuse admission, and have now more inmates than we can conveniently accommodate. We receive children from twelve to eighteen years of age. Nineteen of our children are from the county of Monroe, thirteen from Cayuga, two from Ontario and one each from Seneca, Tompkins and Wayne counties.

"The children have a great respect for the Sisters, and are well behaved. They are not addicted to any special vices. We do not keep any that are refractory, nor do we take any girl with a bad name, lest she should corrupt the others. We never had but one child run away, and she wanted to come back, but was not permitted. We do not allow the children out unless they are accompanied by one of their parents or their guardian. Very few of the girls are entirely destitute of friends. The children are very healthy. No death nas ever occurred among the children in the house.

"We teach the girls the trades of shirt-making and tailoring. We do a great deal in the shirt-making business, and cut out nearly all the shirts we make. If the children stay with us two years they are able to help to support those who are learning. We allow them to live here till they are eighteen. When parents put a girl here to learn a trade we want them to agree to leave her with us three years. If they do not, we expect them to pay for her board. We think the character is well formed by being here that length of time. After leaving us they can readily find places where they may earn from five to eight dollars a week. One of our girls is now in Buffalo. We get very good reports regarding her. The people with whom she lives are greatly pleased with her. When she first came to us she could not read. If the girls are not able to support themselves we feel bound to take care of them. We help to get situations for them, keeping a kind of intelligence office in their interest. Ladies make applications to us, and the girls are thus provided with situations. We watch over them for a couple of years after they leave here, or until they leave town or get beyond our reach. If they do not call to see us we send for them. We hope to make this institution self-supporting. We have consecrated our lives to the work and do not expect to get any earthly reward."

At the date of October 1st, 1875, there were thirty-seven girls in the institution. Fourteen of these were orphans, sixteen were half-orphans, and seven had both parents living. Two had native and thirty-five foreign parents. Five were supported by their parents, and thirty-two wholly by the institution.

The number of children received during the past year was eighteen; the number discharged was six; of these four were returned to parents or guardians, and two otherwise discharged. The average number of inmates in the institution was twenty-eight. The total expenditure during the year was $3,577; its total indebtedness is $3,099.38, of which $1,800 rests upon the real estate.

During our visitation we were shown some very fine *trousseaux* made in the house, which evidenced superior skill in needlework. The work room contained seventeen sewing machines, set very closely. The dining room and dormitories were small, in view of the numbers using them, resulting in some discomfort to the inmates. Notwithstanding these drawbacks, the establishment exhibited commendable housekeeping, and the inmates appeared to be under refining and elevating influences.

More room is greatly needed, not only to accomplish conveniently the work now being done by the Sisters, but also to enable them to enlarge their sphere of usefulness.

Rochester Home of Industry.

Rochester.

The Home was organized in May, 1873, at the suggestion of Right Rev. Bishop McQuaid, and incorporated under the general law February 25, 1874. A two-story dwelling-house, 136 South St. Paul street, was purchased, and Sister Hieronymo, formerly of St. Mary's Hospital, who may be regarded as the founder of that noble charity, assumed its charge. She has three Sisters of the Roman Catholic Order of St. Joseph assisting her in carrying on the work.

The objects of the Home are so well set forth by Sister Hieronymo, that we give them in her own words: "It is an institution designed to make a home for young girls that are homeless, working in shops and yet unable to pay their way in respectable boarding-houses. We charge $2 a week, and besides keeping them from the dangers incident to low boarding-houses, we give them educational advantages and try to elevate them otherwise. This is also a home for our own girls that grow up with us in our asylums. We keep them till we know they are capable of taking care of themselves."

Trades, such as millinery and shoemaking, are taught in the house, besides such matters of housekeeping as every girl ought to be familiar with. The girls who board in the house have also the advantage of obtaining work there when their labor is not needed in the shops. This enables them always to have a home and to keep out of debt.

Tailoring and shoemaking are here carried on. All the different varieties of ladies and children's shoes are made. The girls make the uppers, and the soles are put on by men employed for that purpose. Coats, pants, vests and underwear are also made in the house, and all kinds of fine sewing are done. Ladies leave orders for infants' apparel and for *trousseaux*. In the shoemaking department of the house a1 four sewing machines, a splitting machine, a stock of lasts, and over $500 worth of dies, and in the tailoring department are twelve sewing machines.

In connection with the Home is a shop (124 West Main street), for the sale of the manufactures of the inmates.

"To begin the work," the Sister says, "cost $1,500.00, and yet it was commenced without a dollar of capital, only credit. I am trying to make the business of shoemaking form its own capital. The store now in use was generously furnished me for nine months free of rent.

"Children are taken into the Home from ten years old upward. They come from orphan asylums and from homes wanting father or mother, sometimes both. We do not take any child who is spoiled, nor any street walker." The average age of the girls is fifteen. The

Sister says, "I commenced with twenty-five, taking the oldest girls out of the Asylum. It has always been a rule in the Asylum that no girl be kept there beyond the age of thirteen years. They should be placed out at the age of twelve. The length of time spent at the Home depends, in each case, very much upon the character and disposition of the girl. The aim of the Sister being to form their character and cultivate in them that womanly dignity which will always be a safeguard to them in after-life, it is necessary to deal with each individually.

"Our discipline," says the Sister, "consists in depriving them of pleasure."

The following is the routine of the day as given by the Sister: "Sisters and children rise at five A. M. and prepare for breakfast. After morning prayers they take breakfast, and each one repairs to her particular duties. Those who work in the shops are obliged to leave here at half-past six. They take dinner at twelve o'clock, and then work till six. Now, during vacation, we have two hours' school in the afternoon, from three to five. In the winter the school hours are from seven to nine. The hour for retiring is half-past nine."

"Industrial education," the Sister says, "is too apt to be neglected. It is one of the objections to asylums where they crowd children together without any occupation. They are not sufficiently advanced to be kept in school, without something to divert them, and the teachers are quite likely to crowd their minds with useless knowledge. I found that out before I was two years in St. Patrick's Asylum. I found it to be a pleasure to the children to study in the morning. In the afternoon, I gave them a little amusement."

On the day of visitation, the Sister related several incidents in her experience to show the dangers to which a certain class of girls are exposed from unprincipled men, and the need for her, in the strictest sense of the term, acting the part of a mother toward them. One of these incidents she related in substance as follows:

"A young and pretty girl, quite fond of dress, amiable and good, and yet inclined to frivolity, I allowed to accompany Mrs. ———, a lady of wealth and high respectability, on a trip to New York, to take charge of her little girl on the way. I explained to the lady the character of her charge, and cautioned her to be especially watchful over her interests. While *en route*, on the cars, a well-dressed man, apparently a gentleman, came along, and, unobserved by Mrs. ———, dropped a folded slip of paper into the girl's lap, on which was written, 'When you can get away from the old woman, come into the rear car.' The bait took, and an interview followed, resulting in a correspondence and an offer of marriage. This correspondence came to my knowledge after Mrs. ——— had returned, and the girl had been replaced in the Home. I took pains to quietly inform myself of the standing of the girl's correspondent, and ascertained that he was already married and was an unprincipled character. Shortly after, this man came to Rochester, stopped at a hotel, and sent a message to the girl to meet him there. Becoming informed of this, I undeceived the simple, confiding girl, who was very loth to believe that any thing was wrong. She was thus saved, although plunged for the time into grief. She has since married a respectable farmer, and had her wedding breakfast in the house."

The Sister thought it was remarkable that the girls remained with her so willingly, as there was nothing to prevent them running away, and she was often obliged to deal with them very summarily in the matter of dress or with other weaknesses of character which she thought might injure them. The Sister never relinquishes her maternal care over the girls till they are married, and it is customary then for her to have their wedding breakfast given at the Home, thus carrying out still further the idea of motherhood. Several of the girls have married, and are now well settled in life.

The property is heavily incumbered, and the liabilities of the institution are an obstacle to its usefulness and a source of anxiety to the Sister in charge. Her language is: "I want means to carry on this work. I do not supply the need. I fall far short of it. Two weeks ago our house was so full that two young women who came here had to sit in chairs all night. They had no other place to sleep."

Notwithstanding these discouragements the Sister seems hopeful in her work, and referred to her experience in Buffalo, where she had to contend with as great difficulties as now. Speaking of it she said: "The house we entered was in a fearful condition. We had nothing in it, not even a bed. Our chairs were made by getting nail kegs and putting a board on the top. We got straw and put it into some old skirts, and thus made beds for three of us."

In regard to her present charge, she says: "Here there is much to do and nothing to do with, but the Almighty has placed me here, and if I give it up it would look as if I was depending more on the dollars and cents than on the promises of God."

The Home though small is well arranged, and bears evidence of being in the hands of one who knows how to make the most of every thing, and but for its lack of space would be what it is aimed to make it — a comfortable home and refuge for young girls.

The total expenditures of the Home during the past year were $6,110.50. Its total indebtedness on the 1st of October, 1875, was $12,120, of which $7,000 was upon the real estate. In view of the beneficial results growing out of the work of the institution, it is hoped that the indebtedness, which is an obstacle in the way of its usefulness, may be speedily removed.

The Rochester Orphan Asylum,

Rochester,

Is situated in Hubbell Park, between Greig and Exchange streets. It was organized in February, 1837, and incorporated by special act of the Legislature March 23d, 1838.

The circumstances which led to its establishment are thus stated: "In the winter of 1836-7 it was ascertained by several charitable ladies that there were upwards of twenty orphans in the city who were dependent on private charity, and exposed to all the evils consequent to the loss of parental care. There were also many children of poor widows and others, who were under the most pernicious influences, their parents being extremely poor, and addicted to every kind of vice. In view of all these circumstances the ladies felt that something must be done immediately to rescue these orphans and destitute children from their life of want and sin, and by kind care and judicious training fit them for usefulness here and happiness hereafter. The subject was made general by calling a meeting, at which nearly all the religious societies were represented, and after a free discussion, an association for the relief of orphans and destitute children was formed. Many of the prominent citizens expressed their approval of the objects of the association, and promised their cordial coöperation. A suitable house was rented, a matron procured, and the Asylum was opened with nine children. Fifty-eight were received into the institution during the first year of its existence. In 1839 Mr. John Greig, of Canandaigua, gave to the Asylum the valuable tract of land on which the present buildings were erected in 1843 and 1844, and in April of the latter year the orphans were removed to the new home."

The Asylum is governed by a Board of Lady Managers.

The building was evidently planned with great care, and seems to be well adapted to its uses. The more recent addition is especially well constructed, the comfort and health of the inmates being the great objects aimed at. It is finished in natural wood, is light, airy, cheerful and in every way creditable to its projectors.

The dormitories of the asylum are large, neatly kept and well ventilated. Single bedsteads of iron are used and the bed linen is kept clean by frequent changes. The importance of sleep to the health and comfort of the children is apparently well appreciated by the kind ladies interested in the asylum, and the liberal provision made for their homeless charges is deserving of high commendation.

The nurseries, with all their tiny appurtenances, little cribs, little chairs, toys and happy little children, presented a very cheerful sight.

The infirmary is a fine, well-lighted apartment, furnished with iron bedsteads and all the conveniences for the care of the sick. The room was cleanly kept, and was without an occupant. The health of the children on the day of visitation was good, but during the year scarlet fever had twice entered the house, carrying off several of its little inmates.

The school-room is furnished with patent desks and seats. The children receive a plain English education and remain in the school the hours regularly allotted by the Department of Public Instruction, under whose supervision the educational department of the asylum comes. The girls receive industrial training in general housework and are taught plain and fancy sewing, and the boys are, in various ways, disciplined into industrious habits. The moral and religious edification of the children is carefully considered, biblical instruction forming a prominent feature in the course of teaching. A Sabbath-school is held on the premises, and the children are permitted to attend the city churches, in company with responsible persons.

The dining room is furnished with stools instead of benches. White table-cloths and crockery ware are used at meals. A side table is also kept for the children who are not neat enough to use a table-cloth. The pantry adjoining was in excellent order.

In the lavatory each child has a towel, a basin, brush and comb, and also a tooth brush. The boys' bathing-room is supplied with four tubs, and the girls' with a similar number.

The asylum contains a fine library of six hundred and fifty-five volumes.

On the day of visitation, September 3d, the institution was found to be in the immediate charge of Mrs. L. Clements, Matron. Her subordinates are two nurses, two washer-women, one dining room girl, one girl to take care of the children, a chambermaid and a cook.

The ages of the children were stated to be "all the way from one year to fourteen. They are," the matron says, "brought here by mothers and fathers, and also by the poor-master. Others are children that have been abandoned by their parents. Others, again, are in part supported by their parents."

As examples of the way children have sometimes been treated by parties who were supposed to be trustworthy, the matron said: "We have had two children returned that were abused most shamefully. The custom is to put them out on trial for two or three months. Sometimes farmers take advantage of this, keep them during harvest, and then return them. One boy was taken in this way and sent back, and then taken again and sent back. He was made to work harder than his strength would bear, and it brought on a weakness from which I fear he never will recover. One of our girls was put out, and returned in fourteen months. She ran away from the place, but could not find her way back to us. She got somehow to the Industrial School. One day while there she saw the man who had taken her from here, pass by, and was so frightened at his appearance that she jumped out of the window and ran to Court street, where she met a policeman, and asked him to protect her. Through him she got back here again." "She is," says the matron, "a girl difficult to take care of. She is one that you have to encourage and need to use well. You have to treat her kindly. If you want any work done she will not refuse to obey you, but if you speak kindly to her she will do it more cheerfully."

The number of children in the asylum October 1st was eighty-three. Of these fourteen were orphans, sixty-three were half-orphans, and six had both parents living. The parents of twenty were native; of sixty-three, foreign. Sixty-five were from Monroe county; five from Orleans; four from Wayne; three from Niagara, and one from each of the following counties: Cayuga, Erie, Jefferson, Livingston, Madison and New York.

The whole number of children received during the year was seventy-eight. The number discharged was seventy. Of the latter, six were placed out by adoption; three by indenture; forty-five were returned to parents or guardians; one left without permission; two were transferred to other institutions, and thirteen died. The total expenditures during the year were $10,833.20. The total indebtedness on October 1st was $4,700, of which $3,500 was upon real estate. The invested funds amount to $7,000.

The following additional information as to what is regarded by the managers as being the best methods for furthering the aims of the institution is furnished by one of the ladies of the Society, long an earnest worker in the field. Mrs. W. N. Sage says:

"The policy of this institution has always been to procure for the children, under our care, situations in private families, where they will be apprenticed, or otherwise adopted, and thus brought under the salutary influence of home discipline. We consider this the best method for securing the happiness and usefulness of our children, which are the results aimed at by our charity."

In regard to the manner of placing children out, and the success attending this work, she says:

"The Children's Committee consists of three members of the Board of Managers, whose duty it is to ascertain, as far as possible, the character and condition of persons applying for children. This committee is authorized to place children, given up to the Board, in suitable families, where they will be under good moral and religious influence, and otherwise properly cared for, and they shall cause appropriate indentures to be executed, as early as practicable after the specified time of trial has expired. They shall record in a book, provided for that purpose, and kept at the Asylum, the name and age of each child indentured, the name and residence of the person to whom the child is indentured, whether bound to service or by adoption, the date when such indenture was executed, the date when it will expire, and the name of the member of the committee who bound the child. No child shall be indentured under twelve years of age, unless taken by adoption. Every child, when indentured, shall receive a Bible, in which shall be recorded the name and age of said child, with the date of leaving the Asylum. This committee is required to make a monthly report of the children received and dismissed by them during the month, stating the full name and age of each child, its parentage, place of birth, residence, or any other items of interest in their possession, which may be of use in tracing the history of the child, or identifying it in future years. They are also required to write at least once every year to each person taking a child from the Asylum, thus keeping the Board informed of its condition and prospects.

"The average number of children placed in families for the last ten years has been seventy-six. During the last three years twenty-one children, between the ages of eight weeks and seven years, have been adopted into good families. Nine children, between the ages of ten and fourteen years, have, during the same period, been placed in families, where they will receive a good common school education and be trained in habits of industry, thus fitting them to become good and respectable citizens."

In regard to the general results that have been accomplished by the Asylum, since its beginning, Mrs. Sage further says:

"Since the organization of this Asylum over two thousand children have shared its fostering care. From statistics, and facts which have been gathered in various ways, no doubt is left on the minds of the managers that great good has resulted to the children — that a large majority have been rescued from a life of poverty, beggary, vice and crime, and placed in situations where happier and more elevating influences surrounded them, and encouraged them to cultivate those habits of honesty and industry which would make them a blessing, instead of a curse to society.

"We know of many persons, now occupying prominent positions in society, who passed their childhood in our Orphan Asylum, and who went from our fostering care into good homes, where they received all the advantages of education and culture which could have been bestowed on our own children. Not long since a fine looking and very intelligent lady called at the Asylum with her husband, and asked the privilege of going over the house, saying to the matron, 'I have brought my husband to see where I was so kindly cared for in my helpless childhood.' She now occupies a position of influence in a western city. Another lady is the wife of a successful merchant in our own city. Our protegés are scattered all over the land — lawyers, physicians, merchants, farmers, and happy wives and mothers — the great proportion of whom would have been paupers and outcasts, but for the sheltering care given to their early years by our Asylum. Our policy of finding good homes for our children, as soon as practicable, instead of keeping them within our walls, for so long a period as to give them an institution stamp, has been fully vindicated by its results. I do not mean to be understood that all the children placed in homes by us grow up useful and respectable; hereditary traits will sometimes manifest themselves greatly to our disappointment and sorrow, but the percentage of those who attain to honest and respectable manhood and womanhood is as great as that of an equal number taken from average society."

A review of the work done by this Asylum, during the thirty-eight years of its existence, shows results which could not have been attained without careful management and self-sacrificing Christian effort. The organization has done much to relieve Monroe county from the large accessions to its pauper classes, which would have been made by the poor children of misfortune, that this institution has rescued. It came to their aid at the right time, and before the brand of pauper could be affixed, placed them under healthy family influence and thus absorbed them into the productive portion of society. Now that the almshouse system of rearing and training children has been, by a wise and beneficent law, set aside, the field of usefulness in which its efforts can be utilized will be no less urgent, and it is gratifying to find this worthy charity in the hands of those having large experience and whose benevolence has been well proven.

St. Joseph's German Roman Catholic Orphan Asylum.

Rochester.

The objects of this institution are "the moral and scientific education of orphan, half-orphan and destitute children."

Those familiar with its early history, furnish the following information regarding it:

"In 1862, there were three German Roman Catholic congregations in the city of Rochester, numbering nine thousand souls, the largest of them, St. Joseph's, embracing about six thousand. Up to that time, orphans had readily found homes in families by adoption. But by and by the number of orphans increased, so that homes for all could not be provided at the time of the death of their parents. At this period (1862), a number of the leading members of St. Joseph's congregation organized the Orphan Asylum Society, and on April 23, 1863, it was incorporated by a special act of the Legislature. At first, the Sisters De Notre Dame, under the Superiorship of Sister M. Angelica, took into an old, small and inconvenient frame house one orphan girl. By and by, they took as many as five; for more there was no room; two of these were of Irish parentage. In 1864, two tracts of land were purchased in Irondequoit, outside the city limits (now within), one of fifty-five acres and the other of about thirty-three acres. The latter was laid out in village lots, and sold as opportunity offered for the benefit of the Asylum. From the proceeds of fairs, picnics, concerts, etc., and the sale of the lots, the Asylum work was commenced.

"For a number of years it was able to care for but quite a limited number of children. In 1866, a brick edifice on Andrew street was erected. This, subsequently, proving to be insufficient to accommodate increasing needs, a new and larger edifice, eighty-six by forty-five feet, was constructed on Andrew street, in the year 1874, and was occupied in January, 1875. It cost $25,000, and is capable of accommodating one hundred inmates." This edifice is a three-story brick building, with a basement and an attic. It is a plain, substantial structure of quadrangular shape, with mansard roof. In the basement of the building are the kitchen, pantries and store-rooms. Wide center halls extend longitudinally through the building, on each floor, at each end of which are stairs leading to the top of the building. On the first floor are a parlor, two school rooms and a music room; on the second floor, the chapel and sitting room for the Sisters, etc.; and on the third floor, the children's dormitories. The building is well constructed and has modern conveniences. The windows are large and the sashes suspended by cords, weights and pulleys. It is heated by steam and lighted with kerosene.

The Asylum is under the charge of six Sisters of the Roman Catholic Order De Notre Dame, Sister Mary Gabriel being Superior. At the date of visitation, September 1st, there were thirty-five orphan, and twelve half-orphan children in the institution, and also five whose parents were living, making in all fifty-two. Of this number eighteen were boys. The children were mostly of German parentage.

Some of the children entertained us by singing, accompanied by a piano played by Sister Godbertha, who is remarkably proficient in music. This lady, we were informed, plays on the harp, violin, zithern, guitar, flageolet and piano with equal facility. She also sings well, and is a most useful auxiliary to the Asylum in teaching the children music.

The children were mostly from the city. They are brought in sometimes when only a few months old. In the nursery were eleven little children that had been reared on the bottle, and one little baby who had been taken from the poor-house, all looking clean and nicely dressed.

There are three schools held in the house: A high school for outside pupils, and two schools of a primary character for the orphans. The pupils of the latter are transferred to the high school as soon as they are sufficiently advanced. The high school is carried on in an elegantly furnished school-room, and abundantly supplied with black-boards, globes, maps, charts, etc.

The house contains a very beautiful chapel, with sitting room for about sixty persons.

The nursery is furnished with comfortable little cots, and all necessary appurtenances of such an apartment.

The dormitories for the children are furnished with single iron bed-steads and straw beds. The bed linen is changed once a week.

The children are kept clean, and bathe weekly. All their clothing is made in the house.

The Sister in charge says of the girls: "They remain until eighteen, if they want to, but if they prefer to go sooner they are at liberty to do so." In regard to discipline, she says: "Once in a while we put them in a corner. We aim to get their hearts, and then it is easy enough to manage them." "Boys twenty years old," the Sister says, "bring their money to me regularly to keep for them."

In the rear of the building is a fine yard, with a swing for the children. Across the yard are two large brick edifices, one of which is the parish school for boys, taught by the Brothers of Mary, and the other is the parish school for girls, taught by the Sisters De Notre Dame, who make the asylum their home. This latter school has a daily attendance of about three hundred and fifteen girls.

The number of children received into the Asylum during the year ending October 1st, 1875, was thirty-three. The total number discharged was nine. Of these one was placed out by adoption, four were returned to parents or guardians, and ten, babies, had died. The total expenditures during the year were $23,999.63. Of this sum about $18,500 was expended for buildings and improvements. The value of the personal estate and investments of the Asylum amount to $11,198.60. Its real estate, Asylum buildings, fixtures and furniture are valued at about $87,000. Its total indebtedness is $18,196.64.

The whole number of children that have shared the benefits of the institution since its organization is one hundred and twenty-nine.

The family feeling is quite predominant in this Asylum. There is evidence of good cheer in the appearance of the little ones, and a heartiness and cheerfulness of manner on the part of the older inmates characteristic of the German people, which cannot but have a most happy influence upon the homeless children brought under its beneficent care.

St. Mary's Boys' Orphan Asylum.

Rochester.

This Asylum was removed from South street to its present location in 1866, and its work conducted in a frame building till 1869 or 1870, when the present commodious structure was completed. It is situated in the western part of the city, on the corner of Genesee and West Main streets, on a tract of ground containing five acres. The house is composed of a main and a wing, and the plan contemplates the erection of another wing. It is a stone, stuccoed edifice, two stories high, with also a basement and a mansard story. It is well ventilated, supplied with water from the city, carried throughout the building in pipes, lighted by gas and heated by furnace. Broad halls extend the whole length of the building on each floor. The school rooms are large and pleasant. The chapel will accommodate two hundred persons. The dormitories are large and airy, and the whole building is well constructed, and apparently well adapted to its uses.

The house can provide for one hundred and eighty inmates. When the projected wing is completed, its capacity will be increased to two hundred and forty. At the date of visitation, September 1st, there were one hundred and thirty boys in the asylum.

The institution is under the charge of the Roman Catholic Order of the Sisters of St. Joseph, Sister Stanislaus being the Lady Superior. She has ten Sisters associated with her in the work.

The dormitory walls in this asylum are tinted a soft color. The ceilings are about thirteen feet high. The bedsteads in use are single, of the French pattern, wood color, and varnished, giving the room a cheerful appearance. Straw beds, of good thickness, are in use, and are preferred to mattresses. The Sister in charge says: "The straw can be changed, and the ticks washed as often as necessary." The sleeping apartments of the Sisters communicate with the dormitories. In this way easy access to the children in case of necessity is secured. The Sister says: "Should any child become sick during the night, a Sister is with him immediately."

The wash-room is conveniently arranged, each boy having his own towel, wash-dish, comb and brush. The latter two are kept in a tin box. The Sister spoke emphatically of the importance of giving each child a towel, as a means of preventing the spread of ophthalmia. She says: "It is very easy to let this disease infect them all. Not a child in the house is affected with sore scalp or any skin disease."

Three sewing machines are used in the asylum by the Sisters, in making garments for the children.

The laundry is in the old wooden asylum building, adjoining the new edifice.

The garden is inclosed with a high fence. It contained two acres of potatoes, and about half an acre of onions. A good deal of the work of garden cultivation is done by the boys. There is a small apple orchard upon the place. The supply of apples is not large, as the Sister declares that "they are eaten in the blossom."

The children were found in the orchard playing. They sang several lively rhymes, under the leadership of a little blind boy who was one of the youngest and apparently the happiest among them. They seemed a bright and merry little company, and all appeared to be healthy. There had been no case of sickness or death in the institution during the year. It was stated that the only deaths that had ever occurred in the asylum were among those children who were consumptive when received. The Sister says: "Taking good care of the children makes less trouble in the end."

The St. Mary's Boys' Orphan Asylum was incorporated December 24, 1864, under the general law, soon after its organization. It grew out of the following conditions:

"The number of orphan and destitute boys that wandered in the streets of the city, without any one to control or direct them, and the frequent committal of this class to houses of correction, where they were obliged to remain sometimes for years, caused a few citizens to associate themselves into a corporation, having for its object the care of this class of children. The Right Rev. Bishop Timon, the Very Rev. J. Early, and Sister Stanislaus were the prominent projectors. A small house on South street was opened on the 1st of November, 1864, by the Sisters of St. Joseph, Sister Stanislaus being in charge. The number of orphans received the first week was fifteen, and the number steadily increased."

The average number of inmates during the past year was one hundred and forty-one. Six hundred and seventy-four boys have shared the benefits of this institution since its beginning. They are received from three to sixteen years of age. Their average age on the day of visitation was about eleven years. There were one hundred and seventeen in the asylum October 1st, 1875. Of these eighteen were orphans, ninety-four half-orphans, and five had both parents living. Forty-two had native parents, and seventy foreign parents. Seven of them were partially supported by parents or friends, fifty-five wholly by the institution, and fifty-five in part by the city or county. The municipality of Rochester pays one dollar a week for each child committed from the city, which sum, it is said, is far from covering the expenses of their support. Father Early is of the opinion, however, that it is better that the community contribute toward these charities than that the children should be entirely maintained by the city. He says: "The worst idea that you can indoctrinate into a people is that they should not contribute to the Church or to charity." Eighty-three of the boys were from Monroe county; seven from Cayuga; eight from Livingston; six from Cortland; three from Onondaga; three from Seneca, and one each from Genesee, Oneida, Tompkins, Wayne and New York counties. The number of boys received during the year was twenty-eight. Nineteen were returned to parents or guardians, one was transferred to another institution, and four were discharged otherwise.

The total expenditures of the asylum during the year ending September 30, 1875, were $6,442.96. Of this $1,075 was for building and improvements. The total indebtedness of the institution is $16,000, of which $10,000 is upon the real estate.

The results of the inspection of the institution were very satisfactory. It is believed that, aside from the elevating moral influences which the asylum brings to bear upon the young, its work lessens very considerably the public burdens attached to the support of the dependent and criminal classes.

St. Patrick's Female Orphan Asylum.

Rochester.

This Asylum is located on the corner of Frank and Vought streets, in the northerly part of the city. Its objects are "to provide education, maintenance and trades for female orphan children, and to secure for them homes in respectable families."

The origin of the institution is stated by those familiar with its history to be as follows: "The Asylum was established in the year 1842, by the Rev. Bernard O'Reilly, then Pastor of St. Patrick's Church, at a time when there were few such institutions in the western part of the State. This gentleman, alive to the needs of his parish, concluded that in no way could he be of greater benefit to the people among whom he labored than by establishing an institution which would afford a home for destitute orphan girls, where they could be religiously instructed, afforded a good plain education and taught useful trades, by which at maturity they could support and protect themselves.

"The immediate charge of the institution was assumed by the benevolent Sisters of Charity, under the Superiorship of Sister Beatrice, April 9th, 1845. It has been supported by the charity of the compassionate, aided by the liberality of the State, and has passed through many seasons of great financial difficulty."

The Asylum was incorporated by act of the Legislature April 14th, 1845. A portion of the edifice now in use was erected in 1842, and an addition was made to it in 1864. It is a plain brick structure, three stories high above the basement, erected upon a lot seventy feet in front by one hundred and sixty feet in depth. The basement contains both the children's and the Sisters' dining rooms, pantry, store rooms, children's bath room, wash room and coal cellar.

On the first floor are two parlors, two reception rooms for the use of children's friends when visiting them, the school room, the children's infirmary, Sisters' bathing and clothes rooms. On the second floor are the chapel, the Sisters' sitting room, a school room, a play room, and the children's clothes room. The third floor contains the children's dormitories, also the sleeping apartments of the Sisters.

The building is heated by furnace, lighted with gas, supplied with water from the city works, and will suitably accommodate one hundred and fifty inmates. At the date of visitation, September 1st, there were about fifty children in the Asylum, their average age being nine years. They are taken as young as three years old, and kept till they are about fourteen. The Sister in charge says: "The condition of the children on coming to the Asylum shows more mental than physical poverty. The inclinations of many seem to be to evil, and unless restrained by some controlling power they become quite abandoned.

"There is no fixed period for children to remain at the Asylum. Some stay only a week, others a few months, and others again six, seven, or even eight years. No children are given out unless upon the application of one of our priests. The responsibility then devolves upon him to see that the child is protected. If the influences around her are not such as they ought to be, the Asylum is open for her return. Our success in putting out children has been very great. Some, of course, have fallen away, as will always happen, but the majority have done well. Of late years, we have been more careful to whom we give our children. The persons that formerly applied for children were of a class that had no good homes of their own. This class is now diminishing. There is not such a demand for children as heretofore. When the proper time comes for their disposition, those of the children who wish to learn trades are sent to the Industrial School, under the charge of Sister Hieronymo, the others go out to work. They stay in this institution long enough to get through the common branches of education, but not long enough to learn trades.

They do all the housework, make, mend and wash their own clothes. It requires a careful supervision to render the children orderly, as fully five-eighths are of parents who have neglected their duty to their families. We never use corporal punishment, but discipline by giving additional work and by separating offenders from their playmates. At other times it serves as a punishment, if they are made to work alone. We never deprive them of their food. Singing forms a part of the system of instruction."

A select school was formerly conducted on the premises, but at present the labors of the Sisters are devoted exclusively to the care of the orphan and destitute who come under their charge.

In the infirmary we found one little girl, suffering from heart disease. She had just recovered from an attack of spotted fever. Three deaths had occurred in the Asylum during the year.

The bath-room is furnished with three bathing tubs. Each child has a separate wash bowl, made of tin, and resting in a long wooden sink; also a separate towel and a bag for her combs. The children, it was stated, as a rule, bathe once a week and often twice. The dormitories were furnished with single, wooden bedsteads; the mattresses were of straw, and the counterpanes of snowy whiteness. The Sisters think there is no more trouble in keeping wooden bedsteads clean than iron ones. They say that they find the use of a little insect powder very effectual in keeping away vermin. Two Sisters sleep in each dormitory, one at each end of the room.

The girls do not dress uniformly, except on holidays.

The laundry and bakery are separate from the main building.

The play ground is spacious and paved with brick.

At the date of October 1, there were eighty girls in the institution. Twelve were orphans, fifty half-orphans, and eighteen had both parents living; five were of native parents and seventy-five of foreign. They were from the following counties: Forty-nine from Monroe, thirteen from Livingston, eight from Cayuga, three from Ontario, and three from Seneca. Twelve of the children were supported partially by parents or friends, forty-three by the city and by counties, and twenty-five wholly by the institution. Twenty-five children were received during the past year, thirty-five returned to parents or guardians, and two were otherwise discharged.

Nine hundred and ninety-six children have been received in this institution, and shared its benefits since its organization. So great a work of Christian benevolence speaks its own praise for the reverend founder of the Asylum, and the Sisters in charge, who have borne the burden of the labor.

The entire expenditures of the Asylum during the year ending September 30, 1875, were $4,074.37. Its total indebtedness is $3,000.

Western House of Refuge.

Rochester.

This large institution, established by the authority of the State, for the reformation of Juvenile delinquents, and opened in the month of August, 1848, is so well known through the comprehensive annual reports of its officials, that little, perhaps, can be added to the general stock of information regarding it. The work it is carrying on, however, is of so important a character, that a few notes taken during two of several lengthy visits, may not be out of place.

The Western House of Refuge is situated in the northern part of the city of Rochester. At the time of its establishment, it was without the city limits. The subsequent growth of the city, however, has brought it within the corporation, and it is now being fast surrounded with suburban improvements. The building stands within a walled inclosure, having a street frontage of five hundred feet, and a depth of six hundred and fifty. It is about one hundred feet from the front wall, and shade and ornamental trees embellish the intervening space. Twelve acres in the rear of the walled inclosure are surrounded by a stockade, and devoted to garden purposes.

Boys are received between the ages of seven and sixteen, the average age being about fourteen years. They are detained till the age of twenty-one, unless their good behavior entitles them to an earlier discharge. The greater proportion are committed for petty larceny, but some for graver offenses. By authority of the Legislature, boys from Monroe county may be committed to the Refuge for vagrancy.

The institution is controlled by a Board of Managers, appointed by the Governor, by and with the advice and consent of the Senate, and its current expenses, aside from its earnings, are met by annual appropriations from the State treasury. The title to the property is vested in the State. The institution is under the immediate charge of Mr. Levi S. Fulton, Superintendent.

On the dates of visitation, September 2d and 3d, the Refuge was not filled to its capacity. It then contained about four hundred and twenty-five inmates, but one hundred and twenty-five more could have been accommodated. From the Superintendent, the following information was obtained: Each boy, on entering the institution, is numbered and registered in a book, provided for that purpose. There are also entered in this book his age, weight, height, color of his eyes and hair, complexion, education, occupation, residence, previous arrests, if any, whether ever before in any refuge, reformatory or poorhouse; whether he has step-father or step-mother, and, if so, their habits; the religion and occupation of family; if any one of them was ever arrested, or ever in prison or almshouse; the name and business of the father or mother, or whomsoever he would like to have the Superintendent communicate with in case of sickness. One page of the book is devoted to the record of the subsequent facts ascertained regarding the boy. If he is committed a second time, further entries are made on the same page. A record of the standing of each one is kept, from which the status of any boy is made out for his friends or relatives. The Superintendent says: "We keep no record of the boy's career after he leaves, unless it is of a very interesting character, when we put it in our record." The record having been completed, the boy is then sent to the lavatory with a printed ticket, stating his name and house division, and the shop to which he is assigned. A circular is then sent to the parents or friends of the boy, notifying them of his commitment to the institution; also of the character of the Refuge, its objects; the treatment and discipline adopted for the boys; the rules of the house with regard to visiting days, and especially with regard to the kind of reading matter which the friends of the boys are allowed to send them.

A systematic plan is adopted in the House for the daily routine of even the minutest matters. The Superintendent says: "I always send an order written on a blank form for every thing. If a party comes here, and wants to see a boy, I fill out a blank ticket or order directing the boy to be sent to the waiting room. In the same way, when I want a boy dressed to go home, I also fill a blank order and send it to the shop for him. We give them a citizen's suit of clothes when they go out. We do not give them a trunk. When a boy has attained the standing that entitles him to go home, we send a circular to his friends or parents, notifying them of the fact, and also intimating that by forwarding money to pay his fare and furnishing satisfactory evidence of the home being of such a character that the boy will have constant employment, he will be sent on without delay. We have a blank form that is sent with this letter, to be signed by the county judge, or the police magistrate, which is designed to be a guarantee that the home to which the boy is sent is a suitable one. It certifies that the head of the house sustains a good moral character, is of temperate and industrious habits, and has a good home. We use two sorts of blank forms; one if the boy has parents, the other if he has only friends. If a parent comes and wants to get his son, we fill out a form and send it with him to the discharging committee. The form shows that the boy has attained the requisite standing to entitle him to dismissal. He is then discharged, if the committee see fit.

"We do not bind out boys, because they have an aversion to being bound. If we find places for them, we intrust them to the care of suitable persons during good behavior. Very often boys are not satisfied, and come back. We do not require the parties who take boys to report, but I think there should be some system of that kind. We hear from them very frequently."

The Superintendent, on being asked how the boys turned out, as a general rule, replied: "Some of our boys have turned out finely. Prejudice makes men say, 'A boy comes out of the Refuge worse than he goes in.' But here is a boy who leaves the House of Refuge, and turns out splendidly, makes a good citizen, and is as good a workman as can be found. You hear nothing said about him. Ten such do not make any noise, but the eleventh gets into some scrape and is arrested. He is examined and punished, and a great outcry is made against the House of Refuge. Take the boys we have here now, a large majority of them have been sadly neglected. They never had proper training at home, nor any proper home influences surrounding them. Many boys come here fourteen and fifteen years old, who do not even know their letters. It is not to be expected that we can take these boys and turn them all out unexceptionably good. Because some of them go out and lapse into crime, is it just to say that the House of Refuge is doing no good?"

On being asked his views as to the proper method of treating such cases of boys as are found to be incorrigible, he said: "My own idea is this. I would make this a military school. There is a certain class of boys that will grow up criminals and fill our State prisons. Some are born perverse; it is bred in the bone. They cannot help stealing, and steal they will unless held in check. This class I would drill into military habits. When I found boys of this class, I would take special pains to have them acquire a taste for military life. When this taste is acquired it is very natural for them to enlist. By the adoption of such a course they would not only be saved from crime, but be enabled to render good service to their country." In regard to discipline, the Superintendent says: "I find a system of rewards and punishments works admirably.

"No boy is discharged unless his standing in the house entitles him to go. No influence of any kind can avail. I do not think there is an institution in the world where the managers stand up against political influence like this. The boys know that they are placed here on their good behavior.

"Each boy has a badge of a certain grade. When a boy deserves punishment we change his badge. A boy would rather be flogged than have his badge changed. Sometimes if a boy does any thing mean on the play ground, if he uses obscene language, we let him stay in the shop and deprive him of play for a certain length of time. When this punishment does not suffice, we have a dormitory where a boy can see to read, but cannot look out. We shut him up here for a short time, and have his food brought to him. In extraordinary cases we use the rod. There are cases where you cannot reach a boy except through the skin. When this is necessary it is done privately, so that no other boy knows any thing about it. Should a boy come to me and say I have been 'straight' for so long, and ask to be allowed the time he has lost, I tell him if he does not retrograde during sixteen weeks I will promise to restore the week he has lost. Another then comes in and wants the same favor. They nearly always come back at the end of the sixteen weeks."

The badge system will be better understood by giving the following rules provided by the Discharging Committee:

"A record shall be kept of the conduct of every inmate of the House, in a book designated as the 'Badge Book,' in which No. 1 indicates correct deportment for the week. Any violation of the rules of the House shall be indicated by Nos. 2, 3 and 4, according to the magnitude of the offense. A book shall also be kept in which record shall be made, stating what the offense was for which a change from No. 1 was made.

"Any inmate of the House continuing in Grade No. 1 for sixteen weeks in succession shall be advanced to the First Class of Honor, and wear a badge indicating his standing. This badge, for the First Division, is a copper shield, with the words 'Western House of Refuge,' 'Onward,' across its face; for the Second Division it is a brass shield, with the words 'Western House of Refuge,' 'Onward,' on its face.

"Any member of the First Class of Honor, continuing in Grade No. 1 a second period of sixteen weeks in succession, shall be advanced to the Second Class of Honor, and wear a badge indicating his standing. This badge, for the First Division, is a brass shield, with words 'Western House of Refuge,' 'Upward,' across its face; for the Second Division, it is a German silver shield, with a copper coat of arms of the State of New York in the center of its face, surrounded by the words 'Western House of Refuge,' 'Upward.'

"Any member of the Second Class of Honor continuing in grade No. 1 a third period of sixteen weeks in succession, shall be advanced to the Third Class of Honor, and wear a badge indicating his standing. This badge for the First Division is a German silver shield, with the words 'Western House of Refuge, Excelsior,' across its face; for the Second Division, it is a German silver shield, with a silver coat of arms of the State of New York in the center of its face, surrounded by the words 'Western House of Refuge,' 'Excelsior.'

"This is the highest or graduating class, and until attained, no application for discharge of the inmate will be entertained by the Discharging Committee.

"Any member of the Third Class of Honor continuing in grade No. 1 a fourth period of sixteen weeks in succession, shall be advanced to the Fourth Class of Honor, and wear a badge indicating his standing, and shall be entitled to his discharge from the House when a proper home is provided for him, subject to the approval of the Discharging Committee. This badge is of oriode, round, a figure four in the center of its face, surrounded by the words 'Western House of Refuge, Class Four,' and entitles the wearer to go to the tailor's shop to be measured for a suit of clothes, to be made and in readiness for him to wear out when such home is provided.

"Any member of the Third Class of Honor, entitled to his discharge, must remain No. 1 until a suitable home is provided for him and he be discharged. If for any violation of the rules of the house, his grade is changed from No. 1, he must regain his standing by remaining No. 1 another period of sixteen weeks in succession, before he can be discharged.

"Every offense committed by any member of either of the "Classes of Honor, whereby his grade will be changed from No. 1, must be reported in full, in writing, to the Superintendent, who will investigate the charges, and either forgive the offense or direct a change of grade from No. 1, as he may deem for the greatest good of the inmate and for the best interests of the institution.

"For gross or continued misconduct on the part of any member of either "Class of Honor," his badge may be taken from him at the discretion of the Superintendent."

"Once in a while," the Superintendent says, "we have a boy who loses self respect. I have now a boy seventeen years old who can never get higher than his third badge. He is always falling back."

The partition wall dividing the large yard was originally intended to enable a classification of the boys to be made, according to their moral character. This classification is not maintained under the present system, but one separating the older from the younger boys is substituted.

The outer walls are of stone, eighteen feet high in front and twenty-two in the rear. They are four feet six inches thick at the bottom, and twenty inches at the top, perpendicular on the inside and buttressed on the outward face. Notwithstanding this apparently impossible barrier, the Superintendent informed us that on a recent occasion a very homesick little fellow, finding that neither tears nor entreaties could undo the inexorable bolts about him, had actually scaled the wall, "running up its side like a squirrel."

The Superintendent, on being asked if he thought any changes could be made in the present system, for the better, said: "I think it would be well to have rooms nicely furnished for boys who had proved themselves worthy. I could then hold them out as an inducement to the others to try and earn them by good behavior. Those not thus favored would see the difference made, and I could say to them 'you know why we give these boys those rooms, and when your merits are such as to deserve them, you shall have them too.' I would also make a distinction in their tables. I would have the best boys sit at a table by themselves, like a family, with two of their number to carve. I could, in the same manner as above, explain to the other boys why I made the distinction, thus giving them an additional incentive to work up. I would further allow the best boys to go up town occasionally to church, to attend a meeting or a lecture."

Routine of day's duties.—"The bell rings at five o'clock in the morning, when the boys rise and make their beds. At five-fifteen they go to the bath-room; at five-thirty to the school-room; at seven they march to the breakfast table; and at eight o'clock to the workshop, where they remain till half-past ten, when they have a recess.

They then work till twelve; after which they march to dinner. At one o'clock they march back to the work-shops, and work till three o'clock. They then take a recess for ten minutes, or, if their tasks are done, they are at liberty the rest of the afternoon. Those having unfinished tasks must work till half-past four, when supper is ready. Supper over, all may play until six, when they march to school. After school and closing exercises they have prayers in the school-room, and are then paraded and marched to bed. In winter the boys do not rise as early as in summer."

Industries.— About one hundred and twenty boys are employed in the shoe-making department, the same number in the cane-making, and about twenty-five in the tailoring department. The Superintendent says: "We have a room for making and mending stockings, sheets, pillow cases and towels. Every boy we have is capable of doing something, and all are tasked according to their ability."

Near the door within the entrance to the chair factory is a little fountain, which, with its cooling spray, refreshes one upon entering from the walled yard on a hot summer's day. Small boys were here at work. Each seat is secured in a clamp adjusted to an upright standard, at the proper height for a boy. About sixteen boys do flagging. The rest cane seats.

The work done in the tailoring department is all for the house. The boys dress alike, and wear a dark grey uniform.

In the shoe shop the Superintendent regulates the tasks. "Very little talking is allowed during work, but when the boys get through they can go into the yard and make as much noise as they please." They work "in teams." The cutting and lasting are done in one room, the finishing off in another.

At the time of the visitation made by the President of this Board, together with Commissioner Anderson and the Secretary, in 1868, the expediency of abolishing the contract system was under consideration. It is, however, yet maintained to some extent. The Superintendent says: "You must either be a manufacturer or have a contract system. We are in advance of what we were formerly, yet we still have it. I put one of our officers in every shop, and no man there is allowed to reprimand our boys. This is the only contract we have, and it is, I think, made with an excellent man. There are twelve instructors in this department. One of these, a woman, gives instruction on the sewing machine. We have about one hundred and twenty boys working under contract."

School Rooms.— The school rooms are in each wing and are large, being composed of four adjoining rooms, separated by sliding doors, and are thrown into one room for opening and closing exercises. They are fitted up with modern school furniture. Among the many mottoes on the walls is that from Pope: "Order is Heaven's First Law." Every boy goes to school three hours and a half daily. The institution possesses a spacious chapel where religious services are held; for the Catholic children by the Catholic chaplain, and for the Protestant children by the Protestant chaplain.

In the band room we found twenty boys practicing on cornet-band instruments, under the instruction of a band master. They seemed to have attained creditable proficiency. The oldest boy was about eighteen, the youngest twelve. The band is permitted, under proper supervision, to go to the city on certain occasions; sometimes on the invitation of citizens. The boys, it is said, behave well. At such times they wear a navy blue uniform, and have a wagon appropriated to their use.

At all meals the boys are marched into the dining rooms in double columns, arms folded and cap in hand, headed by martial bands. Military precision is observed in their marching to and seating themselves at the table. The following form of grace is in use: "We thank Thee, our Heavenly Father, for these gifts of Thy promise, and for this expression of Thy kindness. May Thy mercy keep us to Thyself through Jesus Christ our Lord. Amen." The meal consisted of soup, fish, corn, potatoes and bread. The boys, it is said, have all they want, and appearances certainly warranted the statement. The dining room was adorned with pictures and mottoes, and the table was well furnished with table cloths, plates, knives, forks, spoons, water bowls, salt cellars, spice boxes, etc.

The bakery contains a brick oven, in which a batch of about five hundred loaves of bread can be baked at once. On Saturdays, ginger bread is baked for the inmates.

The kitchen is large, the cooking being done by steam. A patent machine is used for chopping meat for hash. It minces twenty-five pounds at a time.

The bath rooms are about one hundred feet long, by thirty wide. They contain stone vats about eighteen by twenty-four feet, and three and a half feet deep. They are heated by pipes passing around the bottom. Another pipe, with fifty jets of water, runs around the inner margin of the vats. The boys stand outside and wash in the jets of water. Every Saturday afternoon, summer and winter, the boys bathe in the vats. A conspicuous motto in this room is: "Cleanliness is next to Godliness."

The boys' dormitories are on long halls with tiers of cells, five hundred and sixty in all, well built, heated by steam and furnished with iron bedsteads. Each door has a strong iron hasp with a padlock. The boys are locked in at night.

The hospital contains nine iron bedsteads, with hair mattresses, and has a bath room and water closet adjoining. We found in it one little boy who had hurt his ankle in the shop. He had been an inmate thirteen or fourteen weeks. There was another who had sprained his ankle jumping. The Superintendent says: "We had only one case of scarlet fever last year, although it was in the families all around the place. Two boys died during the year, one of scarlet fever and the other in an epileptic fit. We have a boy here now who is subject to these fits. We discharged him once, but were forced to take him again by order of the Court.

The washing for the whole establishment is done in three patent cylindrical washing machines. One of the machines is for sudsing the clothes, another is for boiling them, and the third for rinsing. The machines are run by steam power; the drying is also done by steam. The washing is all done by three boys, in two days. The ironing room is about twenty-four feet square; the mangling is done by three of the boys.

The large garden of the institution was found to be in excellent order, not a weed being visible. It supplies all the vegetables used. The garden is sub-drained, the work having been done by the boys.

Eight cows are kept, which yield barely milk enough for the coffee made in the Refuge.

The institution possesses an extensive piggery, which, on the day of visitation, contained about sixty or seventy pigs, and some seventy good-sized hogs. This is conveniently arranged, not only with reference to the proper care of the animals, but to convenience in feeding and slaughtering. The refuse of the kitchen is carried from its repository to each pen upon a tramway. This feature of the establishment, so far from being repulsive, as it is apt to be, through neglect, was quite interesting, from its evidence of thrift and cleanliness.

The closets adjoining the large yards were in excellent condition. They are peculiar in their construction, and are deemed worthy the attention of the managers of large institutions. They embody the principle of earth closets, and their product is utilized, being conveyed to the compost heap by means of a truck and tramway.

In regard to the employés of the institution the Superintendent remarks: "We require all to have a good moral character, and to be of temperate habits — that is to say, strictly temperate. The use of tobacco is forbidden on the premises. The boys will even smell it. They will all chew if they get a chance. With ten plugs of tobacco you could buy any thing of them. I once took a wad out of a boy's bosom containing over a pound. An affectionate mother sent it to her son in the bosom of his shirt. Another mother once wrote to me to furnish her boy with tobacco, the boy not being over eleven or twelve years of age. Mothers will smuggle it in to their children. Every visiting day plenty of it may be found in the yard."

The Superintendent, on being asked if he had ever known the boys to conspire against him, said: "We never have had any organized conspiracy but once, three months after I came. The plan was to tell the patrolman that some one wanted to come in at the back gate, and when he was unlocking it to knock him down and escape. They were armed with knives; a large number refused to obey the officers. I asked the leader to come to me. He at first declined, but at last came. I took him into the office and examined him and examined them all one by one, and they gave up their knives. In the evening, after school, I went in and talked to them. I went to the Executive Committee and had three of the older ones sent to the penitentiary. None of the boys have since had any idea of harming an instructor or an officer. In this case a boy disclosed the plot, as they always will.

"In the spring the boys have great sport with kite flying. They make the kites themselves out of strips of newspapers. The boys in one yard will send up a kite, then those in the other yard send up theirs; the kites become entangled, and one is captured, when the triumphant party are very jubilant.

"The boys also play base ball in the proper season, and have several clubs; among which are the Red and Blue Stockings, and the Spider club. The latter wear a blue spider on their shirts. The Fly club have a red fly for their badge. Another club is called the Excelsior; another the Star. The boys play scientifically, keeping well posted in the latest changes in the game. I believe as much in boys playing well as in their working well. Every Saturday evening for some time they have had games with outside clubs. In fourteen games out of fifteen our boys beat. In cold weather the boys indulge in foot ball and in skating."

The average number of inmates during the year ending December 31, 1875, was about four hundred and four. The total expenditures of the Refuge were \$77,921.45; of which \$64,796.37 was for current expenses. Its real estate comprises forty-two acres of land, which originally cost \$4,200. Its present value, however, is estimated at \$200,000, and that of the buildings at \$165,150.

A visit to this institution impresses one with its orderly and business-like management, and the perfect system which pervades every department. The marching and other movements of the boys are performed with military precision, and with evident pride in excelling in all they do. The school is an admirable one, and is conducted by an efficient corps of teachers.

The Female Reformatory.— By act, chapter 228, passed May 1, 1875, the powers of the Refuge were enlarged to include girls as well as boys, and an appropriation of \$75,000 was made to erect a separate building for them, with a capacity for one hundred inmates. Section five of said act provides that "no part of the moneys hereby appropriated shall be paid by the Comptroller until plans for the erection of the building shall have been presented and approved by the said managers, and a contract made for the erection thereof, at a total cost of not more than $75,000, which contract shall stipulate to complete the building ready for occupancy at once, and without further outlay." Section seven of said act reads as follows: "The managers and Superintendent shall receive and take into said house of refuge all female children under the age of sixteen who shall be legally committed to said House of Refuge as vagrants, or on a conviction of any criminal offense, by any court having authority to make such commitments. The said managers shall have power to place the said children committed to their care, during the minority of such children, at such employments, and cause them to be instructed in such branches of useful knowledge as shall be suitable to their years and capacities; and they shall have power, in their discretion, to bind out the said children, with their consent, as apprentices or servants, during their minority, to such persons and at such places, to learn such proper trades and employment, as in their judgment will be most for the reformation and the future benefit and advantage of such children, provided that the charge and power of said managers, upon and over said female children, shall not extend beyond the age of eighteen years."

The ground on which the edifice is being erected adjoins the Refuge for boys on the south side. It is to be walled in. The building is to be constructed of brick, with a foundation length of two hundred and seventy-three and a half feet, and an average width of about fifty feet. It is intended to combine all modern improvements, and to accommodate one hundred inmates. A matron, a first assistant, two teachers, a dress-maker, a cook and a laundress will be employed in this department. In view of its objects it is intended to secure, at whatever pains, in this department, the very best executive ability, and those specially adapted to reformatory work. The building is expected to be completed and opened for the reception of inmates in or about the month of June, 1876.

Central New York Institution for Deaf Mutes.

Rome.

This institution, organized in April, 1875, is situated at 114 Madison street. The circumstances which led to its establishment, its aims and workings, may be best shown by using the language of the principal, Mr. Alphonso Johnson:

"The need of the existence of our institution has long been felt. The three institutions heretofore established are situated near the borders of the State, two in New York city and one in Buffalo ; and while they have never lacked for pupils, the offered privileges having been availed of by hundreds, still the expense incurred by sending children long distances to school, not to mention the natural reluctance of parents and friends to be so far separated from them at a tender age, has caused a large number, especially in the central portion of the State, to remain at home altogether, or defer going till an age when the advantage is not so great. Thus they lose wholly or in part an education which is of comparatively more importance to them than to those in full possession of their faculties, as avenues of knowledge, that are closed to the deaf, are open to the hearing outside of school-houses and institutions of learning. In view of these facts it was concluded that the establishment of an institution in the central part of the State was what was required. Rome was selected as the most desirable location, it being accessible by the New York Central and Rome, Watertown and Ogdensburgh railroads.

"The citizens of Rome subscribed the sum of $6,000 toward establishing the institution. We started on the 22d of March last with four pupils, which number has increased to fifty-one up to this date."

The regular term of instruction is limited to five years, but the Superintendent of Public Instruction is authorized, at his discretion, to extend the term of any pupil for a period not exceeding three years.

The system of instruction pursued in this institution is the one known as the "combined method," more properly called the "improved method." It consists in imparting instruction to the deaf mutes by means of the sign language and the manual alphabet, and in teaching them articulation and lip-reading.

At the date of visitation the institution had about thirty-five pupils, seventeen boys and eighteen girls. The youngest was a little boy not quite six years of age. The oldest was nineteen years. The principal had the certificates of twenty-two more who were shortly expected.

An examination of the school and methods of instruction left the impression that it was in charge of faithful and enthusiastic teachers.

There were fifty-one pupils in the institution on the 1st of October. Of these two were orphans, twelve half-orphans, and thirty-seven had both parents living. Forty-three were of native parentage, and eight of foreign. Thirteen were from Oneida county, six from Onondaga, from Oswego and Herkimer counties each four, from Cayuga, Chautauqua and Madison each three, from Chemung, Lewis, Jefferson, Washington and Wayne each two, and from Broome, Cattaraugus, Monroe, Orleans and Yates each one. Twenty were chargeable to counties or towns, thirty to the State, and one was supported by friends.

The Home for Christian Care.

Sing Sing.

The Home for Christian Care was incorporated by an act of the Legislature, May 6th, 1874. It is located on a farm of forty acres, donated to the institution, pleasantly situated on the Hudson river, two miles from Sing Sing, and one and a half miles from Pleasantville Station, on the Harlem Railroad. Upon the farm is a commodious dwelling-house. The house was opened for the reception of children January 10, 1874. At the time of our visit to the Superintendent there were fourteen children in the Home under the care of a Matron or House Mother, assisted by her daughter.

The object of the Home is stated by its Superintendent, the Rev. B. B. Leacock, to be as follows:

"Our work begins as a reformatory for neglected and vicious children, and a training school for teachers, nurses, Bible readers and other agencies for benevolent work. We propose to stretch forth a helping hand to the homeless and degraded children that crowd our streets and fill our prisons, and to try upon them the effects of the wholesome, loving discipline of a Christian home. To do this we desire to gather such children as may come under our care into families of about twelve. Each family will occupy its own house. At its head there will be experienced Christian persons, who will hold to the children the relations of father and mother. Associated with them will be several younger men or women, who have devoted themselves to the Lord's work. They will hold to the children the relations of elder brothers and sisters, and through them much of the work of reformation it is hoped will be accomplished. They will have intimate intercourse with the children at all times, be helpers to them in their studies, work and play, and by their example, counsel and admonitions will be insensibly reclaiming these lost ones, and recalling them to the paths of virtue and holiness.

"The means relied upon for effecting this are two-fold. First, removal from the impure atmosphere of the city to the pure, invigorating air of the country. Second, removal from the contaminating influences of their old life to the elevating influences of the Christian home.

"The family at the Home do their own work. In this family are mixed the boys and girls. As soon as we get more means we intend to enlarge the work by building additional houses for families of twelve or fourteen. The influence of the family upon the children is excellent. Many of the children on coming here had the worst of habits, and were addicted to the use of bad language. After a while they were, through the influence of the Home, cured of these, and show now a marked improvement."

In a recent report we find it stated that during the preceding year sixty applications had been made for admission, out of which only sixteen children had been received into the Home, the larger number being rejected because of the lack of accommodations.

The conception of institutions of this kind, having in view the proper training and reformation of homeless and degraded children, under the family system, in the country, is a noble one, and it is to be hoped that the enterprise will fully meet the sanguine expectations of its benevolent projectors.

The Society for the Relief of Destitute Children of Seamen.

West New Brighton (Staten Island).

This asylum is located on the grounds of the Sailors' Snug Harbor, on Castleton avenue. It was organized by several ladies whose attention had been called to the destitute condition of the families of seamen, and in the spring of 1846, an effort was made to provide an asylum for the children of these families who neither came under the head of orphans nor half-orphans. The first house occupied was at Stapleton, Staten Island, and four children were provided for at its commencement.

At the date of visitation, October 21st, we found the children assembled for evening worship. Their average age was about nine years. There were one hundred inmates in the institution, about half of whom were girls.

The children sang very sweetly for us, "Sweet Hour of Prayer."

From the Matron, Miss Drew, we obtained the following information: "We take none but seamen's children. We keep them till they are fourteen years old, when we put them out in homes where it will be convenient for us to visit them. We first put them out on three months' trial, after which papers are signed. We have been very successful in getting homes for our children, especially for the girls. We can accommodate one hundred and twenty. We receive children from two years of age upward. The boys work in the garden during the summer, in which they have flower beds of their own. We teach both boys and girls to sew. The boys sew two afternoons in the week in school, but the girls oftener. The boys are taught to make their own beds, sweep their own rooms and take care of them. We teach our girls to do all kinds of housework; one, about fifteen years old, can bake as nice bread as any housekeeper.

"The best homes for girls are in farmers' families. We do not want them to go out as servants, though we want them to be taught to work. But if they go out as servants, they have to mingle with others who are inferior in character. We make it a point to visit children when placed in homes within visiting distance, and we have a committee who make it their special business to correspond with them after going from here."

The working force of the establishment consists of a matron, three teachers, a care-taker, two seamstresses, two laundresses, a dining room girl, two nurses, two cooks, a gardener and a woman for cleaning — sixteen in all.

A school is taught on the premises, and the younger children attend a *kindergarten*. The Matron says, "the time spent in the *kindergarten* is the happiest period of the day. We get no aid from the county or other public sources. The children are all healthy. We have not a sick child in the house, nor have we had any deaths during the year. We immediately separate the children who are complaining, from the others, when any sickness breaks out. Three years ago we had scarlet fever in the house, but did not lose a child."

The institution possesses a very nice children's library of three or four hundred volumes. "The children go to church every Sunday morning, and attend Sabbath School on the premises in the afternoon at three o'clock. Teachers from outside come in, and are quite regular in attendance. We have a Superintendent who has been here a long time."

The children bathe every Saturday, and wash in running water.

In the dining room were tables and benches. Crockery plates, mugs, knives and forks are used, and the Matron says: "We would like to have chairs."

The dormitories were furnished with iron bedsteads and straw mattresses.

Nine hundred and ninety-three children have shared the benefits of this institution since its organization. The number of children received during the year ending September 30, 1875, was thirty-one. The number placed out by indenture two, and the number returned to parents or guardians, eighteen. There were in the institution October 1, 1875, twelve orphans, fifty-eight half-orphans, and sixty-one children having both parents living. Mrs. J. S. Lowell, the Secretary, says: "Such of the parents as are deemed to be able to contribute toward the support of the children are charged fifty cents per week. There are only a few cases, however, in which that amount s regularly paid."

The total expenditures of the institution during the year were $10,571.11. The value of its invested fund is $14,600.

The class of children coming under the care of this institution are those particularly in need of the help of the benevolent. Left to neglect the consequences are disastrous to society. The work in which the ladies are here engaged is deserving of hearty encouragement. During the past year the invested funds of the Society have been encroached upon, two of its legacies having been disbursed. This was done rather than turn the children away. We were informed that the managers will be obliged to reduce their work still more unless liberal support is forthcoming.

The institution is thought to be well managed, and the children are under elevating influences. It is to be hoped that the attention of the benevolent will be more generally directed toward this worthy charity.

Society of St. Johnland.

St. Johnland, Long Island.

The objects of this Society are—

"*First.* To provide cheap and comfortable homes, together with the means of social and moral improvement, for deserving families from among the working classes, particularly of the city of New York, and such as can carry on their work at St. Johnland; but this provision shall never be used for pecuniary emolument, either to the Society or to any of the agents in its employ.

"*Second.* To maintain a home for aged men in destitute circumstances, especially Communicants, who are deemed entitled to it by the churches to which they belong; to care for friendless children and youths, and especially cripples, by giving them a home, schooling, Christian training, and some trade or occupation by which they can earn their future livelihood; and, generally, to do such other Christian offices as shall from time to time be required, and are practicable by the Society, consistently with its benevolent designs.

"*Third.* To assist indigent boys and young men who desire literary education, with a view to the Gospel ministry, by affording them the opportunity for such education, and at the same time means of self-support by some useful employment. An Evangelical school or college, chiefly for training for the ministry, would come within the scope of the Society.

"*Lastly,* and as embracing its whole, to give form and practical application to the principles of brotherhood in Christ, in an organized congregation or parish, constituted by settled residents of St. Johnland."

St. Johnland is situated on the north shore of Long Island, about forty miles east of New York. It is reached by the Port Jefferson branch of the Long Island Railroad, from Hunter's Point, opposite East Thirty-fourth street, New York. The ride of a mile and a half which must be taken to reach the settlement from St. Johnland station, is a pleasant one, upon a dry road, and affords delightful glimpses of the Sound in the distance. Trees border the highway on either side, prominent among which are the oak and cedar. The latter, in addition to the pleasing effect of contrasted color, particularly noticeable at the time of our visit on the 25th of October, made the air redolent with agreeable perfume.

The view of St. Johnland is abruptly and delightfully presented to the eye upon a near approach to the settlement. The private driveway connecting it with the main road passes a small sheet of water, shaded by large trees and enlivened by aquatic fowls.

The original building of St. Johnland, formerly an old farm house, has by artistic hands been wrought into a bower of sweetness. At the time of visitation the inclosure in front was filled with flowers and fragrant herbs, the porch graced with creepers and flowering plants, and the house within was one of order without stiffness. The outlook from here, upon the commodious buildings of the settlement, scattered here and there upon the slope facing southward and adorned with shrubbery and patriarchal oaks, upon the shady grove of pine, still higher and back of the buildings, affording a fine standpoint from which to scan the wide extent of water beyond was, in view of the objects which prompted the selection and beautifying of this settlement, quite inspiring.

In a recent report of its esteemed and venerable founder, Rev. W. A. Muhlenberg, D. D., the following interesting allusion to its origin is found: "The enterprise was first presented to the public in an imaginary account of it as in successful operation. This was done in the form of two letters, supposed to be written by one who had made a visit to the place when it was some ten or twelve years old. This 'Retro-prospectus,' as it was called, attracted considerable attention as, at least, an entertaining ideal, and some became so much interested in it as to supply the means for beginning its realization."

In October, 1865, after much search in various directions for a suitable locality, a farm was found in Suffolk county, on the north shore of Long Island, about five miles east of the town of Northport, in the purchase of which eight* benevolently disposed gentlemen took a share.

The estate comprises five hundred and sixty-five acres, two hundred and twenty-five of which are arable land, the remainder, woodland and salt meadow.

The property was originally in "an extremely neglected and impaired condition; the first steps in improvement were to restore and renovate it; to convert the dilapidated old farmhouse into a comfortable habita-

---

*** Robert B. Minturn, William H. Aspinwall, Adam Norrie, John Caswell, Percy R. Pyne, John H. Swift, J. F. Sheafe, Franklin Randolph.**

tion, since enlarged into what is now called the Mansion; to repair and add to the farm buildings; to fence in and fertilize the tillable land, and lay out vegetable grounds, etc.

"Husbandry did not enter much into the original plans of the work; but with so many prospective mouths to fill, so much available land could not be allowed to lie fallow. What was possible in the way of agriculture was attended to."

The Society of St. Johnland was incorporated in 1870.

On the day of visitation we found about one hundred and thirty-five children in the place, about equal proportions of boys and girls. One of the buildings is called the "Spencer and Wolfe Home," being given by the ladies whose names it bears, Mrs. C. L. Spencer and Mrs. Catherine Wolfe. The cost of this Home was $7,500, all of which sum these ladies subscribed. There were here forty-two children, ranging in ages from three to fifteen. The Home, with about an acre of land, is inclosed with a picket fence, painted green. It has a great apple tree in front. A little porch is at its entrance covered with morning glory and rambling creepers. Flowers in pots were cherished beneath it, flower culture being one of the amusements of the larger girls. The house is fitted up with dormitories, dining room, bath rooms, and all conveniences. The dormitories are furnished with iron bedsteads, clean white counterpanes and pillow cases, mattresses of straw and husks. Cribs are provided for the babies. Careful provision is made for dolls in a toy house, where are to be found chairs for the dolls to rest their limp and broken limbs upon. In the dining room of this Home the children were partaking of their mid-day meal. They were variously dressed, and seated like a family around a table covered with a snow-white cloth. The room was brightened with pictures of home life, and looked out upon a yard radiant with the bloom of flowers, in the culture of which the children had rendered assistance, the whole presenting a happy sight. "This house provides all things necessary for the comfort and education of the children, most of them former patients of the Children's Ward in St. Luke's Hospital, and brought hither when no longer amenable to surgical treatment. As they become old enough they are transferred to either the Boys' House or the Grown Girls' Department, and taught type-setting or some other occupation whereby they may hereafter support themselves."

West of this is the Boys' House, a frame cottage one story and a half high. It is likewise inclosed with a green picket fence, and accommodates about thirty-six boys, varying in age from twelve to eighteen. A very large oak tree stands on the lawn in front of this house; a flower bed is on each side of the porch, and numerous flower-pots on the porch. In the library, which is used during the day for a school room, is a large photograph of Master John R. Chisholm, a memorial put up by his mother, who built and furnished the cottage at a cost of $8,000. This cottage also contains a school room for the middle and infant classes. The upper part of the cottage is devoted to dormitories. These are furnished with iron bedsteads and the ordinary furniture, including chairs. Each bed has two mattresses. The refectory is in the basement. There is also a place here for the boys' clothing, combs, etc., each boy having a little cupboard. The house is warmed by a furnace and lighted by kerosene. The ceilings are high and supported by iron posts. The Superintendent, Frederick Bridden, and his family, reside here. A brass band, with eight performers, is made up from among the inmates.

The closets are outside the building. Back of the house is a swing.

The printing office is a large two-story frame building. The type setting and printing are done on the first floor. The Superintendent, Mr. Thomas J. Hyatt, asserts that great inconvenience is experienced for lack of a steam press. Back of the printing department is a small building where the forms of stereotyping plates are cast. Twelve boys were employed in the printing rooms, who were thus enabled to earn a support, and who, but for this, would be entirely dependent. The buildings of this department were originally the gift of the late Mr. F. F. Randolph. They have since been enlarged so as to double their business capacity. The first industrial undertaking of the place was "type setting by the boys and girls, mostly crippled, for the manufacture of stereotype plates. Mr. J. J. Golder, the first and faithful Superintendent of the place, undertook the work, being, fortunately, ably qualified for the charge by his previous profession, which he resigned, at pecuniary disadvantage, to take charge of the whole work at its outset."

On an elevated site north of the printing office is the Church of the Testimony of Jesus, "a goodly rural sanctuary, seventy feet long and sixty feet wide across the transepts. It was begun in 1869, and completed in the autumn of the year following, at the cost of $11,000, the sole gift of Mr. Adam Norrie. His daughter furnished the bell, also a beautiful communion service of silver, and other accessories. An elegant marble font was given by Mrs. S. Weir Roosevelt, and through the voluntary agency of her son, Mr. Hilborn Roosevelt, several gentlemen united in the gift of a fine organ. The church accommodates about three hundred persons, and is open regularly for Divine worship by the resident minister."

Another frame building, consisting of a main with two wings, is called "St. John's Inn," or the "Old Man's Home." It was built by the munificence of one gentleman,* at a cost of $30,000. This is the most extensive building on the grounds. It is painted a buff color

* Mr. J. D. Wolfe.

with green blinds, and has porches covered with flowers. About ten crippled people belonging here, were then at St. Luke's Hospital awaiting surgical inspection. An extension northward contains accommodations for ten grown girls, orphans, under training by the Sisters in the several industrial and household departments of the settlement. It is a provision for the care and instruction of unprotected girls from the age of fourteen upwards.

In the boys' department, in a large, well lighted room with a bay window, we found about forty little boys, ranging in ages from four to eleven. The dining room appeared to be general. The old men occupied two tables. The older girls likewise occupied two tables, and the children one. The laundry was furnished with portable washing tubs. The wings of this building are connected with the main by corridors.

The old men's department is a large room with the beds in alcoves around the room, a curtain in front of each forming an effectual screen. A table occupies the center of the room; comfortable rocking chairs and illustrated books are also among its accessories. Each alcove contains a wash-stand, a bureau and an easy chair. Over this room is another corresponding with it. One old man, on being asked what kind of a place St. Johnland is, said with emphasis: "Thank God, it is a good place!"

The house contains a sewing room. All the clothing is made on the place except garments that are donated. The shoes are bought. The kitchen was very neatly kept. Hop yeast is used in making bread.

There is on the grounds a large building designated as the Library and Village Hall. The Hall alone is at present in use.

About three-quarters of a mile west of St. Johnland, on the hill overlooking the Sound, is a house called the "Summer Rest-Awhile," a "summer retreat for poor women and children, given by the late Mr. W. H. Aspinwall. It accommodates from thirty-five to forty guests at one time." During the year 1874 two hundred and eighty-four weeks of country refreshment, divided among one hundred and forty-six city wayfarers, were afforded by this institution. Not only was the board of these poor people defrayed, but in many cases their traveling expenses also, besides contributions of clothing and other necessary aid to the destitute.

On the grounds is a fine old grove, from which a good view of the Sound is obtained. Seats around some of the trees afford opportunity for circles of little girls to sit and chat. Swings are suspended from other trees, which were freely used by large numbers of mirthful children, who, in their bright dresses, heightened the attractiveness of the landscape. A short walk through this grove brings one to the bluff, overlooking a broad expanse of the Sound, from which sea gulls were seen hovering here and there over its surface. The white sails on the dark blue waters faded into indistinctness in the soft haze of a summer afternoon, and the dividing line between ocean and sky was dreamily obscure. In the belt of green foliage fringing the shore, pines, red cedars and Virginia creepers are prominent.

In summer the children are indulged in boating, and the boys bathe in the Sound every day. All enjoy a holiday on the 4th of July, and on September 16th, the birthday anniversary of Dr. Muhlenburgh, the founder of the institution.

The garden is large, and the orchard yields a good supply of fruits. The many facilities here afforded for the best physical development of the young, the wide range of hill and valley, grove and shore, the opportunities for the outflow of exuberant spirits, for healthful sports of all kinds, the bathing, swimming and boating, and rambles after berries in summer, the nut gathering in autumn, the skating and coasting of winter; all partaken of in a pure, moral atmosphere, with wholesome associations, kindly home care, in-door evening amusement, Christian education and training to usefulness in life, seem to leave little necessary to reach the highest moral and physical benefit to the young.

The number of permanent beneficiaries for the year 1875 was two hundred and twenty-five, of whom one hundred and fifty-two were children. The current expenditures were $21,005.70.

As illustrating the nature of the work at St. Johnland, and what is being accomplished there, we quote from a report of the Society:

"As time goes on we feel increasing confidence and encouragement as regards our boys and girls. We have the pleasure to know that most of those who had been any time under our care are doing well outside. Some of them as type-setters are earning very liberal wages. Of others almost ready to be sent off, we are full of hope. One of our orphan Swedes is shortly to be placed with a respectable blacksmith in the neighborhood to learn the trade of his choice. Another is working as out-door man at St. Luke's, and saving up his wages to enable him to pay his board during the first year of his apprenticeship to a city carpenter—the goal of his ambition. Again, another lad old enough to leave us, is so loyal and attached a St. Johnlander that he declines a good opening in the city to become a garden apprentice with us, and so, by and by, to serve us always as a gardener. The girl whom we sent out this year is doing well in the position she has chosen. There has been no stronger illustration of the moral and Christian effect of St. Johnland training than in the case of this young girl. When she came to us three years since, she was so forward and ungovernable that we feared her companionship with our other young charges. When she left us we could not ask a demeanor more modest, dutiful and Christian.

"And so of many another, were it proper to write what is likely to fall under the eye of those portrayed. A sketch of some of our beneficiaries, past and present, would be no dull tale. Many a pathetic story, and even romantic incident, would be unfolded in tracing the circumstances of destitution or bereavement which have made them our charge, while a singularly wide range of nationalities affords continual contrasts and diversities not a little refreshing and enlivening. Thus we have representatives from Norway, Sweden, Russia, Poland, Prussia, Germany, Switzerland, Italy, England, Scotland, Ireland, Cuba, Mexico and Central America, and among our household Christian names are Olga, Lugarda, Ghiradina, Regina, Ottric, Sweyn, Carl, Otto, etc."

From the same source we quote the following: "The children are not dressed alike, nor in any other manner ground into an artificial uniformity by unnecessary routine or cold repression. They have room for spontaneity. They have their own little possessions and predilections, take pride, the little girls especially, in the care and ornamentation of their home, and in the cultivation of their gardens; while the hardier divisions, in true boy fashion, find only too much scope, sometimes, for their free development, in their wide, out-of-door range, and nothing is more commonly remarked by strangers visiting the settlement than the natural, open manners of our young people."

In the report of the Society for the year ending December 27, 1875, it is stated that "the receipts of the past year have not been adequate to the maintenance of the place by about $6,000." * * * Regarding its needs, and one of the methods by which it may be aided, we further quote:

"Miss Wolfe's devoted filial piety and generosity have made a very handsome advance toward an endowment of the Home erected by her father for the old men, but for the poor little children we have no settled provision. An endowment of their Home by means of berths, analogous to the charity beds of St. Luke's Hospital, but less costly, would be a very valuable aid. The sum of fifteen hundred dollars ($1,500) would endow such berth or bed *in perpetuity*—the right of nomination to a vacancy being with the donor, subject to the ordinary regulations of the charity. May it not occur to bereaved parents to find some solace in keeping alive the name of a departed child in a memorial bed of this kind?

"Or again, such berths or beds can be maintained from year to year by annual subscriptions of one hundred dollars each, and churches and Sunday-schools, by combining to support a stated number of these beds, would both assist our income and be themselves gainers in the use of the charity to which their patronage would entitle them."

The Society of St. Johnland is under the control of a board of trustees. Its founder, Rev. Dr. Muhlenberg, is still its Pastor and Superintendent. The immediate work of the charity is committed to the care of the Sisters of the Holy Communion, of whom Sister Anne Ayres is Sister Superintendent, and Sister Jessie Stevens Assistant Superintendent. This community was organized in 1852. The rules of the Order are simple, each Sister binding herself for a term of three years, renewable at her option, while probationers are required to spend a novitiate of six months before admission to the Order. Their habit resembles the ordinary attire of a gentlewoman, and they reside where-ever their work requires their presence.

This Society, though organized but a comparatively short time, has made its work felt upon the afflicted of New York. Its sphere of usefulness is widening, and the work which, by its self-denying effort, has been and is being accomplished in St. Johnland, is one more link connecting it with the grateful thanks of every well-wisher of suffering humanity.

St. Joseph's Asylum and House of Providence.

Syracuse.

This Asylum occupies a large plain brick structure, standing upon a slight eminence a little back from the highway, and approached through an avenue of shade trees. It is about two miles, in a south-westerly direction, from the railroad depot. The farm belonging to the House contains about sixty acres, and its bountiful crops and rich meadows give an idea of plenty quite in keeping with the objects of the institution.

The building now occupied was formerly the City Almshouse. It is three stories high, is supplied with rain water and heated by furnaces. The ceilings are high and the window sashes are hung with cords, weights and pullies. The cellar is used for storing coal and vegetables and for washing. On the first floor are the reception rooms, class rooms, dining room and kitchen. On the second floor are the apartments of the Sisters, sleeping rooms and sewing room. On the third floor are the children's dormitories, the clothes' room and chapel. On the first floor is a broad hall, ninety feet long by twenty-three feet wide, into which open the dining room, kitchen, apartments for adult inmates, school room and the play room for boys and girls. The apartments on the second and third floors open upon a gallery overlooking the lower halls. The gallery is protected by a balustrade.

The House of Providence is the property of the St. Vincent de Paul Society of Syracuse, and was incorporated under the general law of the State. It is conducted by the Roman Catholic Order of the

Sisters of Charity of St. Vincent de Paul. Eight Sisters are engaged in the work, Sister Beata McFaul having principal charge. A farmer is employed to superintend the farm work.

At the date of the visitation, September 6, the house contained a considerable number of adult inmates, including several aged and infirm blind persons. We were informed by Sister Theonetta, that it was not intended hereafter to receive adults, but to confine the work of the house to the care of destitute boys, thus effecting a desired classification. It is thought that the house would accommodate one hundred boys if it had no adult inmates. Sister Theonetta says: "We receive children from four to eleven years of age, and keep them until twelve or thirteen. Some are sent here by the Superintendent or Overseer of the Poor, and come in a very neglected condition. Some of them are adopted into families. The intention of the house is not to receive infants, but we have now three, from six to twelve months old."

Among the boys there was one who was a cripple and had been such from his birth. Another was an idiot and was in his thirteenth year. As we entered the class-room, the boys were kneeling and repeating prayers in response to the teacher. There were between forty and fifty in the school-room, intelligent looking children.

The boys were variously dressed; the older ones in jackets and the little fellows in blue check aprons. Their hair is cut close. After school was over they were permitted a brief season of play in the hall; they then marched around the hall several times, two by two, in company with the teacher, falling into line as they marched and so proceeded to the dining room. The tables here were well supplied and furnished with table-cloths and crockery. The old people ate with the children, the youngest of the latter occupying baby chairs. The usual form of grace was repeated before eating.

The dormitories, of which there were two for the boys, one for the larger and another for the smaller, presented a very cheerful appearance. The beds were very comfortably made up, with plenty of straw in the ticks, covered with blue spreads and supplied with good-sized feather pillows. The bedsteads were single and of iron, two feet four inches wide. The floors were scrupulously clean.

One of the rooms in the house was called the "old ladies' ward." It was a well-lighted, cheerful apartment, having windows on two sides. Colored counterpanes were on the beds, which were furnished with double pillows. Two strips of rag-carpet, made in the house, were laid through the center of the room. Here were a number of old ladies, two of them blind, engaged in knitting or sewing. The stockings that they were knitting were thick and warm.

The clothes room of the house was a very nicely-kept apartment and well supplied. In this room was a chest of clothing just received, which had been donated and which it was intended to make over into garments for the inmates.

The farm land is being improved and brought into a higher condition of productiveness. On the premises is a large barn resting on a stone foundation. It is in contemplation to erect other needed outbuildings, as time and means will permit. A great deal needs to be done upon the house itself to bring it into perfect repair and adapt it to its present use, but a good beginning in this direction has already been made, and the management of its internal affairs are evidently in the hands of zealous and energetic ladies. The asylum is in the way of accomplishing a great amount of good.

The whole number of persons received during the year ending September 30, including children, was seventy-nine; the number discharged, fifty-four; of the latter, three were placed out by adoption, eight returned to parents or guardians, two left without permission, thirty-eight were otherwise discharged, and three died. The total expenditures during the year were $9,833.34. Its total indebtedness was $11,668, of which $9,630 was upon real estate.

The number of children in the Asylum October 1, was sixty-eight. Of these, ten were orphans, fifty-two half-orphans, and six had both parents living. Twenty were of native parents, and forty-eight of foreign. Sixty-three were from Onondaga county; from Albany and Hamilton, each two; from Cortland, one. Ten were partially or entirely supported by parents or friends, forty-six by counties, towns or villages, and twelve by the State.

New York Asylum for Idiots.

Syracuse.

This institution stands upon an elevated site, commanding a view of the city of Syracuse and beautiful country surroundings. Its grounds are extensive and tastefully laid out, being planted with ornamental trees and a great variety of shrubbery. Graveled roads lead from the gateway, right and left, to the main building. A stone wall with embattled comb incloses its front, back of which is a nicely trimmed hedge. Within the gateway is a brick lodge with a slate roof. In front of the main building is a graded lawn, terraced and neatly kept. Luxuriant creepers clamber about the imposing porch at the entrance, which is reached by a flight of stone steps. The building is intended to combine in its construction all modern improvements, and is capable of accommodating about two hundred and twenty inmates. The institution is under the control of a Board of Trustees, of which the Governor, Lieutenant-Governor, Secretary of State, Comptroller and Superintendent of Public Instruction, are *ex officio* members. It is under the immediate superintendence of H. B. Wilbur, M. D., who is aided by a corps of assistants.

The building at Syracuse was completed and occupied in 1855, but the institution was commenced in Albany and conducted there for four years. It was incorporated July 10, 1851.

It is comparatively a recent period since the practicability of the education of idiots was most successfully demonstrated by Dr. Edward Seguin, of Paris, who organized a school for the purpose in 1838. Since his time, institutions for their care have sprung up in most of the older countries. New York was the second State in the Union to establish an asylum for idiots. The first school in the United States for this class, was opened at Barre, Mass., in 1848, by Dr. Wilbur. It was a private institution, begun in the month of July of that year, and continued under Dr. Wilbur's care until he assumed charge of the New York State Asylum in 1851. He remained at Albany until 1855, and then moved to Syracuse, taking with him his corps of trained assistants.

"The design and objects of the asylum, as established by the action of the Legislature, are not of a custodial character, but to furnish the means of education to that portion of the youth of the State not provided for in any of its other educational institutions. Those only will, therefore, be received into the asylum who are of a proper school age, and they for such periods of time as shall, in the estimation of the Board of Trustees, suffice to impart all the education practicable in each particular case.

"Children between the ages of seven and fourteen, who are idiotic or so deficient in intelligence as to be incapable of being educated at any ordinary school, and who are not epileptic, insane or greatly deformed, may be admitted by the Superintendent with the advice and consent of the Executive Committee."

The last visitation to the asylum was made October 28. The house is well arranged, provision being made for every want of the helpless class to which it extends a welcome. There are comfortable beds, clean, airy rooms, well-supplied dining tables and ample arrangements for bathing. The school exercises are suggestive of the wants of this class and of the intelligent and humane efforts that have been made to supply them. In speaking of them, Dr. Wilbur said: "The children in the lowest room, which is provided for those in the lowest form of idiocy, have certain exercises which are adapted to their capacity. Starting from this point, there is a series of exercises so graded that there is no abrupt step experienced in passing up to the ordinary elementary studies of a primary school. Children come in of every grade of intelligence. We put them on the grade to which they belong and then carry them up."

In the primary class were a number possessing the lowest form of intelligence, engaged in their first exercise, which consists in stringing iron rings, the holes in the center of the rings being about half an inch in diameter. The pupil, holding a string with a large needle at the end in one hand, and an iron ring in the other, tries to put the needle through the hole in the ring and so string it on. This affords him amusement, and if he finds himself successful, he receives additional pleasure. Then he is given large beads or wooden buttons to string, each exercise being rendered more difficult than the one immediately preceding by the smallness of the hole. In a more advanced exercise a board is used, in which are a series of holes. The pupil is furnished a number of iron pegs which he puts into the holes in the board. A still more difficult exercise was being practiced, in which some boys and girls were playing with oblong boards, out of which a number of variously shaped pieces had been cut. The pupils were endeavoring to put these pieces back in their proper places, their success or failure in doing so occasioning considerable merriment. The contrivance for teaching boys to walk naturally, without shuffling their feet, is quite ingenious and constructed on the principle of a treadmill. In this two boys are placed, one who can walk and another who does not. The first begins to walk, and in doing so turns the mill. The other is then obliged to lift his feet at regular intervals. A ladder with side-pieces six inches deep, the cross-pieces of which are made of flat boards three inches wide, is laid on the floor and children are taught to step over the cross-pieces, also to walk by stepping from bar to bar.

We witnessed in one of the class rooms an exercise intended to develop the power of attention through the eye and ear. Dr. Wilbur says: "Children on coming here are to a greater or less degree deficient in the power of attention; therefore all our exercises are framed with a view to the development of this power. The gymnastic exercises engaged in are not so much to develop muscular power as to cultivate the attention and bring the muscular system under the control of the will, which is the first step toward bringing the intellectual faculties under such control." The children were seated at their desks, and held in their hands each a pair of dumb-bells. At one end of the room, on a dais, was the teacher who played upon a piano, and before it, facing the pupils, stood a little girl with her back to the teacher, who led the others. As the teacher played, the children marched and performed various evolutions, in which the use of the dumb-bells formed a conspicuous part.

In another room we were treated to a performance by a singing and whistling class. Fifteen boys and girls stood about a piano which was played by a lady teacher. Two of the boys whistled while the others, with the girls, sang. The singing was very good, and the time quite correct. In one of the class rooms the children appeared much interested in a lesson designed to teach them to distinguish color by the use of a series of wooden cups and balls of different colors. For each cup there was a ball corresponding in color. These were placed on a table with the balls misplaced, and the pupils were instructed to take them out and arrange them, each in its proper cup. An amusing exercise was that intended to teach them form and color. A series of cards of different shapes and colors were produced, and a pattern given to the pupils, who were required to put them together so as to make an exact copy of the pattern.

An exercise which, although apparently trivial, yet shows the helplessness of this class and the necessity for the thorough training and drilling to which they are subjected, is that of teaching them how to lace their shoes. A shoe with a stuffed stocking within it, is laced up as it should be when worn, and is then unlaced and the pupils are required to lace it. Simple as is the process, it takes in some instances a great deal of time to inculcate it. In another room the art of writing was being taught. The first lesson is that of making plain strokes. A series of dots in pairs were first made by the teacher, and the pupil was then required to draw lines connecting each pair. This is intended to teach them to place the strokes at equal intervals.

For the second lesson they are taught to make crosses, right angles, triangles, etc., and for the third to write the letters of the alphabet. From letters they proceed to words, and so on to sentences.

A lively scene was witnessed in an exercise on word cards. The children were allowed to select cards out of a bundle, were asked to call out the words upon them, and then questioned a little about the object so represented. For instance: The word "rice" was picked out. The teacher asks, "What is this good for?" "Good to eat," shout the children. "Mitten" is drawn. "What is a mitten used for?" "To put on the hand." Another draws the word "nose." "Show me your nose." They all point to their noses. The word "dumb-bell" is selected. "What is a dumb-bell for?" "To exercise." "Show me how you exercise." There is no mistaking this answer in the energetic swinging of their arms.

Another exercise is practiced by means of picture cards, for object teaching. A card with a butcher shop on it was shown. "What do you see in it?" asked the teacher. "Mutton, beef, knife, chopper," and whatever else the picture includes.

Some of the brighter pupils were exercised in word-making. A word was written on the blackboard, and they were required to make all the words they could out of it, using only the letters it contained. The word selected was "Mediterranean," from which the pupils readily made a number of words, such as "In," "Ida," "Dan," etc. Some of the boys, we were told, could make four hundred and thirty-nine words out of the word "congregationalist," which is capable of six hundred different combinations. A copy-book was shown us in which all these words had been written out by one of the pupils. The boys here were very clean and neat, wrote fairly, and drew creditably. "One of them," the teacher says, "began in the lowest school-room stringing rings. Another, when he came to us, could not talk."

In the sewing-room a sewing-class was receiving instruction. Here were shown us specimens of fancy lettering done by the girls, also pin-cushions, patchwork quilts that they had made, and some stockings that they had knit. The first thing here taught is the cross stitch. This, we were told, was very difficult for some to learn. One girl, it was stated, could read the Bible, but yet could not make a cross stitch. Some of the girls were so far advanced as to be able to make toilet covers, cornucopias, tidies, etc.

The girls are also trained to make beds, to lay tables for dinner, and to do all ordinary housework. The dishes used in teaching them are made out of cards, and when they are receiving lessons in ironing cold irons are used. Some of the girls were in the laundry regularly at work. Some of the boys go out to work on the farm under competent supervision.

Among the pupils was one formerly on Randall's Island. He was at that time very ignorant, in the habit of driveling at the mouth and accustomed to hold his head down. He did not seem to know the name of any object. He now reads, writes, multiplies and subtracts, and has, the teacher says, gone as far as interest in the arithmetic. He can go to the city and buy whatever he is directed to purchase, and he has some money laid by in the bank. Under proper supervision he is now regarded as self-supporting.

Another was a little boy, six or seven years old, familiar to the writer from his having been an inmate of the Erie county poor-house. His left leg, on coming to the institution, was drawn up against the right thigh, and both his lower limbs were greatly contracted. He propelled himself by placing his hands on the ground. His legs were straightened by an operation, and when we saw him he could stand upright and was gradually acquiring their use. He had made remarkable proficiency in every respect since becoming an inmate.

Fifty acres of land are attached to the institution; about fifteen or twenty acres of which are under garden cultivation. Grapes in great abundance are raised and consumed upon the place; also raspberries of different varieties, currants, strawberries and every variety of vegetables. Back of the grounds, on an eminence, is a beautiful grove of forest trees, embracing six or seven acres. In pleasant weather the children are permitted to take exercise here.

On the grounds is also a green-house for starting flowers for the lawn, and vegetables for the garden. The orchard is well stocked with choice fruit trees; plums, cherries, apples and pears all being raised in abundance.

A little rearward of the main building is the farm house, a two-story frame building with a porch in front, extending the whole length and looking out upon the grounds and lawn. Thirteen or fourteen of the older boys work upon the farm, and make their home with the farmer who resides here.

Ample stables, barns and an ice house are upon the premises. Ten cows are kept. The water supply is from the city, and there is a small reservoir in the upper part of the grounds that will serve in case the supply from the city should fail. The rain water is saved in ample cisterns.

The Matron, Miss Woods, says: "Very little trouble is experienced in disciplining the children. Sometimes it is necessary to speak sharply to them, but we can generally restrain them by gentle measures, and by depriving them of something they desire. They are very fond of dress."

There were in the institution Oct. 1st, one hundred and ninety-six children. Of these fifty-six were orphans; eighty-four, half orphans; and fifty-six had both parents living; ninety-two were of native parents, and one hundred and four of foreign. They represented counties as follows: Twenty-eight were from New York; twenty-four from Kings; twenty-one from Onondaga; fourteen from Erie; eleven from Oneida; seven from Chemung; from Cayuga, Columbia, Orange, and Rensselaer, each five; from Albany, Chautauqua, Herkimer, Jefferson, Madison, Monroe, Queens, Ulster, and Westchester, each four; from Cortland, Montgomery, and St. Lawrence, each three; from Broome, Delaware, Dutchess, Fulton, Ontario, Oswego, Schuyler, and Sullivan, each two; and one from each of the following; Chenango, Franklin, Niagara, Orleans, Tompkins, Wayne, Wyoming and Yates. Twenty-two were supported by parents or friends, and one hundred and seventy-four by the State. Beside the number mentioned above, there are fourteen pay-pupils from other States.

The total expenditures of the institution for the fiscal year ending Sept. 30th, were $45,507.20. Of this sum $1,500 was expended for buildings and improvements. The average weekly cost of support of the inmates, exclusive of clothing, was $3.91.

An inspection of the institution and its highly improved grounds confirms the wisdom of the State in making the investment and placing in charge one who is alive to the work and its capabilities. The money expended in purchasing and improving the property has been more than returned to the State in its enhanced value. The humanitarian feature of the work here being carried on, to which all other considerations are secondary, must be a source of gratification to every citizen. The patience and thoroughness displayed in the prosecution of the work, and the successful results with which it is crowned, reflect credit on the able corps of helpers which the superintendent has selected, some of whom have been with him from the very beginning of the undertaking.

The institution, it is believed, has done more than it proposed to do. Its object being, as has been stated, entirely educational, it was not intended to receive any of the idiotic class, but those susceptible of improvement, and these for only a limited period. The State having made no provision for the custodial care of idiots, a large number of both sexes who have received all the benefits that this institution can give them, still remain here for the lack of some other proper provision for them. Consequently, a large number who need its instruction cannot be admitted for want of room. It would seem, in view of the great good which this institution has already accomplished, that the same wise statesmanship and Christian philanthropy that first projected the enterprise should not hesitate to enlarge the work so as to include all of this helpless class that are now inmates of poor-houses where they generally sink into a condition differing but little from that of dumb beasts.

The Onondaga County Orphan Asylum.

Syracuse.

The history of this charity dates back to the year 1835, and is connected with the public school system of Syracuse. A few ladies of the city, then a village, made an effort to furnish a common school education to the poor children of the town, and opened for this purpose a school on the 6th of July. It was taught by Miss Ann Mead, and was held in a vacant room of a store on West Water street. Several hundred dollars being raised by subscription, a building for school purposes was erected on a lot belonging to the Syracuse Salt Company, and opened in 1836. In this building the poorer children of the village for many years received their primary instruction.

This school was under the immediate charge of Miss Mead until the 11th of October, 1839, when adequate provision having been made by the public for all the children of the village, the school-house was sold. The assets of the association were then found to be $427.38.

The condition and wants of the orphan and destitute children of the city and vicinity soon arrested the attention of the benevolent ladies who had been members of this association, as well as others, and various meetings were held for the consideration of this subject. These resulted in forming, on the 21st of October, 1841, an Association for the Relief of Orphans and Destitute Children, and the funds of the former association were paid over to this new organization.

This was sustained by fairs and voluntary contributions. In 1845 the society was merged in the "Syracuse Orphan Asylum," which was incorporated May 10th of that year. A house was immediately rented in South Salina street, and the Asylum was opened with five girls and ten boys. The house was furnished, and the expenses of the year defrayed by voluntary contributions, without encroaching on the funds of the institution already invested, then about $1,500. This house was occupied until the following year, when the present building, which, until then, had been known as the Syracuse Academy, was purchased for the exceedingly small sum of $3,000.

The grounds were spacious, and by the addition, in 1848, of three lots in the north-east corner of the block, at a cost of $1,000, provisions were made sufficiently ample for all the purposes of the Asylum. The comfort of the inmates has since been increased by the erection of a broad piazza on the west side of the building, by the introduction of gas, the addition of blinds, etc. In 1861, through the liberality of the late Horace White, Esq., an ample and convenient building for a school-house was erected on the grounds at an expense of about $3,000. The name of this Asylum was, by an act of the Legislature, passed April 30, 1847, changed to the "Onondaga County Orphan Asylum," its present title.

Its finances are under the control of a Board of Trustees, and a Board of Lady Managers, selected from the various churches in the city, direct and manage its general affairs. The immediate charge of the institution is intrusted to a matron, Mrs. K. M. Woods, who is assisted by three teachers. The subordinate force of the asylum consists of a nurse, three seamstresses, a cook, a kitchen-maid, a dining room girl, two laundresses, two chambermaids and a steward.

The situation is elevated, and affords a fine prospect of the city, but the house being old, and not having been originally built for asylum purposes, lacks many conveniences which are now regarded as important.

The main building is heated by furnaces and lighted with gas. The windows are large, the sashes being suspended by cords, weights and pulleys. Much inconvenience is caused by lack of adequate water supply, as the asylum is not reached by the city works. The rain water is carefully saved, and two wells are on the premises.

The dormitories are furnished with both wood and iron double bedsteads, straw beds and feather pillows. Strips of rag carpet are laid across the middle of the rooms.

Both the boys' and girls' clothes rooms showed ample provision for summer and winter wear. The clothes were all made in the house. The girls, at stated periods, are regularly taught sewing, both by hand and on the machine. The matron says: "I do not mean, however, to have them work for more than one hour a day after school." The children are variously dressed except on Sunday. The boys wear straw hats in summer and caps in winter. The girls have straw hats, with blue ribbons, and felt hats with scarlet velvet trimmings, also pretty sacques and shawls.

During our visit the children gathered in the dining room, which was furnished with long tables, covered with white cloths. Both crockery and tinware are used. The children, before partaking of the food, asked the following blessing: "For these refreshments of Thy mercy, O Lord, we bless and praise Thy holy name, through Jesus Christ, our Lord. Amen."

The school building, a brick edifice near the Asylum, is furnished with patent desks and seats and the usual modern improvements. The school is graded, and children, when they finish the curriculum of studies here, pass into the public schools of the city. It shares the benefits of the singing and drawing masters of the public schools. Many of the children have quite a talent for drawing. The capacity of the school is already quite large, but President White, of Cornell University, has, we were informed, generously offered at any time to increase its accommodations if need be, rather than that the children from this and other counties whom it is desired to send here should be denied admission.

The children entertained us by singing: "Our Father in Heaven," and "Little Boy Blue." Above the school room is a large assembly room, extending the full size of the building, containing an organ and a reading desk. The walls are tinted and illuminated with cards, scripture engravings and mottoes. Sunday-school is held here, in which the ladies of the city take great interest.

The bathing arrangements are inadequate, but this is being remedied by the construction of bathing rooms, to be supplied with rain water. Great pains is taken to keep the children clean. The matron says: "Every morning they are washed, their hair combed with a fine comb, and no child is allowed to go into school until fittingly prepared."

A large apartment on the first floor is used for a children's playroom.

This, at the time of our visit, was clean and airy; flowers were on all the window sills, and several photographic groups of children hung on the walls.

The Nursery is furnished with double bedsteads, cribs and baby chairs. Here a bevy of little ones were encountered, all happy as butterflies, and appearing very natural and noisy. Their hair was nicely combed, and their faces indicated kind and thoughtful attention. The condition of many of these children, on arrival, is very deplorable. Mrs. Woods says: "They show evidence of extreme want and neglect."

A pleasing feature about this institution is the children's reading-room, which contains a library of two hundred volumes. Illustrated papers, such as the Christian Weekly, little picture rhymes and story books, the Saint Nicholas and the Youth's Companion, were found in the room. A benevolent gentleman had left the institution a sum of money, the interest of which is to be yearly expended on the children's periodical, "The Chatter Box." On the walls of the room were quite a collection of prettily framed pictures, presents received by the children at Christmas time. This was, preëminently, the children's apartment, and when any of the little folks, under the temptation of looking at a picture book or reading a story, wished to steal away by themselves, they came here.

Many of the children belong to a temperance society in the city called the "Cold Water Temple;" "and sometimes," Mrs. Woods assured us, "as many as fifty go there at once by themselves, the older ones looking after the younger." "My larger girls," she further says, "I can always trust alone. And I can send my larger boys with money to the bank with entire safety."

The infirmary is a comfortable apartment. It was without any occupant. "The children," Mrs. Woods says, "are usually very healthy; no deaths have occurred during the past year." The closets are detached from the building and adjoin the play-ground.

In connection with the asylum is a vegetable garden and orchard where potatoes, corn, tomatoes and other vegetables are raised, also apples, plums and cherries. The institution possesses two milch cows.

The number of inmates on the day of visitation, September 16, was one hundred and thirty-five, of whom fifty-four were girls. In regard to the latter, Mrs. Woods remarks: "I have made it a special work to see that our girls are properly cared for. It was generally understood, when I came here, that this institution was no place for girls, and few came here. Now the opinion is changed, and the number of girls coming under our care is increasing. We take children at two and a half years old; sometimes in cases of necessity at two years, and in a few instances we have taken them as young as twenty months. The age of fourteen years is the nominal limit for keeping the children, but we generally hold them till good homes are found.

"The usefulness of the institution might be enhanced by making provision to teach the boys trades. Boys need the restraint of a home most when fifteen years old. Many come here and take our boys, not because they love them, but because they want to get work out of them. The girls I can teach myself, but I cannot teach trades to the boys. I have some girls who will become teachers, others that I can qualify for nursery work. I make it a point to instruct them so thoroughly that they shall be able to earn good wages when they leave. We have one young man here in his eighteenth year who is preparing for college. Another of our boys is in a drug store, earning $4 a week. He makes his home in the asylum. I buy his clothing out of his wages, and the remainder I put in the savings bank for him. Some of the larger girls also work outside for wages. I act the motherly part toward them; clothe them out of the money they earn and put the remainder in the bank on their account. One of these, fifteen years of age, has already saved $100.

"I do not believe in shutting children up, frightening them or making them go without their meals. If a child needs a whipping, why I whip it and have it over. As much as possible, however, I let each little child grow up with any little ways and peculiarities it may have. I do not approve of destroying the children's individuality. I never teach these children that they are on charity, and that they must be everlastingly grateful for what is done for them. But I try to impress upon them, especially upon the boys, that it is not what people do for them that is going to avail, but what they do for themselves. I endeavor to convince the boys that they can be any thing they please if they will only try for it. I do not see why they should not fill positions of respectability as well as others. They often go out on vacations. Parties of them are frequently invited out to different places. They always do justice to themselves and behave like gentlemen."

The whole number of children received in the institution since its organization is two thousand and fifty-six. The number received during the past year was one hundred and seven, and the number discharged ninety-two. Of the latter, ten were placed out by adoption, eighty-one returned to parents or guardians, and one was otherwise discharged. The number remaining in the institution October 1, 1875, was one hundred and twenty-three, seventy-one boys and fifty-two girls. Of these, eighteen were orphans, sixty-two half-orphans, and forty-three had both parents living. How many of the children were of native, and how many of foreign birth, has not been reported.

The total expenditures during the fiscal year ending September 30,

1875, were $7,709.13. The value of its invested fund is estimated at $34,578.60.

When it is considered what would have been the results of leaving the large number of children cared for by this asylum to grow up in neglect, some conjecture may be formed of the immense benefits that have accrued to society, as well as the pecuniary benefits to the tax payer by its work, which, it is gratifying to note, is appreciated by the people.

For a long time before the passage of the late law requiring children to be removed from county poor-houses, the people of this county, acting through their Board of Supervisors, took means to place children under better influences than could be afforded them at the county house. This intelligent action, though resulting in great benefit, could not have been carried out without the help of the various asylums in the vicinity, and in this good work the Onondaga County Orphan Asylum largely participated.

St. Vincent's Female Orphan Asylum.

Syracuse.

A narrow belt of green lawn, stretching in front and separating it from the street, appears to the visitor to give to this asylum a hint of seclusion from the busy city life around it. Its location, 20 Madison street, may be considered central. Its building, which is in the Italian style of architecture and is three stories in height with a basement, has been constructed with reference to combining all modern improvements. With a frontage of one hundred and a depth of fifty feet, and with a three-story addition in the rear, thirty by one hundred, it is capable of accommodating one hundred and fifty children inmates, besides two hundred day scholars.

The Asylum is under the charge of twelve Sisters of the Roman Catholic Order of the Sisters of Charity, Sister Tatiana White being Superior. This lady entered upon her duties here in 1856, and has been actively engaged in them ever since.

The history of the Asylum may be briefly stated as follows: "In 1852, the Sisters of Charity came to Syracuse and opened a school for girls. Seventy of these were taught free of charge, and thirty were paid for. There being no institution in the city having for its special object the care of orphan and destitute girls, a want was felt which the Sisters endeavored to meet by the establishment of a Female Orphan Asylum, where the girls might not only be taught the rudiments of an English education, but also those branches of domestic economy, and other important matters so necessary for every young girl to know, in order to become a useful and self-supporting member of society." The work was begun with the care of two children.

The frame building at first used having been destroyed by fire, Bishop McCloskey donated the lot upon which the Asylum now stands, and a citizen of Syracuse, Mr. Cornelius Lynch, who died in 1857, made a generous bequest to the Asylum of $4,000. But as this was not sufficient to meet the needs of the work, an appeal was made to the public and a like amount was raised by subscription, during the years 1860, '61 and '62. This, with the proceeds of fairs and festivals, was carefully husbanded, and, being supplemented by State appropriations of $2,500 in 1864, and of $5,000 in 1867, the institution was enabled to reach its present prosperous condition.

The Asylum was incorporated June 12th, 1860, and the spacious building now in use was erected during the years 1860 and '61. The door of the main entrance is ornamented with carved work and paneled with crown glass. A spiral stairway leads from the hall to the upper floors of the house, and in a niche in the hallway is quite appropriately placed a statuette representing St. Vincent carrying in his arms a little child.

The reception room is tastefully furnished, and has the air of a refined home.

Sister Tatiana says, in regard to the construction of the building: "Were we building again I would suggest some changes. For instance, direct ventilation, by having the windows and doors made opposite each other. A Superior from France, who had visited all our institutions, said that they had one fault, and that was, that while they had a great many doors and windows, scarcely one stood opposite another."

The domestic work of the Asylum is done entirely by the Sisters and the children. "Our girls," says Sister Tatiana, "take alternate weeks in the kitchen. One week a class is learning to make bread; another week the same class is at work in the laundry. The girls go to school in the morning, and the afternoon is devoted to industries and household occupations, under the supervision of the Sisters. Industrial schools and industrial teaching I regard as very necessary. Young girls from fifteen to seventeen years of age are very apt to lack judgment. Then is the time they most need a mother's care. In fact they seem to require more or less counsel until they are twenty-one.

"In imparting this industrial training, care is taken not to overdo it, or to waste the girls' time on work for which they have no capacity or taste." On this point the Sister makes the following very sensible remarks: "We study the capabilities of the children, and endeavor to develop the talents prominent in each. If in one it is for sewing, we train her in that branch of industry. If in another it is for any trade, she is afforded an opportunity to learn it. If her forte seems to be housework, we give her a thorough training in that particular department. We board the girls while they are learning their trades, and then find them good situations in stores or private families."

In regard to the age for admitting children, the Sister says: "We take children at two years old, but we do not like to take them under three years. There ought to be an infant's house connected with every asylum. We object very much to taking a girl in the institution over seven years of age.

"I prefer to have our little ones adopted in families where there are no other children, and in the families of the middle class if possible. We do not like to let any of our girls go as servants into families where other servants are kept. They have to sleep with them, and the influence of this association is undesirable. Nor do we approve of our girls going out exclusively to nurse babies. In such cases they live upon the streets and are exposed to many snares. It is very likely to happen that some unprincipled men whom they meet will give them rings. The consequences to these unsuspecting girls may often be very serious. But one girl has ever reflected discredit upon us by her conduct after leaving. If we hear of any of our children being ill-treated, or in any danger, we write, and find out the particulars from some family living near. We had to bring one back the other day. I received two letters from unknown parties urging me to take one of our young girls away from the family where she was living. Then I received another begging me to take the child away, saying they wanted her out of the neighborhood. There was nothing bad in the family, but the associations of the neighborhood were such that the writer wanted her removed from that part of the city. We took the child away and secured her a good home elsewhere in town.

The Sister's method of looking after the girls when placed out she thus explained: "When people apply for a girl we require them to bring references from the place where they live. Then we make ourselves acquainted with one or two respectable families in the neighborhood, and ask them to let us know how she gets on. It is a continual anxiety to us."

The tables in the dining room were ranged with reference to the sizes of the children, small tables being used for the little ones and for the older children a size larger. All, except the table for the very small children, were covered with neat, white table-cloths. Crockery, plates, knives, forks, spoons and some tinware are used. The children have their food served out to them in portions, except the girls who are preparing to leave; their table is set very much like that of an ordinary family, the viands being placed upon it, and one or more of the girls acting as carvers. The food is of a generous and nutritious character, this being regarded by the Sisters as an important element in fortifying against disease. Near the table for the larger girls is a reading desk. It is customary for one girl to read aloud while the others are eating. Each girl is expected to take her turn as a reader.

In addition to the ordinary meals the little children under ten years of age have lunches of bread at ten and at three o'clock. The children are always given something extra for supper on Sunday.

The custom of reading aloud is not only observed in the dining room, but is also carried into other departments of the house. In the sewing room, when the larger girls occupy it, one reads while the others sew. These girls are as far as possible kept by themselves, have their own sitting room and do not occupy the sewing room except in the afternoon. This department has three sewing machines, and coat making is carried on under the instruction of an experienced tailoress. Sewing, as well as every other industry, is taught in classes. The Sister says: "Every thing in the house is graded according to the ability and age of the children. Girls who are old enough are taught to use the sewing machine, but not before they are perfect with the needle. The older girls do their own dress-making, mending and millinery. They also take care of and clean their own rooms, and in this way prepare themselves for doing all these things after they leave. The ladies, we find, like our girls, because they are prepared to go to work at once."

Perfect system seemed to pervade the house. The clothes room is ample in size and arranged with seats on each side and a table in the center. Both ends are fitted up with closets divided off into compartments. Each compartment contains the clothing of one child, and is marked with her name.

The girls knit their own stockings by hand, and receive ten cents for every pair. They wear woolen stockings in winter. "I think," says the Sister, "the woolen are the better for winter. Children will sometimes get their feet wet when they go out, and are not as apt to catch cold with woolen as with cotton stockings."

The children have three changes of clothing for summer and three for winter. The winter clothing, when not in use, is packed away with camphor.

In regard to the dress of the children Sister Tatiana says: "We do not dress them all alike except when they go out. In winter, on fine days, they wear black sacques, Scotch plaid dresses, and drab colored hats, trimmed with cherry. On very cold days they wear waterproofs. In summer, the girls wear light dresses and black alpaca overskirts, trimmed with double ruffles." With this suit a white bonnet is worn. Another suit is a blue dress, white overskirt and blue bonnet. Yet another dress is the blue parametta, with either a shawl or waterproof cape. A full set of red mittens and red scarfs is also provided."

In the clothes room is an ingenious contrivance, consisting of a number of pockets attached to a piece of cotton fabric, for the pocket-handkerchiefs of the children. Each child has a pocket appropriated to her special use.

The dormitories are furnished with neat French bedsteads, of wood color, varying in size. Those in the dormitory for the largest girls are six feet by three; in that for the younger girls, five feet four by two feet eight, while in the dormitory for the little ones the bedsteads are five feet by two feet and a half, and have side pieces a foot deep to keep the children from falling out. Corn husk mattresses are used for the larger girls and straw beds for the smaller. The straw beds were very thick, some a foot or more deep. White counterpanes were furnished for all the beds, and one or more of the Sisters sleep in each dormitory. The children all sleep singly.

In regard to the relative merits of wooden or iron bedsteads, the Sister says: "We prefer the wooden bedsteads; they are fully as clean as the iron. If there are bugs in the house they must go somewhere. It is folly to say that iron bedsteads keep them out. We use corrosive sublimate in the spring, the middle of summer and the last of November to protect ourselves from them. Saturdays and Sundays we throw all the bed clothes over the foot of the bed and air them, and adopt other devices to keep our beds clean. We do very well with the wooden bedsteads." The white counterpanes are removed at night, and colored spreads substituted. The rooms are swept out with damp saw-dust. The dormitory for the young girls who are preparing to leave contains eleven beds. A large cupboard for spare linen was shown. The linen for each dormitory was neatly folded away and had a separate mark and number.

The infirmary is furnished with beds and small cribs and other requisites for the care of the sick. At the time of our visit the only occupant was a little girl about eight years old who was suffering from paralysis. No deaths had occurred during the year. There was no prevailing sickness among the children. The Sister ascribed this in a great measure to her carefulness to have the children regular in their hours and in all their habits, as much of the sickness from which children usually suffer she attributed to irregularity in these respects.

The Sister says, "The children formerly suffered from frosted feet, but this is now prevented by using a little sperm oil, which we rub on the feet of those who are likely to be affected, with a piece of flannel." In regard to skin diseases the Sister remarks: "We very seldom have any. Should we have any cases of scabies we rub those affected very carefully with sulphur and salt, and put on them a flannel garment fitting closely about the neck, wrists and ankles, and keep them apart from the other children for six or eight days, when they are cured. This disease spreads very easily and needs prompt attention." The Sister related the following touching incident of a poor child whom she had cured of this loathsome disease: "A little girl was once brought to me who had contracted this disease from sleeping with a person thus affected. She came to me in a dreadful condition. She said nobody would take her and begged me to let her in. I took her and put her under treatment, dressed her in flannel and kept her by herself, and in about a week she was able to go with the other children."

The lavatory is large, well lighted and ventilated. The air on our entering was sweet. It contained six bath-tubs, separated from each other by partitions and supplied with both hot and cold water. Provision is also made for warming the room. The children when bathing, we were informed, are furnished with clean bathing gowns, towels and washing cloths, and this they do once a week all the year round. In the center of the room is a double range of porcelain wash basins twelve on a side, and on two sides of the room were places sufficient to accommodate fifty. Every wash-bowl had a cloth, a towel, and a bag for a coarse comb. The Sister says, "It is difficult to make the children keep their combs in the bags. They want to put them in their pockets." Their heads, we were informed, are combed with a fine comb every day. Each child has her own fine comb. This is kept in a little bag and put into a box which the Sister has for the purpose.

The laundry is quite complete; the ironing room is supplied with zinc plates, on which the linen of the Sisters is ironed and which gives it a fine gloss. This, the Sister said, was a French idea.

The school is held in the three-story edifice already referred to. The class-rooms are furnished with double patent seats and patent chairs. This school is under the Department of Public Instruction, which pays the salaries of three of the Sisters. The children sang for us:

"There is beauty all around, when there's love at home."

The Sister remarked that "the children are not allowed to sing any thing that is depressing. Instrumental music is not generally taught, but occasionally when we have a little crippled child, or one who we think could support herself by this means, we make an effort to have her taught."

The chapel is over the school room, and is a large and beautiful apartment, capable of accommodating two hundred persons. It has a central and two side altars. The figure of St. Joseph is on one side of the altar, and that of St. Vincent on the other. On the walls are the fourteen Stations of the Cross, and a large chromo of the Madonna. It also contains an organ, and has connected with it a neat sacristy.

The play-room, which is rather small, is furnished with seats and benches. It contains a little compartment for toys, "to keep the children," the Sister says, "from the habit of hiding things away."

The Sister explained her methods of discipline as follows: "We never lock up a child in a room, and we very seldom have occasion to use corporal punishment. If a child fails in her lesson, or fails in silence—the most frequent failure is failing in silence, for they are obliged to keep silence from the time the bell rings for night prayers till after breakfast next morning—we punish her by putting her behind a small screen, and she cannot see any one till she is released.

"Four Sisters are with the children. They give them good or bad tickets, according to their merits. A Sister in making her report will perhaps say: 'All the children belonging to a certain grade have given satisfaction with the exception of one, who failed in silence, or was disorderly, or was rude to her companions, for which she will take half an hour or an hour's study. Another failed in her geography or arithmetic,' she will remain till she can recite a task perfectly, or perhaps other tasks may be imposed upon them. Then again, those who have failed in any of the various requirements are denied the privilege of going out to walk when the others have an opportunity to do so. If a child behaves very badly we have sometimes to use the rod.

With regard to moral and religious instruction, the Sister says: "We try to awaken the honor of the children as much as possible, and cultivate principle. What we wish to do is to make them lead good Christian lives, and become useful members of society. We endeavor to make them economical and saving. Above all, we aim to train them to be truthful and honest. For this reason we spare no pains in ferreting out the most trivial things."

The children appeared to be healthy and happy. Sister Tatiana says: "We do every thing we can to make the children happy — take them to church twice on Sundays, to picnics during the week, and sometimes to concerts. We try to make Sunday a pleasant day for them. The older girls have a nice library to which they have access."

At the date of October 1, there were in the institution one hundred and twenty-six children, forty of whom were orphans, eighty-two were half-orphans, and four had both parents living. The parents of three were natives of the United States, and the parents of one hundred and twenty-three were of foreign birth. Thirty-two children were partially supported by parents or friends, sixty-two by counties or cities, and thirty-two wholly by the institution. The entire number of children who have been received in this Asylum since its foundation, is about four hundred and twenty-nine, exclusive of the years 1870 and 1875.

The whole number of children received during the year ending September 30, 1875, was thirty; the total number discharged, nineteen. Of the latter, one was placed out by adoption, fourteen were returned to parents or guardians, and four were otherwise discharged. The average number of inmates during the year was one hundred and twenty-five.

The total expenditure during the period named was $7,196.11. The total indebtedness of the institution is $16,229.50. Of this sum, $8,500 rests upon the real estate.

The order and thorough system manifest throughout every department of this Asylum were very noticeable, and suggestive of good results in the formation of habits of personal neatness, industry and methodical work in the girls subjected to its influence.

The House of the Good Shepherd, Rockland County, New York.

Tomkin's Cove.

The House of the Good Shepherd is situated on the west bank of the Hudson river, about fifty miles from New York, and is in the township of Stony Point, Rockland county, Tomkin's Cove P. O. It is one mile above Stony Point, and may be reached by steamboat from the foot of Harrison street, New York, or by the Hudson River Railroad to Peekskill, thence by boats; or by cars of the New York and New Jersey Railroad to Stony Point, and thence by carriage. The property consists of ninety acres of land, rising rather abruptly from the river, on which it borders one-fifth of a mile. Most of the land is wild and uncultivated, and is used for pasture. About fifteen acres have been cleared, and are in grass or under cultivation. The place is well watered by a brook and several springs. From the house — one hundred and sixty feet above the river — an extended view, embracing features of great natural beauty, presents itself; the Hudson river with its shores from Tarrytown to Peekskill, the towns and villages of Tarrytown, Sing Sing, Peekskill, Haverstraw, Stony Point, Tomkin's Cove, Verplank's, Grassy Point, Croton, Montrose Point, and other places are included. On the north and west rise the Dunderberg, Temp, Black, and other mountains, forming the highlands of New York.

The finances of the institution are controlled by a Board of Trustees, and its immediate charge or working is undertaken by Rev. E. Gay, Jr., assisted by his wife.

In connection with this institution, though of a separate organization, is a ladies' association, called the Ladies' Association in Aid of the House of the Good Shepherd, Rockland county, New York. To this organization the institution is largely indebted for its continued prosperity. These good ladies make, or otherwise furnish, almost all the clothing the children wear. Most of the provisions and supplies come also from this source.

The brief history of this delightful home for homeless children is substantially stated as follows: In August, 1865, a German widow died in Haverstraw, leaving three small girls and a little boy. She had been long sick and a pensioner of Trinity parish, Haverstraw. She left the children in the care of the rector of the parish, Rev. J. Breckenridge Gibson, D. D. One girl was in St. Luke's hospital for treatment, being a sufferer from hip disease. Temporary provision was made for the children, pending the solution of the question: What is to be done with them? A few days later the same pastor was called to the death-bed of an English woman, who with her husband was a communicant of his church. She left three little girls entirely destitute; for these also a temporary place was found, but in a home so poor and under such circumstances that they were destitute of the ordinary necessaries of life. The wife of the early rector and founder of the parish previously mentioned, interested herself and friends on their behalf, and, as a result, a benevolent Christian lady donated the sum of $500 with which to rent a house and buy some simple furniture. A widow, Mrs. Sarah A. Waters, was engaged to take care of the children. A house was taken for six weeks in Haverstraw village, and on the evening of February 13th, 1866, the little family was gathered and the work of faith commenced. On Easter Monday, April 1st, the family was removed to a larger house near the church of Garnerville. "Here, as a parish home, receiving also children from abroad, it was continued for five years, depending wholly on the daily gifts of Him who giveth daily bread. Kind friends were raised up to aid the work. A family of twenty or more children was fed, clothed, taught. But the rent was raised; the building was old and unsuitable. The earnest desire had long been felt to have a permanent home. The pastor had become deeply interested in the welfare of poor children. He and his wife determined to devote themselves to the work of caring for and educating such children. God had remarkably blessed their efforts in the work providentially intrusted to them. They looked about for a piece of land which might be purchased for the use of the house. After much time spent in the search and many disappointments, a tract of land was bargained for, and on March 4, 1871, sixty-four and a half acres of wild land was bought for $5,500, and the deed given on payment of $500, which was loaned by a friend, a mortgage being executed for $5,000. In the meantime a Board of Managers had been chosen, and become incorporated under the general laws of the State. A grant of $2,000 was made in the general charity bill of 1870, and on the 7th

30

of March, 1874, with psalms and prayers, the ground was broken for the House, and each member of the household removed a portion of earth for the foundation. A rough building was quickly erected, which gave shelter to the women and girls. The boys were quartered on the hay in the barn, and thus, on April 1st, was the family removed from Garnerville to Stony Point. The pastor and family, with one sick boy, were provided with rooms in a neighbor's cottage.

"The Legislature, in 1872, further appropriated the sum of $15,000, and thus encouraged, the Trustees decided to purchase the remainder of the farm, embracing the river front of sixteen acres, with cottage and barn. The $5,000 mortgage on the first purchase was paid off, $4,000 was paid on the second purchase, and a mortgage of $6,000 given on the same."

The institution is under the immediate care of its founder, the Rev. Ebenezer Gay, assisted by his wife, whose services are voluntary. Associated is a young lady, Miss Brinckerhoff, who, we were informed, not only gives her services without remuneration, but even insists on contributing to meet the regular expenses of the house. A teacher and assistant are hired; also a cook, laundress and seamstress.

At the date of visitation, October 27th, we found the Superintendent, upon our arrival, occupied in the extensive garden of the place with a large force of children variously employed.

There were then forty-three children in the house. They are received at a very early age, and are educated and trained for farm-work, service or trades.

One of the buildings is called the Girls' Home, or "Bee Hive." It contained about twenty inmates, and was provided with all the conveniences of a moderate home. It was under the charge of a lady of refinement and culture. The house was built from the timber of a disused brick-yard shed, and was intended for a work-shop. The lower part is now used as a school-room. A projection was added adjoining the school-room as a chancel, affording a place for service until such time as a church may be built. This building was first used November, 1872.

The grounds also contain a commodious hospital solidly built of stone, with brick trimmings. This is heated and ventilated in the most approved manner, and supplied with purest spring water. It was, we learned, built and furnished by a noble Christian woman * as a memorial thank-offering for Godly parents and beloved children. It was opened with religious exercises July 9, 1873, the founder with her husband and other friends being present, and a few days later its first patient, a teacher of the children, who was stricken with fever,

* Mrs. Dobney.

was admitted. Removed from the bustle and noise of a large household to the delicious quiet of the perfectly ventilated ward, and to the tender care of an experienced nurse and devout woman, who is ever ready in sickness or health to aid the work in every way, she rapidly recovered. Several children have enjoyed its benefits. It is brightened with mottoes, illuminated cards and pictures of a cheerful and elevating character. A nurse's room adjoins. Snow-white curtains and counterpanes and a little table at the head of each bed are also part of the furniture. The only patient was a doll, which was apparently receiving considerable attention from the younger members of the Home. The room was well lighted, having windows on three sides, one of which opened on a pleasant veranda with a delightful outlook. Not only were the stairs carpeted to deaden the sound of footsteps, but the hospital seemed to possess every adjunct to give quiet and comfort to those who might happen to be its inmates.

In the main building, or Nursery Cottage, which is occupied by the Rector and his family, is the children's sitting room, where they spend their evenings, and where family prayers are held. It contains quite a library, also a little conservatory where the children have their own plants. These are kept in little garden patches of their own in summer. The children are taught to weed, water and properly care for their plants, and are instructed how to save the seeds in autumn. The love of flowers is inculcated in the children. The porch of the school building was embellished with them, and boxes for their growth were improvised in the windows of the upper story, in which flowers and creepers were visible.

The grounds are being improved. Here and there a huge rock remains in its original position, giving an air of picturesqueness to the place, as well as a hint of its obdurate character and the difficulties that have been encountered in its subjugation. In the erection of the buildings, and in the clearing and cultivation of the land, the labor of the boys has been employed.

Seven fine milch cows are kept upon the place. The hillsides and garden furnish abundance of summer berries, which, partaken of with the milk, form a healthful diet for the children.

The discipline of the house is thus outlined by Rev. Mr. Gay: "We have no high walls, no bolts or bars. A boy comes to us from the city, village or the country lane. He is, perhaps, perfectly undisciplined and with many bad habits. He is introduced to a boy of his own age, who is to show him the place and inform him of the rules. He finds his days filled from early morning till bedtime with duties, studies and amusements. He is assured of the kind love of those who are over him. He finds himself trusted, his word believed. He is taught his part in our religious services and joins in the hearty singing of God's praise. The result is that the wild, undisciplined boy is transformed to a truthful, trusty, honest youth."

The following extract, from the last report of the Superintendent, affords a living picture of life in the Home:

"We would take the opportunity afforded by this report to introduce our friends to the interior of our house and show them the daily routine. At an early hour, 5 A. M. in summer, 6 A. M. in the shortest days of winter, the family are all astir. In the dormitories the children are taught on rising, first of all, to acknowledge the kind care which keeps them through the night. Immediately after the washing and dressing, each one has some duty to perform — some little work to do. Within the hour all are gathered in the reading room for instruction from God's Word. This instruction consists in the committal to memory of a text illustrative of the Church Catechism, in which the arrangement of texts by the late Bishop Doane, of New Jersey, is generally followed. This text learned in the morning is repeated at each meal before grace, and all the texts of the week are reviewed on Sundays. After the learning of the text, the ringing bell summons the adults, and all join in family prayers. From prayers all proceed to breakfast. After breakfast the girls attend to the housework, the boys to the garden, barn or other out-of-door work, from which, at nine o'clock, they are summoned to school. School duties, with the dinner hour and recesses for play, occupy the day till 3 P. M., when the girls engage in sewing, the boys in outside work till 4.30 P. M., then play till 5.30. Supper is followed by family prayers at 6. The children retire at 7, 8 or 9 o'clock P. M., according to age.

"The evening is spent in reading, sewing, study, music, games. The object in this daily routine is to fill each child's time with some employment which shall occupy his mind, be instructive to him, and mingle with his duties such pleasures as shall make his life what the Creator intended it to be, a cheerful and useful one. In allotting work, care is taken to change the departments once a month, so that each girl may become acquainted with all departments of housework; each boy learns to handle different tools and learns the different kinds of out-door work. In the barn are horses, cattle, pigs, etc. In his turn each boy learns to drive, to milk, to feed the cattle and pigs, to plough, to dig and plant the garden, to hoe and weed, and engages in all the various labors of the farm. On the river he learns to row and to fish. Shad fishing is an important consideration to our family, and the boys have been very successful with the nets. Besides fully supplying the family with abundance of shad, we sold for cash in May, 1874, shad to the amount of $92.32. While erecting the buildings the boys attended the carpenters and masons, and with the young men did most of the painting of the houses both inside and out. They have been also largely engaged in digging drains, in grading the grounds about the house, in clearing the ground of bushes and stones. Our friends who visit us from time to time notice continual improvements. Hill-sides are beginning to be cleared for cultivation. Stone is drawn out ready for the wall layers and builders, the roads are widened and leveled, the hill behind the house has had a large slice cut off, and cast into the hollow in front; banks have been sodded; trees, shrubs and vines planted. The larger portion of all which work, and much more, which, hidden in ditches and drains underground, is unseen, has been done by the boys. * * * * * * *

"The daily religious instruction has been already mentioned. Beyond this, there is the great teaching of the Church's year, in which the life of the Saviour is so wonderfully set before us. We have the full service of the Church on all Sundays and on the principal holy days, with daily service in Lent. The older children learn the Collect and Gospel for each Sunday, and have instruction upon them; also special instruction in classes on the Catechism, and preparatory to Confirmation and the Holy Communion. The religious instruction is, as it were, woven into the life of the family, not as a sanctimonious something to be put on at set times, but as a real part of the constant life, something so real and necessary as to belong to the daily life, so that the child is rather unconsciously influenced by it than absolutely taught. The result is, that all join heartily and of their own free will in the services, both at family prayer and in Church.

"For amusement, the children have all that which plenty of room in the country can afford. The situation of the house on the river bank affords many opportunities for aquatic sports. In the warm summer days there is bathing at high tide. Nearly all, even of the smaller boys soon become ready swimmers, and all who are large enough to handle an oar learn to row. Excursions on the river with the boats form a favorite summer amusement. A row of three to six or more miles is not thought too long a pull, while an occasional visit to West Point, ten miles away, or even farther up the river to Polipel's Island for a picnic, with the pull home by moonlight, affords the highest delight. Several times with crews of the best rowers have excursions been extended as far as the Kaatskills, camping out at night, and on one occasion were tide-waters passed and the boat pushed forty miles above Waterford on the Champlain canal. Such excursions afford the boys a knowledge of the river and the towns upon it, have sufficient of adventure about them to form a theme of conversation during the year, while the hopeful candidates for the next year's excursion find a continual spur in their hope for good conduct and industry. Said a gentleman who accompanied one of these expeditions to the Kaatskills: 'I think these boys are better than the average.

Here have we been for a week with these boys free from restraint, full of fun and frolic, and yet I have not heard an angry or improper word, or seen aught unbecoming a gentleman.'

"In the house and on the winter evenings the reading room, with its bright lights, long tables well covered with books, papers and games, which our friends have so kindly supplied, is a homelike and attractive place. The little girls have their separate sitting room in the 'bee hive,' where they can read or play with their dolls or sew."

In regard to the class of children received, the superintendent says: "We do not take children that are not needy; but if a child is really homeless, we take it. We have children here of all denominations."

A touching picture of one of the little waifs who found a home and kind friends in this institution shows for whom it has been established. "A poor little girl came to our doors — a sickly, deformed, dying child. 'Mother broke my back and didn't love me any more.' 'But my child the dear Saviour loves you.' 'No, He don't; there don't anybody love me.' She suffered much, but no word seemed to touch her. She shrank from all, even the little girls. She would eat alone, nor would she join in any childish sports. The good mother of the family alone seemed to gain any admission to her confidence. One day she was shown a picture of our Saviour weeping over Jerusalem. 'Oh, don't He look sweet,' she said. 'Yes, He is our dear Lord; He is the Good Shepherd; you are one of His little lambs; so He has brought you to this house; you know this is called the House of the Good Shepherd.' 'What, this His house?' 'Yes, my child, this is the House of the Good Shepherd, and He loves you, and has sent you here, where we all love you, and want you to be happy.' She sat and looked long at the picture, and for the first time seemed happy and at peace. An entire change came over her manner. The wildness went away. She desired the other children to be with her. She often said, 'don't send me away; I love to be here.' She wished always to be in at prayers to join in the sweet hymns and praises of the dear Saviour, and on the last day of her life here she was twice brought in her little chair to the family service. Then, in happy trust, she fell asleep."

It is contemplated building a church on the grounds, and some of the stones have, we were informed, been drawn for the purpose, and the corner-stone has been already laid.

The total expenditures for the year ending September 30, were $6,502.11; of this, about $2,000 were expended in liquidating indebtedness previously incurred. The total indebtedness was $10,000, of which $6,000 was upon the real estate.

It is to be regretted that, through lack of means, the benefits of the House cannot be further extended to take in more of the numerous applicants who sadly need its care. From the last report of the Secretary of the Ladies' Association, Mrs. E. Butler, already referred to, it appears that there are "at present one hundred little ones homeless and destitute vainly appealing for admission, there being no funds in the treasury to support them. Can it be possible that any one knowing the needs of these poor little neglected children, will refuse a helping hand in this work which is carrying out spiritually and bodily the command of our Saviour: 'Feed My Lambs?'"

Standing upon this elevated and picturesque spot, with the Hudson and all its varied attractions spread out before us, a grand panorama of marvelous beauty, this house for homeless children, hallowed by unnumbered sacrifices, and by the noble lives devoted to its sacred work, seemed still more beautiful, and we lingered lovingly while tracing its every lineament upon our hearts.

The Day Home.

Troy.

The Home is situated at the corner of Congress and Seventh streets. It occupies an old frame family mansion two stories in height, and has a large yard planted with shade trees. It was organized in 1858, and incorporated April 10th, 1861. It objects are: "To provide a day home for such children as from the poverty or vice of their parents are not fit subjects for the ward schools; also to furnish a temporary home for a day and a night to destitute children who may require such temporary shelter."

The few facts relative to its early history are thus given: "As great numbers of vagabond children roamed about the city begging and idling, a necessity was felt by the ladies for their moral and social elevation. Funds for the purchase of the Day Home were solicited at the same time that the First Regiment from Troy was being fitted out for the late war, in April, 1862. In less than seven weeks $7,000 were raised by the persistent efforts of two ladies. The institution is wholly managed by ladies, being the first one so directed that received a charter in this country. The number of inmates at its opening was one hundred and twenty-five.

At the date of visitation, September 11th, the institution was found to be under the charge of Mrs. Sabra Brainerd. Two teachers, and a woman to do kitchen work, made up, together with the Matron, the entire force of the institution.

The mothers of the children who receive its benefits are those who go out to work, and who, the Matron says; would leave their children in the street to take care of themselves but for this institution. This lady further states: "Many of the parents are drinkers, and many of the children have mothers only. We pick up a great many street wanderers, put them to school, and try to train them up in the way in which they should go.

"We commence school at nine o'clock. We open the gates to admit children at half-past eight, and keep them till four o'clock. They get their dinner every day, and a good dinner it is.

"The school is opened with reading the scriptures, religious instruction and prayers, and then the ordinary English branches — reading, writing, the first principles of grammar and geography — are taught. Once a week one of the Ladies of the Board comes in to give religious instruction to the children. We have always had one hour in the week for music. We can see quite a change in the children after they have been here a while. On first coming they are always ragged and dirty. We get them to appear a little better. We make them clean, and give out clothing, such as shoes and wearing apparel generally, once a month. The number of shoes given out last winter was very large. The clothes are partly donated and partly purchased out of the funds of the institution."

In regard to the ages of the children the Matron says: "The children are of all ages, ranging from the earliest school age upward. A boy eleven years old came last winter, who did not know his letters. We have had some very bright children, and we now have some that are as apt as any children in the city. They look hard and rough when they come first to school. Some of them continue to look so, but there is generally a great change effected in them. Most of them are of German parentage."

The career of the children after leaving the institution, as a general rule, is encouraging to those carrying on the charity. "Some of our girls," the Matron says, "do very well, and nearly all the children do well out of the city."

The behavior of the children was said to be, on the whole, good. "One boy," says the Matron, "we were obliged to expel, but he came back begging to be received again, and he is now doing very well."

In regard to methods of discipline the Matron says: "We try every way we can think of. Sometimes one thing will do, sometimes another. All the dignity one can muster must be assumed at times. Sometimes they are very rude at table, especially when they first come in."

The house appeared to be kept in very good order. The school room had all needed requisites, including an organ.

The dining room was furnished with tables, covered with white enameled cloth. Crockery plates, tin cups and spoons were in use.

In the sitting room were portraits of the founders of the institution — Mrs. C. E. Dickerman, Mrs. Abigail Hagg and Mrs. C. R. S. Ingalls.

"On the holidays," the Matron says, "extra preparations are made to entertain the children. On Thanksgiving they have a dinner of turkey, chicken, pies, etc.; on Christmas, a tree laden with presents. We do not give them a grand dinner then; but at Easter we provide something out of the ordinary routine. Besides these, we have a summer picnic, when we invite the citizens to join us."

The number of children that shared the benefits of the institution during the year ending October 1, was two hundred and twenty-five; the average number was ninety. The total expenditures during the year were $3,539.15. The value of its invested funds at date of October 1, was $32,169.50.

The great number of poor children that have been benefited by the Home since its organization, by taking them from the streets and from the pernicious influences of low homes and putting them in the way of doing something for themselves, must make its value apparent to all thoughtful citizens.

St. Vincent's Female Orphan Asylum.

Troy.

This asylum was organized and known as the St. Mary's Orphan Asylum, Troy, about the year 1850, by the Rev. Father Havermans. It retained this name till the date of its incorporation in 1863, when it assumed its present title. The institution has always been under the charge of the Sisters of Charity. It began with about twelve children, and has been steadily increasing till it has reached its present numbers.

On the date of visitation the asylum was in charge of Sister Sarah A. Baker, who has been connected with it from its very beginning. She is assisted by seven other Sisters of the Roman Catholic Order of the Sisters of Charity.

The present location of the asylum is on the corner of Washington and Fifth streets, in the building formerly occupied by the Troy Hospital. The age of the building and its proximity to the New York Central Railroad render it very undesirable for an orphan asylum. The smoke and sparks from the engines are constantly blown over into the yard, rendering both persons and property unsafe. The Sisters are fully alive to these drawbacks, but, being incumbered with a heavy debt, they are unable to make a change. "We are," says the Sister, "cramped for accommodations. I cannot take in more than one hundred and thirty children, and will have to make room for others by placing some out.

"Children are received between the ages of three and nine years, and when suitable places can be obtained for them they are bound out. They come mostly from the city. The city allows us $1.50, and the county $2, a week for the support of their charges. But we get a great many for whom we receive nothing. There are now in the house over twenty-two that we have to support entirely ourselves."

The utter neglect from which some of the children have suffered is thus described in the words of the Sister: "They frequently come in a very neglected condition. I have had them arrive in so dreadful a state that I was obliged to poultice their heads in order to get them clean."

The girls receive a plain English education, and are taught to wash, iron, sew, cook and make bread. "We make," says the Sister, "all our own clothes, and have a dressmaker in the house to teach dressmaking to the larger girls."

A school is held on the premises. The children are taught vocal music. The class room for little girls and the class room for larger girls are furnished with patent desks and seats, and slate slabs in the walls.

The dormitories were very clean and are furnished with single iron bedsteads. Straw beds and feather pillows are used. Sisters sleep in each room with the girls.

Two were on the sick list in the infirmary, which is furnished with eleven wooden bedsteads, and a Sister's bed.

The Sister says: "We go to a great deal of trouble to preserve the health of the children. It is all the poor children have. Once a week we take them to a hill near here for exercise."

The wardrobes of the children were well supplied. The Sister remarks: "Each girl has seven dresses. Two for everyday wear in summer of calico; two calico suits for Sunday; a light suit to go out in; one suit for winter of Rob Roy flannel; another of green gingham for fall and spring. We buy knit stuff by the yard, and make stockings out of it for the children."

The tables in the dining-room were covered with white enameled cloth. The children sit on benches and use crockery plates, knives and forks, and tin cups. Off from the dining room is the wash room containing a long trough and two bath tubs. The girls wash in running water. The bath tubs were high from the ground to enable the two Sisters who have charge to better endure the fatigue of bathing the children. Both hot and cold water are on supply.

The laundry is separate from the main building, and the ironing is done in the same department.

In regard to the results of the work the Sister spoke as follows: "The children turn out well. Some of them live in the first families in Troy. The money the children earn after they leave I save for them, and even buy them their clothes. Many of them are young and foolish, and if I did not they would spend it all. Some save a good deal. For instance, I had a poor woman's children with me for a long time. Her husband had left her. She went to work, and of her own accord brought her money regularly to me, and in four years' time she had laid up $500 for her children. Many of the girls marry and do well."

The number of children in the institution October 1, 1875, was one hundred and thirty-three. Of these, nineteen were orphans, ninety-one were half-orphans, and twenty-three had both parents living. Fifty were of native parents and eighty-three of foreign. Five were partially supported by friends, nineteen wholly by the institution, and one hundred and nine by public authorities. The number received during the year was sixty; the total number discharged thirty-five. Of the latter eight were placed out by adoption, and six by indenture, eleven were returned to parents or guardians, nine were otherwise discharged, and one died. The average number during the year was one hundred and twenty-eight.

The total expenditures for the year were $15,327.60. Of this sum $1,752.50 was paid out for indebtedness upon the real estate, and about $1,000 for buildings and improvements. The total indebtedness was $24,605.78.

The whole number of girls that have shared the benefits of the institution since its organization is nine hundred and sixty-eight.

The Sister in charge felt the great disadvantage of their present location. In alluding to it, she said: "It is a house difficult to keep clean on account of the smoke from the cars, and from the gas house. The place is badly situated. The noise of freight and passenger trains is very trying, and the sparks from the engines are very dangerous."

The work of this asylum has been, and is now impeded by financial embarrassments. Notwithstanding the efforts of the Sisters to make the most of existing resources, its field of operation has been abridged. The large number of poor girls who have, through its beneficence, been elevated and helped into good homes, and the numerous applicants to whom admission had of necessity to be refused, show that it not only deserves mention among the worthy charities of Troy, but that it should receive hearty encouragement and support from the benevolent.

Troy Catholic Male Orphan Asylum.

Troy.

This institution was organized in 1850, and incorporated under the general law January 5, 1864. Its history is stated to be as follows: "In 1850, Troy had a population of thirty-five thousand, a good proportion of whom were Catholics. There being no institution in the place where Catholic orphan children might be cared for, in accordance with the faith of their church, the Catholics, under the energetic lead of the Rev. Peter Havermans, pastor of St. Mary's church, founded the Asylum. In 1863, the Christian Brothers were called upon to take charge and become the responsible managers, their labors from the beginning having been confined to the care and education of the few children it was able to provide for. From a commencement of three, it kept steadily increasing till its legal organization, when the number reached one hundred and fifty-three, and during the war it had about one hundred and eighty inmates. The exact number cannot be given, as the books have been destroyed by fire. In May, 1866, the old Asylum, a frame building, was burned down, leaving the orphans in utter destitution, and for a time this sad event dispersed them to such places of shelter as could be found among our charitable people. Shortly after, a large shed, which had been used as a barrack for the Union soldiers, was purchased, and made as available as possible for a temporary Asylum. Only those who witnessed the condition of the institution, in these days of trial, can tell the difficulties that had to be overcome and the hardships endured. Shortly after the destruction of the old Asylum, a Board of Trustees was organized, to take measures for the erection of a new building. A proper site having been secured, the new edifice was commenced, and was prosecuted with energy till brought to its present state. Attached to the institution is a farm of fourteen and a quarter acres of land, four acres of which have been generously donated by Rev. P. Havermans."

The new building is of brick, four stories in height, and has a capacity for four hundred children. It is situated on the corner of Hanover and Bedford streets, on an elevated site. The visitation was made on the 13th of September, when the institution contained one hundred and forty-six inmates, ranging from three to seven years old.

A Board of seven trustees control the finances of the Asylum, and its immediate charge is committed to seven Christian Brothers, with Brother Candidus Burke at their head. The employés consist of a woman to take care of the little children, a cook, and a janitor, having a general oversight of the house. The work of the seven Brothers is divided as follows: "Brother Candidus, the Director, has charge of the house and its business affairs; two Brothers are teachers; one, called the Prefect, has supervision of the boys after school hours; another has charge of the linen and clothing department; one Brother superintends the dining room and kitchen, and the seventh superintends the general cleanliness of the house."

The building is spacious, with high ceilings and large windows hung with cords, weights and pulleys. It is lighted with gas and heated by stoves. "Formerly," we were told, "it was heated by furnaces, but these were found unsuitable, and, besides, the roots being stored in the basement, they were liable to decay when furnaces were used, and the smell was carried throughout the house." But since they have used stoves, the basement is kept cool, and it is said the inmates are not now thus inconvenienced.

The building is supplied with city water, and ventilated by flues in the walls.

Most of the children, we were informed, come from the county or city, the former paying $2.00 a week each for their support, and the latter, $1.50. "They remain till we can place them out. We send them either with farmers or with private families. Some of them are put to learn trades, but we do not bind them out.

"In the disciplining of the children we use encouragements, but, when necessary, have recourse to corporal punishment, which is administered on the hands."

A school is conducted on the premises, taught by the Brothers, but under the Department of Public Instruction. A teacher from the public school comes once a week to instruct the children in vocal music, when a piano belonging to the institution is brought into requisition for accompaniments.

In the infirmary was a little infant ill with measles. Two other little children, under five years of age, were on the sick-list. The nurse's room adjoins the infirmary. "We had," says the Brother, "four deaths during the past year. One was from consumption, another from brain fever, and two died from cholera morbus. One of these was six years old, and another was a little German boy, ten years of age."

The dormitories extend the entire length of the building, and are furnished with single iron and wooden bedsteads. The beds are of straw or husks. A Brother sleeps in each room.

The tables in the dining room are made of white wood, oiled. Benches are used for seats. Tin plates, cups, knives, forks and spoons are used at table. A dais is at the end of the room, on which the tables of the Brothers are placed. They eat at the same time with the boys.

The lavatory is fitted up with troughs on three sides, and so arranged that the boys can wash in running water. The washing of clothes, etc., is done in a separate building. The boys wash their own shirts.

A shoe factory is carried on in the basement, in which sixteen boys and three men were at work. The room contained a large machine for sewing uppers, another for sewing on soles, also a splitting machine, an eyelet machine, and a set of dies for making women's, children's and misses' shoes. Most of the boys employed, it is said, have been four or five years in the house. "The intention is to send them out qualified to support themselves by means of a trade."

The number of children in the Asylum Oct. 1, who were orphans, was fifteen; half-orphans, one hundred and twenty; who had both parents living, twenty-four. Thirteen were of native parents. Of one hundred and forty-six, the nativity of the parents was unascertained. Eighteen were partially supported by parents or friends, four wholly by the institution and one hundred and seven by cities or counties. The number received during the year was ninety-eight; total number discharged, sixty-nine. Of the latter fifty-six were returned to parents or guardians; nine were placed out on trial with a view to indenture, and four died. The average number during the year was one hundred and thirty-eight.

The total amount of expenditures for the year ending September 30, was $16,798.26. The total indebtedness was $11,291.06.

The whole number of boys that have shared the benefits of the institution since its organization is about fourteen hundred.

The Asylum is undoubtedly accomplishing a great amount of good and should be well sustained. The Brothers are entitled to much credit in their self-denying and arduous labors. It is thought, however, that if it were possible to secure the aid of the Sisters in the management of the domestic affairs of the household greater economy and neatness might be attained.

The Troy Orphan Asylum.

Troy.

Occupies an elevated site at 294 Eighth street, overlooking the city. A neatly trimmed grass plot extends in front of the building, and flowers embellish its grounds. The edifice is of brick, four stories high with a projecting porch in front and free stone moldings and cornices. The Asylum was established in 1833, and incorporated by the Legislature April 10, 1835. The present edifice building was erected in 1862.

The following scrap of its history has been furnished:

"The object of the founders of the institution was at first to provide for and relieve orphan children alone, but at last the Trustees modified their views, and the exclusive objects of the Association now are to rescue all destitute and orphan children from wretchedness and ignorance and vicious influences; provide for them a comfortable habitation during the period of infancy and early childhood; furnish them with clean and comfortable clothing, and plain but wholesome diet; instruct them in the useful branches of a common education, and form them to habits of industry; and when sufficiently instructed and deemed capable of earning their livelihood, to bind them as apprentices to persons of fair character, and on terms calculated to promote their future welfare.

"Prominent among its founders were the Harts, Merrills, Lanes, Tibbits, Paynes, McCoans, Starbucks, Lockwoods, Vails, Buells, and other families of Troy. Mrs. Richard P. Hart of Troy gave $10,000 toward erecting the present building, the citizens of Troy furnishing the balance, and the school room at the south-east end of the main building was erected by the wife of Hon. George Vail, at a cost of $3,000."

In the hall, observable on entering, are two memorial tablets; one commemorating the gift of Mrs. Richard P. Hart and the contributions of the citizens of Troy toward the erection of the present edifice after the destruction of the former one by fire on the 10th of May, 1862. The other was in memory of Nathaniel Starbuck, which the Trustees, out of affectionate regard for his memory, have erected.

The finances of the institution are controlled by a Board of Trustees — gentlemen; but its domestic and internal concerns are under the direction of an association of lady managers.

The building is lighted by gas, heated by furnaces and supplied with city water.

The Asylum is in the immediate charge of a Matron. The subordinate force consists of one nurse, two chambermaids, three laundresses, two seamstresses, two cooks and a janitor. It is not customary to employ as domestics mothers having children who are inmates of the Asylum. The Matron, Mrs. M. A. Greenman, says on this point: "We do not engage any such now. We found their children always wanted to be with them, and had the idea that they must obey none of the rules that were made, like the other children."

The play-room for little girls is fitted up with compartments for play-things, in which were many little toys. The walls were illuminated with engravings suitable for children, for which the Matron had improvised borders of blue paper, with a view to teaching the children how to make trifles look pretty with little expense.

The boys' play-room is well adapted to its uses, and is so finished with wainscoting that they are able to amuse themselves in full freedom with marbles, balls or tops, without injuring the room.

Ample provision is made for the comfort of the little inmates. The dormitories are airy; the beds furnished with abundance of clothes, suited to the varying seasons. Plain but nutritious food is supplied.

The bath-rooms, in the basement, for both boys and girls, are fitted up similarly and flagged, but covered with wooden racks, to prevent the feet of the children coming in contact with the cold stone. They wash, we were informed, in running water, three or four times a day. Care is taken to separate healthy from unhealthy children, and where there are any suffering with cutaneous eruptions they are bathed by themselves. A care-taker has charge of the girls, and the janitor of the boys.

The school occupies two rooms, one for the little children furnished with the usual infant school gallery, and brightened with picture cards, another with an organ for the larger inmates. The boys and girls sit at opposite sides of the room, facing each other, and the teacher's desk is on a dais between the two.

The floor is varnished, and the apartment neatly kept. The children sang with much spirit: "Hold the Fort." The school is, we were informed, under the Department of Public Instruction, which supplies the teacher. On Sunday a Sabbath-school is held here, the teachers being furnished by the various churches in the city. The school-room opens out on a long piazza extending the entire length of the main building.

Both boys and girls have separate play-grounds with swings. These are inclosed by a substantial brick wall, and are paved with stone flagging, which, the Matron says, "is a great detriment to shoe leather."

The laundry is outside and separate from the main building. The money to build it was donated by Mr. Lockwood. A portion of the rain water is saved but the capacity of the tanks is not sufficient for the needs of the institution. The laundry is supplied from a spring.

In regard to industries, Mrs. Greenman remarks: "The girls are taught to sew and the boys to knit. Every Wednesday afternoon is devoted to this work. The girls are taught to do housework, helping alternately with the washing. We try to teach them to be useful and to cultivate habits of neatness.

"I do not allow the children to think they can go around with their shoestrings hanging in a slack manner. I tell them that the habits they form now will stick to them through life, and that cleanliness prevents sickness."

Ample provision is made for the inmates in the way of dress. Mrs. Greenman says: "The girls have one Sunday and two week-day suits. In summer they are supplied with straw hats and gray cloth sacques.

Their winter suits are uniform; Scotch plaid, worsted goods, felt hats, blue cloaks of beaver cloth, brightened with steel buttons. Skirts of blue flannel and under-skirts made of knitted goods are also worn. The boys in winter wear suits of dark gray woolen cloth."

The various holidays are duly observed: Christmas, Thanksgiving, and the Fourth of July. "We try," Mrs. Greenman says, "to make the children feel that they are in a home while with us, and not in a prison."

The infirmary was without an occupant. The Matron says: "We had no deaths during the past year. We have not had a death since two years ago last May. No children are sick. We do not intend to have any if we can possibly keep them well. Our method is, when any thing is the matter, to attend to them promptly. Regarding the rules for the admission of children, the Matron says: "Children are brought here, and a committee investigate the matter. Some are taken for a number of weeks; others are taken permanently. Those who have friends able to pay for their board are charged $1.50 a week. This committee determines who is to be received, and on what conditions. We are paid $1.50 a week from the city and $2 from the county. Parents or relatives who are able, are charged the same as the city. A few are quite reliable, and pay in advance; others have not paid for years."

The following is the method for disposing of the children: A child is placed out for three months on trial, on the supposition that the party appears, after a reasonable amount of investigation, to be suitable. If the child is not comfortable, or does not suit, it is brought home, and another place for it is procured. "We have had usually," Mrs. Greenman says, "very good fortune with our children. Some of them have married and are doing well, and have nice homes of their own. We do not take children under three years, nor over ten. and we put them out from twelve to fourteen. Those that are given to us permanently we keep till they are of the latter age. In some instances we keep them longer. Others we put out when we can get a chance. If a person comes who is willing to adopt a child, we let him have one, but such cases are very rare. A great many of the children are taken back by their friends."

On being asked what means were taken to look after children placed out, she said: "We have always had a visiting committee to look after them. This committee, it is believed, has been very active in tracing out where children have been ill-treated and bringing them back. As a general thing our children have remained where they have been placed."

As bearing upon what has been accomplished by these earnest workers, who have been so long and zealously engaged in this charity, we quote from the forty-first annual report of the society :

"As the result of their labors, over one thousand children of the class for whom it was established have found a home, with all the comforts and privileges of a home, in this asylum. Many of them have become respected and useful citizens. Some have attained positions of influence, and are blessed with means which enable them, in turn, to act the part of benefactors to those who are their successors in the enjoyment of the benefits conferred by the institution which nourished and cherished them. No labored argument is needed to prove that the orphan asylum is one of the most valuable and important of the institutions which have been reared by enlightened and liberal Christian charity."

From a late report of the secretary of the Ladies' Auxiliary Society, Mrs. E. C. S. Knox, it is inferred that the cordial co-operation of the benevolent is now necessary to carry on the work with efficiency. Her words are:

"While the coming year is likely to be one of increased demand upon all who have any thing to give, it will also be one of many and increased applications here, and while we are endeavoring to use what we have to the best possible advantage, and cut down every unnecessary expense, yet our expenses must still be very heavy. One hundred children cannot be fed and warmed and clothed and nursed on any small sum. Those who provide for small families will readily realize this. We will not believe that our citizens are not ready and willing to support this orphan asylum ; but it is an old story, and like all old stories, becomes tedious at times. The asylum is old, but the children are young, and a fresh reinforcement always at hand; and the Master's test is still the same: 'Lovest thou me? Feed my lambs.'"

The number of children received into the institution since its organization is fourteen hundred and eighty-seven. The number received during the past year was sixty-five; the number discharged, forty-eight. Of the latter, seventeen were placed out by indenture, thirty-one returned to parents or guardians. There remained in the institution, October 1, one hundred and five children. Nineteen were orphans, seventy-six half-orphans and ten had both parents living. Sixty were of native, and forty-five of foreign, parentage. Nineteen were partially supported by friends, sixty-eight by counties or towns, and eighteen wholly by the institution.

The total expenditure for the year ending October 30, was $12,287.67. The amount of its indebtedness was $4,000, and the value of its invested funds was $32,500.

The great sacrifices that have been made in times past by the eminent citizens and friends who have been its patrons, and the large number of destitute and homeless children to whom the asylum has been a stepping-stone to independence and respectability must commend the work to the liberal support of the community in which it is located.

The House of the Good Shepherd,

Utica,

Occupies a healthy situation on elevated ground, in the eastern part of the city, about two miles from the railroad depot.

It was organized through the benevolent efforts of a number of Christian ladies of Utica, in 1872, and incorporated by act of the Legislature, February 8, of the same year. Its property is under the control of a Board of eleven Trustees, composed of gentlemen, who act as an Advisory Committee to the Board of Lady Managers who direct its charitable work and manage its domestic affairs. The house is under the immediate charge of a Matron. A school teacher, two nurses, a cook and a laundress are also employed.

The objects of the society are stated to be "the permanent care of infirm children, and the temporary care of friendless, neglected or destitute children." In the beginning a building for temporary use was secured, and a number of helpless children were soon receiving the kind attentions of the ladies interested. While this work was going on, subscriptions were solicited with a view to the erection of a building for the purposes of the asylum. A handsome sum was at length subscribed to carry out this purpose by the benevolent. The site referred to was secured, embracing an area of two hundred by one hundred and twenty feet. Upon this an attractive building has been erected, seemingly well-fitted to the purposes for which it was designed. The basement is used for kitchen and other purposes. The first floor is divided into apartments for the school and managers' reception rooms, closets, clothes and bath-rooms. On the second floor are dormitories, nursery room for boys and girls, apartments for nurses, clothes rooms, etc. The attic is unfinished, and will enlarge the accommodations of the house when completed. A beautiful view of the scenery around Utica may be obtained from the tower and balconies on the north side of the house. On the 9th of April, 1875, the children were removed from the temporary building to this pleasant home, and the house was formally opened with interesting ceremonies the following June.

From the Matron in charge of the institution, Miss Mary McCune, the following information was obtained in answer to inquiries made on the occasion of a brief visitation, September 14th: "There were thirty-four children in the house, about equally divided as to sex. The youngest was a little girl about four months old; the youngest boy was about two years old. No females over fourteen years of age are admitted into the asylum except in the cases of mothers with infant children. In case of children being received younger than two years, it is customary to place them out in families until they have been weaned, the asylum paying for their maintenance. About eighteen children of the house, and seventeen from outside attend the school, where they receive instruction in spelling, reading, writing, arithmetic and geography.

The work being done here may be best illustrated by quoting the following language from the report of the Secretary, Miss Gertrude H. Coxe, just issued:

"Our work has been from the beginning one of faith, and we have had every encouragement 'to increase that faith in us evermore,' for there has ever been found to aid us kind hearts and open purses. The small tenement house we rented until the completion of the new building, was filled to overflowing with the homeless children who looked to us for shelter, and we were obliged to refuse admittance to many, simply for want of room; a fact which seems to point conclusively to the great necessity for, and worthiness of, our charity. The cases of misery and destitution which we have been able in a measure to alleviate, are numerous and painful, and some instances of suffering and starvation among little children are touching with the pathos of truth.

"One cold autumn evening a little girl came to the house. The Matron asked her what she wanted. She looked up timidly and said: 'Oh! I only want to find the Good Shepherd's Home, and whether they would please let me come in.' She had slept the night before on the back steps of a kitchen, and had nothing to eat all the day, being locked out of doors by her drunken mother. She was received, fed, washed and cared for, her ragged covering exchanged for clean garments; and when she saw the little children kneel to say their evening prayers, she burst into tears, and could hardly believe she was to be numbered with them, and enjoy the comfort of a nice bed, having slept since she could remember 'on the floor in the corner.' Again, a child was brought to the house, found under a canal bridge, where it had cried itself to sleep, while hiding away in fear of its intoxicated parents. In another instance, a child was following its mother, who was being led by a police officer to the station house, the father being already in State prison. The child was observed by a friend, who knew something of her misery, and a home was provided for her in 'The House of the Good Shepherd,' where she was found willing, obedient and grateful for the kindness. Other children have been sheltered who bore evident marks of brutal treatment on their poor, shivering bodies and limbs. Often it is unsafe to give them at once enough to satisfy their hungry cravings. Little ones, who have stayed long enough to become attached to the inmates, and are removed, beg to come back again; and in cases where they have returned, show their delight in ways not to be misunderstood. One little girl said, upon asking admission for the second time, 'This is the only good place I was ever in, and the only place where I ever learned any thing good.'

"Glancing back over the last two years, it seems truly wonderful how much has been accomplished. Beginning with absolutely nothing, save an abiding faith in the everlasting mercy of our Heavenly Father, but with and in that faith beginning, we have, through His blessing, been able to rescue nearly one hundred poor little starvelings from sore distress and destitution — some of them almost from the borders of death itself. Beginning with a small and inconvenient tenement rented for the occasion, we have within this short time erected and nearly paid for a beautiful and durable 'Home,' an ornament in itself and a perpetual monument to the Christian spirit of the noble men and women who have contributed their labor and substance to the undertaking."

The total expenditures of the institution during the past year were $12,102.92. Of this sum, $11,067.66 was expended for buildings and improvements. Its indebtedness on October 1, 1875, was $2,500. It has no invested funds.

It must be stated with regret that the institution is incumbered with a debt of $4,000. It is believed, however, that the zeal shown by the Christian ladies engaged in this work will be fully rewarded by a generous support. This attempt to rescue from degradation a class who have the fewest friends, and who, if neglected, will inevitably swell the pauper and criminal ranks which burden society, cannot be too highly commended

---

St. John's Female Orphan Asylum.

Utica.

Linking together the past and the present of this noble charity, there still remains the simple building in which it commenced forty years ago. To this unpretending structure additions have been made from time to time, till the Asylum now stands forth in the comely proportions in which we found it, on the day of visitation. The growth of this charity, like that of many others of its kind, has called for the exercise of such unflinching perseverance, and for the practice of such rigorous self-denial, as only those who firmly believed in the worthiness and ultimate success of their work could endure. We give a few gleanings from the history furnished by those long familiar with its labors.

"Central New York, in 1834, afforded no sufficient protection to orphan children, whose number was rapidly increasing. Impelled by motives of wise philanthropy, two benevolent citizens of Utica,* brothers, made application to the Mother House of the Sisters of Charity, at Emmitsburgh, Md., for the aid of the Sisters, in opening and conducting a Roman Catholic Orphan Asylum and Day School at Utica. At this time the only means of conveyance between Albany and Utica was by stage or the canal, and the city and surrounding country, as compared with its present condition, was undeveloped. The Asylum was opened in a plain dwelling house, the day school being conducted in an adjoining building, which has been replaced by the large brick Asylum edifice. The day school was principally a charity school. At one time it averaged an attendance of five hundred pupils.

"The early days of the institution were dark and gloomy, often without sixpence in the house, and sixteen or twenty persons to support. Through the mercy of God and the charity of the Devereux family, the zealous labors of the Sisterhood — prominent among which have ever stood forth the zeal and energy of Sister Perpetua — the institution struggled on until March 28, 1849. Since that time it has received aid from the State, and has been liberally supported by contributions from the citizens of Utica. Thousands of destitute females from the tenderest years to eighteen or twenty have been protected within its walls, and received a moral, religious and industrial training which fitted them for respectable positions in society.

"In proof of the good that has been and is constantly being done by this institution, we have but to refer to the generations that have passed through it. There are highly respectable mothers of families, teachers in our district schools, governesses in excellent families, who are esteemed no less for their educational qualifications than for their modest and lady-like deportment, sales and trades-women, domestics of every description, each admirable in her station, not only here in Utica and its vicinity, but also in the east, the south and far west, where they have settled advantageously, and it is not an unfrequent occurrence to have a child brought from those distant parts, whose mother's dying request was to have her little one placed in the care of her own early guardians, in old St. John's."

The location of the Asylum is No. 60 John street.

---

* J. C. & N. Devereux.

The buildings are of brick, three stories high, exclusive of basement. The school-house, employed principally for a charity week-day school, covers an area of about three hundred and fifty square feet. A yard, one hundred and twenty feet wide, connects the Asylum with the school-house. Two covered porches extend the entire length of the rear of the Asylum building.

On the date of visitation, September 14th, the Asylum was in charge of Sister Angelica, a lady who had been engaged in the care and instruction of children for about twenty-eight years, the last seven of which were spent in Utica. Nine other Sisters of charity were associated with her in the present work.

This Sister informed us that the average number of children in the Asylum during the past year had been ninety-seven, sometimes running up as high as one hundred and twenty. The number of inmates received into the institution since its foundation is about three thousand.

"We can accommodate," says Sister Angelica, "two hundred children. We receive them from three years upwards. Sometimes they stay with us only as long as their guardians allow them. Some we place in families, others on leaving go to the Industrial School. We watch over them when they are gone and encourage them to communicate with us. Sometimes we put ourselves to a great deal of trouble and expense in looking after them. We try to provide for the little ones as best we can and trust in Divine Providence that He will not let them suffer for want of any thing. We aim to give them a plain English education, embracing reading, writing, arithmetic and grammar. Those who have superior talent are encouraged to cultivate it. Five hours a day are devoted to secular instruction. But few remain long enough to get a really good education. The parents take them away and endeavor to put them at work. We do not feel quite safe in letting them go till they are fifteen years old. We cultivate whatever talent they have. Some have one kind, some another. If for fancy work, we try to cultivate that. We have some who do not seem to have much talent for any thing. Still we strive to teach them how to work, and all who are old enough to learn, are taught how to use the sewing-machine."

The industrial feature of this institution is very marked, and comprises all kinds of house-work, plain and ornamental sewing, tapestry work, and dressmaking. In reference to this, Sister Angelica remarks, "The girls are taught all branches of domestic economy. Each one has a branch of work allotted her, which she must pursue till she gives satisfaction." Changes are made every two months in the different departments of the house. "Our girls bake nicely, and make very good hop-yeast bread. We try, in our discipline, to be very gentle with them. We never use the switch. We think, in most cases, it does a great injury, as it arouses the animal nature. We reward our children for good conduct by credit marks, and by taking them out frequently."

The children seemed contented, and, we were told, became very much attached to the Sisters. The following incident, related to us by the Sister, shows what is considered the "summum bonum" of happiness by some of these little ones: "Two little girls came here last week, and appeared to be very home-sick. They were crying for their mother. Another little girl went to comfort them, and putting her arms around their necks said, 'Never mind, we have such a happy time here. Why we go out to walk, and even go to funerals!'"

"The very little ones," the Sister says, "take a nap every afternoon, and after that have bread and molasses, which they think very nice." The children were clean, their hair was combed back and tied up with neat ribbons. Among the larger girls we noticed a graduate of the Blind Institution of New York, who seemed to be quite a favorite. We were entertained by the children singing in excellent time "Sweet Heart of Jesus."

The dormitories of the asylum are well lighted apartments, with inside blinds upon the windows. The bedsteads are single, made of wood, in the French pattern, and all the furniture is varnished, showing the natural color of the wood. These rooms presented a very cheerful appearance. Two Sisters sleep in each. The Sister's preferences are for wooden bedsteads. She says: "I like the wooden bedsteads decidedly the best. Some think that iron bedsteads will not harbor vermin. This is a mistake. I am sure we have not a bed-bug in the house. We saturate our bedsteads with poison in the spring, and we brush them carefully every morning." Hair mattresses and feather pillows were on all the beds. The latter were made up with great neatness, and covered with snow-white counterpanes.

The infirmary is a pleasant room, but had no inmates. One death had occurred during the past year. In regard to the health of the inmates, the Sister remarks: "The children's health is uniformly good. We have had but three deaths within eighteen or twenty years. We attribute this great blessing, in a measure, to the free use of sulphur water, a fine spring of which is within the house, and of which the children are extremely fond. Good health being the only heritage of these poor children, every effort is made to preserve it to them. This is done by strict attention to cleanliness, diet, exercise and clothing."

In the sewing-room were two sewing machines. Sister Angelica says of this department: "We have a class in sewing of an hour's duration every day. Some of the girls have two hours' sewing. This depends altogether upon how they get along with their studies. Little girls are engaged on simple work, and the larger ones are taught to make coats and other garments. The children make every thing they wear."

In the sitting room were hung some creditable specimens of needle-work. One was an embroidered picture of "Christ turning the water into wine." This was worked by the girls.

The clothes-room was fitted up with extensive wardrobes, each child having a compartment. The supply of winter and summer clothing was ample. Each child had three changes of dresses for summer, and two of woolen for winter, besides a comfortable sacque.

The lavatory presented an appearance of order and neatness, characteristic of the rest of the house. A sink extends along three sides of this room, over which the children's basins, all brightly scoured, were hung. Above these are little shelves for the combs and brushes. In another part of the room the towels were hung. Each child has her own towel, brush, comb, and basin, and a place for them. Each of these articles was found in its place.

The dining room was supplied with chairs. The tables were spread with neat white table cloths, and well furnished. The larger girls occupied one table; the next in size, another; while the youngest children, who go by the pet name of "frogs," sit by themselves in little baby chairs.

The bakery contained a large brick oven capable of baking, at one time, the loaves made from a barrel of flour. The oven comes into very happy use for another purpose. Sister Angelica says of this feature of the establishment: "The children are very fond of baked potatoes. We now and then throw in a quantity of these and have them served up for supper.

The milk cellar and store rooms were also visited and each bore evidence of superior housekeeping.

The laundry was in a wing extending at right angles to the main building.

The Asylum possessed also a comfortable play-room for the children, suitable school-rooms, and a neat chapel capable of seating one hundred.

The house is heated by three furnaces, and when necessary, stoves are also used. The facilities for bathing are ample, the bath-rooms being supplied with both hot and cold water. Gas is burned throughout the building. The drainage was said to be good.

The work of this institution is divided into different departments, one or more Sisters having charge of each, and Sister Angelica presid ing over the whole. Several were engaged in the school-rooms. One had charge of the dormitories and lavatory; one, the sewing room and clothes room; others, the kitchen and dining room; still others, the laundry. By this means every part of the work is thoroughly supervised by competent persons, and the whole maintained in complete order and cleanliness. By this means also, the children old enough to do any work are well instructed in household labor, and, by the changes of work every two months, in all its varieties. Besides, the Sisters being distributed over the house and mingling with the little bands of children give the house a home-like and family character.

In a small space in the yard of the institution, secluded by an iron railing, is a little piece of ground consecrated by the burial of two of the Sisters, Sister Mary Carr and Sister Mary Angela, who died while serving this deserving charity. In the same space stands a simple block surmounted by a cross, and bearing the following inscription:

"Pray for the soul of John C. Devereux, who died December 11, 1848, founder of this Asylum. He distributed to the poor, he fed these Thy little ones. O Lord, may he receive Thy everlasting benediction!"

The number of children received during the past year was twenty-eight, and the number discharged thirty-one. Of the latter, five were placed out by adoption, thirteen returned to parents or guardians, one was transferred to another institution, and twelve were otherwise discharged. There remained in the Asylum October 1, 1875, seventy-one orphans, thirty-one half-orphans, and seven children having both parents living. Eight were of native, and one hundred and one of foreign parentage. Fifteen were partially supported by friends, twenty-eight by counties, and sixty-six wholly by the institution.

The total amount expended during the year was $7,547.21. The value of its personal estate is estimated at $30,000, and its indebtedness is set down at $2,000.

The visit to this long-established charity was eminently satisfactory in view of the refining and elevating influences to which the children appeared to be subjected, and the home-like character of the institution. It would seem that the characters of girls brought under the influences that surround them here must insensibly be molded into those forms of grace and dignity which constitute the best and most endearing endowment in woman.

St. Vincent's Male Orphan Asylum.

Utica.

The eligible situation of this Asylum, as well as its imposing architectural design, renders it a conspicuous feature of the city of Utica. The edifice, a spacious brick structure, two-stories high, with a basement and mansard attic, is located on Rutger street nearly a mile from the depot, the grounds surrounding it containing five acres of valuable land. The purchase of land was made in 1867, and the corner-stone of the building now in use was laid the same year. The Asylum building is one hundred and fifty feet in length, and its wings are seventy feet in depth. It is wainscoted throughout with chestnut for a space of about four feet from the floor. The windows are large and arranged in keeping with modern improvements. Gas is used for lights, and the supply of water coming from the city is carried to all the floors. Stoves were in use at the time of visitation, but it is intended to put in furnaces. It has a capacity to accommodate one hundred and fifty inmates.

The financial affairs of the institution are controlled by a board of trustees, but the immediate charge and working is assumed by the Roman Catholic Order of Christian Brothers, of whom Brother Jeremiah De Mers is superintendent. The paid force employed consists of a man for out-door work, and a woman in kitchen service.

The garden is large, and yields a good supply of vegetables. Here, in the summer months, when not in school, the boys work, and the necessity of hiring outside help is thus, to a certain extent, obviated.

The dormitories are large, and contain single iron bedsteads. Two Brothers sleep in each of the dormitories with the boys. The Brothers also eat in the boys' refectory, and at the same time, but sit at a separate table, placed on a dais at one end of the room.

The Sunday-school room is furnished with an organ. The chapel has high ceilings and bay windows.

On the day of visitation, September 14th, the number of inmates was fifty-five. Their ages ranged from four to fourteen years.

The institution was incorporated April 21, 1862. An amendment of its charter, made by the Legislature last winter, changed its functions to that of a protectory. It is now suffering from financial embarrassments, which impair its usefulness. If these were removed, the Brothers think its work would be greatly extended in its new field. It has already accomplished large results, through the benevolence of its founders, and the Christian Brothers, who have borne the labor of its management. Five hundred and fifty-two boys have been received in the institution and shared its benefits since its organization. The number of boys received during the year ending September 30, 1875, was twenty-six, the number discharged twenty-five. Of the latter, one was placed out by adoption, fifteen were returned to parents or guardians, four placed out in families, and four returned to counties, and one died. The average number in the institution during the year was forty-four. The number on the 1st of October who were orphans was seventeen, half-orphans twenty-four, who had both parents living, four. The number who were of native parentage was thirty-one, and of foreign parentage, fourteen. Twelve were partially supported by parents or friends, sixteen by counties, towns or cities, and seventeen wholly by the institution.

The total expenditures during the year ending September 30 were $6,500. Of this sum $3,300 was paid upon indebtedness upon real estate. The total indebtedness of the institution is $60,000, of which $30,000 is upon real estate. The value of its real estate, including buildings, fixtures, furniture and all appurtenances, is estimated at $100,000.

Utica Orphan Asylum.

Utica.

About two miles from the depot, at the intersection of Pleasant and Genesee streets, amidst pleasant surroundings and commanding wide views of the beautiful country around, is situated the Utica Orphan Asylum. The grounds upon which the edifice stands contain five acres, are laid out in walks and garden patches, and adorned with shade and ornamental trees. The building, which consists of a main with a tower and two wings, is a commodious brick structure. It is entered by a broad hallway, which soon opens at right angles into the longer hall, extending longitudinally through the whole length of the building, and opening upon the grounds at either end. It was evidently planned with great care, and with a view to combine all modern improvements. Its capacity is for one hundred and twenty-five inmates. The following epitome of its history has been obtained from those well informed of its work:

"The origin of the Asylum dates back as far as 1830, when there existed in the village of Utica a sewing society, conducted by a few benevolent ladies in the interests of the needy. Three little children, having been about this time left utterly destitute by the death of both parents, were thrown upon the pity of the public. One of these ladies, Mrs. Sophia Derbyshire Bagg, imbued with a true motherly feeling, was unwilling to leave these helpless orphans 'to the cold charity provided by public taxation,' and undertook to maintain them in a way that enlisted her heart as well as her hands. She proposed to her associates that they should devote the proceeds of their needles to the support of these three little charges left without any earthly friend. Her proposal was at once acquiesced in, and the children provided for. The distressing fact that no provision existed for destitute children other than the poor-house, soon became apparent, and the degrading influences to which children were there subjected, induced these ladies to think about establishing some asylum for their care, where they might not only enjoy the advantages of a home, but also the benefits of Christian teaching. Accordingly, on the 7th of January, 1830, a meeting was held for the purpose of forming an Orphan Asylum Society, and on the 19th of the following April the present Asylum was incorporated.

"Through the industry and untiring efforts of the ladies a fund of $5,000 was accumulated and placed at interest. In 1844 a legacy of $1,000 was received from Moses Bagg, the husband of the originator of the charity, toward the erection of an asylum building, which was completed and occupied in 1850. Up to this time the asylum was the recipient of several small legacies, but in 1854 a new era of prosperity dawned. Dr. Samuel Healy, of Syracuse, left to the institution $2,500, and a generous citizen of Utica, Alfred Munson, left by his will $5,000 toward the erection of a new and suitable building, and the sum of $25,000 to be securely invested, together with valuable lands in Pennsylvania, on condition that the citizens of Utica should raise and apply the sum of $10,000 toward the purchase of three acres of ground within the city and toward the erection of the building. These conditions were fulfilled by the liberal benefactions of the citizens of the city of Utica, one of whom made a gift of the desirable lot upon which the building now in use was erected in 1860. There have been many noble benefactions to this asylum, including one in 1866 of $25,000, from Mr. Silas D. Childs, conditioned as a permanent fund."

The institution was re-incorporated by special act of the Legislature, March 26, 1856. Its affairs are controlled by a Board of Trustees, consisting of a first, second and third Directress, a Secretary, Treasurer, and nineteen Managers. This Board is assisted by an Advisory Committee of gentlemen. The house is under the immediate care of a Matron, with a corps of assistants made up of a teacher, a seamstress, two nurses, two laundresses, a cook, three female attendants, and a gardener. One of the larger girls attends in the dining room.

At the date of visitation, September 14, there were ninety inmates. This has been the average number during the year. Children are received from two years of age upward. Girls are allowed to remain until fourteen, and boys until twelve. But there is, practically, no specified time for keeping them; this is governed by circumstances. Dependent children are received from the overseer of the poor, the county contributing about $1.25 a week to their support. Surviving parents of children, when able, pay from fifty cents to a dollar per week. A lower rate of board for half-orphan children, however, is fixed when paid by the mother, than when the father pays.

Children are placed out in families, and their interests looked after by a committee, who are said to be active in their duties, corresponding with the children and visiting them periodically.

The Matron, Mrs. F. B. Tufts, said, in regard to the industries carried on: "Our children are mostly too young to be taught trades. The girls learn to do various kinds of domestic work, to wash dishes, make beds," etc.

The routine of the day was given as follows:

"The children rise at six o'clock, dress and wash, after which prayers are said in the sitting room. The children are then exercised in their Sunday-school lessons, the Matron superintending. Breakfast takes place at seven. After breakfast the older children go to their work. The boys clear off the table, sweep the dining room, and the girls make their own beds with the assistance of the superintendent. All assemble in the school at nine o'clock and remain there till twelve, with the exception of an intermission of fifteen minutes. Dinner is served at twelve, after which there is recreation till half-past one, when they enter the school-room again and remain till half-past four. After school they have recreation till five o'clock. Supper is served at five. In winter they have supper very soon after school. The little girls set the tables and assist in light branches of house-work. After supper the children play till bed-time. In winter the younger children go to bed about seven, but the older ones are permitted to stay up a little later. Prayers are said before retiring. Sometimes the children sing; sometimes they repeat psalms. The exercise is varied."

In regard to discipline, the Matron said: "I do not attempt to keep military order. For trifling things I do not punish the children; but for graver offenses I sometimes whip them on the hand and sometimes lock them up. I think children may be governed too much. I find that a little punishment answers the same purpose as a great deal."

The school room is a spacious apartment, with high ceilings. Slabs of slate are paneled in the walls as a substitute for blackboards. The walls are adorned with illuminated cards in frames. The room is furnished with a piano, and the teacher instructs the children in vocal music. There is a separate room for the primary class. The Asylum has a juvenile library, containing nearly four hundred volumes.

The dormitories are furnished with wooden bedsteads, straw ticks and feather pillows. Comfortables are used in the winter. A beautiful feature of the Asylum consists in the custom of allowing a few of the larger girls to have tastefully furnished and pleasant private rooms. These were found to be carpeted, hung with pictures, and supplied with dressing tables, containing drawers; also with comfortable chairs, including rocking chairs.

The nursery for the little boys and girls was nicely furnished. A nurse sleeps in the room with the small children, twenty of whom were found, on the day of visitation, ranging from two to five years.

The children appeared healthy and clean. There were no sick children in the infirmary. It was stated that one death had occurred during the past year, being the only one during the past ten.

The dining room was furnished with stools for the older children, and baby chairs for the little ones.

The laundry is complete in its arrangements, and so separated from the main building as to prevent any vapor from ascending and penetrating the house.

The water-closets are outside the building. There are also night closets attached to the nursery. The bathing accommodations are ample.

The play rooms for boys and girls are distinct, and are located on either side of the building.

The garden supplies all the vegetables except potatoes. Fresh fruit, including apples and pears, is liberally donated by friends of the Asylum. The milk is brought fresh from the country, seventy-five quarts being purchased daily.

Although this Asylum was established for the purpose of caring for orphan and half-orphan children, with a commendable spirit of liberality, destitute children having both parents living are likewise received within its hospitable walls

At the date of October 1, according to the report of the first Directress, Mrs. Cornelia Graham, thirteen of the inmates were orphans, one hundred and fifteen were half-orphans, fourteen had both parents living, and of ten it was unknown whether they had parents living or not. No record designating the nationality of the children's parents having been kept, this point could not be ascertained. One hundred and thirty-six of the children were from Oneida county, and sixteen from Herkimer. Forty-six were partially supported by parents or friends, sixteen by counties, and thirty-one wholly by the institution. The number of children received during the year ending October 1, was fifty-three. Twenty-five were discharged during the year by adoption, thirty-two were returned to parents or guardians, and one was transferred to another institution.

It could not be ascertained with accuracy how many children had received the benefits of this charity since its foundation, but the number falls little short of two thousand. Its receipts during the past year were $13,176.89, and its expenditures $11,768.64. The value of its personal estate is $139,984.24.

It would be impossible to estimate the pecuniary, to say nothing of the moral benefit accruing to society by this charity. To save two thousand children from dependence would be, in itself, a great and noble work, but when the influence for good or evil, which each one of these children is capable of exerting, is considered, the indebtedness of the community to this charitable institution becomes still more apparent.

Thomas Asylum for Orphan and Destitute Indian Children.

Versailles, P. O.

The inception of the humane work now being conducted on the Cattaraugus Reservation in behalf of orphan and destitute Indian children must be attributed to that spirit of love and justice which was the rule of action guiding William Penn in his early intercourse and dealings with the Indians, and which has continued to follow, with its benign influence, this people of unhappy destiny through all the lights and shadows of their history. With watchful zeal the Society of Friends have protected them from the grasping avarice of the white man, stepping forward to vindicate their rights and appealing to the highest tribunal for the redress of their wrongs.

At the time of their settling upon the Reservation, the Friends established in their interest an industrial school, taught them the arts of peace with a view to fitting them for their changed conditions, without which preparation, extinction, inevitably, awaited them.

The following history of the Thomas Orphan Asylum, and of the antecedent work upon the Reservation, with which it is linked, has been gathered from various sources, but in the main has been furnished by Mrs. Wright, widow of the late Reverend Asher Wright, missionary, who during her husband's thirty years of earnest missionary labor among the Indians on this reservation, proved at all times his faithful and intelligent co-worker: "There was originally a boarding or industrial school maintained here by the Society of Friends, and under the charge of a family selected out of its members. It was a free school. Indian girls were here received, and while being educated were also taught to work. This school was in operation, I think, about fifteen years, perhaps longer, and was closed about twenty years ago. Mr. Wright and myself came here in 1845. The school was then in existence, but remained in operation only a short time after that. About the time the Friends closed their school, one of the prominent members of the society, Philip E. Thomas, of Baltimore, who had always taken great interest in this school, and was likewise noted for his benevolence and philanthropy, was here visiting the Indians. I remarked to him that I regretted the closing of the school and wished that it might be reopened as an orphan asylum. This was about the time the Indians made a change in their government from what was called the Chiefs' Government, mainly representing the pagan element, to that known as the New Government, controlled by those who preferred to give up the old wigwam life, sustained by hunting and fishing, for the usages of civilized society and agricultural pursuits. Mr. Thomas and others of the Friends proposed the opening of an industrial school by the new government in the same building in which the Friends had conducted their school. This proposition was accepted, and a small appropriation was made by the new Indian government to begin this school. It was opened by the officers of the new government, with about sixteen scholars, and placed in charge of a Mrs. Hall, a widow lady; but the new government was poor, and it soon became evident that the work must be again taken up and carried on by the benevolently disposed among the whites. The school continued in operation only three or four months.

"About this time, that is to say in the summer of 1854, an Indian died on the Reservation leaving a large family of children in extreme want. The sympathy excited on behalf of the family led to an inquiry into the condition of other poor children who had been left orphans. It was soon ascertained that on this Reservation alone, not less than fifty were in circumstances of great destitution and suffering. The question arose, 'How can this distress be relieved?' The treasury of the Indian Government was empty, and there were no institutions accessible to the poor of this description. Mr. Wright and myself communicated with the Friends through Mr. Thomas. He deeply regretted the closing of the School, and requested that a few of the most destitute children be collected and sustained through the approaching winter at his expense, and in connection with the arrangements for this object a permanent asylum was developed. Ten children were taken into our family, where they remained about a year and a half until the asylum building was ready to receive them. They were all taken from extreme poverty and destitution. One of the little boys, an orphan, was under the care of an aunt. In a fit of anger she tried to destroy him. After beating him severely, she held him under the water in a pool until the poor boy ceased to struggle. He was picked up, providentially, by an Indian who chanced to pass that way, and brought to the Asylum. Several of the children must have perished but for the timely aid thus furnished. These children have since grown up to be men and women, and have turned out well.

"After the children had been thus comfortably provided for, Mr. Thomas suggested that Mr. Wright might secure aid from the State in this charitable undertaking, and enlarge the work. In furtherance of the enterprise to establish a permanent asylum, the Council of the Seneca Nation passed resolutions approving of such a project, and authorizing the use of land. Ten persons, five of them whites and connected with as many different religious denominations, and five Indians associated themselves as Trustees and applied for a charter of incorporation. Mr. Wright proceeded to Albany, and laid the claims of the Indian children before the Legislature, which resulted in an appropriation for the erection of an asylum building of $2,000, and the incorporation, under date of April 10th, 1855, of the "Thomas Asylum for Orphan and Destitute Indian Children."

At the time of the passage of this act nine children were under the care of Mr. and Mrs. Wright, supported principally at the expense of Mr. Thomas. In view of this and of his benevolent work among the Indians, his name was given to the institution. The aims of the trustees were originally confined to the Cattaraugus Reservation, but the Legislature, in view of the aid granted, required them to admit beneficiaries from all the Reservations in the State in proportion to their respective populations. As a means of providing temporary assistance for the Asylum, two brass bands composed of young men (Indians), with a choir of singers, gave a voluntary concert in Buffalo, and a benevolent citizen of the place took it upon himself to insure the pecuniary success of the enterprise, from which an acceptable sum for defraying current expenses was realized.

As soon as practicable after receiving their charter, the trustees procured a lot of ground containing fifteen acres, to which additions have been made, making the whole number of acres at present appropriated to the use of the Asylum about fifty-six. This has been selected from the rich bottom lands of the Cattaraugus Valley, and is pleasantly situated. Preparations were at once commenced for building, but by reason of unavoidable hindrances it was the 14th of September before the corner-stone was laid. Five thousand persons from the surrounding community were present to evince their sympathy with this humane enterprise. One of the State officers, who was present, made an effective speech on the long chapter of Indian wrongs from an incoming and overpowering race, and expressed the hope that this new movement might be regarded as the pledge of a kindlier and more humane policy in future. He was followed by an old Indian, who acknowledged that it was indeed true that formerly the two races met only for purposes of mutual destruction, but now for the exchange of mutual sympathies and deeds of kindness. He then proceeded to describe at length the benefits conferred by the white man upon the Indians, and, in the name of the people, to thank the State for this last and greatest act of kindness in providing for their orphan children.

The lateness of the season and the severity of the following winter prevented the early completion of the building. An additional appropriation was made of $1,500 by the Legislature to enable it to carry out the requirements of its charter, and $500 was sent by the Commissioner of Indian Affairs at Washington. The work was pushed forward on the opening of spring, and by the middle of June the rooms were ready to be furnished.

Soon after the corner-stone was laid certain ladies of Versailles aided the Indian people in the organization of a social circle for mutual improvement. This association resolved to labor for the orphans. The young men furnished funds for the purchase of materials, and the young ladies wrought fancy articles of bead-work, etc., with a design of holding a fair at the opening of the institution. Ladies in Jamestown, Buffalo, and several other places contributed a variety of beautiful articles, and the fair was held on the 18th of June. A generous sum was realized from the sale of the articles, most of which was expended in the purchasing of furniture for the Asylum. With this, and donations from Philip E. Thomas and the Society of Friends, the house was furnished. A span of horses, a double wagon and three milch cows were provided. There were also creditable gifts made from several Sabbath-schools. Altogether the Trustees were enabled to furnish the building sufficiently for immediate occupancy. One additional child had been received during the preceding summer. This and the other ten were removed to their new home, and arrangements made for receiving other beneficiaries. From the commencement, in the fall of 1854, to the 31st of December, 1856, the following sums were received:

From the State, toward erection of buildings............	$3,500 00
From the State, toward support of children.............	215 45
From the Commissioner of Indian Affairs	1,000 00
From Philip E. Thomas and the Society of Friends......	780 00
Proceeds of concert in Buffalo........................	165 72
Contributed at the laying of the corner-stone............	168 02
From the A. B. C. F. M., for Matron..................	145 00
Annuities of children	111 08
Various collections and donations.....................	266 92
Total	$6,352 19

Notwithstanding the aid extended by the State and the benevolent who were interested in this enterprise, it was with very great difficulty that sufficient funds could be raised to carry on the work of this large field, and but for the zeal of the venerable missionary and his wife already referred to, and the earnest efforts of its officers, the enterprise must of necessity have been either abandoned or sunk into comparative insignificance. Their appeals to the public have been frequent, and the work has been followed up persistently through a long period of financial embarrassment.

In the winter of 1875 it was found that in consequence of the recent amendment of the State constitution, the yearly aid that had been customarily given by the State, could not be continued. In this emergency Mr. Wright, then enfeebled by years, again appeared at Albany in behalf of the Indian children. He was accompanied by a tried friend of the Asylum, its treasurer, Mr. E. M. Petit. These gentlemen, in conjunction with the members of the State Board of Charities, brought the critical condition of the Indian children before the attention of their friends in the Legislature. The result was the passage on the 24th of April of the following act:

AN ACT to reorganize the Thomas Asylum for Orphan and Destitute Indian Children, on the Cattaraugus reservation, and to provide for its management and maintenance.

SECTION 1. If, within ninety days after the passage of this act, the trustees of "The Thomas Asylum for Orphan and Destitute Indian Children," a corporation created by chapter two hundred and thirty-three of the laws of 1855, shall transfer and convey to the people of the State of New York, all of the property of said corporation, by a good and sufficient conveyance to the satisfaction of the Comptroller of the State of New York, and shall deposit the same with said Comptroller, the management and control of said Asylum shall be assumed and continued by ten managers on the part of the State, who shall serve without pay, and whose term of office shall be six years, subject to removal at any time by the governor, for cause shown, and all vacancies caused by removal, expiration of term of office or otherwise, shall be filled by the governor, by and with the advice and consent of the senate.

§ 2. The first managers shall be Eber M. Petit, Asher Wright, Elisha Brown, Henry C. Gaylord, Philo H. Carrier, white men, and Lewis Seneca, Sylvester Loy, Hiram Dennis, Joshua Pierce and Zechariah L. Jemeson, Indians.

§ 3. The said managers of said asylum shall, on application, receive destitute and orphan children from each of the several reservations located within this State, and shall furnish them such care, moral training and education, and such instruction in husbandry and the arts of civilization as they shall prescribe by their rules and by-laws.

§ 5. Said managers shall organize and choose one of their number president, and appoint a secretary. They shall also make by-laws and rules and regulations for the transaction of their business, and for the regulation and management of said institution. They shall also appoint a suitable person as superintendent, and such other employés as may be necessary to properly carry on the business of said institution, and fix the compensation of said superintendent and such other employés.

§ 5. The said asylum shall be at all times subject to the visitation, supervision and control of the State Board of Charities; and the managers of said asylum shall annually, on or before the fifteenth day of January, report to the Legislature the condition of said asylum, including a true account in detail of the receipt and disbursement of all moneys that shall come into their hands, the number, age and sex of such destitute and orphan Indian children in said asylum, with the name and reservation to which they belong, and portion of the year each has been maintained and instructed in said asylum.

The institution is located in the southern part of Erie county, New York, on the Cattaraugus Reservation, a little more than a mile from the village of Versailles, its post-office. The grounds are inclosed in front with a neat fence, and the main building is situated a little apart from the road. It is painted a buff color, and has pleasant verandas. A grassy lawn with trees extends in front. Back of the main are grouped the barns and outbuildings, which are lime-washed in a tint corresponding with the Asylum building. A good sized orchard of thrifty grafted apple trees affords shade on its right and in front. In a beautiful grove of oak trees a little distance from the Asylum stands the school-house, a tasteful structure, capable of accommodating all the Asylum children of a school-attending age. The school is under the Department of Public Instruction. The teachers make their home in the Asylum building. The general appearance of the grounds and buildings, as one approaches, makes an agreeable impression on the mind.

The President of the Board of Managers is an Indian, Lewis Seneca. The working force of the Asylum consists of a Superintendent, a Matron, Assistant Matron, a seamstress, housekeeper, assistant laundress, and general assistant. In summer a farm hand is employed, and in winter a foreman in the broom shop.

The most recent visitation was made October 1, 1875. The school was then beginning to organize after the midsummer vacation, which usually lasts six weeks, when those who have friends are at liberty to return to them, but which had been this year protracted on account of the breaking out of measles among the children that remained in the Asylum. Nine were on the sick list, five of whom were convalescent. The Superintendent, Mr. Hall, said: "During the spring eight deaths occurred among the children, all from consumption, save one. The doctor is of opinion that the consumption in every case was traceable to the scrofulous tendencies which the children had inherited. Very few Indian children are without some taint of scrofula."

It is asserted that this taint is generally perceptible in the offensive breath of the children even when otherwise they may appear to be quite healthy. Their constitutions are consequently enfeebled, and they are more liable to suffer from epidemics than white children.

The Asylum is supplied with water by an Artesian well, a hydraulic ram being used to force it through the building. The house is heated by stoves and lighted by kerosene. The ventilation is from the windows, the sashes of which are adjusted by cords, weights and pulleys. The children bathe once a week. The dormitories are furnished with single iron bedsteads.

The children assembled for dinner during our visit. The dining room was furnished with long tables. The boys and girls ate separately. The tables were well supplied with good food. Before partaking, the children repeated in unison the following form of grace, taught them by the Rev. Asher Wright:

"O God we thank Thee for Thy care that keeps us alive and well. Bless us while we are eating this food and feed us with the true bread that comes from Thee that our souls may live forever, Amen."

The meal consisted of meat, potatoes and bread pudding. The girls wore blue check aprons and the boys were variously dressed. The Superintendent says: "The children always have coffee in the morning and bread and milk for supper." The holidays of Christmas, New Years, Independence and Thanksgiving are duly observed.

Children are received at all ages, but it is not considered desirable to admit infants. The youngest inmate on the day of visitation was two and a half years old; the oldest over sixteen. Mr. Hall says: "The boys are more inclined to go back among their people than the girls. There are a good many cases that turn out well, but more that disappoint us.

"We aim to get the girls among the whites. We have two now at the State Normal School, who are being educated for teachers. Their characters are good, and they are quite intelligent. Indian children should be looked after, till they are twenty or twenty-one. Just before then is the most critical time with them as they are so apt to lapse into drunkenness and immorality. The trouble with the boys is that when they are old enough, they go off with the Indians."

Some of the boys, Mr. Hall was very proud of; spoke of them as perfectly reliable and trustworthy, and seemed to think that as a general thing when the boys were put with farmers among the white people, and kept away from evil associates among their own, they turned out well. "Our boys make good farm hands. People like to employ them. They get up early in the morning and work diligently all day. Many Indian boys are ruined by the neighbors giving them cider to drink."

Mr. Hall said: "I do not approve of whipping, as a measure of discipline; I prefer locking the boys up in a room where they may have books and pictures to entertain themselves, or to keep them in from play." The importance of inculcating habits of industry is fully recognized, and forms a principal feature in the asylum training. Mr.

Hall says: "The girls are taught to make themselves useful about the house. Each one has some portion of the house to care for. They do a great deal of the sewing and dish-washing. We attempt every thing pertaining to household duties except bread baking. That is done in a separate building by an outside party. Indian girls may become skillful in housewifery. One of our girls took the premium at the fair for the best bread.

"The boys chop wood, do all the chores at the barn, and in winter make brooms out of the broom-corn that is raised in summer. We made about four hundred dozen last year. They sell well; they do not bring the highest price, but they sell rapidly. The boys, with the hired man, do the work."

The institution has two sewing machines. There is also a library of two hundred volumes, and a melodeon, on which the girls play.

On October 1, 1875, the number of children in the Asylum, who were orphans, was nineteen, half orphans, forty, and who had both parents living, sixteen.

One was from the Onondaga Reservation, seventeen from the Allegany, forty-seven from the Cattaraugus, five from the Tonawanda, and five from the Tuscarora. The total number received since the organization of the Asylum is three hundred and eighty-eight.

During the past year twenty acres of the farm were devoted to broom-corn, three to potatoes, one and a half to corn, and about two acres to garden vegetables, including onions, squashes, carrots, peas, tomatoes and cabbages. "In a good year," says Mr. Hall, "we have one hundred bushels of potatoes." Strawberries and raspberries are raised for the inmates. Seven milch cows are kept, and beeves are purchased and fattened for house supply.

On being asked if the character of the children of the Indians was treacherous, Mr. Hall said: "The Indian children are loving; they are not demonstrative in the expression of their feelings, but when you are in need of help, you can always rely upon them, and they will make large sacrifices to serve you. Indian children are more quiet than other children, but their affections will crop out at times when you least expect it."

Among the inmates were descendants of the distinguished chief Corn Planter, and of the noted Indian orator Red Jacket.

Mr. Hall, on being asked his opinion as to the best way to train Indian children, said: "I have been here seventeen years; I was on the Allegany Indian Reservation before that; I have been altogether twenty-nine years among the Indians, and am of opinion that if the Indian children could be brought into families where they could have a thorough family bringing up, where they would have a seat at our tables and eat the same kind of food as we eat, making no difference between them and ourselves, more satisfactory results would be attained. We do here all that is possible, under our system, still, I think the children realize that they do not enjoy the full sympathy of family membership, so much so that I have been almost tempted to sit down with them and eat at their table. They are, I know, under the impression that their food is not as good as mine, but if I ate at the same table with them, they could not think so."

Mr. Hall, on being asked his opinion of the condition of the Indians on the Reservation, said: "I can see a decided improvement during the last ten years. In fact, I think I can see wonderful improvements. They are better farmers, are more industrious, intelligent and enterprising."

The long experience of Mrs. Wright, while pursuing her self-denying missionary labors among the Indians, renders her opinion on this subject worthy of record: "Within the last half-dozen years a great many Indians who went to the war have come back intemperate. There has been a general relapse all over the country. It seems so to me at least, from the number of drunken people that come to our Indian fairs. But I think, with this drawback, the standard of morals has advanced considerably, and that there has been a great improvement among the Indians, especially in farming. Even among the pagan portion of the people, they have better implements for cultivating the land. There are several families that send their milk to the cheese factory now."

We are indebted to the Superintendent of Public Instruction for the following statistics, showing the number of Indians between the ages of five and twenty-one on the several reservations of the State.

On the Allegany and Cattaraugus Reservation	850
On the Tonawanda Reservation	134
On the Tuscarora Reservation	181
On the Onondaga Reservation	125
On the St. Regis Reservation	267
On the Poospatuck Reservation	17
On the Shinnecock Reservation	43
On the Oneida and Madison Reservation	46

It must be admitted that the most hopeful means of elevating the Indian race is by instructing the children in the industries and usages of white people. This, it has been demonstrated, can be done successfully. More importance is therefore attached to the work of the Asylum, especially as the class relieved by it would, if neglected, largely become outcasts. The humanity and intelligence of the Legislature in making provision for this unfortunate and helpless class, who in view of their lost birthright have strong claims upon the sympathy of the public, is self-apparent.

Jefferson County Orphan Asylum.

Watertown.

The Jefferson County Orphan Asylum is situated on Franklin street, in the city of Watertown. Its object is the "protecting, relieving and educating of orphan and destitute children." It was incorporated May 11, 1859, under the general act, as the "Watertown Home for Destitute, Friendless and Orphan Children." Subsequently, by a special act of the Legislature, chapter 38, Laws of 1864, the charter was amended, and its name changed to its present title.

The building at present occupied was erected in 1864. It is a plain brick structure, resting on a stone basement sixty-five by fifty. Including the basement and attic it is four stories high, and roofed with slate.

In the basement are the kitchen, dining rooms, store-rooms, laundry, cellar and coal room. The first story is traversed by a broad central hall, on the sides of which are a parlor, school-room, a large clothes room, hospital room, waiting room, a girls' bath room, supplied with hot and cold water, and a water closet. Beyond is the boys' bath-room, similarly supplied with water, and connecting with a large clothes room. On this floor is also the nursery, with nurse's bed-room and closet attached.

On the floor above are the dormitories for boys and girls, while the attic is a spacious, unfinished room.

The window sashes are adjusted by cords, weights and pulleys. The ceilings are high. The house is heated principally by furnaces. Several stoves are used in damp weather to take the chill off the halls. The building is airy, cheerful, and seemingly well arranged, and could, with the upper story, accommodate seventy-five or a hundred children.

The edifice stands a little apart from the street upon a lot containing two acres. It is surrounded by the original forest trees.

The institution is under the control of a Board of Nine Trustees, the Chairman of the Board of Supervisors, and the County Judge, being *ex officio* members.

The management of the institution is intrusted to a Board of Lady Directors.

The Asylum is under the immediate charge of Mrs. Torey, Matron, assisted by her husband. Her subordinate aid consists of a teacher, nurse, two girls in the kitchen, and a laundry girl.

The origin of the institution may be stated as follows:

"In 1859, the sudden death of a mother, leaving a family of five little ones with a drunken father, induced a few benevolent ladies to hire a small house, and open it for their reception and for others equally needy In a few days there were some fifteen inmates gathered together under the supervision of Miss Jane Frasier, a lady of untiring zeal and great fidelity and kindness. This small family were, for several years, moved from house to house, as one could be obtained, and were supported by individual liberality, and by means of fairs and festivals, till 1865. About the year 1862, liberal donations were made to procure a permanent location, and the lot of ground on which the present building stands was purchased. There was at the time a small building upon it, which was prepared for the reception of the children and Matron, and occupied till the present building was erected. In 1865, the supervisors of the county decided that 'the Asylum was more fitting in every respect than the poor-house for dependent children,' and authorized the Superintendent of the Poor to send such children to the Asylum, to be there maintained at the expense of the county. Since that period the Supervisors have made an annual appropriation to the Asylum. During the five years following there was a large number of children accommodated, and, up to the present time, between seven and eight hundred have been sheltered within the hospitable walls of this worthy institution."

Children are received under two years or over ten only in exceptional cases. The religious instruction imparted is Evangelical. In the school room the children are under the care of a competent teacher.

On the day of visitation, August 4, there were twenty-eight inmates, the smallest number it ever had. Six were girls and twenty-two were boys. Children are retained only long enough to secure them good homes. They are mainly from Jefferson county. Two of the inmates were daughters of soldiers who had been killed in the war, and came from Clinton county. The following information regarding the asylum was furnished by Mrs. Robert Lansing, its first directress:

"Applications for children are being constantly made to the asylum, thus obviating the necessity of advertising to procure them homes. They are placed out three months on trial, after which a permanent arrangement is made, if desired, by both parties.

"Very few children are now bound out. More than half are adopted into families.

"The Asylum has never suffered from any prevailing sickness, and has rarely had occasion to call in medical aid.

"A careful record of the children sent out is kept, and the institution requires that the parties who take children shall report upon their condition from time to time.

"There is no systematic plan of visiting. This work is deemed to rest properly with the Supervisors in each town.

"The Asylum objects to taking children over ten years of age who have been left to run about the streets. It is thought they have a bad influence on the others. It is considered very important that while children are in the Asylum they should be in school, and special attention is given to their education. The girls are taught needle-work, and the older boys help in the garden.

"We seldom have been troubled with refractory children, and hence the use of harsh discipline is rare.

"The aim of the asylum is to inculcate moral and religious principles. We take great pains to implant the sentiment that they must be loving.

"It is a rule of the house that all the children must bathe once a week.

"Ample time for play is afforded, and the regular holidays are duly observed. On Christmas the children have their Christmas tree, or some entertainment to take its place."

One of the little girls of the Asylum was going to leave on the day of our visitation. A desirable home had been secured for her and her new guardians had come to take her away. The Asylum had provided quite an outfit for the little one, and she appeared to be entering upon her new life under very happy auspices.

In this institution was found a little boy with a club foot. He had been operated upon successfully a short time previous, and was rapidly acquiring the use of his limb.

The total number of children who have shared the benefits of this institution since its organization, is seven hundred and ten. The number received during the past year was thirteen; the number discharged, eighteen. Of the latter, three were placed out by adoption; five returned to parents or guardians; one transferred to another institution; eight otherwise discharged, and one died. The total expenditures during the year were $2,763.07. The invested funds of the Asylum are valued at $10,050. It has no indebtedness.

CONCLUSION.

In closing this report, one cannot well refrain from saying that a general survey of the benevolent work being carried on throughout the State, in asylums, reformatories, aid societies, industrial schools, and other institutions for the care of children, gives one a higher conception of our humanity and its unselfish capabilities. These institutions appear like bright centers from which the goodness of a Divine Being radiates to the homeless and suffering. Dispense with all these benevolent agencies, and society would quickly sink into barbarism. The hands of those engaged in the work should be strengthened, not only with our sympathy, but by our pecuniary aid. The State is now expending millions in the erection of a princely capitol which, when completed, will not equal in value one human life rescued from infamy, and reared to the full stature of virtue and godliness. The individuals engaged in this moral work are, with patient labor, shaping the uncouth outlines of crude characters into forms of grace and beauty, as certainly as are the workmen chiseling the various granite blocks for their places in that stately edifice; and these characters, when completed, will each have its place in the great structure of society, forming an edifice more beautiful, and of greater value, than it is possible to rear by human hands.

To the Commissioners of the Board who have kindly aided me in their respective districts; to the Secretary of the Board and his Assistant, from the first of whom, in addition to valuable service, I have been furnished with considerable historical matter previously collected by him at much pains; to Asylum Officials, and others kindly disposed for whose courtesy I am indebted; and to Mr. Frederick Carman, stenographer, whose faithful labors have been, in part, gratuitous, I beg to tender my cordial thanks.

Respectfully submitted,

WILLIAM P. LETCHWORTH,

Commissioner Eighth Judicial District.

Dated ALBANY, *January* 11*th*, 1876.

APPENDIX.

PAUPER AND DESTITUTE CHILDREN

PAUPER CHILDREN OF NEW YORK COUNTY

REPORT

ON

PAUPER AND DESTITUTE CHILDREN

BY

WILLIAM P. LETCHWORTH

COMMISSIONER OF THE STATE BOARD OF CHARITIES

Transmitted to the Legislature with the annual report of the Board
January 15th, 1875.

REPORT.

To the State Board of Charities:

Gentlemen — In pursuance of instructions from this Board, authorizing me to correspond with superintendents of the poor and with others having jurisdiction in the matter, with the view of removing children from association with adult paupers in poor-houses and city alms-houses, and to use every legitimate means to reform this evil, I beg to submit this report.

I entered upon the task assigned me with more confidence from the knowledge that I was but carrying out long established views of the Board. I find in its second annual report the following language used upon this subject.

" The number of children under sixteen in county poor-houses is 1,222.* The condition of this large number excites the most painful feelings. Many of them are born in the county-house, and pass there the early days of childhood. When we remember how their earliest experience of life is public dependence, under its most unfavorable aspect, in the company of the wretched and depraved; when we recall their education to vicious and filthy habits, we cannot be surprised that they either fill our prisons or furnish a perpetual supply of occupants of our alms-houses. Shall we not in this manner fasten upon ourselves a class of hereditary paupers?

"Some of the counties have adopted the wise course of sending such children to a neighboring orphan asylum. There is no uniform practice in that direction, nor are there any general arrangements for education or training of any useful kind. In a number of the counties indiscriminate intercourse is allowed between paupers of all ages without any attempt to check idleness or the communication of the most corrupt influences."

In subsequent reports I find the same considerations have been advanced.

His Excellency, Governor Hoffman, directed the attention of the legislature to this evil in his annual message, January 3d,

---

* This number did not include the alms-houses in the counties of Kings and New York, and elsewhere in the state.

1871, and again by the same in 1872, and His Excellency, Governor Dix, emphasized its importance in his message, January 7th, 1873. The leading public journals throughout the State have strongly condemned the custom of rearing children in poor-houses, and the members of this board have, in various ways, endeavored to arouse a general public interest in this subject. With such authorities to strengthen my convictions, I have felt that the work was worthy of my best energies.

A systematic effort has been made during the past year to ascertain not only the number of children now remaining in poor-houses and alms-houses, their mental and physical condition, and antecedents, but also to learn as far as practicable how those who were inmates have been disposed of during the year, and whether such as had been placed out in families, were comfortably provided for; whether they have been sent to school, and if so, how long; what proficiency they have made in their studies; whether receiving moral and religious training; what were the influences surrounding them; and what the general results of their treatment. In cases where the child had absconded an effort has been made to learn its subsequent history.

This information has been gathered in part by personal inquiry, but mainly from superintendents of the poor, who at some pains have very kindly filled up blank schedules which were furnished them. Many of these schedules as returned to the Secretary of the Board are quite complete, and show that great care has been taken by the superintendents, aided by keepers and their wives in placing out children; that this duty is discharged conscientiously, and that the children generally have been faithfully looked after in their new homes. In some counties, however, it is evident that the subject does not receive the attention its importance demands; records sufficiently complete of children placed out are not kept, and in such cases a change of officials breaks the thread of personal history, and the little waif which should continue to be an object of solicitude is lost to view.

The importance of keeping records to enable such inquiries to be answered, is generally concurred in by superintendents of the poor and other county officials, and will be obvious even to those less familiar with the subject, since cases are not infrequent ot maltreatment and gross wrongs occurring after the child has passed beyond the control of superintendents. A single illustration of this will suffice.

It has been ascertained that within a few years past, a family from a neighboring Province was in the habit of obtaining from the poor-house in one of the border counties of the State, girls nearly grown up, and keeping them but a short time. The family resided in an out-of-the-way place, and though in apparently good circumstances, were objects of suspicion to their neighbors. It was known that they took children from the poor-house, and that after a time the children would disappear, no one positively knew where, and new faces would be seen about the secluded house. It was currently believed by respectable people in the neighborhood, that for mercenary ends, these homeless girls were consigned to the worst possible fate.

A plan of making inquiries relating to pauper children has been adopted in Massachusetts and is executed through an agent of the State Board of Charities. Every year the condition and moral status of each child placed out are reported upon and such supervision of these "wards of the State," continues until the individual has passed the bounds of childhood. It is thought that among other good effects growing out of such an inquiry, it helps to inspire pride of character in the child, who is thus made to realize that, notwithstanding the loss of natural guardians, it is still an object of human sympathy. It also insures to the child more careful consideration from its guardian, who, by being held accountable, is made to feel a greater sense of responsibility. Some kind of supervision over the friendless child, following up its history until it shall have reached at least the age of sixteen years, would result doubtless, in saving many an individual from vagrancy and crime. This is already accomplished to some extent in certain counties. Westchester county may be mentioned as an example. In addition to the usual covenants prescribed by the statute on the part of the superintendents of the poor and the person taking the child, it is further required that the guardian shall report to the superintendents of the poor, in January of each year during the time of apprenticeship, the condition of the child's health, number of quarter's schooling received, its acquirements, and general conduct.

Not only the spirit of the times, but that of modern legislation seems to tend toward the exercise of greater watchfulness over the welfare of orphans and homeless children. This is evidenced in the humane act entitled "An act to legalize the adoption of minor children by adult persons," passed June 25, 1873. By this statute the interests of the child are not only protected as to its bodily comforts and mental culture, but upon the death of its guardian it becomes, with certain limitations and exceptions, a sharer by inheritance of his estate, thus restoring in the eye of the law a parent and real home to the orphaned and homeless.

In pursuing my work during the past year I have addressed manuscript letters to superintendents of the poor of all the counties in which there were children in the poor-house, setting forth the views and opinions of the Board on the question and the desirability of reform, and also requesting that the subject receive their earnest consideration with reference to a speedy removal of all children from the evil influences of an association with adult paupers.

Previous to the convening of the boards of supervisors, the records of the proceedings of the boards of such counties as had taken action in reference to the care and maintenance of their pauper children elsewhere than in the poor-house were carefully examined, so far as they were accessible, for a period extending back from fifteen to twenty years. The difficulty of reaching the reports of the several boards made the work of compiling this material protracted and laborious. Printed proceedings of the boards of supervisors were in many cases not found on file in the county clerk's office of the several counties, and when found were seldom properly indexed. In consequence of this failure to preserve in printed form these valuable records, the action of certain counties in the matter in question could not be satisfactorily ascertained.

The results of this labor were compiled in pamphlet form, and with them an extract from the message of His Excellency Governor Hoffman, as also an extract from the message of His Excellency Governor Dix, previously referred to in reference to this subject; also extracts from several leading public journals of this state, expressing emphatic condemnation of the evils arising from an association of children with adult paupers in poor-houses and alms-houses; and also an extract from an address touching the same subject, by Commissioner Anderson of this board. A copy of this pamphlet was sent to each member of the various boards of supervisors throughout the state.

STATISTICAL INFORMATION.

The tables appended hereto, and which form a part of this report, show that the total number of children remaining in the various poor-houses of the State, at the several dates of inquiry in 1874, was six hundred and fifteen (615). Of these, three hundred and sixty-two (362) were boys, and two hundred and fifty-three (253) girls. Of the whole number, fifty-one (51) were colored. One hundred and forty-three (143) were under two years of age, three hundred and forty-eight (348) were over two and under ten, and one hundred and twenty-four (124) were over ten and under sixteen. Two hundred and fifty-six (256) were the children of fathers who were natives of the United States; one hundred and fifty-eight (158) of Ireland, seventeen (17) of England, twenty-two (22) of Germany, twenty-seven (27) of other countries. Of one hundred and thirty-five (135), the nativity of the fathers could not be ascertained. Three hundred and thirty (330) were the children of mothers who were natives of the United States, one hundred and sixty-seven (167) of Ireland, seven (7) of England, thirteen (13) of Germany, twenty-seven (27) of other countries. Of seventy one (71), the nativity of the mothers was unascertainable. One hundred and ninety-seven (197) were children of laborers, forty-seven (47) of those following agricultural occupations, eighty-one (81) of mechanical, five (5) of commercial, and sixty-one (61) of various other occupations, twenty-three (23) were children of fathers having no occupations, and two hundred and one (201) were children of parents whose occupation could not be ascertained. One hundred and seven (107) of the children had temperate fathers, three hundred and twenty-nine (329) intemperate. The habits of the fathers of one hundred and seventy-nine (179) could not be ascertained. Three hundred and eighty-seven (387) had temperate mothers, and one hundred and fifteen (115) intemperate. Of one hundred and thirteen (113), the habits of the mothers could not be ascertained. So far as could be learned regarding the relatives of the children, thirty-two (32) were known to be descendants of pauper grandfathers, (47) of pauper grandmothers, one hundred and five (105) of pauper fathers, four hundred and forty-one (441) of pauper mothers. Two hundred and forty-nine (249) had brothers, who, at the time of inquiry, were, or had been paupers, two hundred and twenty-three (223) had sisters who were or had been paupers, forty-five (45) had uncles who were or had been paupers, and forty-seven (47) had aunts who were or had been paupers. Fifty-four (54) of the children had fathers in the poor-house at date of inquiry, and three hundred and forty-two (342) had mothers there. Of the whole number of children one hundred and ninety (190) were born in the poor-house. Two hundred and four (204) were of illegitimate birth.

The following statement shows the length of time the children had been inmates of the poor-houses:

Less than six months	156
Six months and less than one year	85
One year and less than two years	97
Two years and less than three years	68
Three years and less than four years	56
Four years and less than five years	47
Five years and less than six years	31
Six years and less than seven years	23
Seven years and less than eight years	19
Eight years and less than nine years	10
Nine years and less than ten years	7
Ten years and less than sixteen years	16
Total	615

It appears from the examination, that there were about three hundred and twenty-five healthy and intelligent children, over two years of age, then in the poor-houses. The remainder were either under two years, or were defective or diseased, so as to unfit them for family care. Among the latter were included a considerable number of unteachable idiots, epileptics, paralytics and feeble-minded.

The reports made to the board on the 30th of November last, show a considerable reduction in the number of children in the poor-houses of certain counties, since the dates of this inquiry.

During the recent sessions of the various Boards of Supervisors throughout the State, action has been taken, either abolishing the system of rearing children in the county poor-house, or tending to such results, by the counties of Orleans, Ontario, Genesee, Seneca, Essex, Otsego, Clinton, Fulton and Herkimer.

In the various city alms-houses of the State, at the dates of inquiry, there were one thousand seven hundred and thirty-five children. In the alms-house department of New York, principally within the various buildings on

Randall's Island there were	1,344
In the King's county alms-house there were	356
In the Kingston city alms-house there were	14
In the Newburgh city and town alms-house there were	11
In the Oswego city alms-house there were	7
In the Poughkeepsie city alms-house there were	7
Total	1,739

The examination now being made by this board of the children, maintained under the alms-house system in New York, not having been completed, the information gathered in city alms-houses is not tabulated. The facts so far as collected, however, are summarized under the heading of the different counties in the notes relating to pauper children in the poor-houses and alms-houses appended hereto, and to which attention is invited.

The attempt to determine definitely the school acquirements made by the children, has proved so unsatisfactory and discouraging, that this part of the work has been set aside. Suffice it to say, that, in common school studies, poor-house children are, on the whole, far behind children of the same age in the public schools.

CHILD-LIFE IN THE POOR-HOUSE.

The tables appended show among other results, that at the dates of inquiry in 1874, the six hundred and fifteen (615) children then remaining in the various poor-houses of the State, had spent in the aggregate one thousand four hundred and thirty-four (1,434) years of their tender lives in that morally and physically unwholesome atmosphere. When so vast a field is contemplated in reference to the seeds of idleness, shiftlessness, immorality and vice that have been constantly sown in the rich soil of childhood from the older growth about it, and the sad and inevitable results that must be borne to society in the future out from it, as well as its fearful harvest of individual woes, the heart of the benevolent may well be appalled and aroused to an energetic effort to break up a system which works such baneful results.

INFLUENCE OF POOR-HOUSE AND ALMS-HOUSE LIFE UPON CHILDREN.

Travelers in distant lands tell us of a luxuriant island in the tropic seas, among the mountains of which there is a small and desolate valley shut in by volcanic hills and gloomy precipices. The bottom of this valley is covered with the whitened skeletons of birds, beasts, and men. Should the weary wanderer, overcome by fatigue, here seat himself to rest, he finds ere long his breath impeded, the action of his lungs quickened, and his head disturbed with strange pains. On attempting to rise he discovers he has no strength, and energy of purpose forsakes him, and stretching himself upon the barren earth, he soon ceases to struggle and yields to the rigidness of death

Not less subtle than the noxious gases of this dreary valley nor apparently less hurtful to the moral nature of the young is the stagnant atmosphere of the poor-house. Evil associations surround the child, its conscience is weakened, and its moral life almost extinguished, often in a comparatively brief period. Thus reared, it goes into the world, too frequently an object rather shunned than welcomed; indifferent; without hope, self-respect, courage or sense of duty.

The history of the poor-houses and alms-houses throughout the state is replete with instances of children who have been placed out in families or asylums after having been a long time in the poor-house, and have been afterward returned as incorrigible. If such a one be a girl her case is extremely hopeless. She may be placed out repeatedly in good families and as often returned. At length approaching maturity she chooses her natural associates, and in the end returns to the only refuge left where she may lay down her burden of sorrow and shame. If she goes out again it is alone and friendless to mingle with the unfortunate ones with whom her childhood has been spent. It is not strange that she should seek for society among this class, and however good her resolutions may be, her destiny shapes itself into the motherhood and frequently the grandmotherhood of a race of paupers or criminals.

A boy who has been reared under like circumstances, when old enough to work upon a farm or in a shop is "placed out;" but when it is discovered that the vicious influences under which he has been reared have crystallized his nature into obduracy he is returned. The process of placing out may be repeated perhaps several times. But at length he breaks away from all restraint and enters upon a semi-vagrant life, too frequently terminating in crime, and society pays the inevitable penalty of its neglect by supporting him in prison.

REARING OF CHILDREN IN SEPARATE PAUPER ESTABLISHMENTS.

It is sometimes thought that the injurious influences of poor-houses may be avoided by erecting separate establishments on the poor-house grounds, for the care of children, and that within these, they may be properly reared and educated with greater economy than could be secured elsewhere. But these well designed establishments, call them nurseries, juvenile asylums or any other name, although regarded as independent in their functions are nevertheless a part of the poor-house system, and bring children indirectly under its baneful influence, and into association with a greater or less number of the indolent, listless pauper inmates. These establishments are the more dangerous, because of the delusive idea that bad influences are removed, and that a classification is effected, which, in the nature of things cannot be complete, and because the greatest injury they do to society is not immediately demonstrated. The better they are constructed, the more comfortably they are warmed and furnished, the more they attract and tempt families, having children, to become paupers, thereby aggravating the very evil which they were intended to cure. A marked illustration of this is seen in the Kings County Nursery and Richmond County Juvenile Asylum, which are treated in the notes appended to this report.

Some of the reasons why children should be removed from poor-house influence, and why establishments of the kind just named should be set aside, may be summarized as follows:

1st. It is ascertained that children can be kept in asylums under more wholesome influences, and at no greater expense than the public are now subjected to in maintaining them in poor-houses.

2d. That the number at any one time a county charge will be, if they are transferred to asylums, less than if retained in poor-houses, because the officers of such establishments find it difficult to place children in good families with the poor-house brand, so to speak, upon them. Besides if large provision be made for keeping the children by the county, at the county house, its tendency is to repress the efforts to place children out — and that when children are placed out, it is not generally so well done as when they are placed out by orphan asylums, and their committees of ladies and gentleman, who kindly endeavor to find suitable homes for the little ones, and to look after the children placed in them for years afterward.

3rd. That by a vigorous system of "placing out" children in families, they are brought at once under elevating influences, and the county is spared the entire expense of maintaining them.

4th. That under the present system a class of children accumulate, generally boys, who, when placed out, will not remain with their new guardians, but repeatedly come back to their old quarters, becoming all the while more vicious, until at length the superintendent is not unfrequently obliged to shut the doors of his establishment against them, and that they afterward swell the class of vagrants and petty thieves of the street.

5th. That families of children coming in and going out of the establishment, though spending but a short time there, leave with self-respect lessened and largely increase the number in the community tending toward a condition of dependence.

6th. That scholars in the school department of these institutions, though placed under the management of zealous and capable teachers, are lamentably behind other children of the same age in their studies.

7th. That the maintaining of such establishments adds largely to the expenses of the adult pauper department of the county, as many adult paupers come to the county house to be supported who would not come if their children were not provided for at the same time.

8th. That the children, whether in asylums or Christian homes, come directly under the benevolent charge and elevating influences of those whose motives in assuming the responsibility of their care is based upon the highest Christian principles.

PLACING OUT CHILDREN.

The hope of rescuing the child from a life of dependence hinges as much upon the nature of the means employed and the promptness of their application as the cure of the patient does upon the quality and timely administration of remedies for his restoration.

The children should be early removed from the poor-house and placed under influences that are unquestionably good, and, if possible, religious, as these lie inevitably at the foundation of all true reform. If placed in families, great pains should be taken in every instance to ascertain that the family is one of character and respectability. It is not essential that they should be in highly prosperous circumstances, but that they should be industrious and thrifty. It is better, perhaps, that the child should be in a family of moderate means than in one of opulence. Among farmers, mechanics and shop-keepers may perhaps be found the most desirable homes, as the industrious disposition generally lacking in the dependent classes will be best inculcated in such families both by precept and example. It is important that the person taking the child should feel an interest in it beyond a purely selfish one; that he should take it with the hope and desire of benefiting the child and of bringing it up eventually to the standard of useful and respectable citizenship. If this interest is not felt, the child has not found a home in the true sense of the word. It may seem difficult to secure this result under ordinary circumstances, but in a community fully awakened to its importance and with sympathies aroused in behalf of the children, it is a matter of easy accomplishment.

In one of the counties in the State there had been an average of from twelve to twenty children in the poor-house for a number of years. The superintendents of the poor and the keeper of the poor-house had found it difficult to place the children out in good families. The board of supervisors had never made any arrangements for putting them in asylums. The county officials, while desiring to do what was for the best, saw no course of action better than to let the children remain in the county-house, now and then placing one out as a good opportunity presented. During the past year the local press of the county called the attention of the public to the necessity for a reform. A small committee of ladies and gentlemen, who had been appointed by this Board as county visitors to the poor-house, and several members of the board of supervisors in the different towns, took an active interest in the subject, and all lent their aid to the superintendents of the poor in finding suitable homes for the children. The sympathy of the whole community was aroused and directed to the relief and care of these poor little unfortunates, and the result was, that in about two months all the children had been placed in most excellent homes. These children were fortunately, for the most part young, and their prospects are therefore quite promising. It is difficult to conjecture the amount of good that may eventually result from the efforts of the benevolent persons who engaged in this good work.

REMOVING CHILDREN TO OTHER COUNTIES.

I am informed by several superintendents of the poor, that they have derived great advantage from placing dependent children in asylums in other counties than their own where circumstances warranted them in doing so. In numerous cases, where children are placed out within the county to which they belong, it is found that they are in such close proximity to their parents and to the old debasing influences as to retard materially the work of reformation. Their guardians are frequently annoyed with repeated interruptions by parents, sometimes intoxicated, and at length, becoming discouraged, give up their charge, either of their own accord, or upon the demand of its parents. The child thus loses, perhaps, an excellent home, and re-enters its former semi-vagrant life. If placed in an adjoining county, or a little apart from its parents, the reformatory process goes on with less interruption and with far better prospects of complete reformation.

It must be admitted, in view of the enlarged and growing sympathy now felt for destitute children, that in a vast number of cases the welfare of those more nearly concerned, as well as that of society at large, would be promoted by widely removing the child from the associations under which it became dependent.

OPINIONS OF SUPERINTENDENTS OF THE POOR AND COUNTY OFFICIALS.

It is gratifying to be able to state that superintendents of the poor and keepers of poor-houses and county officials, generally throughout the State, desire the removal of children from the county establishments, and direct their efforts to that end. In a very few of the poor-houses, however, an obstacle in the way of removal of the children is found in the school, which must be broken up in case a change is made, or if the number of pupils be reduced so as to make the school too small to warrant the employment of a teacher. The teacher is generally a young lady who occupies a place in the family of the keeper. Her companionship, and the presence of children to whom the family often times become attached, serve in some measure to make the duties of the keeper far less irksome. It is but natural that those who have to discharge the trying and laborious duties of poor-house keepership, should reluctantly yield a feature of their system which cheers and lightens their tasks. The price most generally paid to the teacher is about two hundred dollars a year and board. In most cases the schools are very small.

AID TO SUPERINTENDENTS OF THE POOR.

Throughout the State are a large number of benevolently disposed persons who feel a deep interest in the welfare of destitute children, and who are willing to aid county officials in finding suitable homes for them. Among these may be enumerated the ladies and gentlemen belonging to the State Charities Aid Association, the ladies and gentlemen who have been appointed by this Board as Local Visiting Committees, and also those connected with orphan and other asylums as managers. These persons will serve voluntarily if permitted to do so in this noble work, and when homes have been found, will, it is believed, take the trouble to follow up the personal histories of the children and report to the superintendents of the poor their condition and all that pertains to their welfare. If superintendents of the poor and other officials will call into exercise these beneficent aids, it is believed that it will result in much good to the children and to society at large.

A REMEDY FOR PAUPERISM.

A study into the history of pauperism shows that this condition is rarely reached except through a gradual "letting down" process, sometimes descending through two or more generations before culminating. It seems scarcely reasonable to hope that an evil, or what may possibly be called a moral disease, can be so treated as to bring about an immediate restoration, any more than a fever patient at the height of his malady, can be restored instantly to health by potent remedies. Taking this view of the subject and treating the evil as a disease, it is certainly wise to separate at the outset the incurable from the curable, and while bestowing all necessary care upon the hopeless, spare no exertion to restore to society, in a healthy condition, such as may be considered curable, among whom may be classed the children. These children are born into their degredation through no fault of their own, but are sufferers from the misfortunes or vices of their progenitors, and have the strongest claims upon our sympathy. From the age of two to sixteen, they are forming character; their minds are plastic, and may be easily shaped to good resolves. The surrounding world is a school full of infinite teachings, and they are learning from it. These years of tenderness by their very nature seem designed by Providence as a receptive period. After it has passed character becomes crystallized—the activities of life shut out the opportunities for improvement—the mind does not so readily imbibe knowledge and form moral habits as in its early years. It is found much more difficult to change bad habits when once fixed than to form good ones in the first instance. If these children were taken at the earliest moment practicable, at least before memory began its life-long work, and were placed under the care of those whose primary object in assuming the responsibility would be that of promoting the temporal, moral and spiritual welfare of their wards, rather than seeking any personal emolument, and if, with moral and religious training and fair educational privileges, thorough habits of industry were taught, at the same time that constant practical lessons of personal responsibility were imposed, in most cases the hereditary line of pauperism would be broken off, if it existed, and a healthy, vigorous growth take its place, in which the best aims of society will be reached, and the interests of the State defended.

It is not difficult to accomplish this in cases of illegitimacy. Here the paternal care is absent, the maternal tie is often weakened, and the child is easily separated from its parent. In a great number of instances the child is abandoned by its mother. But in cases where a father and mother become paupers, with a family of children, or either parent is committed to the poor-house or alms-house, with a family of children, an obstacle to improvement arises through the reluctance of kind-hearted keepers or humanely disposed superintendents to separate the children from their parents, notwithstanding it may be evident that the teachings of these natural guardians are, to say the least, in the direction of habits of idleness, shiftlessness and personal neglect. Some times it happens that the family association is absolutely degrading, yet courage is wanting to do what it would seem the law contemplated should be done in making superintendents of the poor the guardians of these children, empowering them to "bind them out," as evidently the interest of the child requires. In some cases it is urged that the family is but to remain a short time —only for the winter, and that it would be hard to separate the children from their parents. But during this short interval the moral natures of the children often become corrupted and energy and self-respect destroyed, and they leave the poor-house well clothed, possibly with ruddy cheeks, perhaps to return the following winter. Could the future be foreseen it might in many instances be demonstrated that it would have been better had these little ones have died than been placed in the poor-house at all. Looking to the best and permanent welfare of the children under such circumstances, is it not due them that they should be taken from those who have been legally proved incompetent to provide for even their bodily comforts? Beyond the well-being of the child has not society a right to demand this much for its own-protection?

The inquiries that have been made, reveal the fact, that while a large number of these children are born of depraved mothers, a great many are the offspring of passion and wrong. Many of the mothers are the victims of deceit and broken vows; some of them have come from distant lands to hide their shame from relatives and friends, and in anguish of spirit and abject repentence, are seeking to recover the position they have lost. The offspring of such, at least, may be regarded as promising subjects for training and culture.

WHAT SHALL BE DONE WITH PAUPER CHILDREN?

Persons of experience whose opinions I have obtained seem to have arrived at the conclusion that the first step to be taken in overcoming the great evils herein treated is to promptly remove all healthy and intelligent children from association with adult paupers and from poor-house life and its stigma, and to place them immediately upon their sinking to the line of public dependence and before being stigmatized as paupers, among such surroundings and under such remedial influences as shall be likely to reclaim them. Aside from the moral benefits of such a course, immense pecuniary saving will result to the public.

In a case of acute insanity, the law now requires that superintendents of the poor shall promptly convey the patient to an appropriate lunatic asylum for treatment. This is done in the expectation, based upon medical authority, that the chances for the recovery of the patient are in the ratio of the promptitude of the application of remedies. Would it not be wise to apply the same principle to the case of an unfortunate child who has been thrown upon the public for support, and thus save it from sinking into pauper life? The statute already makes it obligatory upon county officials to transfer every deaf-mute child of a certain age, becoming a dependent, to asylums for instruction. It virtually does the same with certain other defectives.

I beg to ask, whether a statute extending the benefits of this principle to other dependent children would not be desirable — requiring county officials to place in families or fitting asylums all children over two years of age, excepting unteachable idiots and others unfitted for family care, who become dependent, and prohibiting their being hereafter committed to poor houses.

The following reasons may be stated in addition to those already set forth elsewhere in favor of such legislative action:

1st. It appears from results already reached in the inquiry now being conducted by this Board, and which has been completed so far as it relates to pauper children, except in the county of New York, that there are now only about three hundred and twenty-five healthy and intelligent children, over two years of age, in the various poor-houses of the State. The number being now so reduced, the work of transfer, it is believed, will not inconvenience officials nor cause embarrassment otherwise.

2d. Superintendents of the poor in many counties are now embarrassed in their efforts to dispose promptly and humanely of the children under their charge, and keep the poor-house entirely free from them, for lack of some legislative action.

3d. In case of a change of officials and the multiplicity of cares incident to the closing up of an official term, the work of placing children out is sometimes temporarily suspended by the incumbent in charge of the poor-house, and when the new official has become fairly inaugurated in his position, he finds that a considerable number of children have accumulated in the county-house, and his administration may be near its close before the establishment is again free from them.

4th. It will be seen by the tables herewith submitted that many of the children now in poor-houses were born in them, and have remained there through nearly all their childhood.

5th. There are many mothers now dependents in the poor-houses, who would go out and support themselves if some general regulations were in force, whereby their children would be transferred to places in which they would be properly cared for, and many families that include children would not come under poor-house influences, but for the provision made by the public for rearing children in the county-house.

6th. In a large number of poor-houses in the State there are children that have been committed as truants or vagrants; among these are many girls. Sometimes parents are committed as vagrants, and bring a family of children with them. It is clearly apparent that the poor-house is no fit place for this class of children. If such children are bad, they make their associates in the poor-house worse; if they are not vicious, and are committed in consequence of their parents' faults, and are made worse by poor-house associations, then a manifest injustice is done to the children.

7th. In certain poor-houses of the State, there are sons and daughters of soldiers, who died honorable deaths in their country's service. A grateful recognition of the sacrifice made by their fathers, should secure to them better advantages than poor-house training for pauper life.

8th. A large number of counties in the state have already, through the action of their several boards of supervisors, virtually closed their poor-houses against children by better providing for them elsewhere. The effect of a general law having the same bearing, would be to prevent the stigma or brand of pauperism from being affixed to many homeless, orphan and destitute children.

The information furnished in this report touching the physical, mental, and social condition of pauper children is deduced mainly from the schedules prepared by the Secretary of this Board and his assistants in the inquiry now being conducted under direction of the Board into the causes of pauperism.

In this connection I desire to acknowledge the invaluable assistance rendered me by the Secretary of this Board, as well as the aid I have received from its members, especially from Commissioners

Anderson, Miller, Devereaux and Eastman, and the kindly services of the Secretary of the Prison Association, and members of Local Visiting Committees, and also from many other benevolently disposed and influential citizens throughout the State.

I may perhaps be excused while stating in view of the possibility of my not having met the full expectations of this board in the work allotted me, that if such should prove to be the case it has not resulted from any lack of effort. Since first undertaking it all my own time and that of an assistant has been occupied. A widely extended field has been traveled over. I have found the records relating to this and kindred subjects very incomplete, and sometimes difficult to reach. While prosecuting the special work confided to me I have visited among others a large number of institutions established for the care and reformation of children and have made careful and copious notes containing facts of interest relating to them, which are placed at your disposal.

I beg to tender to this Board the humble services thus rendered, feeling myself amply compensated if my well-intended labors prove acceptable to any considerable number of my fellow-citizens.

Respectfully submitted,

WILLIAM P. LETCHWORTH.

Albany, *January* 12, 1875.

NOTES RELATING TO PAUPER CHILDREN IN THE VARIOUS POOR-HOUSES AND ALMS-HOUSES OF THE STATE OF NEW YORK, CLASSIFIED BY COUNTIES.

ALBANY COUNTY.

In the Albany County Poor-House at the date of December 31, 1874, there were thirty-five (35) children — twenty-two (22) boys and thirteen (13) girls. Three were under two years of age, twenty-five between the ages of two and ten, and seven between the ages of ten and sixteen. There have been in all twenty-four children born in this poor-house during the past year, only three of whom are now remaining. There have been sixty-four received into this institution during the same period.

The fathers of seventeen of the children then remaining were natives of Ireland, seven of the United States, two of England, one of Germany, and one of Canada. The mothers of twenty were natives of Ireland, eight of the United States, one of Germany, and one of Canada. The nativity of the fathers of seven and the mothers of five were unknown. The fathers of twenty-six and the mothers of fifteen were intemperate. The fathers of eleven were moulders by trade. There were seven family groups variously numbering two, three and four children. Nine of the children were reported as having been abandoned by their fathers, two as having been abandoned by mothers, and four by both parents. Three were orphans and six half orphans. All were in fair health.

The dependent children in this county are placed in the various orphan asylums of the city of Albany. The number now in these asylums is between three and four hundred. The price paid by the county toward their maintenance is $1.50 each per week. The county officials are opposed to the keeping of children in the alms-house. The large number now there is accounted for by the fact that a considerable portion are so young that the asylums do not care to receive them.

ALLEGANY COUNTY.

There were five (5) children in the Allegany County Poor-House at the date of December 31, 1874. Two of these were aged four years and the others respectively five, six and eight years. Two had been inmates from birth. The five children had spent an aggregate of fourteen years in the poor-house. Three had been abandoned by fathers, and one, rendered homeless by the death of the mother. The father of one was dead; the mothers of four were in the poor-house; all were healthy save one. Three had been received during the year, and one placed in a family. The one removed is a lad in good health, fourteen years of age, a half orphan. He was born in the poor-house, and had remained there since his birth. He has been placed in the family of a farmer where he is now receiving moral and religious training. The influences surrounding him are good, and he is doing well.

The superintendent of the poor and officials of this county are manifesting a strong interest in the children under their care, and efforts are now being made to find them homes elsewhere than in the poor-house. It is hoped that this will soon be accomplished.

BROOME COUNTY.

At the date of October 27, 1874, there were but two children in the Broome County Poor-House over two years of age, one of whom was a boy nearly fourteen years old. He had been previously placed in the Susquehanna Valley Home and Industrial School, and ran away from there within a few days and came back to the poor-house. He had been reared in the poor-house as it were, before being placed in the home, and his inherited vices had grown by poor-house associations. The superintendent of the Susquehanna Valley Home stated subsequently, in reply to a further inquiry in regard to this lad and his family, as follows: "I think the boy will eventually fetch up in the poor-house. His eyes are bad; he cannot tell a potato from a stone. No glasses that I could find helped him. He is of bad blood. I know the family, always have known them. His father is a strong, able-bodied man, but the town has had to help him always, and his children multiply rapidly. There were four of them here when I came to take charge of the home. This boy's brother was sent to the Idiot Asylum at Syracuse, and is there now. I got a place for his younger sister in town. The family with whom she is placed like her and think she will stay. I think she will take care of herself. The youngest boy is here now and I have a hard subject in him, but I do not despair of making something of him. But the whole of this race are paupers, and they love to be paupers. There are three of the uncles of these children that have to be helped to live." I give this in the graphic words of the superintendent as it is but a type of description that will apply to a very large number of cases that I have met elsewhere.

There have been three children born in the Broome County Poor-House during the year ending October 1, 1874. At date of inquiry there were two in the institution under two years of age.

The indigent children in this county are mainly gathered into the Susquehanna Valley Home from the various towns in the county. This institution is not only the receptacle for destitute children of Broome, but of several adjoining counties. There were collected within it at the time of my visit, October 27, 1874.

	Girls.	Boys.	Total.
From Cortland County	3	6	9
" Delaware "	2	8	10
" Broome "	4	19	23
" Tioga "	2		2
" Sullivan "	1	9	10
Total	12	42	54

The sum charged to these counties for maintenance is two dollars per week. The price originally charged was $1.25, but it has been advanced with the increased cost of living. The institution is not entirely self-sustaining and is aided by charitable donations. It is controlled by a board of managers consisting of nine gentleman and an assistant board of ladies and gentlemen, representing the counties of Broome, Chenango, Cortland, Delaware, Sullivan, Tioga, and Tompkins.

The institution is beautifully located upon an eminence about a mile from Binghamton in one of the graceful bends of the Susquehanna river. It has forty acres of land belonging to it. It appears to be well conducted, and is doing a noble work.

CATTARAUGUS COUNTY POOR-HOUSE.

On the 10th of October, 1874, there were in the Cattaraugus County Poor-House five (5) children — three (3) boys and two (2) girls. Their ages were respectively one year, four years, seven years, ten years, and fifteen years. The boy, aged fifteen, is weak-minded and debased. He is "tongue-tied," incapable of learning, and is thought to be a permanent poor-house fixture, already having been there ten years. The examiner of this board says: "His father was weak-minded and intemperate. His brother was once in this poor-house and was a bright boy. He was bound out to a farmer and is doing well." Two of the children, a boy and a girl aged four years and one year respectively, were born in the poor-house. The other boy and girl aged ten and seven years are brother and sister. Their mother is an inmate and the children have been also inmates seven years. The aggregate child-life in this poor-house of the five children remaining is twenty-nine years. The mothers of four are in the poor-house. Four of the children are healthy and intelligent. The five belong to three family groups, numbering twelve dependents in three generations.

There were in this poor-house, October 1, 1873, seven children, showing a reduction of two during the year. The whole number of children in the poor-house, during the year, was twelve. Two have been placed in families and five removed by their parents.

One of the children placed out, a healthy, bright child, was born in the institution, remained in it seven months, was placed in the family of a farmer where its physical condition has improved and where it is surrounded by good influences. It is reported as "doing well." Of those received during the year, two were brought with their mother, who was committed as a vagrant. She was a thoroughly debased woman. Their older sister had been living previously, and while a member of her mother's household, with a negro, openly regardless of all moral obligations. The younger sister, a girl at that time not over ten years of age, while in the poor-house, by the arrangement of her attire and her languid and inviting manners pitifully displayed in one so young the brazen ways of the wanton. It seems a great mistake to commit such girls to poor-houses to associate with other children. It results in their having made the poor-house children, if possible, worse, themselves worse and they return into the outer world to make it worse. Such a family should certainly be broken up and the children put under correctional treatment and at a distance from their mother. This case, however, is but one of a great many similar cases throughout the State.

CAYUGA COUNTY.

There were no children in the Cayuga County Poor-House over one year of age at the date of September 2, 1874. The dependent children of this county are placed in the Cayuga asylum for Destitute Children at Auburn, whither they are sent directly from the various towns in the county by the overseers of the poor. The system adopted by this institution for the care, training, education and placing out of such children, is efficient, prompt and salutary. It is customary for the board of supervisors to make an annual allowance toward the maintenance of the children in this asylum. This appropriation is not determined per capita, but as circumstances seem to require. It is claimed by the managers that the amount allowed is small as compared with the number of children supported, and the actual cost of maintaining them. The appropriation made at the last session of the board was two thousand five hundred dollars ($2,500).

CHAUTAUQUA COUNTY.

There were seven (7) children in the Chautauqua County Poor-House, October 13, 1874. Two of them were under two years of age; two were six years, and three, two, eight and twelve years respectively. The aggregate time that these children had spent in this poor-house was twenty-two years and eleven months. Five of them had spent twenty-two years in the institution. A boy aged two, and his brother aged six years, were born in the poor-house, and have remained there since birth. The older sister of these brothers, aged eight years, was also born in the poor-house, and has always remained there. Their father and mother are in the poor-house, and both are useful. The children attend the village school near by. The examiner says of the boy, aged twelve years, and who has been six years at the county-house, "that an older brother of his left here, went west, and is now self-supporting. This boy has worked for farmers in the neighborhood. He has had his leg broken, but is now well. The boy is bright enough, and is not lazy, but he seems to gravitate back to the poor-house, partly because his mother is there, and partly from lack of ambition." The mothers of all the infant children are in the poor-house, one of whom is thoroughly degraded and debased, and whose influence upon children must be very injurious. There have been five children born in the institution during the year, and sixteen received born elsewhere. One child under two years of age, and seven between the ages of two and sixteen have been placed in families during the year.

No report is at hand concerning their condition and prospects since leaving the poor-house.

CHEMUNG COUNTY.

In the Chemung County Poor-House, at the time of my visit, October 27, 1874, there was but one child, a young infant. The dependant children in this county come under the beneficent care of the Southern Tier Orphans' Home at Elmira, where they are not only kindly cared for, but receive moral and religious training and secular instruction. As soon as suitable homes are found, they are placed, with great precaution in making the selection, in families. The Board of Supervisors of the county appropriated $750 and all the flour used in the home toward the maintenance of the dependent children of the county during the past year. There are also quite a number of destitute children in this asylum belonging to other counties, for which the institution receives no compensation.

CHENANGO COUNTY.

August 14, 1874, there were in the Chenango County Poor-House eight (8) children, five (5) boys and three (3) girls. Two of them were under two years of age, one seven, one nine, one fourteen, and three thirteen years old. Two were born in the poor-house. Of the children over two years of age, one had been in the poor-house four years, one five years, two six years, and one nine years. The aggregate child-life spent by the children in this poor-house was thirty-two years and two months. One of the boys, aged thirteen, is deformed in his limbs, and has been so from birth. He has a keen bright intellect, but is entirely helpless. Every thing possible seems to be done by those in charge of him to make his condition tolerable. The girl aged fourteen, was received in the house about two months previous to the report, in expectation of maternity. She appears to be confirmed in habits of vagrancy and vice, but is remarkably intelligent. Two of the children are idiots, and one is feeble-minded. Only three of the children in this poor-house are healthy, and one of these is but a year old. Three of them have mothers in the poor-house. Only one child has been placed out during the past year, a little girl two and a half years old, provided for in the family of a farmer. Five children have been taken away by their mothers, and four by both parents The whole number in the county-house during the year was seventeen. As there were twelve in the institution October 1, 1873, and but eight now remaining, it will be seen that a reduction of four has taken place during the year.

CLINTON COUNTY.

There were but three (3) children in the Clinton County Poor-House August 21, 1874, all of whom were boys. One was aged five years, and two were aged each eleven years. The latter are idiots.

The former is healthy and intelligent and has been four years an inmate. The mother of this boy is an inmate, and also the mother of one of the older boys. One of the idiots belongs to the third generation of a family who have all, so far as known, been paupers and inmates of the Clinton county poor-house. He is of illegitimate birth as are also his brother and sister.

There were eight children in this poor-house, October, 1st, 1873. At the date of October 1, 1874, there were two, one having been placed out between the dates of August 21 and the 1st of October. This reduces the number during the year six, and leaves but two, showing a good record for this county. Two children were born in the institution during the year, and seven were admitted, born elsewhere. The whole number in the institution during the year was fourteen. Seven have been placed in families by indenture, and two in the Northern New York Home of the Friendless, at Plattsburgh. One of these was but eight months old and of feeble constitution; the other was ten years old and deformed. Both were orphans. Of those placed in families, six were taken by farmers, and one by a carpenter. Two were girls and five were boys. Six of the children were under two years of age, and one, a boy, was six years of age. All were healthy and either orphans or half orphans. They are said to be well provided for, surrounded by good influences, and doing fairly. The boy six years old is going to school, is making good progress in his studies, and receiving moral and religious training.

The board of supervisors of this county, at their annual session, December 12, 1874, adopted the following resolution relating to destitute children :

Resolved, "That the superintendent of the poor of Clinton county may, in his discretion, place in charge of the institution called the "Home of the Friendless," located at Plattsburgh, Clinton county, such children of paupers, or other paupers as may from time to time come under his charge at the county-house, as would be benefited by being excluded from the influence of county-house associations. The said home to render an account to said superintendent of the number of weeks such children may be kept, and the said superintendent shall audit the same at same rate it would have cost the county had the said children been kept at the county-house, which said amount shall be paid to the said Home of the Friendless, the same to be chargeable to the towns to which they belong, the same as they would be if kept in the county-house."

This considerate action of the board of supervisors of this county, looking to a better care and training of its unfortunate children, warmly commends itself to all persons having the best interests of society at heart, and must result, not only directly, but indirectly, in great and lasting public benefit.

COLUMBIA COUNTY.

There were five (5) children in the Columbia County Poor-House October 5, 1874—four (4) boys and one (1) girl. Two were under two years of age, and one aged each four, eight and one about sixteen years. These three are brothers, and all idiots. The examiner says: "The father of this family died of consumption about two and a half years since. It consisted of six children — two girls and four boys. After the death of the father, the mother, with the four boys, were admitted to the poor-house; one of whom also an idiot, died here. The father is said to have been an intelligent and industrious man; the mother feeble-minded. The two girls (the second and third in this family) are said to be bright and intelligent children. The mother left the county-house after a short stay. The oldest boy is wholly unteachable; the two youngest may be improved under proper training."

Four children from the Columbia county poor-house have been placed during the past year in the Hudson Orphan Asylum, at Hudson. One, a child of three years, has been indentured to a farmer. It is under good influences, and doing well. Five were born in the house during the year. Twenty were received born elsewhere. The whole number in the institution during the year was thirty-two.

CORTLAND COUNTY.

The number of children in the Cortland County Poor-House November 18, 1874, was five (5) aged respectively three months, six months, three years, five years, and fifteen years. They had been inmates only a short time, and but one was born in the institution. Two boys, aged three and five years are brothers, and were abandoned by their parents; they are bright and intelligent children. They had been in the poor-house only one week. A girl aged fifteen is married, and her husband was in jail for drunkenness; she is debased and a vagrant. She never received any training in youth, except what she obtained in a poor-house, which she entered at the age of three years. Her mother, three of her brothers, and one sister have been paupers. Her father is said to have been intemperate. This is one of a multitude of cases, plainly demonstrating the evil effects resulting from rearing children in poor-houses. Her unfortunate mother became a dependent and sought the shelter of the friendly poor-house for herself and her little family. The consequence is that her children have grown up under poor-house influences and this girl is likely to perpetuate a prolific line of of paupers and criminals. Had she been removed with her brother and sister when she first entered the poor-house, at the age of three years, and placed under proper training and good influences, she might have become a useful and respected member of society.

One boy, twelve years old, a half-orphan after having been one month in the county-house, was placed in the family of a farmer. Influences surrounding him are said to be good. A boy aged four years was indentured to a relative and is receiving moral and religious training, and doing well. One boy aged four and another six, were placed in the Susquehanra Valley Home at Binghamton. All were healthy children.

At the time the secretary of this board visited this institution, October 6, 1868, there were nineteen children in the poor-house. In the following year the Board of Supervisors of Cortland County directed the children to be transferred to the Susquehanna Valley Home at Binghamton. At this time there are only nine children maintained by this county in that institution, showing a considerable decrease in the number of pauper children, a county charge since the adoption of this method of disposing of them.

DELAWARE COUNTY.

The destitute children of this county are transferred at once upon their becoming dependent to the Susquehanna Valley Home at Binghamton. The county appropriates two dollars ($2) per week toward their maintenance.

Commissioner Miller's report of the date of December 4, 1868, shows that there were then fifteen (15) children in the Delaware County Poor-House. Under the system that has been adopted of placing them in the Susquehanna Valley Home, there are now no children remaining in the county house over two years of age; and there are but ten, a county charge, in the home. The effect of this humane disposition of the children has been to decrease the number of adult inmates also in the poor-house. Owing in a large degree to the interest taken in this subject by Commissioner Miller during the seven years that he has given it more or less attention, there is but one county in the district represented by him in which there are a large number of children in the poor-house, and this county has taken action, recently, for their removal.

DUTCHESS COUNTY.

The Dutchess County Poor-House contained but five (5) children, November 19, 1874, one an infant boy, aged one month, whose mother died in the institution soon after his birth. She was only fourteen years old at the birth of her child. A girl, aged two years, who was born in the poor-house, is illegitimate, and her mother intemperate. The mother had been previously three months in the Queens county poor-house. She has three children in all, the other two being self-supporting. A girl here, aged eight years old, was born in the poor-house, and has remained there ever since. Her sister, aged twelve, has been there nine years. They are tidy and well-behaved children; the keeper is endeavoring to give them an education, and intends soon to send them out to service. The mother supports herself now by her own earnings. A boy, aged nine years, is deaf and dumb, blind, idiotic, and was born so. His father was a hard drinker. The whole number of years spent in this poor-house by the children now there is twenty-two years and one month.

The Poughkeepsie City Alms-House receives dependent children from the city and town of Poughkeepsie, in this county.

It contained seven (7) children on the 16th of November, 1874; four (4) boys and three (3) girls. One was under two years of age, and six were aged two, three, six, seven, eleven and thirteen years respectively. Five were born in the alms-house. Two had been in the institution two years, two respectively three and five years. Aggregate of child-life of those remaining in the alms-house was fourteen years and four months. One child was idiotic, caused by epilepsy. The mothers of four of the children were with them. One at least is debased. The mother of one of the children appeared to be a respectable and intelligent young woman.

Two children have been adopted in families during the past year and one indentured. One was taken by a shoemaker and two by farmers. Five were removed by their mothers and two of the number went with their mothers to Wards Island. Three of the children have attended school between two and three months during the year. Four are receiving moral and religious training. The influences surrounding six of the children are thought to be good and the same number are considered to be doing well.

ERIE COUNTY.

There were sixty-five (65) children in the Erie County Poor-House, October 1, 1873; forty-nine (49) boys, and sixteen (16) girls. This number became soon after increased to eighty-two. Early in the past year the superintendent of the poor, by authority of the board of supervisors, transferred sixty four of these children over two years of age to orphan asylums, reformatories, and other institutions, as follows : Eight were sent to the State Asylum for Idiots, at Syracuse ; twenty-six to the Buffalo Orphan Asylum ; six to the Evangelical Lutheran St. John's Orphan Home; four to the St. Vincent Female Orphan Asylum ; and twenty to the Society for the Protection of Destitute Roman Catholic Children. Since then other transfers from time to time have been made, so that on September 17th last, when the examination was conducted, there were but two children in this poor-house over two years of age, and these were temporarily there awaiting removal.

All of the institutions to which the children were removed are well conducted, and in addition to other needed teachings, they are properly trained to habits of industry. The latter is an important feature in the system of the last-named institution. A number of those sent there were idle perverse lads, corrupted by poor-house life, and needed industrial discipline. They belonged to a class of boys who, if left in the poor-house, must be pretty sure to find themselves eventually in prisons and penitentiaries. The sum allowed by the county toward the maintenance of these children is but one dollar per week. It was therefore in the exercise of a spirit of large benevolence on the part of the managers of the different asylums that they assumed the irksome charge of these unfortunates. A considerable number of them have already found their way into good homes.

It is difficult to estimate the good done to society through these asylums in thus opening the way for the removal of so many children from poor-house influences.

No children now are retained in the county establishment, in fact they are committed generally by the superintendent of the poor direct to the various asylums, thus avoiding the stigma of having been inmates of the poor-house.

The school-house formerly used at the alms-house for educating the children has been appropriated as a carpenter's shop. The damp basement room with its brick floor, around the limits of which the boys were formerly seated when displayed to visitors is now vacant, and the dormitories where the children slept in iron bedsteads, one over another, are now used for other purposes. The voices of the children no more wake melancholy echoes in the cheerless courts of the massive stone building.

At the last session of the board of supervisors, the committee on poor department recommended to the board "to erect on the poor-house grounds a suitable building adapted to the care of the juvenile poor of the county, with a 'Lying-in Hospital' in connection therewith." The method of placing the children at once under the wholesome influences of the asylums had found so much favor with the people that the proposition was immediately opposed by the local press, and so strong was the interest felt in the subject that a communication was addressed to the board by the Mayor of Buffalo; the three gentlemen comprising the Local Visiting Committee of the State Board of Charities, the County Judge, and the judges of the Superior Court, asking that action be deferred upon the proposition and expressing their conviction, that, "neither the financial interest of the county nor the welfare of the orphan and destitute children would be served by the proposed plan."

A careful consideration of the subject by the board of supervisors resulted in a decisive vote in the negative. It may be safely said that the people of Erie county have made a final decision against the system of rearing children in or about the poor-house.

ESSEX COUNTY.

In the Essex County Poor-House at the date of August, 19th, 1874, there were twenty-seven (27) children—sixteen (16) boys and eleven (11) girls. Only one of them was under two years of age. Fifteen were between the ages of two and ten, and eleven were over twelve years old. Ten of them were born in the poor-house. Eight had been there less than two years. Four had been inmates three years; three had been there each four and six years; five had been there five years; two had been there seven years, and one twelve years.

These children belong to seventeen family groups, which aggregate, so far as known, seventy-four dependents in three generations. The whole time these children had spent in the poor-house was ninety-eight years and eight months. Five of them had pauper fathers; twenty-one had pauper mothers; one had a pauper grandfather; five had pauper grandmothers; eight had pauper brothers; eight had pauper sisters; five had pauper uncles, and five had pauper aunts. Six had been abandoned by their parents. Out of the twenty children over five years old, only three could read and one read and write; ten of the children then present were feeble-minded or idiotic; one was blind; one dumb; one diseased, and two were so mentally and morally perverted as to be unfit to be placed in families. The remainder were healthy and ordinarily intelligent. Two of the girls, one aged four and the other five years, were born in the poor-house and their father and mother were inmates. Both of these children are feeble-minded. Their mother spent her youth in the poor-house — became attached to a negro, also a pauper, " a wandering vagrant," absconded with him and married him. She has had three children, one white and two colored. The mother of her husband is also in the poor-house. She has borne ten children, four of whom were illegitimate. All of these children have been inmates of poor-houses at different times and three of them died in this poor-house. Some are now inmates of poor-houses in adjoining counties. A healthy and intelligent girl, aged fifteen, was brought to the poor-house by one of the overseers of the poor charged with vagrancy and placed there in the hope of reforming her; the prospect cannot be other than discouraging. The mute child referred to is a girl aged twelve. She was also born in this poor house and her mother died there. She is intelligent and healthy, but vicious and depraved. After having been reared in the poor-house she has been placed out several times, but has been as often returned. One of the boys, aged eleven years, has been placed in good families twice, but soon returned. The whereabouts of his parents are unknown — are said to have been intemperate and depraved; he has a sister bound out who is reported to have a good home. If this child had been taken out of the poor-house when quite young he would probably have been saved from a life of dependence. One of the boys stated as feeble-minded is twelve years old. He was brought to Essex county a little over two years ago by his parents; they remained only a short time and absconded leaving this boy. They were said to be from Lower Canada. The child is so weak-minded as to be wholly incapable of improvement and will doubtless remain a permanent dependent.

The number of children in the Essex county poor-house on the 1st of October, 1873, was twenty-two , the increase during the past year being six.

No report is at hand of children placed out in families from this county-house.

The following correspondence and action of the Board of Supervisors of Essex county, in relation to the children in the poor-house, will explain itself:

STATE OF NEW YORK.

OFFICE OF THE STATE BOARD OF CHARITIES,
ALBANY, *November* 2, 1874.

To the Board of Supervisors, Essex county, N. Y.:

GENTLEMEN — At a recent meeting of the State Board of Charities, the secretary was instructed to call your attention to the large number of pauper children in your county poor-house, and respectfully request you to adopt measures for their removal.

The practice of rearing children in county poor-houses, or of allowing them to remain in these institutions, even for a short time, after arriving at the age of understanding, is believed by this board to be a great social evil, resulting in burdensome taxation for charitable purposes. The board, therefore, from its organization in 1867, has constantly directed its efforts to effect a reform in this direction, in which it has received earnest and efficient support.

In 1871, His Excellency Governor Hoffman, in his annual message to the Legislature, called attention to the condition of the pauper children then in the county poor-houses, and recommended their removal, and the matter was also referred to in his annual message in 1872. In the annual message of His Excellency Governor Dix, in 1873, the subject was again brought to public notice in earnest and emphatic language. The press, generally, have condemned in strong terms the practice, and the wise and good throughout the State, seemingly, have co-operated to set it aside. As a result, a large number of counties, through the action of their boards of supervisors, have removed all of their children over two years old from their county poor-houses, and have adopted methods for placing them in orphan and other asylums, and in family homes.

You are urgently requested to give this subject your careful consideration, with a view to determine how a change, so greatly to be desired, may be best accomplished in your county. I will avail myself of this opportunity to forward you an extract from the last annual report of the board relating to this subject.

Very respectfully yours,

CHARLES S. HOYT,
Secretary of the Board.

Extract from the minutes of the Board of Supervisors of Essex county, N. Y.:

Mr. Root presented for the consideration of this board, a communication from the State Board of Charities, in relation to pauper children kept in the county poor-house.

On motion of Mr. Root, the consideration of this subject was set down for eight o'clock P. M.

On motion of Mr. Root, voted that the clerk of this board be instructed to correspond with the Secretary of the State Board of Charities, in relation to pauper children in the county poor-house, as to expense of removal and the course to be pursued in relation thereto.

SUPERVISORS CLERK'S OFFICE,
ELIZABETHTOWN, ESSEX COUNTY,
December 1, 1874.

To Charles S. Hoyt, Esq., Albany:

DEAR SIR — Herewith I send you action taken by the board of supervisors of this county in relation to children in the county poor-house. Please favor the board with your views on or before the ninth of December, and oblige,

Respectfully yours,

GEO. S. NICHOLSON,
Clerk.

STATE OF NEW YORK:

OFFICE OF THE STATE BOARD OF CHARITIES,
ALBANY, *December* 5, 1874.

Geo. S. Nicholson, Esq., Clerk of Board of Supervisors, Essex County, N. Y.:

DEAR SIR — Your communication of the 1st inst., enclosing a copy of a resolution of the Board of Supervisors of Essex county, requesting me to inform them as to the course to be pursued by them for the removal of the children from their county poor-house, and as to the cost of their support in orphan asylums, etc., is received.

The removal may be made by the superintendent of the poor, or by the keeper of the county poor-house, under resolution of the board of supervisors. There are a number of orphan asylums in the State which would receive the children now in your county poor-house, and such others as the county, from time to time, may desire to send. The cost for their maintenance, clothing, education, and care in such asylums would be about two dollars per week. Although this somewhat exceeds the cost for their support in your county poor-house, it is believed that the change would not only largely benefit the children, but that, in the end, it would result in great saving to the county. If your board authorizes the removal, I will cheerfully render such aid in the matter as in my power.

I embrace this occasion to forward to you a copy of a document, showing the action of several counties in reference to their pauper children, which, in every instance, it is said, has proved highly satisfactory.

Yours very respectfully,

CHARLES S. HOYT,

Secretary of the Board.

No official information has been received of any further action in the matter. This county is suffering largely from entailed pauperism, which it is believed can be remedied only by promptly providing for the education and training of its dependent children, otherwise than in the poor-house. The results shown cannot be attributed to any fault of the keeper, but to the evils of the system.

FRANKLIN COUNTY.

In the Franklin County Poor-House there were but four (4) children on the 24th of August, 1874; two (2) infant boys, one three and the other four months old, and two (2) girls, one thirteen and the other fifteen. The two boys were born in the poor-house and are both illegitimate. Both the girls are mentally and morally perverted. These girls have been in the poor-house two years each. They should be placed in some institution specially adapted to their reformation. The father of one of them is reported as "immoral and sensual;" her mother respectable and well behaved. Her older brothers and sisters are self-supporting and occupying respectable situations in life. This girl, the youngest of the family, is thoroughly debased. She has been several times placed in families and returned as incorrigible.

Seven children have been placed in families out of this poor-house during the past year; four girls and three boys. Two were orphans and three, half orphans; two were illegitimate. All were healthy and intelligent, and are well provided for. Five are receiving moral and religious training. The influences surrounding all are good, and five of the number are "doing well." It is not reported whether any are attending school. One is aged two years, two five years, one seven and three nine years. All were remaining in their new homes at date of the report.

FULTON COUNTY.

There were thirteen (13) children in the Fulton County Poor-House October 3, 1874; seven (7) boys and six (6) girls. Four of them were under two years of age, six were over two and under ten, and three between the ages of ten and sixteen. Seven had been in the poor-house less than one year, one sixteen months, three, three years, one, four years, and one ten years, making the aggregate time spent by these children in this poor-house twenty-eight years and ten months. The mothers of three of these children were regarded as being debased, none of them intemperate. Ten of the children are reported as having fathers of idle, shiftless and intemperate habits. Five had been abandoned by their fathers. Four had fathers and seven had mothers in the poor-house. These children belong to families in which there have been thirty-one dependents in three generations. There were three defectives. Three of the children, two boys and one girl, belong to one family. The mother is said to have been under pauper influences, more or less, from childhood, and married a man similarly reared and of intemperate habits. There are three other children, one girl and two boys, belonging to one family, all healthy. A girl, aged ten years, is an idiot. Her grandfather and grandmother were paupers. Of her grandparents, the examiner says, "they were educated and trained as paupers, and have burdened Fulton county for generations past. They belong to the early race of 'backwoods squatters.' Some of the same family are in the Montgomery county poor house."

A communication was addressed to the Board of Supervisors of this county, at its last session, by the secretary of this board, calling attention to the condition of the children in their county poor-house, and pointing out the evils resulting from rearing children under poor-house associations, and urging their removal. It gives satisfaction to state that these suggestions were kindly received and favorably considered by the Board of Supervisors, as shown in the following extract from the minutes of its proceedings:

"FROM THE PROCEEDINGS OF THE BOARD OF SUPERVISORS OF FULTON COUNTY, SESSION OF 1874.

"Mr. Young, presented the following preamble and resolution, which was adopted:

"*Whereas*, A committee of this board, together with the late visitors to the county poor-house, have recommended that a committee be appointed to inquire into the propriety of placing certain children now inmates, and such children as may hereafter become inmates of said county poor-house, in some of the public institutions of charity of this State, for the purpose of maintaining and educating said children at the expense of the county, therefore

"*Resolved*, That a committee of two be appointed, and that said committee be and they are hereby authorized and instructed to correspond and confer with the different institutions of public charities of the State, in accordance with the recommendations aforesaid, and if they deem it to be for the best interests of the county and the public welfare, that the said committee concurring, shall have and they are hereby vested with full power and authority to contract with some one or more of the aforesaid institutions, and to place said children or as many of them as they may deem expedient in such instiutions, and report all proceedings, correspondence and contracts made by them, to the Board of Supervisors of this county, at their next annual meeting.

"The chair appointed as such committee, Messrs. Young and Durfee.

"I hereby certify that the above is a true copy of the original preamble and resolution in my possession.

"GEO. D. HENRY,
"*Clerk of Board of Supervisors, Fulton County.*"

GENESEE COUNTY.

At the date of September 19th, 1874, there were in the Genesee County Poor-House seven (7) children—two (2) boys and five (5) girls—all but one over two years of age. Of these, one had been in the institution three years, one four, one five, and one seven years. The aggregate of child-life spent in the poor-house by the children then remaining there, was twenty-one years and one month All the children are healthy except two, one of whom is epileptic, and the other feeble-minded, and also deaf and partly blind. A deep interest has been awakened in this county regarding poor-house children. The local committee appointed by this board has been zealous in aiding county officials in finding places for children, and it is believed that the general sentiment of the county is opposed to maintaining children in the poor-house. The discussion of the subject has had the tendency to arouse the sympathies of good people in behalf of the children, resulting in making it less difficult than heretofore for the county officials to place them in the better class of families. It is believed that ere long the rearing of children about the poor-house in this county will not be permitted by the people. The children that have been placed out in families during the year are reported as being surrounded by good influences and doing well.

NOTE.—The following resolution relating to pauper children, passed by the board of supervisors of Genesee county, at a recent session, has been received since writing the above:

PAUPER CHILDREN

Moved by Mr. Monell, That the superintendents of the poor be recommended to make arrangements with some orphan asylum for the keeping of the children now in the county poor-house or any that may be hereafter sent there.

GREENE COUNTY.

In the Greene County Poor-House, November 12, 1874, there were twenty-three (23) children; twelve (12) were boys and eleven (11) girls. Seven were under two years of age, fourteen under ten, and two between ten and sixteen. Nine had native fathers, and three foreign; nineteen had native mothers, and two foreign. The nativity of the fathers of eleven, and the mothers of two was unascertained. Eleven of the children were born in the poor-house. Seven of them had remained in the poor-house from six months to one year. Three had been there severally, two and three years; five had been there three years each. One had been there five years, one six, one seven, one eight, and one thirteen years, making an aggregate of child-life spent in the poor-house by these children of seventy-nine years. Twelve had intemperate fathers; four temperate, and the habits of seven were unknown. The mothers of eleven were said to be debased; twelve of the children were illegitimate. Nineteen had pauper mothers, two had pauper grandmothers, three had pauper aunts, two had pauper uncles, ten had pauper brothers, and fifteen had pauper sisters. Seventeen were healthy children; one was idiotic, and two feeble-minded. Five had been abandoned by one or both parents. Twelve had mothers in the poor-house at the date of examination. Three sisters ranging in ages from one to eight years were with their mother, a woman about forty years of age—a vagrant. Her mother was poor, and she was neglected. She had received no advantages of early education, and could not even read or write. She is temperate in her habits; formerly, "lived out" and did housework. She is the mother of five illegitimate children. She is engaged in doing housework in the poor-house, and is a good worker. It has been her practice to leave the poor-house and go out to work, returning soon to add another helpless infant to the list of dependents. This is the history of her life; all of her children were born in the poor-house. Two other children, one aged eleven months, and the other two years, have also a vagrant mother. She is but eighteen years of age; her parents were ignorant and her father intemperate. She had enjoyed no educational privileges, and her moral and religious training in youth had been greatly neglected. She now takes care of her children in the poor-house, and will probably rear a large family there, and no doubt lead a vagrant and pauper life the remainder of her days. She has a sister in this poor-house, aged nine years. One of the boys seven years old who lost his mother three years ago, and whose father was intemperate, was sent here by the poor-master with two little brothers. Two have been given out to farmers, and have good homes. The father of a bright little boy, whose sister is also an inmate and aged eight years, served as a soldier in the late war.

Five children were placed out in families from this poor-house during the year past. Four were boys, aged respectively three, eight, nine and eleven years, and one was a girl, aged eleven years. Four were received in the families of farmers. The girl is engaged in doing housework. No report as to whether they are attending school. Four are receiving moral and religious training under good surrounding influences and are doing well.

HAMILTON COUNTY.

There is no poor-house in this county. No report as to the dependent children has been received.

HERKIMER COUNTY.

There were six (6) children in the Herkimer County Poor-House on the 1st of October, 1873, and five (5) at the date of October 1, 1874, three of whom had been inmates from birth. Three (3) of these were boys, and two (2) girls. One was two years old, two five, one eleven and one thirteen. Three had mothers in the poor-house and two had fathers there. All of the children were healthy and ordinarily intelligent, except a girl aged thirteen who was an epileptic. A boy aged two and one of the girls aged five are brother and sister. Their father, it is stated, is a pauper by habit and preference and their mother was a pauper from childhood and reared in poor-house surroundings. She is a healthy person and able to work. This family has produced eleven paupers in three generations. The five children in this poor-house belong to four families, in which three generations have furnished twenty-seven dependents. All the children, with perhaps one exception, should be placed under good training and active industrial influences.

Two children were taken away from the poor-house during the year, one by the mother and the other by both parents, and placed under influences that were unquestionably bad.

By direction of this board, the secretary addressed a communication to the Board of Supervisors of the county the past year, urging the removal of the children from the poor-house. It has been reported that action was taken in the matter by the supervisors, at their last session, and that the children are to be removed to asylums, and the practice of sending this class of dependants to the poor-house, hereafter, is to be discontinued. This action, it is believed, cannot result otherwise than in a great benefit to the children becoming dependent upon the county, and at the same time tend to lessen the burdens growing out of pauperism, as has already been proved in other counties where similar action has been taken.

JEFFERSON COUNTY.

The number of children in the Jefferson County Poor-House at the date of August 26, 1874, was fifteen (15), nine (9) boys and six (6) girls. Three of these were under two years of age, seven were between the ages of two and ten, and five between the ages of ten and sixteen. Eight were born in the poor-house. A boy aged eleven is feeble-minded, and a girl, aged thirteen has her sense of hearing impaired.

The dependent children of this county are mainly placed in the Jefferson County Orphan Asylum at Watertown; the board of supervisors contributing toward their maintenance the sum of one dollar ($1.00) per week. They are not received in the orphan asylum until they are two years of age, and not permitted to remain beyond the age of twelve.

The children in the Jefferson county poor-house might be further reduced in number by placing some in asylums especially adapted to meet their particular cases. For instance, one of the girls, aged fourteen, has been returned from the asylum at Watertown as unmanageable. It is believed by those understanding her case that if placed in a reformatory institution she might be trained so as to lead ultimately a useful and respectable life.

KINGS COUNTY.

The pauper children of Kings county are provided for in the Kings County Nursery, a department of the Kings County Alms-House, situated near the village of Flatbush, about four miles from the city hall, Brooklyn. The alms-house is under the control of the Board of Commissioners of Charities of Kings county, consisting of five gentlemen. Each commissioner represents one of the five districts into which the county is divided. They are vested with, and exercise the same general powers as county superintendents of the poor.

The number of pauper children in the Kings county nursery over two years of age, in fair health and ordinary intelligence, was, at the date of the inquiry, greater than in all the county poor-houses of this State. The potent influence which this institution exerts over the moral well being, not only of the community in which it exists, but in a degree upon the State at large, makes it seem desirable to present a somewhat minute description of the buildings, and an outline of the system adopted in its management. Several visitations to this institution have been made by me during the past year.

Description of buildings.— The principal building of the nursery is of brick, three stories high, exclusive of a basement. It fronts upon Flatbush avenue, standing a short distance from the street. The ground plan of the main building is E-shaped. The measurement of the front is 200 feet, and the rear projections 82 feet. The principal entrance is in the center of the building. To the right, on the first floor, upon entering, are the superintendent's office, the apartments of the family and officers, and store-room and ironing-rooms. The second and third floors are divided into twenty-four wards, twelve on each floor. Porches about twelve feet wide, inclosed with sash, extend along each floor at the rear of the building, filling the spaces between the rear projections. All the wards and apartments open rearward by means of doors on these porches. There are three separate flights of stairways from basement to upper floors. Two of the wards on the upper floor are occupied by women of the establishment and their children. One ward on this floor is devoted to idiot boys. The twelve wards on the second floor are occupied by male children under seven years of age, and female children of all ages. In the rear of the main structure is a building used for an engine-house, wash-room and carpenter shop. Steam is generated here for warming the entire establishment, being conveyed underground to the main building. A high plank fence incloses a yard in the rear which is about four hundred feet square. This is the play ground of the institution. The fence does not prevent agile lads from finding their way over it occasionally during hours of recreation, much to the annoyance of the neighborhood. The institution is supplied with water from the city, lighted by gas and ventilated by two large air flues, one near each end of the building. They communicate with a system of flues extending throughout the structure. These air flues or stacks are heated by a furnace to facilitate the draught. The large flues which are designed to supply pure air to the building rise but slightly above the foul pavement of the yard. The air introduced into the building is consequently taken from the surface of the ground instead of from ten to twenty feet above it. There are bath-rooms at each end of the building on both of the ward floors. The closets, supplied with water, are located on each floor within the various wards.

Officers and employes.— The institution is under the immediate direction of a superintendent, assisted by a matron, teacher and assistant teacher. There are also employed two nurses, two female cooks, a chambermaid, engineer, gardener and night watchman. The gardener is assisted by pauper adults and the nursery boys in cultivating the garden which contains about three acres.

Adult pauper inmates.—In addition to the employes enumerated there are about the institution ten male and thirty-six female pauper inmates who are mostly engaged in various duties incident to such an establishment.

Four of the adult male inmates are seventeen years of age, and one is nineteen. Two have been inmates of alms-houses, each one year; one six years, and two seventeen years. The ages of the other five male adults vary from twenty-seven to fifty-two years.

Of the thirty-six female pauper adults brought into association with the children in the nursery, the following may be stated: One is under twenty; eleven are from twenty to thirty; twenty-one from thirty to forty, and three from forty to fifty years of age. Seven of the number were single; eight were widows; twenty-one were married; twelve of these had been abandoned by their husbands; two of the number were natives of America; one each was a native of England, Scotland, Germany and Holland; twenty-nine were natives of Ireland, and the nativity of one could not be ascertained. Ten were able to read; seven were able to read and write; nineteen were unable either to read or write. The habits of twelve were stated to be temperate; nineteen were moderate drinkers, and four immoderate. Eighteen assume more or less responsibility in charge of the various wards. The number of children belonging to these female inmates is sixty.

The children.— There were in the institution October 1st, 1874, three hundred and seventy-five (375) children. Ninety-five were reported as having been placed in families during the year previous. The number in the institution on the first of October, 1873, was three hundred and thirty-three (333). It will, therefore, be seen that there was an increase during the year ending October 1st, 1874.

The number of children in the nursery at the date of examination, December 2, 1874, was three hundred and fifty-six (356). Of this number two hundred and forty-three (243) were boys and one hundred and thirteen (113) girls. Of these fourteen were under and two years of age, two hundred and thirty-six were between the ages of ten and twelve, and one hundred and six were between ten and sixteen years of age. The fathers of fourteen of the children were natives of America, twenty-eight of England, one hundred and seventy-seven of Ireland, six of Scotland, thirty-three of Germany, three of France, three of Denmark, one of Italy, one of Hungary, one of Switzerland. The nativity of eighty-nine could not be ascertained. The mothers of six were natives of America, ten of England, two hundred and twenty-eight of Ireland, twenty-seven of Germany, four of Scotland, three of Holland, one of France, two of Denmark, one of Switzerland, and two of Canada. The nativity of seventy-two could not be ascertained. The length of time the children had remained in the institution was as follows: twenty had been there one month, thirty-three two months, twenty-four three months, twenty-two four months, eleven five months, eleven six months, sixty-nine from six months to one year, fifty-nine from one year to two years, eighteen three years, twenty-five four years, twenty-two five years, twelve six years, nine seven years, thirteen eight years, two nine years, three ten years, and one each eleven, twelve, and thirteen years, making an aggregate of child-life spent under alms-house influences by the children then remaining there of seven hundred and ninety-nine years. The average time spent in the nursery at date of report, by each of the children, was two and one-fourth years.

The fathers of one hundred and thirty-two were reported temperate, eighty-nine intemperate, and the habits one hundred and thirty-five could not be ascertained; the mothers of two hundred and six temperate, fifty-one intemperate, and ninety-nine unascertainable. The occupations of the fathers were as follows: laborers one hundred and forty-seven, agriculturists four, mechanics ninety-two, commercial fourteen, and other occupations twenty-eight; unknown seventy-one. The fathers of thirty and the mothers of one hundred and seventy-nine had been or were paupers; the grandmothers of seven were known to have been paupers; one hundred and ninety had pauper brothers, and one hundred and fifty-five had pauper sisters. The fathers of fifteen and the mothers of eighty-nine were in the alms-house or nursery at the date of inquiry; one hundred and one of the children had been abandoned by their fathers, and thirty-three by their mothers; thirty-six were orphan children, and one hundred and sixty half orphans; of the half orphans ninety-five had been bereaved of their fathers, and sixty-five of their mothers. Two of the children were crippled, one each deformed, blind, and deaf, five were blind in one eye, two were dumb, six idiotic, four epileptic, four paralytic, and three feeble-minded. The brothers of twenty-two and the sisters of sixteen had died in the almshouse or nursery. The fathers of eight and the mothers of eight were in the penitentiary.

A few of the children received in the institution come from the alms-house department; they are mainly from the city of Brooklyn; only a few come from the country towns. In the alms-house is a department denominated the "baby ward." Mothers when sufficiently recovered from confinement, are transferred from the hospital with their young infants to this ward or building. The mother is allowed, if she so desires, to remain here with her child until it is old enough to be weaned. She is then required to wean the child, or leave the alms-house and take it with her. Many mothers seek an opportunity of entering the nursery department with their children. This they are permitted to do, if assistance is needed in the nursery. But a small proportion of the children, however, enter the nursery from this source. A majority of them come in family groups, and go out in the same way.

It is not customary to put out in families children between the ages of two and ten unless they are orphans, half orphans, or have been abandoned, or are such as have been neglected for several years, by their parents failing to visit them. It will be seen that there are fewer girls in the institution than boys. The superintendent says: "That of late years he has not been able to supply the demand for girls; while it is difficult to find places for the boys."

Girls are put out readily at all times. Many families in moderate circumstances, will take a little girl when they cannot afford to hire a servant and pay regular wages. Such is the demand, that if the girls who go out are not well treated in their new homes, they leave and find places elsewhere. This is particularly the case after they have had some experience. There are also a great many occupations which small girls may follow, that make them in demand; such, for example, as those carried on in tobacco factories, paper-box factories, patent-medicine factories, and in similar branches of light handiwork. A great many boys go out of the nursery in the summer, and come back to stay during the winter. Formerly a good many were taken out by what are termed "milkmen." These so-called milkmen herd cows on the commons, and along the by-ways, and sell their milk. The boys are required to watch and drive the cows. Two of the boys during the summer have been sent out to lead blind men.

In placing out children no written condition or contract is made. A verbal agreement, or understanding, is entered into with the superintendent on the part of the person taking the child, by which the latter agrees to board and clothe it; send it to Sunday-school; give it, if under twelve years of age, three months schooling in each year, or an equivalent in evening instruction at home. The guardian has permission to return the child, upon obtaining a written consent from one of the commissioners. If the parents of the child desire subsequently to take it back, and can convince a commissioner that they are able to provide for it, the new guardian is required to give it up. In some cases, parties very naturally refuse to relinquish the child upon whom they may have bestowed more care than it ever received before, and to whom they may have become strongly attached. In such cases, an order from the resident commissioner is requisite to compel its relinquishment. A good many boys come back after having been placed out. In such cases, they are repeatedly "put out until they stay out."

Many of the children come in very poorly clad, remain until they are well clothed, and go out soon. This makes the sewing department an active one. It is rendered the more so from the fact that the immediate supervision of so large a number of children is, to a great degree, in the hands of irresponsible persons, that is to say paupers. Upon my first visitation, almost the first child that I saw, a little girl of about ten years, had her clothes almost torn from her. One white shoulder was bare and her torn garments seemed to be merely looped about her person.

Another little girl somewhat younger had her skirt nearly torn out from the waist. There were other evidences of hard treatment of clothing and neglect for which the system and not the matron or officers in charge might be held responsible. One must conclude that such a condition of things is to be expected when girls and boys of all mental and moral grades, including idiots, and of all ages up to sixteen romp and tear about together without intelligent and responsible supervision. This they may do in the high fenced yard, on the porches, in the corridors, wash-rooms and elsewhere. The wash-house occupied by the numerous wash-women of the establishment appears to be a favorite resort and social rendezvous for the boys and girls when tired of play in the yard.

Nursery dietary.— The following is the dietary for the nursery, prepared by the medical superintendent of the Kings county hospital.

	BREAKFAST.					DINNER.							SUPPER.					
	Bread.	Molasses.	Coffee.	Milk.	Sugar.	Beef soup, vegetables.	Bean soup, pork.	Fresh beef.	Salt codfish.	Potatoes.	Bread.	Mutton soup.	Bread.	Butter.	Milk.	Indian meal.	Tea.	Sugar.
	Ozs.					Pts.		Ozs.				Pt.	Ozs.		Pt.	Ozs.		
Sunday	5	½	¼	1	½	½	..	2	..	2	4	..	7	½	½	..	..	..
Monday	5	½	¼	1	½	½	..	2	..	2	4	..	7	½	½	..	..	..
Tuesday	5	½	¼	1	½	..	½	..	..	..	6	..	7	½	½	..	..	..
Wednesday	5	½	¼	1	½	½	..	2	..	..	6		7	½	1-16	..	1-12	½
Thursday	5	½	¼	1	½	½	..	2	..	6	..	..	7	½	½	..	..	..
Friday	5	½	¼	1	½	..	..	..	6	6	2	..	4	..	½	2	..	..
Saturday	5	½	¼	1	½	..	..	..	..	2	6	½	7	½	1-16	..	1-12	½

Extra diet for children under seven years and sick children.— Lunch at 10 A. M., consisting of boiled rice with milk or molasses. Corn starch, farina and sugar in quantities, and at hours ordered by the attending physician. Beef tea daily at $10\frac{1}{2}$ A. M. for children designated by the attending physician. Soda biscuit at any hour.

The school.— The school assembles at 9 o'clock. It is opened by a general recitation of the Lord's Prayer and the Apostles Creed, and is kept in until twelve o'clock, with one intermission of fifteen or twenty minutes. It is called together again at 1, and continues without intermission until 3 o'clock. From this hour until the children retire for the night, the time is mainly taken up in playing about the premises. The retiring hour is about seven in winter and eight o'clock in summer. No industries for children are carried on in the institution. Boys who work in the garden in summer do not attend school any part of the day while so occupied. The ordinary common-school studies are taught in the school-room, that is to say, the alphabet, reading, spelling, writing, history, arithmetic and geography. No class in grammar existed at the time of my visits, although, it was stated, there had been one previous to the last vacation. The principal,. and assistant female teacher appeared to be capable and devoted to their work, but labor under such adverse circumstances that they cannot reach desirable or even satisfactory results. I was informed by a gentleman who had formerly taught the school for six years, and who is now principal of one of the large public schools of Brooklyn, that his labor in this school had always been unsatisfactory and discouraging; that the good imparted while in the school seemed to be neutralized by adverse influences outside of it. A large number of his pupils were always new comers, while others were expecting soon to leave. It took the first some time to get interested, and those about to leave communicated their apathy to a large portion who would but for these hindrances, be more ambitious. But the great cause of demoralization in his school he ascribed to the adult pauper element in the institution.

Sunday-schools. — Upon Sunday afternoon two Sunday-schools are taught. The first commences about a quarter to 1 o'clock and continues until 3. It is conducted by the members of the St. Vincent De Paul Society of Brooklyn. Immediately after this school is over another is called, which is directed by Miss E. J. Cookely, Deaconess, as principal, assisted by other benevolent ladies. It is continued about the same length of time as the former.

Cost of maintaining the nursery. — The cost of maintaining the nursery during the year ending July 31, 1874, according to the report of the Commissioners of Charities, was $39,211.31. The average number of inmates was three hundred and eight-eight (388.) This would make the average, cost of keeping each child $101.06 per year, or $1.94 per week.

If to this sum be added the yearly interest upon the cost of the nursery building and grounds the cost of maintenance will be still further increased.

Influence of the nursery system upon children. — It appears that there have been five hundred and seven children received during the past year into the nursery. As there were only fourteen children under two years of age, at the time of the examination, nearly the whole had arrived at an age when the memory had begun to store up the teachings of its surroundings. Such of the children as come in family groups have, at least, lost some of their self-respect, and some of them will feel little or no repugnance to returning, and as they grow older, will naturally lapse into a life of indolence, ignorance and, perhaps, crime.

This permitting of so many families of children to be brought into the institution, to remain as it were at their pleasure, and then leave after having been corrupted by older children, who have been reared more or less in the alms-house, and whose natures are thoroughly saturated with poor-house vices, is one of the worst features of the system. The listless idle habits of the poor-house are so seductive as to confirm in pauperism the transient adult whom misfortune, for even a short time, brings within its influences How much more is it likely to fasten itself upon children. But families here come and go in almost infinite numbers, and then repeat the process again and again. Who will assume to say that the damaging results springing from these moral contaminations, are not incalculable? Such an institution comfortably warmed, where the inmates are well fed, must have that charm for youth that, standing as it does in sight of a great city, will draw many, who are sure to come again and again, if they can plead an excuse, if for no other reason than to renew the social life begun therein. May it not be properly asked whether such an institution, so related to a large community, does not offer a temptation to individuals to become paupers? It would seem better in cases where a family is tending toward pauperism to extend temporary relief; but if it is found that they must inevitably descend to the grade of dependence, after they have reached that line, and immediately thereafter, would it not be wiser to place the children promptly in good families, or in asylums where they will go into the ascending instead of the descending scale? Would not many parents inclined to thriftlessness and debauchery be stayed in their course by the thought that eventually they must, if they continue on, part with their children, when it shall have been proved that they are unable or unworthy of holding any longer the relation of guardians to them? Would not the certainty of children finding their way into an asylum and from thence into the care of families, under circumstances to preclude their being reclaimed afterward by the parent, prevent many a father from abandoning his family?

An objectionable feature in the Kings county system is that children are not placed out in families until they have arrived at ten years of age, unless they are orphan, half-orphan, have been abandoned by their parents or have not been inquired often after for several years. It would seem to be an easy matter to determine by careful investigation whether there is a probability that the parent will reclaim the child or not; if not, it ought unquestionably to be placed in a family or asylum at once, rather than be subjected to these dragging-down influences. After leaving it but a little time in the establishment, sometimes only a few months, the child acquires habits that preclude its becoming an inmate of the most desirable kind of home. It may be asked who is to assume the responsibility of this degradation, this defacement of those divinely imparted characteristics of humanity?

Another objectionable feature of the Kings county system is that of permitting parents to reclaim their children after having virtually abandoned them for years, and allowing their taking the child from a good home and bringing it into a worse condition, in the promise of what proves to be but a temporary establishment of the old home, under unhappy influences. There seems to be in this not only a manifest injustice to the child, but to its new guardian, who for a few years, while the child is growing and developing under good schooling and proper training, has been carrying a pecuniary burden in the hope of an after return from the grateful service and affection of the child. If a principle already incorporated in the statute were differently applied, this evil would be corrected. In chapter 830, section 10, Laws of 1873, there is a provision as follows:

"Whenever a parent has abandoned or shall abandon an infant child, such parent shall be deemed to have forfeited all claim that he or she would otherwise have, as to the custody of said child, or otherwise against any person who have taken, adopted and assumed the maintenance of such child, and in such case the person so adopting, taking and assuming the maintenance of such child may adopt it under the provisions of this act, with the same effect as if the consent of such parents had been obtained."

It appears that, out of the whole number of unfortunate children in the Kings county nursery, one hundred and six are over ten years of age. A few are imbeciles; but the greater portion at least should be under active industrial influences. Each one of these children in a family, while having its hours of school and play, would, in addition, be performing certain home duties, bearing in accordance with its capacity, a share of household responsibilities, and thus receiving daily lessons in thrift and industry, a knowledge of the value of time and its proper uses, besides learning infinite lessons of manual dexterity, and acquiring habits of order and decency.

If it be necessary to retain so large a number of young persons over ten years of age under these irksome conditions, it would seem their due that they should be actively employed, as well as schooled and taught some useful art or trade. Were this the case, the sense of confinement one feels here, and which oppressed me beyond any other institution I have visited, would be more tolerable. As it is, the close rooms, the enclosed porches, the dim and disagreeable halls, and above all the yard walled by what is intended to be an insurmountable barrier, high as though it enclosed a State prison, and without, so far as I could see, one blade of grass, or green leaf or waving branch of a tree, made the place seem to me like a miniature Bastile. I mentally exclaimed — wherein have these little ones offended that they should be treated as prisioners of State? Many of them are the sons and daughters of honest poverty and misfortune. Is their childhood, which should be the happiest portion of their lives, to be thus spent without human sympathy, without at least occasionally strolling in the green fields and parks or inhaling the sweet breath of flowers? Literally herded together in this confinement, surging hither and thither as a drove of dumb animals in the yard of the farmer, is it to be wondered at if we should see these children sinking into the most degrading and brutish habits?

The sombre features of the Kings County Alms-House Nursery appear the more objectionable, placed, as it is, in striking contrast with the large number of excellent and well-conducted charities in the city of Brooklyn, having for their objects the rearing and training of children to usefulness and respectability. An examination of these institutions, and the great and efficient work they are doing in the cause of humanity, makes it a matter of deep regret that so large a number of children as are in the nursery should be deprived of like advantages. Moreover, when it is considered that the asylums are not the only mediums by which the children may be relieved, but that numberless homes stand ready to receive them as welcome inmates, their unfortunate condition is still further to be deplored.

Conclusions. — Notwithstanding the attention given to this institution by those interested in its management, it becomes painfully apparent to even a casual observer that the King's County Nursery differs but little in all its essential features from the children's department of an ordinary county poor-house. As has been shown, there are forty-six adult paupers who are brought into intimate association with a very large number of impressible children. The individuals thus brought into the relationship of trainers of youth — for they cannot but exercise such function, though it be unconsciously — are not selected with care, nor in view of their peculiar fitness for the great responsibility they assume, but on the contrary are taken entirely from among those who through misfortune, vice or intemperance, have sunk in the social scale to the rank of the dependent class. What can be expected from such teachings and such associations? It would seem that under the system here practiced the institution could not be regarded as other than a nursery to propagate pauperism instead of an institution full of active agencies to neutralize it. If such be true, in even a small degree, this wealthy county, looking at the subject from no other than a pecuniary standpoint cannot afford to sustain the present system. If it should be changed in respect to the employment of pauper attendants, and in the places of those now serving, capable and efficient paid employes were substituted, it would still be found impracticable to shut out all surrounding poor-house influences. If the children are kept in such close confinement as should effect an absolute separation from the other inmates, then such confinement must partake of the nature of imprisonment. Remove these objections and there remain others as insuperable which are presented elsewhere in this report. These objections are so potent as to seemingly admit of no other conclusion than that the rearing of children in connection with pauper establishments is incompatible with the interests of the tax payer and the well being of society. This has already been proved to be the case in other counties in the State where it has been tried and set aside.

By direction of this board, the following letter relating to this subject was addressed to the Commissioners of Charities of King's county:

ALBANY N. Y., *September* 24, 1874.

To the Commissioners of Charities of the County of Kings.

GENTLEMEN — By the direction of the State Board of Charities I address you in reference to the pauper children in the Kings county alms-house. It has been the policy of this board since its first establishment to discountenance the association of adult paupers in poor-houses and alms-houses with pauper children, and its efforts have been directed in every possible legitimate manner toward removing pauper children from these institutions. This has already been done in a large number of counties; a growing interest is generally manifested in the subject, and it is hoped soon to effect in this important particular a complete reform throughout the State. Although Kings county has a separate establishment for children, nevertheless the very large number of adult paupers engaged in and about the children's department creates, it is believed, an evil of great magnitude, making the system differ but little from that of an ordinary county poor-house establishment where no classification is attempted.

Your last report to the State Board of Charities shows that there were at the date of report 341 children in the nursery department of your alms-house. A very large number of these were over two years of age, and a recent inspection convinces the writer that their condition, as regards their moral well-being, is deplorable in the extreme. These children having been reduced through adverse influences to the rank of the pauper class, it would seem that the only hope of elevating them into useful, self-supporting citizens and breaking the line of hereditary tendencies would be in removing them absolutely from the corrupting and debasing contamination of pauperism, and surrounding them not only in school, but when out of it with healthy teachings, and if possible industrial activities. The consequences of adopting an erroneous policy in the treatment of this subject are so vast, whether regarded in a moral or pecuniary view, as should seemingly arrest the attention of every thoughtful and well-disposed person. If there be any force in the conclusion arrived at by the State Board of Charities, that the association of pauper children with adult paupers tends to perpetuate pauperism, then this subject becomes one of great importance to the tax-payers of your county, and not only your county but the people at large.

You are earnestly requested to give this matter you deliberate and careful consideration.

Very respectfully,

(Signed.) WILLIAM P. LETCHWORTH,

Vice-President State Board Charities.

A letter was, at the same time, addressed to the President of the Kings County Local Visiting Committee, respectfully requesting the committee to co-operate with the county officials, and lend such aid in the matter as would be acceptable in the endeavor to reform the evils referred to.

It is gratifying to state that the commissioners gave the subject due attention and it was brought by them to the consideration of the Board of Supervisors of Kings county. This board appointed a committee to confer with the commissioners, who invited the officers and members of the State Board of Charities, and also the Local Visiting Committee of Kings county to a conference. The invitation was accepted and conferences were subsequently held, at which this board was represented by Commissioner Devereux, the Secretary and Vice-President.

It is manifest that the Board of Commissioners of Charities of Kings county and the board of supervisors, desire to reform this evil, but find embarrassments in the way of their doing so. It is believed however, that if it is not done immediately, the interest taken in the matter by county officials — the local press which have given this important subject much attention — and the public generally will at no distant date lead to some reform that shall ameliorate the condition of this class of dependent children and promote the public interest in this regard.

LEWIS COUNTY.

There were in the Lewis County Poor-House, December 31, 1874, six (6) children, four (4) boys and two (2) girls. Two were one year old each and four between four and eight years of age. The fathers and mothers of five were American; one mother was born in Ireland, and the birth place of one of the fathers was unascertained. Two of the children were illegitimate and one was born in the poor-house. The aggregate child-life spent in the poor-house by those remaining at the date of inquiry was eight years and five months. Three of the children had intemperate fathers. Two of them had pauper fathers; three had pauper mothers; four had pauper brothers, and two each had pauper uncles and aunts. Five were healthy and intelligent and one idiotic. Two had been abandoned by their fathers.

There have been six children placed in families from this county poor-house during the past year; all were healthy. One, a boy, aged fourteen, was placed in the family of a farmer, is doing farm work and goes to school; is making proficiency in his studies. The other children were girls all from one to three years old. Four were placed in families by indenture and one by adoption. Two were placed with mechanics and one with a merchant. All except one are doing well. Within the year ending October 1, 1874, two children were born in this institution, and eleven received born elsewhere. The whole number that have been in the poor-house during the year is seventeen.

LIVINGSTON COUNTY.

In the Livingston County Poor-House at the date of August 26, 1874, there were seventeen (17) children, thirteen (13) boys and four (4) girls. Four were under two years of age, nine were between two and ten years, and fonr were over ten and under sixteen. Two of the girls, each aged six years, were born in the poor-house. One of the children had remained in the poor-house three months, four six months, one one year, two one and a half years, three two years, one three years, three six years, one seven years, and one, twelve years, making the aggregate child-life spent in the poor-house of those remaining there fifty-two years and three months. Two of the children had fathers and eleven had mothers in the poor-house. Fourteen were healthy or but temporarily ill. A boy aged fifteen was afflicted with epilepsy and general feebleness of mind. A boy aged eleven years was idiotic. A boy aged ten years was paralyzed upon one side. A boy aged nine, and a girl aged six were brother and sister. The father of these two children was a laborer of "reasonably good habits," and met with an accidental death. The wife was left with five children. She is a good worker, but clings to her children as she says, "to take care of them." The examiner says, "both children and mother should be away; she at work and maintaining herself, as she doubtless could if the children were disposed of as they should be, where they could have educational advantages and proper training for something better than pauper life. A son of this woman was placed in a home from this county-house when six years old, but returned after a couple of years. The reason given, was that his guardians removed to the city of New York, and did not wish to take him with them. The mother of these children renders valuable service in the poor-house establishment."

A girl, aged six years, born in the poor-house, is here with her brother aged nine, and his mother. A boy aged four, and a girl one and a half years are likewise brother and sister. One of the girls here, aged fourteen, was committed to the poor-house with her mother for six months as a vagrant. Her father was a soldier and died in the army; the mother receives a pension. The father of one of the boys, two and a half years old, has separated from his wife. He supports two of his children outside the poor-house. The mother of one of the little boys, now in the poor-house, is stated to have left her husband "because of unkind treatment."

There were in this poor-house, October 1, 1873, fourteen children, showing an increase of three during the year. There have been placed in families during the period named, eight healthy boys, ranging from three to twelve years old, and one girl aged six years; one was an orphan, five were half-orphans, and three had parents living. One, a half-orphan, was provided with a home by its father, the rest were placed in the families of farmers. Eight are well provided for, five of whom are attending school; three of them have had two months schooling, and three have had three months. Eight are receiving moral and religious training under good surrounding influences; four are said to be doing well; three fairly, and the condition of two was unascertained.

MADISON COUNTY.

In the Madison County Poor-House August 12, 1874, there were but three (3) children. Two of these were young infants, both born in the poor-house. One was a girl fifteen years old, temporarily there in consequenee of being severely burned.

At the annual session of the Board of Supervisors of Madison county, held November, 1870, the report received from the committee appointed to consider the best means of providing for the care and maintenance of homeless and destitute children of this county, elsewhere than in the poor-house, contains the following fitting and forcible language: "*No law of the State is more fraught with wisdom than that based upon the idea that it is better to train the youthful mind than support the aged criminal, and no experiment in political economy of more practical value than that which transforms a fruitful source of taxation into a source of revenue — a pauper into a tax-paying citizen.*"

The effect of the principle embodied in the above resolution, and adopted by the county in its treatment of the unfortunate children thrown upon its care, is happily demonstrated in the beneficent workings of the Madison County Orphan Asylum, located at Peterboro. This institution was founded by the late Hon. Gerrit Smith,* who donated the building and furnished it, and also gave ten acres of ground.

---

* The generous deed, referred to above, of this great and good man gave birth to the following touching incident, which took place at his funeral at Peterboro, December 31, 1874.

"About noon the thirty little orphan boys, who were the particular proteges and favorites of Mr. Smith, marched in procession from the asylum which he had established for them, to the grounds and house in which he had frequently entertained them. The majority of them were too young to realize that they were looking upon their benefactor's face for the last time, but the older ones turned away from the casket with tearful eyes. The children formed in a semi-circle and sung a favorite hymn that they had learned to please Mr. Smith.

The children placed in this institution readily find their way into families.

MONROE COUNTY.

In Monroe county the homeless and destitute children are placed at once by the superintendent and overseers of the poor in the various orphan asylums of the city of Rochester, from whence they are absorbed into the better class of the community. The principle is adopted in this county of forbidding the admission of children into the poor-house.

The sum contributed by the board of supervisors toward the maintenance of such children is one dollar ($1.00) per week.

This sum is undoubtedly far below the actual cost of supporting them. It would seem, to say the least but just and fair, that the county should pay for maintaining these children under good influences in the asylums, as much as it would cost to keep them under bad influences at the poor-house; especially in view of the fact that these benevolent efforts directly tend very largely to reduce the burden of taxation for public charities.

The generous spirit shown in relieving the county of the care of these children by assuming the wearisome duty of their proper training, it would seem should be met by a corresponding spirit of liberality on the part of the representatives of the people.

MONTGOMERY COUNTY.

On the 6th of October, 1874, there were in the Montgomery County Poor-House seven (7) children, three (3) boys and four (4) girls. Two were under two years, three were between the ages of two and ten, and two between ten and sixteen. Four were born in the poor-house. All had native mothers. The fathers of four were natives, and three were foreign. One of the children had been in the poor-house six months, one one and a half years, one two and one-half years, two three years, one four, and one fifteen years. The aggregate time spent in the poor-house by all the children was twenty-nine and one-half years. The fathers of four of these children are reported as being of idle habits, and all of them intemperate. Of the mothers three are reported as being idle and two industrious; three as being intemperate, and four temperate. The fathers and mothers except one of all these children were, or had been committed as paupers. The fathers of two and the mothers of six were then in the poor-house. All of the children have brothers or sisters, who are or have been paupers. Four are healthy and ordinarily intelligent. One of the girls, aged fifteen, was feeble minded, and not only her father and mother, but her grandfather and grandmother have been paupers. She is likely to remain dependent during her life. A boy of the same age as this girl is an epileptic. His three brothers and three sisters, as likewise his father and mother, had been committed as paupers. One of the brothers is idiotic and is losing his sight. This family inherit blindness from the mother, and belongs to a race both physically and mentally degenerated by long debauchery and want of elevating influences. The father of two of the children lost his leg at the age of forty-five, became then a dependent upon public charity, and has remained so ever since. He has had four children in the poor-house; two of the girls have been placed in homes, and one of them doing well. The other two are promising children and should be placed in homes. There were three children less in the poor-house at the date of report, than there was the year previous at same date. It is not reported how many have been placed out in families during the year.

NEW YORK COUNTY.

The children that come under the alms-house system in New York county, are mainly in the buildings grouped on Randall's Island and known as the Foundling Hospital, Idiot Asylum, Nursery and Nursery Hospital. The whole number of children reported as being in the alms-house department of New York charities on the 30th of November, 1874, was thirteen hundred and forty-four.

As the inquiry now being conducted by this board into the causes of pauperism, has not been completed in these institutions, conclusions based upon it, conjointly with those drawn from personal inspection, cannot safely be reached until the inquiry which is now being rapidly pushed forward has been wholly completed.

NIAGARA COUNTY.

November 5, 1874, there were twenty-seven (27) children in the Niagara County Poor-House, eighteen (18) boys and nine (9) girls. The aggregate length of time the children remaining there had spent in the poor-house was sixty-two and one-half years. Only four of them are under two years of age, and only one child is classed as a defective, making twenty-two children that should be placed in families or asylums. Nine of them have been abandoned by one or both of their parents, and five are half orphans.

A school is kept at the poor-house by a capable teacher, a daughter of the keeper. The children during the hours of play cannot be prevented from ranging over the premises and intermingling with older inmates, among whom are some who are debased, and cannot be prevented from maintaining social intimacies with the children. The superintendent and keeper say they cannot find places for the children, as there is not much inquiry for them. They would give them out, if opportunity offered, and would be glad to send them, if practicable, to other counties, where the demand exceeds the supply.

No report of this county is at hand of children placed out in families during the past year.

It is with regret that the statement must be made that the number of poor children in this county-house has increased from thirteen to twenty-seven during the year, having more than doubled. I have made several visitations to the Niagara county poor-house, alone as well as in company with prominent citizens of the county, and by direction of this Board, the Secretary addressed a letter to the Board of Supervisors at its last session, calling their attention to the number of children in the poor-house, and asking their consideration of the subject, with a view to removing them. But the way has not seemed to open as yet to remove the children from the evil influences from which they are suffering. If there were some benevolent institutions, in Lockport that would assume the charge of these unfortunate children for the time being, and see to their being placed eventually in families, the difficulty would doubtless be removed, as a strong interest seems to be shown generally in the subject by the people of the county.

ONEIDA COUNTY.

The Board of Supervisors of this county, for a number of years past, have authorized the placing of all the dependent children of the county in local orphan asylums, and appropriated annually the sum of one dollar and twenty-five cents ($1.25) toward the weekly maintenance of each child. This humane policy affecting the welfare of homeless children has been fully carried out during the year past.

ONONDAGA COUNTY.

The Board of Supervisors of Onondaga county, in a resolution adopted December 20, 1869, relating to the disposition and maintenance of destitute children, used the following language:

"*Resolved*, That we recognize in the orphan asylums of the county "the principles of an enlarged Christain charity, which is calculated "to elevate an unfortunate class of our fellow-creatures to a posi-"tion of happiness, respectability and usefulness to which they could "not otherwise attain."

The superintendent of the poor of this county says, Dec. 26, 1874, "That all our children are sent to the county orphan asylums direct; "that is, by the superintendent or overseer of the city and several "towns. The cost is one dollar and thirty-five cents ($1.35) per "week for each child.

"We keep no healthy children at the county poor-house, believing "that it is no place to rear them."

ONTARIO COUNTY.

At the date of October 1, 1873, there were in the Ontario County Poor-House fifteen (15) children. August 11, 1874, at the time of the examination by this board, there were twenty-three (23), the number having increased eight between these dates. Of those remaining at the date last named thirteen (13) were boys and ten (10) were girls. Two of the children were under two years of age, fifteen between two and ten, and six between the ages of ten and sixteen. Four of the girls were born in the poor-house. The fathers of eleven were natives of the United States, the nativity of two were unascertained, and ten were of foreign birth. The mothers of eleven were natives of the United States, ten foreign born, and the birth of two was not ascertained. Three of the children had been in the poor-house six months or less, nine one year, three two years, three three years, three five years, and one each nine and ten years, making an aggregate of child-life spent in the poor-house by the children remaining there of fifty-eight years and eight months. Six had pauper fathers, fifteen had pauper mothers, two had pauper grandfathers, two had pauper grandmothers, thirteen had pauper brothers, twelve had pauper sisters, four had pauper uncles, and two had pauper aunts. These children belong to families which are known to have produced forty-three dependents in three generations. In this collection were six defectives.

By direction of this board the Secretary addressed a communication to the Board of Supervisors of Ontario county during their last session, requesting that body to earnestly consider the propriety of removing the children from the poor-house. The subject received due consideration, and the following copy of a resolution adopted by the Board of Supervisors has been forwarded to this board.

ONTARIO COUNTY:

BOARD OF SUPERVISORS,
October 17, 1874.

On motion of Mr. CHAMBERLAIN, the following preamble and resolution were adopted:

WHEREAS, The influence of the adult paupers as a class at the poor-house, has a tendency to demoralize and corrupt the pauper children while there; therefore,

Resolved, That the superintendents of the poor of this county be requested to consider the propriety of transferring to the Ontario Orphan Asylum, the pauper children which are now at the poor-house, and such as may be sent there hereafter, so far as suitable arrangements can be made with such asylum for the care and education of such children, until they can be placed out in families, as provided by statute, and if suitable arrangements can be made with the orphan asylum, this board respectfully recommend such transfer. And that the superintendents report at our next session, the advisability of such transfer before final action is taken by them.

(A true copy.) HIRAM METCALF,
Supervisors' Clerk.

The superintendents of the poor reported subsequently advising the transfer of the children to asylums, and their removal from the unhappy influences surrounding them is now taking place. This judicious action on the part of the board of supervisors, breaking up the system of rearing children in the poor-house, while bringing new hopes and ambitions to many homeless children, will doubtless result in great pecuniary advantage to tax payers by reducing pauperism in the county.

ORANGE COUNTY.

In the Orange County Poor-House October 19, 1874, there were thirty (30) children; fifteen (15) boys and fifteen (15) girls. Five of this number were under two years of age; seventeen between the ages of two and ten, and eight were over ten years of age. Thirteen were born in the poor-house. Eight had remained there less than one year; four, one year; three, two years; six, three years; four, four years; two, five years; one, six years; one, eight years, and one eleven years — making an aggregate of child-life spent in this poor-house of seventy-nine years. They belong to family groups which number seventy-two dependents in three generations. The fathers of twenty of the children were laborers; four farmers, and three mechanics; the occupations of three were not ascertained. Nineteen of the children had mothers in the poor-house; three of the children had pauper grandfathers; two had pauper grandmothers; three had pauper fathers; twenty-three had pauper mothers; eleven had pauper brothers; seven had pauper sisters; two had pauper uncles, and five had pauper aunts. Three children had been abandoned by parents. Three of the children were idiotic; one epileptic; two afflicted with scrofula; one feeble-minded, and one was a vagrant and debased. Ten over two years of age were regarded as healthy.

Five children have been placed in families during the past year; four of them were boys. One was aged seven years, two were aged respectively ten and fourteen years. Three were placed with farmers, one with a laborer, and one with a painter. One of the boys, aged fourteen, came back after being some time in a situation and was placed out again, but would not stay, and is now at the poor-house. He is an incorrigible case and probably too old now to be reformed. One had attended school three months, and two six months; four were receiving moral and religious training. The influences surrounding the four remaining out are reported "good," and all were doing well. The whole number that have been in the poor-house during the year is fifty-one. The large number that have left the poor-house and not placed in families have mostly been taken away by their parents. In view of the earnest efforts made by the present efficient superintendent, and his desire to have the children removed, it would seem that some action of the board of supervisors in this county is desirable, authorizing the superintendent to place the children in asylums; from whence they might be transferred to families by persons connected with these institutions who make this work a special duty. At the date of my visit, October 19, 1874, the children appeared to be as well cared for as possible under the circumstances, and were attending school. But the construction and arrangement of the poor-house building is such as to prevent any classification, and the well-disposed and debased come, as elsewhere, into intimate association.

There are also in this county a few pauper children, contained in the *Newburg City and Town Alms-House.* At the date of inquiry there were eleven (11) children, three (3) boys and eight (8) girls. One was under two years of age, eight were between the ages of two and ten, and two between ten and sixteen.

Two had been in the house one year each and three two years each. The fathers of six were born in Ireland, and of five in the United States. The mothers of six were natives of Ireland and five of the United States. Six of the fathers were intemperate and five temperate. Three of the children had been abandoned by fathers and three were orphans. One was epileptic; two were temporarily ill. Eight of the children belonged in three family groups.

ORLEANS COUNTY.

There were six children in the juvenile asylum of the Orleans County Poor-house November 6, 1874. Two were under two years, four were aged respectively four, six, ten and thirteen years; aggregate child-life spent in the poor-house by these children was thirteen years and four months. This poor-house has a separate establishment in connection with it, built upon a similar principle to that recently constructed in Richmond county. It has a school-room, and pleasant dining and other rooms. The play-ground is enclosed with a close board-fence to keep the children from intercourse with adult inmates. Notwithstanding this this precaution and the exercise of great vigilance otherwise, circumstances distressing in their nature and annoying to the superintendent were of not unfrequent occurrence, resulting from secret association of the children with adult idiots. The present superintendent, soon after entering upon his duties, became convinced of the wrong of permitting children to remain on the poor-house grounds, and set about at once placing them out in families, thereby reducing them to the present small number. Influential citizens of the county among whom were a Local Committee of three appointed by this Board, also became deeply interested in the subject. The attention of the Board of Supervisors was called by them to this evil. The Secretary of this Board, by your direction, addressed to the board of supervisors a communication on this subject. The result was a consideration of the matter and the adoption of a resolution virtually abolishing the juvenile asylum on the poor-house farm of Orleans county, by authorizing the superintendent of the poor to place the children who were inmates in asylums in adjoining counties, and authorizing the payment of one dollar per week toward their maintenance. As there is no orphan asylum in Orleans county the superintendent finds himself embarrassed in placing them in asylums in adjoining counties at the sum stated.

The influences surrounding the children that have already been placed out from the poor-house, are good. They were receiving moral and religious training, and such as were old enough were attending school. In one instance, a boy was not well-treated, and he was changed to another place, where he is now well cared for.

OSWEGO COUNTY.

There was but one child — a young infant — in the Oswego County Poor-House, October 1, 1874. Three were born in the institution, and four were received during the year, born elsewhere. Two have been placed in families; one taken away by its mother; and four placed in the Oswego Orphan Asylum, showing considerate action upon the subject by the county authorities. The two children placed in families are reported as being surrounded by good influences — one is in the family of a carpenter, and the other in that of a farmer.

The superintendents say: "Our custom has been, and still is, to place children over two years of age in the Oswego Orphan Asylum, where they can have the advantages of early education. We are not much in favor of rearing children in the poor-house, as the influences under which they are naturally brought in such places are not elevating, but deleterious to their moral, social and intellectual growth. We seldom have to keep our children in the orphan asylum a year before we can find places for them."

The *Oswego City Alms-House* receives children from the city of Oswego. This institution contained, October, 1874, seven (7) children, three (3) boys and four (4) girls. One of the children was five months old; the others aged respectively, three, six, seven, nine, ten, and twelve years. None were illegitimate. Four had mothers in the poor-house. One child had been abandoned by its father and two boys had been abandoned by both parents. All were healthy, bright and intelligent and should be placed under different influences than those that now surround them. One child has been placed out from this alms-house during the year in a family, and three were sent to the Oswego orphan asylum.

OTSEGO COUNTY.

There were nineteen (19) children in the Otsego County Poor House, at the date of inquiry, October 28, 1874. Nine (9) were boys, and ten (10) were girls. Three were under two years of age. The remainder were between the ages of two and sixteen. Six were born in the poor-house. Of the whole number, two had been in the poor-house five months; one, each one, five, six, eleven and thirteen years; three, each two and three years; and two, each two, seven and eight years, making an aggregate of child-life spent in this poor-house by the children then remaining there of eighty-nine years and four months. The fathers of twelve of these were reported as being American. One was born in Ireland; three in Germany; three unknown. The mothers of eighteen were American, and the nationality of one was unknown. Five of the children had been abandoned by their fathers; two were idiotic, and one feeble minded. The remaining number were healthy and ordinarily intelligent. Three had pauper grandfathers; three had pauper grandmothers; ten had pauper fathers; sixteen had pauper mothers, six had pauper uncles, five had pauper aunts, ten had pauper brothers, and eleven had pauper sisters. Thirteen were with their mothers in the poor-house. One of the little girls, had been an inmate of the poor-house three years. Her father, mother, and also her younger sisters are now inmates. There have been, at different times, six brothers and sisters of this family here. Their father, the examiner says, "has been in jail several times for vagrancy. He is a man now over seventy years of age, a native of Otsego county and of intemperate habits. In this old man is seen a type of debased humanity, fruitful in a progeny who are likely to follow his footsteps. One of his sons after having served a term in State prison, fled to escape the punishment of later offenses, and his wife and three children became poor-house inmates. She afterward married a pauper, who died in the poor-house. By him she became the mother of two more children, all five being inmates of the poor-house. A half-brother of these children who had been placed out is said to be illegitimate. The mother of the two children first alluded to, is the third wife of the father. She is a woman of middle age, and a moderate drinker. She was born in a neighboring county, and comes from pauper stock; was in the poor-house when a child."

In this county-house may be found other personal histories interesting to those engaged in social studies. The Board of Supervisors of the county was communicated with during its last session by the Secretary of this Board regarding the number and condition of children in the poor-house and action urged for their removal. The subject having been duly inquired into and considered by that board, the superintendent of the poor was authorized and directed to transfer the children to the Orphan's Home at Cooperstown, and ample provision was made for their maintenance in that institution.

The examination made by this board during the past year of all the inmates of the poor-house shows that this county is suffering largely from entailed pauperism, the dependents in a number of instances going back to the third generation.

It is believed that the considerate action of the board of supervisors will result in diminishing the number of paupers in the county and lessen the burden of taxation for charitable purposes.

PUTNAM COUNTY.

The Putnam County Poor-House contained, at the date of November 23, 1874, sixteen (16) children; ten (10) boys and six (6) girls. Two were under two years of age, eleven between two and five years, and three between ten and sixteen. Four had been in the poor-house less than one year, seven, one year, one each three and four years, and three five years, making an aggregate of child-life spent there by these children of thirty-one years. The fathers of nine of the children were born in Ireland, and six in America; eight had mothers who were born in Ireland, and eight in America. The fathers of eight were known to have been intemperate. Eleven of the children had mothers in the poor-house. Eight had been abandoned by their fathers, and two by their mothers. Two were idiotic and one was crippled. The children belonged to five family groups, consisting of two or more children in each. The father of the idiotic child is reported as a constant drinker, and has been in jail for drunkenness. No report has been received from this county of any children being placed out in families during the past year.

There were but four children in the poor-house at the date of vtsitation made by the Secretary of this Board, October 13, 1868. It thus appears that the number has increased since then over three-fold. The conclusion is unavoidable that the welfare of homeless children in this county does not receive, at the present time, the attention its importance demands.

QUEENS COUNTY.

In the Queens County Poor House, there were at the date of my visit, October 23, 1874, five (5) children, two (2) boys and three (3) girls.

So strongly are the superintendents of the poor of Queens county opposed to the rearing of children in the poor-house that they have permitted none to enter the county-house since the last annual convention of the superintendents of the poor, at which time this subject was discussed. In the absence of any authority from the board of supervisors to dispose of the dependent children otherwise, they are being placed in families and provided with homes as opportunities offer.

In addition to the county poor-house there are two Town Poor-Houses in this county, one at Hempstead, and the other near Brockville; the first provides for the poor of the town of Hempstead, and the latter for the towns of North Hempstead and Oyster Bay. In the poor-house at Hempstead there were at the date of examination made by the board, six (6) children, three (3) boys and three (3) girls. One of these was an infant two months old, and one a girl, feeble-minded and crippled.

In the Oyster Bay and North Hempstead town poor-house, there were six children, all under two years of age, excepting an idiot and a boy twelve years of old, who was formerly in the Kings County Nursery.

RENSSELAER COUNTY.

There were in the Rensselaer County Poor-House, December 31, 1874, twenty-one (21) children, ten (10) boys and eleven (11) girls. Nine of these were under two years of age, eleven between two and ten, and one thirteen years of age. Eight were born in the poor-house. Nine of them were illegitimate. The fathers of six six were born in Germany, eight in Ireland, and one in the United States; the birth-places of the remaining were unknown. The mothers of ten were natives of Ireland, one of Germany, and eight of the United States. The fathers of eight and the mothers two of were intemperate. Three of the children had debased fathers, and five had debased mothers. The mothers of all had been inmates of the poor-house, and sixteen were inmates at date of report. Seven of the children had been abandoned by their fathers. One family, consising of a father, mother, and four children, had been inmates of the poor-house since last June. The father is a healthy, temperate man, but by recent misfortune lost his property, and becoming disheartened, sought the poor-house with his family, and they have remained there until the present time. It seems unfortunate that a strong, healthy man could not have found the means of providing for his family and saving them from poor-house degradation. The children are healthy and intelligent.

The following resolution of the Board of Supervisors of Rensselaer county will show the general disposition made of dependent children in this county:

"*Resolved*, That from and after the date of the passage of this resolution, that all the children between the ages of three and twelve years, who shall be pauper inmates of the house of industry of this county, be removed therefrom and placed in one of the orphan asylums of the city of Troy, that such removal and distribution be made as equally as can be done among the several male and female asylums respectively, provided, however, that in all cases where the religious antecedents of the parents of such pauper children can be ascertained, the said children shall respectively be remanded to the orphan asylums under the patronage of Catholic or Protestant directors or trustees according to the religious persuasion of the said parents."

Adopted December 29, 1869.

RICHMOND COUNTY.

October 1, 1873, there were twenty-six children in the Richmond County Poor-House. On the 25th of September, 1874, there were but fifteen children. This large reduction in numbers was owing not only to the efforts of county officials to place the children in families, but to the zealous and voluntary aid rendered them in this good work by the ladies of the Local Visiting Committe for Richmond county. To this organization the county officials acknowledge themselves greatly indebted. At the date of my visit in September, 1874, there were but nine children over two years of age in this poor-house. They were all healthy, bright, intelligent little fellows and fit subjects to be placed under the elevating influences of home life. Notwithstanding this promising condition of affairs it was extremely unfortunate to note in the poor-house grounds and but a few rods from the county-house establishment, a juvenile asylum nearly completed, intended to be used as a home for the children. It was to be enclosed with a fence, and was so constructed as to keep the sexes separate. It had a good-sized school-room on the lower floor. It is intended to place the children there after they shall have reached the age of two years, and rear and educate them. A school-teacher had been engaged at a salary of two hundred dollars per year. It is designed to place one of the pauper women in charge of the establishment as matron, to whom it is expected but a slight compensation need be paid. The building is about the same size and similar in plan to that on the poor-house farm in Orleans county, which, after having been used for a number of years as a juvenile asylum, has, by the action of the board of supervisors at its last session, been set aside and the asylum abolished, by directing the children to be placed in families and asylums, and providing for their maintenance elsewhere than at the poor-house, thus practically condemning the system of rearing children about poor-houses.

It is estimated that this establishment when completed, fenced, and supplied with furniture will cost $3,000. The yearly interest upon this sum is $210, the salary of teacher $200, the board of teacher at $4.00 per week $208, total $618.

This does not include repairs of building, insurance, and the sum whatever it may be which must eventually be paid to some person holding the position of matron. This sum, $618 per year, is $11.88 weekly for merely sheltering the inmates. As before stated there were but nine children old enough to be placed in the asylum, making the weekly cost to each child $1.12; board and clothing cannot be set down at less than $1.50 per week, which will make the total cost of maintenance $2.62 per week. So much had already been achieved in the commendable work of placing children in families that it would seem that a little further effort in that direction would have resulted in saving the county not only this expenditure, but the cost of maintaining the children, and placed them at once under beneficent influences. Had the benevolent spirit controlling the management of orphan asylums been made available they could have thus been disposed of at a cost not to exceed to $2.00 per week, and from these asylums they would soon have found their way into families.

Moreover this attractive building will unquestionably draw families to the poor-house who would not come there but for this feature, and may induce abandonment or neglect by fathers or mothers of children who will thus become a county charge. This in fact has already proved to be the case. A letter from the keeper of the poor-house of Richmond county informs me that at the date of December 28 there were twenty-eight children in the poor-house.

The children that have been placed out in families are receiving moral and religious training, and with one exception are under good surrounding influences.

ROCKLAND COUNTY.

There were in the Rockland County Poor-House November 13, 1874, fourteen (14) children — nine (9) boys and five (5) girls. Two were born in the poor-house. The fathers of five were born in the United States; eight in Ireland; and one in Germany. The mothers of four were natives of the United States; one of Germany; and nine of Ireland. Five of the children had been less than one year in the poor-house; two one year each; one each three and eight years; and two had been there four and six years respectively. The total child-life spent in this poor-house by those remaining there at date of inquiry was thirty-four years and ten months.

Of the fourteen children, ten had intemperate fathers, and four in-intemperate mothers. The mothers of nine had been paupers, and three were then inmates of the poor-house. Thirteen of the children were healthy. One was a deaf mute.

ST. LAWRENCE COUNTY.

There were in the St. Lawrence County Poor-House, August 25, 1874, thirteen (13) children — nine (9) boys and four (4) girls. Six were under two years of age; five were between the ages of two and ten years; and two between the ages of ten and sixteen. One of the girls, aged eleven, is idiotic, and subject to occasional fits of epilepsy. Another girl, aged fifteen, is idiotic. Both of these will, probably, be dependents for life. The aggregate time that these children had remained in the poor-house is nineteen years and nine months. Ten of the thirteen were illegitimate; four were born in the poor-house; eight had mothers in the poor-house. Two of the children are brother and sister, and are there with their mother. Two others are brother and sister, and have likewise their mother with them. These last named were not only born of a pauper mother, but their grandmother had been a pauper.

Three of the children had been abandoned by their parents. The mother of one of the girls is a French Canadian by birth; she is an ignorant woman and owing to her lack of knowledge of our language could not find employment.

There have been nine children placed out by the keeper during the year ending October 1, 1874. They have all with the exception of one been placed in the families of farmers; four of them were boys, and five were girls. One was aged three years, one five, two six, three nine, one eleven, and one thirteen years. Three were orphans, three half-orphans, and one had both parents living. All were healthy children, with the exception of one girl who had been in the poor-house three and a half years; none of the others had remained in it but a few months, and several but a few days. All are believed to be well provided for. It is not ascertained certainly whether they have been sent to school, or if so, how long, nor if they are making any progress in their studies. The child nine years old, is known to have been receiving moral and religious training. It is reported that the influences surrounding all the children are believed to be good, excepting in one case not stated, and in another which is reported doubtful. The keeper of the St. Lawrence county poor-house, says:

" The children placed in families are put there on the recommendation of the supervisor of the town where the applicant resides, stating that the child will be well cared for, schooled, and properly trained. Further than this, we know nothing of them after they are taken away as it is not convenient to see them. I, therefore, cannot answer all questions concerning them as minutely as might be desired.

" Twelve children who came in with their parents were discharged with them, and are not included in the report." There have been thirty-eight children in all, in this poor-house during the year.

SARATOGA COUNTY.

There were in the Poor-House, of this county, December 31, 1874, eleven (11) children, three (3) boys and eight (8) girls. Two of them were under two years of age, five between two and ten, and four over ten and less than sixteen. The father of one of the children was a vagrant, and in the poor-house. Five of the children belonged to one family who had been abandoned by an intemperate father. Their mother was with them. One child had been abandoned by its father, and the mother was dead — another, an illegitimate child, had been abandoned by its mother. The children were generally healthy

Six children have been placed out from the Saratoga county poor-house during the year ending October 1, 1874. Three were boys, and three were girls. All were under three years of age except two boys, aged respectively six and seven years. These two were indentured. Another child was indentured and two were adopted. Four were placed in the families of farmers, one with a mechanic, and one with a laborer. Two boys have been sent to school each three months. Three of the children are likely to receive moral and religious training. One is known to be under good influences, and the influences surrounding two of them are supposed to be good. One of the children is doing well, and two are supposed to be doing well.

SCHENECTADY COUNTY.

Schenectady County Poor-House contained, October, 8, 1874, but two (2) children, one (1) boy and one (1) girl, the former aged ten years and the latter five years. The boy has been in the institution eight months and the girl a year. The boy's father and mother were paupers, and he has a sister a pauper; he is healthy and ordinarily intelligent. The mother is dead, and the father is an unreliable person. The father of the girl is deceased. Her mother is now in State prison. This child is not very intelligent.

During the past year one girl aged nine years has been placed in a farmer's family where her physical condition has improved. She has received two months' schooling, and has made fair proficiency in her studies; she is also receiving moral and religious training. The influences surrounding her are good and she is doing well.

Very few children enter the poor-house of this county. This is mainly attributable to the fact that their interests are protected by the Ladies Benevolent Association, of Schenectady, an organization founded in 1810, and which is very active in looking to the welfare of the children and the indigent. The children are protected before they become dependent.

SCHOHARIE COUNTY.

At the date of December 31, 1874, there were in the Schoharie County Poor-House, seven (7) children, five (5) girls and two (2) boys. Four were between two and ten years of age, and two between ten and sixteen years of age. Three had been there less than one year, two had remained four years, and one each eight and ten years. The aggregate of child-life spent in this poor-house by these children was twenty eight years.

One boy a half-orphan has been taken on trial by a stone-cutter; is doing fairly. He is "choring" and going to school. Has received three months' schooling.

SCHUYLER COUNTY.

There is no Poor-House in this county. The superintendent of the poor says in relation to the disposal of pauper children: "Some we bind out until they become of age; those who have parents we allow, or furnish, a stipulated sum per week for supporting them; where both parents are dead, or have deserted their offspring, we hire the children kept as best we can. We have a few at asylums."

SENECA COUNTY.

On the eleventh of August there were, in the Seneca County Poor-House, seven (7) children — five (5) girls and two (2) boys. One was under two years of age; five were between two and ten; and one between ten and sixteen. Two girls, each aged five and one boy, aged seven, were born in the poor-house. One of the girls is a sufferer from partial loss of hearing; all the remaining children are healthy. Only one of the children — a girl partially deaf — has a mother in poor-house; three of the children have been abandoned by their parents. The aggregate of child-life spent in this poor-house by these children is thirty-four years. No report is at hand of the children placed in families.

At the last annual meeting of the Board of Supervisors of Seneca county, action was taken looking to the removal of the children from the county poor-house to orphan asylums. The sum appropriated toward the support of the children is stated to be $1.50 per week. By this action, the stigma of being paupers is removed from the orphan and destitute children of this county, and these unfortunate ones are brought under happier and better influences

STEUBEN COUNTY.

At the date of October 28, 1874, there were in this Poor-House fifteen (15) children. Ten (10) of them were boys and five were (5) girls. Six of the number were under two years of age. One boy, three years old, was a healthy and intelligent mulatto. A girl eight years old, was healthy, but weak minded. A girl, six years old, was very bright and of good disposition. She was expecting to leave the poor-house soon, with her father, mother and brother. In conversation with the mother of these children, she expressed herself as desirous to have her children, especially the eldest, of whom she seemed very fond, placed in a good home, where they would be well taken care of and educated. Five of the children were born in the poor-house. The longest time any one had been there was five years. The aggregate child-life spent in the poor-house by the children remaining at the time of inquiry was eighteen years and three months. Six were under two years of age; seven between two and ten, and two were ten and less than sixteen. Four were defectives.

These children were found in different parts of the poor-house establishment as is generally the case. Four of them were in a ward with women paupers. Among these was a girl eight or nine years old. One of these women had a child of her own in the same room, and among the children. She had been an inmate twenty months; had a very irritable temper—so violent that she could not retain for any length of time a home outside of the poor house. She was strong and healthy, and a woman of very debased character. Such was one of the hourly companions of these young girls.

A second group of children — boys — were found in the wash-house. They were intermingled with the inmates of the wash-house, around the cauldrons where the dirty clothes were being boiled. Here was an insane woman raving and uttering wild gibberings, a half crazy man was sardonically grinning, and an overgrown idiotic boy of malicious disposition was teasing, I might say torturing, one of the little boys. There were several other adults of low types of humanity. The apartment of this dilapidated building overhead was used for a sleeping room, and the floor was being scrubbed at the time by one of the not over-careful inmates; it was worn, and the dirty water came through the cracks in continuous droppings upon the heads of the little ones, who did not seem to regard it as a serious annoyance. This discomfort was immediately checked when observed by the keeper.

The third group were in a back building called the "insane department." They were the most promising children of all, and yet the place was made intolerable by the groanings and sighings of one of the poor insane creatures, who was swaying backward and forward. She was a hideous looking object, and a great portion of her time was passed in this excited condition. The children are not sent to school, neither is a school sustained upon the premises, the number being too small to warrant the hiring of a teacher. Sad indeed is the lot of one born in destitution, bereaved of natural guardians and forced unwillingly upon the charities of the world, but when, in addition to this, the purity, sweetness and innocence of childhood are subjected to such soul-chilling influences, the deepest fountains of pity are stirred within us, and we hear tender voices of humanity pleading in tones which should reach the inmost chambers of legislative committees at the capitol.

It would be unjust to leave this description with the inference that the superintendents and keeper were at fault for this unhappy condition of the children. The property of the county had the appearance of being well-cared for, and the house was cleanly and in order; but in this case as others less aggravated, no separation of the children from the older inmates is practicable.

SUFFOLK COUNTY.

There were but four (4) healthy and intelligent children in the Suffolk County Poor-House at the date of October 26, 1874, the remaining seven (7) being either under two years of age or defectives. One of the four first named was a boy fourteen years old, who had unfortunately been committed to the poor-house for sixty days as a vagrant. This lad became a vagrant from the necessity of the case; his parents abandoned him. His brother was sent to prison for a misdemeanor—he thus became a wanderer, seeking for work. The examiner very naturally asks, "what is to be the fate of this boy, and who is responsible for his future?"

The superintendents of the poor of Suffolk county, are strongly opposed to the principle of rearing children in poor-houses, and endeavor to keep the county-house, free from them at all times. Not only are those over two years of age, that come in, promptly placed out; but also many under that age. Upon the occasion of a visit made during the early part of the season, there was but one healthy child over two years of age in the county-house.

SULLIVAN COUNTY.

In the Sullivan County Poor-House, at the date of inquiry, there were nine (9) children, six (6) boys and three (3) girls. One was under two years of age, and seven between two and ten, and one over ten; five were born in the poor-house; four had lived there one year each; three, two years each, and two, four years each, making the aggregate of child-life spent in the poor-house by the children there, eighteen years. Two of the children four years old had remained in the poor-house since birth. One child four years old was feeble-minded. Three were orphans; one, a child ten years old, is an orphan and vagrant. Six of the children have mothers in the poor-house, and three had pauper fathers there. One child four years old is reported as having been placed in the family of a farmer by adoption, and is said to be doing well.

The Board of Supervisors of the county, authorized the transfer of indigent children, to the "Susquehanna Valley Home and Industrial School in 1869, agreeing to pay $1.25 per week towards their maintenance. By action of the same board in 1873, the sum to be contributed toward their support was increased to $2.00 per week.

TIOGA COUNTY.

In the Tioga County Poor-House there were six (6) children September 22, 1874, aged respectively one year, four years, six, eight, ten, and eleven years. Two were born in the poor-house and two had remained there from birth. Three other children had been in the poor-house one year each and one nine years, making an aggregate of child-life spent in the poor-house of those then there of seventeen years; three had been abandoned by their parents; four were healthy and one idiotic. The mother of one of these children is a debased woman and was reared and educated in a poorhouse and has other pauper children. Two of the boys, one six and one eight years old are remarkably bright looking and intelligent. The boy aged ten is also a promising lad.

Three children have been placed in the families of farmers from this county house during the year; one an orphan and one a half-orphan. One is reported as having had three months schooling; the influences surrounding one are said to be good and two are doing fairly.

TOMPKINS COUNTY.

There were but two (2) children under two years of age in the Tompkins County Poor-House at the date of November 12, 1874. One was an idiot girl, four years of age; the other, a child, between two and three, who had been abandoned by its parents.

One child, a young infant, has been adopted into the family of a farmer during the past season. It is under good surroundings and doing well.

The officials of this county are adverse to the rearing of children in the poor-house.

ULSTER COUNTY.

There were in the Ulster County Poor-House on the 31st December, 1874, twenty-one (21) children—fifteen (15) boys and six (6) girls. Three were under two years of age; fourteen between two and ten years of age, and four over ten and under sixteen. Seven of the children were born in the poor-house. The fathers of fourteen were of American birth. The birth-place of seven was unknown. The mothers of sixteen were born in the United States. The birth-place of five is not given. The entire time of child-life spent in this poor-house by those remaining at the date of inquiry, was thirty-five years and eight months. Nine of the children were illegitimate, ten had intemperate fathers, and three had imtemperate mothers. The fathers of two are reported as debased; likewise the mothers of ten. Three children had pauper grandmothers; fourteen had pauper brothers; eight had pauper sisters; three had pauper uncles; and four had pauper aunts.

At the date of examination, the fathers of two of the children and the mothers of fourteen were in the poor-house. Nineteen of the children were reported healthy. Two children — a sister and half-brother, the father of one of whom is serving out a term in State prison, are here with their mother. Their grandmother has been an inmate of the poor-house, as was also a brother, who is out and is now supposed to be self-supporting. The father of the children, as well as the grandfather, was intemperate. One girl only fourteen years of age, who had been leading for some time a very abandoned life, had been sent here by her friends. She was the oldest of seven children; her parents are dead, and the other six children are provided with homes by friends. This poor ignorant child has but slight chances of reform unless placed in some correctional institution where habits of self-restraint and industry will be taught, and old associations broken up.

There are several very interesting, and strikingly sad illustrations in this county of the evils resulting from children being permitted to live in poor-houses.

There have been ten boys placed in families out of the Ulster county poor-house, during the past year. They ranged between the ages of seven and twelve years. Five were orphan children; four half-orphan; and two had parents living. All were healthy. Six were placed with farmers; two with boatmen; one with a merchant; and one with a grocer. All were well provided for with bodily comforts. All have attended school more or less, except two. Three are known to have made satisfactory progress in their studies. The influences surrounding five are thought to be good, with four doubtful, and one bad. Five were doing well, four fairly, and one doubtful.

One of the boys placed with a boatman, and who was attending school, recently absconded, and was drowned in the canal.

There are a few pauper children in the *Kingston City Alms-House*, received from the city and town of Kingston.

On the 14th of November, 1874, there were fourteen (14) children, eight (8) boys and six (6) girls. Eleven were between two and ten years of age, and three aged ten, eleven, and thirteen years respectively. Four of the children, all of one family, had been in the institution one year. They were of English parentage and had resided but five years in the United States. The father was a miner, a temperate and industrious man. He was taken ill, came here with his wife and family, and died three months before the date of inquiry; one of his children, a girl, had been placed out in the family of a merchant. It is not improbable but that the future destiny of the children may be unfavorably shaped by this one year of poor-house life to which they have been subjected through the misfortunes of their family. Four other children, two boys and two girls, are here with their mother. The father of these is dead. The mother of these children, as well as their grandmother, was intemperate, The oldest boy was employed on the canal during the summer, and had returned a short time previous to the inquiry, intending to spend the winter in the alms-house. He could neither read nor write. His mother is also equally ignorant. She is strong and healthy, and has passed over five years of her life in poor-houses. The younger children of this family are aged seven, five, and two years respectively. The conclusion is very easily reached that these children must be placed at once under good influence and proper training if they are to be made useful members of society. A third group of four children, two girls and two boys, ranging in age from four to eleven, are of the inmates of this alms-house. Their mother is dead and they have been abandoned by their father who was a mason by occupation. He was intemperate. The mother was reported to have been a respectable, refined, and educated woman. She was of a timid nature and had the misfortune to have had an intemperate husband. She died six months before date of inquiry, of consumption, leaving her helpless children who were abandoned as above stated by their father and consigned to the alms-house for a home. It is intended soon to place these children out, but it is a great misfortune that they should have entered an alms-house even for a single day. A boy seven years of age, born in Connecticut has been a resident of this alms-house three months. Nothing could be learned of his father and mother. He was taken some time since by the wife of a circus manager, and was intended to be educated for a performer, but failing to develop the requisite qualities, he was not retained. Afterward he was adopted in another family, but no papers having been made out, and the family subsequently concluding they did not want him, he was sent to the alms-house. The boy is reported as having no bad habits, and as being clean and obedient. He has had no schooling and can neither read nor write. All of the children in this institution are ordinarily healthy.

There have been three children placed out from the Kingston city alms-house during the past year. One, a girl aged thirteen years, with the family of a sexton. A boy, aged eleven years, with a boatman, and a lad, fourteen, with a farmer. The girl is engaged at housework in good surrounding influences and doing well. No statement has been received of the boys as to their schooling or training. The superintendent says on this point in his report, "It is not in my power to answer the questions left blank, as the general run of the boys coming here are from the canal, and it is difficult to get any satisfactory information. Most of these children are born and brought up on the canal, and my impression is they will die on the canal."

WARREN COUNTY.

There were five (5) children in the Warren County Poor-House, Octobor 19th, 1874, four (4) boys and one (1) girl. Two were under two years of age; one aged respectively six and nine, and two boys ten years of age who are twin brothers, the sons of a soldier. Both of the last named are healthy and intelligent children. Their father died an honorable death in the army. Two children were born in the poor-house. The aggregate child-life spent in this poor-house by the children then remaining, was fourteen years and two months. One of the children had been abandoned by its father, and one by both parents.

Six healthy children have been placed in the families of farmers from this county house during the year past. One male child was taken away by his mother. It is not likely to receive moral or religious training, and the influences that surround it are bad. All the children placed out had been in the institution but a short time; three were boys and three girls. Five are receiving moral and religious training. The influences surrounding five are known to be good. Four are doing well, and two are doing fairly. One, a girl six years old is reported as having attended school two months; she is the only one besides a boy thirteen years of age who was old enough to attend school.

WASHINGTON COUNTY.

The Washington County Poor-House contained sixteen (16) children October 23d, 1874; fourteen (14) boys and two (2) girls. Four were under two years of age, seven between the ages of two and ten, and five between the ages of ten and sixteen. Six were born in the poor-house. Six had remained there since birth. One had been in the poor-house less than one year, six two years, two three years, three four years, and one each five, and seven years, and two six years. The aggregate of child-life spent in the poor-house by the children there at date of inquiry was forty-four and one quarter years. One boy fifteen years old, is a vagrant and intemperate, able to work but will not; one is idiotic, one crippled. The remainder, except two, so far as they are of sufficient age to determine, are healthy and intelligent.

The examiner says of one of the boys, an intelligent lad about sixteen years of age: "This boy has grown up here; is attached to the county house, as to a home, and would never leave, if permitted to have his own way. He manages to come back whenever sent out on trial. This he will do always, unless at once separated from the influences of pauper life; and it is sad to reflect that he is already too far educated to hope for much reform." Of a mulatto boy, aged twelve years, the examiner says: "This is a smart, intelligent, and, apparently, honest-hearted boy, but without a home, and necessarily a vagrant or criminal. He has worked as a cook on a canal boat, and has been turned loose for the winter. In this lad is exemplified the want of proper provision for the care and education, instead of depression, of a certain class."

No report has been received from this county of children placed in families during the year past.

WAYNE COUNTY.

In the Wayne County Poor-House, September 5, 1874, there were six (6) children — three (3) boys and three (3) girls. Three were under two years of age; two, six years; and one fourteen. Five of these six children were born in the poor-house; five had mothers there. The examiner says, "one of the mothers has the appearance of being a respectable girl. Her case is a sad one; she was betrayed under promise of marriage — abandoned by her betrothed — and left a foreign country and came to this, to save her family from her own disgrace." The three over two years of age had been in the poor-house, respectively, seven months, six years, and fourteen years. The aggregate poor-house life of the children was twenty years and seven months. The girl, aged fourteen, is feeble in mind and body, and a dependent for life. Her mother is the youngest of twelve children, and has been fourteen years an inmate. She is likewise weak-minded. Her child is illegitimate.

A healthy, intelligent little girl is here with her mother, a middle-aged woman. The mother is a woman of debased character and rather weak-minded; she has been an inmate of the poor-house about twenty years. She first came with her father and mother who brought with them three children. The father died, the mother of the little girl left, but came back at maturity sick and has remained ever since. She has had two children by pauper inmates — the girl referred to. and a brother nine years old who has been "placed out."

Four children were born in this institution during the year; four were received born elsewhere. The whole number of children in the institution during the year was twelve.

Two children under two years of age and three over two have been placed in families during the year. Two have been taken away by their mothers. One of the children so removed is reported as being surrounded by bad influences.

Of those placed out all are reported as well provided for and doing well. One has been at school one month, one two months, one four months, one five months, and they have made good proficiency in their studies. Four are receiving religious training and the influences surrounding all are believed to be good.

WESTCHESTER COUNTY.

In the Westchester County Poor-House, October 29, 1874, there were forty-five (45) children, twenty-four (24) boys and twenty-one (21) girls. Twelve of them were under two years of age; twenty-nine between two and ten years old, and four between ten and sixteen; seven of this number were colored children, four of them females and three males. Six of the whole number had been born in the poor-house. The fathers of twelve of the children were born in the United States; twenty-six in Ireland; one in Germany; one in Italy, and the birth of one was unknown. The mothers of ten were born in the United States, twenty-nine in Ireland, one in England, one in Germany, one in Italy and the nativity of three was unascertainable.

Two of these children had been in the poor-house seven years each, four three years each, eight, two years each, seven, one year each; and the remainder less than one year.

The aggregate of child-life spent in this poor-house by the children then remaining in it was fifty-six years and seven months. Twenty-nine of the number had intemperate fathers, eight had intemperate mothers. The fathers of twenty-six were laborers; ten mechanics; one commercial, two soldiers and the occupations of six were unascertained.

One of the children had a pauper grandfather, three had pauper grandmothers, seven had pauper fathers, thirty had pauper mothers. The mothers of twenty-five were in the poor-house at the time. Seventeen of the children had pauper brothers; eighteen had pauper sisters; two had pauper aunts.

Only eight of the whole number were illegitimate and yet sixteen had been abandoned by their fathers and four by both father and mother; three were orphans and four half-orphans. There were twelve family groups of two children in each, and two family groups of three children in each. Two of the colored children were twins and were with their mother who had been a slave in Virginia and did field and house work there. She is now employed mainly in kitchen work; is temperate; her children are illegitimate. Two other colored boys here — brothers, one eight and one twelve years old have each lost an eye by small-pox. When the boys recovered partially from this scourge they were sent to the poor-house with their grandmother. They had been in the poor-house seven months. The mother of a little boy and girl here is reported to be in the penitentiary for drunkenness. The father is weak and sickly and unable to support the children, who were sent to the poor-house. The elder two in the family are twins. One of the boys, nine years old, was given by his father to his uncle, the latter agreeing to board him at a certain rate. He, not receiving the board money, brought the lad here. The father is reported to be a very unreliable person.

Two little boys, brothers, are here because the father is intemperate and will not support the wife and children, who have in consequence been sent to the poor-house. He has not run away, but in reality has abandoned his family.

The father of one of the boys, aged fourteen, was killed in the late war. The examiner says: "The boy is pretty intelligent, with a good memory, and gives promise of becoming a useful man if rightly educated." Of a little Italian boy ten years old, the examiner says: "This boy was brought to this country by one of those Italians who bring children here from Italy to play instruments and sing. His mother, the boy says, sent him and his brother away with a man who brought them to New York city and had them play the violin and collect money in the streets. When he came home at night if he did not get much money, his master used to beat him and sometimes hanged him up with a rope (the boy cried when recalling this bit of his history). He lost his way in New York city; some one stole his fiddle when he was sleeping on a door-step. He wandered around until he came into Westchester county. The poormaster not being able to obtain any information regarding him, after advertising him, sent him to the poor-house. He is a very fine bright child, and under proper training may 'become a superior man.'"

A rather bright and promising little lad of about five years old became half-orphaned, it is reported, by the intemperance of his father. After his father died, his mother, who was also intemperate, jumped out of the window and broke her neck, and the boy was then sent to the poor-house. The history of one of the girls (colored), aged about sixteen, shows that through early neglect of parents, she fell into habits of vagrancy. She can read a little, but not write.

The examiner says: "She is bright and neat; has been here six months; has a child now four months old."

The father of one little boy is in Sing Sing — second term, for larceny. His mother is supporting herself and another child outside. This boy is sickly.

An examination made by me of these children a short time previous to October 29, showed that nearly all were in fair health, and such as were old enough to determine, seemed ordinarily intelligent, and some remarkably so.

As there were thirty-seven children in this poor-house, October 1, 1873 — nineteen boys and eighteen girls, it appears that the number has been increased eight between that date and October 29, 1874.

There have been placed out from the Westchester county poorhouse during the past year, three boys and three girls. One boy was sent to the House of Refuge. One of the girls had been in the poorhouse two years, and two of the boys had been there four and three-quarters years. Three were placed with farmers; one with a shoemaker and one with a tradesman. Five of the children were receiving the advantages of school and making fair proficiency in their studies. All were receiving moral and religious training, and it is stated are surrounded by good influences, and doing well. Great care is taken by the superintendents and keeper in placing out children to find good homes for them, and as before stated, they require from the party taking the child a yearly report of what has been done for its improvement and welfare, and a statement of its condition. Fourteen children were born in this poor-house during the year. Sixty-nine have been received born elsewhere. The whole number that have been in the institution during the past year is one hundred and fifteen. Considering the large number of children that come in and go out of this poor-house, its influence upon the community must be considerable either for good or evil.

The school kept at the poor-house is a good one for a poor-house school. It is evidently managed by a zealous teacher. The school-room is large and airy. The keeper of the poor-house is a good disciplinarian, yet with all these desirable accessories it is evident, that the well-being of the children and the interests of the county would be promoted by the people abolishing the system of rearing children in their poor-house.

WYOMING COUNTY.

There were but two children in the Wyoming County Poor House at the date of October 5th; one four months, and the other one year old. This favorable condition may be largely ascribed — in addition to the energetic efforts of the Superintendents of the Poor — to those of a philanthropic member of the Wyoming County Local Visiting Committee appointed by this board. For many years this lady has maintained out of her own purse, and trained under her own direction a small band of destitute children which are selected from the most incorrigible that can be found; her special attention being given to this unpromising class. The people of this county are greatly indebted to her for her self-sacrificing labors; which, while ameliorating the condition of the unfortunate, incidentally lessens the public burden growing out of pauperism.

YATES COUNTY.

There were five (5) children in the Yates County Poor-House, October 1, 1874, two (2) boys and three (3) girls. None were under two years of age. Three were born in the poor-house. One, a girl aged four years, and a boy aged six years, brother and sister, have remained in the poor-house since their birth. The aggregate child-life spent in this poor-house by the children there, was thirteen years and six months. A boy ten years old who was born in this poor-house has been in the county jail for vagrancy. These children with one exception are healthy. Two girls have been placed in families by indenture, one eleven years old and the other thirteen. They are doing housework, are said to be receiving moral and religious training under good surrounding influences, and doing well. No report as to whether they are attending school.

There were seventy inmates, twenty-four of whom were children, in this county-house at the time of the visit made by the Secretary of the Board, June 15, 1868. In the fall of that year the board of supervisors of Yates county directed the children in the county-house to be transferred to asylums, and appropriated two dollars a week toward their maintenance. This action was prefaced with the following preamble:

"Our poor-house is most of the time over-crowded with children, and, in the opinion of the board, said house is a very unfit residence for such children, very deleterious to their physical and moral condition, tending greatly to increase the paupers of our county and of poor-house expenses."

The result of transferring the children to asylums is, that there are but *three* children now maintained at the expense of the county in the Ontario County Orphan Asylum to which institution the children have been subsequently sent, and the number of adult pauper inmates in the county-house has been lessened from seventy, in 1868, to thirty-two, in 1874. This is largely in consequence of those who formerly came to the poor-house to rear their children in idleness, having either left the county or become self-supporting.

TABLE I,

Showing the number, sex, color and ages of pauper children under sixteen years in the various county poor-houses of the State of New York, at the several dates of inquiry in 1874, *with a comparative statement as to the number in the same institutions as shown by the examination in* 1868.

COUNTIES.	Date of inquiry.	Male.	Female.	White.	Colored.	Under two years of age.	Over two years and under ten.	Over ten and under sixteen	Total, 1874.	Total, 1868.
Albany	December 31	22	13	33	2	3	25	7	35	120
Allegany	December 31	4	1	4	1	......	5	......	5	9
Broome	October 27	2	2	4	......	2	1	1	4	21
Cattaraugus	October 10	3	2	5	......	1	2	2	5	6
Cayuga	September 2	4	1	3	2	5	......	......	5	5
Chautauqua	October 13	4	3	7	......	2	4	1	7	31
Chemung	August 13	......	1	1	......	1	......	......	1	12
Chenango	August 14	5	3	8	....	2	2	4	8	12
Clinton	August 21	3	......	3	......	......	1	2	8	9
Columbia	October 5	3	1	4	......	2	2	......	4	10
Cortland	November 18	4	1	5	......	2	2	1	5	19
Delaware	December 24	2	......	2	......	1	1	......	2	15
Dutchess	November 19	2	3	5	......	1	3	1	5	10
Erie	September 17	6	3	8	1	6	1	2	9	65
Essex	August 19	15	12	25	2	1	15	11	27	30
Franklin	August 24	2	2	4	......	2	......	2	4	5
Fulton	October 3	7	6	13	......	4	6	3	13	14
Genesee	September 19	2	5	3	4	1	5	1	7	13
Greene	November 12	11	11	18	4	3	17	2	22	45
Hamilton*	......	......	......	......	......	......	......	......	......	......
Herkimer	September 30	3	2	5	......	......	3	2	5	5
Jefferson	August 26	9	6	14	1	3	7	5	15	20
Kings †	......	......	......	......	......	......	......	......	......	......
Lewis	December 31	4	2	5	1	2	4	......	6	8
Livingston	August 26	13	4	16	1	4	9	4	17	40
Madison	August 12	2	1	3	......	2	......	1	3	22
Monroe	September 22	7	3	10	......	7	2	1	10	20
Montgomery	October 6	3	4	7	......	2	3	2	7	11
New York ‡	......	......	......	......	......	......	......	......	......	......
Niagara	November 5	18	9	25	2	2	20	5	27	46
Oneida	November 23	8	7	14	1	6	6	3	15	28
Onondaga	December 22	2	2	4	......	......	3	1	4	7
Ontario	August 11	13	10	21	2	2	15	6	23	30
Orange	October 19	14	15	28	1	5	18	6	29	40
Orleans	November 6	5	1	5	1	1	3	2	6	16
Oswego	September 10	1	......	1	......	1	......	......	1	2
Otsego	October 28	9	10	15	4	3	12	4	19	28
Putnam	November 23	10	6	16	......	2	10	4	16	4
Queens	October 23	2	3	5	......	2	3	......	5	12
Rensselaer	December 31	10	11	20	1	9	11	1	21	32
Richmond	November 27	11	7	18	......	2	15	1	18	32
Rockland	November 13	9	5	14	......	2	8	4	14	......
St. Lawrence	August 25	9	4	13	......	6	5	2	13	27
Saratoga	December 31	3	8	11	......	2	5	4	11	16
Schenectady	October 8	1	1	2	......	......	1	1	2	14
Schoharie	December 31	5	2	7	......	......	5	2	7	13
Schuyler*	......	......	......	......	......	......	......	......	......	......
Seneca	August 11	2	5	5	2	1	5	1	7	12
Steuben	October 28	10	5	14	1	6	7	2	15	21
Suffolk	October 26	5	6	8	3	4	6	1	11	25
Sullivan	October	6	3	9	......	1	7	1	9	18
Tioga	September 22	5	1	6	......	1	3	2	6	5
Tompkins	November 12	1	1	2	......	......	2	......	2	5
Ulster	December 31	15	6	16	5	3	14	4	21	35
Warren	October 19	3	2	5	......	2	2	1	5	6
Washington	October 23	14	2	15	1	4	7	5	16	30
Wayne	September 3	3	3	6	......	3	2	1	6	7
Westchester	October 29	24	21	38	7	12	29	4	45	100
Wyoming	October 5	......	2	2	......	2	......	......	2	5
Yates	October 1	2	3	4	1	......	4	1	5	24
Total	......	362	253	564	51	143	348	124	615	1222

* No poor-house. † See notes, Kings county. ‡ See notes, New York county.

TABLE II,

Showing the nativity of the parents of the pauper children in the various county poor-houses of the State of New York, at the several dates of inquiry in 1874.

COUNTIES.	UNITED STATES.		IRELAND.		ENGLAND.		GERMANY.		OTHER COUNTRIES.		UNASCERTAINABLE.		
	Father.	Mother.	Father.	Mother.	Father.	Mother.	Father.	Mother.	Father.	Mother.	Father.	Mother.	Total.
Albany	7	8	17	20	2	......	2	1	......	1	7	5	35
Allegany	2	4	1	......	......	......	......	......	......	......	2	1	5
Broome	2	3	1	1	......	......	....	....	......	......	1	......	4
Cattaraugus	3	2	......	......	1	......	......	2	......	......	1	1	5
Cayuga	3	3	......	......	......	....	......	......	......	......	2	2	5
Chautauqua	......	1	4	4	......	......	......	......	2	2	1	......	7
Chemung	......	1	1	......	......	......	......	......	......	......	......	......	1
Chenango	3	4	2	2	1	1	......	......	......	......	2	1	8
Clinton	2	2	......	......	......	......	......	......	1	1	......	......	3
Columbia	2	4	......	......	......	......	......	......	......	......	2	......	4
Cortland	3	2	....	......	......	......	......	......	......	1	......	2	5
Delaware	......	1	......	......	......	......	......	......	......	......	2	1	2
Dutchess	1	2	4	3	......	......	......	......	......	......	......	......	5
Erie	2	4	5	2	......	2	......	......	2	1	......	......	9
Essex	17	18	4	3	......	......	......	......	4	4	2	2	27
Franklin	3	2	......	1	......	......	......	......	1	1	......	......	4
Fulton	11	13	......	......	......	......	......	......	......	......	2	......	13
Genesee	4	4	......	2	......	......	......	......	......	......	3	1	7
Greene	9	18	2	2	1	......	......	......	......	......	10	2	22
Hamilton	......	......	......	......	......	......	......	......	......	......	....	......	...
Herkimer	3	4	1	......	......	......	......	......	......	......	1	1	5
Jefferson	6	7	......	4	1	1	......	......	1	1	7	2	15
Kings	......	......	......	......	......	......	......	......	......	......	......	......	...
Lewis	5	5	......	1	......	......	......	......	......	......	1	......	6
Livingston	5	11	3	2	2	......	......	......	......	2	7	2	17
Madison	1	3	......	......	......	1	......	......	1	......	2	......	3
Monroe	2	4	......	......	......	1	......	......	1	3	7	2	10
Montgomery	4	7	3	......	......	......	......	......	....	......	......	......	7
New York	......	......	......	......	......	......	......	......	......	......	......	......	...
Niagara	2	11	6	7	6	......	1	1	3	1	9	7	27
Oneida	2	2	5	8	1	......	......	......	1	1	6	4	15
Onondaga	......	......	2	2	......	......	1	1	......	......	1	1	4
Ontario	9	11	9	10	1	......	......	......	2	......	2	2	26
Orange	23	23	2	2	......	......	3	2	......	1	1	1	29
Orleans	3	3	3	3	......	......	......	......	......	......	......	......	6
Oswego	1	1	......	......	......	......	......	......	......	......	......	......	1
Otsego	12	18	1	......	......	......	3	......	......	......	3	1	19
Putnam	6	8	9	8	......	......	......	......	......	......	1	......	16
Queens	2	3	3	2	......	......	......	......	......	......	......	......	5
Rensselaer	1	8	8	10	......	......	6	1	......	......	6	2	21
Richmond	2	2	13	14	......	......	2	2	1	......	......	......	18
Rockland	5	4	8	9	......	......	1	1	......	......	......	......	14
St. Lawrence	3	5	......	......	......	......	......	......	......	1	10	7	13
Saratoga	6	7	3	4	......	......	......	......	......	......	2	......	11
Schenectady	......	......	......	1	......	......	1	......	......	......	1	1	2
Schoharie	5	5	......	......	......	......	......	......	......	......	2	2	7
Schuyler	......	......	......	......	......	......	......	....	......	......	......	......	...
Seneca	3	5	1	......	......	......	......	......	......	......	3	2	7
Steuben	9	10	......	......	......	......	......	......	1	2	5	3	15
Suffolk	7	10	2	1	......	......	......	......	......	......	2	......	11
Sullivan	4	7	3	......	......	......	1	1	......	......	1	1	9
Tioga	5	4	......	......	......	......	......	......	......	......	1	2	6
Tompkins	......	......	1	1	......	......	......	......	....	......	1	1	2
Ulster	14	16	......	......	......	......	......	......	......	......	7	5	21
Warren	5	3	......	2	......	......	......	......	......	...	......	......	5
Washington	6	5	1	5	......	1	......	......	5	3	4	2	16
Wayne	3	5	2	1	......	......	......	......	......	......	1	......	6
Westchester	15	11	26	29	......	1	1	1	1	1	2	2	45
Wyoming	1	1	......	1	......	......	......	......	1	......	......	......	2
Yates	2	5	2	......	1	......	......	......	......	......	......	......	5
Total	256	330	158	167	17	7	22	13	27	27	135	71	615

TABLE III,

Showing the occupation of the fathers of the pauper children in the various county poor-houses of the State of New York, at the dates of inquiry in 1874.

COUNTIES.	Total.	Laborers.	Agricultural.	Mechanical.	Commercial.	Other occupations.	No occupation.	Unknown.
Albany	35	6	3	14	1	3	......	8
Allegany	5	2	1	1	......	......	......	1
Broome	4	......	......	......	......	......	......	4
Cattaraugus	5	2	3	......	......	......	......	......
Cayuga	5	......	......	......	......	......	......	5
Chautauqua	7	5	......	......	1	......	......	1
Chemung	1	......	1	......	......	......	......	......
Chenango	8	2	......	1	......	......	......	5
Clinton	3	......	1	......	......	......	......	2
Columbia	4	......	......	2	......	......	......	2
Cortland	5	1	2	......	......	......	......	2
Delaware	2	......	......	......	......	......	......	2
Dutchess	5	5	......	......	......	......	......	......
Erie	9	3	......	2	1	3	......	......
Essex	27	4	......	5	......	1	......	17
Franklin	4	1	......	1	......	......	......	2
Fulton	13	5	3	1	......	......	3	1
Genesee	7	......	......	3	......	......	......	4
Greene	22	4	2	1	......	10	......	5
Hamilton	......	......	......	......	......	......	......	......
Herkimer	5	......	1	......	......	1	2	1
Jefferson	15	......	......	1	......	6	1	7
Kings	......	......	......	......	......	......	......	......
Lewis	6	......	2	......	......	1	2	1
Livingston	17	1	1	5	......	2	1	7
Madison	3	......	......	......	......	......	......	3
Monroe	10	3	......	......	......	......	1	6
Montgomery	7	......	......	2	......	......	......	5
New York	......	......	......	......	......	......	......	......
Niagara	27	12	1	3	2	4	......	5
Oneida	15	7	......	......	......	2	......	6
Onondaga	4	1	1	......	......	......	1	1
Ontario	23	8	1	1	......	7	2	4
Orange	29	18	4	1	......	3	......	3
Orleans	6	5	......	1	......	......	......	......
Oswego	1	......	......	......	......	......	1	......
Otsego	19	2	3	4	......	3	5	2
Putnam	16	7	3	5	......	......	......	1
Queens	5	......	......	......	......	......	......	5
Rensselaer	21	9	......	2	......	5	......	5
Richmond	18	7	......	4	......	......	......	7
Rockland	14	4	1	3	......	......	......	6
St. Lawrence	13	......	1	......	......	......	1	11
Saratoga	11	7	......	1	......	1	......	2
Schenectady	2	1	......	......	......	......	......	1
Schoharie	7	4	......	......	......	......	......	3
Schuyler	......	......	......	......	......	......	......	......
Seneca	7	4	......	......	......	......	......	3
Steuben	15	6	2	......	......	1	1	5
Suffolk	11	3	1	1	......	......	1	5
Sullivan	9	6	......	......	......	......	......	3
Tioga	6	......	1	......	......	1	......	4
Tompkins	2	1	......	......	......	......	......	1
Ulster	21	9	5	1	......	1	......	5
Warren	5	3	1	......	......	......	......	1
Washington	16	3	......	......	......	2	......	11
Wayne	6	......	1	......	......	......	1	4
Westchester	45	23	1	11	......	4	......	6
Wyoming	2	1	......	1	......	......	......	......
Yates	5	2	......	3	......	......	......	......
Total	615	197	47	81	5	61	23	201

TABLE IV,

Showing the habits of the parents of the pauper children in the various county poor-houses of the state of New York at the dates of inquiry in 1874.

COUNTIES.	Total.	FATHERS.			MOTHERS.		
		Temperate.	Intemperate.	Unascertained.	Temperate.	Intemperate.	Unascertained.
Albany	35	5	26	4	17	15	3
Allegany	5	2	1	2	4	......	1
Broome	4	......	3	1	3	1	......
Cattaraugus	5	1	3	1	4	......	1
Cayuga	5	......	......	5	3	......	2
Chautauqua	7	4	......	3	6	1	......
Chemung	1	1	......	......	1	......	......
Chenango	8	1	2	5	3	......	5
Clinton	3	......	......	3	......	......	3
Columbia	4	2	......	2	......	......	4
Cortland	5	......	3	2	3	......	2
Delaware	2	......	......	2	......	......	2
Dutchess	5	......	5	......	5	......	......
Erie	9	1	7	1	5	3	1
Essex	27	3	17	7	13	7	7
Franklin	4	1	1	2	2	......	2
Fulton	13	3	10	......	12	......	1
Genesee	7	2	2	3	5	2	......
Greene	22	3	12	7	20	......	2
Hamilton	......	......	......	......	......	......	......
Herkimer	5	1	3	1	4	......	1
Jefferson	15	1	6	8	13	1	1
Kings	......	......	......	......	......	......	......
Lewis	6	2	3	1	5	......	......
Livingston	17	2	5	10	12	1	4
Madison	3	......	1	2	1	1	1
Monroe	10	....	4	6	8	......	2
Montgomery	7	......	7	......	4	3	......
New York	......	......	......	......	......	......	......
Niagara	27	8	11	8	14	9	4
Oneida	15	1	10	4	8	5	2
Onondaga	4	1	1	2	2	......	2
Ontario	23	2	11	10	14	3	6
Orange	29	13	15	1	24	4	1
Orleans	6	......	6	......	2	4	......
Oswego	1	......	1	......	1	......	......
Otsego	19	1	15	3	11	4	4
Putnam	16	7	8	1	13	......	3
Queens	5	......	......	5	......	......	5
Rensselaer	21	8	8	5	16	2	3
Richmond	18	......	18	......	6	10	2
Rockland	14	1	10	3	6	4	4
St. Lawrence	13	1	2	10	5	1	7
Saratoga	11	2	5	4	3	6	2
Schenectady	2	......	......	2	1	1	......
Schoharie	7	2	......	5	5	......	2
Schuyler	......	......	......	......	......	......	......
Seneca	7	......	3	4	5	2	......
Steuben	15	2	5	8	11	......	4
Suffolk	11	2	7	2	8	2	1
Sullivan	9	2	6	1	8	......	1
Tioga	6	... ..	2	4	2	1	3
Tompkins	2	......	2	......	1	1	......
Ulster	21	7	11	3	16	3	2
Warren	5	1	4	......	2	3	......
Washington	16	1	12	3	10	4	2
Wayne	6	....	......	6	5	......	1
Westchester	45	10	29	6	31	8	6
Wyoming	2	......	1	1	2	......	......
Yates	5	......	5	......	2	3	.....
Total	615	107	329	179	387	115	113

TABLE V,

Showing the number of children in the various county poor-houses of the State of New York, at the dates of the inquiry in 1874, who had pauer relatives, and the degree of relationship for three generations as far as could be ascertained; the number of each of the parents of such children then in these institutions, and also the number of such children born in poor-houses and the number of legitimate birth.

COUNTIES.	HAD PAUPER								Fathers in poor-house.	Mothers in poor-house.	Born in poor-house.	Legitimate.	Illegitimate.	Not stated.
	Grandfathers.	Grandmothers.	Fathers.	Mothers.	Brothers.	Sisters.	Uncles.	Aunts.						
Albany	......	......	2	24	20	17	......	......	1	16	5	26	7	2
Allegany	......	......	1	3	......	......	......	......	......	4	2	3	1	1
Broome	1	......	......	3	......	......	......	1	......	3	2	1	3	3
Cattaraugus	......	1	1	4	4	3	......	......	......	4	2	2	2	1
Cayuga	......	......	......	3	......	......	......	......	......	3	1	1	3	1
Chautauqua	......	......	3	7	......	......	......	......	3	7	3	4	2	1
Chemung	......	1	......	1	......	......	......	......	......	1	1	......	1	......
Chenango	......	1	......	5	......	......	......	......	1	3	2	1	1	6
Clinton	......	1	......	2	1	1	1	......	......	2	1	1	2	......
Columbia	......	......	......	4	2	......	......	......	......	1	1	2	......	2
Cortland	......	......	......	3	4	1	......	......	......	3	1	4	1	......
Delaware	1	1	1	2	......	......	1	1	......	1	1	......	2	......
Dutchess	......	......	......	4	......	2	1	......	......	1	3	3	2	......
Erie	......	......	1	7	2	2	......	......	......	7	6	6	2	1
Essex	1	5	5	21	8	8	5	5	3	14	10	13	10	4
Franklin	1	......	......	2	......	......	......	1	......	1	2	1	2	1
Fulton	4	1	4	12	8	8	3	1	4	7	2	12	1	......
Genesee	......	......	2	6	3	4	......	......	2	5	3	2	5	......
Greene	......	2	......	19	10	15	2	3	1	12	11	3	12	7
Hamilton	......	......	......	......	......	......	......	......	......	......	......	......	......	......
Herkimer	2	3	2	3	2	3	3	3	2	3	3	2	3	......
Jefferson	1	1	5	13	3	4	2	1	4	12	8	8	7	......
Kings	......	......	......	......	......	......	......	......	......	......	......	......	......	......
Lewis	......	......	2	3	4	......	2	2	......	2	1	4	2	......
Livingston	......	......	1	13	7	4	......	1	2	11	2	10	7	......
Madison	......	......	......	2	......	......	......	......	......	2	2	......	2	1
Monroe	......	......	2	8	2	......	......	......	2	8	5	4	5	1
Montgomery	1	1	6	7	4	7	......	......	2	6	4	5	2	......
New York	......	......	......	......	......	......	......	......	......	......	......	......	......	......
Niagara	1	1	2	16	16	11	1	1	2	15	2	16	8	3
Oneida	......	......	1	9	3	5	......	1	......	4	4	11	2	2
Onondaga	1	1	2	3	1	1	......	......	......	2	2	1	3	......
Ontario	2	2	6	15	12	12	4	2	5	14	4	15	5	3
Orange	3	2	3	13	10	7	2	5	......	20	13	15	14	......
Orleans	......	......	2	3	5	1	......	1	2	3	1	5	1	......
Oswego	1	1	......	1	......	......	1	1	......	1	1	1	......	......
Otsego	3	3	10	16	10	11	6	5	2	13	6	13	6	......
Putnam	......	......	1	12	11	6	......	......	1	11	2	13	3	......
Queens	......	......	......	......	......	......	......	......	......	......	......	......	......	5
Rensselaer	......	3	5	19	13	12	2	......	4	16	8	10	9	2
Richmond	1	......	2	13	14	7	......	......	......	13	......	13	5	......
Rockland	......	......	......	9	9	5	......	......	......	4	3	13	1	......
St. Lawrence	......	2	......	7	2	2	1	......	......	8	4	......	10	3
Saratoga	......	1	2	10	5	6	1	1	1	7	1	10	1	......
Schenectady	......	......	1	1	......	1	......	......	......	......	......	2	......	......
Schoharie	1	1	4	3	3	3	......	......	2	......	......	4	3	......
Schuyler	......	......	......	......	......	......	......	......	......	......	......	......	......	......
Seneca	1	......	3	6	2	3	......	......	1	1	3	3	3	1
Steuben	2	2	2	9	3	1	1	1	1	6	5	8	6	1
Suffolk	......	......	1	9	1	3	......	......	......	8	7	7	4	......
Sullivan	......	......	3	7	4	4	......	......	......	6	5	2	6	1
Tioga	......	1	1	3	2	1	......	......	1	3	2	3	2	1
Tompkins	......	......	......	......	......	......	......	1	......	......	......	2	......	......
Ulster	......	3	4	18	14	8	3	4	2	14	7	8	9	4
Warren	......	1	0	4	1	......	......	......	......	1	2	2	3	......
Washington	......	......	2	11	4	11	......	......	......	9	6	8	8	......
Wayne	2	2	1	6	2	1	2	2	1	5	5	2	4	......
Westchester	1	3	7	30	16	19	......	2	1	24	9	33	8	4
Wyoming	......	......	......	2	......	......	......	......	......	2	1	1	1	......
Yates	1	......	2	5	2	3	1	1	2	3	3	3	2	......
Total	32	47	105	441	249	223	45	47	54	342	190	352	204	59

TABLE VI,

Showing the length of time spent in the various county poor-houses of the State of New York, by the pauper children in these institutions, at the dates of inquiry in 1874.

COUNTIES.	Number of children.	Less than six months.	Six months and less than one year.	One year and less than two years.	Two years and less than three years.	Three years and less than four years.	Four years and less than five years.	Five years and less than six years.	Six years and less than seven years.	Seven years and less than eight years.	Eight years and less than nine years.	Nine years and less than ten years.	Ten years and less than sixteen years.	Aggregate length of time spent in poor-houses. yrs.	mos.
Albany	35	13	8	4	6	1	...	2	...	1	...	...	...	43	9
Allegany	5	...	...	2	...	...	3	...	...	...	...	...	...	14	
Broome	4	...	...	2	...	...	...	...	1	1	...	...	...	12	6
Cattaraugus	5	...	...	1	...	...	1	...	...	2	...	...	1	29	
Cayuga	5	4	1	...	...	...	...	...	...	...	...	...	...	1	6
Chautauqua	7	2	1	...	1	...	...	...	2	...	1	...	...	22	11
Chemung	1	...	...	1	...	...	...	...	...	...	...	...	...	1	
Chenango	8	1	...	2	...	...	1	1	2	...	...	1	...	32	2
Clinton	3	1	...	...	...	...	1	...	...	...	...	...	1	15	3
Columbia	4	1	1	2	...	...	...	...	...	...	...	...	...	2	11
Cortland	5	3	1	...	1	...	...	...	...	...	...	...	...	2	8
Delaware	2	...	1	...	1	...	...	...	...	...	...	...	...	2	8
Dutchess	5	1	...	1	...	...	1	...	...	...	1	1	...	22	1
Erie	9	7	...	1	...	...	...	...	...	1	...	...	...	8	8
Essex	27	5	1	2	1	4	3	5	3	2	...	...	1	114	8
Franklin	4	2	...	...	2	...	...	...	...	...	...	...	...	4	7
Fulton	13	2	5	1	...	3	1	...	...	...	...	...	1	28	10
Genesee	7	...	3	...	...	1	1	1	...	1	...	...	...	21	1
Greene	22	1	2	4	3	5	3	1	...	1	1	...	1	73	
Hamilton	...	...	...	...	...	...	...	...	...	...	...	...	...	...	...
Herkimer	5	...	...	1	1	1	...	2	...	...	...	...	...	16	
Jefferson	15	2	2	...	5	...	2	1	...	1	...	...	2	55	2
Kings	...	...	...	...	...	...	...	...	...	...	...	...	...	...	...
Lewis	6	1	3	1	...	...	...	1	...	...	...	...	...	8	5
Livingston	17	1	4	3	3	1	...	...	3	1	...	...	1	52	3
Madison	3	3	...	...	...	...	...	...	...	...	...	...	...		5
Monroe	10	9	...	1	...	...	...	...	...	...	...	...	...	1	5
Montgomery	7	...	1	2	...	2	1	...	...	...	...	...	1	29	6
New York	...	...	...	...	...	...	...	...	...	...	...	...	...	...	...
Niagara	27	7	1	1	8	4	4	...	...	...	2	...	...	62	6
Oneida	15	7	2	2	1	3	...	...	...	...	...	...	...	14	9
Onondaga	4	1	...	...	...	2	...	...	...	...	...	1	...	15	1
Ontario	23	1	3	8	3	3	...	3	...	...	...	1	1	58	8
Orange	29	4	4	3	3	6	4	2	1	...	1	...	1	78	
Orleans	6	1	...	3	...	...	1	...	1	...	...	...	...	13	4
Oswego	1	1	...	...	...	...	...	...	...	...	...	...	...		5
Otsego	19	2	...	2	2	3	2	1	1	2	2	...	2	89	4
Putnam	16	1	3	7	...	1	1	3	...	...	...	...	...	31	
Queens	5	5	...	...	...	...	...	...	...	...	...	...	...	...	...
Rensselaer	21	9	7	2	1	2	...	...	...	...	...	...	...	15	9
Richmond	18	4	1	...	4	...	2	2	2	1	...	2	...	64	10
Rockland	14	4	2	2	...	1	2	...	2	...	1	...	...	34	10
St. Lawrence	13	4	3	...	2	3	1	...	...	...	...	...	...	19	10
Saratoga	11	9	...	2	...	...	...	...	...	...	...	...	...	2	11
Schenectady	2	...	1	1	...	...	...	...	...	...	...	...	...	1	8
Schoharie	7	...	2	1	...	...	2	...	...	...	1	...	1	28	
Schuyler	...	...	...	...	...	...	...	...	...	...	...	...	...	...	...
Seneca	7	1	...	...	...	1	1	2	...	1	...	...	1	34	
Steuben	15	4	4	5	...	...	...	2	...	...	...	...	...	18	9
Suffolk	11	2	3	3	1	1	...	...	1	...	...	...	...	18	2
Sullivan	9	...	...	4	3	...	2	...	...	...	...	...	...	18	
Tioga	6	...	...	4	...	...	1	...	...	...	...	1	...	17	
Tompkins	2	1	...	...	1	...	...	...	...	...	...	...	...	2	1
Ulster	21	6	3	3	4	2	1	1	...	1	...	...	...	35	8
Warren	5	1	2	...	1	...	1	...	...	...	...	...	...	7	5
Washington	16	1	...	5	1	2	3	1	2	1	...	...	...	44	3
Wayne	6	3	1	...	...	...	...	...	1	...	...	...	1	20	9
Westchester	45	15	9	7	8	4	...	...	...	2	...	...	...	56	7
Wyoming	2	2	...	...	...	...	...	...	...	...	...	...	...		9
Yates	5	1	...	1	1	...	1	...	1	...	...	...	...	13	6
Total	615	156	85	97	68	56	47	31	23	19	10	7	16	1434	3

REPORT

ON

PAUPER CHILDREN

OF NEW YORK COUNTY

BY

WILLIAM P. LETCHWORTH

COMMISSIONER OF THE STATE BOARD OF CHARITIES

Transmitted to the Legislature with the annual report of the Board
January 14th, 1876.

SUPPLEMENTARY REPORT

RELATING TO PAUPER CHILDREN IN NEW YORK COUNTY.

To the State Board of Charities:

GENTLEMEN — The report relating to pauper children in the various poor-houses and alms-houses of the State, submitted by me to this Board, January 12th, 1875, was based not only upon extended personal visitations to the poor-houses, but mainly upon the information gathered by the Board in its examination into the causes of pauperism, directed by the concurrent resolution of the Senate and Assembly of 1873.

As the examination was not then completed in New York, that county could not be included in the report. Since then, however, the inquiry has been finished, and the facts obtained have been placed at my disposal. This supplementary report is, therefore, now submitted, and with it the task assigned to me by the Board, in 1874, of reporting upon the condition of the children in the poor-houses and alms-houses of the State, is fully completed.

The establishments of New York for the care of pauper children, are located on Randall's Island, and practically constitute the children's department of the alms-house of that city. During the past year I have made several visitations to these establishments, accompanied on one occasion by Commissioner Roosevelt. These visits were made with a competent stenographer. The buildings and inmates were carefully inspected, and a minute inquiry made into the methods of administration. The report is based upon the information gathered during these vistations, and upon the facts elicited in the examination of this Board above referred to.

The children's department of the alms-house on Randall's Island comprises:

1. The Infant or Foundling Hospital, an imposing brick structure on the city side of the island, with spacious grounds about it, containing at date of October 1, 1875, two hundred and seventy-six infants.

2. The Idiot Asylum, a large brick building easterly from this, with an extensive pavilion ward, containing at date of October 1, 1875, one hundred and seventy-three children.

3. The Nursery Hospital, a group of three buildings a little beyond the last named, in the same direction.

4. The Nursery, a group of eight buildings, beyond the Nursery Hospital, and on the opposite side of the island.

Although divided in name and superintendency, the third and fourth groups, comprising eleven buildings, should be considered as one, and to these our attention will be mainly directed.

In order to understand so much of the New York alms-house system as relates to the care of children in the Nursery and Nursery Hospital, it will be necessary to state the relation of the buildings to each other, and their uses, also for the reader to keep these usually unimportant details in his mind. This relation is shown by the accompanying diagram which comprises the following:

A. Warden's office, school-rooms and work-house women's lodging rooms.

B. Reception house and department for small girls.

C. Dining-room and dormitories for large boys.

D. Large girls' department.

E. Large boys' quarters.

F. Small boys' department.

G. Infants' department for quite small boys and girls.

H. Main kitchen, laundry, tailor's shop for boys and sleeping apartments for paid nurses or domestics.

I. South hospital building.

J. North hospital building.

K. Superintendent's office, etc.

Building "A" is constructed of gray stone, quarried upon the island. It is two stories high with attic and basement. It contains the warden's office, class-rooms of the school, and sleeping apartments for the work-house women. In front of this building is a grass plat extending six hundred and seventy-three feet to the East river.

All the other buildings belonging to the Children's Nursery and Nursery Hospital groups, are built of brick, are three stories high, and are shaded a light buff color. The size of each and distance apart are given upon the diagram. Nearly all of these buildings, at least the larger ones, have piazzas extending their whole length on one side, and some of them on two sides. Two of the buildings in the Nursery Hospital group, have their porches inclosed with sash.

During a visit made October 13, 1875, the buildings of the Nursery and Nursery Hospital were inspected in the following order:

Building "B"—Reception House and Department for Small Girls.

On entering the building we found the little girls just passing from the play-room into the dining-room. The table was set with crockery

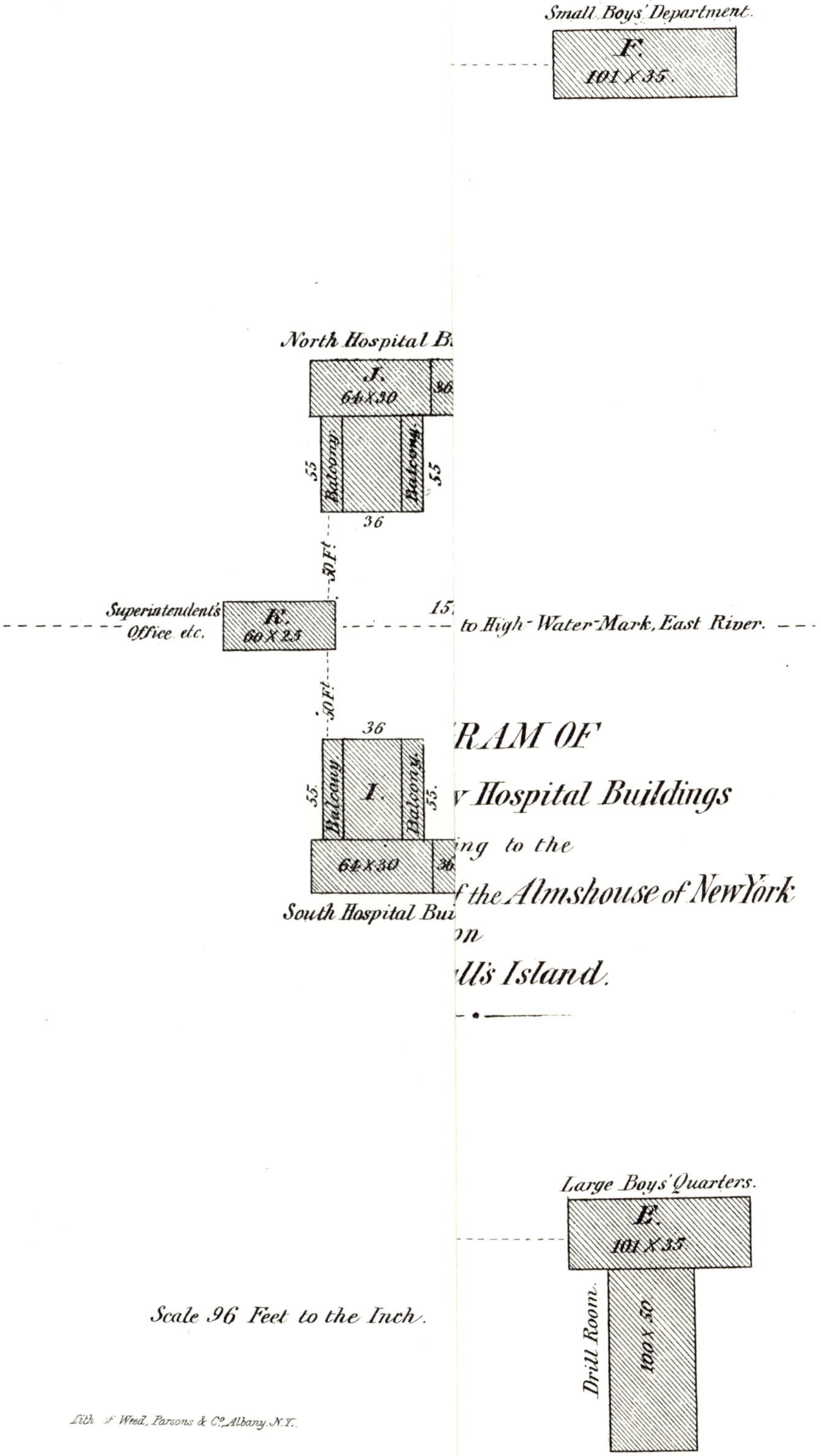
Small Boys' Department.
F.
101 X 35.
North Hospital Bi
J.
64 X 30
36
55
Balcony
Balcony
55
36
50 Ft.
Superintendent's Office etc.
K.
60 X 25
15
to High-Water-Mark, East River.
50 Ft.
36
55.
Balcony
I.
Balcony
55.
64 X 30
36
South Hospital Bui
RAM OF
Hospital Buildings
ing to the
f the Almshouse of New York
on
ll's Island.
Large Boys' Quarters.
E.
101 X 35
Drill Room.
100 X 50.
Scale 96 Feet to the Inch.
Lith of Weed, Parsons & Co. Albany, N.Y.

plates and mugs, with spoons, knives and forks. The meal for each child consisted of a plate of soup, with an ample supply of potatoes and meat, also a large slice of bread. A work-house woman dressed in blue jean, the common dress of this class here, was serving the food to the children.

The dresses of all the children were of blue gingham with white linen aprons. Cotton stockings and shoes were worn. The winter dress was stated to be a woolen or flannel underskirt, and a cotton chemise. In summer a canton-flannel underskirt and a cotton chemise are worn. Only such cases as are directed by the attending physician, wear shoes and stockings in the summer. Sometimes these are furnished by parents. Children on leaving are dressed in the same clothing they wore when admitted. It was observed that the dresses were, many of them, ludicrously out of proportion; some too short, others much too long; some too large and loosely gathered, others looking as though the children had out-grown their clothes. This was unavoidable where so many were coming in and going out, and wearing clothes not made for them.

The matron in charge, in reply to our inquiries, said: "We keep the children here but a short time after their arrival. We dress and wash them, and after the doctor has examined them, they are transferred to their proper places. We keep here the smaller girls. We can accommodate eighty by putting two in a bed. To-day we have seventy-one; their ages ranging from four to eight years."

In the dormitories were double bedsteads of iron, three feet six inches wide. Straw beds and pillows were in use. The straw was said to be changed as often as the matron considered necessary. Each bed had two sheets and a double pair of blankets.

The floors of the room were clean, and connected with each was a bath-tub and a night-closet, the air of the apartment, however, did not seem sweet and wholesome. In this building six adult persons including matron, were employed. Two were work-house women, and one was from the alms-house.

Building "C"—Dining-room and Dormitories for Large Boys.

Here the dinner was being served for about two hundred and fifty boys. It consisted of meat, potatoes, pudding and gravy. Each boy had two pieces of bread. The bread is baked in the Blackwell's Island department of the alms-house. The meal seemed ample. The boys marched across the yard into the dining-room, in companies of about twenty-five. They beat time with the right foot, marched in close column with the lock step, and in the same manner as the convicts march across the yards at Auburn and Sing Sing. The drill-master said he had "forbidden the use of this step, but the boys seemed to prefer it, and would use it when they could." This feature of the institution is doubtless owing to the association of the children with the convict class. Each company had a boy at its head who was termed a non-commissioned officer. He has a blue uniform. The best behaved boys, we were told, were selected as officers, and the effect was said to be good. The boys all stood at the table except ten or twelve who were crippled. The boys were mostly dressed in jackets and pants of gray cassimere. Forty of them have a blue uniform.

The dormitory above the dining-room was furnished with double bedsteads, iron, and heated by a cast-iron stove. Three of the women doing the work in the building, received wages, and two were from the work-house.

Building "D" — Large Girls' Department.

There were in this building ninety-one girls, ranging in ages from eight to fourteen years. The matron in charge, in answer to our inquiries, said: "I have one paid assistant. I am usually allowed eight women from the alms-house and work-house, but I have only six to-day."

The dormitories here, as well as those afterward visited, were furnished similar to those last named. In the bathing-room was a large oval vat about ten feet long, by four feet wide. The person in charge complained that the supply of water was insufficient. She said: "We have not been able to wash in running water since last April." The children are not furnished with towels. It is customary to put clean linen aprons on them every morning at about nine o'clock. These supply the place of towels, etc., during the day, and are changed the following morning at the same hour.

Building "E" — Large Boys' Quarters, etc.

This building contained a play-room, gymnasium, and drill-room, on the first floor. In one of the rooms was a large wooden vat for bathing. The boys wash in running water, and in summer time swim in the river daily. The upper part of this building is used for dormitories and store-room for boys' clothes.

The boys, on leaving the institution, are dressed in the same clothes they wore when they were admitted, if they have not outgrown them. The drill-master sleeps in this building. He designates three boys to act as monitors and report every case of disobedience of orders. Six females do the work, three of whom are work-house women.

Building "F" — Small Boys' Department.

One hundred and thirty-six boys occupied this building. All, excepting a few, were between the ages of five and eight years. On the first floor are gymnasium, play-room, bathing-room and water-closets. The upper part of the building contains two dormitories. Six women were employed. One of these received wages, and the other five were paupers or criminals sent from Blackwell's Island. A woman, we were told, "always remains on watch during the night; she is one of the prisoner women." The assistant matron sleeps in the building.

Building "G" — Infants' Department.

Here we found seventy-two children, mostly boys, ranging from two and a half to five years of age. Six females were employed. One of them received wages and five were "prisoners" sent up from Blackwell's Island. The assistant matron lives in this building.

Building "H" — Main Kitchen, etc.

Here the paid nurses and work-house women take their meals. The dining-room contained tables and stools sufficient to seat fifty persons.

In this building the cooking is also done for the whole nursery department. The food is cooked by steam. Six large iron caldrons are used. The cook, on being questioned, said: "I have been here three years and a month; I have three children here; I came here to work for them; I cannot tell where my husband is; he got drunk and I left him; I have not seen him for six months."

In the laundry there were eight women from the work-house, and one who was receiving a small remuneration. They appeared to be about the average class of women that are committed to work-houses. In the upper part of this building is a tailor shop, where we found thirteen boys seated cross-legged on broad tables upon either side of the room. The official in reply to our questions, said: "We usually have about twenty-four boys here; some of them now are sick, and some of them are kept in school. When the school is out the force will be increased. The boys are taught to mend their own clothes." This shop was said to be under the charge of a man from the work-house, assisted by another committed by one of the magistrates. On the bench also was a simple-minded person who had been about fourteen years on the island. He was said to be a "tolerably good tailor."

Building "I" — South Hospital.

In this building were ninety-seven boys, ranging from four to fifteen years. They all slept singly on iron bedsteads of good width. Bath tubs and water-closets are attached to each ward. About half the pauper and work-house women belonging to the hospital department sent up from Blackwell's Island, sleep in this building.

Building "J"—North Hospital.

Here were one hundred and eighteen inmates. This building is used for girls and for small boys under five years old. Adjoining one of the children's wards is a sleeping apartment for some of the work-house women. It contained nine beds, and owing to the crowded condition, two beds were put together for three to sleep on. One of the wards in this building was said to be used for contagious diseases.

Administrative Force.

The eight nursery buildings, and the affairs connected with them, excepting the school department, are under the charge of a warden. He is assisted by a drill-master, clerk, head matron, and three assistant matrons. There were also attached to the establishment thirteen nurses and paid domestics, and a large force of male and female "helpers" who had been sent up from the alms-house and work-house departments of Blackwell's Island. Of these we shall speak hereafter. The paid domestics receive $10 per month. Quite a number of these had formerly been inmates of the alms-house.

The three nursery hospital buildings, and the affairs connected with them, are under the charge of a superintendent. He is assisted by a matron with a corps of paid assistants, and a large force of "helpers," likewise from the alms-house and work-house departments of Blackwell's Island. A physician resides at the Infant Hospital who devotes a share of his attention to the Nursery, Nursery Hospital and Idiot Asylum, as well as to the Infant Hospital. He is aided by an assistant.

The examination of the inmates directed by this Board was finished in the early part of the season. The subsequent visitations were made in the month of October last. At the latter period the number of children in the Nursery and Nursery Hospital, did not differ materially from the number who were inmates at the time of the examinations made by the Board. At the date of October 13th, the warden stated there had been no material change in their methods since the particular examination referred to, and that the system he directed was practically the same.

Owing to the incompleteness of the records kept at the Randall's Island Nurseries, the lack of knowledge on the part of officers regarding the personal histories of the children, in many cases, the ignorance and lack of interest in the children themselves as to their family relations, and their extreme youth, it was found very difficult to obtain as full information as desirable.

Statistical Information Relating to the Nursery and Nursery Hospital.

The result of the examination, made by the Board, may be stated as follows:

There were, in the Nursery and Nursery Hospital, 769 children; 545 were boys, and 224 were girls.

Ages of the Children.

Between 2 and 3 years	5
" 3 " 4 "	37
" 4 " 5 "	60
" 5 " 6 "	94
" 6 " 7 "	98
" 7 " 8 "	87
" 8 " 9 "	94
" 9 " 10 "	68
" 10 " 11 "	63
" 11 " 12 "	52
" 12 " 13 "	50
" 13 " 14 "	24
" 14 " 15 "	22
" 15 " 16 "	15

Length of Time Inmates.

Had been inmates one week	8
" " two weeks	3
" " one month	100
" " two months	54
" " three "	64
" " four "	34
" " five "	24
" " six "	62
" " seven "	23
" " eight "	23
" " nine "	14
" " ten "	6
" " one year	112
" " two years	94
" " three "	47
" " four "	40
" " five "	30
" " six "	12
" " seven "	10

Had been inmates	eight years	....	1
" "	nine "	....	2
" "	ten "	....	2
" "	eleven "	....	2
" "	twelve "	....	2

Making an aggregate, as near as could be ascertained from the sources of information at hand, of a little over one thousand one hundred and fifteen years of child-life spent in the alms-house. The average length of time each one of the children had been inmates, was a fraction more than one year and five months.

Nativity of the Parents.

The fathers of	128	and mothers of	136	were natives of the	United States:
" "	23	" "	25	" "	England.
" "	2	" "	3	" "	Scotland.
" "	220	" "	246	" "	Ireland.
" "	61	" "	49	" "	Germany.
" "	2	" "	2	" "	France.
" "	1	" "	1	" "	Italy.
" "	21	" "	20	" "	Other coun's.
" "	311	" "	287	" "	Unascertain'd

Of the 769 children, 84 were born in foreign countries, that is to say, 22 in England, 40 in Ireland, 3 in Scotland, 12 in Germany, 5 in the Canadian provinces, and 1 each in France and Italy.

Occupation of the Fathers.

The fathers of	149	were	....	Laborers.
" "	4	"	....	Sailors.
" "	219	"	....	Mechanics.
" "	26	"	....	Commercial pursuits.
" "	5	"	....	Agricultural.
" "	1	"	....	Professional.
" "	58	"	....	Other occupations.
" "	307	"	....	Unascertained.

Habits of the Parents.

The fathers of	196	and the mothers of	312,	were	temperate
" "	178	" "	102	"	intemperate
" "	395	" "	355	"	habits unascert'd.

Family Condition.

The condition of the families to which these children belonged, was as follows:

The fathers of 12 and the mothers of 30 were known to be in prison.
" mothers of 85 were in some of the institutions on Randall's Island.
" brothers of 247 " " "
" sisters of 151 " " "

Were orphans	53
Were half orphans by death of father	185
Were half orphans by death of mother	108
Had both parents living	393
Were unascertained	30
Had been abandoned by both parents	40
" " the father	122
" " the mother	34

Children Boarded.

The board of 201 of the children was to have been paid for either wholly or in part, as follows:

By both parents	19
By the father	80
By the mother	93
By other relatives or friends	9

The Superintendent of Out-Door Poor states that about half of those that agree to pay for the children's board, fail to do so.

Mental and Physical Condition.

701 of the children were regarded as being of average mental capacity—some of them " very bright "— 48 below the average, 17 feeble minded, and 3 idiotic.

Of the 599 children in the nursery proper, 551 were considered healthy.

The physical condition of the remaining number, 48, appeared to be as follows: Four were suffering from temporary sickness, six from general feebleness of body, six from some form of skin disease, three from sore eyes, three from blindness, ten from loss of sight in one eye, and sixteen from being deformed or crippled.

Among the cases of disease and affliction in the hospital there appeared to be the following. Some of the children suffering from more than one disease at the same time:

Diseased scalp	29
Itch	19
Other diseases of the skin	25
Diseased eyes	57
Blindness	7
Loss of sight in one eye	3

It is sad to state, that the inquiry at the Hospital closed with the belief in the mind of the examiner, that five of the children who were placed in the Hospital in consequence of some temporary sickness, had, by coming in contact with other children suffering from sore eyes, been inoculated with virus producing disease of the eye and, it was thought, would become blind, and that in two cases out of the five the calamity was certain.

There were also, in the Nursery and Nursery Hospital, 18 inmates who were over 16 and under 20 years of age; 11 of these were males and 7 were females. Nine were orphans and 6 were half-orphans. All of these were fairly intelligent. The general health of 3 was good. Six were crippled, 2 were deformed, 3 paralytic; 1 was an epileptic and 3 were suffering from temporary sickness.

One of the number, a girl just passed her 16th year, was the eldest of a family of seven children. They had come upon Randall's Island with their mother, a woman 37 years of age, having recently arrived from England where the father still remained.

Adult Female Helpers.

Seventy-four adult females were employed in the Nursery and Nursery Hospital; 50 in the former, and 24 in the latter.

Their ages were as follows:

Between 20 and 30 years	18
Between 30 and 40 years	39
Between 40 and 50 years	14
Between 50 and 60 years	2
Seventy-four years old	1

Their social condition may thus be stated:

Single	17
Married	24
Widows	33

Their nativity was as follows:

Natives of the United States	10
" " Canada	2
" " England	5
" " Ireland	54
" " Scotland, Germany and France, one each	3

One of those, given as natives of the United States, was a young negress, whose parents were natives of Africa. Another was a quadroon.

Twenty-nine were unable to read, 28 could read, 9 could read and write, and 8 had a fair education. One was known to be of thrifty habits, and 9 were said to be idle and shiftless.

The habits of 7 were temperate; 13 were moderate drinkers; 35 were periodical drinkers, and 19 were constant drinkers.

Twenty-three of these females belonged to the pauper class, and 51 to the work-house class that had been sent up from Blackwell's Island. Of the former, 1 was a pauper in consequence of a permanent disabling disease; 2 from destitution; 4 by abandonment of husband; 8 by death of husband; 7 were self-committed, and 1 was placed in the Nursery when a child.

Of the 51 that belonged to the criminal class, 13 had been committed as vagrants, 2 for disorderly conduct, and 36 for drunkenness and disorderly conduct. The number of times they had been committed was as follows:

Committed once	7
" twice	18
" three times	4
" four "	10
" five "	3
" six "	5
" seven "	1

and of 2, it could not be ascertained how many times they had been committed. One of them had been committed a number of times, and the other repeatedly during the last forty years. To use her own language, "times past counting part of the time for the last forty years." She had been thirty years a dependent, either committed as a pauper or as a criminal.

Twenty-six of these females were employed in the Nursery department to wash and scrub, 3 to iron, 1 to cook; 12 worked in the kitchen, 2 in the dining room, and 10 in the dormitories; 3 were engaged in sewing, 10 in the immediate care of children, 2 were nurses, 4 were night-watchers, and 1 was unemployed.

Thirty had children; 42 of their children were on Randall's Island, 5 were in asylums, 34 were self-supporting, and 14 were supported by friends.

There were 40 adult males registered on the books of the Nursery and Nursery Hospital, 24 in former, and 16 in the latter. They were employed in the performance of various duties, under the direction of the warden or superintendent.

Twenty-two of these men were self-committed to the poor-house, 17 had been committed to the work-house for drunkenness, and one for assault and battery.

Placing Children Out.

The manner in which the children are disposed of at the Nursery is, according to the statement of the Warden, substantially as follows: Applications are made to the central office. If the applicant obtains an order for a child, he comes to the Nursery and makes his own selection. He has four months to try the child. If he is satisfied, the child is then indentured to him. There is a greater demand for girls than for boys. The boys are hard to dispose of. Upon subsequent inquiry at the central office, in regard to the method of placing out children, it was found to differ materially from the method generally adopted by asylums, though doubtless as perfect as could well be in an office overburdened with poor-house business, and with this business crowded into a few hours daily. Further, it was understood that there is no systematic plan for visiting the children, after they have been placed out, to ascertain if they are properly educated or humanely treated, nor does it appear that any attempt is made to maintain a correspondence with the children, or to place them under disinterested benevolent surveillance. As stated, any person taking a child is at liberty to return it at the end of four months, if not satisfied. It is believed that this privilege is not unfrequently availed of by parties who merely desire to obtain the services of a child during pressure of work.

The practice of taking children for merely selfish purposes, is verified in the large experience of the Right Rev. Bishop McQuaid, who says: "Many of the persons who take children from the orphan asylums, regard them as mere money-making machines, to be used while they pay, and to be cast off when they cease to pay." It is the opinion generally expressed by asylum managers, that the returning of a child, but a few times even, to an asylum, greatly injures it. Some go so far as to say that "it ruins the child."

One of the great evils in every poor-house system, and that of New York cannot be regarded as an exception, has been found to be the facility with which children may repeatedly be admitted to and discharged from the alms-house. After going in and coming out a few times a don't-care feeling takes hold of the child, and it loses whatever self-reliance of character it may have possessed.

The School

under the Department of Public Instruction, designated as Grammar School No. 6, contains a primary and grammar department. The former is very well attended, the latter has but few scholars.

But notwithstanding the laborious efforts of the teachers to interest and advance the pupils, it was painfully apparent that an air of listlessness, common to pauper institutions, was prevalent here.

Sunday Schools

for both Roman Catholic and Protestant children are conducted; for the former by members of the society of St. Vincent de Paul, and for the latter by the ladies and gentlemen of the Protestant Episcopal Church. An occasional Mass is also celebrated.

Industrial Training.

It will be seen, by reference to the ages of the children, that a very large number were old enough to be susceptible of industrial training, and yet, in this immense establishment, no general systematic plan for inculcating even the simplest forms of industry is adopted. As to industries, the official remarked: "We carry on nothing, except that a number of the boys repair clothes under the direction of a tailor, who works with them. In the girls' department they do their own repairing. We have about 30 boys in the tailor shop and possibly about 25 girls in their department."

In view of the fact that a large proportion of the inmates have probably fallen into this condition of dependence and pauper life, through lack of habits of persevering industry on the part of their parents, and that the object of this institution should be to train these children to be self-supporting and to fit them for useful stations in life, the absence of efficient industrial training is, evidently, a fundamental error in the system. If these children were in industrious families, or in appropriate asylums under the charge of benevolent persons especially devoted to the work, this essential element of their education would not be neglected.

The Boarding System.

It will be seen that, at the time of the examination, about 200 of the children were nominally boarded by their parents, the latter agreeing to pay for all or at least a part of their board, although only one-half of the number kept their promise. The price fixed, however, is in no case sufficient to cover the entire cost of maintenance. Poor and worthy families, becoming impoverished and looking upon Randall's Island as a refuge for their children, regarding it as a fitting place for their little ones in view of the respectability thrown around it by official sanction had, unsuspectingly, placed their children under the unhappy influences which surround them here, learning only, too late, perhaps, that a deadly virus had infected the innocent nature of their offspring. It is believed that the Nursery is also made a convenience of by many shiftless families on the verge of pauperism. The facility with which they can place their children on the island by the payment of a small sum for their board, or by agreeing to pay it, favors rather than otherwise the pauperism against which they should struggle.

As an illustration of the dangers of the boarding system, and the evil associations growing out of it, we will allude to one of the almost numberless cases appealing for sympathy that came under our notice on the 13th of October.

In one of the wards of the North Hospital Building, our attention was arrested by a very attractive face. It was that of a young girl of 14 years. She was half-reclining on her bed, having just been waited on by one of the ward women. Her hair was very neatly dressed, and her transparent face was rendered beautiful by its intelligence and earnestness. Over her shoulders was drawn a blue-trimmed invalid's sacque, the gift, it appeared, of her mother. There was something in the lines about her lips and the introverted expression in her eyes, that seemed to tell of the soul within as being busy with its forlorn hopes. In the other beds of the ward were eight sick children, and, gathering about us, was a large group, afflicted with skin and other unsightly diseases. One of these children stood close against the bed of the invalid girl, and was suffering from red and bleeding abrasions in the joints of her arms and hands. She was excitedly endeavoring to allay the irritation of a troublesome, and in her case — seemingly — dangerous disease. The air seemed to be tainted with exhalations from the skin, producing an unwholesome odor, against which nature revolted. The girl first mentioned, said she had been five years in the nursery, and that her father paid $5 a month towards her support; that she had been in the hospital nearly two months, and had had intermittent fever. She said, "I got up and caught cold. My mother put me here. Father went to look for work." The ward was under the charge of a female, a former inmate of the alms-house, said to be "a faithful nurse," assisted by two work-house women, sent up from Blackwell's Island. These appeared to be the only adult associates to whom, during her convalescence and moments of weariness, she could look for entertainment and companionship. Aside from the moral contamination to which this interesting child was subjected, she was liable, at any moment, to inoculation from some of the repulsive skin diseases around her, and, while in the hospital under treatment for intermittent fever, was exposed to infections, which might result in total blindness — an experience not unknown here.

Criminal and Pauper Associations.

From what has been stated it will be seen that, in the dense buildings of the Nursery and Nursery Hospitals, grouped quite closely together, there were at the time of the examination of this Board, 773 girls and boys under 16 years of age. Brought into more or less intimate association with these tender natures, were 23 females that had, either through misfortune or some controlling weakness of character, sunk into the rank of the dependent class. There were also 51 females who had drifted downward, and had sunk into the rank of the criminal class, many of them, as has been shown, having been committed again and again for drunkenness and disorderly conduct, for street brawls and other offenses which had rendered them amenable to penal servitude. There were also, going and coming on various duties, 40 male adults belonging to the pauper and criminal classes, making in all 114 persons, who were either at the time actually paupers or criminals, or had been committed at some time as such, and of whom, it is safe to say, belonged to the pauper or criminal classes of society, brought more or less into contact with the children. Even with the strictest rules forbidding it, the association of the children with these persons must, from the nature of the case, be inevitable; but, so far as our observations went, the rules did not appear even to forbid it. The older girls were seen passing in and out of the laundry, and assisting in carrying linen to the dormitories, and work-house women were found dealing out food to the children, and otherwise engaged in serving them.

The county poor-houses, it has been demonstrated, were not the places for the rearing and training of children, and yet, it is believed, the influences to which the children were subjected in these places were not so debasing as those under the alms-house system of New York, for there they were brought into familiar association with the school teacher residing in the institution, and with the family of the keeper, thus counteracting, to some extent, the effect of the evil association with adult paupers. But under the poor-house system of New York county, vast numbers of children are literally herded together, and brought into association with the degraded and debased; not only with those belonging to the pauper class, but largely with the criminal condemned to penal servitude. Over this vast congregated body the personal influence of the very few officials superintending, can hardly be felt. A distressing feature about this association is, that its influence does not end with the brief time spent by the child in the Nursery, but continues to exert its baleful effect even after it has been put into a respectable family, or restored by its parents to its place in its former home. In many cases it is aggravated by personal contact with former associates, and this often occurring after a long interval of separation. But even where this does not happen the influence may be still insidiously operating to the defilement of the child. As bearing upon this point, it may be stated that, during the time of the examination made by the Board, it was ascertained that a lady from Connecticut had called to make complaint that a girl whom she had taken from the Nursery, some time previous, was being contaminated by the letters she was then receiving from one of the women whose acquaintance the child had formed while an inmate of the Nursery.

In regard to the effects of these paupers and criminal associations, it may not be out of place to quote here the language of an English lady,* widely known by her life-long efforts to elevate the unfortunate in her own land. At the congress of the State Boards of Charities, held in Detroit in May last, a paper giving the conclusions on her observations made upon Randall's Island, during a previous and recent visit to this country, was read. She says:

"I visited the pauper establishment on Randall's Island. The site afforded every facility for developing an admirable institution, where agricultural labor and the salutary influences of nature might have been given to the inmates. But nothing of the kind was done, and seldom have I witnessed a more soul-sickening spectacle than the degraded women and incapable men having the charge of these children. The mere sight of them must have a demoralizing effect on the children; and though the intellectual instruction was fair, yet there was a painfully distressed and spiritless look among them. The system of employing the lowest women in the care of the young, is most injurious, and if done from motives of false economy, cannot be too greatly reprobated."

As bearing also upon this feature of association with criminals, the chairman † of the committee on children of the State Charities Aid Association, a frequent visitor to Randall's Island, says:

"Two among the many crying evils on Randall's Island are the employment of prison labor in the care of the children, and the want of thorough industrial training. The children are diseased through neglect, and degraded in character under such influence. They become useless, idle and pauperized. How can such children become self-supporting men and women?"

It may not be out of place to state here that the evils existing in the Randall's Island Nurseries have long been familiar to the ladies of the State Charities Aid Association, who have made complaint regarding them to the Commissioners of Public Charities and Corrections, as well as to this Board, and who have, for the last two years, displayed a generous zeal in their attempts to ameliorate the condition of the children, and direct public attention to this matter.

Home Life.

The absence of any thing like home-life, or the best orphan asylum life, in the nursery is painful. The unfitting dresses of the little

* Miss Mary Carpenter, of Red House Lodge.
† Miss A. P. Cary.

ones, giving them a grotesque appearance; the habit of standing in great rooms to eat; the bare floors and walls without a picture or article of furniture to suggest home-life; the moving to and fro in great masses, destroying, as it does, all individuality, are among the conditions which should awaken sympathy for this tender class.

Ways for Disposing of the Children.

The question may naturally be asked, what disposition can be made of the children of the Nursery. A review of the whole system adopted in the State for the care of dependent children, such as has recently been made by a member of this Board, leads to the conclusion that no difficulty need be apprehended on this score. There are in the city of New York well-managed asylums for the care of children, which are not filled to their capacity, and a considerable number in other parts of the State. These benevolent agencies are, it is believed, sufficient to provide for all the dependent children of the State without the aid of the Nursery, and would, doubtless, be glad to receive them, were they permitted to do so. There are also organizations directed toward ameliorating the condition of unfortunate and homeless children, and some who make it their special work to find good homes for such in the country about New York or the West, and who, it is believed, would take and properly dispose of all the children that might be assigned to them. The children, disposed of in either of these ways, would be far better off than in the Nursery; the county of New York would be a gainer by being relieved, in some cases, of a portion of, and in others, of the entire cost of, their support.

Expense of Maintaining the Nursery and Nursery Hospital.

The warden, who has had 15 years, experience on the island, on being asked his opinion as to the employment of pauper women in the establishment, replied: "Most undoubtedly I would work to better advantage with the aid of hired help, but you can't get them for $10 a month to come up here. During the month of August, it cost us five cents, five mills and four-tenths of a mill per day for each inmate. The month cost us $5, 15 cents, nine mills and nine-tenths of a mill. Multiply that by 12 and it will give you the average yearly cost. Some months it costs more, but this is the average. The monthly cost of salaries is 77 cents, seven mills and six-tenths of a mill. The average of keep for last year was 16 cents a day including food, fuel, clothing and salaries."

This, it will be seen, is $1.12 per week. But it must be borne in mind that it is the warden's estimate on the cost per capita of the children in the Nursery. The cost of support per week, per capita, in the Nursery Hospital, is stated by the Commissioners of Public Charities and Corrections to be $1.41 weekly, not including vegetables. This estimate is independent of the school department. The cost of maintaining the school department of Randall's Island is stated to be as follows:

Salaries	$15,000
Repairs	100
Books and stationery	650
Fuel	500
	$16,250

No estimate upon the average cost of keeping the children can be considered a correct one, without embracing the sick with the well, in the average. Neither does the warden include in his present calculation, certain general expenses borne by the whole department of Public Charities and Corrections, a share of which should be charged to the Nursery. Neither does it include interest upon the large sum invested in the Nursery and Nursery Hospital.

If the warden was obliged to employ, at remunerative wages, in place of the large force of assistants under him, brought up from the work-house and alms-house, competent, responsible persons, selected with reference to their fitness as associates for the dependent class who need to be elevated both by precept and example if they are ever to be intrusted with the rights of citizenship, it would be found that the cost per capita per week, would be largely in excess of his estimate.

An important omission in the warden's estimate, and which may be fairly considered are the expenses attending the pauperizing effects of the nursery system, or in consequence of the diseases which it is likely to entail. As bearing upon this point, and showing how the poor-house system brings about pauperized conditions, the following is taken from the report of the State Charities Aid Association:

"In the hospital the ignorance and incapacity of the paid nurses are painfully evident; and in their absence the prison helpers are left in sole charge of the wards. The following extracts are from the note-books of the Randall's Island visitors:

"'Found the nurses and prison helpers all away, and a crippled dwarf the sole attendant.'

"'The children in one ward had been without any care for several hours, until a Roman Catholic priest notified the matron of the fact.'

"Nov. 26, 1875.—'Found wards four and five of the nursery hospital in a deplorable state. Some of the children were ill in bed, and two very ignorant prison women had the care of them. The nurse had gone about a week before, and after several days her place was filled by a woman who remained only one night, leaving every thing in confusion.'

*   *   *   *   *   *

"One of the most fruitful sources of infection is the imperfect laundry work. The hospital clothing is kept separate from that of other departments, but all infected garments are washed together, no matter what the disease may have been, and used in common for all hospital children. The pretense of washing through which they go only facilitates the spread of contamination through all the garments. The supply of towels is usually insufficient. There is great carelessness in keeping the sponges and cloths used for ophthalmic patients apart from those used by the other children, and even if conveniences were supplied, the nurses and helpers are too ignorant and careless to use them properly. It can be readily understood that children brought in for the cure of trifling and temporary ailments contract loathsome maladies, entailing upon them life-long suffering, and unfitting them for the homes into which they might be received."

The following testimony in the same direction will be found in the yearly report of the Visiting Physician to the Nursery and Nursery Hospital, made December 31, 1869, to the Commissioners of Public Charities and Corrections:

"The repeated occurrence of these contagious diseases must be expected while such large liberty of communication with the city is allowed, and I earnestly recommend that special provision be made for the isolation and care of such cases. The present quarantine is not available for such purposes. It only serves as a house of temporary detention, to give time to examine the children and see that they are not the subjects of contagious disease. If it happens that they are suffering from such disease, they must be transferred at once to the general wards of the hospital, and as soon as this is done the danger of contamination of the other inmates commences.

"A former epidemic of scarlet fever in this Institution, I am informed, destroyed *sixty* lives, and it is a wise and humane precaution to guard against such disastrous occurrences."

Ophthalmia, it has been found, has existed in a virulent form in the poor-houses of the State, and is one of the sad features of poor-house child life. It was fearfully prevalent in the Kings county Nursery, at the time that institution was abolished. It will be seen by reference to the examination of the Board, that in the Nursery there were three cases of sore eyes, three children were blind, and ten were blind in one eye; and in the Nursery Hospital that fifty-seven children had sore eyes, seven were blind, and three blind in one eye, making in all eighty-three children that were either suffering from diseased eyes, or were blind in one or both eyes. The precise number of these children who were sufferers in consequence of the poor-house system, it could not be determined. But it was believed by the examiner, that five of these children had been inoculated with virus producing sore eyes while in the hospital, and after being sent there and while under treatment for other ailments. Three of these poor children it was thought would become blind, while of the other two it was regarded as a matter of certainty. The expense of maintaining a single blind person from childhood upwards, is a grave consideration in a pecuniary sense, and one which must be brought into these particular estimates to arrive at a just conclusion. In a humanitarian view, however, the relative expense of various systems are not to be considered.

We read of a boy prince pleading on his knees before his keeper, that his eyes might not be put out with red-hot irons; and that his cruel tormentor, looking into those beautiful windows of the soul, lost heart to perform his fearful commission. The bare mention even of such a horrid conception causes the cheek to burn with indignation; but it is believed, that here, in the 19th century, at one of the few central points of the wealth and civilization of a continent, we find an evil tolerated that permits the light of day to be shut out forever from the eyes of orphan children. This sounds strange, and yet it is no nursery tale, but an ugly fact.

It is deemed proper to say that any system which needlessly exposes a single child, whether it be an orphan, or the offspring of honest poverty, or even a child of misfortune, to the deprivation of its sight, should not only not be tolerated, but be so entirely displaced that the memory of so great an act of inhumanity might be utterly forgotten.

Evils Underlying the System.

We have seen this strangely-conglomerated system of poor-house, boarding-house, public school, work-house and penitentiary on a summer's day, when the pleasant voices of children came to our ears across the grounds, and as we beheld, looking down the broad walk under the ailantus trees, through which golden bars of light were flitting, the white sails gliding dreamily to and fro on the distant water; and as we felt the courteous attentions of the intelligent officials placing us at our ease, it was easy for one to imagine that here, indeed, was a favored spot of earth. But let us contemplate it, when the warm night has thrown its weird shadows over the scene, and when the agents of mischief that dare not work by day, creep into activity. The men from Blackwell's Island are marched away to a building some "four hundred yards distant" from the grounds, designated by the official as a "branch penitentiary;" it is supposed, to be locked up for the night. The work-house women have gone to their quarters over the school-rooms; the warden has retired to his family residence upon the island; the paid nurses, cooks and domestics find their quarters over the kitchen. The male idiots, including all the older portion, have been marched over from the Idiot Asylum, and are occupying a dormitory in one of the large boys' buildings which should be locked, but which the drill-master admitted he had never found secured. Over this large community, with a considerable extent of harbor shore, one night-watch holds guard. The abuses which may result during the night hours to the helpless and unprotected, may be easily imagined. On being questioned, the watchman said: "I walk around the hospital, and go through every building except the girls' department. The work-house women are not locked up at night. They go up at 7 o'clock in the evening. There is nothing to prevent their going out and getting around the grounds, unless I am around. When I came here first, I was disturbed by the boats coming to assist the women away."

It will be borne in mind that here is an island with miles of shore, abundance of ambush, subject to abuse within and without, and, as stated, one night watchman over the Nursery. In consequence of this lack of proper custodial attention to the defective, pauper and criminal classes, this freedom from restraint and general looseness characteristic of the institution, how far Randall's Island Nursery contributes to swell these classes throughout the country, and to supply those vast and overgrown receptacles for their care and custody in New York must be left to conjecture.

CONCLUSION.

After a patient and impartial examination of this subject, the conclusion seems to be inevitable, that the whole Randall's Island nursery system should be set aside agreeably to the statute, and that the children should be placed in asylums suited to their various needs under the charge of those devoted to the interests of the young, or into good families where they may be trained and educated to useful and respectable citizenship. The Kings county nursery system was bad enough, but this is infinitely worse. That was not abolished by force of legal enactment alone, but by the exercise of an enlightened public sentiment.

This institution, like poor-houses generally, will always be under the control of party organization which must necessarily influence its management in the selection of subordinates, and being under the control of public officials the voluntary efforts of benevolent people to minister to the needs of unfortunate children must, in consequence, be shut out from this field of labor and the children deprived of what experience has demonstrated as being the very best agencies for their elevation.

If an attempt should be made, with even partial success, to remove the objectionable features that exist in the pauper and criminal attendants, it would result in larger expenditure than would be incurred in providing for the children in orphan asylums and other institutions for their care. Besides, a large portion of the labor performed, for the pay, by the employees, under an improved alms-house system, would, in asylums, be cheerfully rendered, for the children, by benevolent people, free of cost to the public.

It is believed that whatever may be done to improve this system, it will still have the same general characteristics, and retain about it the indolent atmosphere peculiar to all institutions having the care of the pauper classes, and that all attempts in this direction will only serve to gild over or cover up a radical evil without effecting a cure. Wherever the experiment has been tried, elsewhere in the State, to improve the condition of the children of pauper institutions by building for them good school-houses, or by separating them from the adult inmates in entirely distinct departments, the results were disappointing, and were found not only to work disastrously to the children, but to be against the interests of the poor.

The proper mental and moral improvement of so large a number of children as are inmates of the Nursery is not a question of immediate cost of keeping only, but it involves the future well-being of society. It is believed that the attempt to afford to these homeless children the best possible advantages, at whatever cost, will be found in the end to be true economy. Every child preserved from a life of pauperism and crime, adds so much to the productive forces of society, and, at the same time, lessens greatly the public burdens. It has been said by a citizen of Madison county, "that no law of the State is more fraught with wisdom than that based upon the idea, that it is better to train the youthful mind than to support the aged criminal, and that no experiment in political economy is of more practical value, than that which transforms a fruitful source of taxation into a source of revenue — a pauper into a tax-paying citizen."

There is a vein of wisdom in this simple passage, which is well worthy of thoughtful attention, particularly when the public mind seems to be directed towards dealing with existing evils by preventive means, and at a time when pauperism and crime are so alarmingly on the increase.

It is but just to say that, so far as our observation went, the impression was made that the officials and matrons connected with the institution were faithful in the discharge of their duties, and were endeavoring to do the best they could under the circumstances; but they were working under a system established at a time when it was customary to load the insane with chains, and to fasten them to the floors in darkened cells; when the blind and the deaf and dumb received less humane care than at present, and when the whole criminal and alms-house administration admitted practices that would not, at this day, be for a moment tolerated. This system for the care of homeless children has stood till the present, a time-honored abuse, embarrassing the action, and dissipating the energies, of the officials in immediate charge.

Since writing the foregoing, and before closing this report, it is gratifying to be able to state that the Commissioners of Public Charities and Corrections, have declined to receive children over three years of age, excepting idiots, epileptics, paralytics and those otherwise diseased; have notified such parents and guardians as have children in the Nursery, to remove them, and have taken other action looking to the closing up of that institution.

The Legislature and the charitably disposed who are stepping forward in this emergency to the relief of the helpless and the unfortunate.

are entitled to the thanks of a grateful people; and when the work has been fully accomplished, as it is believed it soon will be, the beneficent results growing out of this important change in the alms-house department of the great metropolis, will not only be felt in some degree throughout the entire State of New York, but also in adjoining States.

That jealous and almost affectionate care with which the State now enfolds its dependent children, and preserves them from the stigma of pauperism, enables its citizens virtually to say, with a just pride, that in no county within her borders does there exist a system, under legal sanction, that brands the orphan or homeless child, a "pauper."

Respectfully submitted,

WILLIAM P. LETCHWORTH,
Commissioner Eighth Judicial District.

ALBANY, *December* 27, 1875.

CHILDREN AND YOUTH
Social Problems and Social Policy

An Arno Press Collection

Abt, Henry Edward. **The Care, Cure and Education of the Crippled Child.** 1924

Addams, Jane. **My Friend, Julia Lathrop.** 1935

American Academy of Pediatrics. **Child Health Services and Pediatric Education:** Report of the Committee for the Study of Child Health Services. 1949

American Association for the Study and Prevention of Infant Mortality. **Transactions of the First Annual Meeting of the American Association for the Study and Prevention of Infant Mortality.** 1910

Baker, S. Josephine. **Fighting For Life.** 1939

Bell, Howard M. **Youth Tell Their Story:** A Study of the Conditions and Attitudes of Young People in Maryland Between the Ages of 16 and 24. 1938

Bossard, James H. S. and Eleanor S. Boll, editors. **Adolescents in Wartime.** 1944

Bossard, James H. S., editor. **Children in a Depression Decade.** 1940

Brunner, Edmund DeS. **Working With Rural Youth.** 1942

Care of Dependent Children in the Late Nineteenth and Early Twentieth Centuries. Introduction by Robert H. Bremner. 1974

Care of Handicapped Children. Introduction by Robert H. Bremner. 1974

[Chenery, William L. and Ella A. Merritt, editors]. **Standards of Child Welfare:** A Report of the Children's Bureau Conferences, May and June, 1919. 1919

The Child Labor Bulletin, 1912, 1913. 1974

Children In Confinement. Introduction by Robert M. Mennel. 1974

Children's Bureau Studies. Introduction by William M. Schmidt. 1974

Clopper, Edward N. **Child Labor in City Streets.** 1912

David, Paul T. **Barriers To Youth Employment.** 1942

Deutsch, Albert. **Our Rejected Children.** 1950

Drucker, Saul and Maurice Beck Hexter. **Children Astray.** 1923

Duffus, R[obert] L[uther] and L. Emmett Holt, Jr. **L. Emmett Holt:** Pioneer of a Children's Century. 1940

Fuller, Raymond G. **Child Labor and the Constitution.** 1923

Holland, Kenneth and Frank Ernest Hill. **Youth in the CCC.** 1942

Jacoby, George Paul. **Catholic Child Care in Nineteenth Century New York:** With a Correlated Summary of Public and Protestant Child Welfare. 1941

Johnson, Palmer O. and Oswald L. Harvey. **The National Youth Administration.** 1938

The Juvenile Court. Introduction by Robert M. Mennel. 1974

Klein, Earl E. **Work Accidents to Minors in Illinois.** 1938

Lane, Francis E. **American Charities and the Child of the Immigrant:** A Study of Typical Child Caring Institutions in New York and Massachusetts Between the Years 1845 and 1880. 1932

The Legal Rights of Children. Introduction by Sanford N. Katz. 1974

Letchworth, William P[ryor]. **Homes of Homeless Children:** A Report on Orphan Asylums and Other Institutions for the Care of Children. [1903]

Lorwin, Lewis. **Youth Work Programs:** Problems and Policies. 1941

Lundberg, Emma O[ctavia] and Katharine F. Lenroot. **Illegitimacy As A Child-Welfare Problem, Parts 1 and 2.** 1920/1921

New York State Commission on Relief for Widowed Mothers. **Report of the New York State Commission on Relief for Widowed Mothers.** 1914

Otey, Elizabeth Lewis. **The Beginnings of Child Labor Legislation in Certain States;** A Comparative Study. 1910

Phillips, Wilbur C. **Adventuring For Democracy.** 1940

Polier, Justine Wise. **Everyone's Children, Nobody's Child:** A Judge Looks At Underprivileged Children in the United States. 1941

Proceedings of the Annual Meeting of the National Child Labor Committee, 1905, 1906. 1974

Rainey, Homer P. **How Fare American Youth?** 1940

Reeder, Rudolph R. **How Two Hundred Children Live and Learn.** 1910

Security and Services For Children. 1974

Sinai, Nathan and Odin W. Anderson. **EMIC (Emergency Maternity and Infant Care):** A Study of Administrative Experience. 1948

Slingerland, W. H. **Child-Placing in Families:** A Manual For Students and Social Workers. 1919

[Solenberger], Edith Reeves. **Care and Education of Crippled Children in the United States.** 1914

Spencer, Anna Garlin and Charles Wesley Birtwell, editors. **The Care of Dependent, Neglected and Wayward Children:** Being a Report of the Second Section of the International Congress of Charities, Correction and Philanthropy, Chicago, June, 1893. 1894

Theis, Sophie Van Senden. **How Foster Children Turn Out.** 1924

Thurston, Henry W. **The Dependent Child:** A Story of Changing Aims and Methods in the Care of Dependent Children. 1930

U.S. Advisory Committee on Education. **Report of the Committee, February, 1938.** 1938

The United States Children's Bureau, 1912-1972. 1974

White House Conference on Child Health and Protection. **Dependent and Neglected Children:** Report of the Committee on Socially Handicapped — Dependency and Neglect. 1933

White House Conference on Child Health and Protection. **Organization for the Care of Handicapped Children, National, State, Local.** 1932

White House Conference on Children in a Democracy. **Final Report of the White House Conference on Children in A Democracy.** [1942]

Wilson, Otto. **Fifty Years' Work With Girls, 1883-1933:** A Story of the Florence Crittenton Homes. 1933

Wrenn, C. Gilbert and D. L. Harley. **Time On Their Hands:** A Report on Leisure, Recreation, and Young People. 1941